MW01045484

# COMPLETE GUIDE TO PLANT OPERATIONS MANAGEMENT

MICHAEL MUCHNIK

PRENTICE HALL
Englewood Cliffs, New Jersey 07632

Prentice-Hall International (UK) Limited, *London*
Prentice-Hall of Australia Pty. Limited, *Sydney*
Prentice-Hall Canada, Inc., *Toronto*
Prentice-Hall Hispanoamericana, S.A., *Mexico*
Prentice-Hall of India Private Limited, *New Delhi*
Prentice-Hall of Japan, Inc., *Tokyo*
Simon & Schuster Asia Pte. Ltd., *Singapore*
Editora Prentice-Hall do Brasil, Ltda., *Rio de Janeiro*



10 9 8 7 6 5 4 3 2 1

**Library of Congress Cataloging-in-Publication Data**

Muchnik, Michael.
Complete guide to plant operations management/Michael Muchnik.
p. cm.
Includes index.
ISBN 0-13-636903-0
1. Production management. 2. Production control. I. Title.
TS155.M7698 1992 92-5429
658.5—dc20 CIP

ISBN 0-13-636903-0

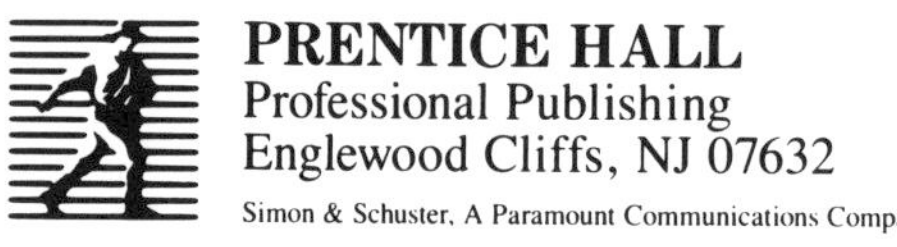


Printed in the United States of America

# About the Author

Michael Muchnik is the president of Integrated Management Systems (IMS), a manufacturing education and consulting firm specializing in consulting, executive development and training. IMS provides services in the areas of Just-in-Time and Total Quality Management applying an Integrated Business Management approach. IMS is based in Houston, TX.

Previously he served on the faculty of Western Illinois University teaching production/operations management, and later at the University of Houston-Downtown teaching production/operations management and business management. He continues to teach production and materials management on an adjunct basis at the University of Houston-Clear Lake and at the University of St. Thomas.

Prior to becoming a university professor, he spent 18 years in manufacturing and 8 years in executive development and consulting. He held management positions with a record of significant accomplishments in product design and development, production and inventory control, materials management, purchasing, quality control, plant maintenance, and projects.

His experience in industry includes equipment and machine tool manufacturing, automotive products, steel production, consumer goods, agricultural machinery production, continuous flow industries and plastic extrusion, rubber, textile, food processing, defense, electronics, petro-chemical, and mining industry.

Dr. Michael Muchnik is a recognized authority on manufacturing systems and Just-in-Time systems. As a trainer, he has developed and regularly presented more than 60 management training seminars and workshops such as "Production

Synergy Workshop" and "How to Gain the Competitive Edge in the 1990s"—A workshop on World-Class Performance.

He has assisted many companies in improving their performance in today's competitive business environment. Dr. Muchnik is a dynamic lecturer, educator, and researcher. He is a prolific author who has conducted executive programs around the world.

Michael Muchnik holds a Ph.D. degree in Production/Operations Management, a Masters degree in Economics, and a B.S. in Mechanical Engineering.

# What This Book Will Do for You

Operations managers face unparalleled challenges, and their role in an organization is changing, for recent experiences have dramatically modified business priorities calling for interactive relationships between production and other business functions.

Manufacturers have discovered that not all improvements in functional areas of operations are turned into general improvements of the manufacturing system and a business as a whole. For example, suppose that an inventory reduction or product quality improvement has been achieved but sales are not increasing because the product is still expensive. Usually, business improvements require simultaneous refinements in quality, cost, and customer service.

Nowadays, functional systems are being replaced by comprehensive integrated business systems featuring functional interrelationships of various business professions acting within multifunctional teams and business teams. This attribute of business emphasizing integration of business functions deserves special attention.

*Complete Guide to Plant Operations Management* has been written in response to a perceived need for instruction in developing an integrated manufacturing strategy. It cuts across functional areas of manufacturing with particular emphasis placed on functional business interactive relationships. It is written for managers requiring broader cross-functional skills and ability to fulfill integrated business strategies.

The contribution of each function to the total integrated business objective is emphasized. An *integrated business management* approach recognizes that improvements in business functional areas are compounded into an overall business improvement program.

Companies in which services and decision making are diffused among functional subunits are alarmed at their productivity stagnation. Such companies need different measures for being competitive and to stay in business. Where do we start? Customer needs outline the changes you will require: quality control problems, warranty complaints, after-sale services, product price, appearance, and durability. Your improvements should be *product centered* rather than *function centered.* This product-based information will direct you to specific business areas requiring improvements.

This is a reference book in which the reader finds a fast and comprehensive answer to a particular problem. For this purpose, the book is structured into four parts:

Part 1—*Organization of Operations Management System.* In this part, Chapters 1 and 2, you will find information explaining how to organize a production system and how to discriminate between diverse organizational structures and production frameworks.

Part 2—*Production Planning and Control Systems.* Chapters 3–7 concern hierarchical production planning and control systems, based on proven practices of high-performance manufacturing companies.

Part 3—*Just-in-Time Manufacturing Systems.* This part, Chapters 8–11, adopts a structured approach to a JIT system, explaining its step-by-step development and implementation. Four stages of JIT are distinguished here and are illustrated with numerous examples of advanced JIT organizations. This part is based on the survey of 4,000 American manufacturing companies.

Part 4—*Production Support Systems.* This part, Chapters 12–16, offers an in-depth discussion of purchasing, cost accounting, quality control, plant maintenance, and project control, stressing their functional interrelationships.

*Complete Guide to Plant Operations Management* is written for production managers and general practitioners in industry both at the beginning and advanced stages of their careers. Anybody who is involved in developing an integrated business management system will benefit from reading this book.

This book should be of interest to executive branch managers willing to get a better grasp on production, to the people on the shop floor, and to everybody working toward business improvements, applying organized resources of the profession.

This book will help you manage the following functions:

*Production Planning.* This book will show you how to adopt a coordinated approach to productive systems improvements and how to be a member of a cross-functional team, considering the dynamics of group behavior. As a production-operations manager, you are the focus of a business multifunctional team, and you work in close cooperation with business units, such as product design, manufacturing engineering, cost accounting, and other production and support services. See Chapters 1 and 2.

*Purchasing.* A purchasing price reduction is not the main concern of the purchasing function. Your concern is in the cost reduction of the *total purchasing contribution* to the manufacturing function, not just an upfront price you pay. This book explains how to organize a purchasing function as part of materials management and stresses the purchasing relationship to production planning and control, product design, and process engineering. See Chapter 12.

*Quality Control.* How to deal with quality issues. You work with production, plant maintenance, design and manufacturing engineering, and cost accounting when improving quality and the product value. Quality issues discussed here include the means of organizing a quality control system and improving quality, as well as estimating and reducing four quality costs categories. Discussed in the book are; Quality standards and quality instructions used by exemplary total quality control (TQC) companies including a quality manual developed in compliance with International Standard Organization (ISO) and international quality standards required for acceptance into the European Economic Community's market. See Chapter 14.

*Plant Maintenance.* The maintenance function contributes to the product value by making an equipment available when it is needed and assuring its performance to standards and specifications at no extra cost. You need to know how to work with the production planning and control; in order to schedule your preventive maintenance tasks; with the design department, and cost accounting in order to timely write off an equipment; and how to compile and control an optimized preventive maintenance schedule. See Chapter 15.

*Cost Accounting.* Cost accounting is a vital part of operations management and a formidable tool for production managers assisting in improving the product value by revealing concealed problems. The basics of cost accounting are described here accompanied by real-life examples of an activity-based cost accounting system (ABCS). ABCS system applies cost drivers successfully used by progressive world-class manufacturers cost accounting is a good example of production and engineering cross-functional task. See Chapter 13.

*Product Design.* A product designer works with manufacturing, engineering, production planning and control, purchasing, and other functions in an organization in order to maintain an acceptable product value throughout the product life. Interrelationships of all these functions are explained in this book. See Chapters 1, 10 and 11.

*Engineering*. The role of an engineering profession is changing in a JIT environment that depends on a meaningful involvement of a labor force. This book explains how to reduce line employees' boredom, stress and labor fatigue; how to design jobs for a better work force motivation; how to reduce production costs; and how to compile work standards that enhance planning and job control. This book teaches you how the engineering function works in alliance with other production and business functions to increase the product value, such as improvements to design and to manufacturing processes. The techniques and examples of successful world-class organizations discussed will help you to gain a competitive edge. See Chapters 10 and 11.

*Project Management*. In manufacturing, an essential part of production is controlled as projects. It has been found that up to 95 percent of product life expenses on product development and maintenance are spent even before a single product is produced. These are project-related activities. Advanced project management techniques, explained in this book, will help you to control time, resources, and project cost. See Chapter 16.

*Production and Administrative Services*. In contributing to product value, production and administrative services are business activities which are undergoing intensive restructuring, to maximize their contribution to the production function. Everybody, ranging from the personnel manager to the marketing manager, should know their specific contribution and how their specific activities relate to other functions of an integrated business system. See Chapters 12–16.

This book describes operations management and its role in contemporary business systems. The most compelling business requirement is that you should have a grasp of a whole, while selecting important areas and work with details. This book provides you with new refinement of management applications in establishing a balance between often contradictory realities of a multifunctional business environment. This book captures the dynamics of the operations management beyond its rudimentary topics and thus is ideally suited for members of cross-functional teams. It teaches how to make cross-functional decisions on competitive choices and tactics by building efficient business relationships and organizational structures. By referring to this book, you will have a clear understanding of various types of manufacturing systems. You will be able to discriminate among the strategies explained in the book and select the ones most likely to succeed.

You will find a brief listing of the functional areas of operations covered in the book in the chart that follows.

*Michael Muchnik*

# COMPLETE GUIDE TO PLANT OPERATIONS MANAGEMENT

*Table of Contents—Overview*

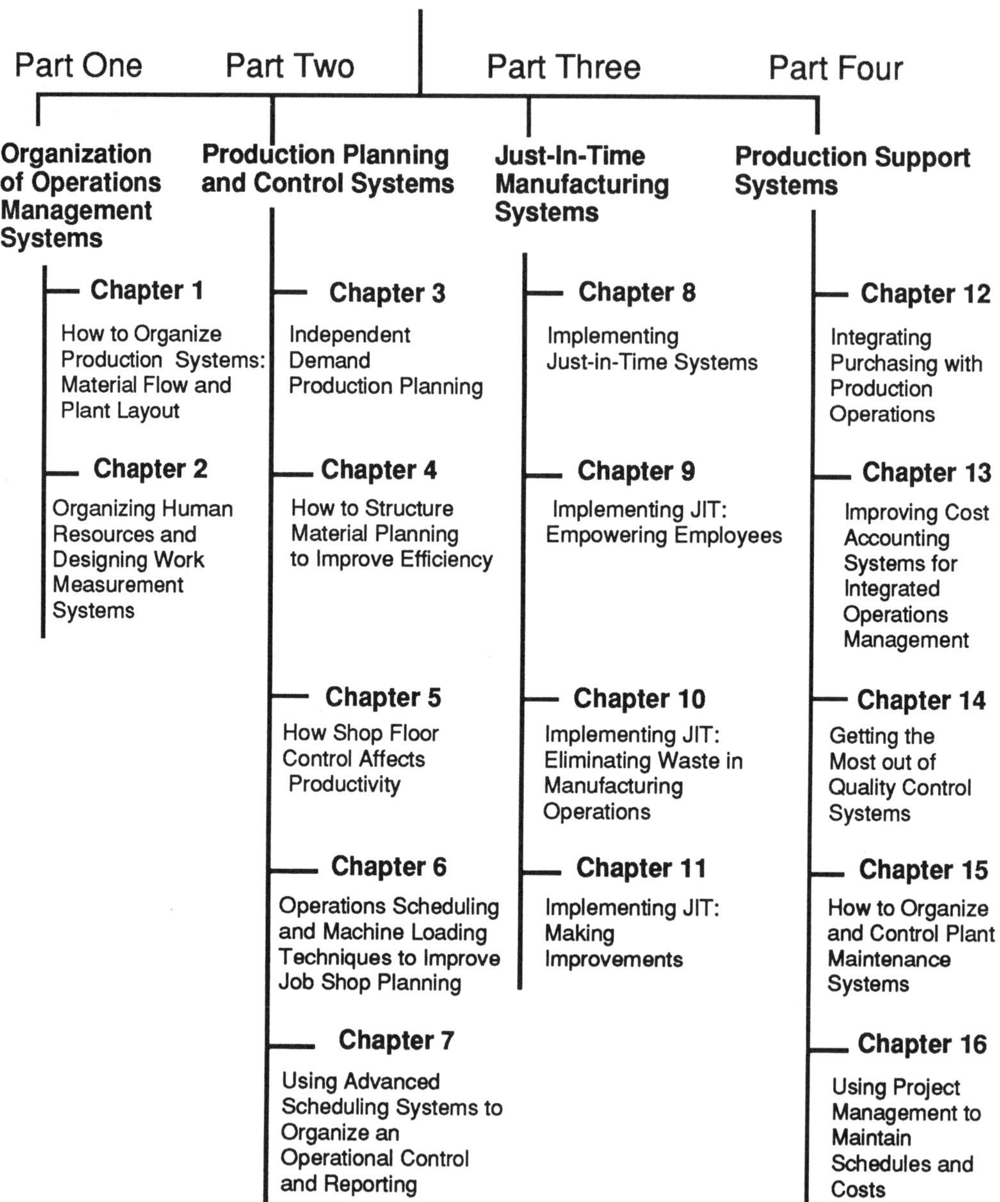
Complete Guide to Plant Operations Management
Part One
Part Two
Part Three
Part Four
Organization of Operations Management Systems
Production Planning and Control Systems
Just-In-Time Manufacturing Systems
Production Support Systems
Chapter 1
How to Organize Production Systems: Material Flow and Plant Layout
Chapter 2
Organizing Human Resources and Designing Work Measurement Systems
Chapter 3
Independent Demand Production Planning
Chapter 4
How to Structure Material Planning to Improve Efficiency
Chapter 5
How Shop Floor Control Affects Productivity
Chapter 6
Operations Scheduling and Machine Loading Techniques to Improve Job Shop Planning
Chapter 7
Using Advanced Scheduling Systems to Organize an Operational Control and Reporting
Chapter 8
Implementing Just-in-Time Systems
Chapter 9
Implementing JIT: Empowering Employees
Chapter 10
Implementing JIT: Eliminating Waste in Manufacturing Operations
Chapter 11
Implementing JIT: Making Improvements
Chapter 12
Integrating Purchasing with Production Operations
Chapter 13
Improving Cost Accounting Systems for Integrated Operations Management
Chapter 14
Getting the Most out of Quality Control Systems
Chapter 15
How to Organize and Control Plant Maintenance Systems
Chapter 16
Using Project Management to Maintain Schedules and Costs

# Contents

# Foreword to Complete Guide to Plant Operations Management

America's competitive edge in industry is still deteriorating. These results are both disappointing and paradoxical for they are a measure of the results of fifteen years of a revitalized and highly motivated manufacturing sector.

The turnaround has been massive and widespread, effectively amounting to an industrial renaissance replete with broadly accepted new concepts and techniques such as Just-in-Time, Total Quality Control and Computer-Integrated Manufacturing. But in spite of all this heroic effort, during this same period much of American industry has failed to gain ground on its important foreign competitors.

While there are exceptional companies and industries, the overall picture whether measured in productivity, quality, market shares, new product lead times, or exports and imports—shows that we are still chasing after all these years.

Why do we show a consistent sluggishness in bringing about essential changes such as in work-force management, innovating new processes, and compressing the times required for new product development?

The need for such fundamental improvements was clear fifteen years ago. The management literature of that period was rife with articles arguing that such changes were needed for the survival of western industry. In spite of nearly total agreement that such basic improvements were necessary, the rate of change has been dismal. What internal brakes have been holding us back in doing what is clearly important to do?

What is still wrong with much of western manufacturing is that in spite of the adoption of many new techniques and restored vitality, the basic "fixes" identified as needed back in the 70s have been too slow in coming. Furthermore, as a result of the wholesale application of off-the-shelf techniques, industry is full of internally inconsistent systems and infrastructures. In contrast to the hodge-podge of ideas adopted without a strategic vision, fundamentally sound and needed strategic management approaches have penetrated only slightly. As a result many industries are not competitive.

By 1975 we had slipped, over twenty years, into a devastating loss of world market shares in manufactured products, losing ground in dozens of industries from steel to autos to consumer electronics to machine tools. Business media and academic literature of the times pointed up serious but obvious needs for major competitive improvements in cost reduction, quality, delivery cycles, and customer service. These performance criteria in turn demanded a return to historic annual productivity improvements which had deteriorated badly in the 60s and 70s, shorter new product development cycles, more devotion to quality and better inventory and shop floor controls. And at the most fundamental level, it was widely recognized that we had to automate more quickly, improve work force morale and participation to unleash energies and ideas, and break down organizational walls, particularly between engineering and manufacturing.

These needs were obvious and so generally accepted that articles in both the academic and periodical literature generally focused more on how to accomplish these tasks than on what the tasks should be. But in spite of the enormous motivation for survival, the clarity of what was needed to be done, and the urgency involved in many industries, the slow progress obtained—both absolutely and relative to aggressive overseas competitors—is surprising and revealing.

Industry did best in the productivity race, getting back on the 75-year track of annual gains which had been interrupted for about 15 years. Even so, the rate of productivity gains failed to match those of Japan, West Germany, and most Pacific Basin nations during the past 10 years, leaving us "still chasing."

The story is the same in "quality," where, driven by ever more intense global competition for consumer acceptance, great effort was expended to improve results. And quality performance has improved substantially throughout the bulk of US industry. But the problem is that competition—especially Japanese competition—has made equal or greater gains. In the auto industry, for example, *Consumer Reports* noted in April 1991 that US quality had moved up in ten years, reducing new buyer problems by two thirds but that meanwhile Japanese carmakers had improved also. As a result the quality gap was almost as bad as before, with American cars having two and a half times as many problems as those of the Japanese.

Progress in automation has been modest relative to the need and opportunities for CIM, robotics, laser process controls, and FMS. We have moved ahead with slow but continuous improvements and thereby improved output per employee, but nowhere enough to have gained significant competitive ground. And the proportion of annual investment in process development relative to product R&D is typically very modest.

Progress in reducing lead times, inventories, and customer dissatisfaction over poor service has generally been a real plus competitively. Use of computer-based scheduling and production control systems, "short-interval scheduling," smaller lot sizes, techniques for faster changeovers, and Just-in-Time and Kanban had shortened production cycle times.

This book offers a clear comprehensive coverage of the "New operations management." I like Michael Muchnik's approach because it can provide a concise review of the different fundamentals of operations management for all levels of managers. It can help a manager learn a new concept or technique and it can help a general manager understand better the functions under his/her supervision.

There is an urgent need for the upgrading of many production managers because of so much change in the field and because too many general managers (in my opinion) delegate excessively and do not either understand or coordinate the uses of the concepts and techniques covered in this book.

There is much work to be done if we are to perform better in global competition.

Wickham Skinner
Harvard Business School
March 9, 1992

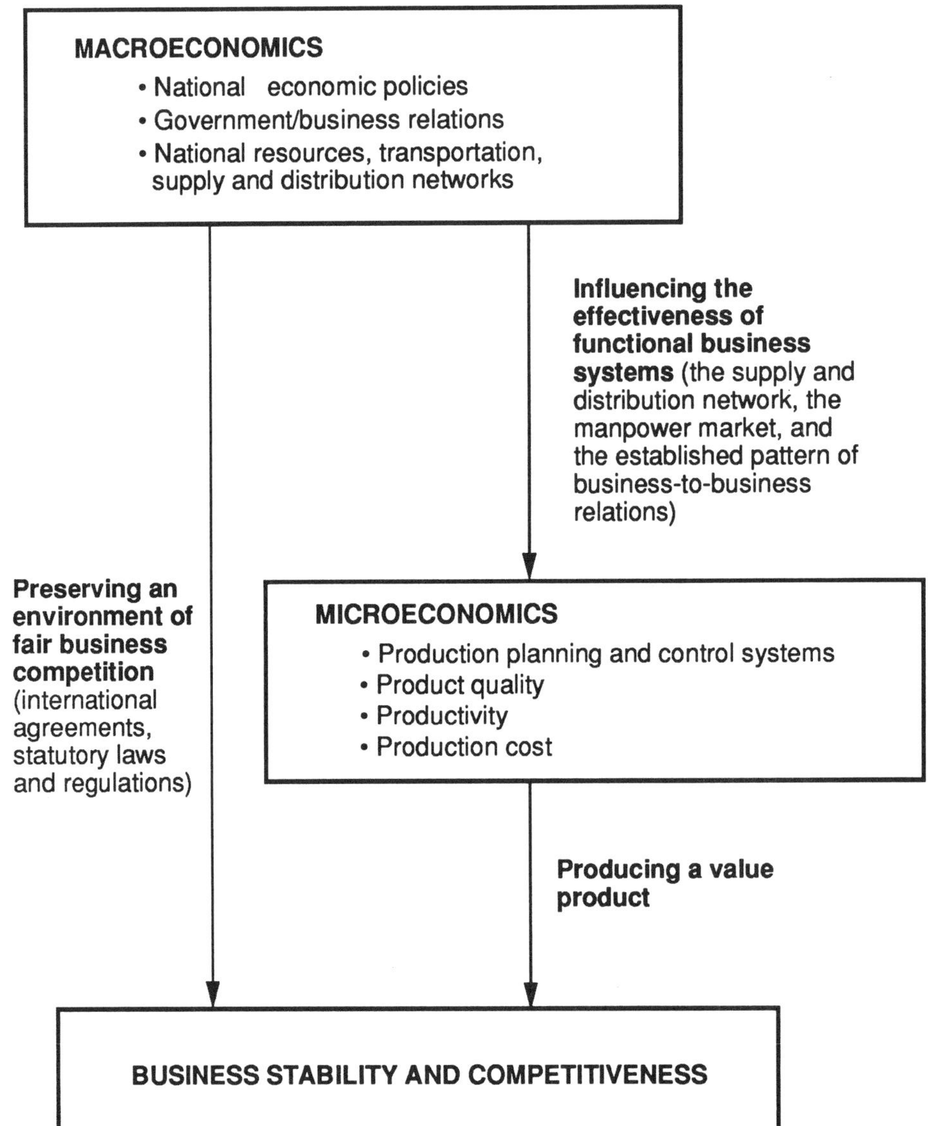


**Figure 1**

**Macroeconomics and Microeconomics are Two Requirements For Business Stability and Competitiveness**

# Preface

> The old excitement of managing a complex mix of people, machines, and materials is now being supplemented with a major new challenge, that of system planning and control.
>
> —Wickham Skinner, *Manufacturing: The Formidable Weapon*

The very survival of many firms and entire industries depends largely on their ability to develop effective business management systems able to produce competitively priced quality products.

Present industrial conditions are characterized by the diversification of products, wide selection of options, and more frequent changes in models. The emerging reality in industry is the restructuring from mass production to smaller production runs and the shorter product life. Such changes are due to a more sensitive response to individual customer orders. These conditions call for more dynamic and efficient manufacturing operating systems capable of managing regular job changes and more frequent setups.

Every sector of the economy—including services—has close ties with manufacturing. Consumers, suppliers of raw materials, and providers of services all benefit from manufacturing. Now we have realized that manufacturing is the foundation on which tomorrow's prosperity rests.

The decline in manufacturing can be attributed to a failure to coordinate marketing strategies, to improve productivity and efficiency, and to overcome the concomitant resistance to invest in the new technology. American competitiveness will rely greatly on our ability to adopt an industrial philosophy encompassing team-oriented flexible production systems supported by advanced planning and control techniques, as well as the ability to adopt coordinated manufacturing strategy. Concurrently, the human behavior factor should be taken into account in the world of changing industrial relations, emphasized with the on-the-job satisfaction stemming from the increased work force involvement into basic decision making.

Questions many ask are: "Where do we stand today?" "What is the policy direction in production management?" Sometime ago, the experts voiced an opinion that our failure to invest in the new equipment is the reason for our lagging behind the Japanese. The Japanese, in contrast, have been installing modern equipment since the end of World War II and are constantly updating and changing it, as conditions demand.

But, recently, it was stated that the $200 billion poured by American companies into new facilities and the equipment between 1980 and 1985 has scarcely slowed the erosion of our global competitiveness. Thus the investment in the new technology and equipment does not necessarily resolve problems in production. At present, the world leadership opportunities depend not so much on the technology as on the quality of management.

Manufacturers are realizing now that production problems cannot be resolved through automation alone; business strategies based on throwing new hardware at old performance problems are unlikely to work. The solution is to integrate the technology with manufacturing and marketing strategies and to link them to organizational changes that promote teamwork, training, and continuous learning.

Some companies view the solution in the improved quality attack called *total quality management* (TQM). Others see the solution in the reduction of inventory (zero stock) and in employee motivation through practicing bottom-up management. Advanced management methods which apply improved and innovative techniques should be a major contributor to any enhanced productivity plan. Developing such an enhanced productivity plan is the challenge faced by many companies in the present competitive world in this climate of ever-increasing competition from both the established international competitors and the newly industrialized countries.

## THE ROLE OF PRODUCTION/OPERATIONS MANAGEMENT IN TODAY'S INDUSTRIES

The significance of the production-operations management function is widely appreciated. There is a growing consensus among experts that inefficiency in management systems, and particularly in operations management tactical planning and control, is the major reason behind our dilemmas in the world economic competition. Thus, there is a need for management methods amenable to present-day goals and objectives.

The resurgent interest in manufacturing is apparent. What is required now is a blend of the scientific theory and practice for production management that provides standards for planning, coordination, production control, and analysis and contributes to the industrywide productivity improvement through more efficient management.

## GLOBAL INTEGRATED SYSTEMS AND AMERICAN INDUSTRY

Individual businesses exist within a framework of a larger industrywide structure. Industrial competitiveness is affected by two factors:

1. *Macroeconomics*—business external factors that largely refer to the national economic policies and government-business relations.
2. *Microeconomics*—internal organizational factors, such as product quality, production planning and control, productivity, and production cost.

Figure 1 on page xxviii shows that business stability and its competitiveness depends upon both macroeconomic and microeconomic conditions. The United States has been losing ground to international competition in both these areas.

### Macroeconomic Conditions

An organizational macroenvironment includes numerous external business factors which are beyond that individual business control—society, technology, statutory laws, national supply and distribution infrastructure, and national transportation networks used for movement of goods and materials. These conditions are influenced by business interactions and alliances and, to a large extent, by the government-business relations.

Government affects businesses through stimulating small-business development; conducting fiscal and budgetary policies; introducing and maintaining laws and regulations, imposing surcharges, import levies, and tax breaks; protecting businesses from unfair practices of local and foreign competitors; and based on the forecasts, outlining further opportunities for expansion of selected sectors of economy as well as stimulating and assisting such an expansion.

In the United States, foreign competitors have succeeded in capturing some of our industries. For example, the American share of the consumer electronics market has dropped in the past two decades from nearly 100 percent to a mere 5 percent. Similar conditions are observed in the textile industry and such industries as pharmaceuticals and semiconductors which are now being challenged by foreign competitors.

One of the reasons for weakness in American industry is how the industry interacts with government. In contrast, the Japanese government has played an important role in the remarkable progress of Japanese industry by establishing the Ministry of International Trade and Industry (MITI) in the late 1950s.

MITI has been spearheading the efforts of individual companies in the purchasing of raw materials, developing new products and technology, and marketing. MITI has created an environment conducive to efficient management of Japanese manufacturing systems. In the United States, this task has failed, due to the administration's stand against government intervention in economy and its excessive reliance on the controlling mechanism of the free market economy. Japanese government-business relations are a good example of the constructive role the administration plays in assisting businesses in the worldwide competition.

There are many people who understand that this trend cannot continue for much longer. In this regard, a committee of Massachusetts Institute of Technology scholars has suggested developing a structure that will facilitate intelligent communication between corporations and the government and would permit establishing business alliances.

Future prospects are not so bright. While we are lagging due to the gap in management methods, we also are going to be confronted with the superiority in Japanese technology. The Japanese are currently investing twice as much as the United States in developing new technologies and new products, despite the fact that their gross national product is less than two-thirds that of ours. This is significant for the technology, especially the process technology, is more difficult to transfer than management systems.

It is accepted now that all countries are part of the integrated world economy and that there is a single world market, which we share with others. Our common task, the alliance of business and administration, is to find our rightful place in the world integrated economic system.

### Microeconomic Conditions

Suzanne Berger and her colleagues in *Scientific American* write that

> Macroeconomics alone cannot adequately explain why some businesses thrive in the very same sectors where others are failing, nor why Japanese manufacturing plants in U.S. have often achieved better results than comparable American plants. (S. Berger, M. L. Dertouzos, R. K. Lester, R. M. Solow, and L. C. Thurow, "Toward a New Industrial America," *Scientific American*, Vol. 260, no. 6, June 1989, pp. 39–47)

Leaders of the American machine tool industry justify the decline in machine tool production by reasoning that the "Japanese are enormously competitive because there is a single national industrial policy directed by a government body" (Y. M. Rohan, "Tools in Trouble," *Industry Week*, May 21, 1990).

In reality, the lack of coordinated government-business policy in the United States is not the only reason for the downfall of this industry. In the opinion of machine tool users, this industry is characterized by long lead times—sometimes one needs to wait for several years for an order to be delivered—as opposed to Japanese deliveries in a matter of three to four months. Lead time is a major indicator of a company's efficiency and the effectiveness of its planning and control system. It affects inventory level, quality, and costs in a major way.

Why do American car manufacturers, who designed the first automobile mass production lines, now have a hard time competing locally and internationally with their overseas competitors? Elizabeth Haas writes that the American auto industry, which alone has invested $40 billion in capital improvements, continues to lose ground to Japanese automakers who produce subcompacts at a cost of $1,800 less per unit than that of Detroit (Elizabeth Haas, "Breakthrough Manufacturing," *Harvard Business Review*, March–April 1987, p. 75).

The competitive position of American companies continues to deteriorate. Our competitors are harvesting many financial benefits and are able to devote larger amounts of resources to research and development, thereby increasing the gap even further. Many markets are lost due to our inefficiency in managing manufacturing operations and our inability to develop efficient organizational structures and manufacturing planning and control systems.

## IMPROVING PERFORMANCE IN TODAY'S MARKETPLACE

Conclusive evidence indicates that the distinction between a company losing ground to its competitors and a company that stands up successfully to its competitors lies in the fact that the latter effectively structures its manufacturing function, a major part of which is production planning and control. American companies, most successfully competing abroad, are mainly those of the process-type industry. These companies have a standard productive flow and are not amenable to frequently changing environments requiring stringent production planning and control. Problems are experienced mainly in the manufacturing of engineered assembly products that have various degrees of customization—*job shop production*.

Nowadays, many industries are restructuring into business organizations with increased customization of orders and thus are becoming more like job shop–type organizations. Industrial organizations fully benefit from modern technological progress—powerful microcomputers, automation, and industrial robotics—when reliable production planning and control methods are developed. Compiled plans are the basis and the standard for good performance and reliability. Productivity is ensured by adjusting performance levels to correspond to the predetermined standards. Companies may need different remedies for improving their performance: some need to improve quality; others must beef up plant maintenance or develop planning and control methods; and still others should invest in R&D and the new technology, improve on organization, employee motivation, or tightening up the discipline. Thus, for various companies, there are different solutions for the improvement in performance.

There is a need to develop a standardized management methodology in order to assist companies in improving their planning and control systems. The development of such planning and control is a major business undertaking which, in an individual organization, requires thousands of work-hours with no assurance for success. In many instances, the outcome of these undertakings is a major factor behind the success or failure of an organization. Experience indicates that many such developments are unsuccessful.

Only large organizations have the resources and expertise for developing custom-made manufacturing control systems. In the United States, we need to pay attention to assisting mid-to small-sized manufacturing companies in developing efficient manufacturing practices, including planning and control methods. These small, 30- to 200-employee organizations, known as *subcontractors*, are a major driving force behind the success of Japanese industry.

## THE LESSON OF THE MRP CRUSADE

The performance of our economy over the past two decades deserves a special assessment. These times were marked by the inception of the advanced system the material requirements planning (MRP) featuring zero-stock calculated, time-phased ordering. Although skillfully designed as a zero-stock ordering system, MRP was not intended for companywide production planning and control and certainly not for operational control and optimization. These MRP installations, which were expected to perform as manufacturing planning and control systems, have either completely failed or did not rise to the expectations (M. Muchnik, "Bill of Integrated Tasks and Functional Control of Intermittent Job Shop Operations," *Production and Inventory Management Journal*, Fourth Quarter 1988, p. 43).

Job shop planning and control are the most unsettled of all the industrial and business applications. In any type of production, if a job shop is part of the process, it is responsible for the majority of production control problems. Production planning and control of job shop production is an issue of controlling a large number of interrelated intermittent operations. The failure of the "MRP crusade," as it was termed, is largely due to an inability to organize operational control over material flow.

### Just-in-Time (JIT): A Possible Solution?

The questions many ask are: "What happens next?" "What comes after the MRP crusade?" Management has recently learned a new term, *Just-In-Time* (JIT). Is this a method for planning and control? JIT is a collection of various principles, most of which are related to human factors. R. C. Walleigh writes: "Despite the extensive publicity and interest, few companies have implemented JIT in their manufacturing operations. If JIT provides all the benefits claimed for it, why have so few factories adopted it?" (R. C. Walleigh, "What's Your Excuse For Not Using JIT?" *Harvard Business Review*, March–April 1986, p. 38).

How many companies are introducing JIT? Industrywide, it isn't an impressive figure. A recently concluded survey of 4,000 American manufacturing companies shows that only 4.6 percent of manufacturers have reported that they installed or considered Just-in-Time systems. From these, about 45 percent have realized some conclusive advantages from the JIT development.

While there are many reports claiming successes in JIT, you should exercise caution for, in reality, there are often improvements in functional areas of operations such as quality control, inventory control, and plant maintenance, which are attributed to Just-in-Time.

In talking to people about JIT, you can get the impression that you should reduce inventory at any cost—JIT is a zero-stock philosophy—and that quality should be improved to match that of Japanese products. However, we need to define explicitly and standardize JIT methods, set up priorities in its development and implementation, and relate these to different applications, organizational structures, and objectives.

To date, we have not overcome the consequences of the MRP crusade. The objective should be to address this predicament and to prevent it from turning into another failure with the "JIT crusade."

## HOW ANSWERS TO PRESENT ORGANIZATIONAL PROBLEMS CAN BE FOUND IN HISTORICAL CONTRIBUTIONS TO PRODUCTION-OPERATIONS MANAGEMENT

### What Was Left Unnoticed in the Heritage of Scientific Management?

There is an old saying that states in order to see the future, one should look into the past. In this regard, past contributions to production management should be reexamined because many modern production-operations management (POM) practices have their roots in developments which can be traced back to the late 1800s.

The recognition of operations management (OM) as a systematic field of knowledge originated a long time ago, but in a refined form, it can be traced to the development of the scientific management of Frederick Taylor, the organization of production lines by Henry Ford, and the contributions of such others as Henry Fayol, Frank and Lillian Gilbreth, Abraham Maslow, and Frederick Herzberg.

Taylor is known as "the father of scientific management." According to his view, management should take the responsibility for planning and organizing the division of work in a firm. The beginning of the century was marked by the division of labor—breaking down jobs into simple repetitive tasks. This was done at the broad scale and has resulted in substantial increase in productivity in industry.

Frederick W. Taylor went further by introducing the separation of labor production activities and management functions. At the time, workers were relatively free to set their own pace for the work assignments and to apply their own methods to carry out these assignments, but Taylor stressed that a worker must be in charge of physically doing the job, whereas such activities as planning and control should be assigned to managers and planners, people who are better qualified to perform these functions.

Taylor highlighted the significance of having a systematic, rational, and deliberate scientific approach to all jobs and problems in an organization. The four principles of scientific management, as they have been seen by Taylor, are still not entirely understood. Here is a brief review:

1. *Develop a science for each element of a person's work, which would replace the old rule-of-thumb method.* F. W. Taylor initiated a detailed analysis of human movements, applying the time and motion study, which has resulted in establishing progressive work standards.
2. *Scientifically select, train, teach, and develop a worker.* This principle requires a scientific selection of workers for their tasks, highlighting human factors and the need to motivate employees. Next, comes training, teaching, and developing workers. This is more than simply training workers in the specific skills required to perform specific work tasks. To teach also means to give a worker a scientific knowledge of affiliated functions in related areas of technology and production.

Taylor had envisaged the development which we are engaged to accomplish now, namely, the Just-in-Time method. Taylor emphasized respect for people and seeing people as an extraordinary resource. If workers are not challenged to improve their skills and to advance professionally and intellectually, they are likely to have a low morale.

3. *Ensure hearty cooperation between management and workers, so that all work is being done in accordance with the developed scientific principles.* Here, the question of training and development of workers is related to the hearty cooperation between the management and the work force. With respect to the cooperation between management and workers, Japanese distinguish themselves from American managers. In Just-in-Time circumstances, this concept is defined as people-oriented management.

4. *Divide work and responsibility equally between management and the workers.* Taylor's fourth principle deals with sharing the responsibility between the management and the workers.

These principles are summarized in the accompanying table. Twenty years ago Herzberg said that the only way to motivate employees is to give them challenging work in which they can assume responsibility. This opinion is also shared by Drucker who says: "We need to do what IBM did 25 years ago when it determined that the job of its 'managers' was to bring out the strength of the work force: competence and knowledge and capacity to take responsibility."

The employees' initiative, combined with the new management approach, makes scientific management so much more efficient than the previous practice. We are still puzzled by the esoteric meaning of Taylor's principles. Their intriguing message deserves further attention. Scientific management had a great impact on industrial advancement through scientific approach to job design, industrial engineering, and work study techniques.

Up to now, scientific management has been applied mainly as a means for estimating workers' productivity. We have reached the stage when the productivity of an individual workstation is at its best, and it can be quantitatively measured and controlled. Is this the only change that Taylor had in mind?

| Principles | Stage of Development | What Is Accomplished |
|---|---|---|
| 1. Develop the science for each element of a person's work | Division of labor<br>Industrial engineering<br>Work study standards | Significant improvement in workers' productivity |
| 2. Scientifically select and train, teach, and develop workers | Human factors related to JIT | Part of the JIT development |
| 3. Ensure hearty cooperation between management and workers | Same as above | JIT people-oriented management |
| 4. Divide the work and responsibility equally between management and workers | Human factors involving workers in a decision making | Management and workers functional partnership |

Taylor's model of management-labor relations stipulates that the management assumes the function of training, teaching, and developing workers. Training of workers blends the technical knowledge with their experience into innovative methods. He envisaged that the relationship between management and workers will be developing into a full partnership manifested in the equal division of work and shared responsibility—the fourth principle. This was outlined at the beginning of this century, but only now some consideration has been given to sharing the responsibility between managers and workers.

Scientific management is a coherent, evolutionary program comprising four consecutive steps; four principles required for developing advanced methods of industrial management. The first principle of scientific management has resulted in the startling increase in productivity through improvements in workers' performance. The remaining three principles concerning management functions were not attended to the same extent. Thus, the development of these principles is still in progress. The principles of scientific management should not be counted out as outdated theories; they are, in fact, relevant to the present attempts to improve production by applying the people-oriented Just-in-Time approach.

Companies experiencing the erosion in sales and the dismal increases in productivity are those who did not move beyond Taylor's first and second principles, rigidly assigning to managers function of planning and supervising and viewing workers as those who do the work according to prepared plans.

In successful high-performance companies, the work force is involved in planning at all levels, and, conversely, managers take greater interest in the execution of what they have planned. In one such company, Baylor, power equipment manufacturer, there are several teams in which the work force is self-supervised and responsible for planning their jobs within the parameters set by the central planning. Managers and workers effectively share the authority and responsibility over the execution.

Baylor's JIT-type magnets production cell had remarkable productivity gains which have been improved by 30% without change in equipment or process. Roger Riley, Production Manager, says he believes that more is attributed to the increased spirit of team work and to being involved in jobs planning. Team members are now magnet builders rather than individual welders, assemblers, and machinists. Each person sees results of his or her work as part of the final product.

Riley recalls that when implementing the cell, the greatest emphasis was on the people solution. Trying to identify a list of volunteers who had a cooperative attitude was the greatest challenge for the manufacturing cell. The selection of personnel was based as much on attitude as was on skill. For example, the person doing the final machining operation was a forklift operator. He was, however, motivated to make the transition because he saw the need to advance in the company.

Now into the second year of operations of JIT cell, 3 main categories of self-determination and JIT-type management began to take shape:

1. *Employees involvement in planning*. There is only one work provision in jobs submitted—the final due date rather than traditional detailed operations scheduling procedures determining up to 40 operation sequences stipulated

in the work centers' dispatch list. Production planning and scheduling is done by team members, planning the work sequences themselves. This has resulted in hot jobs and expediting being eliminated.

2. *Work force cross-training*. Team members are involved in employee cross-training. The training schedule is determined by the team members themselves, including setting the training budget and scheduling time convenient to the team members.

3. *Involvement in production services*. Team relations with engineering has been changed in such a way that the team members themselves define process engineering characteristics and do their industrial engineering studies. Whenever engineering assistance is required, this is initiated by the team members working in close cooperation with the engineering staff. Such a work organization develops process ownership and is a strong factor enhancing motivation.

## Why the Management Principles of Henry Fayol Are Applied in Recent High-Performance Systems

A significant early contribution to management was done by a French mining engineer and business executive, Henry Fayol. Fayol was the first to recognize that management activities in organization are not homogeneous actions, but are purposeful and intentional activities aimed at fulfilling specific management functions. For the first time, Fayol had formulated such separate management functions as planning, organizing, coordinating, directing, and controlling, which are similar to what is recognized now. Another significant finding of Fayol is that all activities in an organization are interrelated and must be coordinated for achieving the best results.

His definition of coordination is to harmonize activities by

1. Meshing activities by sequencing and timing
2. Allocating the rightful properties of resources
3. Adapting means to end

*Coordinating* means laying out the timing and sequence of activities binding together, unifying, and harmonizing all activities and efforts. This management function has recently attracted special attention. The message was to establish a harmony among the various parts of an organization through continuous coordination, instead of taking narrowly conceived actions and threatening the running of the whole. Fayol's outlines are as relevant as ever, reflected in the contemporary practice of integrated systems such as JIT, also known as the synergistic approach to business functions.

## FUTURE TARGETS: THE INTEGRATED MANAGEMENT APPROACH

Should we pave our way to economic decline or should we attempt to reverse recent events and accelerate our economy by injecting yet unused reserves of efficient operational management through the integrated management approach?

The question is how to direct people's efforts into an integrated business system. in order to ensure business stability and competitiveness. This requires developing the means for measuring productivity of any functional unit of an organization. The task, is to acquire the ability to appraise the performance of separate functional units. Often, top executives who compile strategic plans fail to recognize that the execution of their plans on the shop floor plays a major role in the success of these strategic plans.

The emphasis should be on coordinating work centers so that they operate harmoniously in achieving common organizational goals. There is a sense of urgency to develop a generalized methodology, a framework for the integrated systems approach resulting in production of more competitive products. Some needed improvements are already underway. We are witnessing an unprecedented restructuring of American companies in two major areas of their operations: organizational structures and management-labor relations. In the first area, companies compress their organizational structures along with stimulating cross-functional activities; while in the second area, the emphasis is on the employee empowerment—work-force involvement in decision making and taking greater repsonsibility for company performance.

To succeed, American industry should be able to adopt a management approach that addresses present industrial needs for operations control—a standardized production planning and control method capable of benefiting a wide spectrum of manufacturing companies, rather than high-resource organizations only. A concerted effort is required to forge such individual contributions to be able to meet the challenge of the international competition. The question asked is: "Who will take the lead?"

# Acknowledgments

The publication of a contemporary text on production/operations management (POM) requires extensive professional and personal support. Many individuals and organizations extended their extraordinary support throughout all stages of preparation and production of this book.

The author cannot emphasize enough the contribution of the management of the following companies, whose functional systems developments are described in the book:

Dresser Industrial Tool Division; CAMCO, Inc.; Siecor-Keller Corp.; Ruska Instrument Corp.; Presision Mold and Tools; Browning-Ferris Industries; Compaq Computers; ASK Computer Systems; Lotus Development Corp. and Ashton-Tate Corp. My depth of gratitute goes to Professor Wickham Skinner whose encourgaement goes back to before this project was considered, and who has contributed to this book his valuable comments and many suggestions.

Also, I am grateful to the Prentice Hall editorial and production staff, Ruth Mills, Zsuzsa Neff, and Audrey Kopciak who assisted, guided and advised me throughout the preparation and production stages, suggesting many valuable improvements to this book, and produced it on time, despite the sometimes strenuous schedule.

A special appreciation goes to my wife Bella and to my daughter Yolanda, for their willingness to put up with the ordeal of having the husband and father whose primary attention for a long time was detracted from family matters and household commitments.

Along with my wife, who helped me with the graphical part of the book, many thanks go to all my friends, who in so many small ways have assisted and supported me in this endeavor.

Michael Muchnik

# Part One

## ORGANIZATION OF OPERATIONS MANAGEMENT SYSTEMS

# 1

# How to Organize Production Systems: Material Flow and Plant Layout

A production system exists in every private or public enterprise engaged either in manufacturing or the dispensing of services. A production system produces a specific tangible product. A service system provides services to an individual consumer or organizations.

All product information is structured into three categories, corresponding to the three stages of product life: product design, product manufacture, and product use. Figure 1-1 shows the three stages of the product life: product design and product manufacture are the stages of a manufacturing system, while product use is the stage in the product life when the consumer utilizes the product.

Products can be in one of these three states: fabrication, transportation, or storage. Three types of capital production resources correspond to the three states of production:

1. *Plant and machinery* serve the production stage
2. *Transport* and *material handling equipment* serve the transportation stage
3. *Storage facilities* serve the need for storing semiproducts during intermediate stages of production and warehousing a final product.

Any analysis of production systems involves the examination of production processes. A process is a predetermined sequence of actions instrumental in achieving the desired output. Two groups of processes present in any productive

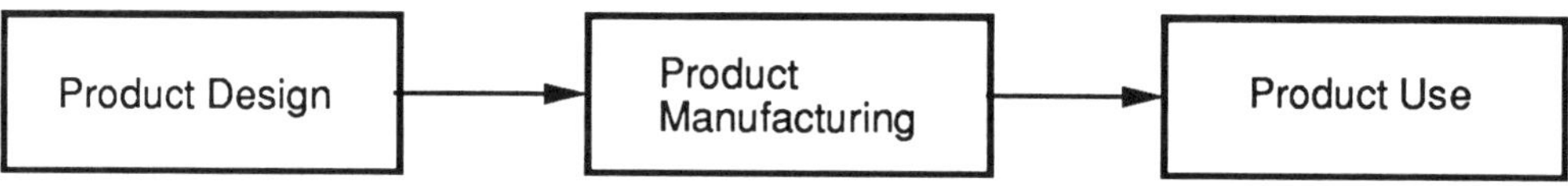


**A. Three Stages of Product Life**

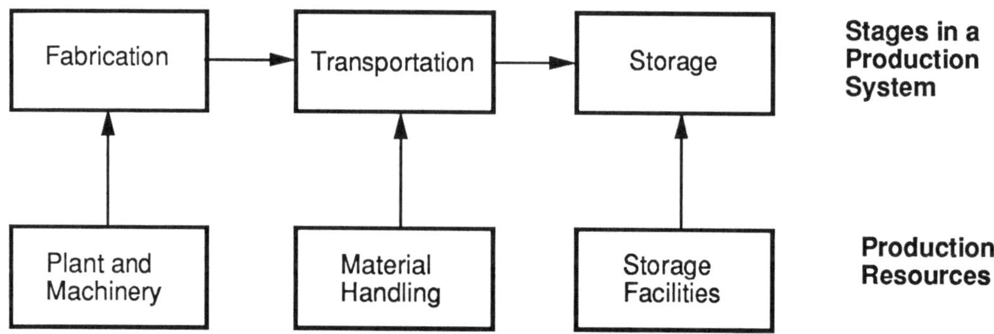


**B. Three Stages of Production Systems**

**Figure 1-1**
**Three Types of Capital Resources Serving Three Stages of a Production System**

system are primary processes and secondary processes. A production system comprises *primary* or *line processes* directly involved in producing the specialty of a firm, whether it is a tangible product or a service and *secondary* or *service processes,* providing service to production.

Primary processes are represented by

- *Forming processes,* such as casting, forging, stamping, rolling and extrusion
- *Machining processes*, such as removing metals, machine shop production, boring, milling, turning, drilling, planing, and grinding
- *Joining and assembly processes*, including the assembly of parts and components applying mechanical joining, welding, and soldering
- *Finishing processes,* such as painting, electroplating, and galvanizing

- *Heat treating processes*, such as hardening and annealing
- *Nonmetal industries processes*, such as plastic and woodworking

The production function is accompanied by a wide range of business activities, such as forecasting, sales, marketing, engineering services, finance, purchasing, capacity planning and production control, supervisory management, personnel, and labor relations. These service processes are further classified into

- *Clerical processes*, such as those applied in office type operations which often interrelate with other service-type processes
- *Expert-advisory processes*, such as professional services supporting primary production functions, which require high degree of specialization, for example, engineering, legal services, laboratory
- *Maintenance processes*, which differ from professional services in that they involve manual operations or the use of tools or machines

Some service processes grow into autonomous service systems.

It is important to pay attention to the distinction in production processes, because of the differences in supervision and the distinctive features of planning and control. For example, planning and control of machining processes, which are conventionally accepted as *job shop production*, are essentially different from the assembly processes known as *line production*.

A manufacturing system should also take into account the difference in managing primary processes and service processes in various types of production.

## CLASSIFYING PRODUCTION SYSTEMS

Production systems are classified according to

1. Category of produced products
2. End product type and quantity
3. Type of a producer-customer relationship

### Classifying Productive Systems According to Category of Produced Products

According to produced products or services, productive systems are further broken down into four categories:

1. Manufacturing systems
2. Process industry productive systems
3. Services systems

4. Project systems

Material flow in manufacturing, process industry, and projects are identified as *productive flow*. The productive flow in manufacturing is a flow of materials. In services, it is a flow of services. As far as operations management is concerned, the dissimilarities of manufacturing processes, services, construction, and projects are blurred because a similar operational productive flow is present in all of these applications. Nevertheless, due to their dissimilarities, all categories of productive systems require distinctively different production planning and control approaches.

## THE MANUFACTURING SYSTEMS

*Manufacturing systems* refer to productive systems where a number of materials and semiproducts are assembled into finished products. Engineering-type production, such as a production line or an assembly line, are examples of manufacturing. Manufacturing is also known as synthetic production, a type of production engaged in production of discrete products. Unless there is mass production of selected few products, such production systems are referred to as *job shop*.

## THE PROCESS INDUSTRY PRODUCTIVE SYSTEMS

The term *process industry* usually refers to continuous production lines producing fluid materials, such as petrochemicals, or production lines producing bulk materials or continuous sheets such as steel, plastics, and paper.

In process industry, raw material is transformed into component parts and ingredients. Petroleum refineries are an example of such a production system. In petroleum refineries, crude oil is processed into various products: gases, motor fuels, kerosene, gas oil, diesel fuel, fuel oil, and a number of by-products used in the production of asphalt and plastic materials.

Process industry production systems are often characterized as analytical production. In most applications, analytic production produces flow products. An analytic conversion process begins with relatively few raw materials, which are broken down into a variety of end products. Manufacturing and process types of productive systems are illustrated in Figure 1-2.

## SERVICE SYSTEMS

*Service systems* do not produce a tangible product; instead there is a service to a customer, such as with retail stores and health care organizations. The distinction of such productive systems is in the involvement of a customer in planning and executing service operations. There is no inventory in service systems, and thus services planning should accommodate increases and declines in demand, often on an hourly basis.

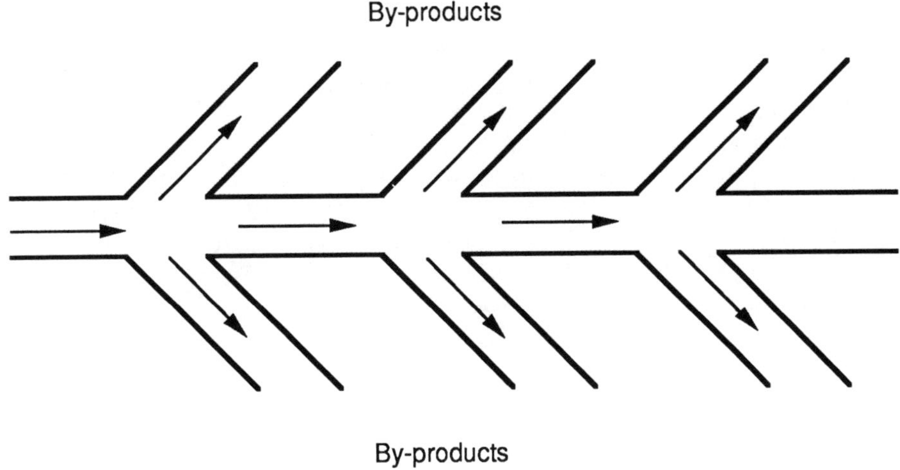


**A. Process Type Production -- an Analytical Production System**

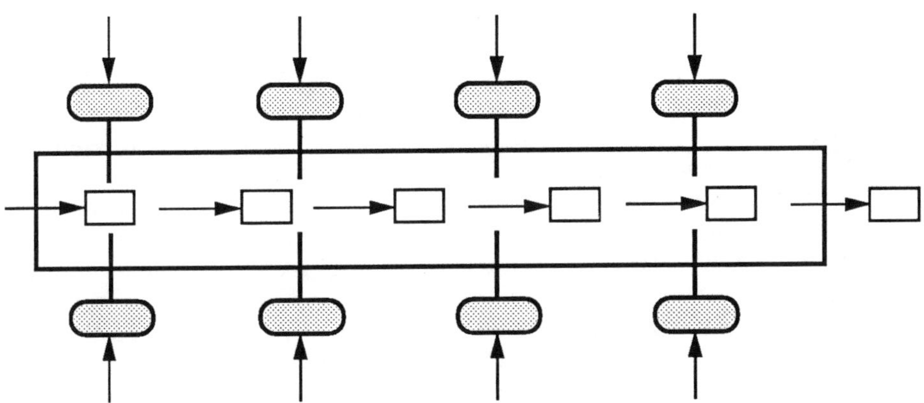


**B. Manufacturing System -- Synthetic Production**

**Figure 1-2**
**Synthetic and Analytic Production**

PROJECT SYSTEMS

*Projects* include a type of production where the frequency of orders is one-off—each project has a unique end product which is never repeated again in the same product form and organizational structure. In reality, few productive systems feature only one type of production or service. For example, fast-food organizations, such as McDonald's, feature both production of food products and serving these products to an end user. Conversely, pure manufacturing systems include many services of a technical, engineering, and clerical nature, similar to projects which involve many production and service activities. Consequently, production planning and control systems must take into account the mix of various categories of productive systems.

## Classifying Production Systems According to End Product Type and Quantity

End products are classified according to the *type of products* (engineering, electronics, food processing, rubber, and paper) and the *degree of standardization* of the product:

- A *standard product* is a product with options, which is produced to customer specification, run on established production lines.
- A *nonstandard product* is a custom-made product with a number of options or a product engineered to customer specifications: engineer-to-order production.

*An order quantity* is one of the primary characteristics of production systems shaping a material flow and configuring planning and control. Diverse production systems, such as lot production, batch production, and jobbing, call for distinct production planning and control systems.

Often companies elect to manufacture both standard and nonstandard products, each one calling for a different planning and control system. For best results, planning and control of different products should be reconciled within an integrated production planning and control system. In practical terms, this calls for an additional customization of standard manufacturing computer-based systems, such as master production scheduling (MPS) and material requirements planning (MRP).

## Classifying Production Systems According to Producer-Customer Relationship

Depending on a specific producer-customer interrelationship, namely, how the production orders are initiated (order intake), there are two basic types of production systems: open shop and closed shop.

An *open shop* is open for outside customer orders. This type is also called *make-to-order* or *assemble-to-order* production. A *closed shop* is closed for individual customer orders. This type is also called *make-to-stock* production.

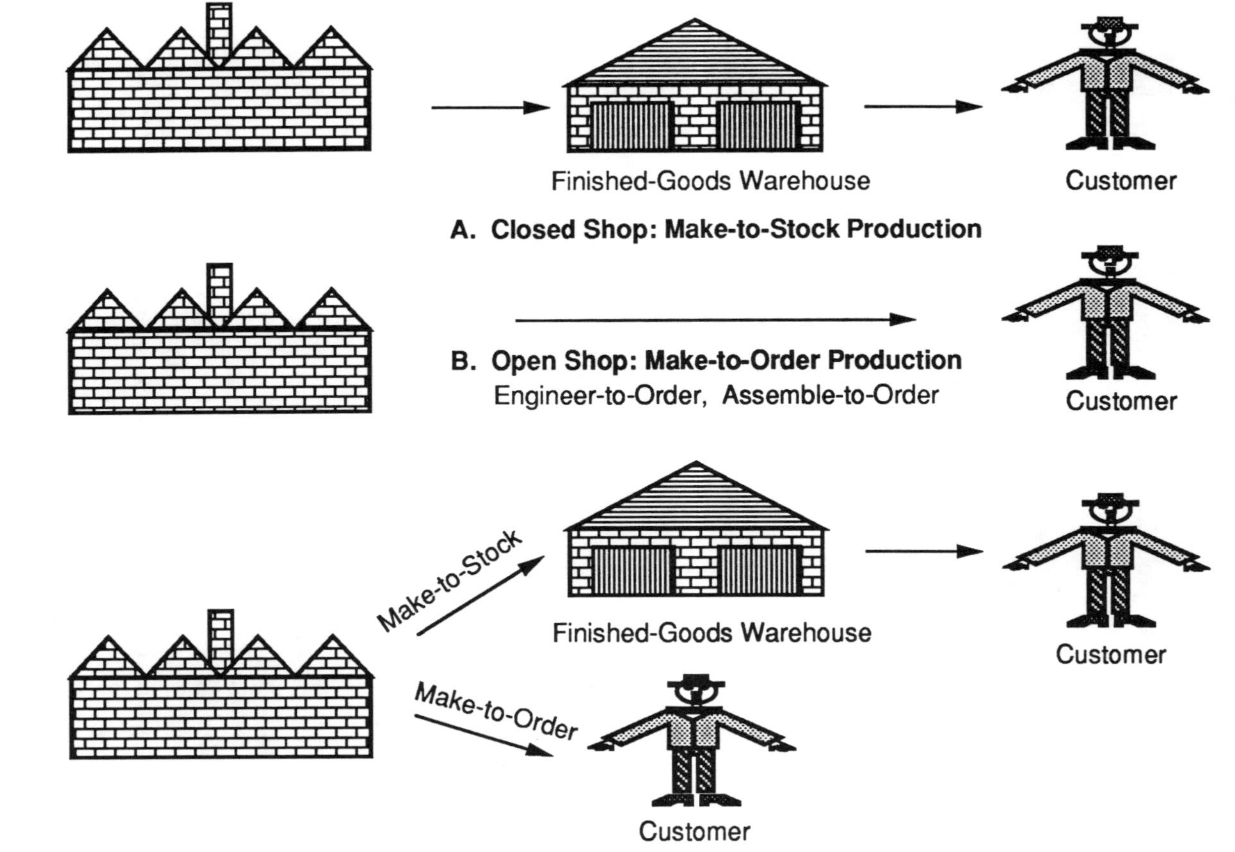


**Figure 1-3**
**Types of Production-Customer Relationships**

Here, production is initiated by the long-term and midterm plan, and the production output is placed in inventory.

A closed shop does not necessarily mean that individual customer orders are not accepted. A customer order can be satisfied from the inventory. The main condition considered in identifying a closed shop is how a customer order affects the current production program. In a closed shop, an individual customer order has a negligible impact on the production plan: the inventory acts as a buffer.

The type of a production system prescribes production planning and control: in an open shop, production control over a material flow is emphasized, while in a closed shop, production control is focused at inventory control. Closed shop companies applying inventory-based production control find themselves in a difficult position when they send a customer order to production. Production control over such a customer order can interfere with the established in such companies inventory-based planning and control procedures.

Often, companies do not have a strictly open shop or closed shop, which means that they are accepting individual customer orders which are satisfied through inventory, or, depending on the stock position, these orders can be placed directly with production. These types of production systems are classified as a *generic shop*. Such companies are not able to restrict their planning and control to only one type material flow control or inventory level control. In reality, such a manufacturing application requires a hybrid of the two planning and control systems—inventory control based and material control based—which is more complex than any one of these two types of planning systems. Three types of producer-customer relationships are illustrated in Figure 1-3.

## THE THREE STAGES OF MATERIAL FLOW

A material flow is organized in stages structured around assembly lines, depending upon their relationship to the final product, as shown in Figure 1-4. These include the components production stage (stage 1), the components assembly stage (stage 2), and the final assembly (stage 3). Each stage of production is conducted at different types of production units, namely, job shop–type and line production, and therefore there is a different type of material flow.

There are three main types of material flow—continuous, intermittent, and stationary assembly, each of which is illustrated in Figure 1-5.

1. *A continuous material flow* is organized for a standardized product with high-quantity, repetitive orders. A material flow is unidirectional and uninterrupted by other jobs. A continuous material flow is typical to process production.

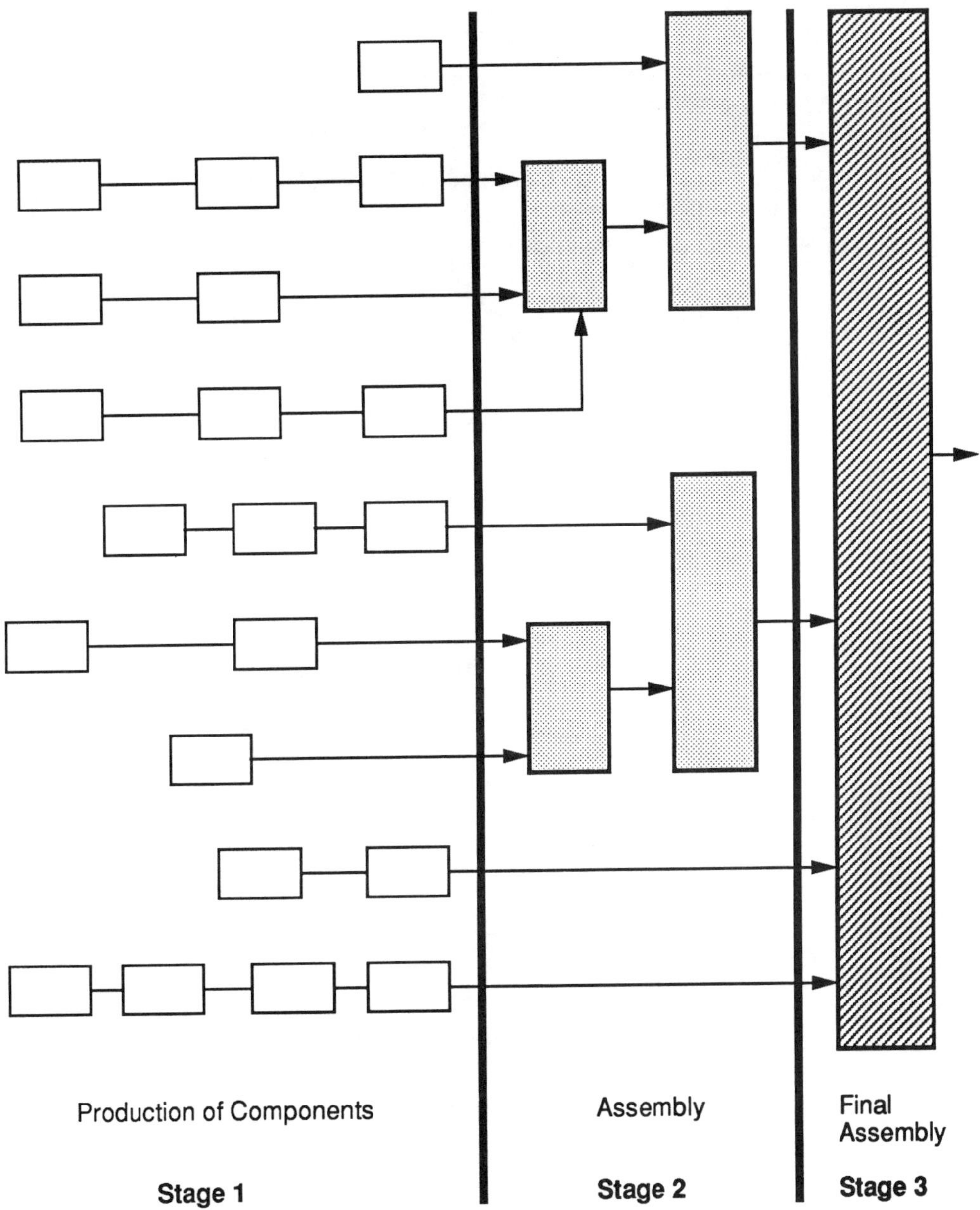


**Figure 1-4**
**The Three Stages of Material Flow in Productive Systems**

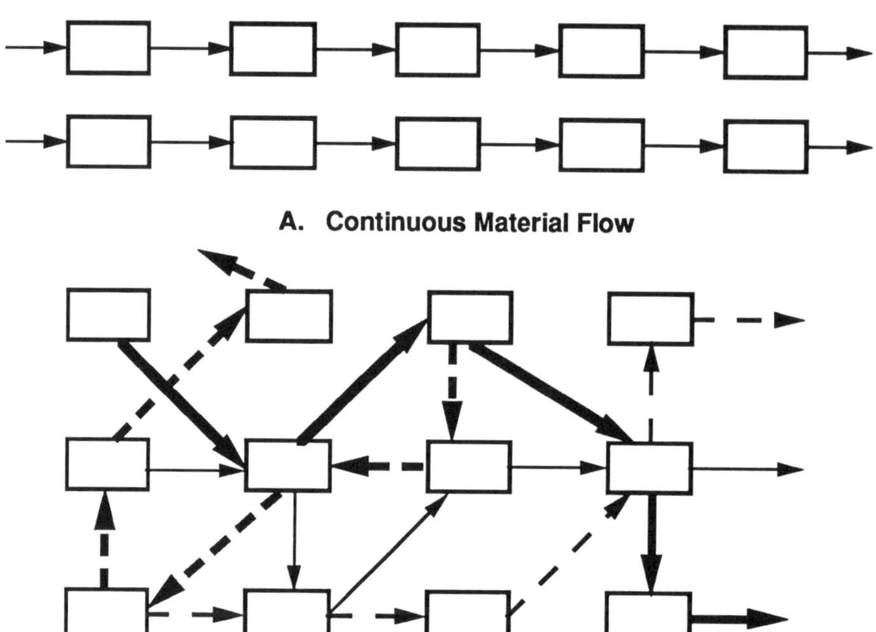


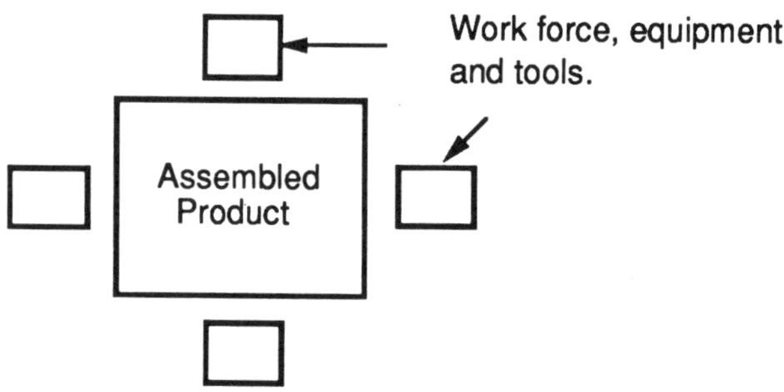


C. Stationary Assembly

**Figure 1-5**
**The Types of Material Flow**

2. *An intermittent material flow* is a job shop–type operation producing small quantities to a customer order. An intermittent material flow is synonymous with job shop production. Continuous production systems usually yield lower unit costs than intermittent systems.

3. *Stationary assembly* is used in production of bulk and heavy products, such as sea liners and airplanes, which otherwise is not possible to place on moving assembly lines.

The majority of manufacturing companies feature more than one type of material flow, the so-called *mixed flow production.* The listed features of production and a material flow are interrelated in that various product quantities call for a different material flow type and for a different production cycle and phases, discussed in the next section.

## ORDERING AND PRODUCTION CYCLES AND PHASES

A *cycle* is defined as the time period elapsed between two orders. A *phase* defines how ordering cycles of product components correspond to each other. *Single-phase ordering* means that components are ordered in corresponding quantities to satisfy a specific customer order. *Multiphase ordering* means that components are ordered in economic order quantities or according to individual components stock position.

An ordering phase and cycle are shown in Figure 1-6. In the first case, components A, B, and C are ordered in uniform cycles—order frequency and the uniform phase of orders—meaning that all components cycles correspond due to the fact that these components are required by assembly processes at the same time. In the second case, there is a discord in ordering cycles of components A, B, and C, which means that ordering is out of phase, namely, multiphase ordering. The first case is typical to make-to-order production systems where components are ordered to satisfy specific customer order; the second case is typical to assemble-to-order production, where production of components is inventory bound.

Figure 1-7 exhibits single-cycle and multicycle ordering situations. Single-cycle ordering is typical to make-to-stock situations, whereas multicycle is used in make-to-order applications.

Figure 1-8 exhibits the relationship between an ordering cycle and a production cycle. The uniformity of an ordering cycle and a production cycle is observed in continuous production. By contrast, it takes a major effort to relate the ordering stage to the production stage in job shop production.

The variance of the ordering cycle and the production cycle takes place, due to an intermittent material flow which causes a variability in the ordering phase and the production phase, as well as a buildup inventory and delayed assembly processes. These variances are attributed to the deficiency in production planning and production control.

An ordering cycle and a phase are major variables affecting a material flow. For example, one producer of automotive components, being an identical

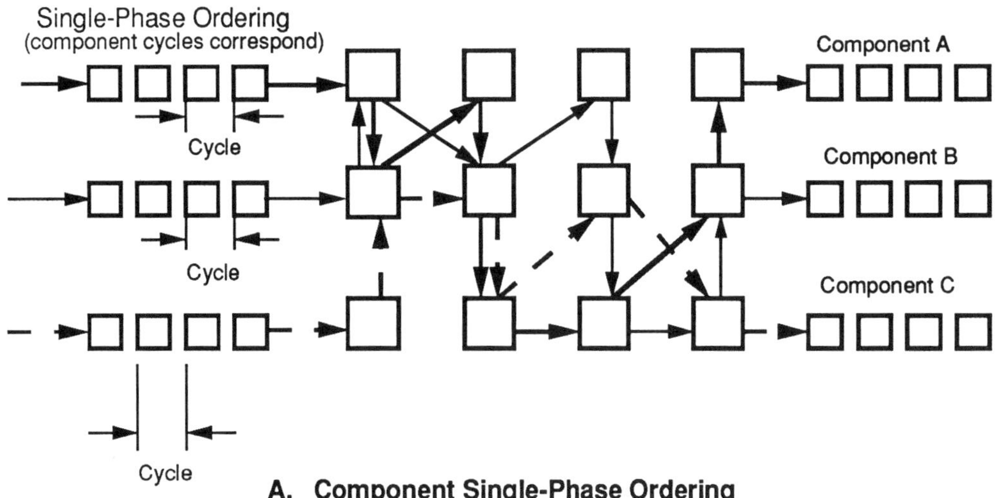


**A. Component Single-Phase Ordering**

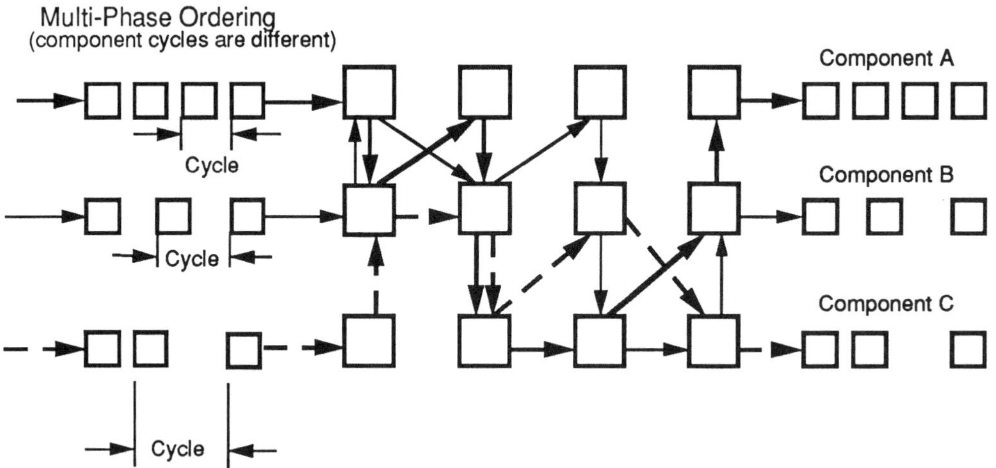


**B. Component Multi-Phase Ordering**

**Figure 1-6**
**Cycle and Phase Ordering**

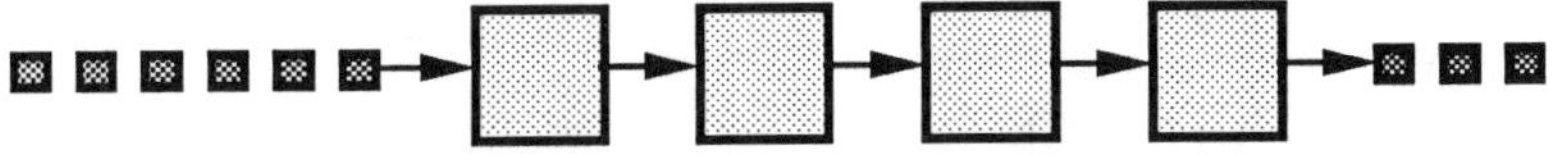

**A. Components Ordered In a Single-Cycle**

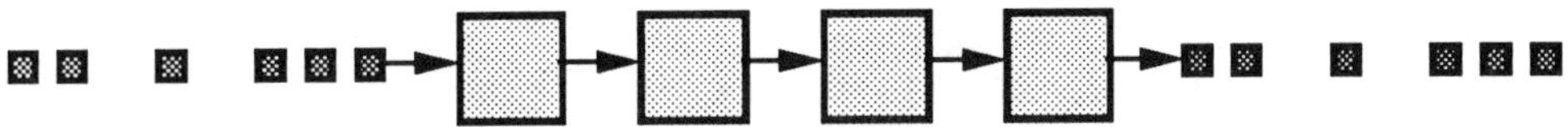

**B. Components Ordered In a Multi-Cycle**

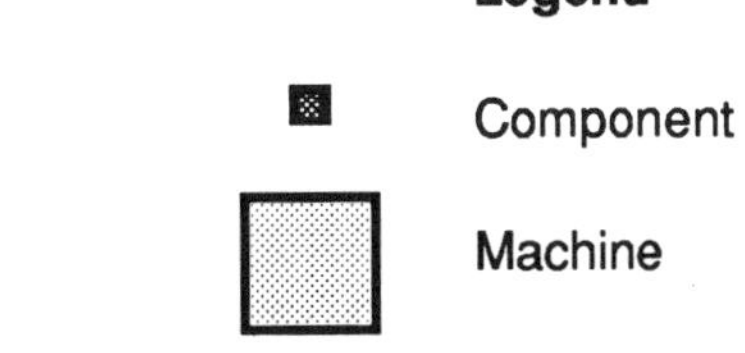


**Figure 1-7**
**Cycle Ordering**

twin company to its overseas holding company (same products, drawings and specifications, production technology, equipment, and even plant layout) found to his surprise that the computer-based planning and control package that the firm hoped to utilize did not work. The author has been involved in investigating such a phenomenon and has found that all the conditions being equal, the ordering cycle and phase were different, due to the smaller size of production orders. Thus such a seemingly insignificant difference changed the production system to the extent that the production planning and control programs required modification.

The lesson to be learned is the following: you should pay attention to the characteristics and differences of the ordering and production cycle as well as to the ordering and production phase.

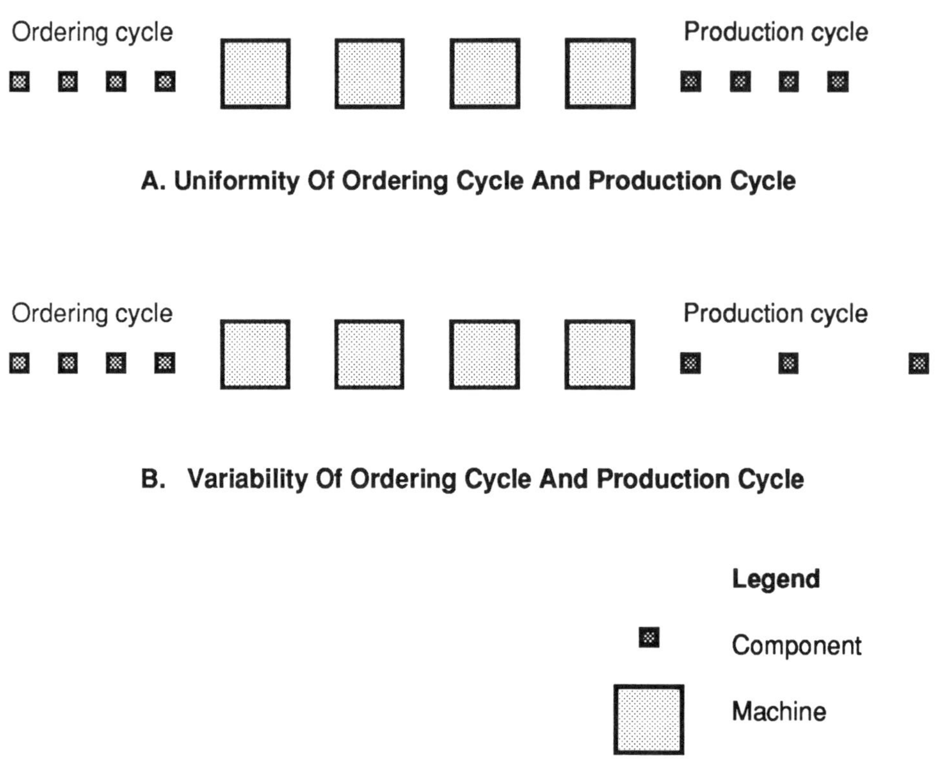


**Figure 1-8**
**The Relationship Between the Ordering Cycle and the Production Cycle**

## PLANNING FOR PREPRODUCTION

Production flow, the essence of an operation system, is a sequence of events in space and time during which a value-adding transformation of resources into finished products takes place. A production system is a framework of activities relating a production flow to the material, information, and human efforts. Productive systems are designed before a firm starts production. This management function is called *preproduction planning.*

Decisions made at the preproduction system design stage relate to the plant layout, material handling, information systems, planning and control systems, and human factors. The foundation of the highest productivity of production units is laid at this stage of production planning. It includes the product consideration and an analysis related to the type, quantity, and quality of product and the desired degree of automation within the limits of available financial resources. The material flow should be examined, in regard to the elements affecting this flow: queueing, stores, material handling, and operational scheduling and expediting practices.

The design of a productive system is an ongoing process that requires a continuous redesign effort and improvement on product quality and cost reduction. The system enhancement is achieved through better planning and effective control over the material flow, and through the coordination of manufacturing activities.

Just-in-Time continuous improvement programs discussed in Chapters 8 through Chapter 11 are a perfect example of the lead time reduction due to reduction and even elimination of queueing, storage time, material handling, and expediting.

## MAKING EFFICIENT PRODUCT DECISIONS

### Start With a Good Product Design

Production means producing goods or services for a customer. Production starts with product design. Customer needs are identified, and a plan is devised to create a quality product to be delivered to the customer. Thus *product design* is the first stage or operation in the product development and production.

The design stage of a product, as is the manufacturing stage, is aimed at the continuous improvement of the product value. The product design is an iterative process in improvement of the product's functions, appearance, durability, and, certainly, from the point of view of the productive system, the quality improvement and cost reduction.

Often, designers see their task accomplished with the commencement of regular production of the product, and they seldom return to examine and audit the design. Due to the continuity in the development of a product, a product value improvement through the improvement in product design should be considered throughout the life of the product.

A study of the U.S. industrial performance conducted by a distinguished group of experts from the Massachusetts Institute of Technology reveals that many U.S. companies fail to coordinate the product design and the manufacturing process. The observation is that it is a standard practice for design engineers to end their involvement with a new product once they have accomplished its design. They hand over the design to manufacturing engineers, who are then supposed to come up with the process for the product's manufacture. The study concludes that such a segmentation of tasks has led to serious problems. Product-design groups often neglect manufacturing considerations.

In comparison, Japanese engineers design the product concurrently with production processes, and they are involved in maintaining product and process design throughout the product's life. Benefits from such an approach are substantial, since design determines about half the product's controllable cost. Callie Berliner of Arthur Andersen & Co. reveals that product planning and product design combined (the cost incurred before production of a new product commences) are responsible for 95 percent of product life-cycle cost. The designers' ultimate function is a synergistic contribution to the development of the product so that the customer is satisfied with the product value received.

Design is part of a production process, as exhibited in Figure 1-9. It commences with the detected need for a product and continues throughout the product life. The design is depicted as part of the product *lead time*, defined as the time a customer discovered the need for the product through the time the product is delivered to the customer. Thus, a reduction of time required for design and development reduces the lead time and enhances the effectiveness of an organization. The same study of MIT professors reveals that American car builders have been taking about five years to carry a new design from the conceptual stage to the commercial introduction, whereas Japanese manufacturers complete the cycle in three and a half years.

It is realized that the best product ideas are coming from listening to customers. This includes the considerations of consumer preference along with the considerations of available resources. The greatest value of a product comes as a result of matching these two concepts—consumer needs and available resources.

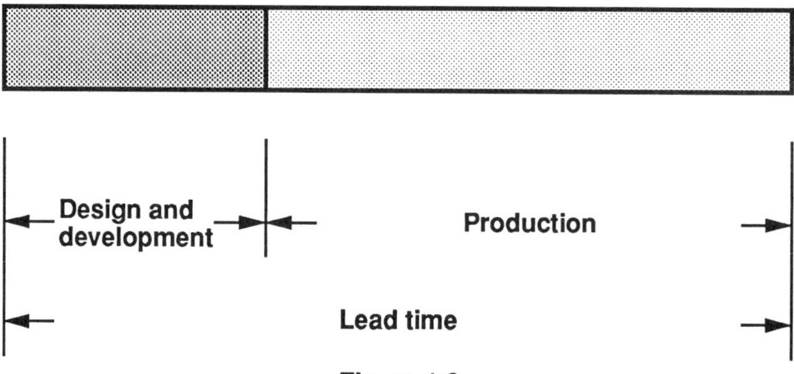


**Figure 1-9**
**Product Design Is Part of Product's Lead Time**

The value of a product is constantly changing due to the competition and changing consumer preferences and fads. Hence the designer's task is to update continuously the product value, revising and auditing the initial design. The revision of design takes advantage of rapidly changing production and improvements in industrial processes. The designer's task is to increase the product value by improving the quality and reducing the production cost.

Design is a production function. Designers should take a keen interest in how the product value is created by production throughout the product's life. For example, it was found that Japanese automotive engineers had incorporated quality—enhancing features into the design itself, to the extent that the product quality, to some degree, tolerates variability in the manufacturing process.

The concept of product value recognizes that the value is created by combined efforts of all functions and services involved in production of a product, each function or service contributing synergistically to this business objective. The synergy in marketing, product design, and production presents an unmatched opportunity for constant improvements in the product value.

## Using Product Information

Product information is structured based on three stages of the product life:

1. Product description
2. Product manufacturing information
3. After sale information

### PRODUCT DESCRIPTION

A *product description* consists of graphical and descriptive information concerning the final appearance of a product. Design drawings giving two-dimensional views of the product and its components and assembly drawings giving an exploded view of the assembly unit showing its component parts, schemes, and blueprints—all are part of the product description. Specifications, product description or composition, and batch ingredients should all be set forth in the product description.

### PRODUCT MANUFACTURING INFORMATION

*Product manufacturing information* includes:

- Production standards and information for quality control inspections
- Information required for production planning:

  Bill of materials

  Route sheet

  Operation process charts and

  Flow process charts

**Bill of Materials** *The bill of materials* (BOM) is a list of components required in order to produce an assembled product. BOM presents parts and components the way they are related in the product's structure—divided into levels or stages of assembly. A BOM has two formats: an explosion type and an implosion type.

An *explosion BOM* is a breakdown of a top-level assembly into its constituent parts—subassemblies, parts, and components. An *implosion BOM* is the reverse: it shows the usage of parts. A BOM can contain such information as total quantities per product as well as a component's highest level, when such a component goes into several assemblies. Other formats for BOM are a single-level bill of materials, an indented bill of materials, and an indented-where-used bill of materials.

- *A single-level bill of material* shows the relationship at one level down—only those components required in a parent item.
- *An indented bill of material* explodes different levels in bill of materials by indenting them from left to right of the margin.
- *An indented-where-used bill of material* lists a parent item for a single component and all other product assemblies where this component is used, as well as all the assemblies where the parent items are used, and so on until the ultimate level zero is reached, along with the quantity of the component that each parent-level assembly calls for.

**Route Sheet** A route sheet provides information about processing individual parts. Individual operations are specified in the sequence the material flows. A route sheet is compiled for each individual part. A route sheet includes information for product identification—part number, part description, drawing number, material, description of operations, departments and work centers, machines performing the operations, and basic information about these machines, such as the repair priority level, alternative routes, tools, and standard run time and setup time.

**Operation Process Chart** An operation process chart is a graphic representation of operations and inspections carried out during the manufacturing process. This chart shows the material flow step by step, showing how material is introduced into the process, and assists in the visual assessment of operations, starting with the initial one through the final operation in an assembly.

An operations process chart shows operations, such as quality inspections, but excludes material handling. An operation process chart includes information required for planning, such as time standards, type of equipment, and its location. Along with the route sheet, an operation process chart contains essential information required for planning.

### INFORMATION ASSISTING IN THE PRODUCT USE

The mission of serving a customer continues after a product is sold, during and after the warranty period. Product specifications, unpacking instructions, warranties, service instructions, and maintenance schedules assist in the after-sale service of the product.

### Using Process Information

Process information is divided into two categories: information describing a process unit and information required for planning.

#### INFORMATION DESCRIBING PROCESS UNITS

Process information about production lines, conveyors, and individual machines includes the description of equipment and information required for maintenance, such as service instructions, maintenance schedules, maintenance job specifications, and so on (this information is discussed in Chapter 15). This information includes the factory register, descriptions of production lines, maintenance instructions, and manuals.

#### INFORMATION REQUIRED FOR RELATING PROCESS TO PRODUCT

This is information about the availability of equipment—the available capacity. For example, the summary of the available capacity is shown for the duration of 3 to 4 months at weekly intervals. The capacity is calculated per machine center in each department in the form of a list of resources or as a capacity matrix.

## DETERMINING THE ORGANIZATION STRUCTURE OF PRODUCTION OPERATIONS

The management mission in a firm is the task of organization and supervision as well as assisting in an effective and uninterrupted transformation process. In manufacturing, people and facilities make up a company. Here, an organization means a deliberate grouping of people and facilities established to accomplish goals and objectives of the enterprise. Organizing, as a management activity, includes identifying the functions necessary for achieving these goals and objectives.

An organization is a structural framework of line departments, service departments, and administrative units, a blend of human and material resources enabling a business to function as an integrated unit. Managers control operating results of an organization by developing teamwork, achieving efficient performance, and reducing the operating cost.

*An organizational structure* involves establishing a formal structure of authority and responsibilities built around the company's major functions—production, marketing, finance, and administration. In an organization, these functions are broken down into various departments and work centers—organizational hierarchical structure.

An organizational structure is the manner in which the entire company resources are organized into the business units—a hierarchy of divisions, departments, work centers, and organizational levels of authorities and responsibilities.

Setting organizational structures, sometimes called simply organizing, involves choosing the technology, the degree of automation, the departmentalization, the job design and plant layout as well as how the plant and equipment are assigned among various production units, and how these production units are integrated. Also, organizing envisages an operational relationship among people with the various degree of authority. This is the framework through which the strategic, tactical, and operational objectives can be accomplished. Organizing is performed in two stages—tactical and operative.

*Tactical* organizing involves setting up an organizational structure of business and productive units comprising human and material resources. These business and productive units are divisions, departments, and work centers. Divisions are defined as multifunctional business units involving more than one business activity. Examples are production, marketing, finance, and administration. Some business activities can be shared by two or more divisions (e.g., marketing or some administrative services). *Departments* are functional units specializing in the performance of a single business function. These units comprise human and material resources performing a single business function (e.g., production, purchasing, and accounting). *Work centers* are business units involving human and material resources performing a specialized activity of a single business function (e.g., an inspection center, an assembly line, receiving and shipping department, tooling shop).

*Organizing material resources* involves setting up plant, equipment, and labor force into productive units within departments and work centers. Organizing operative production units, also known as *operative organizing,* includes setting up a labor-machine production unit—the basic production unit—and establishing the plant layout (discussed further in this chapter). Existing organizational structures come under the scrutiny in new manufacturing systems as part of cost reduction programs. Each company requires its own customized organizational structure.

## TYPES OF ORGANIZATIONAL STRUCTURES

### How Divisions Are Organized

An organization is a dynamic entity which is changing constantly. Designing an organization is not a goal in itself. The mission of an organization is to facilitate the transformation process and the exchange of goods or services. Organizing is a pragmatic segmentation of human and material resources into productive units, according to their relationship to the transformation process.

Organizing, defined as putting an organization in place, is a management function of designing, developing, maintaining, and improving organizational structures. Like any planning function, organizing is an ongoing process of changing and improving.

Large multilocation and multiproduct companies are structured around business divisions according to the following principles:

- The function the company performs
- The market it serves
- The product it produces

***Division according to functions*** The divisions are set according to the functional business relationship: production, finance, marketing, administration, and services divisions.

***Division according to market served*** The divisions are set according to the location and customers served or are structured to take advantage of the existing distribution channels. Such organizations stay closer to the customer and, therefore, are able to provide a better service. The division according to the location of a business unit is a convenient way to separate it as an autonomous business unit or a cost center. The division according to market can result in the suboptimized use of resources and the duplication of efforts by various divisions in an organization, both technical and advisory services (e.g., personnel, R&D, finance, accounting, marketing, and distribution).

***Division according to product*** This is made on the basis of major products or product lines produced by the company. Such division results in simplified coordination, since all the expertise, know-how, and human skills in the product design and production are organized under the common management. The specialization leads to the proficiency and constant improvements. An important factor is defined as the relationship between the authority and responsibilities. Decision making is improved, since the managers are both physically and organizationally close to the productive lines. The accountability is apparent here, and productivity and efficiency figures are easy to define. The disadvantages include a "clannish attitude" created by such division and a competition for resources between the divisions. Such division also inhibits the vision of organizational objectives—the managers' vision of an organization is centered around their respective products. Organization according to product, where people deal with one product or product type, contributes to a self-centered attitude, as managers tend to overemphasize the contribution of their respective products to the accomplishment of total organizational objectives. Such organization increases the product cost due to the need for dedicated service units and functional specialists in divisions.

Structural arrangements of product-focused and process-focused organizations are illustrated in Figure 1-10.

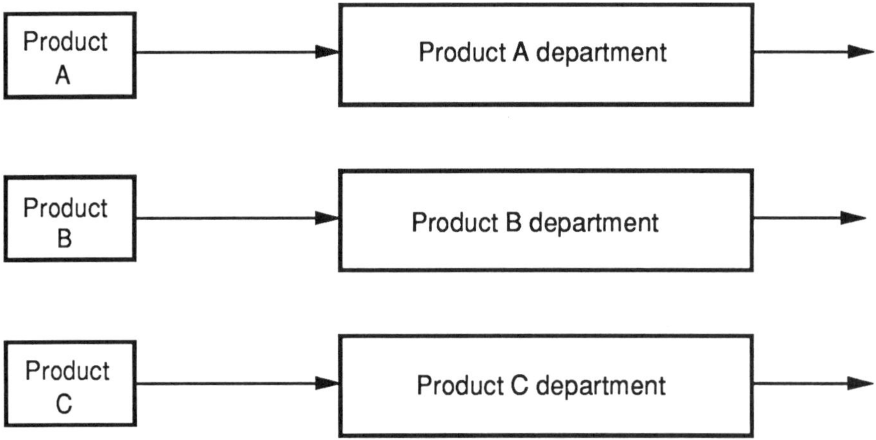


**A. Product-Focused Organization**

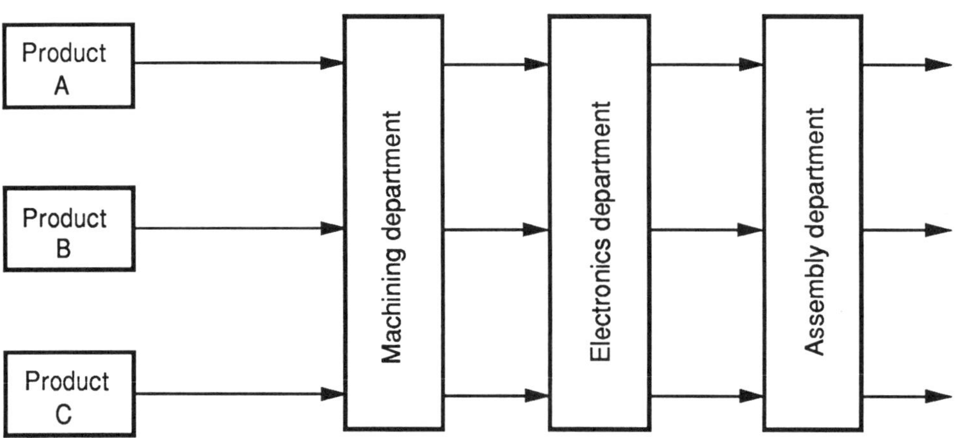


**B. Process-Focused Organization**

**Figure 1-10**
**Product-Focused and Process-Focused Organizations**

## Organizing Departments and Work Centers According to Product and Process

The next level in organizational structures is the subdivision of business divisions into departments. There are two principles applied in departmentalization: according to process or according to product. Product or process orientation significantly affects production planning and control, management and personnel, production services, financial services and cost accounting, vendor relations, and distribution. A process-focused organization is structured around different functional units or processes, namely, production and service departments that serve a variety of different products.

### FUNCTIONAL DEPARTMENTALIZATION

The division according to process is known as *functional departmentalization*. Functional departmentalization is defined as the function a specific unit (it can be a department or a work center) performs in the production process. People with the common expertise are grouped together. This results in a better specialization in technical areas of expertise and in the efficient problem solving.

Products undergo processing in different functional units, under different authorities and responsibilities (line and function responsibility). A process-focused organization is a multifunctional organization in which priority is assigned to organizing processes, usually at a significant capital cost.

Management in a process-focused organization is heavily involved in coordinating a multifunctional material flow and logistics between production units due to the fact that nobody in particular is responsible for individual products or customer orders.

The functional departmentalization significantly complicates planning and control, increases the interdepartmental production flow and the accompanying flow of information, and increases the need for communication and coordination. Above all, the functional departmentalization decreases the accountability for the timely completion of products or services, due to the complex job tracking and complex productivity analysis.

Along with the planning function, the cost accounting function constitutes a major task of centralized management in a process-focused organization. The total product cost can vary due to production units being structured according to cost responsibility and longer production cycle time.

The advantages are similar to those of the division according to function. There is a narrow specialization contributing to efficiency improvement through better utilization of equipment and human skills.

### PRODUCT DEPARTMENTALIZATION

The departmentalization according to product simplifies the coordination in an organization and improves decision making because the authority in a product organization is highly decentralized and decisions are made closer to production lines. Production planning and control are significantly improved, inventory is reduced, and product quality is highlighted in a product-focused organization. There is a tight rein over the product cost and profit, due to the fact that departments are often organized as profit centers, with the responsibilities well defined. Profit or return on investments are routinely estimated. Such organization requires less initial capital outlay.

## HOW DEPARTMENTS RELATE TO THE PRODUCTION PROCESS

The departmentalization according to the relationship to a production process concerns departments which are organized into line departments—*primary departments* and service units or *secondary departments.*

*Line departments* are organizational units directly engaged in production of the business specialty, either a specific product or a service. These departments are regarded as the primary ones. There are three types of line departments: functional departments, production departments, and assembly departments. *Functional departments* do not produce completed components. Instead, they perform one or several operations on these components. Usually, functional departments perform a specific function, a single process, or type of production operation, such as milling department, forging department, extrusion, annealing, or painting department. *Production departments* produce completed components for an assembly, and *assembly departments* engage in assembling these components. Three types of line departments are engaged in different types of operations requiring different planning and control approaches. A production planning and control system should take into consideration such differences in production units, since these units are involved in different stages of production: functional and production departments are involved in the stage 1 production of components, while assembly departments are responsible for components assembly and the final assembly, stages 2 and 3 in the material flow (refer to Figure 1-4).

*Service departments* do not contribute directly to production of a product but, rather, serve the line departments. Service departments such as industrial engineering, R & D, or plant maintenance are also known as *secondary departments.* There are two categories of service departments: departments providing service to line departments and departments providing service to management.

*Service to line departments* are service departments that are assigned specific duties, such as plant maintenance, quality control, purchasing, material handling, wharehousing, and engineering. *Service to management departments* are departments that provide assistance for decision making. These departments are divided into three categories:

1. *Advisory service departments*—serving as groups of specialists assisting in decision making and having little or no authority (i.e., legal, public relations, and labor relations departments).

2. *Control and coordination departments*—providing advice, such as production planning and control departments and quality control departments, with various degree of authority in an organization.

3. *Administrative departments*—having authority over what they are doing. These are personnel, budgeting, and accounting departments. Later in the text, services to line departments will be referred to as the production services, while services to management decision makers will be referred to as the administrative-clerical services.

## HOW TO ORGANIZE OPERATIVE PRODUCTION UNITS

### Designing a Plant Layout

A layout is the way in which machines, equipment, labor, services, and materials are divided among the divisions, departments, and work centers in an enterprise. A layout involves planning of production facilities so as to minimize the costs of processing, material handling, and storing.

There are two types of plant layout: overall *interdepartmental* and work centers layout, which largely depends on the organizational structure and the products produced, and *intradepartmental* layout, reflecting the way the equipment is arranged within a single department.

There are four types of plant layout:

1. Line layout
2. Functional layout
3. Group layout
4. Fixed position layout

These are arranged in two groups: product-focused layout and process-focused layout. The functional type layout belongs to a process-focused layout category. Product-focused layouts are line layout, group layout, and fixed position layout.

### Using a Process-Focused Layout

#### THE FUNCTIONAL LAYOUT

In the functional layout, identical types of machines are positioned together. In an example of functional layout applied in a machine shop, exhibited in Figure 1-11, all lathes are together, all milling machines, drilling machines, welding machines and presses are together, also the equipment and labor required for assembly processes are grouped into one work area. A functional layout is regarded as a general type layout, practical in producing a variety of products.

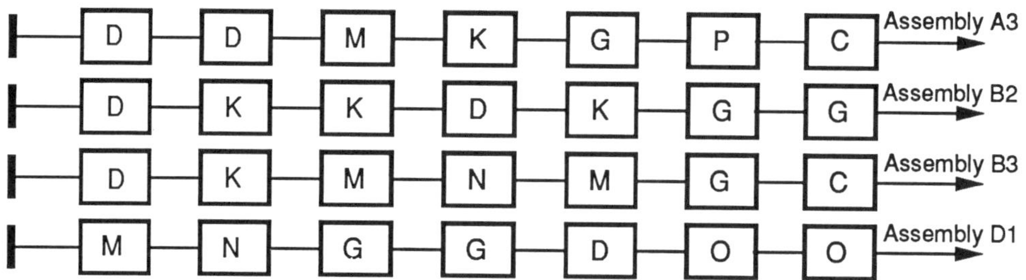


**A. Line Production - Continuous Material Flow**

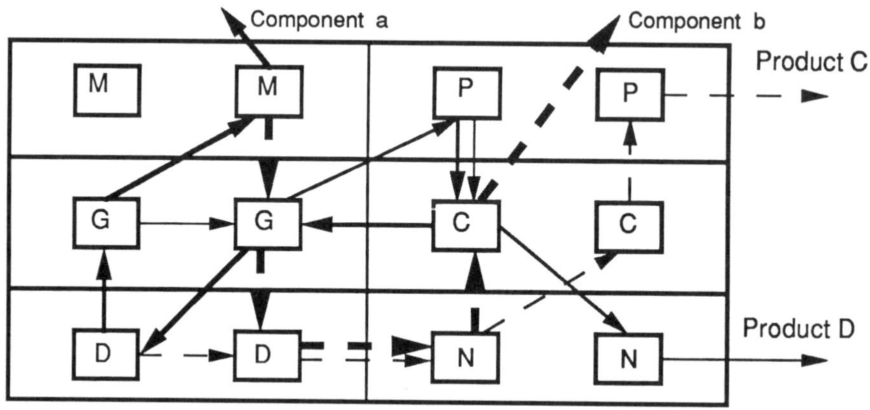


**B. Functional Layout**

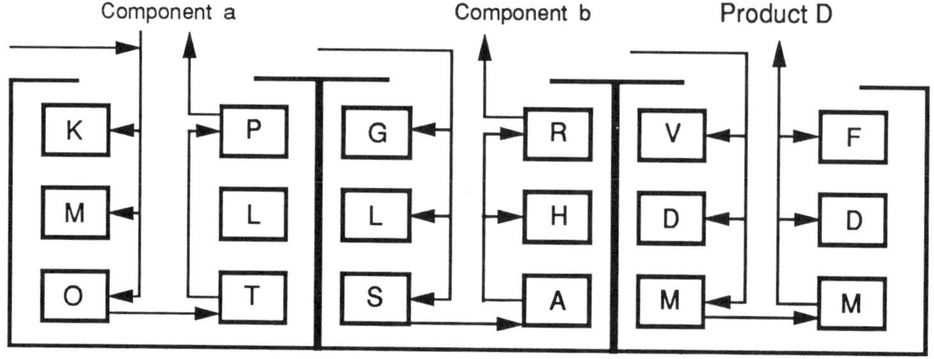


**C. Group Layout**

**Figure 1-11**
**The Three Types of Layout**

A functional layout allows the specialization of supervision and labor force, as well as the flexibility in planning products and order intake, along with the ability to accommodate a wide variety of products. A functional layout is distinguished by a better motivated labor force and a lower investment in equipment.

A functional layout is widely used due to its advantages of lower initial investments and flexibility in product/orders planning. A uniform labor force allows for easier supervision and a greater span of control. It is used when the low volumes produced do not justify a specialized product-focused layout. Consequently, this type of layout is the choice for newly established companies.

The disadvantages of the functional layout are complicated material flow control, a higher production cost due to the need for expediting, and frequent delays due to waiting lines. A functional layout entails material handling involving the cross-hauling and backtracking; the routing and scheduling is difficult, the inventory investments are larger, and the cost accounting is elaborate.

In the production line, the processing time at each station varies. The material flow is intermittent, contested at each workstation—one of the features of a job shop. A series of queueing systems is taking place here—the waiting-line problem which is often buffered by in-process inventories. The majority of production systems, to a various degree, include fragments of the functional layout.

As companies grow, the problem of production control is becoming a major obstacle in increasing productivity. In many instances, the disadvantages of vague production control outweigh the benefits of the functional layout.

## Using a Product-Focused Layout

### THE LINE LAYOUT

In line layout, the production equipment is arranged so as to facilitate the production of a single specific product. As illustrated in Figure 1-11, a line layout results in the continuous material flow because the material follows the same route. The line layout, also known as continuous production, is distinguished by the high productivity due to its use of special-purpose machinery. The line layout often utilizes a conveyor for moving the material from one workstation to another.

Line layout is applied in assembly processes and in some high-volume production of individual components. The assignment of jobs to individual workstations is not contested—there are no waiting lines—but there is a need to balance the production line. The requirement is to setup the line production in such a way as to divide the work into operations performed by workstations having the same cycle time.

The term "line layout" implies that machines should be arranged in a straight line. This is not always the case, since with the line layout, the equipment also can be arranged in a variety of shapes, such as circles, U-shapes, L-shapes, or S-shapes. Such arrangement of equipment reduces the material handling cost and results in saving the floor space.

The main feature of line layout is a continuous uninterrupted material flow. The *advantages* of the line layout include the fact that it does not require a skilled work force: rather, it utilizes high-productivity equipment. Line layout has low work-in-process, and easy planning and control. A balanced material flow and the reduction in setups results in low unit cost and shorter lead time.

The *disadvantages* of the line layout is that there is a need to have a high production volume and continuity of demand to substantiate higher investments in the special-purpose machinery that may become obsolete with the termination of the product. The product mix is limited to few basic standard types. A breakdown of one machine leads to shutting down an entire line. The division of labor and the subdivision of operations into even smaller repetitive tasks affects the productivity by creating work monotony and boredom, stemming from performing the same operation for a long time. Line layout production has recently undergone a revision, responding to the need to improve workers' motivation.

***How to Balance Assembly-Line Production*** A well-known application of line layout is an assembly line where the components are put together in a series of work tasks. Assembly-line production requires balancing of work tasks to obtain a high degree of labor and equipment utilization and to minimize the idle time by grouping work tasks into equalized operations. This leads to line production often being mechanically paced and synchronized. In other words, the production time of each workstation is constant and is equally proportional to the cycle time.

Synchronizing a production line (*line balancing*) is achieved in five steps:

1. Estimating the cycle time according to the following formula:

$$\text{cycle time} = \frac{\text{production time available per day}}{\text{output units required per day (production rate)}}$$

   The cycle time is the time between completion of two components.

2. Estimating the minimum number of workstations using this formula:

$$\text{Minimum number of workstations} = \frac{\sum_{i=1}^{m} \text{time required to complete task } i}{CT}$$

where:

$m$ = number of assembly tasks
$CT$ = cycle time
$i$ = work tasks, = 1, 2, 3, ...., $m$
$t$ = time per operation/task

3. Compiling a precedence diagram according to the precedence data
4. Assigning individual tasks to workstations by grouping them according to the precedence requirements (all the predecessors should be completed before any task can begin)
5. Estimating the efficiency of an assembly line using the following formula:

$$\text{Efficiency} = \frac{\sum_{i=1}^{m} t_i}{(\text{assigned number of workstations}) \times (\text{actual cycle time})}$$

Here is an example of assembly-line balancing:

| Task | Time (sec) | Preceding task(s) |
|---|---|---|
| A | 12 | - |
| B | 20 | A |
| C | 16 | A |
| D | 47 | A |
| E | 12 | C |
| F | 11 | C |
| G | 25 | B |
| H | 9 | E, F |
| I | 22 | G |
| J | 15 | D, H, I |
| K | 26 | J |
| L | 19 | K |

Line-balancing rules are applied in developing the solution shown in Figure 1-12. The work elements are assigned to five workstations in the following order:

| | | |
|---|---|---|
| Station 1 | Elements A, B, C | Total time, 48 sec. |
| Station 2 | Element D | Total time, 47 sec. |
| Station 3 | Elements E, F, G | Total time, 48 sec. |
| Station 4 | Elements H, I, J | Total time, 46 sec. |
| Station 5 | Elements K, L | Total time, 45 sec. |

Operation time of 48 seconds is scheduled for stations 1 and 3. Station 2 is underutilized by 1 second per cycle, station 4 is underutilized by 2 seconds per cycle, and station 5 is underutilized by 3 seconds per cycle. Further balancing

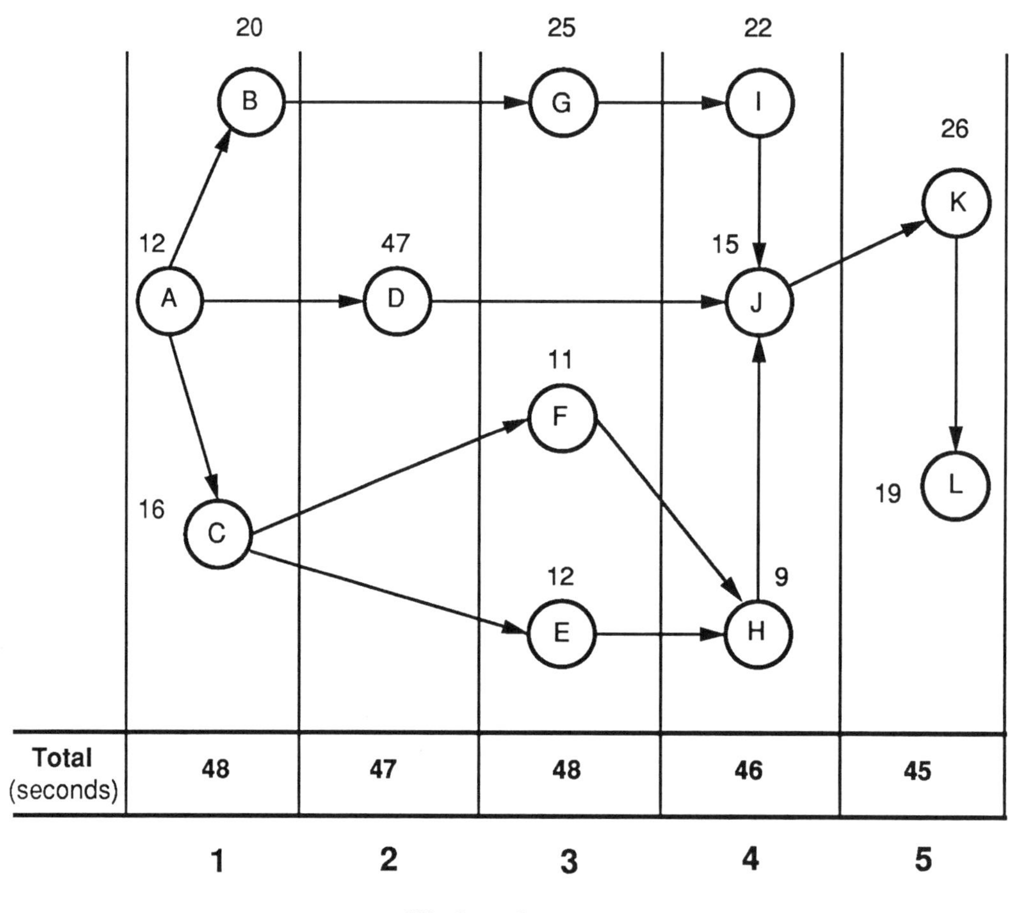


**Figure 1-12**
**Balancing an Assembly Line**

is possible, but it requires a further detailed subdivision of tasks into the subtasks. Not all the subtasks have the same restrictions as their higher-level tasks have, and thus, at more detailed level of work, additional choices are available.

Efficiency is estimated by dividing the total task time of all workstations, which is 234 seconds, by the product of the number of workstations, five stations in our example, times the cycle time, which has been selected as 48 seconds.

$$\text{efficiency} = \frac{48 + 47 + 48 + 46 + 45}{5 \times 48} = \frac{234}{240} = 97.5\%$$

***How to Organize the Mixed Model Production Line*** Mixed-model line balancing is becoming popular due to the need to produce a greater variety of products in small quantities. High-volume assembly lines simultaneously producing several models of products are an example of mixed model lines. One of the first examples of such lines is successfully applied in the automobile production, where several models of an automobile are coming from the same assembly line. Line balancing in mixed-model assembly lines can be an improvement as compared with a single-model assembly line, because more product mix choices are available.

Examples of the assembly line balancing, especially the mixed-model line balancing, and their applications in JIT production are discussed in Chapter 9.

### THE GROUP LAYOUT

*Group layout* is also known as a group technology (GT) layout. A GT layout is illustrated in Figure 1-11. Here machines are grouped into cells, each containing an equipment required for processing a family of components. GT is a product-focused layout for a family of parts having common characteristics, such as form similarity requiring comparable machining operations, similar labor requirements, similar machine setup, or the same raw material.

Group technology has the benefit of a product-focused layout, such as labor specialization, and at the same time, the benefit of the functional layout capable of dealing with a variety of jobs, and improving the motivational factors. The material handling is significantly reduced, along with setup times, and planning and control procedures are improved.

### THE FIXED POSITION LAYOUT

*Fixed position layout* is applied for heavy, large-sized items stationed in one location. In the fixed position layout, the work is organized in such a way that the people and the equipment are brought to the product site. Resources flow to the item being produced or served. A condition leading to the use of the fixed position layout would be a situation where product handling on a moving assembly line is not possible due to its large size and weight. Production requires that the labor, equipment, and materials are moved to the assembly place as they are required.

Shipbuilding and large aircraft assemblies are examples of the fixed position layout. The toughest task here is scheduling operations in such a way as to achieve a higher degree of equipment and labor force utilization. Integrated task management (ITM), discussed in Chapter 7, presents a new solution for the fixed position layout scheduling and control.

### THE MIXED LAYOUT

*Mixed layout*, where two or more layout types are used in a single facility, is commonplace in manufacturing industry. For example, there can be a process layout, a product layout, and a group layout arranged in different sections of a company. Often, the supply of a continuous assembly line with high-volume production is provided by production units arranged in a functional layout or group layout. Here, departments are arranged according to the general product flow representing the product-focused layout, coupled with the process-focused functional layout within the departments and the line layout at the assembly lines.

## PLANNING AN EFFECTIVE PLANT LAYOUT

It is clear that a unidirectional material flow is easier to control than is a multidirectional intermittent operational material flow as with the job shop environment. A flow-line layout is the most convenient case as far as a production planning and control system is concerned. The flow of material is one directional. Operational routes are balanced providing an uninterrupted material flow. A functional layout features a multidirectional material flow. The job shop application of an intermittent material flow is an example of counterflow operational paths featuring waiting lines.

One of the most obvious methods of improving a material flow is to reduce the number of operational paths. This leads to a lower production cost, due to the reduction in the inventory level, material handling operations, and lead time.

The plant layout should come under a periodical review, due to the changes in products, product design, technology, quantity produced, and any subcontracting which would lead to change of capacity and space requirements, including the space provided for storage of work-in-process (WIP) and material handling operations. Facilitating the flow of information is important for better communication and decision making.

The establishment of an effective plant layout starts with organizing an individual workstation, providing a worker with the convenience of being able to reach all the needed items during operations and the convenience and safety in operating and maintaining the equipment.

An observed trend in the plant layout features attempts to achieve a higher utilization of resources through consistent material flow, with minimum backtracking of material, minimum material handling, and a reduction of manufacturing spaces—more compact factory layouts, positioning workstations closer to each other, and reducing spaces allocated for storage and services.

## How to Prepare a Plant Layout

The objective in establishing a plant layout is to minimize the interdepartmental material handling cost. Also, consideration should be given to production support services, the disposition of administrative units, and the management information systems (MIS) in place.

We will discuss the steps in planning a plant layout when we consider the example of the Tool and Implement Co., a tool and agricultural implement manufacturing company comprised of eight departments, exhibited in Figure 1-13.

Determining a plant layout means applying a load-distance cost analysis, and it involves the following steps:

1. Compile a materials movement schedule and determine which departments have the most frequent links. The annual sample of the interdepartmental material flow is compiled into a table. The number of loads is multiplied by the distances. This step determines the intensity of the material handling traffic compiled as a of load-distance matrix.
2. Determine the cost of material handling by multiplying the number of loads-distance figures by the cost per one load. This information is presented in the form of a load-distance matrix. The total material handling cost is found by multiplying the numbers in the load-distance matrix by the cost per load.

This information is presented in the cost matrix. This matrix can also be presented in a semimatrix format, where the *to* and *from* load-distances between two departments are presented as a sum, as shown in Figure 1-14.

3. Identify possible changes to the layout, which reduce the cost. The initial solution can be improved by highlighting the high interdepartmental handling cost and attempting to reduce it. Figure 1-15 identifies high-volume costs which can be reduced if departments are placed adjacent or closer together.
4. Arrange departments so as to minimize the total cost. A revised plant layout is exhibited in Figure 1-13. The cost matrix shows an improvement of $10,280, from $57,910 down to $47,630.

In this improved layout, departments responsible for high material handling cost are located closer together. For example, placing departments 2 and 4 and 2 and 1 closer to each other reduced the material handling cost from $9,000 to $4,200 and from $4,000 to $2,000, respectively. Similar results have been accomplished by shifting departments 5 and 8—an improvement from $3,200 to $1,400—and 4 and 8—an improvement from $2,500 to $1,300. The material handling cost is estimated as follows:

$$\text{material handling cost between all pairs of departments} = \sum_{i=1}^{n} \sum_{j=1}^{n} L_{ij} C_{ij}$$

| 4<br>Milling | 1<br>Stamping | 5<br>Shipping | 6<br>Grinding |
|---|---|---|---|
| 3<br>Cutting | 8<br>Inspection | 7<br>Final Assembly | 2<br>Turning |

**A. Initial Layout**

| 1<br>Stamping | 2<br>Turning | 6<br>Grinding | 7<br>Final Assembly |
|---|---|---|---|
| 3<br>Cutting | 4<br>Milling | 8<br>Inspection | 5<br>Shipping |

**B. Improved Layout**

**Figure 1-13**
**Tool and Implement Co. Improvements to the Plant Layout**

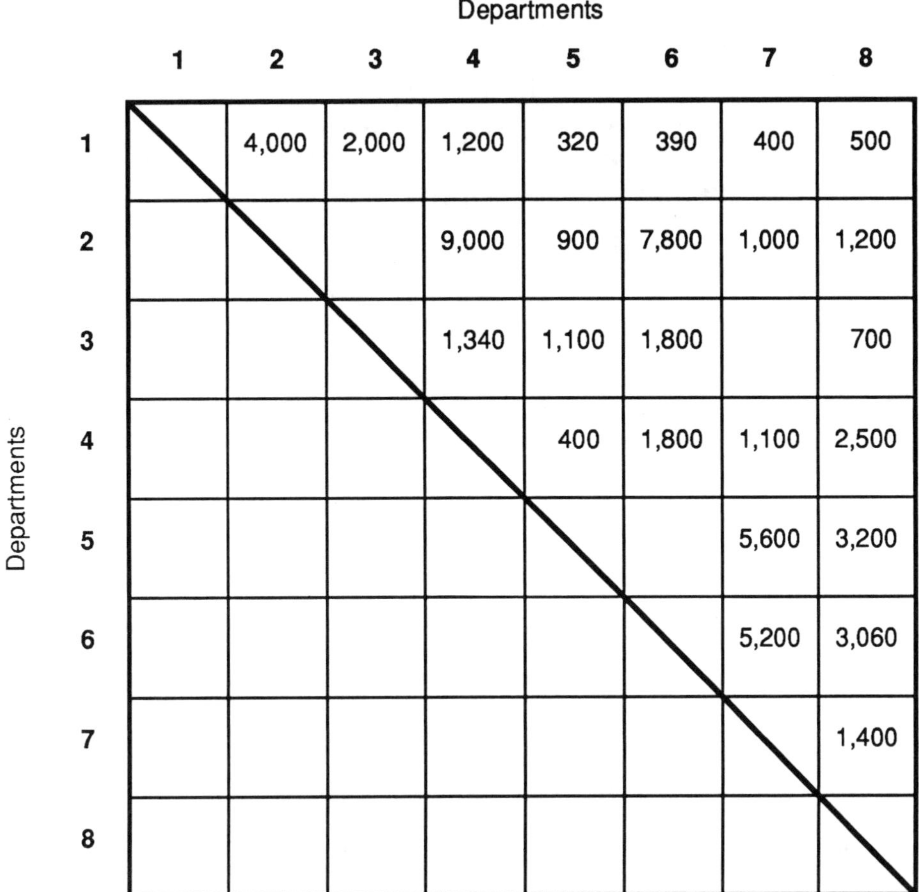

Departments (rows) / Departments (columns)

| | 1 | 2 | 3 | 4 | 5 | 6 | 7 | 8 |
|---|---|---|---|---|---|---|---|---|
| 1 | | 4,000 | 2,000 | 1,200 | 320 | 390 | 400 | 500 |
| 2 | | | | 9,000 | 900 | 7,800 | 1,000 | 1,200 |
| 3 | | | | 1,340 | 1,100 | 1,800 | | 700 |
| 4 | | | | | 400 | 1,800 | 1,100 | 2,500 |
| 5 | | | | | | | 5,600 | 3,200 |
| 6 | | | | | | | 5,200 | 3,060 |
| 7 | | | | | | | | 1,400 |
| 8 | | | | | | | | |

The initial cost matrix of material handling between departments

**Figure 1-14**
**Material Handling Cost of the Interdepartmental Material Flow. Initial Layout**

| Material Handling Cost | |
|---|---|
| Departments | Cost ($$) |
| 2-4 | 9,000 |
| 2-6 | 7,800 |
| 5-7 | 5,600 |
| 6-7 | 5,200 |
| 1-2 | 4,000 |
| 5-8 | 3,200 |
| 6-8 | 3,060 |
| 4-8 | 2,500 |
| 1-3 | 2,000 |
| 3-6 | 1,800 |
| 4-6 | 1,800 |
| 7-8 | 1,400 |
| 3-4 | 1,340 |
| 1-4 | 1,200 |
| 2-8 | 1,200 |
| 4-7 | 1,100 |

**Figure 1-15**
**Highest Material Handling Cost**

where

$n$ = total number of work centers

$i,j$ = individual departmental links = 1, 2, 3, ...n

$L\ i,j$ = number of loads moved from department $i$ to department $j$

$Ci,j$ = cost to move a unit load between department $i$ and department $j$

Due to the complexity of layout problems, some simplifying assumptions are made in this example by paying primary attention to work centers' "nearness"/disposition pattern, without considering the size and the shape of work centers.

One assumption made is that the cost per unit/distance depends on "nearness" of work centers. An analysis of a plant layout can be based on considerations other than materials handling costs, such as technological factors or health and safety regulations. For example, the welding department should be segregated in order to protect people and the property from sparks and flames, just as painting processes should be separated to protect people and property from toxic fumes and fire hazards.

Manual applications by trial and error sometimes are required before arriving at the best layout solution. In recent years, computer programs have been written for solving complex layout problems. The best known of these are GRAFT, COFAD, ALDER, and PLANET.

## HOW THE PLANT LAYOUT AFFECTS PRODUCTION PLANNING AND CONTROL

Plant layout is a direct function of the level of demand. Changes in demand, product changes, and modifications call for a change in the layout. It is especially relevant to present fluctuations in demand and variations in customer orders. Consequently, the concept of a flexible layout and *flexible manufacturing systems* (FMS) is a popular subject.

A change in the layout is required especially when companies decide to embark on the automation of production lines. This could be coupled with significant changes in material handling systems. In general, any change in product design, work methods, job design, cost reduction, and productivity improvement programs or any change resulting from improvements in human factors eventually affects the plant layout. All contemporary manufacturing systems call for continuous improvement and flexibility in the plant layout.

## USING A FLEXIBLE LAYOUT TO FACILITATE QUICK CHANGES

A flexible layout is becoming a real issue in establishing JIT production systems. A flexible layout allows for quick changes to different product models or

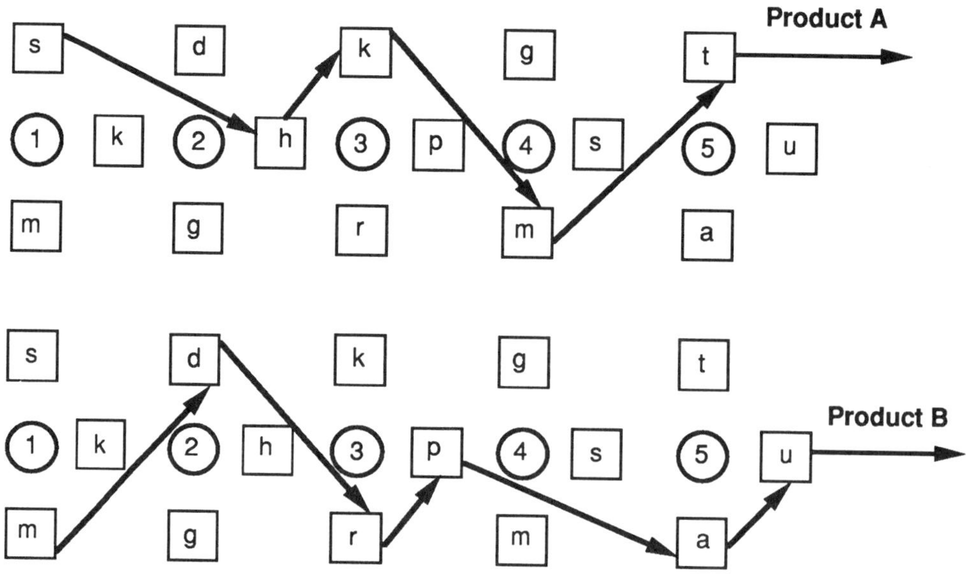


**A. One Operator Serves Several Workstations**
(Different products are produced on the same production line)

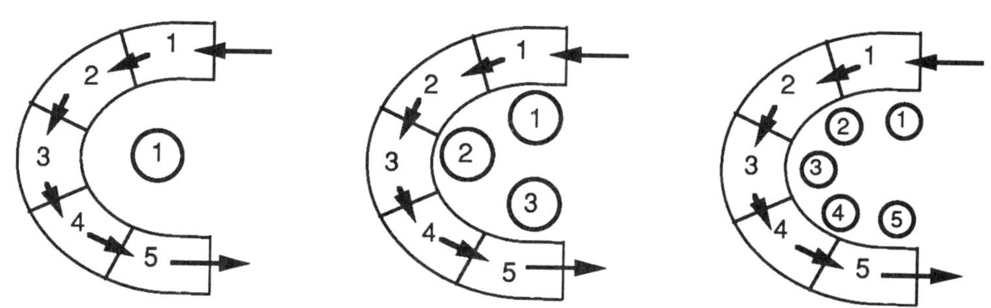


**B. U-shaped Short Lines -- Flexible Staffing**
(Varying number of operators on the same production line)

**Figure 1-16**
**Tool and Implement Co. Flexible Manufacturing Systems**

different production rates and organizing a unidirectional material flow. There are different approaches to flexible layouts, but all of them have one point in common: these layouts, each in a different way, aim at achieving the flexibility in planning.

A flexible layout envisages setting up a production line with existing equipment for different products and customer orders as a product-based type layout. The two basic approaches to the flexible layout are:

1. Changing the sequence of machines for each contract or customer order by physically rearranging the layout
2. Arranging the necessary sequence of machines among the stationary equipment

This is a multi-product group technology with a product-focused layout. Figure 1-16 illustrates various approaches to the flexible layout based on changing characteristics of workstations ranging from one to one through one to many. Such flexibility is accomplished due to multiskilled workforce.

Another approach to flexible manufacturing systems is to utilize a transient equipment. Industrial companies having light equipment, such as companies in the garment industry, are making use of such flexibility so as to arrange a product-focused line layout for different customer orders.

## THE FUNCTIONS OF MATERIAL STORES

Material stores provide facilities with both long-term and temporary storage of materials and components until the time they are required, in accordance with the production schedule. Stores change the character of the material flow and perform the following functions:

1. Releasing function—to act as a buffer for unpredictable variations in supply
2. Accumulating function—to isolate the supply side from the demand side while the components are in the store. Here, stores perform dividing and combining operations, and change the material flow frequency.
3. Preassembly collection function—to combine product sets ready for assembly.

The two categories of stores are in-process stores and finished-components stores. To justify their existence, stores contribute to the buildup of inventories. Companies resort to stores in an attempt to eliminate orders input-output imbalances, and to balance ordering and production cycles. If stores are overcrowded with inventories, this is the evidence of inefficiency of the production planning and control system.

Figure 1-17 illustrates how stores change the material flow.

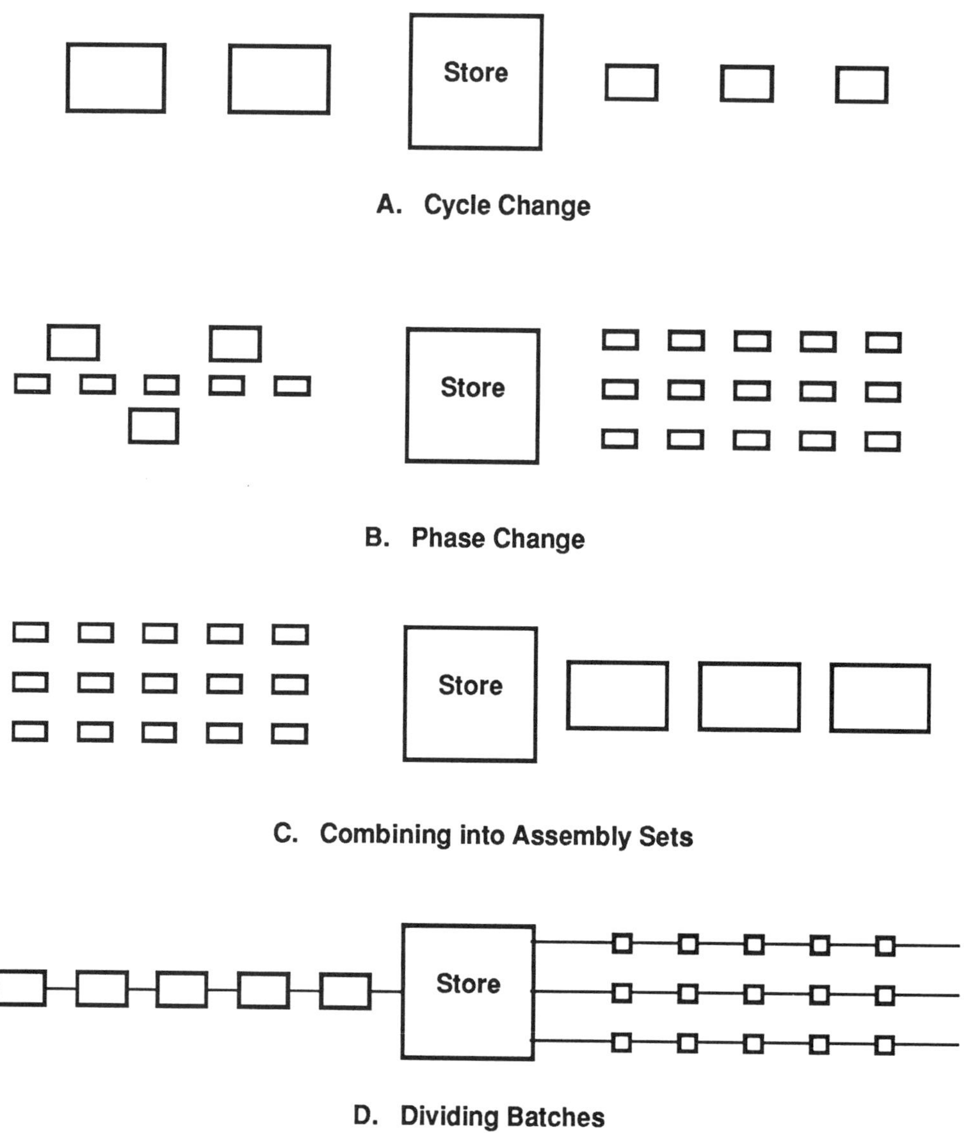


**Figure 1-17**
**The Functions of Stores**

# 2

# Organizing Human Resources and Designing Work Measurement Systems

The next step in organizational design is to relate various functions to specific positions in an organization. This is known as structuring the company's human resources. The principle of grouping capital resources into specialized departments has been discussed previously, when we covered line layouts. The departmentalization relies on the specialization and is linked to organizing human resources into line and staff authority.

## TYPES OF ORGANIZATIONS

### Line Organization

The fundamental principle in the *line organization* is the unity of command, the line of authority where every subordinate has only one superior or receives only one set of instructions at a time. The direct line of flow of authority from a superior to subordinates sets up the channels of communication formed according to the unity of command as shown in Figure 2-1.

In organizations where the producing function is regarded superior to all other functions, line managers are those who are directly involved in the primary operation. Here, the designation of line managers and staff managers refers to the line of functional responsibility, structured as primary and secondary functions. The line of command and the line of functional responsibility should not be confused because they are different factors in organizational structures.

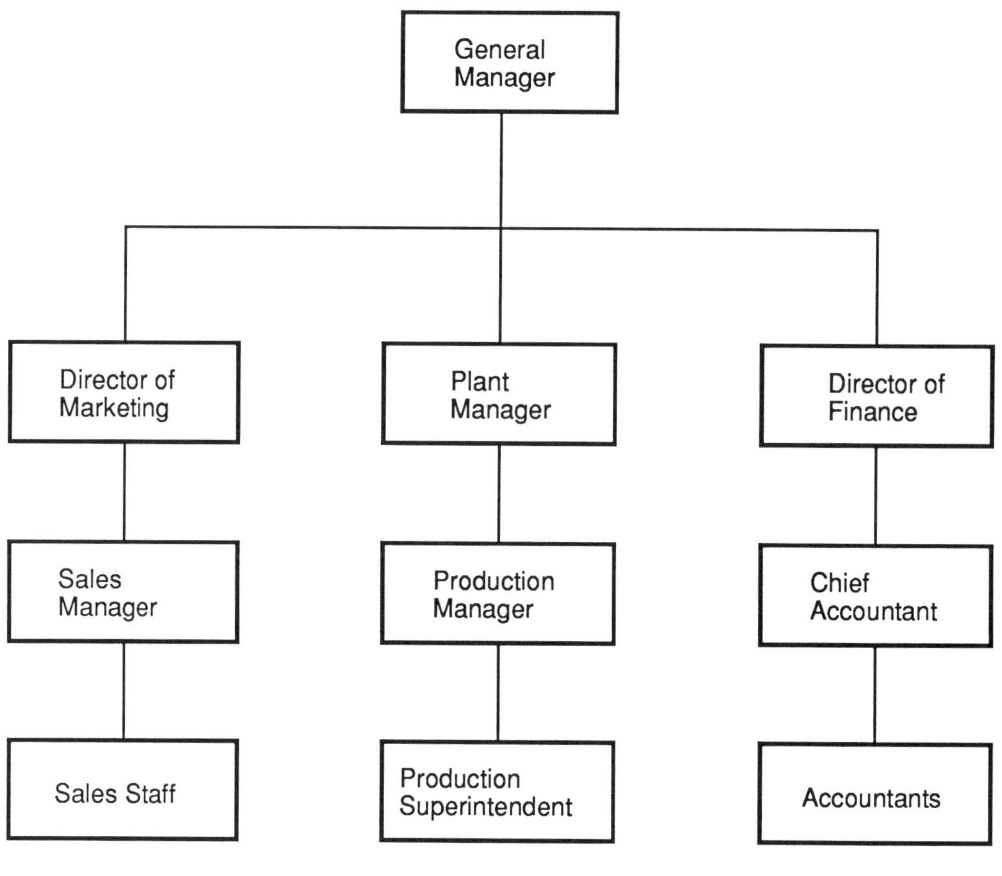


**Figure 2-1**
**Line Organization**

### Staff Organization

*Staff organiations* serve line officers by providing specialized knowledge and advice. Staff personnel do not have the authority to give orders to line managers. However, staff organizational units include expert, advisory, and clerical processes, such as engineering, legal, and production support services, which can offer suggestions to the line officers. A staff organization is also known as a functional organization. Schematically, a staff or functional organization is shown in Figure 2-2.

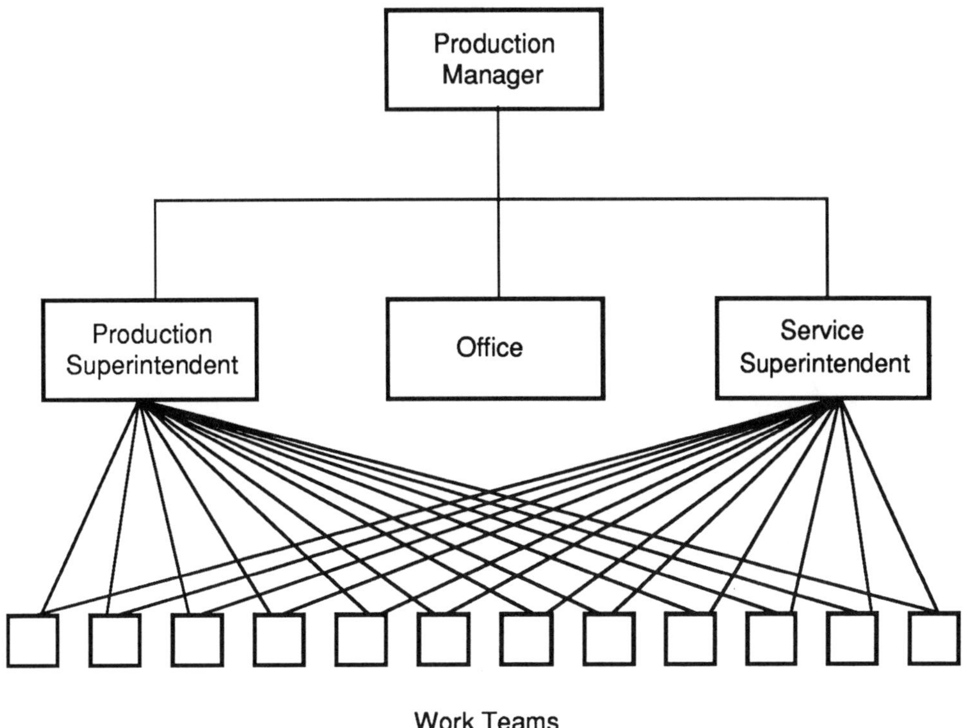


**Figure 2-2**
**Staff or Functional Organization**

## Line-Staff Organization

Often staff specialists possess a specialized knowledge but do not have an integrated approach to the entire operation. Staff units are used in the line organization to advise line officers and to relieve them of similar specialized functions. A conflict exists between line officers and staff positions with regard to the responsibility and accountability of jobs. The basic structure of a line organization still exists, due to the fact that management has authority for making and implementing decisions, while staff personnel gathers information required for these decisions. The *line and staff organization* are shown schematically in Figure 2-3.

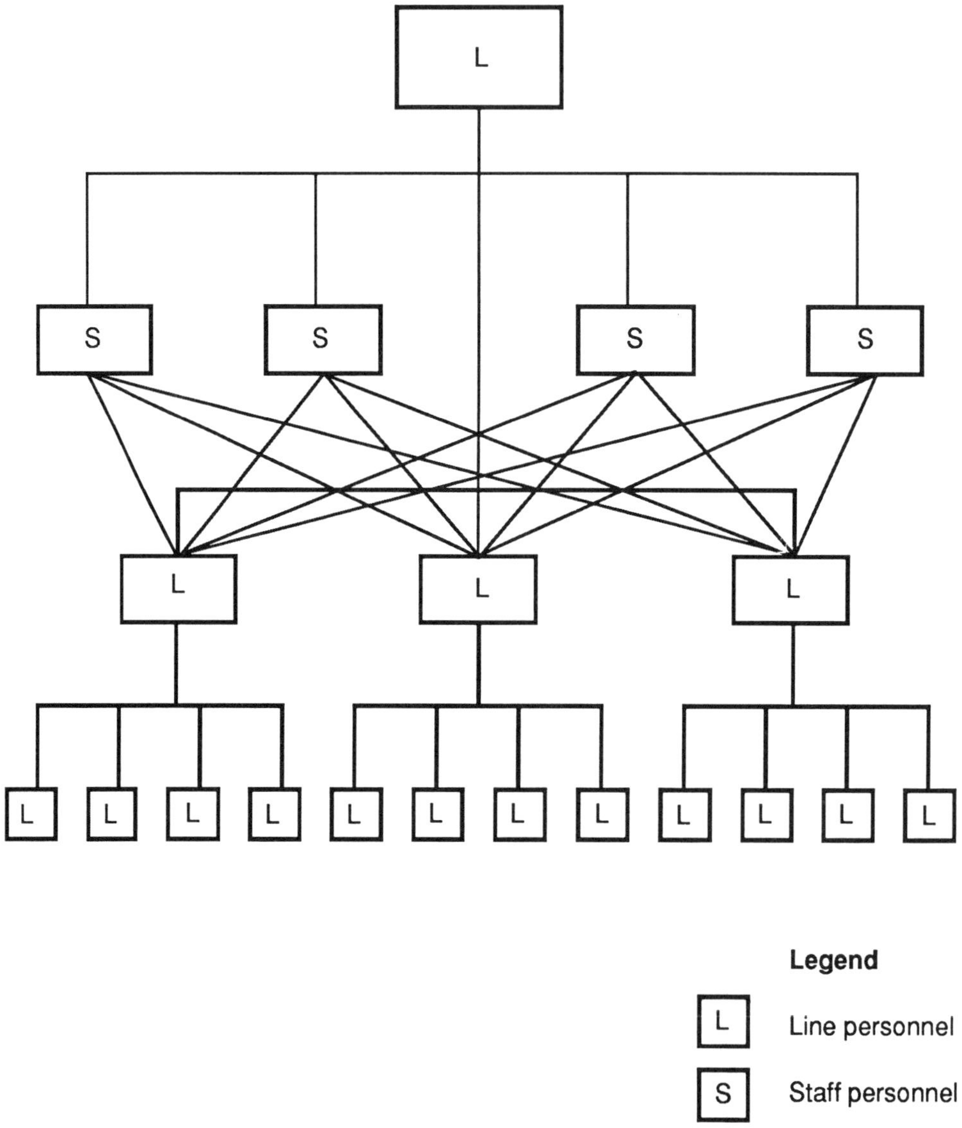

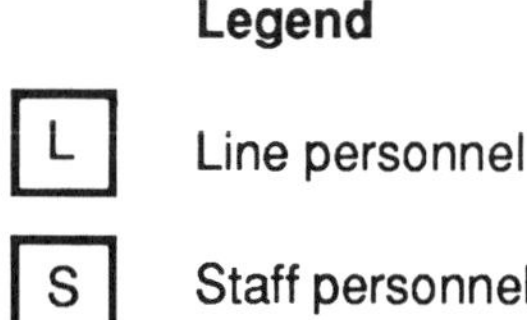


**Figure 2-3**
**Line and Staff Organization**

## Project Organization

A *project organization* is aimed at facilitating the execution of particular project activities and their management—design, planning, and control. The major task here is the efficient use of resources, along with the on-time delivery. A project is a one-time affair, and the project organization is phased out as soon as the project is completed.

In a project organization, people from different units of the organization, having different skills, are assembled together for the execution of a one-time undertaking. For the duration of the project, these employees work as a team. A project manager has authority over the team members, along with the responsibility for the job performance, maintaining the due dates, resources, and keeping it all within the budget, as shown in Figure 2-4. Projects management will be discussed in Chapter 16.

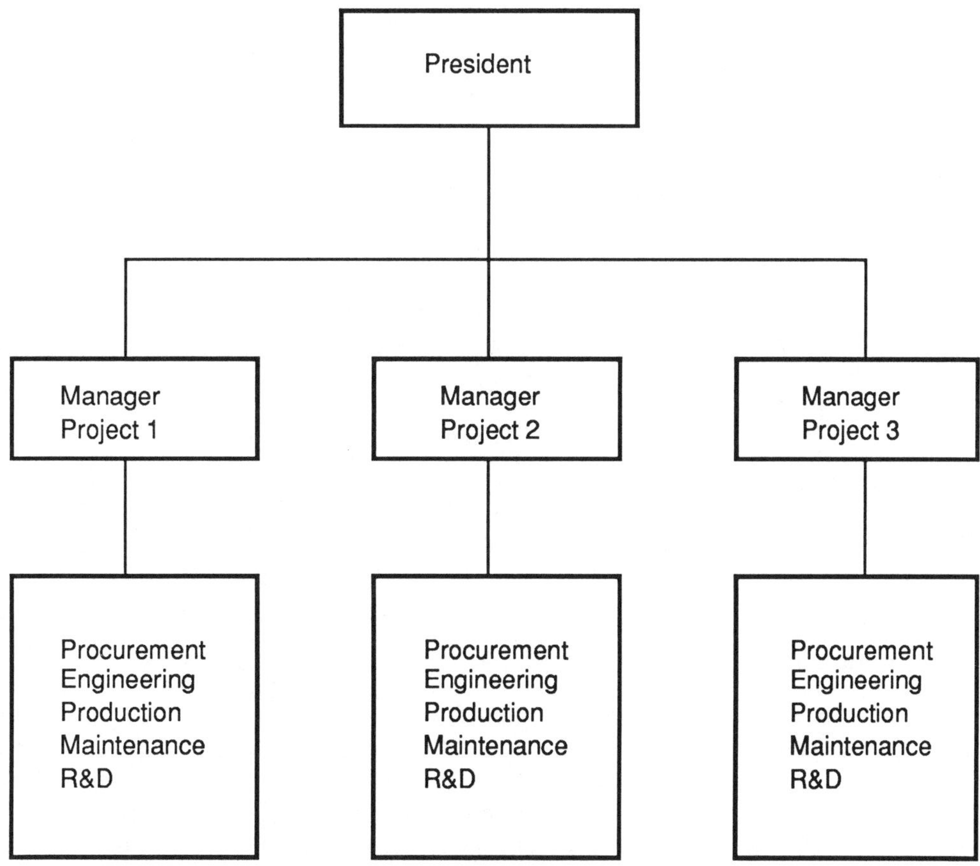


**Figure 2-4**
**Project Organization**

## Matrix Organization

A *matrix organization* is a kind of hybrid between a project organization and a functional organization. A matrix is an organizational structure associated with project management. This type of organization can be represented by a graphical model of a two-dimensional matrix. The ultimate authority lies with the project manager assigned for this particular project. During the project, the project manager requests the functional staff to be assigned at various stages of the project, often temporarily having limited authority. These personnel return to their functions as soon as their tasks are accomplished. In Figure 2-5, a row represents an independent product or project, while columns are support units (operating departments).

In the matrix organization, each employee has a dual accountability, first, to the program manager for the assignment he or she is responsible for, and second, to the departmental superior for the matters related to this functional department. Such a dual accountability is reflected in Figure 2-5 by criss-crossing the lines of command (the crossing pattern of authority). The matrix has recently come under criticism from various sources because of the dual authority problem.

The idea of making use of experts for a short period of time and then sending them back to their corresponding departments appeals to some managers, because it makes the project more cost effective. The total organizational benefit, however, is not so obvious, because it is not always possible to arrange for the coordination of all projects so as to make the utmost use of human resources.

There are three areas of conflict in a project organization:

1. *The authority over the utilization of resources*—a conflict between functional managers and project managers over planning and allocation of resources.
2. *The difference in priorities*—projects are one-time affairs, while the functional personnel has a continuous time perspective, more concerned with the long-term perspectives of their organization.
3. *The unity of command*—a conflict of alignment of advisors to project managers and to functional managers. This often requires the involvement of a higher line of command in order to resolve conflicts.

## Committees

A *committee* is a variation of a line and staff organization. The organizational authority and responsibility are assigned to a group of individuals—to a committee rather than to a single decision maker. A committee can act as an advisory body to a manager who ultimately holds the responsibility and makes decisions based on this advice. Decisions made by committees take into account diverse views of the participants. It is a long process to reach a compromise. Committees vary by the degree of authority assigned to them.

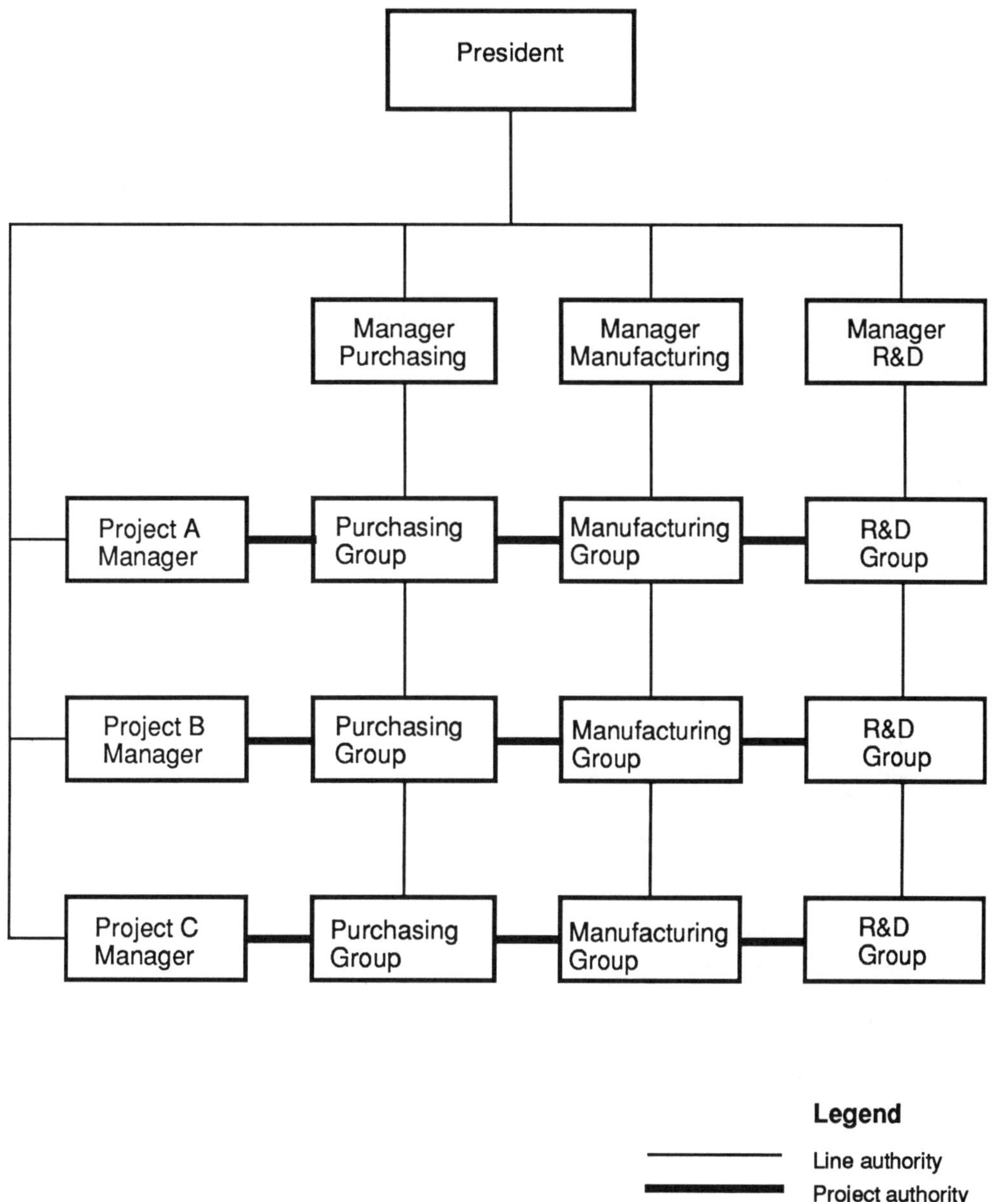


**Figure 2-5**
**Matrix Organization**

### Flexible Organization

In many organizations, there is no clear line or staff systems. An example is the area of production planning and control. Here, a production planning department is in charge of planning and issues orders to the work centers. This flexible organization case is classified as the functional authority, distinct from the line authority in a line organization or the staff authority as with a staff organization.

Many staff activities require decision making. The concept of a line-staff organization explains such a case because the decision point, the strategic decision-making position in organization, requires the staff expertise with the line authority. More staff is forced into decision making, while before they have only gathered information and have provided advice to the line decision makers.

## ASSIGNING FUNCTIONAL AUTHORITY AND USING DECISION CENTERS

A traditional practice of authority is changed into the concept of functional authority. *Functional authority* means to assign staff employees authority to act with regard to activities for which other persons are responsible. This is the feature of the integrated system approach to decision making. The expertise of line and staff personnel serves decision centers without regard to their position in the organizational hierarchical structure. Everyone involved in the decision center activity can contribute to decision making regardless of the functional boundary, the line of command, and the organizational hierarchy.

These decision-making centers represent a whole new concept, where employees of an organization gather at a single point, where all the ranks and distinctions are not important. A team atmosphere prevails in which everybody can express his or her feelings, talents, ideas, and worries. The team acts as a decision group functioning on a continuous basis.

## USING LIMITED AUTHORITY

The "limited authority" takes place when the supervisory staff has partial authority over the subordinates, thus assigning to the subordinates some decision-making role in the matters affecting their operational performance. This specifically relates to the first-line supervision, where some supervisory management functions are overtaken by the subordinates: the authority over planning, execution, and control of the tasks they perform (e.g., services such as quality, plant maintenance, and individual tasks scheduling applying priority rules). The supervision is reduced due to the decentralized decision making and self-supervision exercised by the work force.

## Simplifying Authority in T-Organizations

Some organizations restructure from having tall organizational structures with the increased vertical chain of command relationships into flat organizational structures having a horizontal as well as a vertical collaboration. The trend is to promote an environment where employees have an equal opportunity for utilizing the best of their abilities. The collaboration, both vertical and horizontal, as shown in Figure 2-6, is identified as T-organizational structures (the shaded area has a form of the letter "T").

In a T-organization, the chain of command is overlapped. The horizontal and vertical interrelationship produces the common authority and responsibility. The horizontal collaboration is especially beneficial, because it goes alongside the material flow lines. A horizontal interrelationship is applied in the just-in-time-kanban type material flow control.

Taylor's fourth principle of functional partnership takes place here. In Figure 2-6, such a horizontal and vertical interrelationship is shown by shaded areas. T-organizational structures are applied in quality circle-type productive systems.

### Using Centralization and Decentralization for Faster Decision Making

The degree of *centralization* in decision making is the degree to which control resides at the top levels of management. A high degree of centralization is typical for small organizations. Policy decisions are getting decentralized as a company grows. There are advantages and disadvantages to the decentralization. The need for communication and coordination of decision making is greater with the decentralization.

A person has a limit on the ability to work and make decisions, and the decision effectiveness is reduced if these limits are stretched. The efficiency in various organizations depends on the degree of centralization of decision making. It has been found that most efficient companies are of medium size, those having an equilibrium between the centralized and decentralized decision making.

*Decentralization* leads to faster decision making at autonomous centers. The disadvantage is that these decisions are not always properly coordinated and streamlined for achieving total organizational objectives.

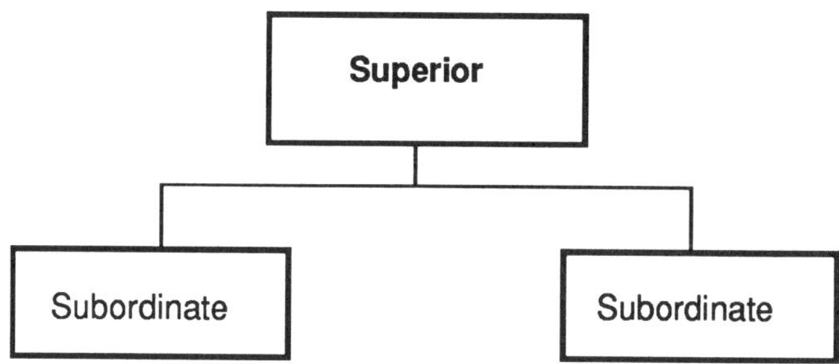


A. Traditional Organization

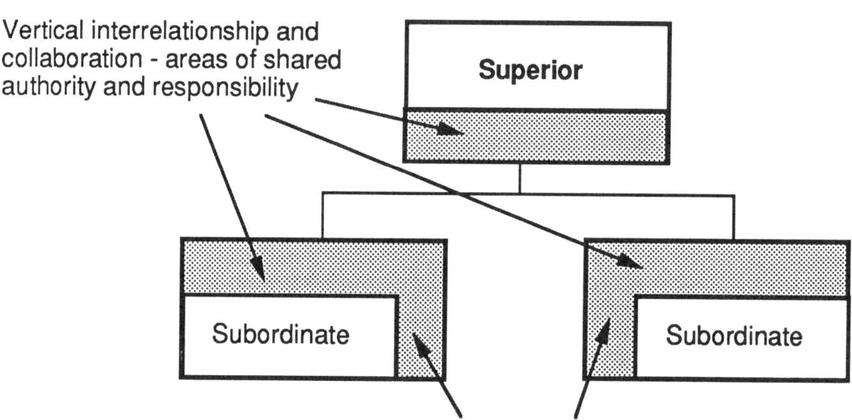


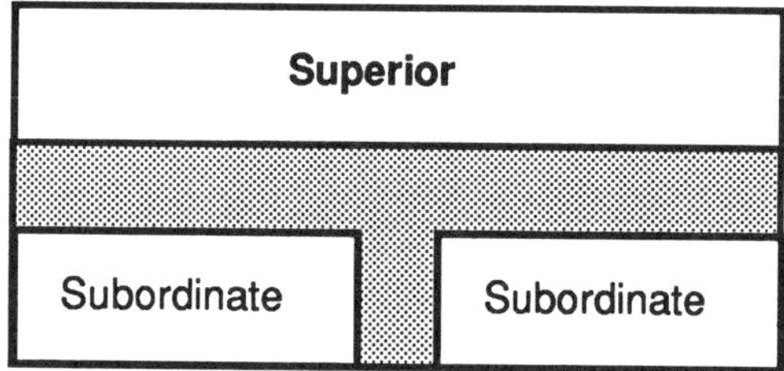


B. T-Organizational Structures

**Figure 2-6**
**Traditional and T-Organizational Structures**

The solution that produces good results is the decentralization applying a set of programmed decisions, although a certain balance between the centralized and decentralized planning is required for achieving the synergistical effect in operations. An example of such a balanced centralized-decentralized planning and control system is discussed in Chapter 7.

## Understanding the Span of Control

The degree of centralization is reflected in the organizational span of control, also called the span of management. The *span of control* is the number of subordinates who can be effectively controlled per one management position. Given the type of task, the type of production, and the working environment, this is shown by the ratio of the subordinate-superior relationship. The question of the span of control basically boils down to how many subordinates it is possible to supervise efficiently. This question profoundly affects the organizational structure. Higher up in a hierarchical structure, the span of control decreases as the responsibility increases. Having too many levels in an organization creates problems in communication and particularly in coordination of the decision-making red tape.

### TALL AND FLAT ORGANIZATIONAL STRUCTURES

Structure A in Figure 2-7 illustrates an example of an organizational structure with the span of supervisory control of four. Structure B represents an organization with the span of supervisory control of six. Structure A has a total of four organizational levels. Structure B has a total of three organizational levels. One level of the organizational structure is eliminated.

It should be pointed out that the majority of problems are experienced in the vertical communication, which in this instance is reduced. There are fewer organizational levels here, since the span of control for the given organization increases. When the number of subordinates directly reporting to the given supervisor increases, the ability of this supervisor to maintain tighter control is diminishing, because proportionally less time will be available, and each subordinate will be more free to act independently on his or her own.

The span of control affects the delegation of activities and directly influences the organizational centralization. The trade-off should be made between the effective supervision, resulting in the smaller span of control, and the desire to have fewer hierarchical levels in an organizational structure. The choice is between a tall structure with a short span and tight supervision and a flat structure with a wide span of control, and increased delegation, resulting in higher morale, improved human relations, and greater motivation.

The span of control gets a new dimension in the systems approach. The concern here is with the information channels and the nature of information, the degree of modeling and standardization of decision making, the impact on decision-making centers, and the employees' motivation.

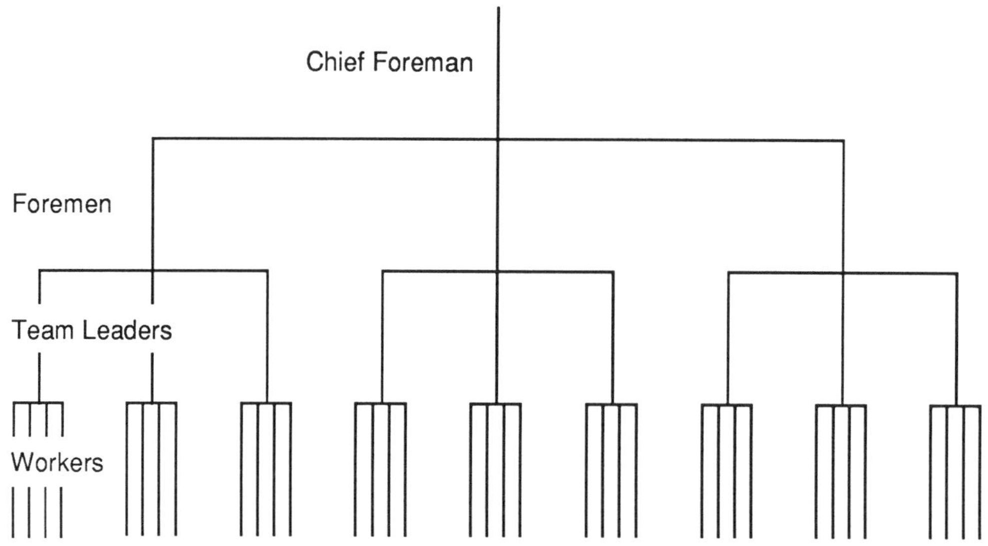


**A. Four-Workers Span of Control**

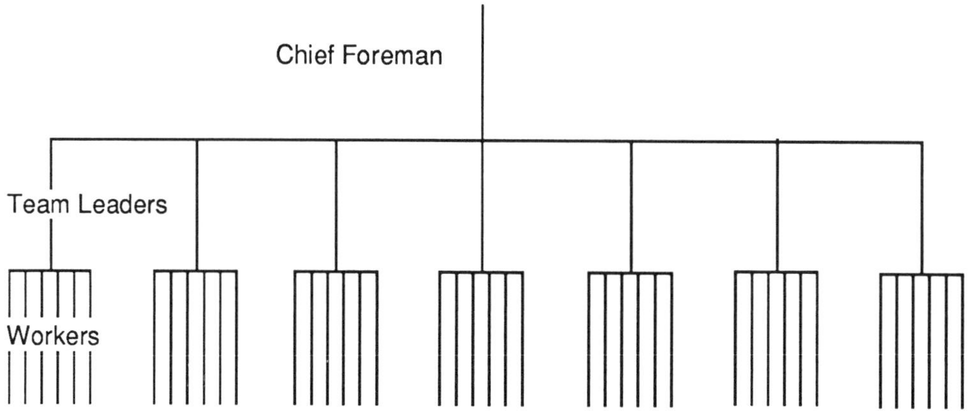


**B. Six-Workers Span of Control**

**Figure 2-7**
**How the Span of Control Affects Organizational Structures**

## HORIZONTAL AND VERTICAL RELATIONSHIPS

Each position in an organization serves not only for decision-making purposes but also for communication of information. For example, a team of three with one supervisor has seven interpersonal links. Vertical interrelation links are more complex than the horizontal ones in achieving free communication, complete cooperation, and coordination.

The upper-management echelon has a smaller span of control, because they, to a greater extent than other management levels, are involved in decision making. Reducing the number of tiers in an organization leads to more efficient communication and to bringing management closer to production. Reducing the number of tiers eliminates the high-level less productive communication links and improves the motivation of those in execution, as they regard their increased significance in the lower organizational pyramid.

A greater span of control can be achieved by applying T-organizational structures and limited authority. The increased span of control reduces overheads and production costs. Vertical communication in decision making is decreasing and is replaced by horizontal communication and coordination. Horizontal, cross-functional communication improves control over the material flow because the coordination of activities is done where the action takes place. Now the supervisor of the machining department communicates directly with the supervisor of the next production process—grinding department—instead of using formal intermediaries—the managers of both these departments.

Horizontal communication is particularly beneficial at the shop floor operational level, bypassing supervisory authority. The JIT-*kanban* system applies such shop floor horizontal communication.

## TAKING CONTROL: HOW TO IMPROVE THE EFFICIENCY OF ORGANIZATIONAL STRUCTURES

The purpose of organizational structures is to serve the execution. Some organizational structures are monuments to the extravagance of their creators, the Eiffel towers of business. This is known as *empire building*—a sociopsychological phenomenon resulting in the expansion of functional units beyond their needs and expanding the staff units even if the work load does not justify this expansion.

In some organizations, it is becoming a critical issue significantly affecting the functioning of the organization and particularly diminishing the product value. Large organizations with complex organizational structures have more difficulties in managing their activities. Applying the departmentalization by division, many companies split their operations into smaller self-sustained production units—as smaller business entities which are easier to manage.

Organizational units, entities, or individual positions, which completely or partially perform a useless function, can be called *redundant* organizational units or redundant positions. Redundant organizational units or individual positions fall under Parkinson's law, which states that work expands to fill up the available time. For example, a job requiring five hours can be expanded into 8 hours if there are no other jobs scheduled for this day. Organizational structures also expand to a higher degree when the output of the organization increases.

Managers execute their function by receiving and communicating information to the peers, subordinates, and superiors, both in line and staff authority. Redundancy in management means redundancy in communication and information processing. Managers do not do work themselves but organize other people to do the work, which managers accomplish through communication of information and planning. Decision making often is done in groups by communicating these decisions to others farther down the line of command. Managers, as well as other members of an organization, are not restricted to their specific areas in an organization. People at various levels of organizational structures are working in association, providing each other with information and ideas and communicating their decisions or advice, thus affecting the decisions and work of others in an organization.

Consequently, the redundancy in management is much more damaging than the redundancy in the work force. One redundant position in an organizational structure involves others. Such redundancy in an organization increases overheads and production costs. Nevertheless, there is seldom an obviously redundant position in an organization. The real redundancy problem is disguised and is deeply-rooted in organization's functions when a position is "partially redundant," meaning that not all, but some, of the activities performed by the person in this position are redundant. The redundancy in this instance is difficult to detect. The task is then to prevent such a "partial redundancy" from occurring in an organization.

The present trend of flattening organizational structures is having a beneficial effect on the reduction of redundancy. Flattening organizational structures start with taking off the "fat" of redundant and partially redundant functions. There are reported cases when the management and the supporting staff is reduced up to 20 to 25 percent, yielding improved performance and even an increased output. The effectiveness of various levels of organizational structures is increased when the organizational structures are flatter and the decision making is done closer to the production lines.

## DESIGNING WORK SYSTEMS AND WORK MEASUREMENTS

An important step in designing work systems is specifying the most efficient work methods for accomplishing various tasks that must be performed in order to support production.

Job design considerations fall into three major categories:

1. Sociopsychological job considerations
2. Ergonomics, which refers to physical job environment
3. Analysis of work methods and work measurements

*Sociopsychological considerations* refer to designing a workplace where employees are satisfied with what they are doing. This is achieved when employees function at the level of their skills and mental ability.

*Ergonomics* include studies of the interface between a worker and a machine, designing a workplace according to physical job environment, and creating working conditions conducive to efficient work performance.

*Work methods and work measurements* refers to an analysis of how the job is done. This means identifying and sequencing work tasks to perform the job in the most efficient way and in shortest possible time.

Job design involves designating and sequencing specific work tasks, selecting work methods, and identifying responsibility. Initially, the division of labor and the specialization of job tasks was the source of remarkable productivity improvements accelerating industrial progress. But when the division of labor has reached its peak, it induced monotony, boredom, and workers' fatigue and caused job-related illnesses. A drastic decline in productivity on assembly lines has compelled managers to pay more attention to workers' motivation and improving job design.

Factors involved in sociopsychological considerations depend on the task and skill variety within each job, that is, the task identity—when it is possible to identify the task performed by an individual or a team as a meaningful or at least recognizable part of an entire product. Many behavior investigations have mounted the evidence that workers satisfaction has a primary effect on productivity, quality, and cost.

## Job Design

Two approaches to job design are job enlargement and job enrichment.

### JOB ENLARGEMENT

Job enlargement intends to make a job more interesting by increasing the job variety and reducing the monotony. At first, attempts to improve motivation and the work force morale through better job design were directed at assigning more tasks to a single workstation. This is known as the *horizontal job increase*, or *job enlargement* (i.e., workers at the production line perform several tasks instead of doing one task).

Another common practice of job enlargement is to rotate workers between jobs, either daily or weekly. This is often used on factory production lines where jobs are performed on comparable machines.

Job enlargement does not lead to more satisfaction and personal growth and does not lead to increased skills or knowledge. In some way, it improves the workers' attitude but not to the extent that it makes a significant improvement in job satisfaction and efficiency. Despite larger number of tasks performed by a worker in job enlargement, the work skill level remains the same.

### JOB ENRICHMENT

Job enrichment, which means giving an employee a greater responsibility for a single task, proved to be more rewarding. *Job enrichment* is a vertical job increase, adding more responsibility to the same job in production and services and assigning to workers some management supervisory and planning functions. This contributes to satisfying the self-esteem and self-actualization needs. In job enrichment, broader responsibilities require workers to exercise a greater number of skills and abilities or to operate a more sophisticated automated equipment that requires higher-level operating and programming skills.

The desire of the work force to perform at the highest skill level and to take charge of additional responsibilities is satisfied when, for example, the workers are entrusted with inspecting their own work, thus eliminating the need for a quality control inspector, or with sequencing/scheduling the jobs they perform, within the broad constraints set by centralized planning and scheduling.

The case of CAMCO FMS, where workers were shifted from operating conventional machines to operating automated, computer-based manufacturing cells featuring robots and autonomous guided vehicles (AGV), is an example of job enrichment.

Self-supervisory teams become a widely accepted reality in an industrial organization, to the extent that supervision is seen as an extinguishing profession. There is an opinion that we can no longer afford to have people merely controlling other people as a function of their jobs: the function of controlling a job should be assigned to the person executing the job. In fact, the opinion about the extinguishing profession does not reflect the reality because it refers to one supervisory function only, namely, controlling the work of others. The remaining supervisory functions, such as planning the work and organizing, are more important than ever, due to the increased significance of planning in production management.

Often, job enlargement and job enrichment merge. The example is the team-minigroup approach in line production where moving assembly lines with 80 to 120 workers reorganize into a team assembly of 6 to 8 people having added responsibility for quality and production control. Combined job enlargement and job enrichment, as often is the case in self-supervisory teams, produces the best results in the sociopsychological approach to job design.

## ERGONOMICS

Studies of work environment and its effect on humans is known as human factors engineering or *ergonomics.* Ergonomics means fitting the job to the worker. It includes the physiological study as well as anatomic considerations of muscular work studied for the purpose of improving design of the workplace according to the characteristics of humans.

Chemical processes taking place in the human body continuously produce heat. And heat is produced at an increased rate during work activity. The body temperature stays constant if it loses heat to the surrounding environment at the same rate as the body produces heat. But if this excess heat is not absorbed by the surrounding environment, the body temperature starts to rise, causing physical and mental fatigue. To avoid the heat stress, temperature, humidity, and ventilation should be balanced in the work environment.

Researchers have found that, although blood is restored during the period of muscular relaxation, during a work activity, the time of muscular contraction, the muscular blood supply must be increased up to 20 times the resting value.

A work environment, including the level of illumination and noise and the surrounding air conditions, such as temperature and humidity, affects the body's internal conditions and the employees' safety, influences the energy use, and causes muscular fatigue and employee health problems in general.

Maintaining the body's internal conditions is one of the tasks of ergonomics.

### Physical Job Environment

A workplace environment contributes directly to the fatigue rate and eventually has an effect on employee motivation. Tasks exertion is of two types: physical and mental. As a worker becomes physically and mentally fatigued, the quantity and quality of his or her work output diminishes. The results of an exertion are measured experimentally and are highly dependent on the individual worker.

Job design involves structuring work into tasks requiring no exertion of physical ability. For example, the use of a particular muscle group for an extended period of time can precipitate the fatigue.

Ergonomics are involved in machine design where humans and machines each have certain functions, dividing the job into elements and assigning each function to the person who does it best. In production, a human being, the primary component of a productive unit, interacts with one or more machines. An interface between a worker and a machine can have the following relationships: one to one, one to many, or many to one, as illustrated in Figure 2-8.

Workplace design includes considerations of anthropological characteristics of the human body, body geometry and height, size and movement of arms, for both females and males in either sitting or standing position. Structuring the worker-machine interface includes design of the workplace, tools, and other work assessories.

One-to-One Relationship

One worker serves one machine.

A. Machine-Limited Relationship

One-to-Many Relationship

One worker serves several machines.

B. Worker-Limited Relationship

Many-to-One Relationship

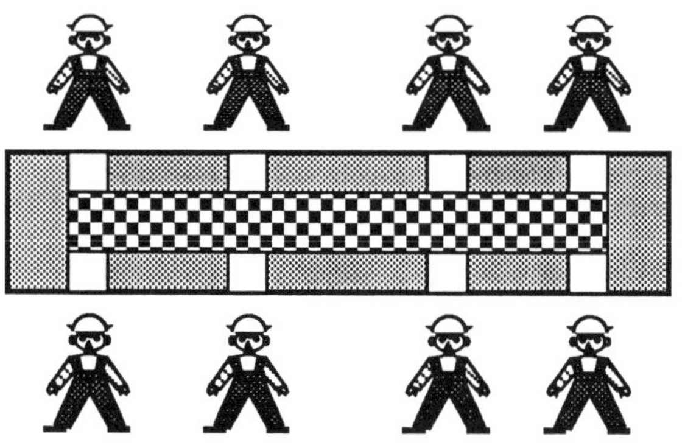

Several workers serve one workstation.

C. Machine-Limited Relationship

Figure 2-8
Worker-Machine Relationship

### Safety Considerations in Job Design

Organizations carry an overall responsibility for the safety and health of employees. This includes eliminating hazardous conditions and correcting unsafe and unhealthful conditions organizationwide through various safety programs, one of which is the health and safety training program. Also conducting periodic physical examinations of employees is a part of the preventive health maintenance program.

Monitored physical exercises often are part of an employee wellness program, just as weight reduction and nonsmoking programs are helpful in reducing stress and improving the employees general health condition. Machines equipped with guards, protection devices and electronic safety censors, along with good lighting and noise reduction features are important for safe working conditions.

Making a workplace safe and healthy is an important responsibility shared jointly by both employer and employees. Employees are responsible for developing safe work habits, using safe work methods, and following safe work rules.

## WORK STUDY: WORK METHODS ANALYSIS AND WORK MEASUREMENTS

Work study consists of two basic activities: work methods analysis and work measurement. This is illustrated in Figure 2-9.

The aim of the *work methods analysis* is to develop more efficient work methods and reducing job contents. This is accomplished through the systematic recording and analysis of present and proposed work methods.

*Work measurement* is determining the time required to accomplish a specific work task acceptable in terms of quantity, quality, and safety.

### Work Methods Analysis

The work methods analysis starts with a general overview of the entire job (macroanalysis), and then proceeds to examine specific elements of the job down to the detailed elements of the job, such as tasks and movements. All productive and nonproductive elements of the job are examined.

The method analysis, both design of new products and improvements and modification of existing ones, follows the revision of product design and the design analysis. The purpose of the design analysis is to try to simplify the design by reducing the number of parts and assembly units, making use of better materials, and to explore the possibility for relaxing tolerances and limits without reducing the quality. Design simplification is an opportunity to improve on both product design and process design.

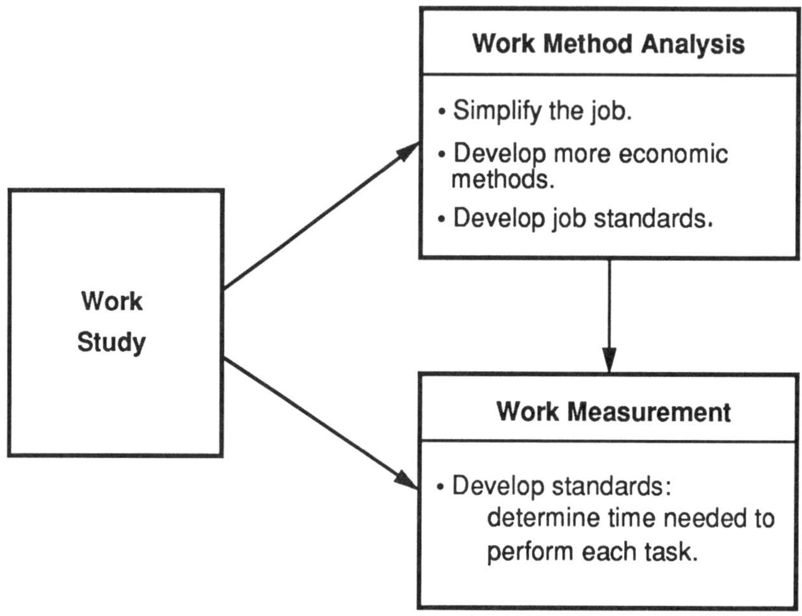


**Figure 2-9**
**Work Study Activities**

The design analysis is followed by the operation analysis which is carried out for each product element.

The rule, when conducting the operations analysis, is to attempt to eliminate an operation before trying to improve it. Often operations are set at the inception of the product and continue throughout the product life disregarding changes in the manufacturing technology, machines and tool design, or changes in the product design. Often the reason for an operation is to ensure the quality of the preceding operations. The rational for such an operation does not exist anymore when the JIT-based quality at source is applied, where the responsibility for the quality is assigned to the person performing the job.

Improvement in production planning and operations scheduling leads to the elimination of many nonvalue-adding operations, such as storing, material handling, and quality control. Also changes in the plant layout, being part of JIT programs, often call for changes in operations and, in fact, present an excellent opportunity for improvements. The operation analysis may involve introducing more efficient tooling and setup time reduction or improving manufacturing processes and eliminating production tasks by using new materials.

## Techniques Used in Work Methods Analysis

A number of tools are used in the work methods analysis, both in the charting form or graphical form and in the table format. Main aids are the operations charts, process charts, and assembly charts, and operator-machine charts.

### THE ASSEMBLY CHART

The process flow design is reflected in the *assembly chart*, also known as a *gozinto chart*. It shows the sequence in which parts are assembled into the final product. An example of an assembly chart is shown in Figure 2-10.

A double-panel desk consists of four major components: FF4RR.4, FF4RR.3, FF4RR.2, and FF4RR.1. Assembly unit FF4RR.4, box drawer pedestal, assembled of parts FF4RR.4.1 through FF4RR 4.8, proceeds to assembly with component FF4RR.3, modesty panel, and further, with component FF4RR.2 double panel. The final assembly is completed by assembling top—FF4RR.1—cleaning the desk, painting and drying, and providing the final inspection.

The assembly chart shows all product components, the sequence of their assembly, and auxiliary operations such as cleaning and inspections.

### THE FLOW PROCESS CHART

The *flow process chart* is a presentation of the sequence of tasks required to do the job. Tasks are coded by means of graphical symbols, and distances are indicated along with time. Coding activities allow visual evaluation of the sequence and the frequency of activities taking place. An example of the flow process chart is shown in Figure 2-11.

### THE OPERATOR-MACHINE ANALYSIS CHART

The *operator-machine analysis chart*, compiled for each individual operation, assists in analyzing the interaction between the worker and the machine. Along with the operations analysis, performance improvement requires examining each operation step in detail so that every worker's action while performing the task is analysed. An example of the operator-machine analysis chart is shown in Figure 2-12.

The purpose of this form is to identify the rationale, timing, and duration of each motion, to eliminate extraneous motions, reduce motion time, and select and replace those motions causing fatigue. The operator-machine analysis chart is further analyzed with the aim of achieving motion economy, known as the *micromotion analysis*. The micromotion analysis is done applying a *simultaneous motion chart* or *simo chart*. The simo chart is used to compare the movements of each hand during an operation.

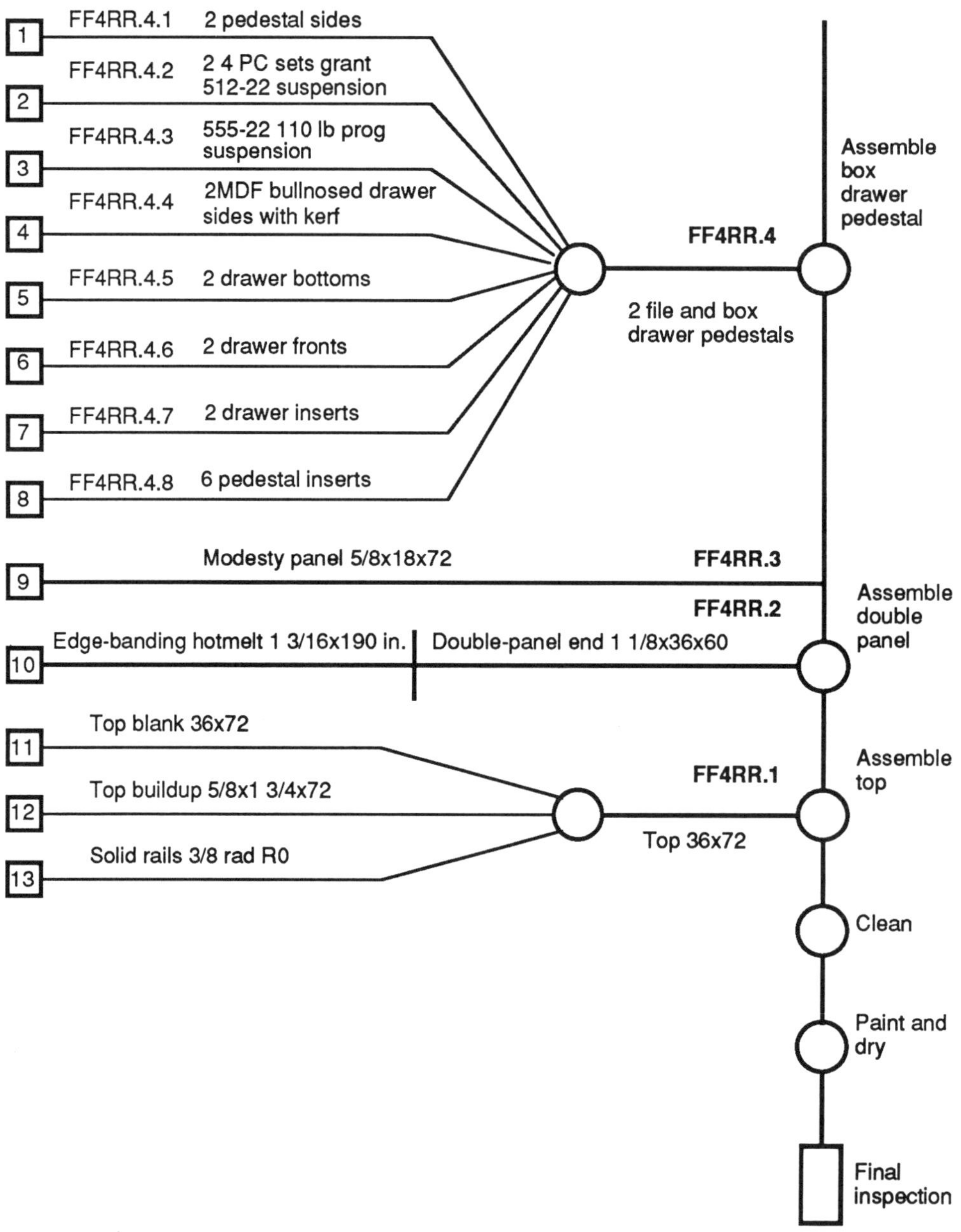


**Figure 2-10**
**Assembly Chart for a Double Panel Desk**

| Department | | Study # | Date |
|---|---|---|---|
| Division | | Taken by | |
| Section | | Chart Commences | |
| Present/Proposed Method | Man/Material Chart | Chart Ends | |
| Task Description | | | |

| Step # | Details of Operation | Operation | Inspection | Delay | Transport | Storage | Quantity | Destination | Time | Remarks |
|---|---|---|---|---|---|---|---|---|---|---|
| | | ○ | □ | D | ⇨ | △ | | | | |
| | | ○ | □ | D | ⇨ | △ | | | | |
| | | ○ | □ | D | ⇨ | △ | | | | |
| | | ○ | □ | D | ⇨ | △ | | | | |
| | | ○ | □ | D | ⇨ | △ | | | | |
| | | ○ | □ | D | ⇨ | △ | | | | |
| | | ○ | □ | D | ⇨ | △ | | | | |
| | | ○ | □ | D | ⇨ | △ | | | | |
| | | ○ | □ | D | ⇨ | △ | | | | |
| | | ○ | □ | D | ⇨ | △ | | | | |
| | | ○ | □ | D | ⇨ | △ | | | | |
| | | ○ | □ | D | ⇨ | △ | | | | |
| | | ○ | □ | D | ⇨ | △ | | | | |
| | | ○ | □ | D | ⇨ | △ | | | | |
| | | ○ | □ | D | ⇨ | △ | | | | |
| | | ○ | □ | D | ⇨ | △ | | | | |
| | | ○ | □ | D | ⇨ | △ | | | | |
| | | ○ | □ | D | ⇨ | △ | | | | |
| | | ○ | □ | D | ⇨ | △ | | | | |
| | | ○ | □ | D | ⇨ | △ | | | | |
| | | ○ | □ | D | ⇨ | △ | | | | |
| | | ○ | □ | D | ⇨ | △ | | | | |
| | | ○ | □ | D | ⇨ | △ | | | | |

| Summary | Total number of steps | Operation | | Inspection | | Delay | | Transport | | Storage |
|---|---|---|---|---|---|---|---|---|---|---|
| | | | Time | | Time | | Time | | Time | |
| | | | | | | | | | | |
| | | | | | | | | | | |

**Figure 2-11**
**Flow Process Chart**

| Task No. | Task Description | Operator | Machine |
|---|---|---|---|
| 1 | Withdraw material from stack | 0.15 minutes | Idle |
| 2 | Put plate on machine table | 0.08 minutes | 0.08 minutes |
| 3 | Tighten bolts | 0.65 minutes | 0.65 minutes |
| 4 | Light cut of plate (one run) | 2.40 minutes | 2.40 minutes |
| 5 | Release bolts | 0.35 minutes | 0.35 minutes |
| 6 | Remove part from machine | 0.18 minutes | 0.18 minutes |
| | **Total cycle time** | **3.81 minutes** | |
| | Work time | 3.81 minutes | 3.66 minutes |
| | Idle time | -- | 0.15 minutes |

**Figure 2-12**
**An Operator-Machine Analysis Chart**

## Work Measurements

After method studies have been completed, the next step is to identify the job/task durations and establish the production rates so essential for production planning and control. It is often said that time standards motivate employees because they serve as a guideline for performance. Nobody likes to be behind. Standards show how we are performing, where we stand now, and what it takes to get ahead. Usually, a little bit of forward planning will distinguish those who are ahead from those lagging behind. In this respect, standards are motivators that bring assurance to the work force by showing the direction.

The work methods analysis and work measurement are not just independent preproduction planning activities; they are conducted iteratively, with the purpose of identifying the way of producing a product of highest value where product quality is complemented by its lowest possible cost.

Work measurement is a critical input into production planning, including the capacity planning and the vital function of operations scheduling and machine loading. It is also essential for cost accounting, budgeting, and performance measurement.

There are four techniques used in developing the time standards:

1. Historical data
2. Time studies based on the number of observations of an operator
3. Predetermined motion-time data, that is, making use of existing timetables of the motions generic to all jobs
4. Work sampling

### MAKING USE OF HISTORICAL DATA FOR DEVELOPING TIME STANDARDS

Historical data time standards are developed based on the previous performance. Even nonrepetitive job shop production consists of standard job elements constantly repeated for a variety of jobs. Time standards for these job elements are relatively simple to develop, based on production records—work reports and time cards. In some make-to-order production systems, this technique, often sufficiently accurate and producing by far the lowest cost, is the only way to determine the standard time to perform work tasks.

These so-called nonengineered techniques find wide use in nonstandard-type production applications and in modern production systems where planning and control, at an increasing rate, become the responsibility of the people performing the work tasks.

The work force is involved in planning, shouldering the responsibility for the work they do, and taking an active part in setting their work standards. Usually, worker-developed work standards are higher than the engineered ones set by time study analysts.

### HOW TIME STUDY IS USED FOR DEVELOPING TIME STANDARDS

Time study, that is, timing a worker performing the task, involves the following steps:

1. Dividing work into commonly performed tasks
2. Periodically observing a task being performed and establishing time standards for each element, applying the stopwatch work measurement
3. Assessing the level of performance exhibited by an operator, according to a specific rating criterion being developed for each work situation
4. Adjusting the time standard according to the observed cycle time, operator's level of performance, and time allowances

When observing a task, the observer must make a judgment of the speed at which the work is being performed—the speed rating. The *speed rating* is a performance evaluation method measuring the work speed—the amount of work done per unit of time. To do this, one must compare the speed of work with the acceptable standard speed. A standard speed of work is set at a production level that qualified workers will maintain for the entire working day without getting overtired.

Speed rating is expressed as a ratio of the observed performance standards to the performance speed, assumed to be 100 percent. The standard speed is usually depicted by a person walking without a load at 3 miles per hour. Performance rating of 115 percent or 92 percent, for example, indicates that the observed speed is, correspondingly, above or below the normal speed. Despite the fact that the time study analyst applies a subjective judgment to determine the speed rating, these ratings become accurate enough with experience. The computation of three times used in the time study analysis—cycle time, normal time, and standard time—follows:

*Cycle time* (*CT*) is an average of the observed cycle times:

$$CT = \frac{\text{sum of observed cycle times}}{\text{number of observations}}$$

When computing the average cycle time, uncommon nonrecurring observations are not taken into account. For example, if the task observations are as follows: (in minutes) 6, 8, 7, 8, 9, 17, 7, then the average cycle time is computed as

$$\text{cycle time} = \frac{6 + 8 + 7 + 8 + 9 + 7}{6} = 7.5 \text{ minutes}$$

Cycle time is 7.5 minutes. (An odd observation of 17 minutes is discarded since there could have been unusual circumstances, such as delays or job interruptions.)

*Normal time* (*NT*) is equal to the cycle time adjusted for operator's performance rating:

$$NT = \text{cycle time} \times \text{performance rating}$$

*Standard time* (*ST*) is equal to normal time adjusted for the delays expressed by the allowance factor:

$$ST = \text{normal time} \times \text{allowance factor}$$

The *allowance factor* consists of an allowance for personal needs, fatigue, and unavoidable delays.

*Allowance for personal needs*, for example, allows employees to maintain general body functions, such as trips to the restroom and drinking fountain. Personal needs allowance is usually assigned from 3 to 5 minutes per hour.

*Allowance for fatigue* largely depends on the work environment, such as noise, temperature, humidity, and light conditions and the type of work performed by the operators. *Allowance for unavoidable delays* includes interruptions by the supervisors for giving instructions, delays due to the time study, personal telephone calls, and so on.

Total allowance (*TA*) estimated as sum of all allowances:

$$TA = \text{allowance for personal needs} + \text{allowance for fatigue} + \text{allowance for unavoidable delays}$$

For example, total allowance at Dresser Industrial Tool Division consists of personal allowance, allowance for fatigue, and miscellaneous allowance: 1.8 minutes, 2.4 minutes, and 1.8 minutes per hour, respectively:

$$TA = 1.8 + 2.4 + 1.8 = 6.0 \text{ minutes per hour}$$

which is 10 percent of the working time:

$$\text{Allowance factor} = \frac{100\%}{100\ \% - \text{total allowance (in \%)}}$$

$$= \frac{100}{100 - 10} = 1.11$$

PREDETERMINED TIME STANDARDS

*Predetermined motion time standards* (PMTS) use elemental motion time for developing time standards. PMTS systems deal with times for the manual part of work tasks—basic motions rather than job elements.

The average time for performing a basic manual work element is relatively constant for any type of operation. These times of predetermined motion elements are compiled into tables of standard time values, like the ones shown in Figure 2-13A and Figure 2-13B. These motion elements could be such as reach, grasp, move, position, and release, each one, in turn, further subdivided according to the moving distances. The duration of basic elements is estimated in terms of time measurement units (TMUs), which is equal to 0.00001 hour or 0.0006 minute.

To estimate a time standard, a particular operation is subdivided into these elementary movements, and their duration found in the tables is summarized. This involves considerable details for compiling a time standard.

Many predetermined motion-time data systems are currently available, the main ones representing a family of time measurement methods developed by the Method Time Measure Association (MTM)—MTM-1, MTM-2, MTM-3,

| Distance moved inches | Time TMU | | | | Hand in motion | |
|---|---|---|---|---|---|---|
| | A | B | C or D | E | A | B |
| 3/4 or less | 2.0 | 2.0 | 2.0 | 2.0 | 1.6 | 1.6 |
| 1 | 2.5 | 2.5 | 3.6 | 2.4 | 2.3 | 2.3 |
| 2 | 4.0 | 4.0 | 5.9 | 3.8 | 3.5 | 2.7 |
| 3 | 5.3 | 5.3 | 7.3 | 5.3 | 4.5 | 3.6 |
| 4 | 6.1 | 6.4 | 8.4 | 6.8 | 4.9 | 4.3 |
| 5 | 6.5 | 7.8 | 9.4 | 7.4 | 5.3 | 5.0 |
| 6 | 7.0 | 8.6 | 10.1 | 8.0 | 5.7 | 5.7 |
| 7 | 7.4 | 9.3 | 10.8 | 8.7 | 6.1 | 6.5 |
| 8 | 7.9 | 10.1 | 11.5 | 9.3 | 6.5 | 7.2 |
| 9 | 8.3 | 10.8 | 12.2 | 9.9 | 6.9 | 7.9 |
| 10 | 8.7 | 11.5 | 12.9 | 10.5 | 7.3 | 8.6 |
| 12 | 9.6 | 12.9 | 14.2 | 11.8 | 8.1 | 10.1 |
| 14 | 10.5 | 14.4 | 15.6 | 13.0 | 8.9 | 11.5 |
| 16 | 11.4 | 15.8 | 17.0 | 14.2 | 9.7 | 12.9 |
| 18 | 12.3 | 17.2 | 18.4 | 15.5 | 10.5 | 14.4 |
| 20 | 13.1 | 18.6 | 19.8 | 16.7 | 11.3 | 15.8 |
| 22 | 14.0 | 20.1 | 21.2 | 18.0 | 12.1 | 17.3 |
| 24 | 14.9 | 21.5 | 22.5 | 19.2 | 12.9 | 18.8 |
| 26 | 15.8 | 22.9 | 23.9 | 20.4 | 13.7 | 20.2 |
| 28 | 16.7 | 24.4 | 25.3 | 21.7 | 14.5 | 21.7 |
| 30 | 17.5 | 25.8 | 26.7 | 22.9 | 15.3 | 23.2 |

**Case and Description**

**A.** Reach to an object in a fixed location, or to an object in other hand or on which other hand rests.

**B.** Reach to a single object in a location which may vary slightly from cycle to cycle.

**C.** Reach to an object jumbled with other objects in a group so that search and select occur.

**D.** Reach to a very small object or where an accurate grasp is required.

**E.** Reach to an indefinite location to get a hand in position for body balance or next motion or out of way.

**Figure 2-13 A**
**Methods Time Measurements (MTM). Data for Reach Motion**

| Distance moved inches | Time TMU | | | | Weight allowance | | |
|---|---|---|---|---|---|---|---|
| | A | B | C | Hand in motion B | Weight (lb.) up to | Factor | Constant TMU |
| 3/4 or less | 2.0 | 2.0 | 2.0 | 1.7 | 2.5 | 0 | 0 |
| 1 | 2.5 | 2.9 | 3.4 | 2.3 | | | |
| 2 | 3.6 | 4.6 | 5.2 | 2.9 | 7.5 | 1.06 | 2.2 |
| 3 | 4.9 | 5.7 | 6.7 | 3.6 | | | |
| 4 | 6.1 | 6.9 | 8.0 | 4.3 | 12.5 | 1.11 | 3.9 |
| 5 | 7.3 | 8.0 | 9.2 | 5.0 | | | |
| 6 | 8.1 | 8.9 | 10.3 | 5.7 | 17.5 | 1.17 | 5.6 |
| 7 | 8.9 | 9.7 | 11.1 | 6.5 | | | |
| 8 | 9.7 | 10.6 | 11.8 | 7.2 | 22.5 | 1.22 | 7.4 |
| 9 | 10.5 | 11.5 | 12.7 | 7.9 | | | |
| 10 | 11.3 | 12.2 | 13.5 | 8.6 | 27.5 | 1.28 | 9.1 |
| 12 | 12.9 | 13.4 | 15.2 | 10.0 | | | |
| 14 | 14.4 | 14.6 | 16.9 | 11.4 | 32.5 | 1.33 | 10.8 |
| 16 | 16.0 | 15.8 | 18.7 | 12.8 | | | |
| 18 | 17.6 | 17.0 | 20.4 | 14.2 | 37.5 | 1.39 | 12.5 |
| 20 | 19.2 | 18.2 | 22.1 | 15.6 | | | |
| 22 | 20.8 | 19.4 | 23.4 | 17.0 | 42.5 | 1.44 | 14.3 |
| 24 | 22.4 | 20.6 | 25.5 | 18.4 | | | |
| 26 | 24.0 | 21.8 | 27.3 | 19.8 | 47.5 | 1.50 | 16.0 |
| 28 | 25.5 | 23.1 | 29.0 | 21.2 | | | |
| 30 | 27.1 | 24.3 | 30.7 | 22.7 | | | |

**Case and Description**

**A.** Move object to other hand or against stop.

**B.** Move object to approximate or indefinite location.

**C.** Move object to exact location.

**Figure 2-13 B**
**Methods Time Measurements (MTM). Data for Move Motion**

and MTM-4—computer-aided systems, each providing a varying degree of time estimate precision.

## DEVELOPING TIME STANDARDS APPLYING WORK SAMPLING

Work sampling is a method of compiling time standards by randomly observing a portion of a work activity or a task over a period of time. Brief observations of an activity yield data about idle time and the nature of work interruptions. Along with setting labor standard times and determining allowances, work sampling is used in ratio-delay studies—determining the percentage of time and the nature of delays and measuring workers' performance. Work sampling is often used in employees' evaluations and when compiling job descriptions.

Work sampling is especially useful in the analysis of nonstandard jobs when identifying job elements and skill levels involved. Work sampling technique is based on the statistical certainty and thus is prone to errors. The maximum value of sample error is

$$E = Z\sqrt{\frac{p(1-p)}{n}}$$

where

$E$ = maximum value of the sampling error

$Z$ = the value of the standard normal random variable representing the number of standard deviations required for reaching the desired confidence level

$n$ = the sample size

$p$ = proportion of time worker is observed

The confidence level of obtained data depends on the number of observations which sometimes can be fairly large when a degree of accuracy is required. The size of the sample is estimated according to the following formula, derived from the previous equation:

$$n = \frac{Z^2\, p\,(1-p)}{E^2}$$

where

$n$ = sample size

$Z$ = number of standard deviations required for reaching the desired confidence level ($Z$ = 1 for 68% confidence, $Z$ = 1.96 for 95% confidence, and $Z$ = 2.58 for 99% confidence)

$h$ = acceptable sample error (here percentages interpreted as decimal fractions)

For example, at Dresser Industrial Tool Division, CNC Turret Lathes Work Center, when developing time standards, the average idle time per workstation is assumed to be approximately 10 percent of work time. You must determine the number of observations, applying the work sampling method, if the desired confidence level is 95.45 percent and the acceptable sample error is 4 percent.

According to the previous equation, the result is

$$n = \frac{Z^2 p(1-p)}{E^2} = \frac{(2)^2(0.10)\ (0.90)}{(0.04)^2} = 225 \text{ observations}$$

The result is 225 observations, which must be taken at any time during working hours. This is not a time study as such but an observation of the work/idle condition of a workstation. Work sampling requires a fairly large number of observations according to the statistical rule of large numbers. These observations do not need to be deliberate and can be done while passing by or working in this work area on other tasks.

## SUMMARY

The organizational structures of the four types of productive systems, both strategic and tactical ones, discussed in this chapter—manufacturing, process industry, services, and project—are often mingled so that two or more system types are integrated within a single organization. For example, there is no pure manufacturing system or process industry productive system as such, as these systems require all kinds of services and often include project activities. And conversely, service systems often include manufacturing and project activities. Dissimilarities of these productive systems are blurred when they are approached from the operational optimization perspective of the productive flow.

Product flow is affected by plant layout as well as ordering cycle and phase, which vary according to type of product or services and order quantities. Variances between planning cycles and production cycles depend entirely on the effectiveness of planning and control procedures. The latest trend in industry is in flexible manufacturing systems (FMS). These systems rely on a multiskill work force and on assigning the responsibility to those who do the work. An example of such an organizational structure is a T-organization in which employees are involved in decision making and share the responsibility with their bosses.

Design of work systems also relies on efficient work methods. Considerations in job design fall into three major categories: sociopsychological job considerations, ergonomic considerations which refer to the physical job environment, and the analysis of work methods and work measurements.

Sociopsychological considerations for job design include job enlargement and job enrichment. Ergonomics focuses at creating work conditions conducive to efficient work performance and safety. Finally, work study consists of two basic activities; work methods analysis and work measurement, and is aimed at developing more efficient work methods and reducing work contents as well as developing and maintaining time standards.

Our next discussion concerns production planning and control systems and their differences and similarities in various productive systems.

# Part Two

## PRODUCTION PLANNING AND CONTROL SYSTEMS

# 3

# Independent Demand Production Planning

## USING PRODUCT AND PROCESS PLANNING TECHNIQUES

Production management involves continual decision making, decision making as to the best use of productive resources and creating a balance between the desired results and the available resources within time and cost constraints. Production management achieves its purpose through controlling the material flow and its accompanying productive services flow. Production management accomplishes its purpose largely through the production planning and control system. *Balancing* could be the synonym for planning.

Balancing in planning means finding the equilibrium—balancing what is required (product requirements) with the means (resources) available. In Figure 3-1, the product represents the final result of a production activity, the product itself, while resources are the means of production: labor, equipment and machinery, tools, and raw materials. Please note that raw materials are considered part of resources.

### Recognizing the Two Types of Production Resources

There are two categories of resources. First, there are resources controlled by the inventory control system. These are known as *dedicated resources*—raw materials and purchased components. Second, there are resources controlled by

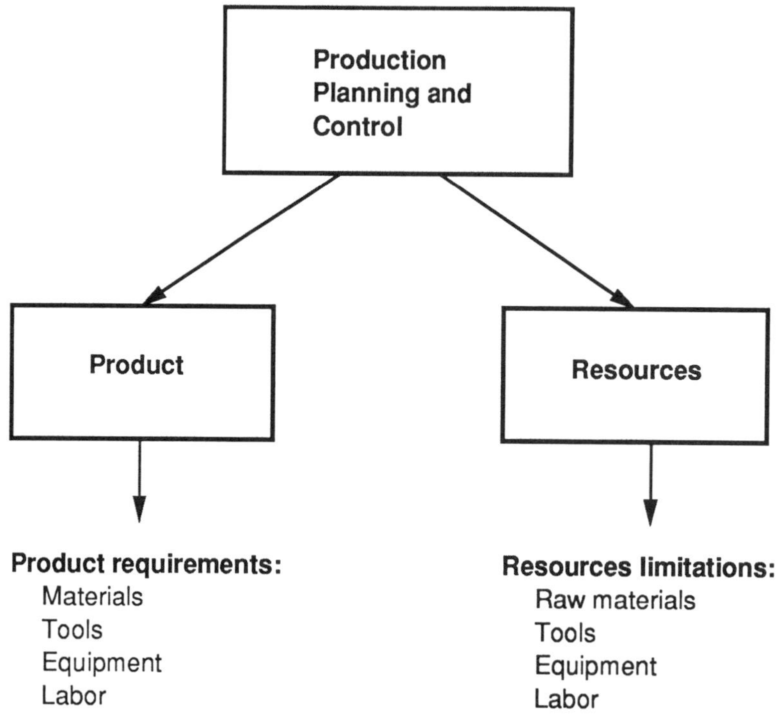


**Figure 3-1**
**The Concepts of Production -- Product and Resources**

the capacity planning and control system. These are called *shared resources*—labor, equipment, tools, and services. Figure 3-2 illustrates the separation of resources into the dedicated and the shared categories.

## DEDICATED RESOURCES

Dedicated resources have their one-time availability. Dedicated resources are used once in the production of a specific item. Examples include such items as a piece of a steel bar that is used exclusively for the manufacture of one gear. Another piece of a steel bar is required in order to produce another gear. A welding rod is used to weld two pieces (a shaft and a pin) together into a one-shaft assembly unit. To produce another shaft assembly unit, another shaft and pin are needed, as well as another welding rod. Dedicated resources are controlled by the inventory control system. The primary concern here is the availability of a resource at the first stage of its usage.

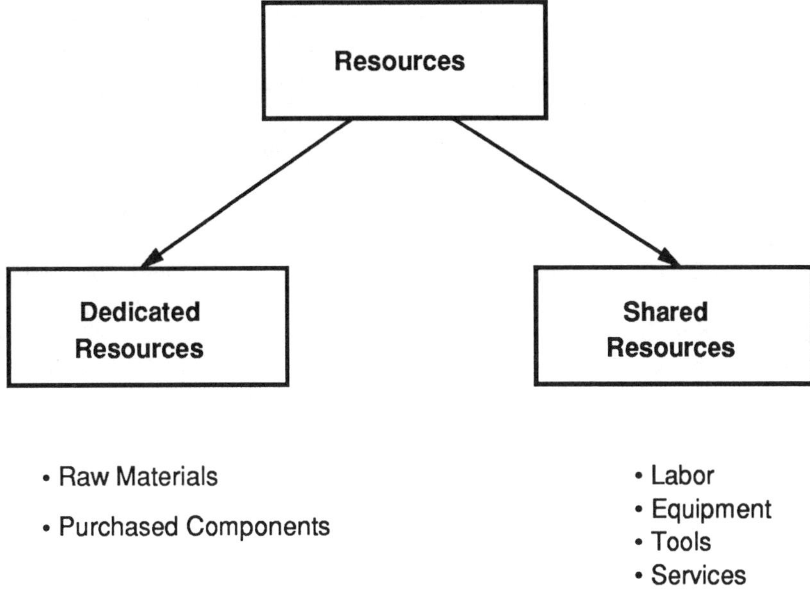


**Figure 3-2**
**Dedicated and Shared Resources**

Resource planning ceases after a dedicated resource has entered the first production stage because the resource is already used, becoming part of work-in-process. Dedicated resources are used exclusively for producing a product, and at the end of the production process, they appear as the final product. Supply items, tools, and raw materials are also dedicated resources when they are used exclusively for this product. Planning and control over dedicated resources aim at the one-time availability of these resources. Dedicated resources represent the product concept. For example, steel used in the manufacture of an automobile is the automobile itself.

SHARED RESOURCES

Shared resources include the plant, the equipment, and the labor force used to make a product. Shared resources are "reusable" resources. Proper control over shared resources is targeted at their increased utilization, requiring time-phased planning. Shared resources are more difficult to plan and control because they "reappear" in each phase of the time-phased planning. Production planning is largely concerned with the efficient sharing of these resources by many products—the so-called "time sharing." Planning and control over shared resources —labor, machines, and services—are structured as a time-phased program aimed at the maximum utilization of these resources over extended periods of time. Control over shared resources is continuous or time phased. Planning is done in "time slot" units.

Two concepts are paramount in production: product and process. *Product* is the result of a production activity, while *process* includes all the means of production to make this product. Product includes dedicated resources, such as raw materials and bought out components. Process includes shared resources involved in the production of this product, such as equipment and labor.

Everything involved in production is attributed to one of these concepts. Production planning and control can be defined as the balancing of product requirements with process limitations. The relationship of product and process is shown in Figure 3-3. Product comprises everything contained in the final outcome of production, including raw materials and purchased components. These are dedicated resources as is shown in Figure 3-4.

Process comprises the means of production—shared resources. The concepts "product" and "process" are essential to any production system: product requirements are subject to process restrictions.

Shared productive resources—labor, materials, machines, and services—have features/characteristics different from dedicated resources and thus require different types of planning and control systems. The availability of dedicated resources can be effectively controlled by a traditional inventory control system. Shared resources, such as machines and labor, require time-phased production planning and control system, as well as detailed operational scheduling and machine loading. To optimize the utilization of resources, process restrictions and product requirements must be continuously evaluated and analyzed within the framework of the production planning and control system. Production planning is important

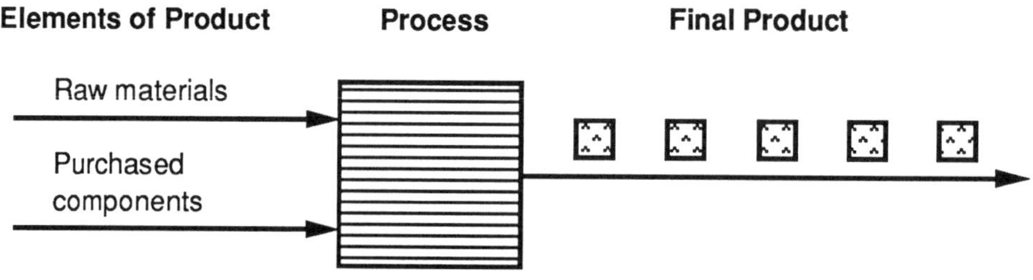


**Figure 3-3**
**The Relationship of Product and Process**

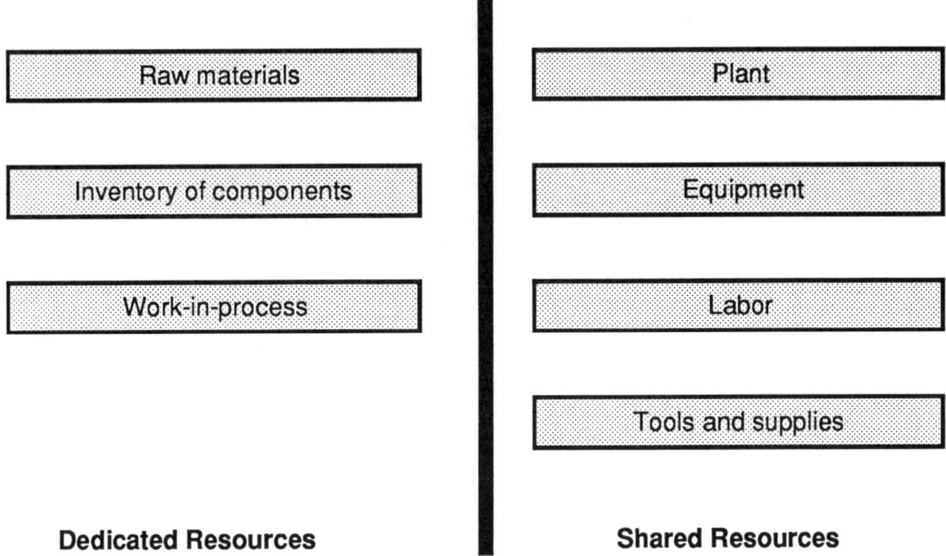


**Figure 3-4**
**Dedicated and Shared Resources**

in that it specifies/delineates company's major performance indices, such as lead time, product cost, productivity, and efficiency.

## Two Stages of Production Planning

Two stages are recognized in production planning:

1. Establishing the *set of objectives*
2. Specifying the *course of actions* needed to achieve these objectives

Figure 3-5 illustrates how production planning is broken into two stages.

All planning should have a clear set of objectives. Establishing objectives should be your main task. The next stage is to balance the available resources needed to satisfy your customer demand. Existing or expected customer demand, the basis for planning, is satisfied within the limits set by the existing level

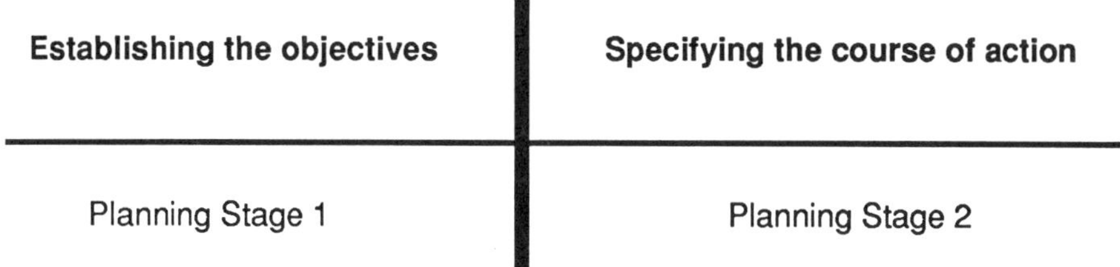

Establishing the objectives
Specifying the course of action
Planning Stage 1
Planning Stage 2


**Figure 3-5**
**The Two Stages of Production Planning**

of resources. This definition applies equally to any type organization, manufacturing or services.

### USING THREE TACTICAL PLANNING ALTERNATIVES TO ACHIEVE EQUILIBRIUM

There are two possible states that may occur during planning. First, your requirements may exceed your resources; second, your resources may exceed your requirements.

Three alternatives are possible for achieving the equilibrium between product requirements and process limitations.

### ALTERNATIVE 1: ADJUSTING STAFF AND MATERIAL RESOURCES

Alternative 1 consists of balancing your planning by *adjusting your human and material resources* to suit given requirements. Alternative 1, state 1 is to hire an additional work force when your demand exceeds your resources, while alternative 1, state 2 is to lay off the work force when the demand declines. Such a policy is not always cost effective, if the decrease in demand is temporary. To retrench the work force requires expenses, such as unemployment insurance and severance pay. Even greater expenses are needed for training when rehiring the work force. Another strategy is to increase your inventory levels or simply subcontract the work.

### ALTERNATIVE 2: ADJUSTING PRODUCTION REQUIREMENTS TO MATCH YOUR RESOURCES

Alternative 2 consists of balancing by *adjusting your requirements* to suit your resources. Alternative 2, state 1 is to satisfy only this part of demand for which the resources are available. Alternative 2, state 2, increasing demand, is a significantly more complex task because it can be accomplished only by increasing the product value. Increasing the product value often can be achieved by reducing the selling price, which should be supported by the increased productivity and the reduction in production costs. Often advertising and promotions assist in influencing the demand, despite the fact that production function is still a supreme factor in influencing the customer acceptance.

### ALTERNATIVE 3: RECONCILING PRODUCTION REQUIREMENTS AND RESOURCES

Alternative 3 consists of balancing by *reconciling both your requirements and your level of resources*. The best result in planning—the efficiency improvement—is achieved by planning adjustments to both your product and process, not only by plain leveling of one or another variable.

All these alternatives require advanced forecasting and integrated product and process planning and control. Adjusting product and resources is achieved through establishing a product-focused layout. In this regard, flexible manufacturing systems (FMS) are becoming increasingly popular, especially as they relate to operational planning, where manufacturing cells have a strong capability to respond instantly to operational fluctuations in demand (i.e., to expand instantly in one shop floor area and to contract its capacity in another shop floor area).

## RECOGNIZING THE SPECIFIC FUNCTIONS OF PRODUCTION PLANNING AND CONTROL

A production program is a course of actions, a standard for execution. At the execution stage, it seldom happens that everything goes as planned. There are numerous disruptions to the production program, such as equipment breakdowns, power failures, absenteeism, lack of materials or supplies, and labor strikes. Production plans are verified against the actual performance at the execution stage. This is the function of production control. A production plan is the standard with which production control performs.

The relationship of planning and control functions is often compared with an electronic "feedback" process control device controlling the temperature in a building. It is a self-adjusting system designed to monitor the temperature and adjust it to the predetermined level when a deviation occurs. The basic principle is that the sensing mechanism measures the actual output and sends the data to the controlling mechanism, which compares it with the desired planned output. The variance data are sent back to plan a corrective action by triggering an electrical impulse instrumental in bringing the temperature back to normal.

In production planning and control, the "thermostat's" corrective actions are comparable with that of management monitoring performance and taking corrective actions when a deviation occurs. Here, the process adjustment requires a human intervention—decision making—due to the large number of interrelated variables/activities involved in the process and the dispersion of the events in time and place.

There are two types of control: corrective and preventive. Corrective control is depicted as feedback control that takes place after the action has occurred. Preventive control is directed at preventing the undesired performance before a deviation occurs.

## Using Corrective Control

*Corrective control* is a postevent action aimed at adjusting the process to the predetermined standard of performance. As a result, a deviation occurs before the action is taken, and the plan is affected. In corrective control, adjustments can be done to the future performance. There are two types of corrective control: interfunctional control and execution control.

### INTERFUNCTIONAL CONTROL

In *interfunctional control*, shown as case A in Figure 3-6, the deviation is communicated back for replanning. The adjustment of the process is done through varying the production plan, which requires communication of information and involves outside process decision makers. Because interfunctional control involves revising and issuing the updated plan such an updated plan is invariably the second best choice after the initial plan.

### EXECUTIONAL CONTROL

*Executional control*, shown as case B in Figure 3-6, is a self-regulating system where the adjustment is done by those executing the process, without communicating the information to outside decision makers. This is, for example, represented by programmed decisions taking place when the developed standard procedures, policies, and rules allow the subordinates to make on-the-spot decisions, without waiting for the involvement of a higher echelon decision maker. The need for forward and backward communication of information and the need for outside decision making is reduced. Nevertheless, in this example, a deviation from the plan has still occurred, and it requires further replanning. Executional control requires timely operational information.

*Advantages* include cost effectiveness because (1) communication and outside decision making are eliminated and (2) this method, when well organized, leaves the production plan intact.

*Disadvantages* include a danger of management by crisis due to the excessive expediting.

Execution control is contrary to expediting practice where dedicated expeditors struggle through the jungle of functional production units to move toward the assembly of components of the products for which they are responsible. An example of execution control occurs in T-organizations, where functional production

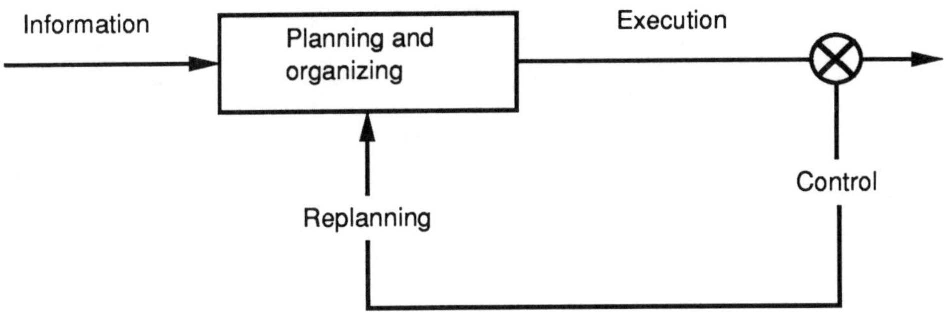


**A. Interfunctional Control**

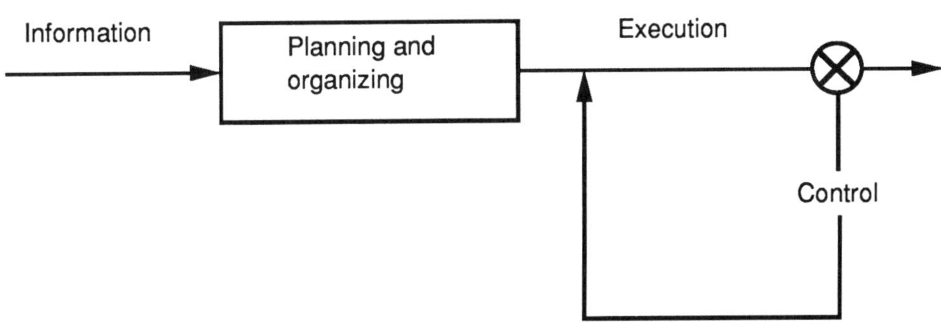


**B. Executional Control**

**Figure 3-6**
**Interfunctional and Executional Control**

departments receive daily/weekly operational work orders and work in concert with other functional, production, and assembly departments, identifying job priorities and adjusting their operations accordingly.

Production control cannot exist without production planning. Planning outlines your standard for performance, while control compares your performance against the setup standards. Flexible manufacturing systems utilizing manufacturing cells are a good example of executional control. These systems are discussed in Chapter 8.

## Using Preventive Control

*Preventive control* is often called *feed-forward control,* where the anticipation of future problems and the development of contingency plans are undertaken to overcome these problems. Preventive control occurs when work orders are issued only after making sure that no backlog exists and that the required production capacity is available. Steven Covin, originally head of management information systems, and now in charge of training at Compaq's Houston factory, says: "We ensure the availability of capacity all the way through to the shipping and dispatching area, and a job is not scheduled unless there is capacity available."

Corrective and preventive production control can be expressed by the following models:

*corrective control:* information→planning→execution→control→planning
*preventive control:* information→planning→control→planning→execution→control

A preventive production planning and control model usually produces better results than the corrective control one because the plans are verified prior to the execution. Thus less control and fewer adjustments are required at the execution stage. Executional control is routinely exercised in well-developed preventive control production systems. A diagram illustrating preventive planning and interfunctional control is shown in Figure 3-7. As an example, production planning by means of master production schedule will be associated with corrective planning.

Production planning that involves operational scheduling, and machine loading is an example of preventive control. The availability of capacity is ensured there. As a result, such production planning produces a smoother material flow and requires less adjustments and replanning.

## Using Compounded Control

Compounded control includes both preventive and executional control, which means that production programs are verified and balanced at the planning stage prior to the execution. This effectively reduces variances at the execution stage and makes it possible to apply operational executional corrective control, eliminating the need for the feedback and replanning as is illustrated in Figure 3-8. Compounded control has proven to be successful in many Just-in-Time systems. Later, in Chapter 7, there will be an example of a manufacturing planning and control system known as the integrated task management (ITM). ITM applies compounded production planning and control in which operational schedules submitted to production and functional departments are centrally verified for the availability of capacity. This is followed by enforcing execution control and taking the responsibility for timely job deliveries to downstream work centers.

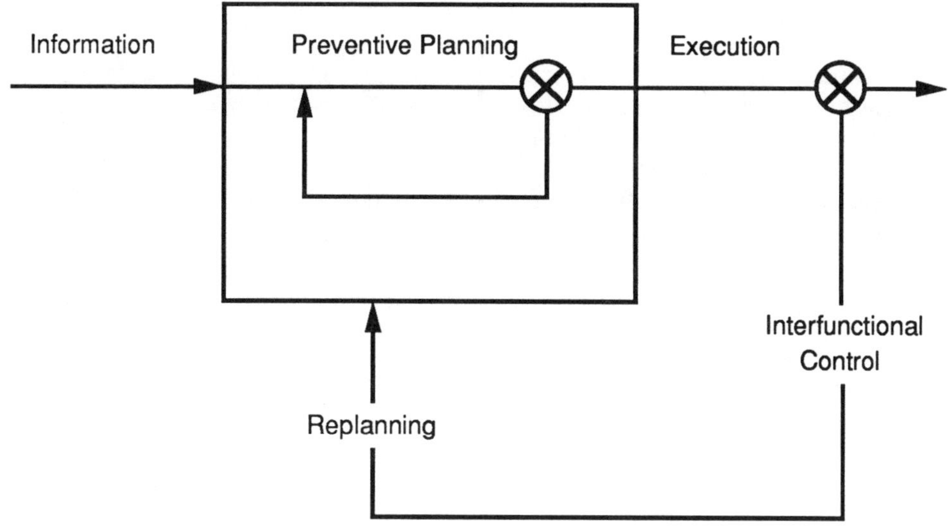


**Figure 3-7**
**Preventive Planning and Interfunctional Control**

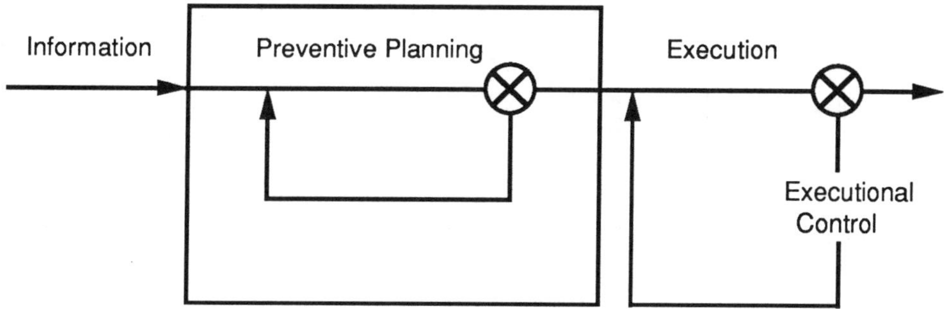


**Figure 3-8**
**Preventive Planning and Executional Control**

## QUALITY AT SOURCE IN PLANNING—WHICH PLAN IS BEST FOR YOU?

The concept of "quality" is obvious in production processes. Lately, numerous plans have arisen to ensure quality. They are collectively known as *quality-at-source plans.* These plans have been producing remarkable results. The concept of quality at source should be enforced in all production planning. This means you will need to verify the validity of your production plans even before the execution takes place.

How can you compile a good quality plan? Your production consists of people whose primary responsibility is the quality of your product and effectiveness of the entire production system in satisfying customers. Your mission and responsibility as a manager is not so much in producing plans but in producing commodities. Thus, any plan is only as helpful as the extent to which it facilitates the production. In other words, it can be said, that planning undergoes a test during the execution. How does your plan work in your day-to-day work environment? The bottom line of the production planning and control system is the total of completed work orders. A good plan will produce a good quality product or service. Every step in your plan is important. No details should be omitted. One planner states that they ensure the availability of every tool and every single bolt before issuing a production order. In many companies, productivity increases up to 20 to 25 percent when preventive control is introduced, as compared with the practice of using corrective control. Still others report productivity improvement through the use of corrective control.

What kind of control is best for you and your company? The majority of planning and control systems practice a mixture of both preventive and corrective control. To achieve the best results in performance, planning and control are fermented into a system comprising a balanced blend of preventive and corrective control. Such examples of preventive planning and control are applied in Just-in-Time systems, which we discuss later on in Chapters 8 through 11.

## LAYING OUT YOUR OBJECTIVES FOR OPTIMUM PRODUCT AND PROCESS PLANNING

For any production to be effective, resources should be utilized to their maximum and the product should be produced within the given time limits at minimal production cost. *Product objectives* can be achieved through the effective management of material flow, for example, completing each stage on time without interruption throughout production stages until the last operation is completed. *Process objectives* are to maximize the utilization of resources by ensuring that all machines and labor are occupied. The purpose of production planning is to reconcile these two diverse tasks. Since these are two distinct concepts with quite different set of objectives, two planning procedures are applied, namely, *product planning* aimed at maximizing production of your product or services and *process planning* aimed at increasing the usage of your resources. Your product and process considerations should be consolidated into a uniform coherent operational optimization methodology and targeted at the common objective of higher productivity and cost reduction.

## Why Time Phasing Is the Principal Factor in Planning

Planning is defined by the measure of how far it extends into the future—the so-called planning horizon or time span. A *time span* consists of time increments, smaller time units in which planning is accomplished. For example, some strategic planning has a 10- to 12-year time span with increments of 1 year. In a shorter duration plan, these are monthly or weekly increments. Planning levels are identified by the time span. Time increments are *time periods*, also known as *buckets*, as shown in Figure 3-9.

The accumulation of data according to time periods is known as *timephasing*. Time is used as a measure of resources (e.g., a machine-hour is a one-hour unit of capacity or a labor-day is an eight-hour capacity of one worker). A time unit multiplied by resource unit-hours of production (labor or machine) is a measure expressing both product requirements and available resources.

time unit x resource unit = capacity unit

The time measurement becomes a general planning unit to the extent that sometimes the time itself is seen as the resource of utmost value. Nevertheless, the time value is established by the resource it measures. On its own, time

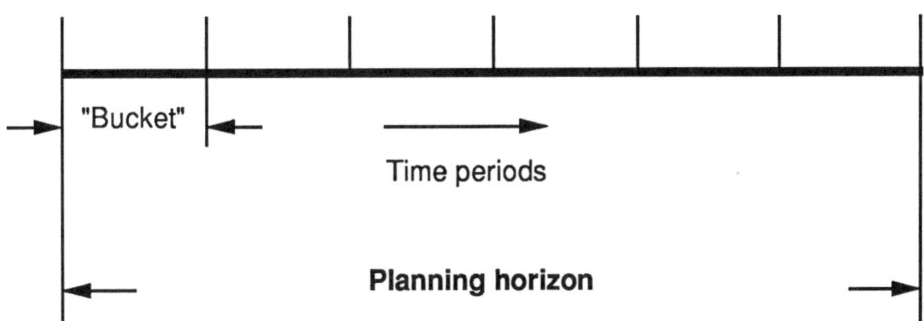


**Figure 3-9**
**Planning Time Units: Planning Horizons and Time Periods**

does not have value. A machine-hour has the value of the machine's hourly running cost. The same could be said about a labor-hour which depends on the worker's hourly rate.

Time phasing is an essential attribute in production plans. It is a major component in any plan. The concern of a routine plan is to ensure the availability of planned items. Time phasing elevates our plan to a preventive production plan. A general plan is, for example, 12,800 components will be required per year. A time-phased plan breaks down the need for these units over a 12-month period as follows:

| Jan. | Feb. | Mar. | Apr. | May. | Jun. | Jul. | Aug. | Sept. | Oct. | Nov. | Dec. | Total |
|---|---|---|---|---|---|---|---|---|---|---|---|---|
| 1,150 | 1,080 | 850 | 880 | — | — | 920 | 960 | 1,120 | 1,060 | 1,200 | 1,220 | 12,800 |

The advantage of the time-phased planning is obvious. During each time period, components can be produced to satisfy just one-period demand instead of keeping 12,800 components in stock to satisfy one-year demand. Time phasing standardizes planning by allocating jobs to various time buckets time periods. Such job allocation simplifies decision making and makes it possible to apply preventive control and corrective executional control of performance.

## USING DEMAND MANAGEMENT TO PREDICT CUSTOMER NEEDS

One purpose of an enterprise is to satisfy customer needs in goods or services. Identifying customer needs is a function known as demand management. Further, demand management interprets the customer demand into a production program outlining the best use of resources to satisfy the demand.

Marketing information is a primary input to a production program. Marketing contributes to a production program the knowledge of what is actually happening to the demand and what can be expected to happen in the future, due to changes in the general economy, the consumer behavior, and the competition. Marketing information is used in forecasting.

Planning deals with the future activities—balancing the future product demand with the process limitations which can be imposed on satisfying this demand. The role of forecasting is to formulate information about the future demand to assist production planning. Forecasts are conducted to serve each stage of planning: a long-term plan, a middle-term plan, and a short-term plan. In essence, every significant management decision is based on some forecast of the future. Long-range, medium-range, and short-range forecasts are known as the *demand forecasts*. A current demand forecast is the shipping forecast.

A long-range demand forecast does not have specific details. The details are not essential at this stage, and the capacity requirement is defined in general terms. A medium-range demand forecast is generated from sales forecasts and combined on-hand customer orders. A short-range shipping forecast is more accurate, it is the latest (last week) demand which is submitted to production departments as a final product mix program.

Demand is an essential and basic component of production planning, since the demand tends to invariably fluctuate due to a number of reasons, such as the seasonal influence, the product life cycle, cyclical elements, and random fluctuations.

Figure 3-10 shows that the components of demand include seasonal variations, cyclical variations, and random variations. Also, demand is distinguished by trend.

demand = trend + seasonal variations + cyclical variations + random variations

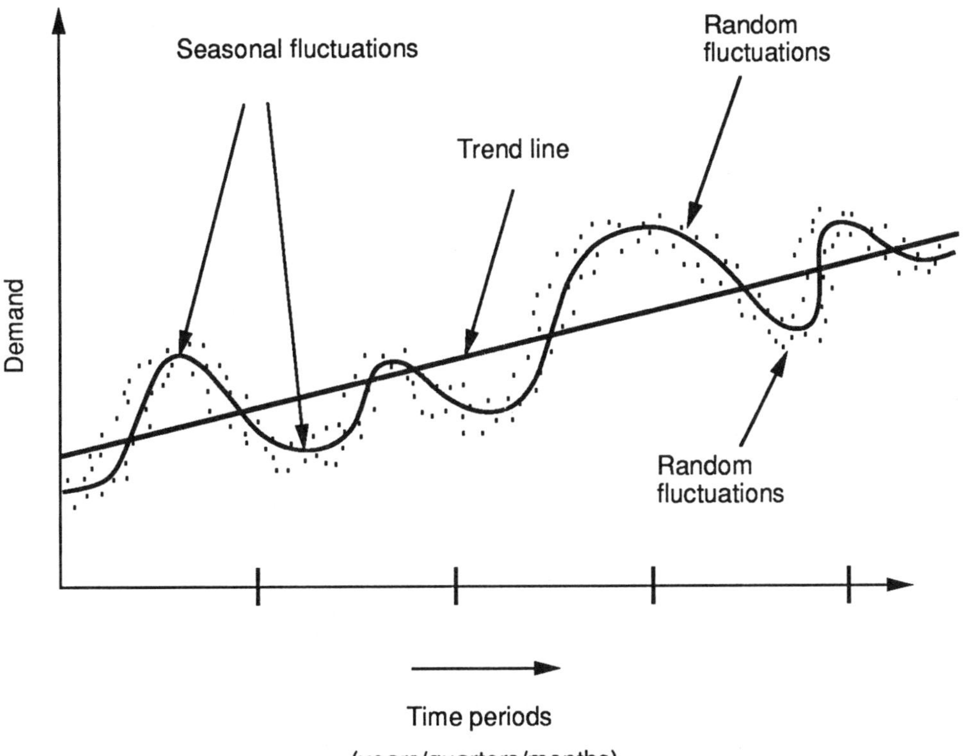


**Figure 3-10**
**Components of Demand**

## Taking the Product Life Cycle into Account

The demand for product or service is not consistent during its lifetime—time elapsed from the inception of a product till its production is terminated. A product life is usually shown graphically as a curve divided into four segments corresponding to the four stages in the product life: introduction, rapid growth of demand, steady state demand or maturity, and product decline. Stages in the product life cycle are exhibited in Figure 3-11.

### THE INTRODUCTION STAGE OF NEW PRODUCT

The initial demand for a new product depends to the great extent on marketing. The initial production stage is the most critical time for a product from its *introduction* through the consumer acceptance. Along with the product development, there is an increased marketing cost, including advertising, pro-

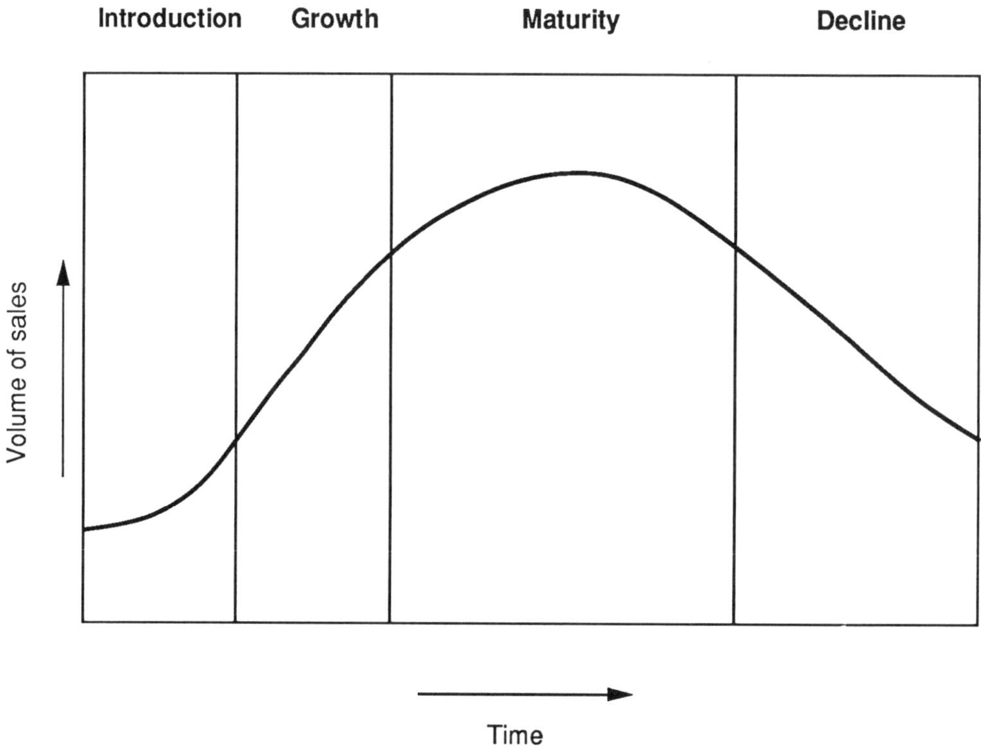


**Figure 3-11**
**Stages in the Product Life Cycle**

motional programs, market trials, surveys, and consumer orientation. Marketing information—the feedback to production—is instrumental to further development and product design improvements.

### THE GROWTH STAGE

The *growth stage* is reached when the number of customers increases: new customers are added, and the existing ones are repurchasing the product. An increased volume of production is observed at this stage through expansion of facilities, increased productivity, and better planning and control. The product cannot sustain the growth unless customers continue to support it through repeating orders. There is no question about the significance of the marketing function in building up the customer demand. Through advertising, promotions, and customer orientation, marketing creates awareness about the product and is instrumental in organizing initial sales. Repeated sales come solely through customer satisfaction with product value, which is realized during the product use. The growth stage relies on production to the great extent.

### THE MATURITY STAGE

When product succeeds on the market, and the initial expenses have been incurred, the competitors try to cash on the product and to grab some market share. Although the volume of sales increases at the initial stages of *maturity*, it starts to decline when the market reaches the saturation point and competition increases. The strategy at the growth stage is to continue increasing productivity, improving planning and control and inventory systems, and eventually reducing production costs.

### THE DECLINE STAGE

In the *decline stage*, the sales volume continues to decrease due to the fading consumer support and appearance of new products on the market. The product value is changing from one stage to another in the product life cycle, and due to the fluctuations in consumer demand. Here the forecast is used to foresee the influence on demand by various factors such as changes in consumer behavior and a policy change of competitors.

When the product reaches the stage of largely satisfying consumer demand, the volume of production is gradually declining and is eventually phased out. The product and process strategy and marketing programs are changing as the product line ages.

The cyclical influence relies upon the political climate, events, social, and economic conditions of prosperity and depressions. Random variations are those which fluctuate the demand without an obvious reason. Random variations do not have a consistent pattern of timing or magnitude characteristics, but they are largely responsible for the inaccuracies in forecast. An intricate problem in preparing forecasts is to reduce the effect of random deviations contained in historical data used in the forecast.

Demand can be defined by predicting and forecasting. *Predicting* is identifying future demand, based on the intuition and personal experience; predicting is used where the historical data of demand are not available in any form.

## Using Forecasting Techniques to Estimate Demand

*Forecasting* is defined as estimating future demand by applying expert judgments and past history of events to predict the future. There are four approaches to forecasting:

- Qualitative/subjective
- Quantitative
- Causal relationship
- Simulation models

### QUALITATIVE/SUBJECTIVE TECHNIQUES

*Qualitative techniques* apply subjective inputs and the individual judgment when forecasting the expected level of demand. Qualitative judgmental methods are used to develop medium- and long-range forecasts. These are all kinds of market surveys, expert opinion, and sales force estimates used as the main source of the forecast.

***Executive Committee Consensus*** The *executive committee consensus* is an effective and widely used method of the sales forecast by high-ranking managers from various departments in an organization, such as sales and marketing, financial, production, or product engineering. Compensating views of managers provide a good cross section of opinions. Such forecast is done on a consensus decision as a compromise which eliminates extreme opinions of individuals. This is the most common, cost-effective, fast, and accurate forecast method, provided there are qualified individuals doing the forecast.

***Delphi Method*** The *Delphi method* entails a group or panel of experts responding anonymously to the series of questionnaires in rounds. The coordinator of the procedure provides the original questions. The summary of responses is fed back to the coordinator or the group of decision makers who clarifies and edits them, tabulates them, and then makes them available to all the participants.

The answers and comments on questions are used to formulate the next round of questions. The forecast is done through the average of up to six rounds of questions, until the consensus among the panel members is reached.

***The Consumer Market Survey*** The *consumer market survey* is conducted for the purpose of eliciting the response from customers or potential customers on the question concerning the quantities of product they intend to purchase in the upcoming time periods. These questions can be asked by mail, by telephone, or through personal interviews. Other useful information that can be surveyed at the same time is related to the customer opinion and preferences in product design, product quality, price, appearance, number of options, and so on. These surveys can answer some questions at the introduction stage of product.

***The Survey of the Sales Force*** The *survey of the sales force* is an estimate of future demand through preparing future sales estimate by each salesperson. These estimates are combined into the sales force composite, which presents data for those making the final decision. This is a valuable data, since salespeople are usually aware of customers' future plans.

Qualitative forecasting techniques are intuitive and rely on the experience and skill of people performing the forecast. More detailed and accurate forecasts use quantitative methods, causal methods, and simulation.

### QUANTITATIVE TECHNIQUES

Quantitative techniques rely on the set of observations and use mathematical and statistical means of interpreting such historical data.

***Time Series Analysis*** *Time series analysis* is a staged sequence of observations taken at successive intervals of time. The forecast is based on the assumption that the future demand has some correlation to the past value of the series, assuming that what has happened in the past will continue in the future. Some forecast techniques accept the series at face value, often without attempting to identify variables that influence the series. Collecting time series values is followed by an analysis intended to compile a time series forecasting model.

The time series forecast attempts to detect internal and external factors affecting the underlying demand pattern in the past and attempt to project it into the near future. Time series analysis forecasts are applied in short-term forecasts.

The techniques of time series forecasting are the following:

***The Naive Approach*** *The naive approach* to forecasting assumes that demand in the next period will be equal to the demand observed in the most recent period. The philosophy behind this method is such that if, for example, there were 420 units sold in June, then one can expect the same amount to be sold in July. It is apparent that this is a very inaccurate forecast since it does not take into consideration seasonal, cyclical, and other fluctuations in demand. Nevertheless, due to its simplicity, this can be an inexpensive alternative to other methods in such instances where the accuracy of forecast can be compromised.

***Averaging Forecast Techniques*** *Averaging forecast techniques* smooth random variations in data. These are simple average, moving average, and weighted moving average. *Simple average* is an average value of the time series for a certain number for the most recent periods:

$$\text{average} = \frac{\sum d}{n}$$

where: $d$ = demand in previous time periods
$n$ = the number of periods

The simple average where $n = 1$ produces the same result as the naive approach.

*Moving averages* achieve the effect of smoothing random variations. This method emphasizes the recent experience. Each time period, a new set of variables becomes available, including the latest figures for the time period, prior to the forecasted one and excluding the oldest period figures. An example of a moving average is shown in Table 3-1. The longer the moving average time period is, the greater is the effect of smoothing random deviations. A shorter smoothing time period leaves more of demand oscillations, while a longer smoothing time period produces a smoother response, but lags the trend.

*Weighted moving averages* is a simple moving average method where equal weights are assigned to all the time periods. Nevertheless, it is often

| Period | Actual demand | Three-month moving average | Five-month moving average |
|---|---|---|---|
| 1 | 2 | 3 | 4 |
| Jan. | 12 | -- | -- |
| Feb. | 11 | -- | -- |
| Mar. | 13 | -- | -- |
| Apr. | 15 | (12+11+13)/3=12.00 | -- |
| May | 14 | (11+13+15)/3=13.00 | -- |
| Jun. | 12 | (13+15+14)/3=14.00 | 13.00 |
| Jul. | 10 | (15+14+12)/3=13.67 | 13.00 |
| Aug. | 9 | (14+12+10)/3=12.00 | 12.80 |
| Sept. | 11 | (12+10+9)/3 =10.33 | 12.00 |
| Oct. | 8 | (10+9+11)/3 =10.00 | 11.20 |
| Nov. | 9 | (9+11+8)/3 = 9.33 | 10.00 |
| Dec. | 12 | (11+8+9)/3 = 9.33 | 9.40 |

**Table 3-1**
**Three and Five-Month Moving Average**

found that the most recent time periods show performance that more accurately reflects the expected demand than the older time periods included in the demand estimate. Thus, it is quite justifiable to place a heavier emphasis on most recent data, to increase the weight of most recent data, and to reduce the weight of remote time periods data. Allocating such weights is accomplished by assigning different coefficients to time periods and allowing most recent data to influence the demand forecast.

In the example exhibited in Table 3-2, a three-month moving average is compared against the three-month weighted average. A greater smoothing effect is achieved when averaging is done over a longer period of time. The moving

| Period | Actual demand | Three-month moving average | Three-month weighted moving average |
|---|---|---|---|
| Jan. | 12 | -- | -- |
| Feb. | 11 | -- | -- |
| Mar. | 13 | -- | -- |
| Apr. | 15 | (12+11+13)/3=12.00 | [(12*2)+(11*3)+(13*5)]/10=12.20 |
| May | 14 | (11+13+15)/3=13.00 | [(11*2)+(13*3)+(15*5)]/10=13.60 |
| Jun. | 12 | (13+15+14)/3=14.00 | [(13*2)+(15*3)+(14*5)]/10=14.10 |
| Jul. | 10 | (15+14+12)/3=13.67 | [(15*2)+(14*3)+(12*5)]/10=13.20 |
| Aug. | 9 | (14+12+10)/3=12.00 | [(14*2)+(12*3)+(10*5)]/10=11.40 |
| Sept. | 11 | (12+10+9)/3 =10.33 | [(12*2)+(10*3)+(9*5)]/10 = 9.90 |
| Oct. | 8 | (10+9+11)/3 =10.00 | [(10*2)+(9*3)+(11*5)]/10 =10.20 |
| Nov. | 9 | (9+11+8)/3 = 9.33 | [(9*2)+(11*3)+(8*5)]/10 = 9.10 |
| Dec. | 12 | (11+8+9)/3 = 9.33 | [(11*2)+(8*3)+(9*5)]/10 = 9.10 |

**Weights applied:**

| | |
|---|---|
| Last month | 5 |
| Two months ago | 3 |
| Three months ago | 2 |
| **Total weight** | 10 |

**Table 3-2**
**Comparing Three-Month Moving Average and Three-Month Weighted Moving Average**

approach is useful in instances when there is a probability that the market demand will not have significant fluctuations and it does not have seasonal characteristics.

***Exponential Smoothing*** The deviation between the forecasted and actual demand is largely attributed to random variations. *Exponential smoothing* forecast techniques are intended to reduce the effect of random variations. Exponential smoothing is a type of moving average technique with the continuous revising of the estimates by using a forecast error as a variable in establishing the demand.

The equation for a simple exponential forecast is as follows:

$$F_t = F_{t-1} + \alpha\,(A_{t-1} - F_{t-1})$$

where

$F_t$ = exponentially smoothed forecast for period $t$

$F_{t-1}$ = the exponentially smoothed forecast for previous t-1 period

$A_{t-1}$ = the actual demand for previous time period

$\alpha$ = smoothing constant

The concept is simple: the latest estimate of demand equals the latest estimate of demand plus the portion of an error in the previous time period. The discretion in this forecast is in selection of the exponential smoothing constant, which is usually accepted as equal to 0.01 to 0.4. Smaller exponential smoothing constant produces smoother forecasting curve, as is shown in Figure 3-12. There, smoothing constant 0.3 produces a smoother exponential curve than smoothing constant 0.5 does. The exponential smoothing requires relatively little record keeping of past data. This is an especially valuable point when there is a large number of forecasted items involved.

*Example*: Forecast the demand for August, if sales for July were 11,270 instead of 10,500 forecasted. Use smoothing constant $\alpha$ = 0.4.

*Solution*:

$$\begin{aligned} F_{Aug.} &= F_j + \alpha\,(A_j - F_j) = 10{,}500 + 0.4(11{,}270 - 10{,}500) \\ &= 10{,}500 + 308 \\ &= 10{,}808 \end{aligned}$$

All previously discussed forecast methods are not, in fact, the extrapolation of data beyond the current demand date. These are the most current up-to-date smoothed averages. It is a statement of the most current demand and not a forecast as such. As one can see, the time series forecasting techniques are two-step techniques:

1. Averaging performance over previous time periods

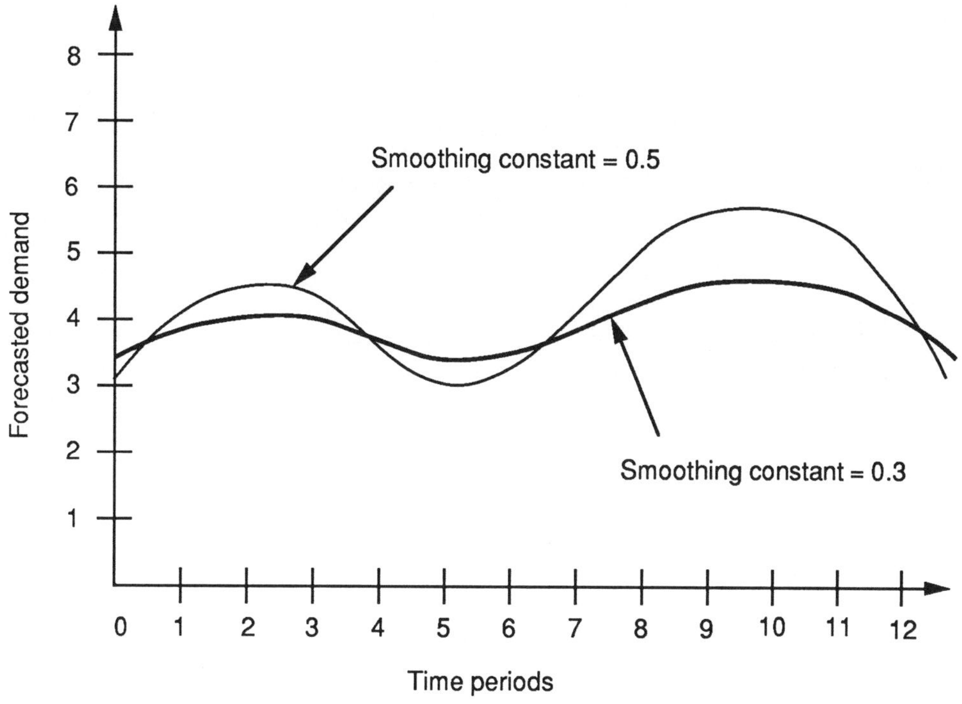


**Figure 3-12**
**Exponential Forecasts -- the Effect of the Smoothing Constant**

2. Applying the naive approach—assuming that the demand in the immediately following time period will be the same.

***Trend Adjusted Exponential Smoothing*** Exponential smoothing forecasts can be improved by incorporating *trend projections* in the forecast. When the trend of the previous demand is not reflected in the forecast, it causes a persistent deviation from the actual performance.

A trend refers to a gradual long-term propensity in the data. A trend is the difference between the successive values of forecasts

$$T = F_t - F_{t-1}$$

where:
$T$ = trend
$F_t$ = forecasted time period
$F_{t-1}$ = forecast for previous time period

Forecast including trend (*FT*) is composed of two elements—a forecast and a trend factor

$$FT_t = F_t + T_t$$

where

$FT_t$ = trend-adjusted forecast for period $t$
$F_t$ = forecast for period $t$
$T_t$ = trend adjustment for period $t$

A forecast including a trend—also known as *double smoothing*—is conducted in two stages, namely, estimating the exponential smoothing forecast and calculating the trend. Here is an example:

| Period | Demand | $F_t - F_{t-1}$ |
|---|---|---|
| 1 | 79 | 0 |
| 2 | 82 | 5 |
| 3 | 86 | -2 |
| 4 | 97 | 10 |
| 5 | 109 | 8 |
| 6 | 105 | 6 |
| 7 | 118 | 12 |
| 8 | 124 | -4 |

Forecast for $F_8$ = 120
Trend adjustments $T_8$ = 2

At Stage 1,

$$F_9 = F_8 - \alpha\ (A_8 - F_8) = 120 + 0.4(124 - 120) = 121.6$$

In this example, the long-term trend in sales is going up, notwithstanding periodical ups and downs. Such trend is sometimes called a *secular trend*, and it can run in both directions. In our example, the sales trend shows the progression at which the sales are increasing. Trend projections can be improved by considering latest variations in demand. For this, a smoothing constant β is applied in the trend projections:

$$T_t = T_{t-1} + \beta\ (F_t - F_{t-1})$$

where:

$T_t$ = current trend estimate
$T_{t-1}$ = trend adjustment for previous time period

$\beta$ = trend smoothing constant
$F_t$ = current time period exponential smoothing forecast
$F_{t-1}$ = previous period exponential smoothing forecast

$T_9 = T_8 + ... \beta (F_9 - F_8) = 2 + 0.4(121.6 - 120) = 2.64$

Finally, a forecast including trend is computed:

$FT_9 = 121.6 + 2.64 = 1244.24$

## Causal Forecasting Methods

*Causal forecasting methods* apply an analysis of events which influence the demand of the item being forecasted (for example, the economics and the competition affecting demand). A causal forecast attempts to establish the relationship between these factors and their individual and collective effect on the forecasted events. A causal forecast is based on the assumption that a mathematical relationship exists between the demand for one product and some leading indicators/activities known to be independent variables or correlations. An example of correlators is: demand for furniture that is proportional to the number of houses sold. The technique for establishing mathematical relationship and developing forecasting model is the *linear regression analysis*.

### LINEAR REGRESSION ANALYSIS

A regression analysis establishes the series to be forecasted in relation to the series of other variables which are believed to be in control or at least influencing the demand for the item in question. For example, sales of new homes can be directly related to the level of employment, or sometimes correlation is found between the demand for housing and the number of marriages.

The simplest form of a regression model is the one that establishes the relationship between the two variables. In this technique, one variable is known and this known variable is used to forecast the unknown variable through establishing a linear functional relationship between them. The regression analysis forecast establishes a linear regression of the parametric coefficients of the equation of a straight line, minimizing the sum of squared vertical deviations of points of an independent variable.

This equation of a straight line through a parametric coefficient of the independent variable assists in computing the value of the dependent variable.

$Y = a + bx$

$a = y - bx$

$$b = \frac{\sum xy - n\bar{x}\,\bar{y}}{\sum x^2 - n\bar{x}^2}$$

where

$y$ = value of the dependent variable
$a$ = intercept of regression line with y-line
$b$ = slope of regression line
$x$ = forecasted time period
$y$ = value for period $x$

The task is to find values of $a$ and $b$. The forecast for any period can be estimated by either inserting the value of $x$ in the equation or by indicating $x$ number of time periods: $x$ = 1, 2, 3, 4. . . . . n

In the multiple regression analysis, the combined effect of several independent variables is forecasted. Here, causal factors are established applying the concept of simple regression analysis. This problem is usually resolved with the help of computers. A regression analysis requires a considerable historical data, for the forecast to be accurate, if it is projected into a distant future.

*Example*: You are a production manager for a small tool manufacturer, and you are asked to predict the number of estimated sales of special machine tool fixtures for 1991. Forecast your demand for 1991 based on the previous demand over the period of 1984 to 1990:

| Year | Sales |
|---|---|
| 1984 | 19 |
| 1985 | 22 |
| 1986 | 20 |
| 1987 | 24 |
| 1988 | 26 |
| 1989 | 28 |
| 1990 | 23 |

*Solution*: The first step is to compile a table where time periods are transformed into simpler numbers, then plug the values into our formula. The table also includes the computed values for $x^2$ and $xy$:

| Year | x(period(s) | y(sales) | $x^2$ | $xy$ |
|---|---|---|---|---|
| 1984 | 1 | 19 | 1 | 19 |
| 1985 | 2 | 22 | 4 | 44 |
| 1986 | 3 | 20 | 9 | 60 |
| 1987 | 4 | 24 | 16 | 96 |
| 1988 | 5 | 26 | 25 | 130 |
| 1989 | 6 | 28 | 36 | 168 |
| 1990 | 7 | 23 | 49 | 161 |
| Total | 28 | $y = 162$ | $x^2 = 140$ | $xy = 678$ |

$$y = a + b(x)$$

$$b = \frac{\sum xy - n\bar{x}\bar{y}}{\sum x^2 n\bar{x}^2} = \frac{678 - (7 \times 4 \times 23.14)}{140 - (7 \times 4^2)} = \frac{30.1}{28} = 1.075$$

$$a = \bar{y} - b\bar{x}; = 23.4 - 1.075 \times 4 = 19.1$$

The forecast for 1991 (period 8) is

$$Y_8 = 19.1 + 1.075 \times 8 = 27.7 \approx 28$$

So you have estimated that you will sell 28 special machine tool fixtures for 1991 (period 8).

## Forecasting Simulation Models

Forecasting simulation models are computer-based programs able to analyze the effect of many independent variables on the expected performance of one or more dependent variables. These programs are able to answer "what-if" questions pertaining to what would happen with the dependent variable if there are different inputs to the problem. A spreadsheet program is extensively used in forecasting simulation models. Simulation techniques and spreadsheets are discussed further in Chapter 7.

## Forecasting Errors

It is accepted that forecasts contain errors because the demand for a product is constantly changing due to the changes in the many components, both internal and external. Forecasting techniques should be tested to ensure the fairness of assessments. There are two basic sources of forecast errors:

1. Inaccurate information used in the forecast along with the errors in the assessment and estimating the forecast
2. Random deviations

The simplest technique for testing a new forecast method is to apply this method to the historical data and compare the estimates with the actual past results. The judgment can be made if the difference between the forecast and the past performance is within the acceptable limits.

Forecast is controlled by estimating forecast errors. A forecast error is the difference between the forecast and the actual demand. A forecast error is measured by the mean absolute deviation (MAD).

The mean absolute deviation, MAD, is computed as the sum of the absolute values of the individual forecast errors for the previous time periods divided by the number of periods:

$$\text{MAD} = \frac{\sum_{t=1}^{n} |D_t - F_t|}{n}$$

where

$n$ = total number of periods
$t$ = period number
$D$ = actual demand for the period
$F$ = forecast demand for the period
$|\ |$ = a mathematical symbol indicating the absolute value disregarding positive or negative signs

The relationship between the standard deviation $\sum$ and the mean absolute deviation MAD is approximately $\sum = 1.25 \times \text{MAD}$.

MAD estimates an average forecast error without an indication of the direction of errors. Often, forecast errors are a random both negative and positive value, mutually canceling when the average is calculated.

For planning purposes, the direction of a forecast error is helpful in preparing contingency measures. *A tracking signal* gives an indication about the direction the forecast errors had in the past. A tracking signal is used to compute a moving sum of forecast errors. There, the average deviation (MAD) is divided into the cumulative deviation often called a *running sum of forecast errors* (RSFE).

$$\text{tracking signal} = \frac{\sum \text{(actual demand in period i - forecast in period i)}}{\text{MAD}}$$

A tracking signal limits of -3 to +3 or -8 to +8 are set up subjectively. If these action limits are exceeded, the forecasting technique should be reevaluated.

*Example*: The estimation of the MAD and tracking signal shown in a Table 3-3 is a case based on Precision Mold and Tool Co. The table set up in monthly periods (column 1) showing actual sales (column 2) is compared against the forecasted five-months moving average. The forecasted error (column 4) is the actual difference between the forecast and the actual performance for a specific month. For example, a forecasted error for July is computed as a difference between the actual sales of 10.00 and the forecast of 13.00 (10.00 - 13.00 = -3). The running sum of forecast errors is shown in column 5. The

| Period | Actual | Forecasted five-month moving average in $100,000 | Forecasted error | RSFE | Absolute error | Sum error | $(Error)^2$ | MAD | Tracking Signal |
|---|---|---|---|---|---|---|---|---|---|
| 1 | 2 | 3 | 4 | 5 | 6 | 7 | 8 | 9 | 10 |
| Feb. | 12 | -- | -- | -- | -- | | | | |
| Mar. | 11 | -- | -- | -- | -- | | | | |
| Apr. | 13 | -- | -- | -- | -- | | | | |
| May | 15 | -- | -- | -- | -- | | | | |
| Jun. | 14 | -- | -- | -- | -- | | | | |
| Jul. | 12 | 13.00 | (10-13) =-3.00 | -3.00 | 3.00 | 3.00 | 9.00 | 3.00 | -1.00 |
| Aug. | 10 | 13.00 | (9-13) =-4.00 | -7.00 | 4.00 | 7.00 | 16.00 | 3.5 | -2.00 |
| Sep. | 9 | 12.80 | (11-12.80)=-1.80 | -8.80 | 1.80 | 8.80 | 3.24 | 2.94 | -2.99 |
| Oct. | 11 | 12.00 | (8-12) =-4.00 | -12.80 | 4.00 | 12.80 | 16.00 | 3.20 | -4.00 |
| Nov. | 8 | 11.20 | (9-11.20) =-2.20 | -15.00 | 2.20 | 15.00 | 4.84 | 3.00 | -5.00 |
| Dec. | 9 | 10.00 | (12-10.00)=+2.00 | -13.00 | 2.00 | 17.00 | 4.00 | 2.83 | -4.59 |

$$\text{MAD} = \frac{\text{Sum Error}}{n} = \frac{17.00}{6} = 2.83$$

$$\text{Tracking signal} = \frac{\text{RSFE}}{\text{MAD}} = \frac{-13.00}{2.83} = -4.59$$

Tracking signal/ MAD = -4.59/2.83 = -1.62

**Table 3-3**
**Estimates of MAD and Tracking Signal**

absolute value of the forecast error is shown in column 6, and the running sum of absolute errors (RSAE) is shown in column 7. Column 8 shows the squares of absolute errors. The computed MAD is shown in column 9, and the tracking signal is shown in column 10.

For example, in December, MAD is computed by dividing the running sum of absolute errors (17.00) by 6—the number of forecasted periods (17.00/6 = 2.83), and the tracking signal is computed by dividing RSFE (-13.00) by MAD (2.83). The estimated tracking signal varying between -1 (July forecast) and -5 (November forecast) shows the consistency of demand being lower than the forecast.

## SETTING UP A PRODUCTION PLANNING AND CONTROL SYSTEM

Planning is organized as a hierarchical system, each level of the hierarchy itself being a subsystem interacting with other system elements in contributing to the total planning function. An integrated planning system in Figure 3-13 shows the interrelationship among the business strategic plan, the aggregate production plan, the master production schedule, and the materials planning.

The levels of a hierarchical planning system correspond to three levels of management hierarchy: executive, tactical, and operational management level.

Planning activities are distinguished by two characteristics: the time span and the planning unit. *Planning units* are the measuring units of product and resources in which the balancing is conducted. Each planning level is distinguished by the *time span*—how far into future the planning is done, and the time increments—the duration of planned time periods.

### Hierarchical Planning

Customer demand fluctuates in real business situations. Such fluctuations affect productivity and increase the production cost due to the uncertainty in demand and the need to keep buffer stocks. Sometimes, companies find themselves struggling to respond to an unforeseen, sudden increase in short-term demand.

What would you do if your demand were anticipated to increase about 30 percent over the next six months? A proper management decision would be to respond to this demand by increasing the capacity—plant, equipment, and labor force. This capacity should be in place in six months time when your new orders are expected. However, the times required for increasing your capacity are as follows:

- Equipment purchasing—18 months
- Labor hiring and training—9 months
- Equipment installation, commissioning, and introduction—3 months

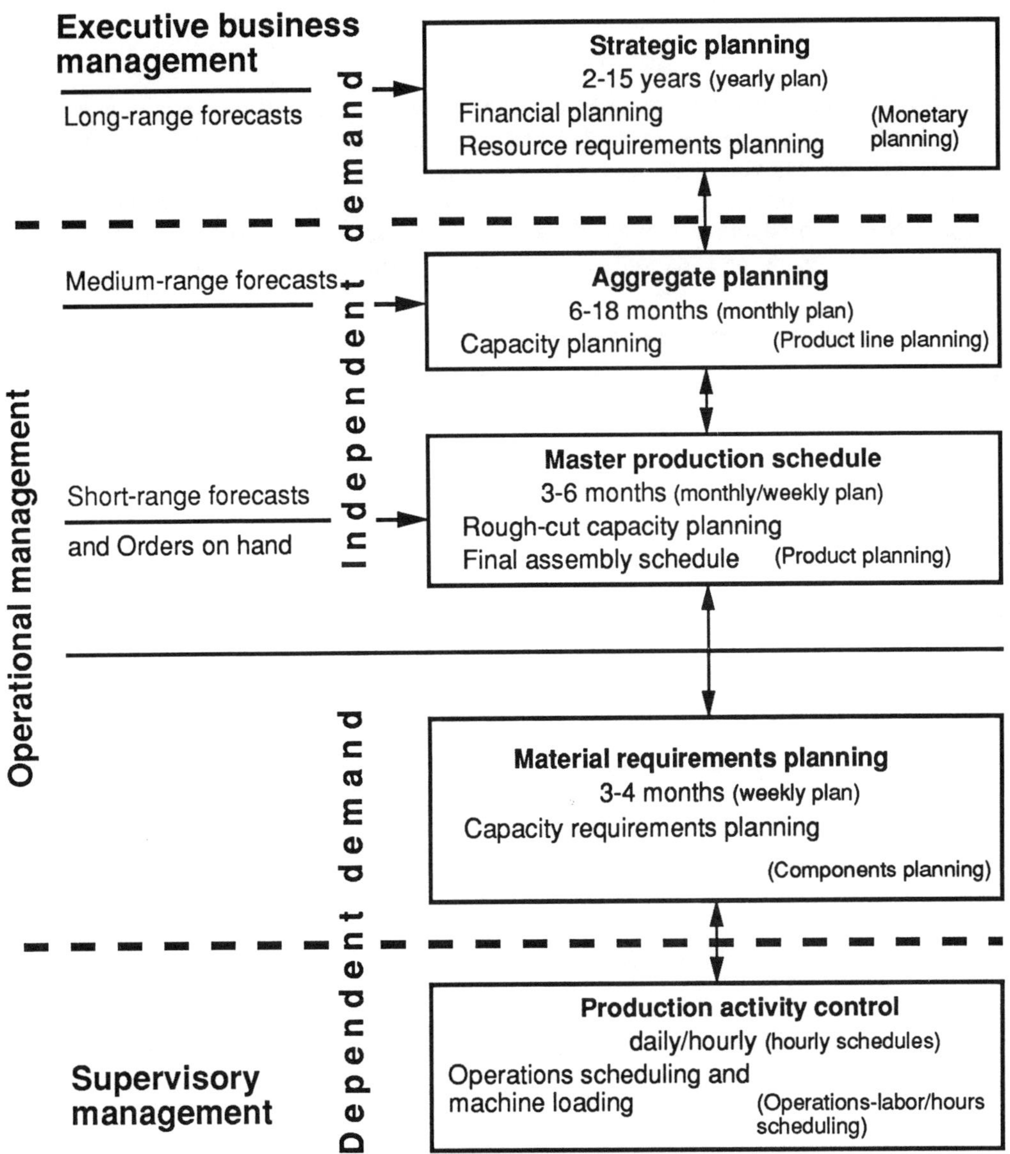


**Figure 3-13**
**Time Units and Planning and Control Units of a Production Planning and Control System**

- Materials on order—3 months

for a total of 33 months.

Some of these times can overlap. Elements of lead time capacity expansion are illustrated in Figure 3-14. Sometimes, long lead time of capacity expansion can prevent you from accepting new orders.

Companies experiencing a debilitating competition can manage to trim their preproduction activities substantially by overlapping purchasing and commissioning a new capacity and training employees. Steve Covin of Compaq

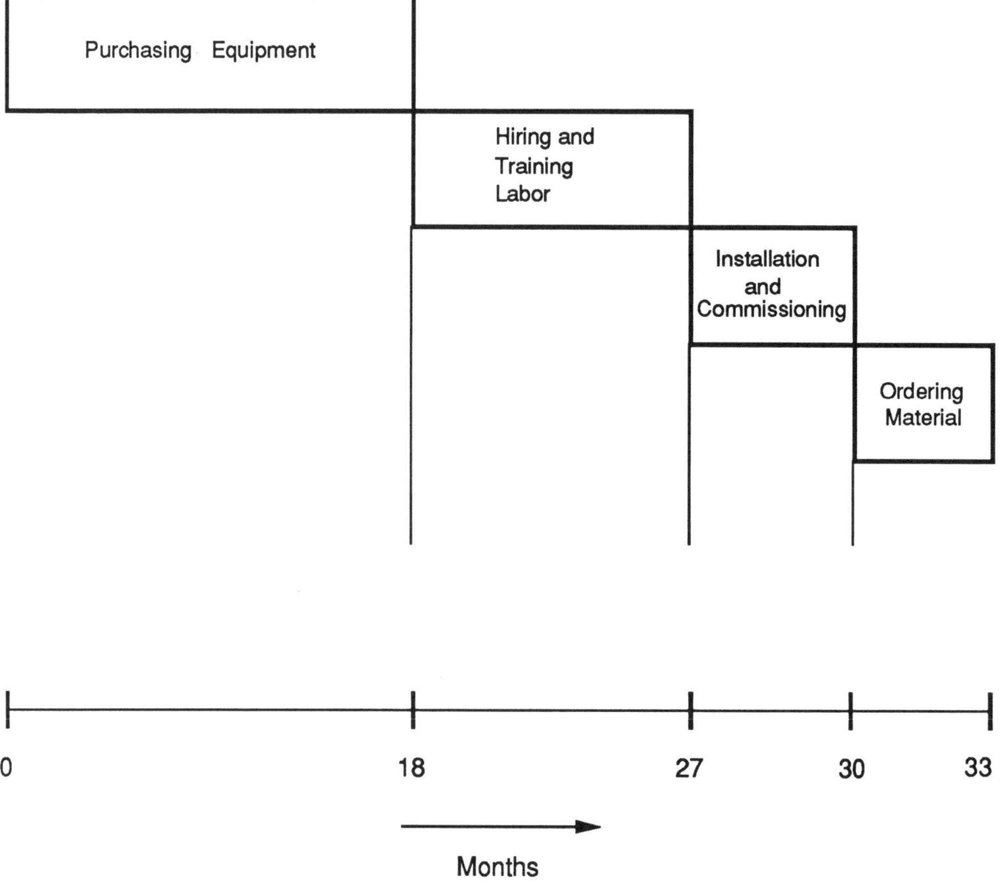


**Figure 3-14**
**The Lead Time of Capacity Expansion**

says, "These are traditions. I wonder how factual they are now! Such capacity expansion takes not more than 9 months at the Compaq."

The span of long-term planning depends on the delivery dates of the production equipment and the training of the new labor force, not to mention budgeting, approval, and obtaining funds required for the expansion. It varies from one year, in industries applying a standard type and general-purpose machinery to four to six years in heavy industry (for example, steel mills).

In planning systems, *strategic planning* is derived from these delivery dates, the span of *medium planning* depends on the individual order's lead times, and a *short-term planning* horizon is derived from the average processing time of components. The three stages of production planning are illustrated in Figure 3-15. Production planning and control systems vary in organizations depending on a lead time of their products.

## Strategic Business Planning

Executive management is involved in outlining the strategic policy of an organization—the *strategic business planning.* Long-range planning, known as *corporate strategic planning*, includes a statement of organizational objectives for the next 2 to 15 years.

A strategic business plan outlines the allocation of production based on the analysis of market's changing environment. Strategic management develops strategies and contingency plans capable of meeting organizational objectives, utilizing available resources, and avoiding obvious pitfalls in such unpredictable events affecting the world economy, as well as responding to changes in national and local economies. Strategic management is an instrument linking the organizational external strategy with its internal capability.

Strategic decisions are made based on forecasted demands and involve such areas as a new products phase in or an old products phase out; capacity expansion or capacity contraction; the labor policy—hiring and training or laying off; setting up a subcontracting policy; and corporate decisions on purchasing of raw materials, acquisition or divestiture; revenues and expenditures, stocks and shares, and profit planning.

The corporate strategic plan, based on demand forecasts, may include a long-term program outlining business strategic issues, such as the capacity expansion or holing up, a facility location, a product policy and a new product development, adding new product lines and terminating old ones according to the business marketing strategy, and investment decisions.

The time horizon of strategic planning is determined by the lead time for the acquisition of new plant units and training employees to run these production facilities. Sometimes, a strategic plan is developed specifically for the production function, based on the strategic business plan and the sales forecasts.

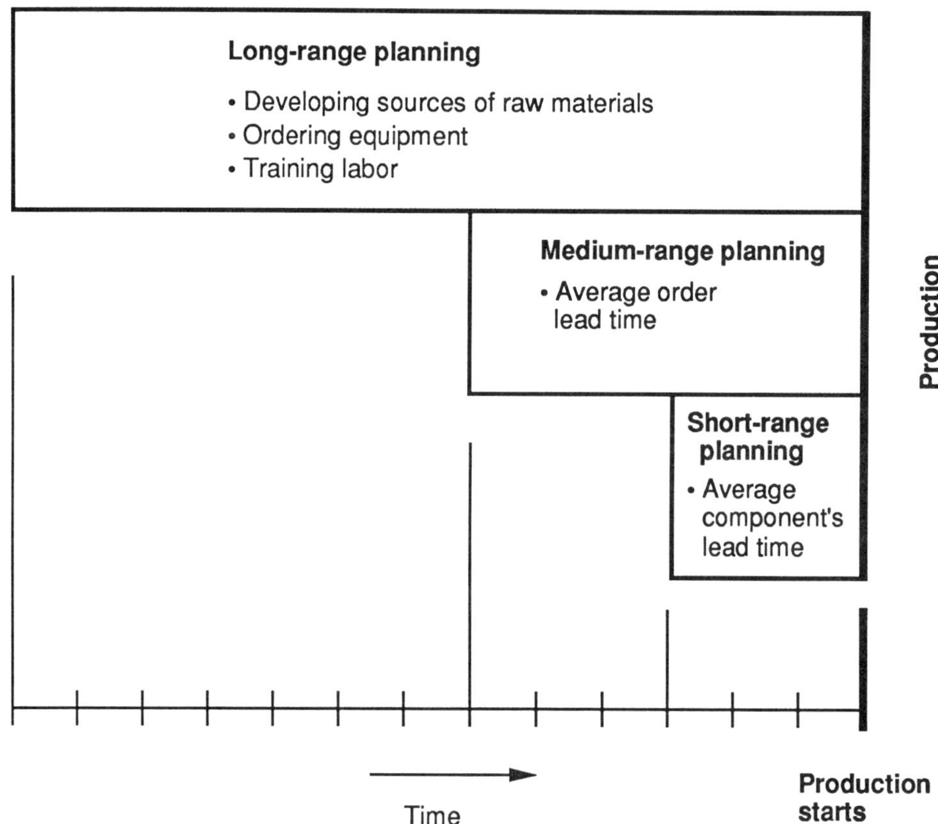


**Figure 3-15**
**The Three Stages of Production Planning: Time Horizons Depend on the Lead Time**

The measuring unit in strategic planning is the value of the output estimated as the total output monetary value in millions of dollars, or in some instances, an average "synthetic" product.

In multiproduct companies, at the strategic planning level, the measuring unit can be an average product—the product having an average price, or an average capacity, or other resource required to produce one unit.

For example, a company producing a number of different car models can choose one which has an average engine size and requires an average production capacity. In some companies, electronic distribution systems automatically select and update such an average product, for example, by using a Lotus 1-2-3 computer program.

Long-term plans translate a business forecast into the individual markets and product lines objectives. Long-term plans are reconciled with financial planning and the available resources. This is long-range capacity planning; resources planning; and planning of facilities, equipment, and personnel.

### STRATEGIC PLAN—JOHNES ELECTRIC COMPANY

Johnes Electronic Components, Inc. (JEC), produces electrical and electronic components for industrial manufacturers and automakers as well as pneumatic tools and home appliances. JEC strategic plan starts with stating a present volume of sales, material cost, *earnings before tax* (EBT), and *return on investments* (ROI). Excerpts form JEC strategic plan are exhibited in the appendix. This is followed by market status and market-product strategy, major economic planning assumptions, statement about competitive environment, and key business objectives. Strategic concerns are a declining aircraft market and increasing fringe benefit costs and legal costs. Sales in other markets—motor vehicle, energy, and general industry are on the increase. Based on the foregoing conditions, the strategic four-year plan is broken down into yearly product line plans adjusted by the expected rate of inflation. Organizational strategy in various markets is stated as quality, service, and technical support.

JEC strategic plan is divided into international and domestic markets. International market is divided further into individual country's plans. As an example, strategic plans for Mexico and Germany are shown. The strategy is designed around capital spending, inventory trend, depreciation, and accounts receivable. A four-year inventory trend schedule is shown as an example.

Expenses in strategic plan are divided into major categories, namely, manufacturing, selling, and administrative. These expenses are compiled in the headcount and salary strategic plan according to domestic and international market and according to individual countries. Separate strategic plans are compiled for capacity cost categories, namely, manufacturing capacity costs, selling capacity costs, administrative capacity costs, and engineering capacity costs. Finally, geographical sales plans are broken down into sales of individual product lines, as shown on the example of the products K-20-25 through K-20-61.

In strategic planning, the first planning alternative is applied, namely, adjusting resources to correspond to demand because a strategic plan allows time for expanding or contracting the capacity. At JEC, headcount and salary reports and capacity cost reports are used in long-term resource requirements planning. The strategic business plan is a basis for compiling an aggregate production plan.

## Resource Requirements Planning

The purpose of the *resource requirements planning* (RRP) is to determine long-term capacity needs. Resource requirements planning translates long-range sales forecasts and production plans into acquisition and development plans of key resources, such as facilities/plant, work force, raw materials, inventory levels, energy, and information.

The time horizon should be sufficient to cover the lead time. Planning measuring units are machine-hours per year per one capacity item, or they can be expressed as an output rate, such as a discrete number of items. In process-type industry, these units can be the bulk volume produced per year. Product load profiles or bills of resources are used in RRP for estimating the need for resources.

RRP deals with long-term lead acquisition time resources, serves as a guideline and the limit for the next stage—aggregate production planning—and is a basis for capital budgeting plans.

In process industries, long-term RRP is followed by a more detailed complete five-year plan. RRP is regarded as a rough check on resources, which is followed by capacity planning—a more detailed and accurate review of capacity requirements.

## Aggregate Production Planning

Usually, aggregate production planning is done 6 to 18 months into the future in 1-month increments. Planning units at this stage are the quantities per product line. The second and third alternative/option of adjusting demand to suit the existing capacity levels is used in aggregate planning because at this stage time does not allow for expansion of capacity.

An aggregate production plan derives from a wide strategic outline. A plan for one period is exploded further into more detailed time periods and more specific units of output—product lines. Often, an aggregate production plan accommodates fluctuations in demand by building up an inventory or considering a backlog, in order to keep a stable capacity/labor force level.

Normally, the aggregate production plan is compiled in monthly increments, in product units as is shown in Figure 3-16, illustrating production planning stages in the Tools and Implement Co. There a production plan is a hierarchical sequence of plans beginning with the strategic business plan. The current year strategic business plan envisages $160 million value of output in total. The next planning stage, aggregate plan, divides a broad business plan into two main product lines, namely, tractors and garden appliances. The time span of this aggregate plan is one year, and the time increment is one month. For example, January production is planned as 220 tractors and 600 garden appliances, February production is 210 tractors and 600 appliances, and March production amounts 220 tractors and 590 appliances. An aggregate plan is compiled so that the 12-month production amounts to $160 million in total.

An aggregate production plan is prepared through the iterating process of planning and replanning, involving individuals from each business functional area. First, there is an adjustment in accordance with the demand forecast error (preventive planning and control takes place here). A capacity is acquired according

**A. Strategic Planning -- Four Year Plan**

| Current year | Second year | Third year | Fourth year |
|---|---|---|---|
| $160 million | $185 million | $195 million | $200 million |

**B. Aggregate Planning -- Current Year, First Quarter**

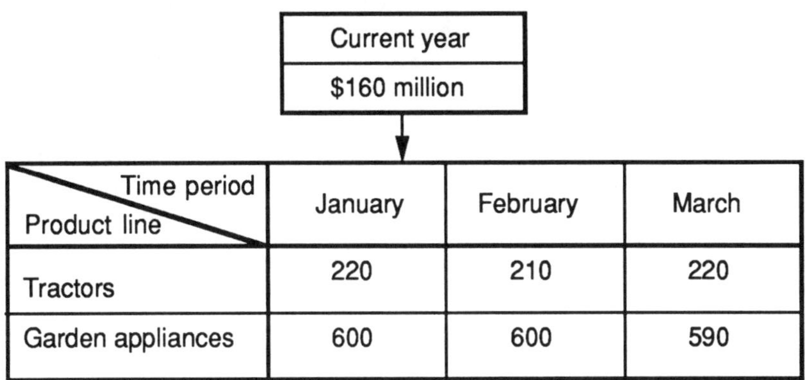

| Current year |
|---|
| $160 million |

| Product line \ Time period | January | February | March |
|---|---|---|---|
| Tractors | 220 | 210 | 220 |
| Garden appliances | 600 | 600 | 590 |

**C. Master Production Schedule -- Current Year, February**

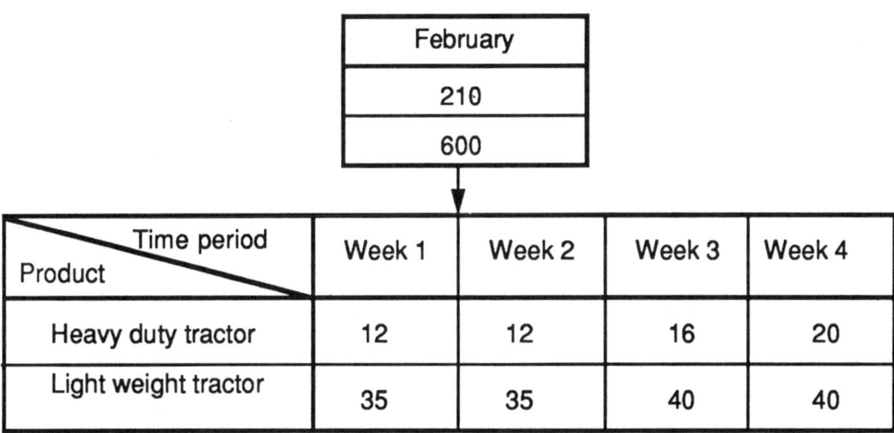

| February |
|---|
| 210 |
| 600 |

| Product \ Time period | Week 1 | Week 2 | Week 3 | Week 4 |
|---|---|---|---|---|
| Heavy duty tractor | 12 | 12 | 16 | 20 |
| Light weight tractor | 35 | 35 | 40 | 40 |

**Figure 3-16**
**Stages of Hierarchical Planning at Tool and Implement Co.**

to the strategic plans or aggregate plans and according to the lead time for delivery, commissioning, and labor training. Most of this falls within the range of strategic plans based on long-term forecasts.

Second, the use of this capacity is an element in the medium-range adjustable capacity planning. For example, there is a greater flexibility with a general-purpose equipment and a cross-trained labor. The essence of this concept is to plan broad capacity groups and later on convert the group capacity into a detailed plan applying more detailed capacity units.

The primary concern of aggregate planning is to outline the organization's general policy and define the direction of the future growth and markets, as well as to define the capacity required to satisfy ever-changing market requirements, with the perspective of making a profit, expanding the market share, or developing new product lines.

Production planning units used in preparing the plan vary considerably among companies. In some firms, an aggregate plan is prepared in labor hours or in units of production, or it can be expressed in terms of the number of units to be produced on each major product line. Some make-to-order companies producing short lead time items prepare the aggregate production plan in annual aggregate time units corresponding to the subsequent MPS disaggregation. In this instance, the aggregate plan and the MPS are compiled iteratively, in order to arrive at the optimum solution.

Figure 3-17 illustrates capacity planning in Precision Mold & Tool. This is an aggregate production plan compiled in labor/machine-hours.

Inputs into aggregate planning are as follows:

- Strategic business plan
- Market plan
- Product forecast
- Sales performance
- Customer orders

All this information is compared with available resources—production, engineering, and materials planning— and information is provided for budgetary decisions and long-term decisions regarding the acquisition of capacity.

An aggregate production plan is a guideline for a master scheduler for preparing an itemized production program, by setting the overall level of a manufacturing output. It provides guidelines and constraints for production, analysis, and at the same time, it is the basis for budget control and marketing.

Some companies compile an aggregate production plan on a monthly basis, using up to two years of forecasts. Such a plan is a detailed instruction fed directly into master production scheduling. This detailed production plan is a yardstick for measuring the performance.

The aggregate planning strategy is accomplished by various techniques, such as changing the work force size—hiring labor when demand increases

**Product Line #1**
(standard hours)

| Activity \ Time | Jan. | Feb. | Mar. | Apr. | May | Jun. | Jul. |
|---|---|---|---|---|---|---|---|
| Production Forecasts | 1,200 | 1,200 | 1,300 | 1,300 | 1,350 | 1,350 | 1,350 |
| Orders on hand (included in production forecasts) | 600 | 550 | 400 | 100 | -- | -- | -- |
| In stock | 400 | -- | -- | -- | -- | -- | -- |
| Balance | 800 | 1,200 | 1,300 | 1,300 | 1,350 | 1,350 | 1,350 |

**Figure 3-17**
**Aggregate Plan for Product Line 1 at Precision Mold and Tool Co.**

and laying off when demand is lower, carrying an excessive inventory, making use of subcontractors, making use of overtime, and accepting the underutilization of equipment when demand fluctuates.

The most common techniques used in compiling an aggregate plan are:

- The trial and error method
- Mathematical approaches
- Graphical and charting methods

### TRIAL AND ERROR METHOD

The main tasks addressing aggregate planning are balancing supply and demand, optimizing resources, and reducing the cost of production. Three plan balancing strategies are applied for finding the optimum solution. The alternatives considered are affecting demand by the pricing and promotion strategy, back-ordering, changing size of work force—hiring and firing workers, using part time workers, and subcontracting. Eventually, the effectiveness of each alternative is measured by the total cost comprising the production cost, the inventory holding cost, the cost of changing the capacity level, and the cost of backordering. Production cost alternatives are evaluated based on fixed and variable cost information, production rates, make or buy decisions, and purchasing.

- *Inventory holding cost.* The decision is made here as part of the trade-off between attempts to lower the inventory level and provide an adequate customer service.
- *Changing capacity level.* Here, decision alternatives are concerned with acquiring resources, new technologies and automation, hiring and training an additional personnel, or laying off workers.
- *Backlog orders.* Backlogging means negating on a promise to a customer. This carries additional costs resulting from irregularities in the material flow and expediting, as well as reduction of sales revenues as a result of diminished customer support.

***An Example of the Trial and Error Method*** Your forecast for the next six months ranges from 550 units in the months 2 and 3 to 700 units in month 4 and 900 units in month 5. Your production rate is 650 units per month. Your production cost per unit varies as follows:

- Regular production cost = $6
- Overtime production = $8
- Inventory cost = $2
- Backorder = $9
- Subcontracting = $10

There are two available alternatives here.

***Alternative 1*** Alternative 1 would be to produce at the regular production rate at the cost of $6 per unit, assuming the backlog cost of a negative inventory balance. This is shown in Table 3-4A. Production starts with a zero inventory and builds up the stock during the first three periods. The negative difference exists in periods 4 and 5, and the backlog of 50 items exists in period 5. Average inventory is computed as follows:

$$\frac{\text{beginning quantity} + \text{ending quantity}}{2}$$

The total cost for this alternative is $25,100.

***Alternative 2*** Alternative 2 is to cut inventory by planning the capacity at the lowest demand rate and making use of overtime (to apply backordering and subcontracting would be more expensive than overtime). Alternative 2 is

| Periods | 1 | 2 | 3 | 4 | 5 | 6 | Total |
|---|---|---|---|---|---|---|---|
| Forecast | 600 | 550 | 550 | 700 | 900 | 600 | 3,900 |
| Prod. rate (regular) | 650*6= =3,900 | 650*6= =3,900 | 650*6= =3,900 | 650*6= =3,900 | 650*6= =3,900 | 650*6= =3,900 | 23,400 |
| Overtime | | | | | | | |
| Subcontract | | | | | | | |
| Difference | 50 | 100 | 100 | (50) | (250) | 50 | |
| Inventory: beginning | | 50 | 150 | 250 | 200 | | |
| ending | 50 | 150 | 250 | 200 | | | |
| Average | 25 | 100 | 200 | 225 | 100 | | |
| Inventory cost | 50 | 200 | 400 | 450 | 200 | | |
| Backlog | | | | | 50 | | |
| Backlog cost | | | | | | | |
| **Total per period** | 3,950 | 4,100 | 4,300 | 4,350 | 4,500 | 3,900 | 25,100 |

**Table 3-4A**
**The Trial and Error Method -- Alternative 1**

shown in Table 3-4B. This alternative results in overtime production in periods 1, 4, 5, and 6. Total cost of this alternative is $24,600, which is less than in the previous plan.

MATHEMATICAL METHODS

***Linear Programming*** Linear programming (LP) is used in applications where there are two or three products competing for a few common restricted resources. In aggregate planning, this resource is the capacity. However, often this method is used for planning the use of raw materials. There are several steps which must be followed in resolving the LP problems.

1. First, identify the objective of the problem. Usually, the objective is to maximize the profit or to minimize the cost.
2. Second, identify those variables over which the decision maker has control.

| Periods | 1 | 2 | 3 | 4 | 5 | 6 | Total |
|---|---|---|---|---|---|---|---|
| Forecast | 600 | 550 | 550 | 700 | 900 | 600 | 3,900 |
| Prod. rate (regular) | 550*6= =3,300 | 550*6= =3,300 | 550*6= =3,300 | 550*6= =3300 | 550*6= =3,300 | 550*6= =3,300 | $19,800 |
| Overtime | 50*8= =400 | | | 150*8= =1,200 | 350*8= =2,800 | 50*8= =400 | 4,800 |
| Subcontract | | | | | | | |
| Difference | | | | | | | |
| Inventory: beginning | | | | | | | |
| ending | | | | | | | |
| Average | | | | | | | |
| Inventory cost | | | | | | | |
| Backlog | | | | | | | |
| Backlog cost | | | | | | | |
| **Total per** period | 3,700 | 3,300 | 3,300 | 4,500 | 6,100 | 3,700 | 24,600 |

**Table 3-4B**
**The Trial and Error Method -- Alternative 2**

3. Third, identify the parameters which are beyond the decision maker's control.
4. Fourth, formulate the objective function.
5. Fifth, formulate the constraints on the decision variables.

*Example*: An engineering company produces two components/products—gears and shafts—for a major car manufacturer. The capacity demand in hours in three work centers is as follows:

| Work Center | Gears | Shafts | Capacity |
|---|---|---|---|
| | Hours Required for Production in Units | | |
| Machining | 5 | 2 | 3800 |
| Grinding | 3 | 6 | 5400 |

The two products contribute different amounts to profit: each gear contributes \$10, while each shaft contributes \$8.

*Solution*:

1. The objective is identified as to maximize the profit.
2. The decision variables are identified as follows: gears—$X_1$; shafts—$X_2$.
3. The parameters are measured in machine-hours required for the gears $X_1$ and the shafts $X_2$. These parameters are identified as $5X_1$ and $2X_2$ in the machining work center, limited by 3,800 machine-hours total capacity. In the grinding department with the 5,400 machine-hours total capacity, these figures are $3X_1$ and $6X_2$, respectively.
4. The constraints of the problem are formulated as follows:

$$\begin{aligned} &\text{maximize} && Z = 10X_1 + 8X_2 \\ &\text{with} && 5X_1 + 2X_2 \leq 3{,}800 \\ &&& 3X_1 + 6X_2 \leq 5{,}400 \end{aligned}$$

and

$$X_1,\ X_2 \geq 0$$

Graphical linear programming techniques start with allocating each product to each of the graph axles. Take the first constraint (for example, the machining WC) and calculate the maximum number of gear units $X_1$ that might be possible to machine there if it were the only product served in this WC, in other words, assume $X_2 = 0$. Then 3,800/5 = 760. Plot this number on the $X_1$ axis. This is exhibited in Figure 3-18. The same procedure is repeated for the shafts $X_2$, yielding 3,800/2 = 1,900. Join the two points plotted so far with the straight line. The property of this line is such that every point on it stands for such a product mix ($X_1$ and $X_2$) that will exactly absorb the capacity of the WC. For example, point *A* yields a product mix of $400X_1$ and $900X_2$, which requires the total of

$$(400X_1 \times 5) + (900X_2 \times 1) = 3{,}800 \text{ machine-hours.}$$

This line contains the maximum production possible in the machining WC. Any point taken on the left side area of the line will denote a product mix consuming less than the maximum capacity of 3,800 machine-hours. Conversely, any point on the right side of the line will exceed the maximum capacity available.

The graph area on the left side of the line is known as the *feasibility area*. The same procedure is repeated for the second constraint—the grinding WC. The second line identifies the feasible area for the second constraint. The area on this graph, common to both constraints, represents the area of the feasible solution to this problem.

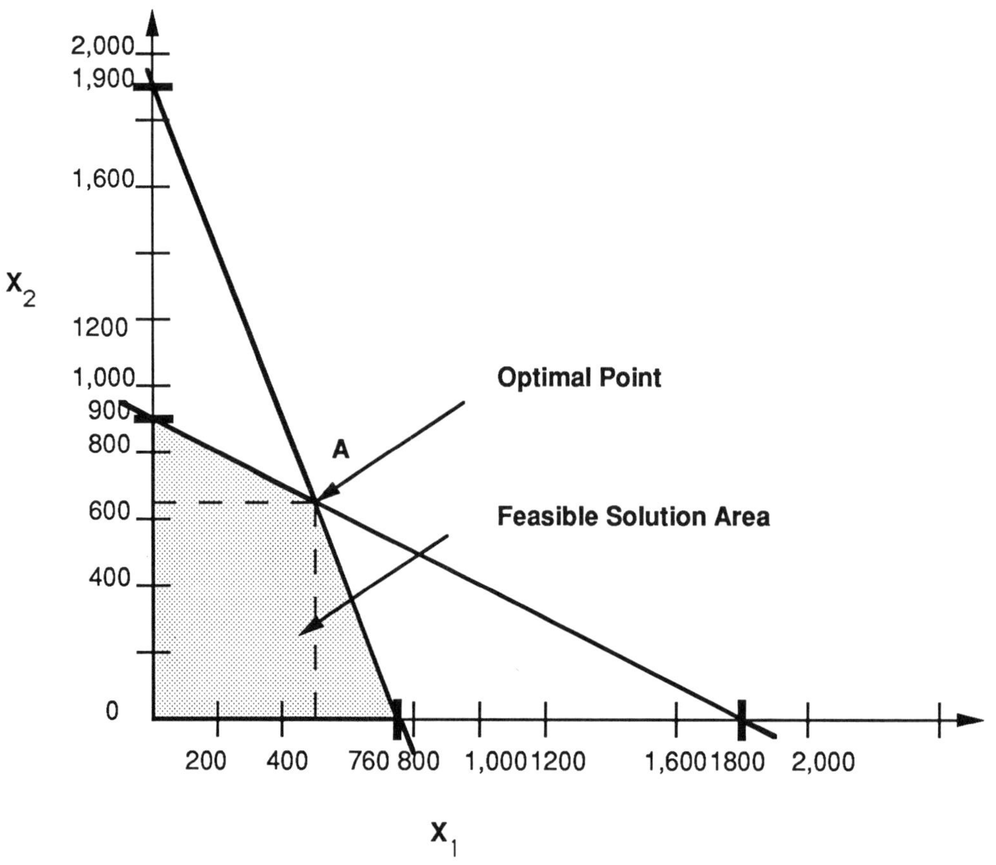


**Figure 3-18**
**Linear Programming**

The optimum product mix yielding the maximum profit is found at one of the corners of the area of the feasible solution. In the aforementioned problem, this corner is at the intersection *A* of the two lines representing the two constraints. This solution requires production of 500 gears ($X_1$) and 650 shafts ($X_2$) at the maximum profit of (500 * 10) + (650 * 8) = $10,200.

The optimum point can also be found mathematically by solving the system of equations representing the two constraints. Here we have converted the inequalities into equalities in order to maximize the utilization of capacity.

$$5X_1 + 2X_2 = 3{,}800$$
$$3X_1 + 6X_2 = 5{,}400$$

*Solution:*

$$(5X_1 + 2X_2 = 3{,}800) \times 3$$
$$(3X_1 + 6X_2 = 5{,}400)$$

$$15X_1 + 6X_2 = 11{,}400$$
$$-\ (3X_1 + 6X_2 = 5{,}400)$$

---

$$12X_1 + 0X_2 = 6{,}000$$

$$X_1 = 500$$

$X_2$ is found by substituting $X_1$ by its value:

$$(5 \times 500) + 2X_2 = 3{,}800$$
$$2X_2 = 1{,}300$$
$$X_2 = 650.$$

***Linear Programming Transportation Method*** The linear programming transportation method is used when aggregate planning deals with allocating capacity to meet the forecasted demand. The assumption of the LP transportation method is that all capacity types should be utilized in full until the demand is satisfied.

*Example*: The assumption of the transportation problem is that supply equals demand. Thus, in a transportation matrix, the unused capacity column is introduced as having zero cost of capacity. Data for clamp production is presented in Table 3-5. Table 3-6 (on page 123) illustrates the solution to this problem using a linear programming matrix. The unused 250 units of the subcontracted capacity in period 1 are transferred to period 2, and 220 units of the subcontracted capacity from period 2 are transferred to period 3. The final unused capacity is 200 units of subcontracting.

## GRAPHICAL METHODS

These methods are relatively straightforward to use and often are sufficiently adequate for aggregate decision making, unless there are many other constraints involved which cannot be reconciled in the graphical form. The traditional way

**Clamps Production**

| Period | Regular capacity | Overtime capacity | Subcontract capacity | Demand |
|---|---|---|---|---|
| 1 | 1,300 | 100 | 400 | 1,600 |
| 2 | 1,450 | 120 | 300 | 1,900 |
| 3 | 1,600 | 130 | 400 | 2,150 |

Initial inventory = 50
Regular time cost/unit = $40
Overtime cost/unit = $52
Subcontracting cost/unit = $58
Inventory carrying cost = $2 per unit per month
Back order cost = $10 per unit per month

**Table 3-5**
**The Transportation Problem**

is to use a Gantt chart, which is usually sufficient for aggregate production planning.

Aggregate production planning makes uses of linear programming and simulation. Also, rough-cut capacity planning discussed later on in this chapter is used in preparing an aggregate production plan.

## Master Production Scheduling

Master production scheduling (MPS) is the last stage of independent demand production planning where the forecast demand for an item is considered. The inputs into MPS are the aggregate plan and the adjusted demand. MPS is the

| Supply | | Demand | | | | Total capacity available |
|---|---|---|---|---|---|---|
| | | Period 1 | Period 2 | Period 3 | Unused capacity | |
| Beginning inventory | | 50 [0] | | | | |
| 1 | Regular | 1,300 [40] | [40] | [40] | [40] | |
| | Overtime | 100 [52] | [52] | [52] | [52] | |
| | Subcontract | 150 [58] | 250 [58] | [58] | [58] | |
| 2 | Regular | [40] | 1,450 [40] | | | |
| | Overtime | [52] | 120 [52] | | | |
| | Subcontract | [58] | 80 [58] | 220 [58] | | |
| 3 | Regular | [40] | [40] | 1,600 [40] | | |
| | Overtime | [52] | [52] | 130 [52] | | |
| | Subcontract | [58] | [58] | 200 [58] | 200 | |
| Demand | | 1,600 | 1,900 | 2,150 | | |

**Table 3-6**
**Linear Programming -- The Transportation Method**

anticipated production program, which differs from the sales forecast in that, along with the forecast, it takes into consideration the latest demand (for example, orders on hand, inventory, backlog, available capacity, and materials). MPS blends customer orders with forecasts as shown graphically in Figure 3-19.

MPS establishes production rates expressed in the final product configuration and the quantity assigned to monthly or weekly time buckets. In make-to-stock closed shop companies, MPS controls finished-goods inventory based on the production rates and the actual shipping data. In a make-to-order open shop, MPS applies available to promise planning techniques. In both instances, the aim of a master scheduler is to reconcile variations in demand with the variability

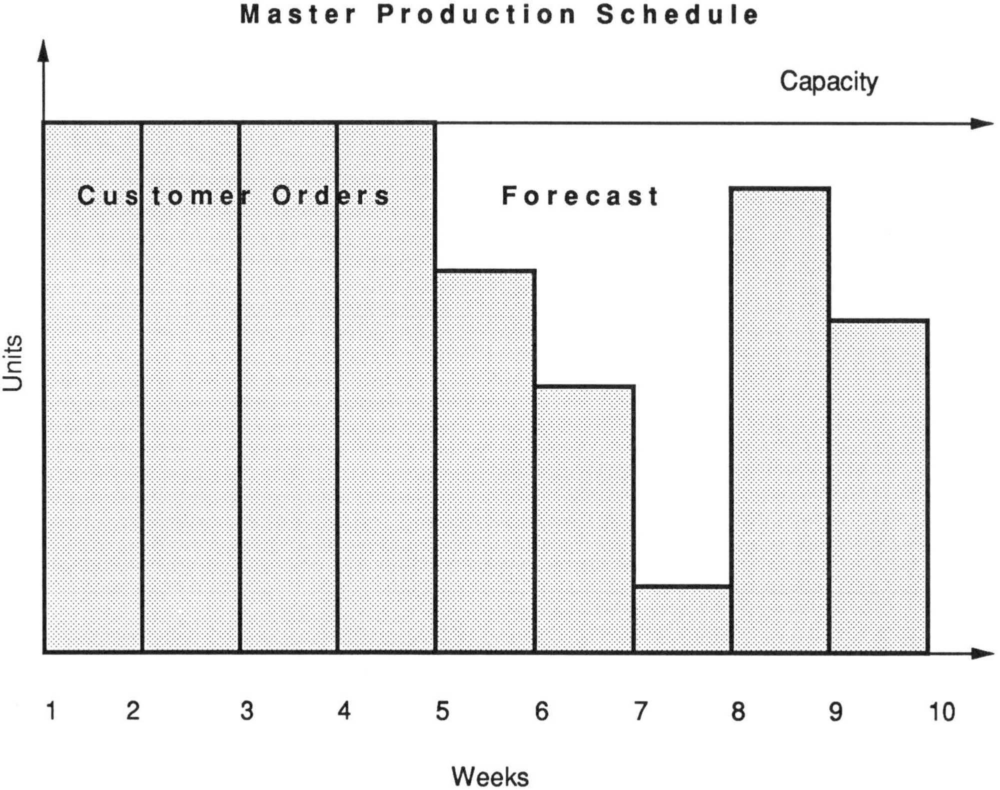


**Figure 3-19**
**How MPS Blends Customer Orders with Forecasts**

in the production output by maintaining and controlling the inventory level for each produced item and creating a stable production schedule. Relationships of MPS to other production planning activities are illustrated in Figure 3-20.

MPS is a disaggregation of an aggregate plan into a time-phased schedule compiled in end product quantities. MPS is a statement of the anticipated built schedule indicating specific product configurations in quantities to be manufactured per time period.

The master production schedule prorates monthly plans into weekly buckets of specific products in a product line. For example in Figure 3-16, 210 tractors in the February MPS plan are alloted to heavy duty tractors and light weight tractors weekly production plans. This plan is further interpreted into tactical operational schedules. On the resources side, MPS is expressed by a period

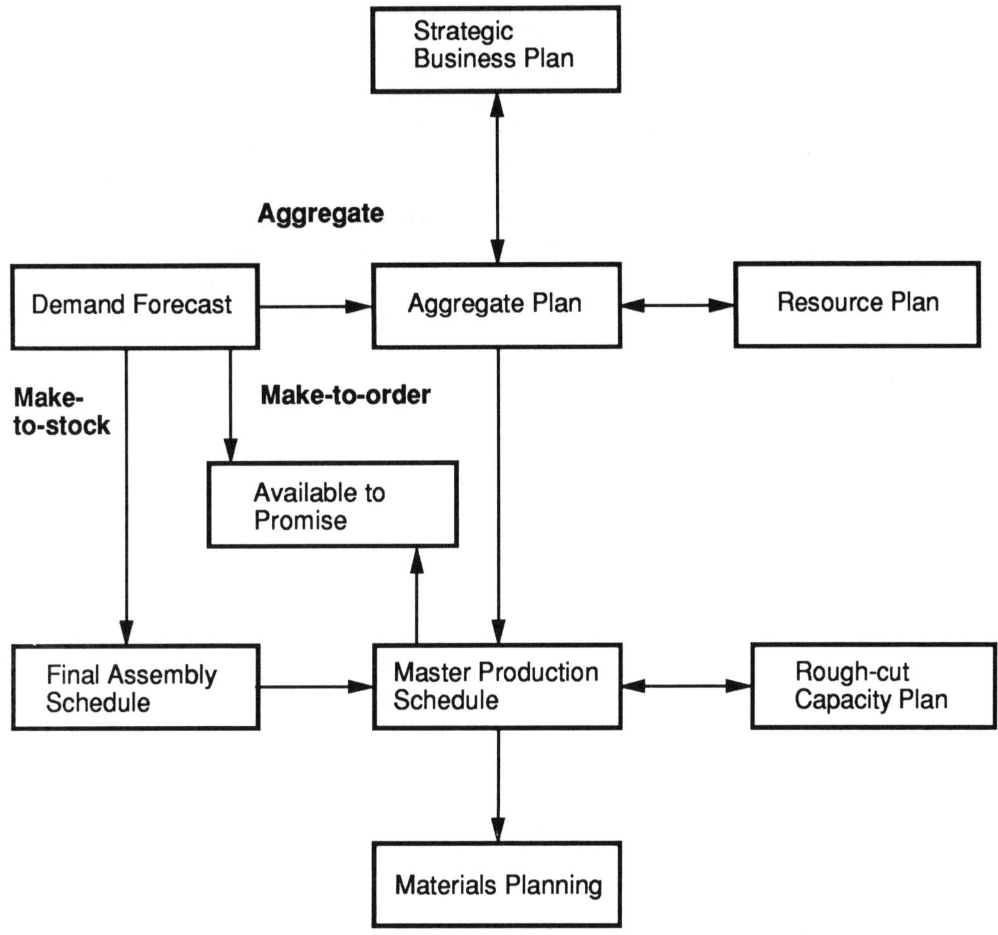


**Figure 3-20**
**How Master Production Schedule Relates to Production Process**

and by a capacity group. The time horizon is up to 18 weeks, with weekly increments, and the measuring unit is a specific product in a product group. In make-to-stock companies, MPS can be expressed in terms of end product items, major assembly units, or component parts which are distribution items.

The MPS planning horizon must extend far enough to avoid any produced or purchased components being scheduled in past due buckets. MPS is an aggregate demand planning system.

*Example*: You are a production manager of a small cellular phone manufacturer. You've drawn up an MPS plan to accommodate your orders. In its final form, a conventional MPS format consists of four lines of information on quantity and time. Figure 3-21 shows MPS compiled in weekly buckets over the 10 weeks' time horizon. There is a deviation between your sales forecasts and the MPS schedule (line 3) due to the inconsistency in demand and your available capacity. The projected available products are shown in line 4. You should make your adjustments to the available-to-promise column when stock falls below demand.

| Activity \ Weeks | 3 | 4 | 5 | 6 | 7 | 8 | 9 | 10 |
|---|---|---|---|---|---|---|---|---|
| Sales forecast | 35 | 35 | 30 | 30 | 35 | 35 | 40 | 40 |
| Customer order backlog | 45 | 25 | 20 | 15 | 30 | | | |
| Master production schedule * | 45 | 100 | | | | 120 | | |
| Available-to-promise | | 10 | | | | | | |

* Scheduled receipts -- the quantity has been released to the "in-process" status

**Figure 3-21**
**Available-to-Promise Calculations**

*Available to promise* (ATP) is computed for each time period by subtracting from the current available MPS level your total of customer orders backlog for all time periods until next MPS receipts. For example, your total customer order backlog for weeks 4, 5, 6, and 7 (90 in total), until next MPS order of 120 is due in week 8, is subtracted from the fourth week's schedule (100 units). The available to promise in week 4 is 10 items. Your ATP is the product quantity which is not yet committed to customer orders and is thus available to promise.

MPS is the last planning stage which applies a final product as a measuring unit. To prepare an itemized production plan, a master scheduler has to conduct a detailed analysis of capacity requirements and measure them against ever-changing itemized production rates. This is accomplished through rough-cut capacity planning.

## ROUGH-CUT CAPACITY PLANNING

In *rough-cut capacity planning*, the capacity required for a product is stated in collective terms of a group of equipment, without identifying specific types of equipment in this group. This is done according to the departments' or functional work centers' capacity profile.

Rough-cut capacity planning breaks down the plan into functional capacity categories. This plan is itemized in work hours of major production units or labor categories. It involves an analysis of MPS, along with the detection of potential bottlenecks, based on developed key resource profiles for each product family or group of products. Rough resource requirements are compared with available resources and are reviewed against the MPS plan for any obvious capacity constraints. Subcontracting alternative may be considered at this stage.

Rough-cut capacity planning is done by simulating the load on critical resources through interaction with resource requirements planning—the "what-if" planning analysis. This analysis includes both dedicated and shared resources. A rough-cut capacity is also known as the product resource profile. Compiled time-phased resource requirements are compared with available resources. A further resource load and constraints are determined through the simulation of alternatives. A product mix is developed at this stage through the interactive trial fit process. The selected product mix should total the demand for each product line in the aggregate plan updated with the latest forecasted demand and orders on hand. Figure 3-22 illustrates the distinction between the traditional master production schedule and the two-level MPS featuring the "what-if" analysis and rough-cut capacity planning.

Rough-cut capacity planning involves an analysis of several alternatives that may be posed by management when compiling the master production schedule. These alternatives, such as involving an overtime or subcontracting an alternate routing of work, and employment level changes, are considered when selecting the right one. In every organization, there are several critical processes building

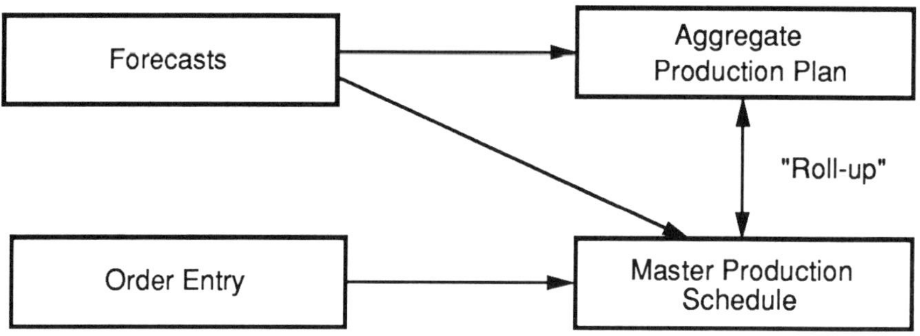


**A. Traditional Master Scheduling**

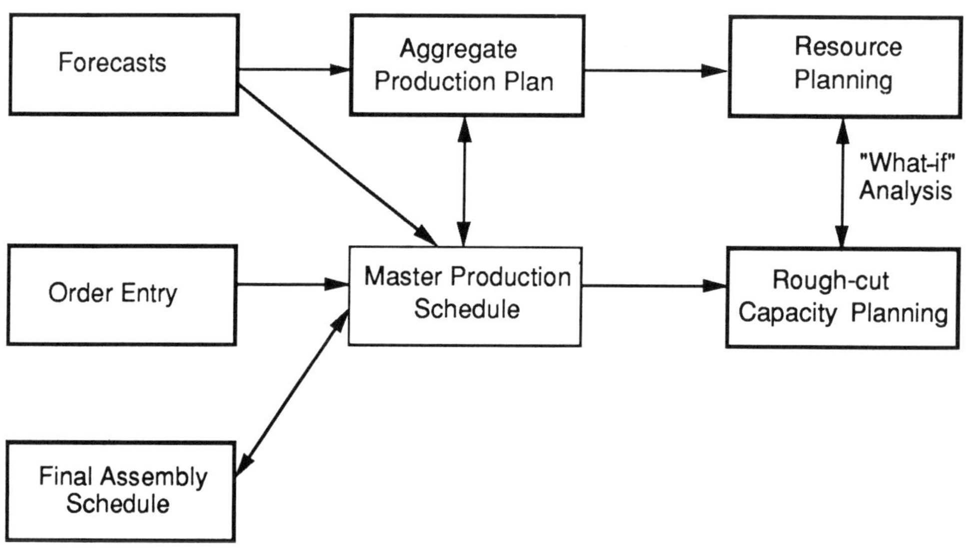


**B. Two-Level Master Scheduling**

**Figure 3-22**
**Traditional Versus Two-Level Master Scheduling**

up queueing lines and idle operations. These "bottleneck" processes can be both internal or external, vendor-supplied components or raw materials not readily available from other sources. In other companies, the final assembly process, the testing operations, or the operations conducted on special purpose machines which are run on a three-shift basis can represent such critical processes that must be closely monitored.

Rough-cut capacity planning simulates the load on these critical resources. At the MPS stage, rough-cut capacity planning attempts to ensure that there are no apparent capacity constraints for the projected production level.

The significance of rough-cut capacity planning is in that it is instrumental in determining the "optimal" product mix, through the "what-if" analysis of possible alternatives. Rough-cut capacity planning sometimes calls for changes in MPS, in order to accommodate the capacity limitations and to keep MPS realistically balanced. Nevertheless, such MPS plans are still inadequate for the execution because products are still not related to specific resources—no balancing as such has been performed as yet. The planning is not detailed and is still done in general terms.

The master scheduler is a focal point of reconciling sometimes contradicting requirements, such as to provide a quality customer service while at the same time, avoid building up unnecessary inventory, to respond to the fluctuations in demand while at the same time, reduce the production cost.

Along with rough-cut capacity planning, other techniques have been developed in master production scheduling, such as applying a bill of labor, a planned bill of materials, and the final assembly scheduling.

***Applying a Bill of Labor*** *Bill of labor* or *bill of capacity*, as it is sometimes called, is a product capacity profile prepared from BOM and a route sheet in the following sequence:

1. Explode BOM.
2. Compile time-phased BOM.
3. Use a route sheet to determine run times in work centers.

Following is a listing of a typical amount of capacity required to produce one item. Such a list is *bill of capacity*. Bill of capacity is not an accurate or detailed time-phased capacity requirement. It is compiled according to major capacity categories and sometimes on critical processes only.

*Example* : Consider this bill of capacity (by major work centers or major labor categories).

| Capacity | Product A (hours) | Product B (hours) |
|---|---|---|
| Welding | 1.2 | 0.4 |
| Machining | 3.8 | 8.5 |
| Hot treating | 0.8 | — |

| | | |
|---|---|---|
| El Discharge Machine (EDM) | 3.6 | 4.5 |
| Grinding | 2.7 | 3.9 |
| Assembly | 2.5 | 3.1 |

The multitude of combinations of special options, BOL contains information required for the rough-cut capacity planning.

## MASTER PRODUCTION SCHEDULING WITH PLANNED BILL OF MATERIALS

In make-to-order companies, MPS is often compiled at the option BOM level based on the "planned" bill of materials, where end items have a large number of options assembled from few basic subassembly types.

Planned BOM, comprises a multitude of product options which configure various end product assemblies. A planned BOM is an input into the final assembly schedule when the configuration of the assemblies is not known in advance. The final assembly schedule structures the end product and assists in product costing.

Establishing demand prior to the MPS being compiled is not always possible, since customer options become known later. The planning bill of materials differs from the conventional engineering BOM in that it is structured in two BOM levels—namely, the final assembly and the major subassemblies—making it possible to select the appropriate components from the storage, according to customer preferences.

*Example*: Long Reach Manufacturing has several options for the produced product LOB25: having three options of bale arms—18 * 36, 18 * 32, and 18 * 40, in quantities of 3,000, 5,000, and 2,000, respectively: two options of mounting kit—LOB ITA "A" and LOB ITA "A" QH, in quantities of 7,000 and 3,000, respectively; and two options of common parts F/NON S/S LOB25 and S/S LOB25, in quantities of 5,500 and 4,500, respectively. There is only one possible option of common parts group F/ LOB25 requiring a full quantity of 10,000. The planning bill of materials for LOB25 is shown in Figure 3-23 and graphically illustrated in Figure 3-24.

The planning BOM breaks down the standard BOM into combinatory options of the final product. This is also known as the *single-level planning BOM* or the *super bill of materials*.

Due to rough-cut capacity planning, there can be many variations in processing time requirements. For example, a situation can occur when a required specific machine in the group is not available, even though there is idle capacity in this machine group. For such a situation, a provision is made to balance the product requirements with the process limitations by shifting the actual production slightly forward or backward—the so called *time fences*.

Time fences also serve the purpose of accommodating hot orders and unexpected jobs. MPS is a connection between an aggregate plan and a stiff detailed operational plan. MPS disaggregates loose plans into structured time-phased

**Single Level Bill of Materials** **Review Bill**

| Review WU | Review Route | Add Struct | Add Part | Printed Report | Both |
|---|---|---|---|---|---|

**Part Number** SUPR LOB25

| Description | Unit of Measure | Part Class | Part Status |
|---|---|---|---|
| Super Bill for LOB25 | EA | F | |

| Component Part | Config Code | Description | UM | Quant Per | Prior Flag | Expl Code |
|---|---|---|---|---|---|---|
| CMNSURPLOB25 | | COMMON PARTS GROUP F/LOB25 | EA | 1.0000 | Y | Y |
| GBL-01055-LOBTG | | LOB25/35 LH/RH BALE ARMS 18X36 | EA | .3000 | N | Y |
| GBL-0126-LOBTG | | LOB25/35 LH/RH BALE ARMS 18X32 | EA | .5000 | N | Y |
| GBL-0128-LOBTG | | LOB25/35 LH/RH BALE ARMS 18X40 | EA | .2000 | N | Y |
| HKS-0011-LOBTG | | LOB ITA "A" MOUNTING KIT | EA | .7000 | Y | Y |
| HKS-0011-LOBTG | | LOB ITA "A"QH MOUNTING KIT | EA | .3000 | Y | Y |
| HYDLOB25NN | | COMMON PARTS F/ NON S/S LOB25 | EA | .5500 | Y | Y |
| HYDLOB25NS | | COMMON PARTS F/ S/S LOB25 | EA | .4500 | Y | Y |

1016

**End of retrieval**

**Figure 3-23**
**Planning Bill of Materials**

Reprinted with permission from Long Reach Manufacturing Company.

operational schedules. MPS is a standard against which an actual production output is measured.

The three types of time periods are as follows:

1. *Frozen*—indicating that no changes are possible; for example, six weeks prior to the execution date
2. *Firm*—indicating that changes are possible after review and plans evaluation
3. *Adjustable*—indicating that changes are possible if the capacity is available, demonstrating the possibility of making changes in scheduled orders

Time fences beyond the cumulative lead time are not restricted as much as these three time periods. Time fences of MPS are illustrated in Figure 3-25.

The duration of MPS time fences depends on the production lead time. A substantial lead time reduction in JIT systems reduces time fences corre-

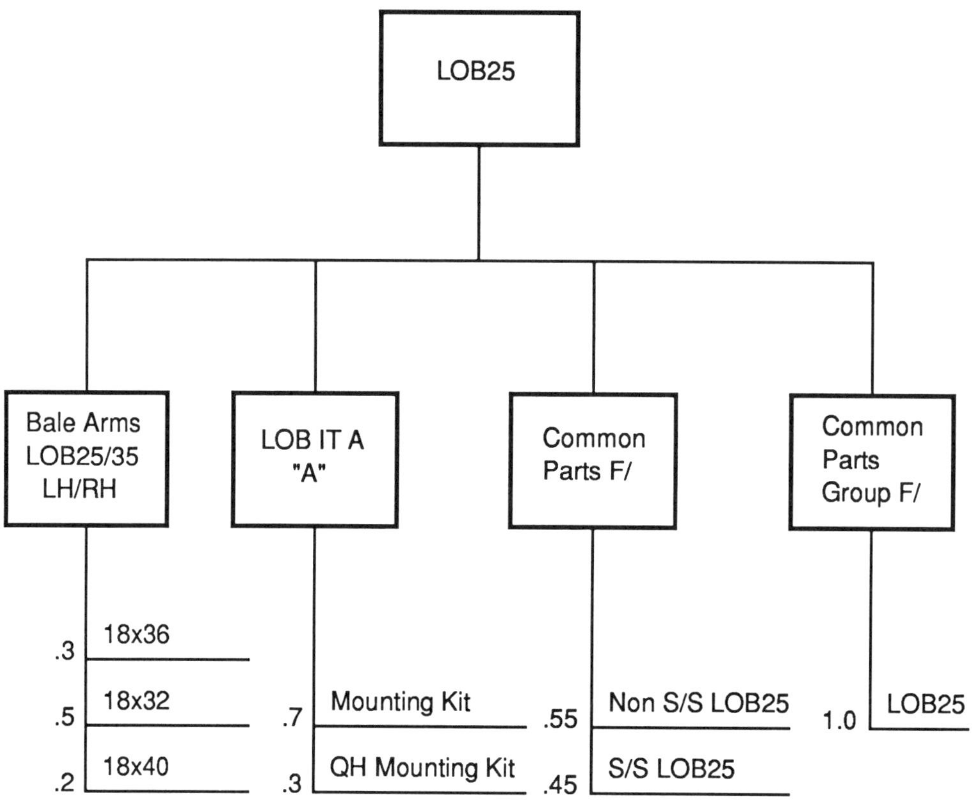


**Figure 3-24**
**A Single-Level Planning Bill of Materials for Product LOB25**

Reprinted with permission from Long Reach Manufacturing Company.

spondingly. High-performance JIT system companies apply two- to three-week time fences. Some companies estimate time fences in days rather than weeks. For example, at Compaq, time fences are on a six-day time period.

Despite that the items are scheduled outside of a firm time fence, the manufacturing of components is included within this fence. Consequently, changes made within the *firm* time fence period can affect the production schedule of the frozen time fence. Some companies have a rule that any changes made within the firm time fence require an authorization from the top management and even involve the accounting function to compare the cost of changes against the benefits derived from these changes.

The practice of some companies to charge more for "hot orders" is a simple reflection that these orders are more expensive to produce. Probably,

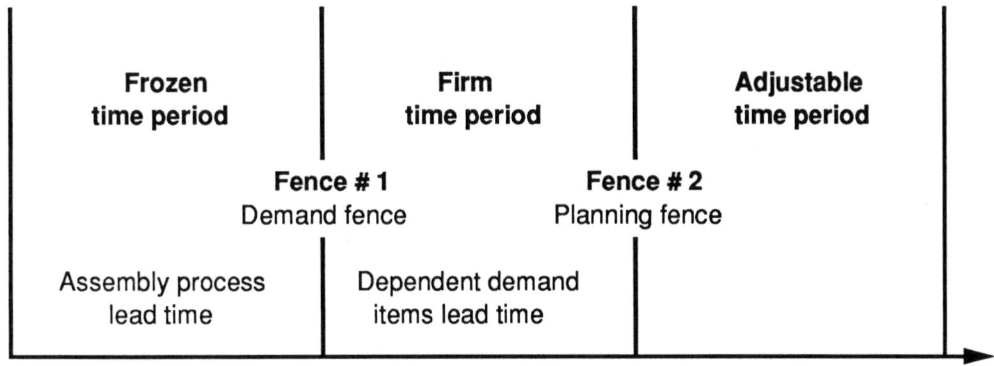


Time fences divide production planning horizon into three time periods according to lead times:

- period 1 -- **Frozen time period --** depending on lead time for assembly processes
- period 2 -- **Firm time period --** depending on lead time for components manufacturing and purchasing, small changes are possible
- period 3 -- **Adjustable time period --** changes are possible during this time period.

**Figure 3-25**
**Master Production Schedule -- Time Fences**

in such a case, all customers should be charged more due to the fact that all orders are getting more expensive to produce.

Any disruption to the production plan increases the production cost. The problem is that quite often we do not realize the extent of the disruption caused by a "hot job." If we are able to estimate and quote customers a real cost of disruptions to production and to the material flow, then the number of these disruptions would be significantly reduced, since few customers will agree to pay such high charges.

Applying time fencing in MPS creates stability for MRP by accommodating customer demand through leveling the load on facilities. Unbalanced work orders are simply reshuffled by shop floor planners, who then schedule jobs according to their priority. The significance of MPS is in that it presents a rescheduling basis.

The rule stating "Never reschedule at the component level" is accepted by many manufacturing firms. Rescheduling should go back to the product level, and the delay or progress, if at all possible, should be verified and arranged to include an entire set of components, thus avoiding partial production and building up work-in-process inventories. You should ensure that for each work order, a capacity is available since a delay of one or several components prevents assembling the product and again will increase work-in-process.

In general, more resistance to change must come as the due date approaches. The trend is to compress time fences along with the lead times. Customer orders provide a basis for final assembly schedules.

The master production schedule is the last independent point in production planning which takes into consideration an input from other functions of the business—sales, marketing, and finance. The next planning stage is materials planning. A system widely used in materials planning is the material requirements planning (MRP). MRP and production activity control (PAC) are based entirely on the MPS decision. MRP and PAC are known as dependent demand planning stages and will be discussed in the next chapter.

The operations plan provides feedback to ensure the validity of strategic plans. MPS translates aggregate plans into specific end items and, through rough-cut capacity planning, converts it into specific material and capacity requirements. Time intervals used in MPS correspond to the time buckets, later used in MRP.

Unless there is an electronic integration with the customer (for example, job ordering is linked directly to the customer inventory and sales information, where sales at the distribution level trigger an electronic replacement order), MPS is compiled for subassemblies or groups of options, not for finished products because it is difficult to forecast an end item configuration in option-sensitive products. MPS disaggregates an aggregate plan into specific products. The final product configuration is planned by the final assembly schedule. The final assembly schedule (FAS) makes final commitments to the end items.

## FINAL ASSEMBLY SCHEDULING

In a hierarchical planning system, final assembly scheduling is the last production program to include end product options. The name of the final assembly scheduling perfectly explains its meaning. The final assembly schedule is the MPS considering product options stated in a component configuration below the final assembly level of BOM. It is used in make-to-order firms to satisfy the actual customer option configuration.

Planning of the final assembly schedule is detached from MPS, so it takes over where MPS ends. Figure 3-26 shows that an input into the final assembly schedule comes from the order entry and MPS. MPS covers the time span from the acquisition of raw materials until all individual components and subassemblies are ready for the final assembly, including testing, packing, and shipping to customer.

In companies working with a sufficient backlog, the final assembly schedule is a commitment to the completion of each customer order. In companies where customer orders on hand do not sufficiently cover an entire MPS program, it is desirable to hold back on the commitment as to when to build a specific final product configuration.

Final assembly scheduling is becoming increasingly popular, due to its response to the order customization—although a product is built to the forecast, the final assembly is done after the customer order is received specifying the unique product configuration.

The first stage of production is conducted under a *planned order*, while the second stage—when the product assembly begins after the end product configuration is defined—is conducted under a *firm order*. In order to reduce an inventory, many companies use the final assembly schedule to order production of short lead time components, while long lead time components are controlled by MPS.

Still other companies reduce inventory costs by controlling high-cost components by the final assembly schedule. Often, the final assembly schedule is used to level the production plan when demand varies from period to period. In this case, MPS smooths out the plan to correspond to the production capacity, then the final production schedule reflects the incoming customer orders which

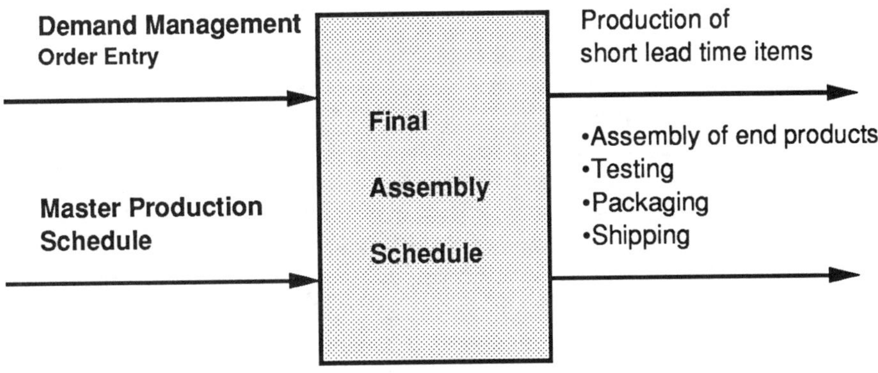


**Figure 3-26**
**Final Assembly Schedule**

can be already on hand or in process. Here, the final assembly schedule achieves the leveled load of capacity and the improved customer service. The final assembly schedule is the ultimate stage of MPS. It is a production order which has a shorter time horizon (one to three weeks in advance) and shorter time increments (twice weekly or even daily). The final assembly schedule, thus, has a higher revision frequency than MPS.

MPS concludes independent demand planning. Further production planning is dependent on demand, which means interpreting prepared plans into specific work order instructions. The next planning stage is MRP, where MPS is further "exploded" into assembly units and components. The final stage, *production activity control*, requires a detailed operational plan compiled in machine/hours. PAC applies operational planning.

## Master Production Scheduling at Dresser Industrial Tool Division: A Case Study

"Master production scheduling at Dresser Industrial Tool Division (ITD) is designed to address our type of business and business objectives on service," says Bob Collins, manager of manufacturing, at the Houston plant. However, some items are built to stock while others are specifically designed and built for a specific customer. On service, a major Houston plant objective is to operate with less than 10-day backlog, which, of course, requires quick response to incoming business. This causes an emphasis on customer orders over forecast items.

The MPS covers a two-year horizon with 36 weekly buckets followed by 17 four-week buckets. Service parts are forecast with a computer model and automatically scheduled across the planning horizon. Tool assemblies are forecast based upon the annual profit plan with product mix determined by marketing. Level loading for a planning horizon uses capacity requirements planning simulation. Actual sales to forecast are reviewed and adjusted monthly, while minor adjustments are made weekly.

Prior to material requirements planning, which is run weekly, the customer backlog and MPS are merged. That is, backlog is matched to the MPS, and for matching items, the MPS is reduced by the backlog quantities for a period of up to eight weeks. No "past due" is carried in the MPS. If an item is sold, it becomes backlog and is assembled and shipped. If an item is not sold as forecasted, the first-week quantity is simply "dropped" on the next MRP run. Since products are primarily assembled to order, the major function of MPS and MRP is to ensure quick availability of components, particularly longer lead time items such as castings, forgings, and bearings.

On the final assembly schedule, as assemblies are "kitted," they are moved to an available assembly area and a visual card system is used to assign work to assembly personnel in sequence according to priority. Shelf stock assemblies are used as a buffer to level the load in assembly against day-to-day fluctuations on incoming customer orders.

## MASTER PRODUCTION SCHEDULES IN VARIOUS TYPES OF PRODUCTION

Types of production are distinguished by their material flow patterns. Discrete assembly-type production typically begins with many raw materials and purchased components converted into few finished types of products. This type of production is illustrated in Figure 3-27.

High-volume manufacturing companies producing assemble-to-order products have a structure shown in Figure 3-27. There, many raw materials and purchased components inputs are used to make few types of subassembly units. These units are put together in a number of different combinations, in order to make many types of finished products. The famous example of such a production type is an automobile manufacturer producing many end options

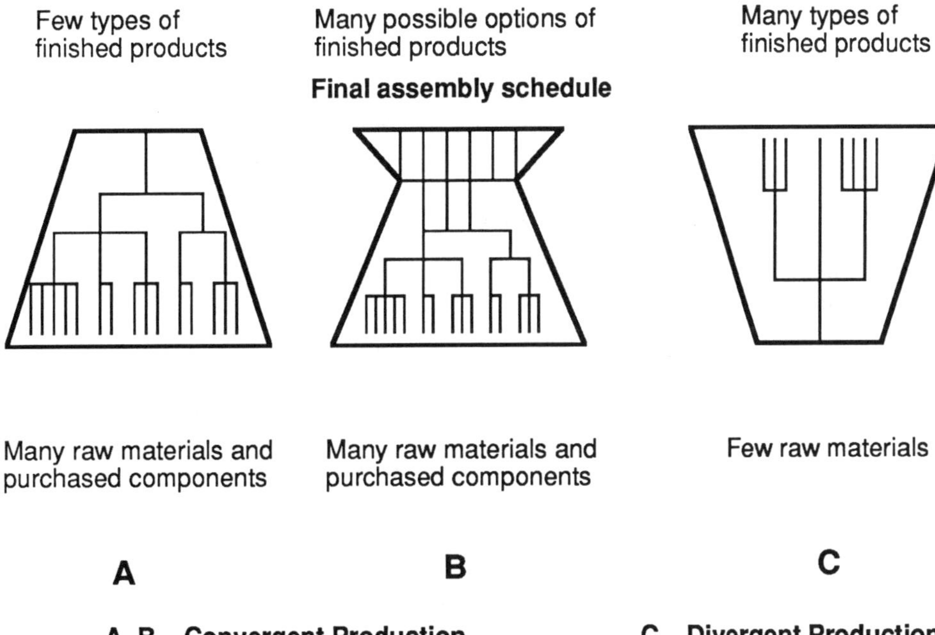


**Figure 3-27**
**MPS in Various Types Of Production**

from the lesser number of subassemblies. Type of production processes shown in Figure 3-27A and B, are known as *convergent production.*

A reverse arrangement is observed in process-type industries where few types of raw material inputs are converted into many types of finished products—*divergent production.* This is an analytic production process, such as seen in petro-chemical industry. This type of production is illustrated in Figure 3-27C.

The experience has shown that MPS is more effective when it deals with a smaller number of items. This leads to the improved accuracy of forecasting, better planning and control, and the reduced information cost.

In the application here, MPS is positioned at the narrow part of structures. Thus, discrete assembled products are master scheduled at the end items level, since it requires to schedule the least number of items. This type of MPS is compiled in final product units based on the forecasted demand.

Companies producing discrete products with options plan their MPS at the subassembly level. These companies build their products according to the final assembly schedule.

Process industry applications are master scheduled at the raw material level on the input side of the narrow part of the structure. Here, the variety of possible outputs leads to uncertain capacity requirements, since various end products require different production facilities. This operational planning and control over WIP and finished goods inventory is more complex.

## MPS IN CONTINUOUS FLOW PRODUCTION

MPS in a repetitive manufacturing firm is closer to the final assembly line and has an even greater significance, since materials planning and PAC are standardized to a various degree. Often, MPS goes directly to production, with orders, especially in nondiscrete conversion processes.

Lead time is shorter and uniform in every repetitive run, due to stable material flow and the significant reduction of waiting lines. A steady material flow is also facilitated by the fact that open orders are not interrupted: work orders advance as soon as they are started. Also, a single work order will often satisfy several customers because the customers submit their requests well in advance, and production control, job tracking, and expediting are reduced. Production planning departments have a less critical function in continuous production, while the significance of planning and executing of plant maintenance is emphasized.

The master production schedule, or "production bible," as it is often called on the shop floor, is the last stage of independent demand planning. It is a final revision of a production plan, which must be correlated with inventory control, capacity planning, production activity control, purchasing, engineering services, cost accounting, marketing, sales, and customer relations. A list of functions performed by the MPS planner indicates that this is really a key position in the organization who needs strong interactive and communication skills and flexibility in order to perform his or her important function successfully.

# 4

# How to Structure Material Planning to Improve Efficiency

As a production manager, your job is to establish adequate control over the material flow. Proper materials management can help you to achieve improved efficiency and cost reduction. The basic cost of materials is fast becoming a dominant part of the final product cost. Consequently, this area of manufacturing has been given particular attention in recent years by highlighting the materials management function. Materials management is singled out as a separate business function which integrates a number of activities affecting material flow control. Inventory control is a major activity of materials management. Designing an efficient inventory management system will aid in your cost control.

## DESIGNING PRODUCTIVE INVENTORY MANAGEMENT SYSTEMS

Materials planning breaks down the master production schedule (MPS) program into a basic components' level and ensures the timely delivery of components for assembly processes from three sources: vendors, inventory, and production departments. Inventory orders, production orders, or purchasing orders are ordering media at this stage. Schematically, sources of supply are illustrated in Figure 4-1.

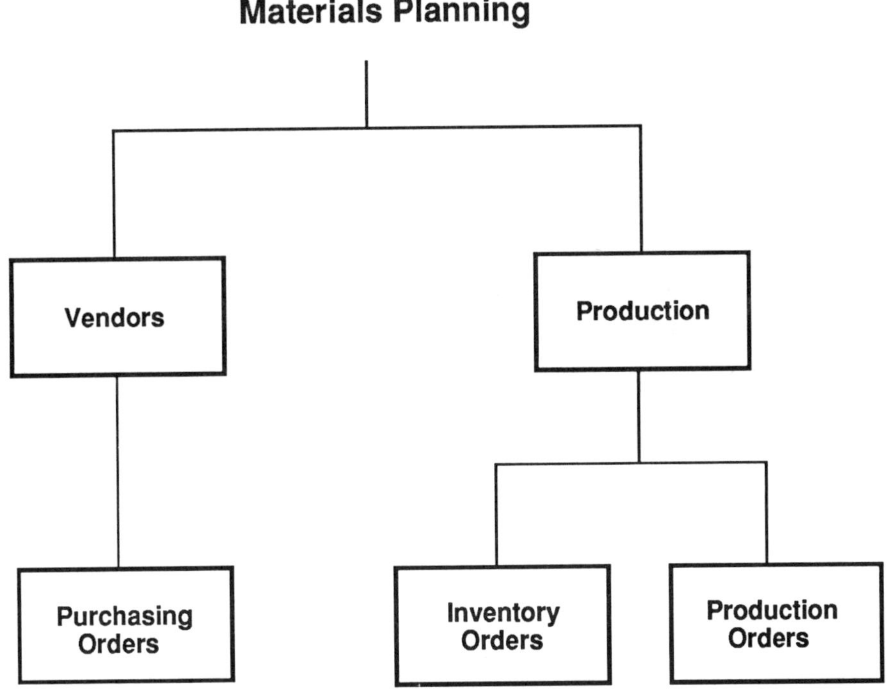


**Figure 4-1**
**The Three Sources of Components Supply**

This chapter deals with ordering of components and materials from the inventory system and production departments. Purchasing is discussed later on in Chapter 12. In an open production system, after the MPS firmed up your production program, the next step is to verify the availability of end products, semiproducts, components in stock, and on-order items against your inventory. Manufacturing orders or purchase orders then can be placed for the balance of these items.

Inventory represents the difference between the input and the output of a system. This difference remains in the system.

inventory = input - output

A basic inventory equation is as follows:

$$X = H + O + P - R$$

where
$X$ = quantity available
$H$ = quantity on hand
$O$ = quantity on order
$P$ = quantity planned for future order release
$R$ = quantity required

*Example*: The status of an inventory of bearings in General Industries Co.:

| | |
|---|---|
| On hand | 120 |
| On order | 90 |
| Planned orders | 130 |
| Required | 420 |

available: 120 + 90 + 130 - 420 = -80

There are only 120 bearings in an inventory, 90 bearings are in production, and another 130 bearings are scheduled for production. An additional 80 bearings should be ordered to satisfy demand.

An inventory is seen as an idle resource. Some people regard capacity (for example, equipment and labor) as being part of an inventory system; others see inventory as a source of a short-term capacity (for example, items in stock can buffer the shortages of labor and equipment). Is capacity a part of an inventory, or is an inventory a part of capacity? The answer is that an inventory belongs to dedicated resources, while a productive capacity belongs to shared resources. The inventory and the production capacity are controlled by two distinctive systems: Inventory (dedicated resources) is controlled by the inventory control system, while capacity (shared resources) is controlled by capacity planning, a part of the production planning and control system, as shown in Figure 4-2. In other words, an inventory is part of a product, while a productive capacity represents a process.

An inventory is dedicated resource prior to entering the next stage of the material flow, that is, the inventory of materials and components before entering the production stage and the inventory of finished goods awaiting delivery or in the process of delivery to a customer.

## Recognizing the Three Stages of Inventory

There are six basic classes of inventory:

1. Raw materials
2. Bought-out components

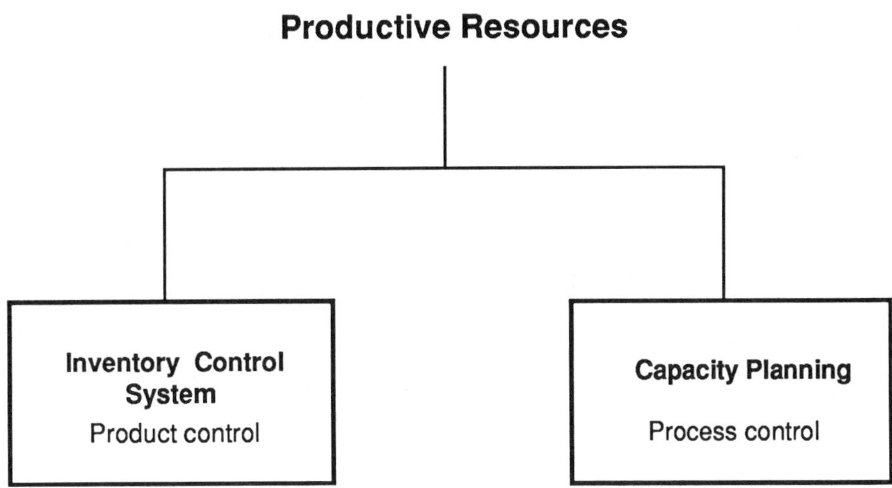


**Figure 4-2**
**The Two Systems Used in Controlling Productive Resources**

3. Supplies
4. Work-in-process (WIP)
5. Finished goods
6. Goods in transit

Three stages of inventory are distinguished: acquisition, production, and distribution.

- Stage 1—From vendors and suppliers to acquisition inventory or purchasing
- Stage 2—From purchasing to WIP inventory
- Stage 3—From production to distribution inventory (finished goods inventory and goods in transit)

The three categories of inventory, corresponding to the three states of product—acquisition, production, and distribution—are illustrated in Figure 4-3.

An inventory is considered a dedicated resource deposited between the adjoining production stages with the purpose of buffering any existing or future discord in their production cycles. Thus, an inventory is a function of planning and control of production cycles at various stages of production as well as a function of acquisition and distribution. The primary purpose of inventory is decoupling/buffering the main stages of material flow.

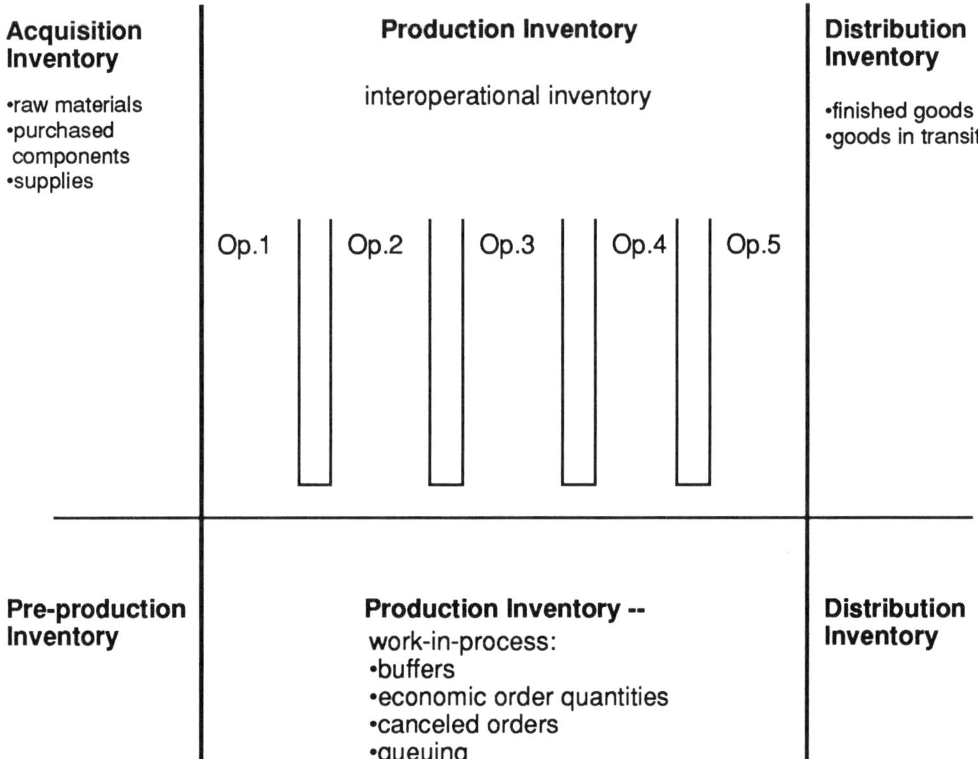


**Figure 4-3**
**Pre-Production, Production, and Distribution Inventories**

## ACQUISITION INVENTORY

An acquisition inventory consists of *raw materials* and *bought-out components*. The latter are items purchased from outside suppliers or vendors and temporarily stored prior to entering production stages. An acquisition inventory is often justified as a protection from unreliable suppliers. An acquisition inventory is also regarded as a preproduction inventory. *Supplies* can be regarded as an inventory required for some production and technical services. An acquisition inventory also includes supplies, such as spare parts required by maintenance. Various inventory categories require different inventory control approaches: raw material and bought-out standard components are controlled by independent demand inventory models based on the average rate of demand.

#### PRODUCTION INVENTORY

The main concern of operations management, and by far the greatest source of production problems, is controlling the interoperational inventory of materials and components entering production stages—work-in-process (for example, inventory between the stages of raw material and finished goods). The effectiveness of any enterprise is largely determined by how effective their WIP control is. WIP is an inventory which is most difficult to control due to its ever-changing product state, changing costs of labor, and the overhead rates. Work-in-process requires more complex empirical models, discussed later in the text.

#### DISTRIBUTION INVENTORY

*Finished-goods inventory*, often classified as distribution inventory, are products completed and ready for delivery or at any stage of delivery. Finished-goods inventories are justified as the tool for better customer relations or for smoothing out shop overloads and underloads. Goods in transit are items at the stage of delivery to customers. A manufacturer holds the title for these goods for which payments have not yet been made.

### Classifying Inventory by Function

There are various reasons for having inventory:

1. To reduce purchasing costs or production costs. This is known as the *lot-size inventory.*
2. To be used as a buffer from an unexpected increase in demand or a reduction in supply. This is called *fluctuation inventory.*
3. To attempt to level the load on production. This is known as a *load-leveling inventory.*

#### LOT-SIZE INVENTORY

Lot-size inventories have the purpose of achieving the economical effect of purchasing in lots classified for quantity discounts. In production, the purpose of lot sizing is to produce a larger number of components using the same setup time.

For example, a crankshaft neck machining operation requires 3.5 hours setup time. Run time is 5 minutes per shaft. If there are 20 shafts on order, the operation time is as follows:

$$T = \frac{210 + (20 \times 5)}{20} = 15.5 \text{ minutes}$$

If the lot size is 100 shafts, the operation time is as follows:

$$T = \frac{210 + (100 \times 5)}{100} = 7.1 \text{ minutes}$$

This example is illustrated graphically in Figure 4-4. Increasing the lot size from 20 shafts to 100 shafts reduces operation time from 15.5 minutes to 7.1 minutes.

Ostensibly, productivity is more than doubled, but there is a hidden holding cost and in the long run there are many instances where productivity gains are depleted due to the pilferage and obsolescence caused by product modifications.

FLUCTUATION INVENTORY

A fluctuation inventory intends to buffer up demand or supply variations. These are inventory items held as a reserve or a safety stock to cover an unforeseen upsurge in demand or disruptions in supply. For example, an industrial transformer manufacturer experiences a fluctuation in demand from 300 to 400 units per month. In order to satisfy demand, the manufacturer might decide to keep 80 transformers in inventory if maximum production capacity is 320 units per month. These 80 transformers are the fluctuation inventory.

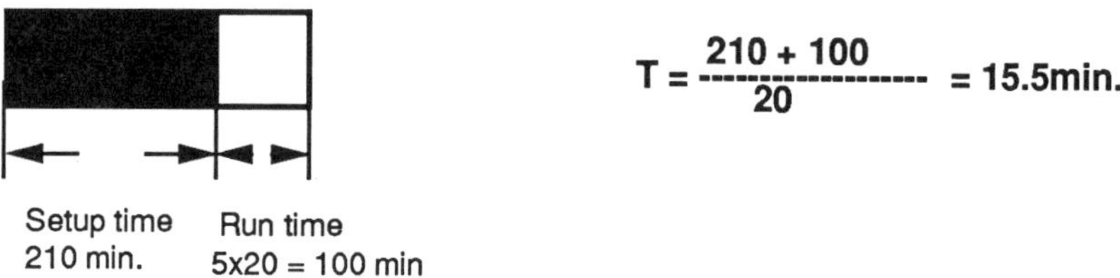


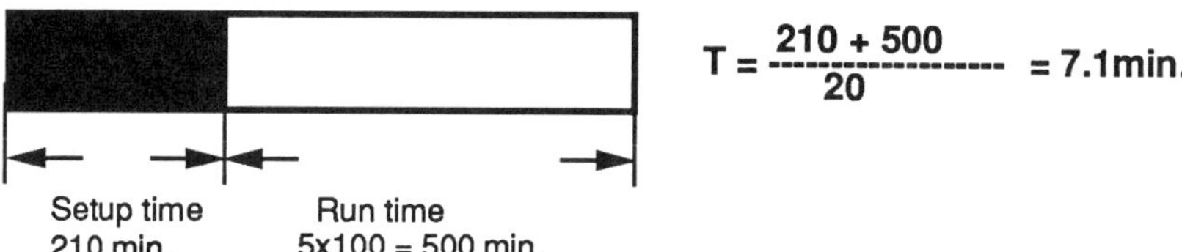


**Figure 4-4**
**The Correlation Between the Lot Size and the Operation Time (T)**

### LOAD LEVELING INVENTORY

A *load-leveling inventory* is built up in advance of future requirements, in order to distribute the load evenly on production facilities or to utilize idle productive resources. It is also used to act as a buffer: supplying workstations with components between the stages of material flow. This type of inventory is similar to the fluctuation inventory. The difference is that in the *fluctuation inventory*, the objective was to satisfy customer demand—a *product-focused inventory*, while the *load leveling inventory* is the result of the desire to keep the equipment occupied—*process-focused inventory.*

Often the question is asked: Are inventories assets or liabilities? Inventories are classified as assets on a balance sheet and thus there are taxes paid on them, in addition to the expenses already incurred plus the storage costs. Collectively, all expenses for the inventory are borrowed capital investments on which an interest is paid. Consequently, there should be a very good reason for keeping an inventory: the benefit gained from keeping an inventory should outweigh all the earlier mentioned expenses. The contemporary trend toward a zero-inventory production system calls for offsetting inventory costs. Demands for the inventory cost reduction are more imperative than ever before.

## THE CONNECTION BETWEEN INDEPENDENT AND DEPENDENT DEMAND INVENTORY

A dedicated resources inventory is divided into two categories:

1. Resources waiting to enter the production process—the preproduction inventory
2. Resources which have already entered the production—the WIP inventory.

Raw materials, bought-out components, and standard components fall into the first category. The value of the inventory does not change significantly because no value is added. In the second category, an inventory enters production, adding to the cost of the item. A preproduction inventory is controlled by the *independent demand* system, while work-in-process is controlled by the *dependent demand* system.

### Setting Up Independent Demand Inventory—Stock-Controlled Systems

Product elements of different levels of the BOM structure are planned and controlled by different levels of the production planning and control system. The highest product level, the zero level in BOM, is planned by an MPS and aggregate production planning. This is identified as independent or random demand. In general, *independent demand* items are those whose requirements are forecasted or established by a customer order. An independent demand product level is not related to demand for other BOM items. An independent demand quantity decision is based on considerations other than the parent-level requirements. Independent demand is typical to distribution-type inventory systems. An independent demand item can be a finished product or a service. Independent demand items are forecasted rather than calculated because the requirements are derived from various sources. An example of independent demand is when an ordering decision is made based on the forecasted demand and the current inventory position. Figure 4-5 shows BOM of Product 20-12. There, aggregate

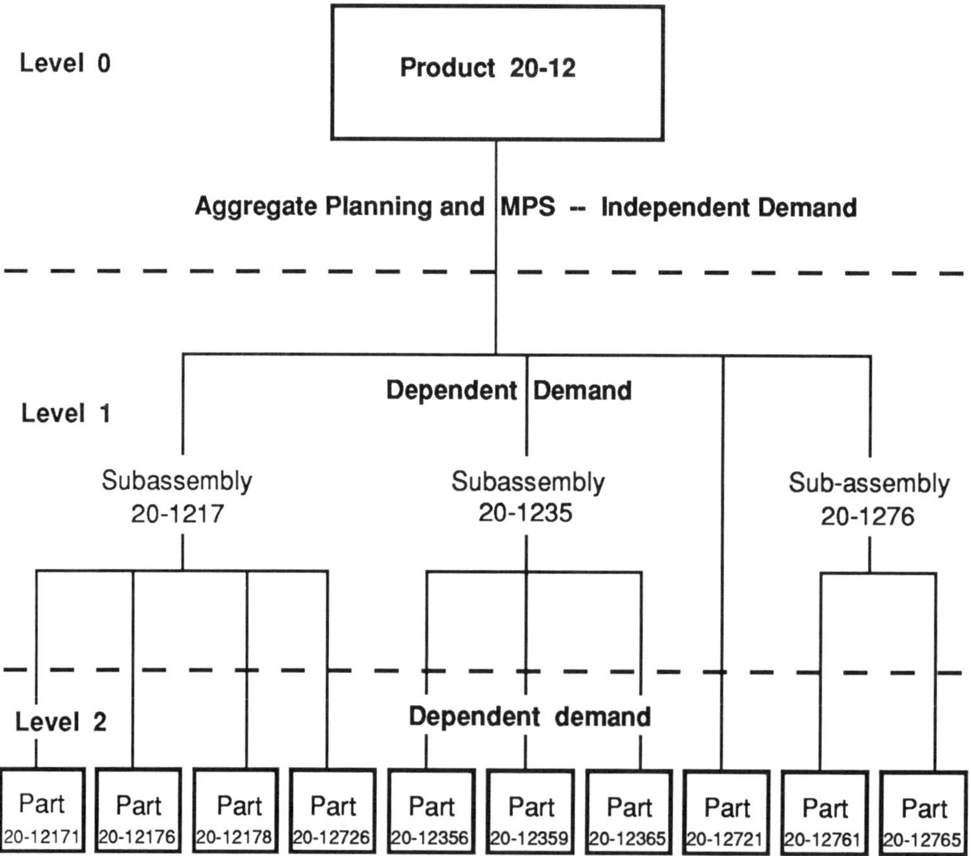


**Figure 4-5**
**Dependent and Independent Demand Items of BOM**

planning and MPS decisions concerning the product quantity are based on a number of strategic and tactical business considerations. As soon as such a quantity decision is made, demand for any lower BOM level component is defined by the place of this component in the BOM product structure.

Ordering of components for independent demand items is dependent on defined product quantities.

## Setting Up Dependent Demand Inventory Systems

A dependent demand inventory occurs where demand can be derived from a known product structure relationship. The demand is dependent upon the quantity on an order of their BOM's parent items. The value of a dependent demand inventory is constantly changing as components undergo operations and constantly add value.

*Dependent demand* quantities of inventory items are generated from demand for the higher-BOM-level items. Dependent demand is calculated typically based on the MPS rather than being forecasted. An example of a dependent demand item is an assembled product in which each component is ordered in quantities corresponding to the order on the final product or parent items.

*Example*: ABC Woodcrafters sells a handpainted pine wagon used mainly for decoration. The wagon has two sides, a front and a back base, and four wheels. In the ABC's production plan, the quantity of wagons represents the independent demand, while all the components of a wagon represent the dependent demand (they are dependent on the quantity of wagons in the production plan). If there are 100 small wagons on an MPS order, this figure represents independent demand. The ordering decision can vary. Instead of ordering 100 wagons, for example, a production planner could combine several orders into one single order (for example, order 400 wagons instead of 100 or split one order into two by placing two orders for 50 wagons each). Once the order amount has been decided upon, all further ordering of components will depend on the quantity decided upon. This ordering of components represents the dependent demand (for example, the ordering of 400 wheels, 200 side panels, 200 front and back panels, 100 bases, and 100 handles). Dependent demand can be calculated based on the higher BOM assembly level requirements.

This type of inventory undergoes multiple planning and operations scheduling stages. Dependent demand inventory categories include:

1. Semifinished component parts in stock
2. Semifinished component parts in process
3. Finished component parts in stock
4. Subassemblies in stock
5. Subassemblies in process

Generally, items on the BOM structure, other than those at the zero level, represent dependent demand. Some dependent demand components can be independent demand items when they are stated as separate items on a customer order or in the production plan (for example, spare parts production).

## What Are the Three Types of Stock Controlled Ordering Approaches?

According to quantity and time ordering considerations, independent demand inventory control systems can be divided into three categories: lot-for-lot ordering, fixed-time period ordering, and fixed-order quantity ordering.

### LOT-FOR-LOT ORDERING

Lot-for-lot inventory systems are an example of ordering where both quantity on order and timing are non-standard, and the ordering decision is made regarding *quantity on order and time* at the time when the order is placed. A lot-for-lot ordering quantity is equal to the quantity of withdrawal, at the time of withdrawal. For example, many stockrooms have regulations stipulating that a work order must be issued on the amount of components withdrawn from the inventory. There is no standard quantity and standard timing of orders in the lot-for-lot ordering system. Inventory replenishment and ordering systems are illustrated in Figure 4-6A.

### FIXED TIME PERIOD ORDERING SYSTEM

A *fixed time period ordering system* is applied when demand fluctuates. The order quantity varies depending on the usage rate. Here a stock counting inventory control model is used, where the inventory is counted at predetermined time periods and the order is placed for the number of items needed in order to replenish the stock to the predetermined level. The replenishment occurs periodically, within fixed time periods: weekly, monthly, quarterly, or semiannually. Orders with manufacturing departments are placed at the time when the counting takes place. Such methods usually require a higher level of stock, and there is a probability of being out of stock during the review period or during the lead time after the order is placed. This condition is considered by setting up a higher level of safety stock to protect against stockouts.

In a fixed time period ordering system illustrated in Figure 4-6B, ordering time is standardized, there is monthly ordering, but the order quantity fluctuates depending on demand.

| Part Number | Jan. | Feb. | Mar. | Apr. | May | Jun. | Jul. | Aug. | Sept. | Oct. | Nov. | Dec. |
|---|---|---|---|---|---|---|---|---|---|---|---|---|
| AQ-12-60 | 60 | | 80 | | 45 | | 50 | 40 | | 55 | 65 | |
| AQ-14-86 | 80 | | | 85 | 95 | | 55 | | 65 | | 75 | |
| AQ-14-92 | 110 | | 100 | | 95 | | 130 | | 145 | | 120 | |
| KL-8-37 | 140 | | | 130 | | 145 | | 125 | | | 130 | |
| KL-18-43 | 220 | | | 240 | | 190 | | 185 | | | 215 | |

**A. Lot-for-Lot Ordering System**

| Part number | Jan. | Feb. | Mar. | Apr. | May | Jun. | Jul. | Aug. | Sept. | Oct. | Nov. | Dec. |
|---|---|---|---|---|---|---|---|---|---|---|---|---|
| AQ-12-60 | 20 | 20 | 30 | 40 | 50 | 50 | 50 | 40 | 30 | 35 | 35 | 30 |
| AQ-14-86 | 30 | 20 | 40 | 45 | 60 | 50 | 65 | 40 | 40 | 35 | 30 | 40 |
| AQ-14-92 | 40 | 40 | 50 | 70 | 85 | 60 | 90 | 85 | 55 | 60 | 50 | 70 |
| KL-8-37 | 45 | 40 | 60 | 35 | 45 | 40 | 75 | 60 | 40 | 45 | 55 | 65 |
| KL-18-43 | 55 | 45 | 70 | 50 | 50 | 65 | 45 | 55 | 55 | 65 | 60 | 55 |

**B. Fixed Time Period Ordering System**

| Part number | Jan. | Feb. | Mar. | Apr. | May | Jun. | Jul. | Aug. | Sept. | Oct. | Nov. | Dec. |
|---|---|---|---|---|---|---|---|---|---|---|---|---|
| AQ-12-60 | 40 | | 40 | 40 | | 40 | | 40 | 40 | 40 | | 40 |
| AQ-14-86 | 40 | | 40 | 40 | | 40 | | 40 | 40 | 40 | | 40 |
| AQ-14-92 | 80 | | 80 | 80 | | 80 | | 80 | 80 | 80 | | 80 |
| KL-8-37 | 40 | | 40 | 40 | | 40 | | 40 | 40 | 40 | | 40 |
| KL-18-43 | 80 | | 80 | 80 | | 80 | | 80 | 80 | 80 | | 80 |

**C. Fixed Order Size Ordering System**

**Figure 4-6**
**Inventory Replenishment and Ordering Systems**

## FIXED ORDER QUANTITY ORDERING SYSTEM

A *fixed order quantity ordering system* is an inventory system in which the quantity on order is standard and the decision is made concerning the *time when to place an order*. A fixed order size ordering system, illustrated in Figure 4-6C, is characterized by a standard quantity on order and a fluctuation of ordering time. A feature of the fixed order size ordering system is that the work order is placed in assembly sets according to item quantities in BOM structure. This is a single-phase ordering system.

## HOW TO COMPUTE YOUR REORDER LEVEL AND REORDER POINT

A stock control ordering system establishes a certain stock level. This is known as the *reorder point* inventory system (ROP). The fluctuations in usage are adjusted by the time between the orders. The placement time of an order depends on the lead time or procurement time of the order and the demand during this period—the reorder level. *Reorder level* is established so that the quantity is sufficient to satisfy demand, until an order arrives. When a stock reaches a zero level, the order should arrive, and then the stock is back to the maximum level. The reorder point and reorder level are illustrated graphically in Figure 4-7.

reorder level = lead time in days × demand per day

$$ROP = T_p \times D$$

where

$T_p$ = lead time (the time between placing and receiving the order)

$D$ = rate of demand

A new order is triggered whenever the stock level reaches the predetermined reorder level. When the demand is constant, the reorder level can be estimated fairly accurately. In cases where demand fluctuates, the situation shown in Figure 4-7 may occur, resulting in shortages of components during lead time. ROP is valid when the consumption rate is constant and delivery is on time. Whenever one of these conditions fails, a shortage or a stockout occurs.

In a reorder point system, the inventory position is checked at fixed regular time intervals, at which time the replenishment order is placed so as to restore inventory to the specified inventory level. A *buffer stock* is introduced to protect the inventory from stockout situations when demand or supply fluctuates. A safety stock inventory model is shown in Figure 4-8. ROP is applied in inventory control of critical items of class A; average inventory is smaller due to the fact that record keeping is done every time the items are withdrawn or introduced to stock. This method is more accurate than fixed time period control systems because the order is placed exactly at that time when the quantity on hand reaches the reorder level. In a fixed time period control system, the order is placed when the review period arrives. In the fixed order quantity system,

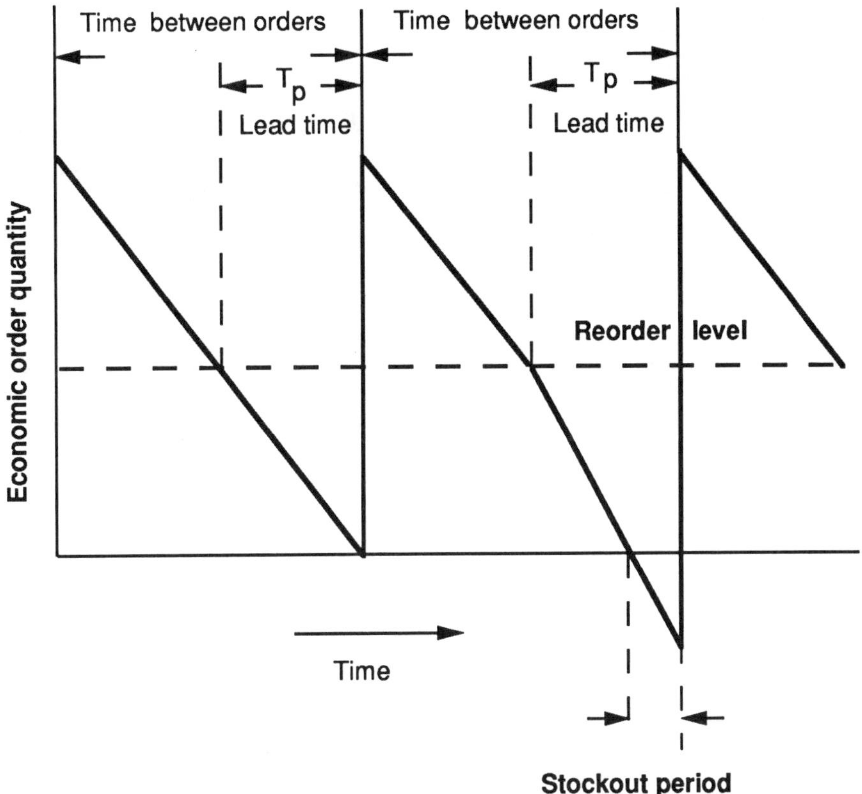


**Figure 4-7**
**Reorder Level and Economic Order Quantity**

the order quantity is constant, while in the fixed time period system, the order quantity is different for each order. The reorder point system was the most widely accepted system of stock replenishment for inventory control and ordering, before the alternative plan of material requirements planning (MRP) came into existence. The reorder point estimates include both demand forecasts during lead time and safety stock to buffer the fluctuation in demand.

ROP inventory systems are applied in continuing demand applications or when orders are repeated. One of the major disadvantages of ROP is its insensitivity to the specific timing for future demand.

reorder point = average lead time × average demand per time period + safety stock

$$\text{ROP} = LT \times D + S$$

where
$LT$ = lead time
$D$ = demand
$S$ = safety stock

A *safety stock* is often expressed in daily, weekly, or monthly supply quantities. Supply time is the time period identifying the length of time the stock satisfies the demand. The calculation is as follows:

$$\text{supply in period of time} = \frac{\text{safety stock}}{\text{demand}}$$

For example, if a component's safety stock is 12 units and the quarterly demand is 60 units and the lead time is 4 weeks, compute the supply time and the reorder point:

$$\text{supply} = \frac{12}{60/3} = \frac{12}{20} = 0.6 \text{ month supply (2.4 weeks)}$$

In constant demand inventory systems, lead time can be expressed in terms of units of stock.

$$\text{ROP} = LT \times D + S = 1 \times 20 + 12 = 32$$

When the probability factor is taken into consideration, statistical properties of normal distribution are introduced, namely, the standard deviation, the forecast error (MAD) and the desired service level. A statistical service level is subjectively selected as an index of the degree of certainty that there will be no stockout. For example, a service level of 0.97 means that inventory items are available on order 97 percent of the time. There is a probability of a stockout 3 percent of the time.

The service level is directly related to the number of standard deviations or MAD forecasts errors. Assuming that a forecast error is normally distributed, statistical tables of standard normal distribution are used.

A statistical safety stock is computed based on the desired service level, lead time, and the standard deviation of demands.

$$SST = Z\sqrt{LT \times s}$$

where
$SST$ = safety stock
$Z$ = the number of standard deviations based on the desired service level
$LT$ = lead time
$s$ = standard deviation

$Z$ is found from the table depicting areas of standard normal distribution.

*Example*: Demand for the component of 180 units per week varies by a standard deviation of $s$ = 25 per week. Production lead time is 2 weeks. Estimate the safety stock, if the desired service level is 98 percent. Ninety-eight percent certainly corresponds to 2.1 standard deviations.

*Solution*:

$$SST = 2.1\ \sqrt{2 \times 25} = 15$$

The reorder point is

$$ROP = (180 * 2) + 15 = 375$$

USING THE SUPPLY-TIME ORDERING RULE

*Supply time-ordering* is a priority rule applied in scheduling the batch production in inventory-based production systems. Supply time is the time period identifying the length of time during which the stock satisfies the demand.

$$\text{supply time} = \frac{\text{inventory level}}{\text{demand rate}}$$

Those items having the shortest supply time are assigned the highest priority. An example of the supply-time priority rule used in Tool and Implement Co. is shown in Table 4-1.

| Product/ Component | Inventory Level | Demand per Week | Lead Time | EOQ | Production Time (Weeks) | Supply Time |
|---|---|---|---|---|---|---|
| 1 | 360 | 210 | 1.71 | 800 | 0.2 | 360/210 = 1.71 |
| 2 | 680 | 320 | 2.13 | 1,200 | 0.32 | 680/320 = 2.13 |
| 3 | 1,200 | 480 | 2.5 | 1,800 | 0.53 | 1,200/480 = 2.5 |
| 4 | 450 | 270 | 1.67 | 1,300 | 0.24 | 450/270 = 1.67 |
| 5 | 890 | 230 | 3.87 | 900 | 0.85 | 890/230 = 3.87 |
| 6 | 490 | 320 | 1.53 | 2,000 | 0.36 | 490/320 = 1.53 |

Table 4.1
Estimating Supply Time and Order Priorities

Component 6 has the shortest supply time of 1.53 weeks and, therefore, this job has the highest priority. But when the following week's work order for 2,000 units of component 6 is completed; the stock position has changed, from 1.53 to 7.48 of supply time, see Table 4-2.

| Product | Inventory Level | | Supply Time |
|---|---|---|---|
| 1 | 360-(210 × 0.3) | = 297 | 1.41 |
| 2 | 680-(320 × 0.3) | = 224 | 0.7 |
| 3 | 1,200-(480 × 0.5) | = 960 | 2.0 |

| | | | |
|---|---|---|---|
| 4 | 450-(270 × 0.7) | = 189 | 0.7 |
| 5 | 890-(230 × 0.6) | = 752 | 3.27 |
| 6 | 490-(320 × 0.3)+2000 | = 2,394 | 7.48 |

Table 4-2
How Supply Time and Order Priorities Have Changed One Week Later

Components 2 and 4 have the shortest supply times of 0.7 weeks. However, component 4 should be selected first because it has the shortest production time of 0.2 week. After the work order for component 4 is completed, component 2 still has 0.5 week supply, and 0.3 week is sufficient for its replenishment.

## HOW TO USE A TWO-BIN ORDERING SYSTEM

A two-bin system is a kind of a reorder point system. Component inventory is placed into two adjacent storage bins marked bin 1 and bin 2. The second bin holds the ROP quantity required to cover the lead time. A two-bin inventory system is graphically illustrated in Figure 4-9. Initially, components are used from the first bin until it is empty. When the first bin is empty, the reorder point is reached and it is time to place the order. At this point, the order is issued to replenish the empty bin. At the time when the second bin is emptied, the first bin should be refilled and the second order is placed.

The two-bin system works best when there is the same person in charge of the inventory and withdrawals. The JIT-*kanban* system, discussed in Chapter 10, has many similarities to the two-bin inventory system.

## USING BACKORDERS TO SOLVE A STOCKOUT SITUATION

The stockout situation can be resolved by backorders of independent demand items. In this instance, an outside customer accepts a waiting time period until the item becomes available. A shortage, or a stockout situation, can be planned when the inventory holding cost is high. Trade-offs should be made between reducing the cost of the inventory and providing a satisfactory service to a customer.

## REDUCING INVENTORY COSTS WITH AN EFFICIENT INVENTORY CONTROL SYSTEM

The cost of inventory is one of your major investments. An inventory constitutes a substantial part of your total product cost. Thus reducing your inventory should be part of your organization's efforts to reduce production costs. An ideal situation is to have an inventory of dedicated resources available when they are needed according to the zero-stock policy. This is not always possible due to fluctuations in both demand and supply.

The cost of inventory includes the following constituent parts:

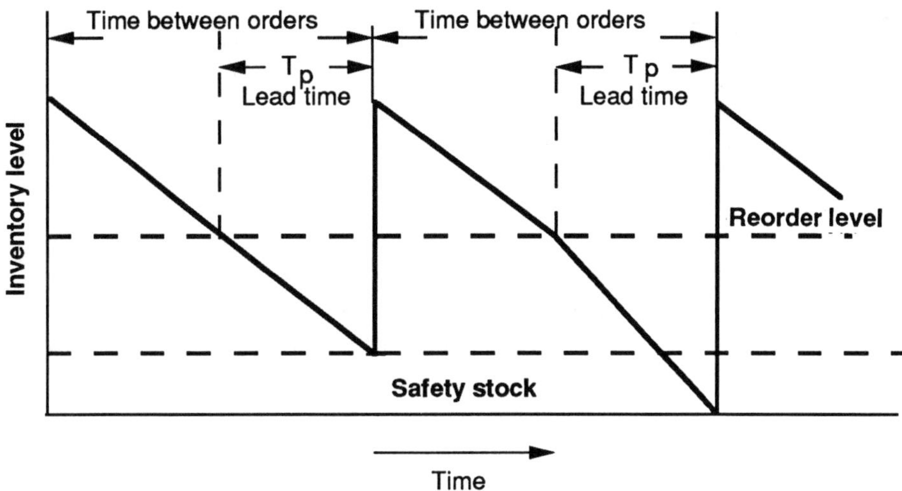


**Figure 4-8**
**An Inventory System with Safety Stock**

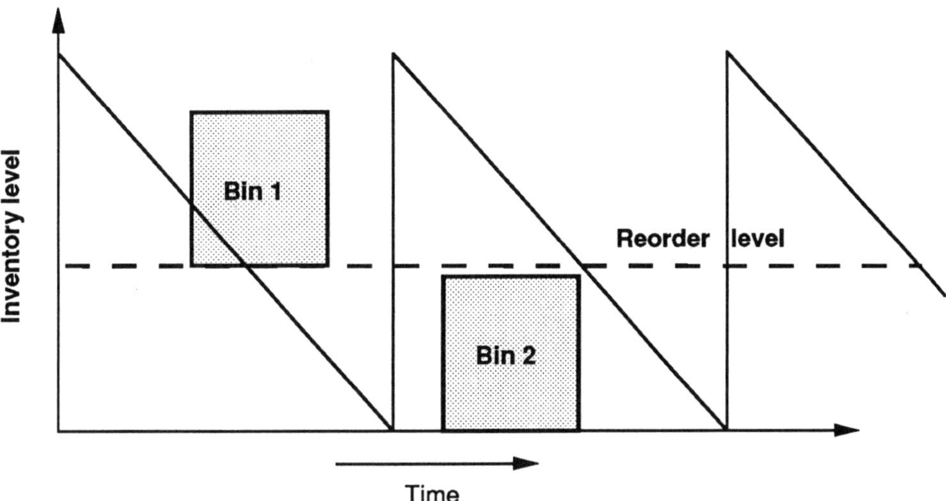


**Figure 4-9**
**A Two-Bin Inventory System**

- *Item cost* which is the cost of producing or purchasing an item.
- *Order replenishment costs.* These are expenses for issuing purchase orders or internal production orders. These expenses include management decision making and the clerical cost.
- *Annual ordering cost.* This is the function of the number of orders per year $D/Q$ and the cost of placing a single order $S$:

$$\text{cost of replenishment} = \frac{D}{Q} \times S$$

where
$D$ = annual demand
$Q$ = the quantity on order
$S$ = the cost of one order
$T_C$ = ordering cost + holding cost

Remember that the ordering cost of internal manufacturing is known.

- *Setup cost.* This cost includes the cost of changing over the production process to produce the required item. The elements of the total inventory cost are illustrated in Figure 4-10. The ordering cost is lower when $Q$ is larger.
- *Holding cost.* This includes the cost of storage, including material handling, pilferage, obsolescence, insurance, taxes, and depreciation. The holding cost is lower when the order quantity is smaller.

The cost of carrying an inventory is linear related to the order size and is equal to the average inventory level times the carrying cost.

The average stock level is one-half of the order quantity:

$$\text{average stock level} = \frac{(Q_{max} + Q_{min})}{2} = \frac{Q}{2}$$

$$C = \frac{Q \times H}{2}$$

where
$C$ = total cost of carrying inventory
H = holding cost of one unit of inventory per year
$Q$ = stock level

USING THE ECONOMIC ORDER QUANTITY MODEL TO REDUCE THE COST OF MAINTAINING INVENTORY

The *economic order quantity* (EOQ) is a simplified model of an inventory system aimed at reducing the total cost of maintaining an inventory. The EOQ model assumes constant demand, a leveled uniform depletion, and instant replenishing. The maximum stock level is equal to $Q$, which is a standard order quantity.

The EOQ depends on the trade-off between two factors: the cost of carrying inventory ($I_c$); and the cost of replenishment ($I_r$). So

total annual item cost = annual holding cost + annual setup cost + annual purchase cost.

$$\text{Total inventory cost} = \frac{Q}{2} \times H + \frac{D}{Q*} \times S + PD$$

where
P = purchase or production cost per item

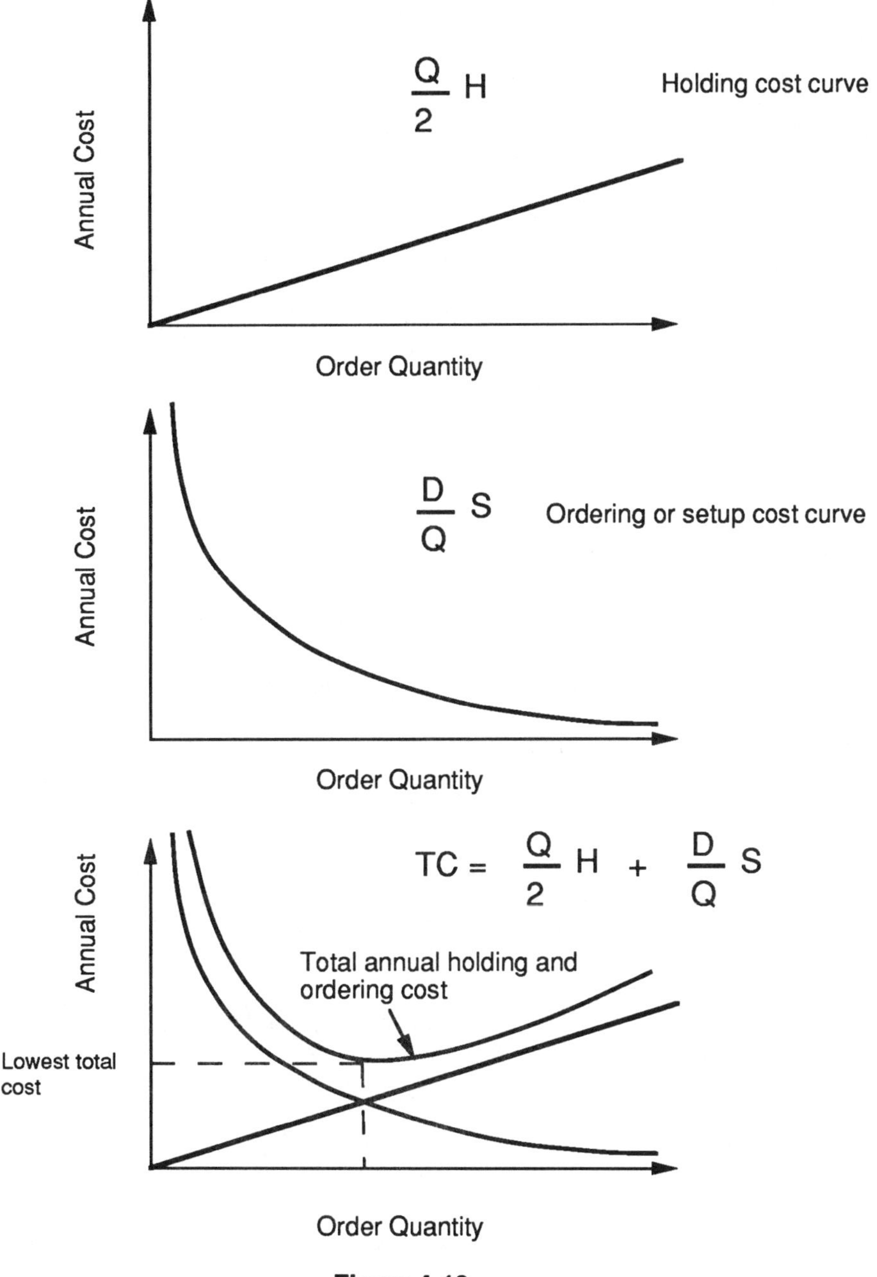


**Figure 4-10**
**Total Inventory Costs**

The economic order quantity $Q$ is directly related to the size of an order that minimizes the total inventory cost. The lowest inventory cost occurs when carrying the cost equal to the replenishment cost.

$$\frac{Q}{2} \times H = \frac{D}{Q*} \times S \qquad Q^2 = 2D \times \frac{S}{H}$$

$$Q = \sqrt{\frac{2DS}{H}}$$

*Example*: Find the economic order quantity if your annual demand is $D = 80$, your ordering cost is $S = \$20$ per order, and your holding cost is $H = \$ 2.5$ per unit per year.

$$\text{EOQ} \sqrt{\frac{2 \times 80 \times 20}{2.5}} = 36$$

USING THE ECONOMIC PRODUCTION QUANTITY MODEL

Instant replenishment inventory systems are typical to acquisition inventories. In a production environment, the replenishment and the depletion rates are steady. A gradual restocking takes place while the consumption is steady. Here production takes place concurrently with satisfying daily demand. The annual inventory holding cost in the production inventory order quantity model is estimated as equal to the annual inventory holding cost plus the annual setup cost:

annual inventory holding cost = average inventory level × holding cost per unit

An inventory is built up gradually by the difference between the daily production rate, $p$, and the daily demand, $d$. The maximum inventory level is equal to the daily inventory balance multiplied by the production time $t$.

$$(p - d) \times t$$

Q, the inventory level, is the order quantity produced during the $t$ time period:

$$Q = p \times t$$

where $t = Q / p$, Then

$$I_{max} = (p - d) \times \frac{Q}{p}$$

where

$I_{max}$ = maximum inventory level
$p$ = daily production rate
$d$ = daily demand rate

$Q$ = economic production order quantity

Graphically, the elements of the production order quantity are shown in Figure 4-11.

$$\text{holding cost} = \frac{(p - d) \times \frac{Q}{P} \times H}{2}$$

$$\text{Setup cost} = \frac{D}{Q} \times S$$

Optimal order quantity is found when annual holding cost = annual setup cost:

$$\frac{D}{Q} \times S = \frac{(p - d) \times \frac{Q}{P} \times H}{2}$$

$$2DS \times p = (p - d) \times Q^2 \times H$$

$$Q = \sqrt{\frac{2DS \times p}{H \times (p - d)}}$$

This equation can be used for identifying the optimum quantity when a gradual delivery or production takes place.

*Example*: Continental Flags and Pennants, Inc., produces all types of flags, banners, and pennants for nationwide distribution. Calculate the economic order quantity of flags, $Q$, if the annual demand rate is 4,500, the daily production rate is 40, the setup cost is $50, and the inventory holding cost is $2 per item per year.

$$Q = \sqrt{\frac{2DS \times p}{H \times (p - d)}} =$$

$$= \sqrt{\frac{2 \times 4{,}500 \times 50 \times 40}{2(40 - \frac{4500}{300})}} =$$

$$= \sqrt{360{,}000} = 600$$

The economic production order quantity is 600 flags.

## HOW TO USE ABC ANALYSIS IN INVENTORY CONTROL

The ABC analysis, also known as the *Pareto principle*, named after its inventor. Vilfredo Pareto, an economist, discovered that some things are not equally distributed among the population, so that for any given group, a small

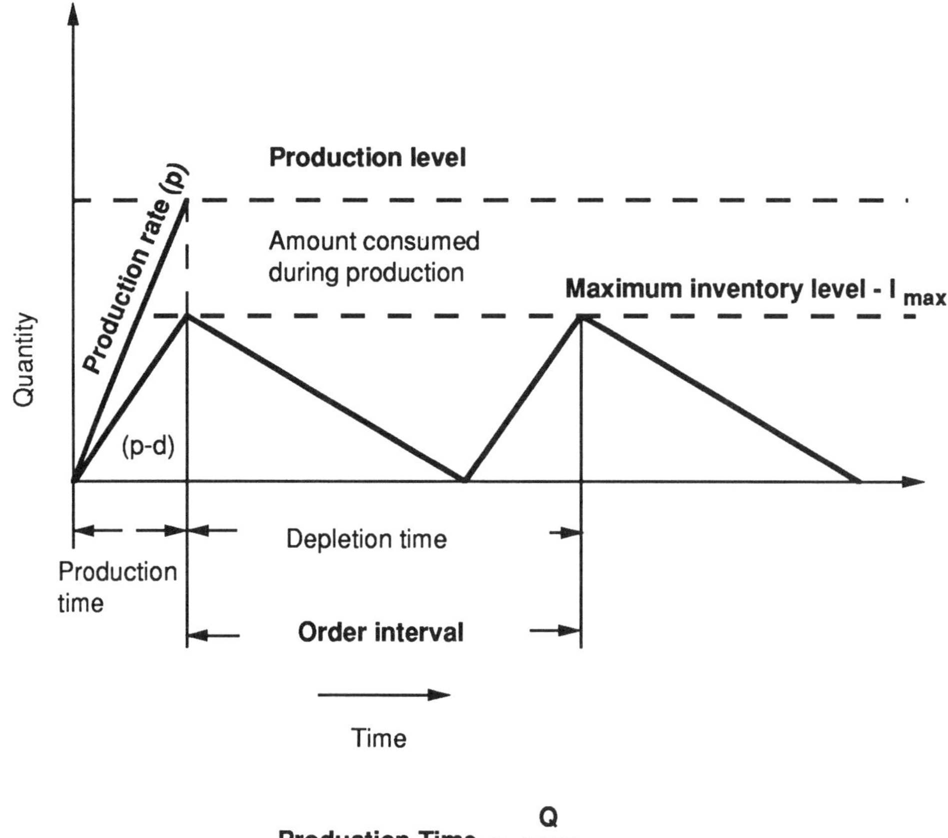


$$\text{Production Time} = \frac{Q}{p}$$

**Figure 4-11**
**Production Order Quantity**

number of items in that group will account for the bulk of the total value. Applied to the business environment, this principle will translate into such situations, for example, as few customers are responsible for most of your company's orders, few parts are responsible for the majority of your breakdowns, and a small number of quality problems is responsible for the majority of your total losses attributed to quality. ABC classifications have found a broad application in many inventory control systems.

According to the Pareto law, a small number of inventory items is responsible for most of inventory costs. This is group A, a "wealthy" group of the statistical population, group B is the middle group of the population, and group C comprises of "poor" group of the statistical population. The ABC analysis is graphically illustrated in Figure 4-12.

According to the Pareto law, inventory systems are divided into three categories/classes:

1. *Class A*—high-value items which involve a large amount of expenditure. Items of this category represent 15 to 20 percent of all the items and account for 65 to 80 percent of the total inventory value. In an inventory system, these items must be rigidly controlled.
2. *Class B*—medium-value items which involve a moderate amount of expenditure. Items of this category represent 35 to 40 percent of all the items, and account for 15 to 30 percent of the total inventory value.
3. *Class C*—low-value items. Items of this category represent 40 to 50 percent of all the items and account for only 5 to 10 percent of the total inventory value. In inventory systems, class C items attract only a minimum amount of control.

There are different ordering procedures for the three inventory categories, namely, various order quantity, order frequency, and safety stock permitted.

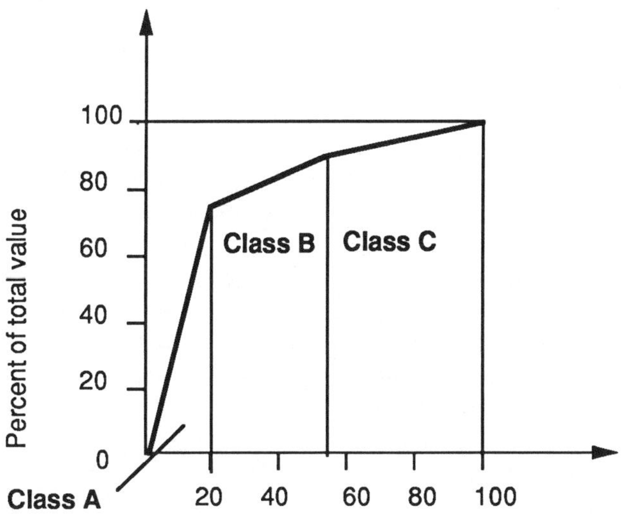


**Figure 4-12**
**An ABC Analysis**

There are few variations to this approach, especially in large systems having "AA" group of items or "D" group of items.

## USING INVENTORY PERIODIC PHYSICAL COUNTING AND CYCLE COUNTING FOR ACCURACY

The effectiveness of an inventory planning and control system depends on the accuracy of inventory records. Operations decision making is going to err if the information provided is unreliable, namely, the actual inventory level will deviate from the inventory record. Inaccurate inventory records lead to missed schedules due to late deliveries, shortages of some items while there are excesses of other items, obsolescence, and excessive expediting. It is clear that all these causes increase production costs and do not add to the quality improvement.

The accuracy of inventory records should be close to 100 percent if the computerized inventory system is to be efficient.

Two types of inventory counting are used for auditing inventory records: *periodic physical counting* and *cycle counting*. A *cycle* is the time it takes to count all items in an inventory. For example, each inventory item will be counted at least once a year if there is a yearly cycle. Items will be counted twice a year if there is a semiannual cycle. The number of times each item is counted per year is called the *annual count frequency*.

Periodic physical counting is conducted once or twice a year, often during holiday time or on some other occasions when the plant is shut down. Cycle counting is continuous physical counting of the inventory throughout the year, and inventory records are periodically reconciled with the actual data. A small percentage of the total number of items is counted every day. Measures are taken when significant variances are detected, the uncovered inaccuracies are rectified to prevent them from happening again in future. So, along with detecting the variances, cycle counting leads to eventual improvements in the inventory system. A typical cycle counting report is illustrated in Figure 4-13.

There are several approaches to cycle counting. Often, the ABC classification is used to determine the frequency of item counting. High-value class A items are counted more frequently than are lower-value class B items. Class C items can be counted once or twice per year. Then the differentiated fixed interval of the inventory control period for three inventory categories is established. Also various standards for accuracy are applied. For example, if a class A item requires adherence to ± 0.3 percent of accuracy, then class B items can have ± 1 to 2 percent of accuracy, and class C items would only need ± 5 percent of accuracy.

Another approach is to conduct your inventory counting at the same time that changes to your stock position are taking place (for example, when orders are placed or received, when the record or stock is zero, or when the record is negative). This approach is also known as *event-based counting*. A variety

RE,105,2.MDATABAS ASKON CAMERA COMPANY -- MANUFACTURING
MON, APR 15, 1991, 12:40 AM

CYCLE COUNT REPORT

STORES LOCATIONS

PAGE NO : 9

CYCLE COUNT START DATE: 04/15/91

LOCATION: 23-1-B

| * | PART NUMBER | DESCRIPTION | LOT NUMBER/ PROJECT ACTIVITY | DATE OF LAST CYCL CNT | CYCLE COUNT DUE DATE | LAST 3 MONTHS USAGE | UOM | CLASS CODE | ABC | COUNTED | STAMPED |
|---|---|---|---|---|---|---|---|---|---|---|---|
| * | 1008B | GRADE 2 BATTERY | 1 | 04/05/90 | 04/27/90 | 366.00 | EA | 6 | A | ------- | ------- |
| * | 1014 | 50MM LENS 1.5 FSTOP | 1 | 03/19/90 | 07/29/90 | 149.00 | EA | 1 | C | ------- | ------- |
| * | 1027 | 50MM LENS 1.2 FSTOP | 1 | 04/04/90 | 06/09/90 | 33.00 | EA | 1 | B | ------- | ------- |

LOCATION: 23-1-C

| * | PART NUMBER | DESCRIPTION | LOT NUMBER/ PROJECT ACTIVITY | DATE OF LAST CYCL CNT | CYCLE COUNT DUE DATE | LAST 3 MONTHS USAGE | UOM | CLASS CODE | ABC | COUNTED | STAMPED |
|---|---|---|---|---|---|---|---|---|---|---|---|
| * | 1049 | VARIABLE RESISTOR | 1 | 04/11/90 | 08/21/90 | .00 | EA | 3 | C | ------- | ------- |

LOCATION: 23-2-A

| * | PART NUMBER | DESCRIPTION | LOT NUMBER/ PROJECT ACTIVITY | DATE OF LAST CYCL CNT | CYCLE COUNT DUE DATE | LAST 3 MONTHS USAGE | UOM | CLASS CODE | ABC | COUNTED | STAMPED |
|---|---|---|---|---|---|---|---|---|---|---|---|
| * | 1047 | SILVERED MIRROR | 1 | 03/12/90 | 07/22/90 | .00 | EA | 1 | C | ------- | ------- |

LOCATION: 23-2-B

| * | PART NUMBER | DESCRIPTION | LOT NUMBER/ PROJECT ACTIVITY | DATE OF LAST CYCL CNT | CYCLE COUNT DUE DATE | LAST 3 MONTHS USAGE | UOM | CLASS CODE | ABC | COUNTED | STAMPED |
|---|---|---|---|---|---|---|---|---|---|---|---|
| * | 1001 | ASKON 10 CAMERA | 1 | 02/01/90 | 06/13/90 | 693.00 | EA | 5 | C | ------- | ------- |
| * | 1002 | 70-210 ZOOM LENS | 1 | 05/02/90 | 05/24/90 | 194.00 | EA | 1 | A | ------- | ------- |
| * | 1003 | 130MM WIDE ANGLE LENS | 1 | 03/26/90 | 04/17/90 | 43.00 | EA | 1 | A | ------- | ------- |
| * | 1004 | TRIPOD | 1 | 04/30/90 | 09/09/90 | 153.00 | EA | 5 | C | ------- | ------- |
| * | 1005 | HARD CASE | 1 | 03/26/90 | 08/05/90 | 128.00 | EA | 5 | C | ------- | ------- |
| * | 1007 | SOFT CASE | 1 | 04/16/90 | 08/26/90 | 58.00 | EA | 5 | C | ------- | ------- |
| * | 1014 | 50MM LENS 1.5 FSTOP | 1 | 08/17/89 | 12/27/89 | 149.00 | EA | 1 | C | ------- | ------- |

**Figure 4-13. Cycle Counting Report**

Reprinted here with the permission of ASK Computer Systems, Inc.

of continuous counting methods are location based, where all inventory items placed in one location are counted.

Team of stock counters are on the job year round. By specializing, they are able to maintain a sufficient standard of records accuracy, the timely detection and correction of variances, and the timely resolution of inventory system problems.

## MAKING INVENTORY DECISIONS

An inventory control system functions as a direct input to your production control, while at the same time, it is a system on its own requiring information from production control, scheduling, purchasing, and costing.

Decision making regarding inventory should be made by considering the cost of keeping an inventory against the possible benefits. These benefits include the following:

1. *Shorter product lead time.* Stocking a long-lead-time item can reduce WIP for an entire assembly unit. Every product has such long-lead-time assembly units or components which extend the lead time of the entire product. Usually, it is one or two components which are responsible for a long lead time of an assembly unit. Such a situation is graphically depicted in Figure 4-14. Lead time of 5.5 weeks for component 3 is responsible for the 6-week-long assembly unit lead time. Stocking component 3, as shown in Figure 4-14B, reduces the lead time of the assembly unit to 3.5 weeks. Consideration should be given to the holding cost of this item for the benefit of reducing the lead time of the final product. Additionally, a process analysis often reveals that a single operation is responsible for the long lead time of a component. In instances when these are rough machining operations, for example, a frequent solution is to keep semifinished components in stock. This reduces the lead time and keeps the holding cost to a minimum, as finishing machining, not a component's initial operations, are responsible for most of the manufacturing cost.
2. *Trade-offs regarding the effect of inventory on the product value.* Trade-offs should be made between the options of keeping WIP and increasing the equipment utilization and attracting a customer by providing a speedy delivery.

The benefits should be compared against the expenses, such as overhead, holding costs, taxes, and insurance. Another consideration is a *stockout cost*—the cost of lost opportunities due to the items being out of stock at the time of demand or due to lost production (for example, idle equipment or staff labor occurring as a result of such shortage). Keeping a large inventory is justified if the benefits offset the expenses. Considerations of a dependent demand WIP inventory managed by the production planning and control system differ from raw material inventory considerations. Use inventory control ratios. Remember

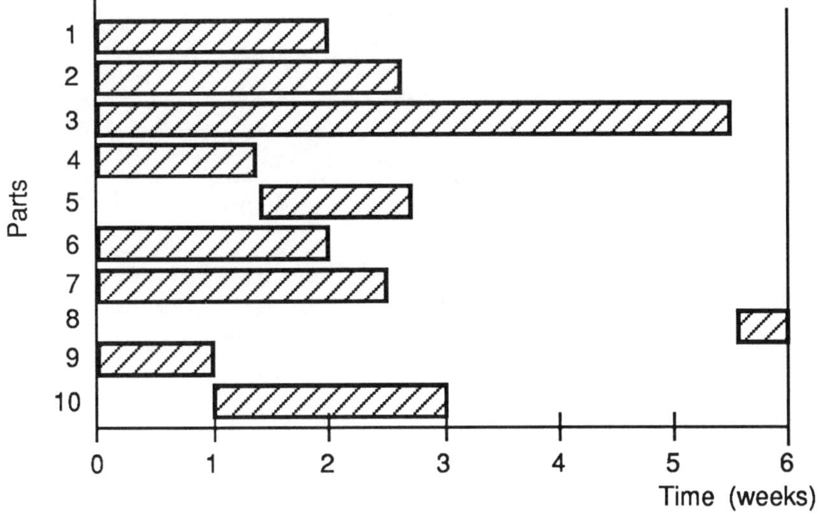


**A. Zero-Stock Production**

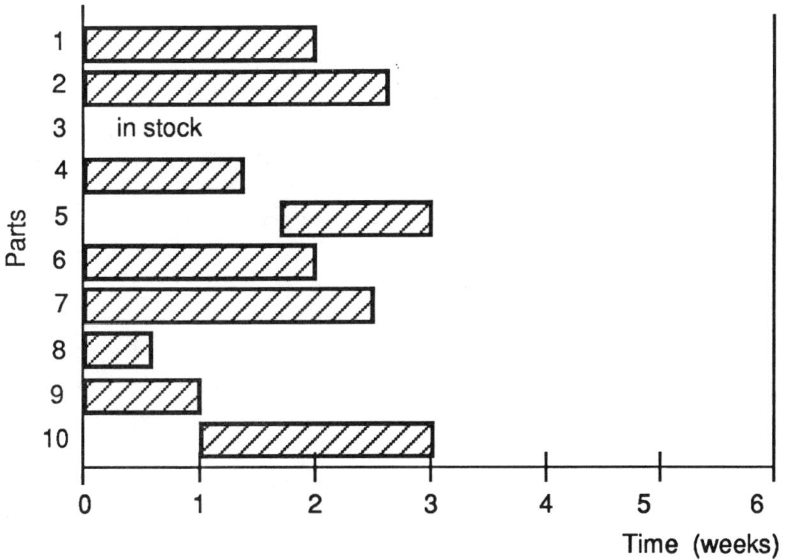


**B. Component 3 Is in Stock**

**Figure 4-14**
**How an Inventory Can Reduce the Lead Time**

that inventories are money which should be put to best use. One measure of your inventory efficiency is your inventory turnover. An inventory turnover indicates how often per year the company sells its average inventory. An inventory turnover is calculated as follows:

$$\text{inventory turnover} = \frac{\text{annual cost of goods sold}}{\text{average value of inventory}}$$

Consider the example of Tool and Die Co., which has $2,800,000 in annual sales and an average inventory of $350,000 in the dollar value. The inventory turnover is $2,800,000/$350,000 = 8 turns/year.

## Types of Dependent Demand Inventory Systems

### TAPPING THE POWERS OF MATERIAL REQUIREMENTS PLANNING

There are definite distinctions between the manufacturing and nonmanufacturing inventory. Nonmanufacturing inventories are mainly independent demand systems, while manufacturing inventories are mainly dependent demand inventory systems. Manufacturing inventory systems are inseparable from production planning and control systems.

The statistical order point and EOQ are insensitive to the timing of actual demand. They are based on the assumption of steady demand, gradual depletion, and instantaneous replenishment. A stock replenishment system compensates the inability to determine the precise quantity and the time of demand. A ROP system is an ordinary component-based inventory system, whereas an MRP is a time-phased product-based system in which the position of an item in the product structure is considered. So you can see that *independent demand* is based on forecasts, while *dependent demand* items are calculated based on the end-product requirements.

Order point and material requirements planning are two methods of ordering components. *Order point* is based on an average usage and forecasts, while MRP is based on the actual orders on hand. MRP is an ordering and inventory control method which has become associated with almost mythical powers of zero-stock production. The significance of MRP becomes obvious when it is compared with the economic order quantity approach and inventory-based production systems.

Management of a discontinuous (time-phased) demand is largely concerned with timing of the requirements, replacing the then-prevailing philosophy concerned mainly with the quantity. ROP implies timing based on the past average. EOQ deals solely with the quantity. The priority in EOQ lies with the cost of ordering and storing an item, and it is largely insensitive to both timing and actual discrete demand which can be expected during this period.

Inventory control is activated when the disbursement is taking place by calculating quantity on hands, *X*, as the inventory position, +*A*, plus the quantity on order, –*B*, minus the quantity required, *C*:

$$X = A + B - C$$

MRP is calculated when an order is placed with production. MRP is the final plan which goes directly to production, and any changes will result in various degrees of production losses.

MRP implies time phasing and adds the time dimension to the equation by distributing these estimates over time periods by calculating your item demand versus your forecasts applied in ROP inventory systems. ROP and EOQ exercise control over the inventory, while MRP is the first step toward controlling actual orders sent to production.

MRP was, and still is, the most significant development in production operations management in the past three decades. MRP, for the first time, has introduced the concept of zero-stock production. Each year, more and more firms have joined the MRP "bandwagon." Yet statistics show that not all these firms have been able to incorporate MRP successfully into their overall planning and control strategy. The answer for this phenomenon is by no means simple. But one can understand the expectations and the excitement behind the so-called "MRP crusade" and its zero-inventory approach.

MRP is a series of computer programs which essentially matches material requirements with the inventory levels. It operates a master schedule indicating the requirements for end items by time periods, exploding an end item into its constituent components specified in bill of materials, and then checking the availability of components currently on hand and on order contained in the inventory file.

MRP was seen primarily by its inventors as a component planning system for plants that have or can have MPS. These inventors have outlined the conditions for the successful MRP functioning as follows:

1. The existence of a master production schedule should outline the production program of quantity and timing of end items. The MPS is the main input. It is the point of departure for the MRP system.
2. The master production schedule should be stated in components' time-phased requirements derived from the bill of materials.
3. Product information should be available in time of planning indicating the lead time of a product and lead times for all its constituent components.
4. All inventory records should be available, indicating the current inventory status and outstanding orders.

5. Ordering and receiving procedures should be in place and enforced even for the short-duration stocking. Monitoring the succession of production stages is the requirement for MRP.

MRP is driven by an independent demand master production schedule in conjunction with the structured product data base—the bill of material and lead times. MRP relationships within manufacturing management system (MANMAN) developed by ASK Computers is illustrated in Figure 4-15.

MRP requirements are correlated with the availability of components in the inventory and placed on order with the processing departments and with vendors. It is seen here that during a single time period, the actual input is less than planned, while in the succeeding time period, the input has exceeded the capacity. A sample of the input-output report is shown in Figure 4-16. The shop input, output, and deviations from the plan are monitored on a continuous basis. This provides input into the ever-changing job priorities based on cumulative deviations from planned and actual input and planned and actual output. The ordering to the shop floor is accomplished by issuing a dispatch list, weekly, biweekly, or even daily, based on MRP and including latest job priorities.

***How to Use MRP Record*** A conventional MRP record displays the following information:

- Part identification
- Level in the BOM structure
- Lead time
- Lot size

The first row of an MRP table displays time periods that can vary from one day to several months, depending on lead time and other factors, such as the MRP fencing approach and the final assembly scheduling policy. An example of an MRP inquiry report is shown in Figure 4-17. The second row, "Total Gross," is a time-phased statement of anticipated demand for the item, directly derived from the master production schedule. The third row, "Scheduled Receipts," reflects open orders and the dates of the expected completion by vendors or work centers. The fourth row, "Proj On Hand," indicates the inventory status at the end of a time period, after the replacement orders have been received and gross requirements have been satisfied. The number at the beginning of the row shows an initial inventory status at the start of the period 1. The last row, "Planned Orders," is computed from the values in the "On Hand" row. An order is released as soon as the on-hand quantity becomes negative. A negative on-hand quantity is converted into a planned order by offsetting lead time and taking the lot size or safety stock restrictions into consideration.

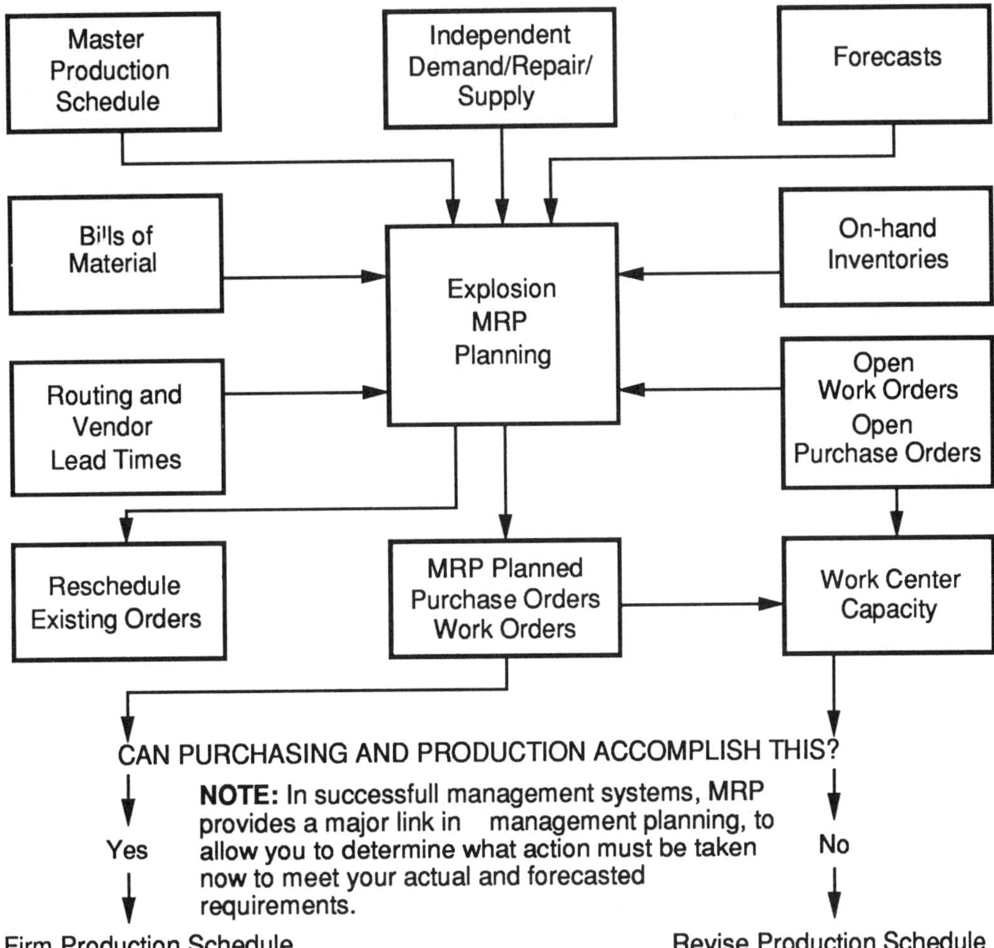


**Figure 4-15**
**The Interfaces of the MANMAN Material Requirements Planning Module with Other Modules**

Reprinted here with the permission of ASK Computer Systems, Inc.

Planned order releases are not shown in the scheduled receipts row until they are released to production or purchasing. Planned order releases are further exploded into components' gross requirements throughout the BOM structure. Dresser MRP report format is generated in 52 weekly buckets followed by 12 monthly buckets.

Standard Hours

| Week (Ending Date) | W1 (1/2/84) | W2 (1/9/84) | W3 (1/16/84) | W4 (1/23/84) | W5 (1/30/84) | W6 (2/6/84) |
|---|---|---|---|---|---|---|
| **Planned input** | 340 | 370 | 390 | 390 | 385 | 380 |
| **Actual Input** | 340 | 360 | 375 | 390 | 380 | 365 |
| **Cumulative deviation** | -- | -10 | - 25 | - 25 | - 30 | - 45 |
| **Planned output** | 390 | 390 | 380 | 380 | 380 | 390 |
| **Actual output** | 390 | 370 | 375 | 390 | 385 | 395 |
| **Cumulative deviation** | -- | - 20 | - 25 | - 15 | - 10 | - 5 |

**Figure 4-16**
**Sample Input/Output Report**

Additional rows containing information about orders submitted to work centers or vendors may be included in MRP reports. In Dresser MRP reports, such an additional information shows open orders, where used, and made from.

***Understanding MRP Logic*** The MRP logic is similar to a perpetual inventory system of keeping a running account of incoming and outgoing components. MRP has replaced stock inventory systems by the zero-stock time-phased demand approach. MRP time-phased ordering uses the following equation:

quantity on order = quantity on hand - time-phased requirements

Gross requirements and allocations against the inventory on hand and scheduled receipts become net requirements. Net requirements, offset for lead

# REQUIREMENTS EXCEPTION REPORT

08/22/91 REPORT TYPE: INQUIRY PAGE 2

| PART NUMBER | PART DESCRIPTION | SUP CODE | PLANT CODE | ORD POL | UNIT STD COST MAT | UNIT STD COST LAB · OH | UNIT STD COST TOTAL | SET UP COST | SET UP HRS | COST METH | SOQ | SAFETY STK |
|---|---|---|---|---|---|---|---|---|---|---|---|---|
| 000423 | 3/8 RND SOLAR CR | P | C-C | A | 1.02 | .00 | 1.02 | 25.00 | .0 | A | 1 | 0 |

| ON HAND | BACKLOG | OWED PROC | SURPLUS | AVAILABLE | OTHER LOC | OTHER ACCT | ANN USE 2 | DOLLAR VOL | RANGE | DATE OBS | PCY MODIFIER | STD COST SOQ | LOW L CODE |
|---|---|---|---|---|---|---|---|---|---|---|---|---|---|
| 0 | 0 | 0 | 0 | 0 | 0 | 0 | | 0 | 0 | NONE | | 1.02 | 4 |

| ON ORDER | LEAD TIME | ACUM L/T | CUS BACKLOG | CON BACKLOG | GROUP CODE | TOQ | ANN USE 3 | 1ST ORD COST | 2ND ORD COST | 3RD ORD COST | TOT ANN REQ | LOT SIZE CODE | PROD CENTER |
|---|---|---|---|---|---|---|---|---|---|---|---|---|---|
| 180 | 8.0 | 8.0 | 0 | 0 | 0 | --- 13 | 114 | .00 | .00 | .00 | 137 | 1 | |

| | PAST DUE | | | | | | | | 1 | 2 | 3 | 4 | 5 | 6 | 7 | 8 | 9 | 10 | 11 | 12 |
|---|---|---|---|---|---|---|---|---|---|---|---|---|---|---|---|---|---|---|---|---|
| WEEK START DATE | | | | | | | | 08/12 | 08/19 | 08/26 | 09/02 | 09/09 | 09/16 | 09/23 | 09/30 | 10/07 | 10/14 | 10/21 | 10/28 | 11/04 |
| TOTAL GROSS | | | | | | | | | | | | | | | 1 | | | | 2 | |
| SCHED RECEIPTS | | | | | | | | | | | 180 | | | | | | | | | |
| PROJ ON HAND | | | | | | | | | | | 180 | 180 | 180 | 180 | 179 | 179 | 179 | 179 | 177 | 177 |
| PLANNED ORDERS | | | | | | | | | | | | | | | | | | | | |

| | 13 | 14 | 15 | 16 | 17 | 18 | 19 | 20 | 21 | 22 | 23 | 24 | 25 | 26 | 27 | 28 | 29 | 30 | 31 | 32 |
|---|---|---|---|---|---|---|---|---|---|---|---|---|---|---|---|---|---|---|---|---|
| WEEK START DATE | 11/11 | 11/18 | 11/25 | 12/02 | 12/09 | 12/16 | 12/23 | 12/30 | 01/06 | 01/13 | 01/20 | 01/27 | 02/03 | 02/10 | 02/17 | 02/24 | 03/02 | 03/09 | 03/16 | 03/23 |
| TOTAL GROSS | | | 2 | | | | 2 | 6 | | | 2 | 4 | | | 2 | 5 | | | 2 | |
| SCHED RECEIPTS | | | | | | | | | | | | | | | | | | | | |
| PROJ ON HAND | 177 | 177 | 175 | 175 | 175 | 175 | 173 | 167 | 167 | 167 | 165 | 161 | 161 | 161 | 159 | 154 | 154 | 154 | 152 | 152 |
| PLANNED ORDERS | | | | | | | | | | | | | | | | | | | | |

| | 33 | 34 | 35 | 36 | 37 | 38 | 39 | 40 | 41 | 42 | 43 | 44 | 45 | 46 | 47 | 48 | 49 | 50 | 51 | 52 |
|---|---|---|---|---|---|---|---|---|---|---|---|---|---|---|---|---|---|---|---|---|
| WEEK START DATE | 03/30 | 04/06 | 04/13 | 04/20 | 04/27 | 05/25 | 06/22 | 07/20 | 08/17 | 09/14 | 10/12 | 11/09 | 12/07 | 01/04 | 02/01 | 03/01 | 03/29 | 04/26 | 05/24 | 06/21 |
| TOTAL GROSS | 4 | | | 8 | 8 | 2 | 8 | 9 | 8 | 11 | 3 | 7 | 8 | 8 | 7 | 7 | 8 | | 4 | |
| SCHED RECEIPTS | | | | | | | | | | | | | | | | | | | | |
| PROJ ON HAND | 148 | 148 | 148 | 140 | 132 | 130 | 122 | 113 | 105 | 94 | 91 | 84 | 76 | 68 | 61 | 54 | 46 | 46 | 42 | 42 |
| PLANNED ORDERS | | | | | | | | | | | | | | | | | | | | |

| USAGE PERIOD | MAD | AVERAGE | CUR MON | 1 MON | 2 MON | 3 MON | 4 MON | 5 MON | 6 MON | 7 MON | 8 MON | 9 MON | 10 MON | 11 MON | 12 MON | | | | | |
|---|---|---|---|---|---|---|---|---|---|---|---|---|---|---|---|---|---|---|---|---|
| BOOKINGS | 0 | | | | | | | | | | | | | | | 0 | 0 | 0 | 0 | 0 |
| INVOICE | 0 | 9 | | 8 | 6 | 14 | 7 | 13 | 11 | 13 | 7 | 6 | 13 | 7 | 9 | 113 | 113 | 128 | 152 | 123 |

| OPEN ORDERS | ORDER NO. | DATE DUE | QTY DUE | ORDER NO. | DATE DUE | QTY DUE | ORDER NO. | DATE DUE | QTY DUE | ORDER NO. | DATE DUE | QTY DUE | ORDER NO. | DATE DUE | QTY DUE |
|---|---|---|---|---|---|---|---|---|---|---|---|---|---|---|---|
| | 39759-01 | 09/02/91 | 180 | | | | | | | | | | | | |

WHERE USED

| CODE | DESCRIPTION | QTY | CODE | DESCRIPTION | QTY | CODE | DESCRIPTION | QTY |
|---|---|---|---|---|---|---|---|---|
| 202866 | RESET SPRING DISC | .02 | 833691 | PIN | .14 | 863020 | REV VALVE BUSHING | .10 |
| 867951 | PIN | .10 | 867957 | WS-620 B PIN-SOCKET RET. | .09 | 869384 | CAM FOLLOWER PIN | .07 |

MADE FROM

| CODE NO. | DESCRIPTION | UNIT QTY | ON ORDER | ON HAND | BACKLOG | OWED PRO | SURPLUS | AVAILABLE | OTH LOC | OTH ACCT | GROSS REQD |
|---|---|---|---|---|---|---|---|---|---|---|---|
| | | | | | | | | | | | |

**Figure 4-17**
**The MRP System Inquiry Report at Dresser LTD.**

time, become planned orders verified with CRP. This becomes an input into production activity control (PAC) and operational scheduling.

Inventory transactions are updated starting from the top of the product structure and exploding downward, level by level. The data is accessed according to time periods—time buckets where the availability of components is estimated.

The projected stock balance is the projected balance at the end of the period after receiving replenishment orders and satisfying gross requirements. The planned order release is determined from the net requirements (netting) by means of offsetting and lot sizing.

MRP is a computerized ordering system applying two different updating methods, namely, regenerative and net change. According to the *regenerative method*, MRP batch processing is carried out regularly based on demand, supply status, engineering changes, and exceptions. Regenerative reports use the MRP network logic and netting and require long computer processing time due to the large amount of data involved. It is not unusual for a regeneration plan to take 6 to 12 hours of processing time, due to the need for records updating, despite the fact that much of the information processed has not changed. Due to its long processing time, MRP regeneration reports are generated weekly or biweekly. The new updated MRP program includes the rectified deviations from the previous plans.

According to the *net change method*, a production program is continuously updated as deviations occur. This method is more accurate and requires less data processing because it deals with changes and variances one by one.

There are three types of data used in MRP: the bill of materials, the inventory data, and the master production schedule. This data correspond directly to the three types of MRP files: the bill of materials file, the item data file, and the master production file. These three types of MRP files are shown in Figure 4-18.

***Bill of Materials File*** A BOM file identifies the composition of a product and stages in product manufacturing. A BOM file contains information about the product structure, all the components and how they relate to each other in this structure, the parent level, the component level, and the quantity of each component. Material requirements planning priorities are calculated based on the BOM structure. Both indented and exploded format of BOM can be used, but the latter is more widely used in a single-level explosion. These estimates of components relations are directly used in an assembly unit. Here each item is listed showing its quantity required for the assembly level. A BOM file controls all the components making an assembly and quantities of these components required for the final product assembly. This is achieved by translating the final assembly planned order requirements into gross requirements for each component.

A BOM explosion explodes the product structure based on dependent demand for an item, breaking down an order for the end product into elementary

**Bill of Material File**

| Parent | Component | Quantity |
|---|---|---|
| S-10 | S10-1 | 1 |
| | S10-2 | 3 |
| | S10-5 | 6 |
| | S10-8 | 1 |
| T-41 | T41-3 | 10 |
| | T41-5 | 10 |
| V-30 | V30-4 | 5 |
| | V30-7 | 5 |
| | V30-11 | 1 |
| | V30-15 | 1 |

**Item Data File**

| Description | Item No. | Order Policy | On Hand | Safety Stock | Low-Level Code | Cost Cntr. | Lead Time |
|---|---|---|---|---|---|---|---|
| Wear strip plug | S-10 | A18 | 0 | 0 | 0 | A | 3 |
| Body strap plate | T-41 | BB3 | 30 | 15 | 1 | B | 1 |
| Cyl. Tube Weld. | V-30 | A70 | 100 | 10 | 2 | D | 2 |

**Work Order Master File**

| Item No. | Order Number | Quantity | Due-Date | Prior | Compl. | Scrap | Mater. Cost | Labor Cost |
|---|---|---|---|---|---|---|---|---|
| S-10 | AA-37 | 200 | 5/6/90 | | 50 | 2 | 0.50 | 2.5 |
| T-41 | CC-5 | 200 | 5/12/90 | | 10 | 1 | 0.70 | 1.5 |
| V-30 | EE-85 | 50 | 5/18/90 | | 15 | 1 | 2.5 | 2.3 |

**Figure 4-18**
**MRP Files**

component gross requirements. Bill of material files are compiled in the same end items as the master production schedule and contain, among other data, pointers to other files enabling to locate the parent or parents of each component in the product structure. An indented bill of material report, as one shown in Figure 4-19, highlights such a component-parent relationship.

#### Modular BOM

A modular BOM file is a reference file in which the product structure is organized around product modules, rather than end products. A modular BOM is a form of the MPS planning file discussed in Chapter 3. In MRP, some higher-level components at the assembly and subassembly levels are controlled as a single unit or module. This is a so-called modular bill of materials item stocked as a single unit which can appear in different end items. This simplifies control over the inventory.

A modular BOM is shown in Figure 3-26. There are 12 product modules which are assembled in various combinations to make LOB25 end product. A modular BOM is an effective planning tool in conjunction with the final assembly schedule.

*Low-level coding* is used in MRP systems when identical items occur at various levels of BOM. Here identical items are placed at the same BOM level. The advantage of the low-level coding is that only one-level scanning is required for estimating the requirements of a component.

#### Costed Bill of Materials

A costed bill of materials file contains costing information relevant to cost accounting. This includes the material cost, overhead cost, and labor cost for each component. An example of a costed bill of materials is shown in Figure 4-20.

***The Item Data File*** An item data file contains information related to manufacturing as well as the inventory status. This includes part description; item number; item characteristics (for example, a low-level code indicating the lowest level at which the item appears in the BOM structure); planning factors, such as lead time including setup time and run time; costs; and inventory status information, safety stock and quantity on hand. All this information is presented in a time-phased format or as a list of items. The inventory status data are maintained up to date through inventory transactions when changes in inventory are taking place.

***The Master Production File*** A master production schedule is a basic input into MRP initiating all further processing. A master production file is also known as a work order master file. A work order master file contains data related to a shop order: order number, quantity on order, due date, priority, costing information, and the latest status indicating quantity completed and quantity scrapped.

```
LI,201,1.MDATABAS  ASKON CAMERA COMPANY -- MANUFACTURING            DISTRIBUTION: MANAGER - ASK COMPUTERS
MON, APR 15, 1991,  3:57 AM                                INDENTED BILL OF MATERIAL                          PAGE NO:  1
                                                           =========================
                                                              AS OF ALL DATE

   CLASS CODE GROUP: 1    COMMODITY CLASS
   CLASS CODE:       5    FINISHED GOODS
                                                                                          OP: ORDER POLICY CODE
1001            OPCODE: 4 REV: F    ASKON 10 CAMERA
MODEL: 100-00-01
ECO NO: ECO-1012
DATE OF LAST ECO: 10/14/88

                                                                                     DAYS
                                                           O     ITEM  QTY PER YIELD       OFF REFERENCE  EFFECTIV OBSOLETE
 PART NUMBER                        DESCRIPTION            P RV   NO. ASSEMBLY FACTR UM SC SET DESIGNATOR  DATE     DATE
 1-2-3-4-5-6-7-8-9----------------- ---------------------- - -- ----- -------- ----- -- -- --- ---------- -------- --------

 1010                               ASKON 10 BODY ASSEMBLY  1 B     1    1.000 1.000 EA M   0             00/00/00 99/99/99
   1026                             FINISHED CASTING        1 B    11    1.000 1.000 EA M   0             00/00/00 99/99/99
     1025                           RAW CASTING             3 A     0    1.000  .990 EA B   0 CAD         00/00/00 99/99/99
                                                                                              DRAWING
                                                                                              J6662
   1030                             SPEED CONTROL BRIDGE    1 A     1    1.000 1.000 EA B   0             00/00/00 99/99/99
   1031                             FLASH/SYNC ASSEMBLY     1 A     2    1.000 1.000 EA B   0             00/00/00 99/99/99
   1032                             DBL EXPOSE ASSEMBLY     1 A     3    1.000 1.000 EA B   0             00/00/00 99/99/99
   1033                             SHUTTER CHANGE ASSEMBLY 1 A     4    1.000 1.000 EA B   0             00/00/00 99/99/99
   1034                             MIRROR BOX ASSEMBLY     1 A     5    1.000 1.000 EA B   0             00/00/00 99/99/99
   1035                             WIND/SPROCKET ASSEMBLY  1 A     6    1.000 1.000 EA B   0             00/00/00 99/99/99
   1037                             BLACK FRONT             1 A     7    1.000 1.000 EA B   0             00/00/00 99/99/99
   1038                             BACK DOOR RELEASE       1 A     8    1.000 1.000 EA B   0             00/00/00 99/99/99
   1039                             REWIND ASSEMBLY         1 A     9    1.000 1.000 EA B   0             00/00/00 99/99/99
   1040                             COUNTER ASSEMBLY        1 A    10    1.000 1.000 EA B   0             00/00/00 99/99/99
 1011                               METER DRIVE BACK ASSEMBLY 1 C   2    1.000 1.000 EA R   0             00/00/00 99/99/99
   1020                             CIRCUIT ASSEMBLY        1 A     1    1.000  .990 EA B   0             00/00/00 99/99/99
   1021                             LINKAGE ASSEMBLY        1 C     2    1.000 1.000 EA M   0             00/00/00 99/99/99
     1043                           MOTOR ADVANCE GEAR      2 A     1    1.000  .990 EA B   0             00/00/00 99/99/99
     1044                           SHEAR GEAR              2 B     2    1.000  .980 EA B   0             00/00/00 99/99/99
     1045                           SHUTTER RELEASE LEVER   2 B     3    1.000  .980 EA B   0             00/00/00 99/99/99
*    1046                           CUSTOM SHOULDER SCREW   2 B     4     .028  .950 GS B   0             00/00/00 99/99/99
 1012                               PRISM/METER ASSEMBLY    1 A     3    1.000 1.000 EA M   0             00/00/00 99/99/99
   1022                             BATTERY LEADS           1 A     1    1.000  .860 EA B   0             00/00/00 99/99/99
   1023                             BATTERY BOX             1 B     2    1.000  .920 EA X   0             00/00/00 99/99/99
     1041                           BATTERY CAP             1 B     1    2.000 1.000 EA B   0             00/00/00 99/99/99
     1042                           BATTERY CONTAINER       1 A     2    1.000 1.000 EA B   0             00/00/00 99/99/99
   1024                             ASA CONTROL ASSEMBLY    1 B     3    1.000 1.000 EA B   1             00/00/00 99/99/99
 1013                               VIEW/FRESNL SCREEN      1 B     4    1.000 1.000 EA B   1             00/00/00 99/99/99
 1014                               50MM LENS 1.5 FSTOP     1 K     5    1.000 1.000 EA B   1             00/00/00 99/99/99
 1015                               RTV BONDING CEMENT      1 KK    6     .300 1.000 OZ F   0             00/00/00 08/30/88
*1046                               CUSTOM SHOULDER SCREW   2 B     8     .020 1.000 GS B   0             10/14/88 99/99/99
 1050                               RTV GLUE                1 A     7     .005 1.000 OZ F   0 SEE         05/31/88 10/29/92
                                                                                              DRAWING
                                                                                              5536G
```

**Figure 4-19**
**The Indented Bill of Materials**

Reprinted here with permission from ASK Computer Systems, Inc.

LI,205,1.MDATABAS ASKON CAMERA COMPANY -- MANUFACTURING DISTRIBUTION: MANAGER - ASK COMPUTERS
MON, APR 15, 1992, 3:58 AM

COSTED BILL OF MATERIALS

PAGE NO: 1

STANDARD COSTS AS OF 04/15/91

CLASS CODE GROUP: 1 COMMODITY CLASS
CLASS CODE: 5 FINISHED GOODS

1001 REV: F ASKON 10 CAMERA
MODEL: 100-00-01
ECO NO: ECO-1012
DATE OF LAST ECO: 10/14/88

| PART NUMBER | DESCRIPTION | RV | ITEM NO. | QTY PER ASMBLY | UM | SC | EXTENDED BURDENED ASSEMBLY MATL COST | EXTENDED COMP MATERIAL OVERHEAD | EXTENDED UNBURDEND COMPONENT DIR LABOR | TOTAL EXTENDED COMP OVERHEAD | EXTENDED BURDENED COMPONENT OUT PROC | EXTENDED UNBURDEND ASSEMBLY DIR LABOR | TOTAL EXTENDED ASSEMBLY OVERHEAD | EXTENDED BURDENED ASSEMBLY OUT PROC |
|---|---|---|---|---|---|---|---|---|---|---|---|---|---|---|
| 1010 | ASKON 10 BODY | B | 1 | 1.00 | EA | M | 15.230 | 6.092 | 19.100 | 24.830 | .000 | 4.200 | 5.460 | 7.200 |
| 1011 | METER DRIVE BA | C | 2 | 1.00 | EA | R | 1.700 | .680 | 1.755 | 2.282 | .000 | 4.035 | 2.789 | .000 |
| 1012 | PRISM/METER AS | A | 3 | 1.00 | EA | M | 3.990 | 1.596 | .000 | .000 | .000 | 2.925 | 3.803 | .000 |
| 1013 | VIEW/FRESNL SC | B | 4 | 1.00 | EA | B | 6.650 | .000 | .000 | .000 | .000 | .000 | .000 | .000 |
| 1014 | 50MM LENS 1.5 | K | 5 | 1.00 | EA | B | 28.700 | .000 | .000 | .000 | .000 | .000 | .000 | .000 |
| | | | | | | | 56.270 | 8.368 | 20.855 | 27.112 | .000 | 11.160 | 12.051 | 7.200 |

| | |
|---|---|
| MATERIAL COST: | 46.170 |
| ASSEMBLY MATERIAL OVERHEAD COST: | .000 |
| COMPONENT MATERIAL OVERHEAD COST: | 18.468 |
| COMPONENT DIRECT LABOR COST: | 32.015 |
| COMPONENT FIXED OVERHEAD COST: | 15.063 |
| COMPONENT VARIABLE OVERHEAD COST: | 21.088 |
| COMPONENT THIRD OVERHEAD COST: | 3.012 |
| COMPONENT OUTSIDE PROCESSING COST: | 3.000 |
| COMPONENT OUTSIDE PROCESSING OVERHEAD COST: | 4.200 |
| ASSEMBLY DIRECT LABOR COST: | 8.155 |
| ASSEMBLY FIXED OVERHEAD COST: | 3.027 |
| ASSEMBLY VARIABLE OVERHEAD COST: | 4.239 |
| ASSEMBLY THIRD OVERHEAD COST: | .605 |
| ASSEMBLY OUTSIDE PROCESSING COST: | .000 |
| ASSEMBLY OUTSIDE PROCESSING OVERHEAD COST: | .000 |
| STANDARD FROZEN COST: | 159.042 |
| SUM OF INDIVIDUAL COMPONENTS' STANDARD COSTS AND STANDARD ASSEMBLY COSTS: | 159.042 |

**Figure 4-20**
**The Costed Bill of Materials**

Reprinted here with permission from ASK Computer Systems, Inc.

MRP is driven by the master production schedule in conjunction with the structured product data base: bill of materials and lead times. On the other hand, these requirements are correlated with the availability of these components in inventory and on order with the processing departments and with vendors.

### Pegging

MRP allows for the creation of a *peg record file*, including the material requirements for an item for all planned order releases. Pegging involves taking gross requirements and determining where they come from. Pegging information is regarded as a where-used file where information on an item can be traced to particular customer orders (as opposed to the order explosion) and is sometimes called an implosion. Pegging is used in replanning when shortages of material occur or when attempts are made to reduce inventory.

A useful feature for job control is "job chaining"—applying the multilevel pegging which links requirements to the sources by the job number. This allows for detailed control of work orders and identifying the status of each component in the order.

***Bucketed and Bucketless MRP Systems*** One of the advantages of MRP, the time-phasing feature, sets up ordering and due dates to the time periods or time *buckets*. In bucketed material requirements planning, all requirements are accumulated and then grouped into a fixed number of time buckets.

Such a planning system does not compute precise dates for new planned orders because planning is done in a fixed number of weekly buckets. A bucket accumulates the total of individual gross requirements, without identifying the individual requirements.

A *bucketless* MRP system stores individual records by fixed dates rather than in time periods or buckets. Advanced production planning systems, such as Just-in-Time, require daily and even hourly planning, so a bucketless MRP system can be applied. In a bucketless system, gross requirements, scheduling receipts, and planned order releases are stored in records containing individual due dates. All computations of planned orders are conducted on individual dates, as opposed to total gross requirements of bucketed dates in a bucketed MRP system.

***Horizontal and Vertical MRP Reporting*** An MRP output has two basic formats: horizontal by buckets and vertical by date. A *bucket report* is a matrix that contains weekly information. This report shows the positive projected net available which takes into account open orders. A *horizontal display* is the most general format type used in MRP. An MRP horizontal report is shown in Figure 4-21.

The MRP *vertical format* is used in the bucketless MRP system where replenishment, requirements, and other data are presented in the vertical format by date as shown in Figure 4-22.

```
RE,906,1.MDATABAS  ASKON CAMERA COMPANY -- MANUFACTURING
MON, APR 15, 1991,  3:52 AM    MRP RUN: 01/21/92          HORIZONTAL MRP REPORT                                              PAGE NO:   4
                                                          =====================

PART: 1013                               MINQTY:      38.75  FLTIME:       20  INVLOC: 11-2-B        DEMRND: UP    QOH      :     1409.00
DESC: VIEW/FRESNL SCREEN                 SAFETY:     228.00  ULTIME:    .0000  VENDOR: V-104         SUPRND: DOWN  GROSS RQ:      945.00
BC/PC: DC REV: B  UOM: EA SC: B          SHRINK:      2.000  DTSTCK:        1  UNCOST:       6.65    PLNRND: UP    OPEN ORD:         .00
CC:       1 OPCODE: 1 ABC: C             NDAYS :          5  MULTPL:     1.00  VALUE :    9369.85

             PAST DUE 04/15/91 04/22/91 04/29/91 05/06/91 05/13/91 05/20/91 05/27/91 06/03/91 06/10/91 06/17/91 06/24/91 07/01/91
GROSS REQTS:       20        0        0        0        0       24        0        0        0        0        0        0       19
OPEN ORDER :        0        0        0        0        0        0        0        0        0        0        0        0        0
ORDER DUE  :        0        0        0        0        0        0        0        0        0        0        0        0        0
ORDER START:        0        0        0        0        0        0        0        0        0        0        0        0        0
PROJ AVAIL :     1389     1389     1389     1389     1389     1365     1365     1365     1365     1365     1365     1365     1346
RESCHED TO :        0        0        0        0        0        0        0        0        0        0        0        0        0

             07/08/91 07/15/91 07/22/91 07/29/91 08/05/91 08/12/91 08/19/91 08/26/91 09/02/91 09/09/91 09/16/91 09/23/91 09/30/91
GROSS REQTS:       20        0        0        0        0        0        0        0        0        0        0        0        0
OPEN ORDER :        0        0        0        0        0        0        0        0        0        0        0        0        0
ORDER DUE  :        0        0        0        0        0        0        0        0        0        0        0        0        0
ORDER START:        0        0        0        0        0        0        0        0        0        0        0        0        0
PROJ AVAIL :     1326     1326     1326     1326     1326     1326     1326     1326     1326     1326     1326     1326     1326
RESCHED TO :        0        0        0        0        0        0        0        0        0        0        0        0        0

             10/07/91 10/14/91 10/21/91 10/28/91 11/04/91 11/11/91 11/18/91 11/25/91 12/02/91 12/09/91 12/16/91 12/23/91   FUTURE
GROSS REQTS:        0        0        0       20        0        0        0      150       22        0      125        0      545
OPEN ORDER :        0        0        0        0        0        0        0        0        0        0        0        0        0
ORDER DUE  :        0        0        0        0        0        0        0        0        0        0        0        0        0
ORDER START:        0        0        0        0        0        0        0        0        0        0        0        0        0
PROJ AVAIL :     1326     1326     1326     1306     1306     1306     1306     1156     1134     1134     1009     1009      464
RESCHED TO :        0        0        0        0        0        0        0        0        0        0        0        0        0

>>>>>>>>>>>>>>>>>>>>>> D E M A N D <<<<<<<<<<<<<<<<<<<<<<    >>>>>>>>>>>>>>>>>>>>>>>> S U P P L Y <<<<<<<<<<<<<<<<<<<<<<
DEMAND TYP  WHERE REQUIRED      QUANTITY       DUE DATE      *  ORDER NO.  STATUS    QUANTITY       DUE DATE  NEED DAT
----------  -----------------   -------------  --------      -  ---------- --------  -------------  --------  --------
ORDER       S.O.  10003                20.00   03/20/91
W.O.SHORT.  S.W.O.  WO-1002            24.00   05/15/91
W.O.SHORT.  S.W.O.  WO-1007            19.00   07/02/91
W.O.SHORT.  S.W.O.  WO-1112            20.00   07/12/91
ORDER       S.O.  10020                20.00   10/29/91
W.O.ALLOC.  1001                      150.00   11/29/91
W.O.SHORT.  S.W.O.  WO-1003            22.00   12/06/91
W.O.ALLOC.  1001                      125.00   12/20/91
W.O.ALLOC.  1001                      150.00   02/18/92
ORDER       S.O.  10020                20.00   02/25/92
W.O.ALLOC.  1001                       50.00   03/09/92
W.O.ALLOC.  1001                      200.00   03/25/92
W.O.ALLOC.  1001                      125.00   09/02/92
```

**Figure 4-21**
**The MRP Report—Horizontal Format**

Reprinted here with permission from ASK Computer Systems, Inc.

```
RE,900,1.MDATABAS  ASKON CAMERA COMPANY -- MANUFACTURING
MON, APR 15, 1991,  3:07 AM                  MATERIAL REQUIREMENTS PLANNING REPORT                            PAGE NO:   1
                                             =====================================

   CLASS CODE GROUP: 1    COMMODITY CLASS
   CLASS CODE:       1    OPTICAL
                                             DUE DATE                          SCHEDULED
                                    DEMAND   /ACTION  MRP NEED   QUANTITY       ORDER    WO OPEN ORDER       QUANTITY    BALANCE
                   WHERE REQUIRED    TYPE      DATE     DATE     REQUIRED     QUANTITY   PO   NUMBER   STA   ON ORDER    QUANTITY
                 ----------------- ---------- -------- -------- ----------- ----------- -- ---------- --- ----------- -----------


PART: 1013                          UM SC FLT DTS  ULT O  OP/SS     EOQ    SF PAN SIZE NDS UNIT CST    NONNET        QOH      STRT BAL
DESC: VIEW/FRESNL SCREEN            -- -- --- ---  ---- - -------- -------- -- -------- --- -------- ---------- ----------- -----------
REV : B                             EA B   20   1  .00 1  228.00    38.75  2      1.00  5   6.650       64.00      1409.00     1409.00

                 S.O.   10003       ORDER                 03/20/91     20.00                                                  1389.00
                 S.W.O.  WO-1002    W.O.SHORT.            05/15/91     24.00                                                  1365.00
                 S.W.O.  WO-1007    W.O.SHORT.            07/02/91     19.00                                                  1346.00
                 S.W.O.  WO-1112    W.O.SHORT.            07/12/91     20.00                                                  1326.00
                 S.O.   10020       ORDER                 10/29/91     20.00                                                  1306.00
                 1001               W.O.ALLOC.            11/29/91    150.00                                                  1156.00
                 S.W.O.  WO-1003    W.O.SHORT.            12/06/91     22.00                                                  1134.00
                 1001               W.O.ALLOC.            12/20/91    125.00                                                  1009.00
                 1001               W.O.ALLOC.            02/18/92    150.00                                                   859.00
                 S.O.   10020       ORDER                 02/25/92     20.00                                                   839.00
                 1001               W.O.ALLOC.            03/09/92     50.00                                                   789.00
                 1001               W.O.ALLOC.            03/25/92    200.00                                                   589.00
                 1001               W.O.ALLOC.            09/02/92    125.00                                                   464.00

PART: 1014                          UM SC FLT DTS  ULT O  OP/SS     EOQ    SF PAN SIZE NDS UNIT CST    NONNET        QOH      STRT BAL
DESC: 50MM LENS 1.5 FSTOP           -- -- --- ---  ---- - -------- -------- -- -------- --- -------- ---------- ----------- -----------
REV : K                             EA B   15   1  .00 1  180.00    18.23  1      1.00  5  28.700      450.00      1149.00     1149.00

                 S.W.O.  WO-1002    W.O.SHORT.            05/15/91     28.00                                                  1121.00
                 S.W.O.  WO-1007    W.O.SHORT.            07/02/91     19.00                                                  1102.00
                 S.W.O.  WO-1112    W.O.SHORT.            07/12/91     20.00                                                  1082.00
                 1001               W.O.ALLOC.            11/29/91    150.00                                                   932.00
                 S.W.O.  WO-1003    W.O.SHORT.            12/06/91     22.00                                                   910.00
                 1001               W.O.ALLOC.            12/20/91    125.00                                                   785.00
                 1001               W.O.ALLOC.            02/18/92    150.00                                                   635.00
                 1001               W.O.ALLOC.            03/09/92     50.00                                                   585.00
                 1001               W.O.ALLOC.            03/25/92    200.00                                                   385.00
                 1001               W.O.ALLOC.            09/02/92    125.00                                                   260.00
                                             06/01/92 99/99/99                           PO PO-B1002            400.00      656.00
                                             07/02/92 99/99/99                           PO PO-B1002            500.00     1151.00
                                             10/29/92 99/99/99                   BLANKET PO PO-B1002           1000.00     1151.00
```

**Figure 4-22**
**The MRP Report—Vertical Format**

Reprinted here with permission from ASK Computer Systems, Inc.

**MRP Exception Reports** Due to the fact that MRP has no ability to control the material flow, often deviations from the MRP plan occur. These are reflected in *exception reports*. The validity of input data is checked along with the adjustment of MRP output reports, due to the deviation in performance. The ability to adjust an MRP is an essential production planning and control tool representing the only means of how MRP can rectify deviations that have occurred at the shop floor.

An example of the MRP vertical report on shortages is shown in Figure 4-23. The *shortages report* indicates the order number and work center, quantity due, due date, and promised date. The delay report, also known as due date maintenance, is another example. Due date maintenance means that proper due dates are being met as jobs progress through work centers.

A *reschedule report* compiled by part number shows the status of a job, quantity completed, current work order due date, and the MRP rescheduled need date either backward or forward. An example of the reschedule report is shown in Figure 4-24.

There are problems in synchronizing MRP with the physical flow of material, despite all its powerful features and the zero-stock philosophy. The MRP time-phasing and zero-stock philosophy are the mandatory features of any modern production management system, along with planning priorities which are transformed into the detailed order releases and the scheduled-receipt due dates.

A *job costing report* is another example of MRP reports. In addition to maintaining the status of a part in the inventory, on order, and in work-in-process, MRP provides cost accounting information. This includes the standard material costing, burden cost, labor and outside cost, and work in process cost inquiry, including labor charges to work in process. A costed bill of materials compiled according to the product structure was shown in Figure 4-20. Figure 4-25 shows another example—an open work order cost report. In this report, costing information is grouped according to three cost items—material, labor, and overheads—and it includes the WIP cost.

**The Advantages of MRP** Among the advantages of an MRP program the following can be pointed out:

- Time phasing adds the time dimension to the inventory status data, which in an inventory system was previously shown only as the quantity on hand and the quantity on order. In ROP, an order is activated as soon as the reorder point is reached, regardless of whether there is immediate demand or not.
- The gross-to-net feature of MRP translates gross requirements into net requirements by taking into account items on order and completed components, as well as components already assembled into products.

```
RE,302,2.MDATABAS  ASKON CAMERA COMPANY -- MANUFACTURING
 MON, APR 15, 1991,  3:54 AM                          ALL SHORTAGES                                            PAGE NO:  1
                                                      =============

    CLASS CODE GROUP:  1     COMMODITY CLASS
    CLASS CODE:        4     MECHANICAL PARTS

                                                 WORK ORDER WO QUANTITY QUANTITY  PROMISED MRP   ORDER NO./ QUANT IN QUANTITY PROMISED
 PART NUMBER          DESCRIPTION          UM SC   NUMBER   RE  SHORT   ON HAND     DATE   DATE  WORK AREA REC/INSP   DUE      DATE
 -------------------- -------------------- -- -- ---------- -- -------- --------- -------- ----- ---------- -------- -------- --------

 1010                 ASKON 10 BODY ASSEMBL EA M WO-1002    F    29.000  2277.000 11/15/91 99/99
                                                 WO-1007    F    19.000  2277.000 09/01/91 99/99
                                                 WO-1112    F    20.000  2277.000 07/16/91 99/99
                                                                                                 WO-1006        .000  200.000 02/02/92
                                                     ** SUBCONTRACTED PURCHASE ORDERS FOR REFERENCE ONLY **
                                                     VENDOR NAME: ASK COMPUTER SYSTEMS,INC       PO-1007       1.000  177.000 09/11/91

 1033                 SHUTTER CHANGE ASSEMB EA B WO-1006    C   200.000  1421.000 02/02/92 99/99
                                                     VENDOR NAME: US CAMERA SUPPLY               PO-1003       2.000  346.000 05/28/91
                                                     VENDOR NAME: GORDON ELECTRONICS             PO-B1001       .000  500.000 07/15/92
                                                     VENDOR NAME: GORDON ELECTRONICS             PO-B1001       .000  500.000 07/31/92
                                                     VENDOR NAME: GORDON ELECTRONICS             PO-B1001       .000  500.000 08/09/92

 1034                 MIRROR BOX ASSEMBLY   EA B WO-1006    C   200.000  2038.000 02/02/92 99/99
                                                     VENDOR NAME: US CAMERA SUPPLY               PO-1003     420.000     .000 01/01/91
                                                     VENDOR NAME: US CAMERA SUPPLY               PO-1003     100.000  250.000 05/07/91
                                                     VENDOR NAME: US CAMERA SUPPLY               PO-1003        .000  650.000 06/25/91

 1038                 BACK DOOR RELEASE     EA B WO-1006    C   200.000  9457.000 02/02/92 99/99
                                                     VENDOR NAME: PRECISION METAL                PO-1006   65000.000********* 02/27/92

 1039                 REWIND ASSEMBLY       EA B WO-1006    C   200.000   788.000 02/02/92 99/99

 1040                 COUNTER ASSEMBLY      EA B WO-1006    C   200.000   926.000 02/02/92 99/99
```

**Figure 4-23**
**The MRP Shortages Report**

RE,905,1.MDATABAS ASKON CAMERA COMPANY -- MANUFACTURING DISTRIBUTION: MANAGER - ASK COMPUTERS
TUE, JAN 21, 1992, 3:54 PM RESCHEDULE BUY REPORT PAGE NO: 1
** 3 DAYS LEEWAY ALLOWED **

CLASS CODE GROUP: 1 COMMODITY CLASS
CLASS CODE: 4 MECHANICAL PARTS

| BC | PART NUMBER | DESCRIPTION | REV | UM | SC | OPC | P.O. NO. | VENDOR | QUANTITY IN INSP | BALANCE TO BE RECEIVED | VENDOR'S ORIGINAL PROMISED DATE | LATEST PROMISED DELIVERY DATE | MRP REQUIRED DELIVERY DATE | STOCK DUE DATE |
|---|---|---|---|---|---|---|---|---|---|---|---|---|---|---|
| GM | 1030 | SPEED CONTROL BRID | A | EA | B | 1 | PO-1008 | V-103 | 11.00 | 100.00 | 10/15/91 | 10/15/91 | CANCEL | 10/15/91 |
| | | | | | | | PO-1008 | V-103 | .00 | 80.00 | 01/13/92 | 01/13/92 | CANCEL | 01/13/92 |
| | | | | | | | PO-1008 | V-103 | .00 | 100.00 | 04/14/92 | 04/14/92 | CANCEL | 04/14/92 |
| | | | | | | | PO-1008 | V-103 | .00 | 100.00 | 07/14/92 | 07/14/92 | CANCEL | 07/14/92 |
| | | | | | | | PO-1008 | V-103 | .00 | 100.00 | 10/14/92 | 10/14/92 | CANCEL | 10/14/92 |
| GM | 1031 | FLASH/SYNC ASSEMBL | A | EA | B | 1 | PO-1008 | V-103 | 15.00 | 300.00 | 10/15/91 | 10/15/91 | CANCEL | 10/15/91 |
| | | | | | | | PO-1008 | V-103 | .00 | 300.00 | 02/11/92 | 02/11/92 | CANCEL | 02/11/92 |
| | | | | | | | PO-1008 | V-103 | .00 | 300.00 | 06/14/92 | 06/14/92 | CANCEL | 06/14/92 |
| | | | | | | | PO-1008 | V-103 | .00 | 300.00 | 10/14/92 | 10/14/92 | CANCEL | 10/14/92 |
| GM | 1032 | DBL EXPOSE ASSEMBL | A | EA | B | 1 | PO-1008 | V-103 | 8.00 | 250.00 | 09/10/91 | 09/10/91 | CANCEL | 09/10/91 |
| | | | | | | | PO-1008 | V-103 | .00 | 250.00 | 11/12/91 | 11/12/91 | CANCEL | 11/12/91 |
| | | | | | | | PO-1008 | V-103 | .00 | 250.00 | 07/12/92 | 07/12/92 | CANCEL | 07/12/92 |
| DC | 1033 | SHUTTER CHANGE ASS | A | EA | B | 1 | PO-1003 | V-104 | 2.00 | 348.00 | 03/19/91 | 05/28/91 | CANCEL | 05/28/91 |
| | | | | | | | PO-B1001 | V-105 | .00 | 500.00 | 06/14/91 | 07/15/92 | CANCEL | 06/15/91 |
| | | | | | | | PO-B1001 | V-105 | .00 | 500.00 | 07/31/92 | 07/31/92 | CANCEL | 08/01/92 |
| | | | | | | | PO-B1001 | V-105 | .00 | 500.00 | 08/09/92 | 08/09/92 | CANCEL | 08/10/92 |
| DC | 1034 | MIRROR BOX ASSEMBL | A | EA | B | 1 | PO-1003 | V-104 | 420.00 | 420.00 | 01/01/91 | 01/01/91 | CANCEL | 01/01/91 |
| | | | | | | | PO-1003 | V-104 | 100.00 | 350.00 | 04/15/91 | 05/07/91 | CANCEL | 05/07/91 |
| | | | | | | | PO-1003 | V-104 | .00 | 650.00 | 04/23/91 | 06/25/91 | CANCEL | 06/25/91 |
| | 1038 | BACK DOOR RELEASE | A | BX | B | 1 | PO-1006 | V-107 | 130.00 | 450.00 | 02/27/92 | 02/27/92 | CANCEL | 02/27/92 |
| | 1043 | MOTOR ADVANCE GEAR | A | BX | B | 2 | PO-1006 | V-107 | 100.00 | 100.00 | 12/07/91 | 12/07/91 | CANCEL | 12/07/91 |
| DC | 1044 | SHEAR GEAR | B | BX | B | 2 | PO-1006 | V-107 | 3.00 | 250.00 | 03/18/92 | 03/18/92 | CANCEL | 03/18/92 |
| | | | | | | | PO-1014 | V-107 | 20.00 | 20.00 | 06/20/91 | 06/20/91 | CANCEL | 06/20/91 |
| | | | | | | | PO-1014 | V-107 | 46.00 | 50.00 | 07/10/91 | 07/10/91 | CANCEL | 07/11/91 |
| | | | | | | | PO-1014 | V-107 | 50.00 | 50.00 | 07/19/91 | 07/19/91 | CANCEL | 07/19/91 |
| | | | | | | | PO-1015 | V-107 | 37.00 | 40.00 | 07/20/91 | 07/20/91 | CANCEL | 07/22/91 |
| | | | | | | | PO-1015 | V-107 | 40.00 | 40.00 | 10/10/91 | 10/10/91 | CANCEL | 10/10/91 |
| | | | | | | | PO-1016 | V-107 | .00 | 40.00 | 10/18/91 | 10/18/91 | CANCEL | 10/18/91 |
| | | | | | | | PO-1016 | V-107 | .00 | 40.00 | 10/31/91 | 10/31/91 | CANCEL | 10/31/91 |
| | | | | | | | PO-1016 | V-107 | .00 | 40.00 | 11/08/91 | 11/08/91 | CANCEL | 11/08/91 |
| | | | | | | | PO-1016 | V-107 | .00 | 40.00 | 12/31/91 | 12/31/91 | CANCEL | 12/31/91 |

**Figure 4-24**
**The Reschedule Buy Report**

Reprinted here with permission from ASK Computer Systems, Inc.

RE,313 .MDATABAS ASKON CAMERA COMPANY -- MANUFACTURING DISTRIBUTION: MANAGER - ASK COMPUTERS
MON, APR 15, 1992 3:55 AM

OPEN WORK ORDER COST REPORT PAGE NO: 1

| PART NUMBER: 1021 | | DESC: LINKAGE ASSEMBLY | RE: C UM: EA SC: M | ACCOUNT NO: WIP | |
|---|---|---|---|---|---|
| WORK ORDER NO: WO-1013 | RE: A | ORDER QUANTITY: 50.00 | AOQ: 70.00 | START DATE: | 11/06/91 |
| COMPLETED QTY: .00 | | SCRAP QUANTITY: .00 | EOQ: 71.94 | DUE DATE: | 11/08/91 |
| | | | | COMPLETED: | 06/03/91 |

MATERIAL

| PART NUMBER/ DESCRIPTION | SEQ | RE | UM | SC | QUANTITY SCHEDL'D | QUANTITY ISSUED | UNIT COST | SCHEDL'D COST | STANDARD AMOUNT ISSUED | EXTENDED USAGE VARIANCE | ACTUAL USE VAR OVERHEAD |
|---|---|---|---|---|---|---|---|---|---|---|---|
| 1043 MOTOR ADVANCE GEAR | 10 | A | EA | B | 50.00 | 51.00 | .45 | 22.40 | 22.85 | .32 | .13 |
| 1044 SHEAR GEAR | 10 | B | EA | B | 50.00 | 52.00 | .17 | 8.40 | 8.74 | .24 | .10 |
| 1045 SHUTTER RELEASE LEVER | 10 | B | EA | B | 50.00 | 52.00 | .29 | 14.70 | 15.29 | .42 | .17 |
| | | | | | | | | 45.50 | 46.88 | .98 | .40 |

LABOR

| | | | | ACTUAL HOURS | | EARNED HOURS | | WORK-IN-PROCESS CHARGES | | | | | EFFICIENCY VAR | |
|---|---|---|---|---|---|---|---|---|---|---|---|---|---|---|
| SEQ | OPER | WORK CENTER | QUANTITY COMPLT'D | SET UP | RUN | SET UP | RUN | ACT LAB | ACT OVHD | ERND LAB | ERND OVHD | ERND O.P. | LABOR | OVERHEAD |
| 10 | GP/LNK | 50-601 | 0 | .00 | .00 | .00 | .00 | .00 | .00 | .00 | .00 | .00 | .00 | .00 |
| 9999 | TRANST | TRANST | 0 | .00 | .00 | .00 | .00 | .00 | .00 | .00 | .00 | .00 | .00 | .00 |
| | | | | .00 | .00 | .00 | .00 | .00 | .00 | .00 | .00 | .00 | .00 | .00 |

| TRANSFERS IN AND OUT | MATERIAL | MATERIAL OVERHEAD | LABOR | FIXED OVERHEAD | VARIABLE OVERHEAD | THIRD OVERHEAD | OUTSIDE PROCESSING | OUTSIDE PROCESSING OVERHEAD | TOTAL |
|---|---|---|---|---|---|---|---|---|---|
| ASSEMBLY IN AT STD: | | | .00 | .00 | .00 | .00 | .00 | .00 | .00 |
| COMPONENT IN AT STD: | 33.48 | 13.39 | .00 | .00 | .00 | .00 | .00 | .00 | 46.87 |
| *TOTAL IN AT STD: | 33.48 | 13.39 | .00 | .00 | .00 | .00 | .00 | .00 | 46.87 |
| M LESS USAGE VARIANCE: | .98 | .40 | .00 | .00 | .00 | .00 | .00 | .00 | 1.38 |
| M LESS CONFIGURATION VAR: | .00 | -.01 | .00 | .00 | .00 | .00 | .00 | .00 | -.01 |
| LESS METHODS CHANGE VAR: | | **AVAILABLE AT JOB CLOSE** | | | | | | | |
| LESS LOT SIZE VARIANCE: | | **AVAILABLE AT JOB CLOSE** | | | | | | | |
| LESS ASSEMBLY SCRAP: | .00 | .00 | .00 | .00 | .00 | .00 | .00 | .00 | .00 |
| LESS TRANSFERS OUT : | .00 | .00 | .00 | .00 | .00 | .00 | .00 | .00 | .00 |
| RESIDUAL VALUE: | 33.48 | 13.39 | .00 | .00 | .00 | .00 | .00 | .00 | 46.87 |
| M*EFFICIENCY VARIANCE: | | | .00 | .00 | .00 | .00 | | | .00 |
| *RATE VARIANCE: | | | .00 | | | | | | .00 |
| TOTAL ACTUAL COST: | 33.48 | 13.39 | .00 | .00 | .00 | .00 | .00 | .00 | 46.87 |

**Figure 4-25**
**The Open Work Order Cost Report**

- MRP reduces inventories while the customer service is improved: components are ordered in required quantities. Time phasing makes it even more efficient, as parts are ordered to be available in time for an assembly.
- MRP improves control over the availability of components.
- MRP generates material net requirements, bucketed tool requirements, and initiates corrective actions to eliminate imbalances.
- Provides on-hand information for adjusting MPS.

***The Disadvantages of MRP*** There is an opinion that many MRP users are unhappy. MRP is a component ordering system rather than a material flow control, which some companies expect it to be. MRP is a product planning and control system. An inventory-type planning and control system can only analyze past production events and the accomplished operations, if at all possible, once holdups call for improvements in the material flow. This type of control has little positive influence on current shop floor activities; it is focused on control of the availability of physical elements of the product structure, represented in discrete manufacturing by parts and components, and is defined as structural control.

Systems utilizing this type of control are, basically, inventory-type manufacturing systems with an emphasis on stores control rather than shop floor control. They are associated with dispatching and expediting certain holdup jobs at the expense of other jobs, sometimes affecting the entire production program. MRP controls inventory items. It has no means to control shared resources, such as labor and equipment.

The MRP system has been based on the assumption of an infinite capacity; that is, machines, labor, tools, services, and finance are available whenever they are required to satisfy the needs of the MRP plan. The only balancing done up to now is the rough-cut capacity check ensuring the general conformance of MRP with resources, without considering timing, specific operations, and uniqueness of intermittent flow of materials.

MPS planning establishes production rates for product families based on rough-cut capacity planning. MPS planning can answer the question of how many refrigerators per week can be built in the established standard-type production, but it is not a sufficient plan for companies in which make-to-order jobs interfere with established products. For example, if the standard production of refrigerators is concurrent with the make-to-order air-conditioning sets and make-to-order ventilation systems, all of them are competing for the same shop capacity in various combinations—product mixes. MRP is effective in assembly-type operations where control of availability of components to assembly processes is a vital requirement.

It is not always possible to execute a detailed MRP plan, due to the shortages of capacity, materials, or numerous interruptions on the shop floor. The essence of MRP is that it presents a components ordering program where only the ordering date and due date are highlighted regardless to the availability of capacity. Practice shows that this is the major reason behind the so-called "MRP failures." The MRP logic is standing up to such a test of zero stock, while the execution of such detailed time-phased programs is invariably the reason for messing up the program.

The failure of an ordering system, be it an order point system or MRP, is manifested in the shortage of components required for the subsequent processes. An ineffective system requires reinforcements to support it. Such reinforcements are a shortage list, a list of overdue components, and the concomitant dispatching activities often disrupting MRP programs. The MRP solution is in the detailed operations scheduling—preventive planning and control.

## MRP ENHANCEMENTS

MRP changes have resulted in a number of improvements to the system. One such improvement is the MRP II closed-loop system.

***MRP II—The Closed-Loop System*** Many failures of MRP systems stress the need for control of capacity and the need to extend a narrow function of MRP as an exclusively component ordering system into more of a shop control system. This need gave way to MRP enhancements, which include capacity planning and control. This extended manufacturing control system became known as *manufacturing resource planning* or MRP II.

MRP II includes master production scheduling, which is reconciled with capacity requirements planning, and detailed scheduling, along with the feedback from vendors and the shop floor for rescheduling the operations. An MRP II flow diagram is illustrated in Figure 4-26.

The MRP component ordering feature has been reviewed in such a way as to permit checking the availability of capacity through *capacity requirements planning* (CRP). This way, MRP and MPS are validated through the CRP feedback. At the same time, CRP is constantly updated through the feedback from execution of the capacity plan—process control—while MRP is updated by the shop floor and purchasing feedback on execution of material plans. This is called a closed-loop MRP, the system which makes it possible to validate MRP and MPS to effect the necessary changes and to replan, in order to have a sufficient capacity to execute the MPS plan.

The progress in computer technology opens an opportunity to evaluate both tactical and strategic business policies by using a common data base. MRP II expands MRP into the areas of sales and marketing, accounting, cost control, personnel, and engineering. MRP II interfaces the business strategic plan with the aggregate production plan, MPS, MRP, and CRP to develop validated execution and procurement planned order releases. In a classical MRP II environment, the job contents are fed directly to the payroll, and they are tied out daily throughout the payroll data file. Accounting and cost accounting files are also integrated with shop data information.

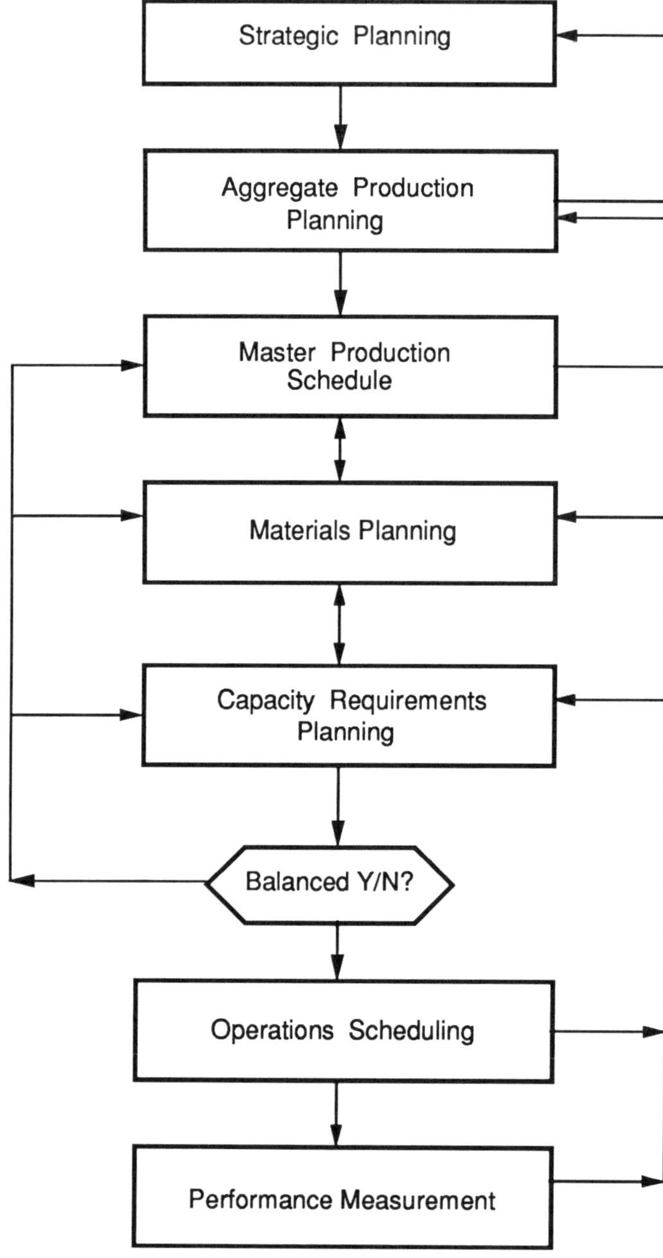


**Figure 4-26**
**A Closed-Loop MRP System**

MRP II defines key resources—product resource profiles—and provides inputs to the long-range business acquisition or disposition decisions. However, MRP II does not go beyond the point of planning order releases. Further operation scheduling is done based on MRP II orders.

MRP II expands MRP horizontally into other business functions, but not vertically onto the execution stage. Further operational scheduling and optimization are done separately as part of shop floor control, by applying assorted scheduling techniques, priority rules, and simulation. Shop floor control is examined in Chapters 5, 6, and 7.

MRP II deals with the MRP system nervousness that occurs when changes to MPS regarding quantity and timing are initiated. There are different causes and solutions to the nervousness in the execution of MRP plans, but the most frequent reasons are recurrent changes in customer orders.

MRP II reduces the nervousness by applying the MPS zoning. The solution is to reduce the underlying causes for changes to the MRP plan by restricting changes to the master production plan.

MRPII is a system intended for integrating control over business resources, such as capacity requirements planning: labor-hours and machine-hours; tooling; support services, such as plant maintenance and engineering support; and cash flow. Closed-loop manufacturing means that there is a feedback from shop floor and vendors to MPS and MRP and all the deviations are rectified in an orderly manner.

## WHAT'S NEXT IN MRP? MRP III?

Material requirements planning has grown from a small material subsystem to a fully integrated company system. A communication system links major departments of a corporation together from inventory, purchasing, and manufacturing to sales, engineering, and accounting.

MRP regeneration (updating the item data file and work order master file) is the common system bottlenecks: it has always been, at best, hours in a major manufacturing company. This precludes any real-time simulations. Long computer run times required to generate the data have affected planning and execution and have also hindered proper functioning of the system. It has always been assumed that the material plans were not connected to the capacity and shop floor plans automatically. In other words, it was thought that you could load as much as required according to the master schedule, and MRP would generate plans regardless of their chances of being executed on the factory floor. Now, specialized multiprocessors can regenerate MRP files in seconds.

The evolution to total quality management (TQM) and Just-in-Time (JIT) manufacturing practices drives a company to reduce the cost and cycle times. PC local area networks will allow the intricate sublogic between departments to be streamlined, then automated. This can drop purchase order release cycle times down to days rather than weeks and factory reaction times to hours rather than days.

What happens in the next evolution is that the real-time simulation will become possible (MRP regenerates in seconds). One problem with execution has always been the "You really don't know if the plan is executable until you execute the MRP." The rough-cut capacity tools just aren't good enough. Remember, it only takes shortage of one part to blow your entire plan if you are an assembly manufacturer. The "quick gen" is going to add more reliability to planning process, as well as more flexibility to the delivery of goods and services.

The new word, MRP III, is coined through the network solutions (PCs) that help speed up the decision logistics of information feeding and reduce the data entry to a minimum. We don't need to duplicate the functionality at the department level, but we do need a minimal duplication of data files and elements. This will call for a different philosophy toward the data base architecture as well as security. But these systems will speed up the decision making and adjustment cycle, make them more accurate, and will further integrate areas that have not been efficient (for example, capacity and material requirements plans).

We do need to make sure that these departmental or subsystems fit a holistic worldwide corporate system. We don't need a shortage list coming from five different places. We have enough trouble expediting one shortage list.

Scheduling data and execution plans could also be incorrect, if these subsystems do not use the latest information. The data base administration, security, and data architecture need to be viewed holistically, not separately.

Steve Covin of Compaq Computers states that we have upgraded the regeneration of information from what used to take over 48 hours to 19 seconds. However, we still have the same old clerical interface, data entry, and administrative systems that support the MRP infrastructure. We have to get light-year improvements in this area to really take advantage of all other improvements. The best place to streamline these is in a LAN-based sublogic system. In the end, MRP III will be here before we know it. Companies that can use it wisely will have a competitive advantage over those who cannot.

***Don't Overlook Capacity Requirements Planning*** *Capacity requirements planning* translates an MRP program into capacity requirements for each work center by exploding MRP in order to translate various products and orders into congruent units related to time. CRP is a detailed plan verifying the MRP time-phased capacity lot-sized requirements for both open shop orders (scheduled receipts) and planned work orders and applying gross to net requirements techniques. CRP is, therefore, a detailed updating of MPS and rough-cut capacity plans.

Most important, CRP adjusts MPS rough plans to correspond to the available capacity on the time-phased basis. CRP applies the backward scheduling in work centers loading. CRP makes use of routing information, time standards, setup time and run time and considers average queueing time.

Capacity requirements planning converts the production plan into demand for capacity in each of the work centers. CRP considers lot sizes and scheduled receipts. This is expressed in labor-hours required for each operation against labor-hours available on the time-by-time basis. An example of a CRP report at CAMCO, Inc., is shown in Figure 4-27. Department 01, work center 0141, Bridgeport Mill, is overloaded during weeks 1 and 2. This means that further balancing is required. CRP is not a final schedule as such—further operations scheduling is required, which is done at a work center prior to execution. Capacity requirements planning is an extension of an MRP. The main purpose of CRP is to compute and verify the future MRP-based work load.

## PLACING ORDERS FOR INDEPENDENT AND DEPENDENT DEMAND ITEMS

Most manufactured end products are composed of many parts and components, each one being an item in either an independent or a dependent demand inventory control system and being controlled by various inventory management techniques. An inventory control system fulfills the function of ordering components from outside sources and internal manufacturing departments so as to have them available on time for the next production stage or a final assembly. Ordering and reordering is an essential part of an inventory control system and of production planning and control as a whole. Independent demand inventory control systems are functionally separated from production lines. Work orders for independent demand inventory items compete for the production capacity against outside customer orders, as illustrated in Figure 4-28.

Usually, replenishment work orders have priority over outside orders as "internal customers," but this is not always the case. Orders for independent demand items are placed both with production and with outside suppliers and vendors.

## INVENTORIES ARE TWO-DIMENSIONAL SYSTEMS

During your decision making in inventory planning, you have to answer two questions: "How much do you need?" and "What are the time constraints?" (for example, *quantity and time*, or how much to order and when).

While making a *quantity decision* you have two alternatives: to order the quantity required at present time, or to order a larger quantity and save on reordering in the future. You can base your decision on your future requirements.

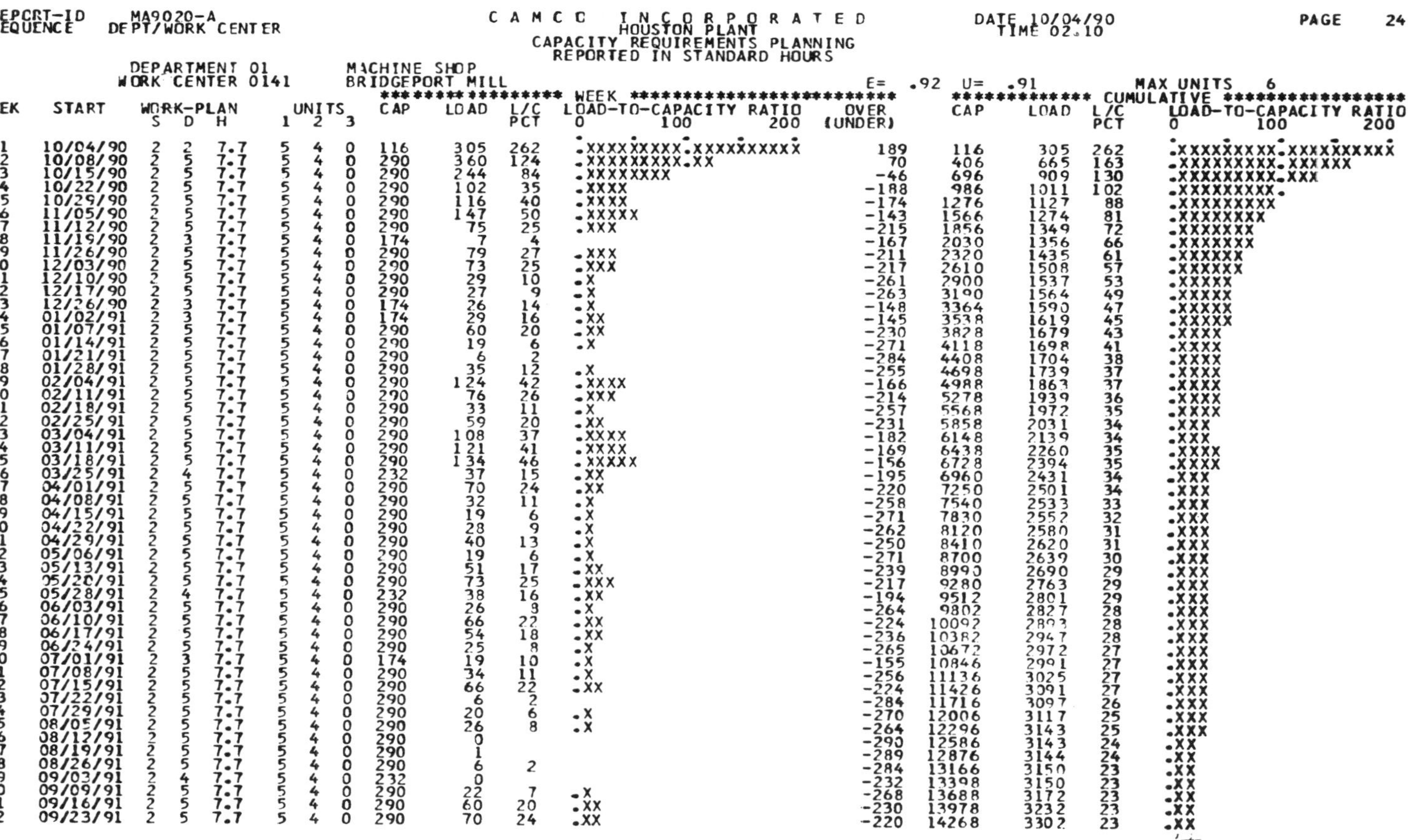

REPORT-ID MA9020-A                C A M C O   I N C O R P O R A T E D                DATE 10/04/90        PAGE 24
SEQUENCE DEPT/WORK CENTER                HOUSTON PLANT                TIME 02.10
CAPACITY REQUIREMENTS PLANNING
REPORTED IN STANDARD HOURS

DEPARTMENT 01        MACHINE SHOP
WORK CENTER 0141        BRIDGEPORT MILL        E= .92   U= .91        MAX UNITS 6

| WEEK | START | WORK-PLAN S | WORK-PLAN D | WORK-PLAN H | UNITS 1 | UNITS 2 | UNITS 3 | WEEK CAP | WEEK LOAD | WEEK L/C PCT | WEEK LOAD-TO-CAPACITY RATIO (0 100 200) | OVER (UNDER) | CUMULATIVE CAP | CUMULATIVE LOAD | CUMULATIVE L/C PCT | CUMULATIVE LOAD-TO-CAPACITY RATIO (0 100 200) |
|---|---|---|---|---|---|---|---|---|---|---|---|---|---|---|---|---|
| 1 | 10/04/90 | 2 | 2 | 7.7 | 5 | 4 | 0 | 116 | 305 | 262 | .XXXXXXXXX.XXXXXXXXX | 189 | 116 | 305 | 262 | .XXXXXXXXX.XXXXXXXXX |
| 2 | 10/08/90 | 2 | 5 | 7.7 | 5 | 4 | 0 | 290 | 360 | 124 | .XXXXXXXXX.XX | 70 | 406 | 665 | 163 | .XXXXXXXXX.XXXXXX |
| 3 | 10/15/90 | 2 | 5 | 7.7 | 5 | 4 | 0 | 290 | 244 | 84 | .XXXXXXXX | -46 | 696 | 909 | 130 | .XXXXXXXXX.XXX |
| 4 | 10/22/90 | 2 | 5 | 7.7 | 5 | 4 | 0 | 290 | 102 | 35 | .XXXX | -188 | 986 | 1011 | 102 | .XXXXXXXXX. |
| 5 | 10/29/90 | 2 | 5 | 7.7 | 5 | 4 | 0 | 290 | 116 | 40 | .XXXX | -174 | 1276 | 1127 | 88 | .XXXXXXXXX |
| 6 | 11/05/90 | 2 | 5 | 7.7 | 5 | 4 | 0 | 290 | 147 | 50 | .XXXXX | -143 | 1566 | 1274 | 81 | .XXXXXXXX |
| 7 | 11/12/90 | 2 | 5 | 7.7 | 5 | 4 | 0 | 290 | 75 | 25 | .XXX | -215 | 1856 | 1349 | 72 | .XXXXXXX |
| 8 | 11/19/90 | 2 | 3 | 7.7 | 5 | 4 | 0 | 174 | 7 | 4 | | -167 | 2030 | 1356 | 66 | .XXXXXXX |
| 9 | 11/26/90 | 2 | 5 | 7.7 | 5 | 4 | 0 | 290 | 79 | 27 | .XXX | -211 | 2320 | 1435 | 61 | .XXXXXX |
| 10 | 12/03/90 | 2 | 5 | 7.7 | 5 | 4 | 0 | 290 | 73 | 25 | .XXX | -217 | 2610 | 1508 | 57 | .XXXXXX |
| 11 | 12/10/90 | 2 | 5 | 7.7 | 5 | 4 | 0 | 290 | 29 | 10 | .X | -261 | 2900 | 1537 | 53 | .XXXXX |
| 12 | 12/17/90 | 2 | 5 | 7.7 | 5 | 4 | 0 | 290 | 27 | 9 | .X | -263 | 3190 | 1564 | 49 | .XXXXX |
| 13 | 12/26/90 | 2 | 3 | 7.7 | 5 | 4 | 0 | 174 | 26 | 14 | .X | -148 | 3364 | 1590 | 47 | .XXXXX |
| 14 | 01/02/91 | 2 | 3 | 7.7 | 5 | 4 | 0 | 174 | 29 | 16 | .XX | -145 | 3538 | 1619 | 45 | .XXXXX |
| 15 | 01/07/91 | 2 | 5 | 7.7 | 5 | 4 | 0 | 290 | 60 | 20 | .XX | -230 | 3828 | 1679 | 43 | .XXXX |
| 16 | 01/14/91 | 2 | 5 | 7.7 | 5 | 4 | 0 | 290 | 19 | 6 | .X | -271 | 4118 | 1698 | 41 | .XXXX |
| 17 | 01/21/91 | 2 | 5 | 7.7 | 5 | 4 | 0 | 290 | 6 | 2 | | -284 | 4408 | 1704 | 38 | .XXXX |
| 18 | 01/28/91 | 2 | 5 | 7.7 | 5 | 4 | 0 | 290 | 35 | 12 | .X | -255 | 4698 | 1739 | 37 | .XXXX |
| 19 | 02/04/91 | 2 | 5 | 7.7 | 5 | 4 | 0 | 290 | 124 | 42 | .XXXX | -166 | 4988 | 1863 | 37 | .XXXX |
| 20 | 02/11/91 | 2 | 5 | 7.7 | 5 | 4 | 0 | 290 | 76 | 26 | .XXX | -214 | 5278 | 1939 | 36 | .XXXX |
| 21 | 02/18/91 | 2 | 5 | 7.7 | 5 | 4 | 0 | 290 | 33 | 11 | .X | -257 | 5568 | 1972 | 35 | .XXXX |
| 22 | 02/25/91 | 2 | 5 | 7.7 | 5 | 4 | 0 | 290 | 59 | 20 | .XX | -231 | 5858 | 2031 | 34 | .XXX |
| 23 | 03/04/91 | 2 | 5 | 7.7 | 5 | 4 | 0 | 290 | 108 | 37 | .XXXX | -182 | 6148 | 2139 | 34 | .XXX |
| 24 | 03/11/91 | 2 | 5 | 7.7 | 5 | 4 | 0 | 290 | 121 | 41 | .XXXX | -169 | 6438 | 2260 | 35 | .XXXX |
| 25 | 03/18/91 | 2 | 5 | 7.7 | 5 | 4 | 0 | 290 | 134 | 46 | .XXXXX | -156 | 6728 | 2394 | 35 | .XXXX |
| 26 | 03/25/91 | 2 | 4 | 7.7 | 5 | 4 | 0 | 232 | 37 | 15 | .XX | -195 | 6960 | 2431 | 34 | .XXX |
| 27 | 04/01/91 | 2 | 5 | 7.7 | 5 | 4 | 0 | 290 | 70 | 24 | .XX | -220 | 7250 | 2501 | 34 | .XXX |
| 28 | 04/08/91 | 2 | 5 | 7.7 | 5 | 4 | 0 | 290 | 32 | 11 | .X | -258 | 7540 | 2533 | 33 | .XXX |
| 29 | 04/15/91 | 2 | 5 | 7.7 | 5 | 4 | 0 | 290 | 19 | 6 | .X | -271 | 7830 | 2552 | 32 | .XXX |
| 30 | 04/22/91 | 2 | 5 | 7.7 | 5 | 4 | 0 | 290 | 28 | 9 | .X | -262 | 8120 | 2580 | 31 | .XXX |
| 31 | 04/29/91 | 2 | 5 | 7.7 | 5 | 4 | 0 | 290 | 40 | 13 | .X | -250 | 8410 | 2620 | 31 | .XXX |
| 32 | 05/06/91 | 2 | 5 | 7.7 | 5 | 4 | 0 | 290 | 19 | 6 | .X | -271 | 8700 | 2639 | 30 | .XXX |
| 33 | 05/13/91 | 2 | 5 | 7.7 | 5 | 4 | 0 | 290 | 51 | 17 | .XX | -239 | 8990 | 2690 | 29 | .XXX |
| 34 | 05/20/91 | 2 | 5 | 7.7 | 5 | 4 | 0 | 290 | 73 | 25 | .XXX | -217 | 9280 | 2763 | 29 | .XXX |
| 35 | 05/28/91 | 2 | 4 | 7.7 | 5 | 4 | 0 | 232 | 38 | 16 | .XX | -194 | 9512 | 2801 | 29 | .XXX |
| 36 | 06/03/91 | 2 | 5 | 7.7 | 5 | 4 | 0 | 290 | 26 | 9 | .X | -264 | 9802 | 2827 | 28 | .XXX |
| 37 | 06/10/91 | 2 | 5 | 7.7 | 5 | 4 | 0 | 290 | 66 | 22 | .XX | -224 | 10092 | 2893 | 28 | .XXX |
| 38 | 06/17/91 | 2 | 5 | 7.7 | 5 | 4 | 0 | 290 | 54 | 18 | .XX | -236 | 10382 | 2947 | 28 | .XXX |
| 39 | 06/24/91 | 2 | 5 | 7.7 | 5 | 4 | 0 | 290 | 25 | 8 | .X | -265 | 10672 | 2972 | 27 | .XXX |
| 40 | 07/01/91 | 2 | 3 | 7.7 | 5 | 4 | 0 | 174 | 19 | 10 | .X | -155 | 10846 | 2991 | 27 | .XXX |
| 41 | 07/08/91 | 2 | 5 | 7.7 | 5 | 4 | 0 | 290 | 34 | 11 | .X | -256 | 11136 | 3025 | 27 | .XXX |
| 42 | 07/15/91 | 2 | 5 | 7.7 | 5 | 4 | 0 | 290 | 66 | 22 | .XX | -224 | 11426 | 3091 | 27 | .XXX |
| 43 | 07/22/91 | 2 | 5 | 7.7 | 5 | 4 | 0 | 290 | 6 | 2 | | -284 | 11716 | 3097 | 26 | .XXX |
| 44 | 07/29/91 | 2 | 5 | 7.7 | 5 | 4 | 0 | 290 | 20 | 6 | .X | -270 | 12006 | 3117 | 25 | .XXX |
| 45 | 08/05/91 | 2 | 5 | 7.7 | 5 | 4 | 0 | 290 | 26 | 8 | .X | -264 | 12296 | 3143 | 25 | .XXX |
| 46 | 08/12/91 | 2 | 5 | 7.7 | 5 | 4 | 0 | 290 | 0 | | | -290 | 12586 | 3143 | 24 | .XX |
| 47 | 08/19/91 | 2 | 5 | 7.7 | 5 | 4 | 0 | 290 | 1 | | | -289 | 12876 | 3144 | 24 | .XX |
| 48 | 08/26/91 | 2 | 5 | 7.7 | 5 | 4 | 0 | 290 | 6 | 2 | | -284 | 13166 | 3150 | 23 | .XX |
| 49 | 09/03/91 | 2 | 4 | 7.7 | 5 | 4 | 0 | 232 | 0 | | | -232 | 13398 | 3150 | 23 | .XX |
| 50 | 09/09/91 | 2 | 5 | 7.7 | 5 | 4 | 0 | 290 | 22 | 7 | .X | -268 | 13688 | 3172 | 23 | .XX |
| 51 | 09/16/91 | 2 | 5 | 7.7 | 5 | 4 | 0 | 290 | 60 | 20 | .XX | -230 | 13978 | 3232 | 23 | .XX |
| 52 | 09/23/91 | 2 | 5 | 7.7 | 5 | 4 | 0 | 290 | 70 | 24 | .XX | -220 | 14268 | 3302 | 23 | .XX |

**Figure 4-27**
**Capacity Requirements Planning at CAMCO, Inc.**

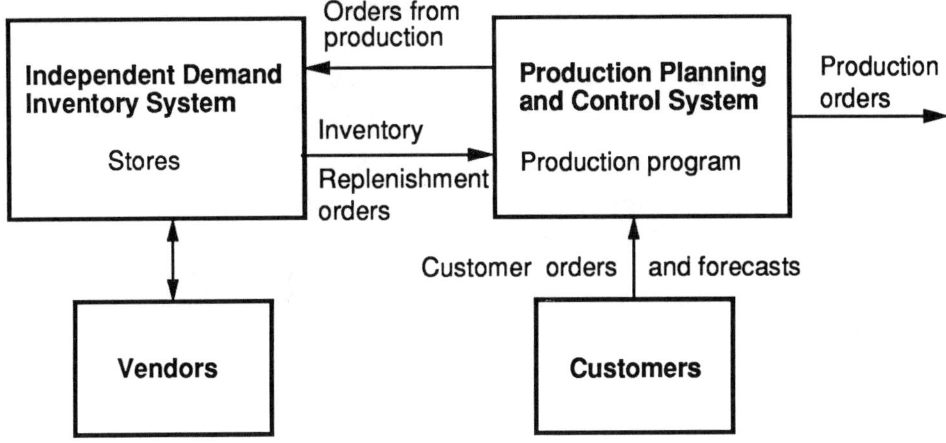


**Figure 4-28**
**Placing Production Orders**

When your future requirements are known, estimates can be made applying the trial and error method. It is possible to determine the exact stock required so as to give you the lowest possible production cost. If your future requirements are unknown, the uncertainty factor is introduced. You will have to base your decision on statistically estimated figures based on past experience.

Good *timing of orders* has an objective of creating a minimum inventory and even a zero stock. Ordering time is directly related to an item's lead time. Work orders should be planned considering the available production capacity and demand for components, assuring their availability at each production stage. This is known as *time phasing*. Time phasing is a major consideration in WIP dedicated resources because as soon as resources enter the production process, they accumulate an increasing amount of production costs. These costs should be recovered promptly and redirected back into the system.

## SUMMARY

There are two categories of inventory management systems, namely, independent demand, stock-controlled systems and dependent demand inventory systems, also known as the calculated demand systems. There are different ordering/replenishment methods used in inventory systems. We have discussed three ordering approaches in independent demand stock controlled inventory systems, namely, lot-for-lot ordering, fixed time period ordering, and fixed order quantity ordering.

Ordering in dependent demand inventory systems, quantity, and time is calculated based on bill of material quantities and the dates of assembly processes. Material requirements planning is the main system used in dependent demand ordering.

Both independent demand and dependent demand inventory systems are two-dimensional systems which do not consider the availability of capacity. These inventory systems assume that there are limitless capacities available. An improvement of MRP is the MRP II, which includes capacity requirements planning and detailed scheduling with a feedback to MRP and MPS. However, MRP II production plans still require detailed scheduling at work centers prior to execution.

# 5

# How Shop Floor Control Affects Productivity

*Planning* means predefining the future actions of your organization and preparing a program of how to apply your resources in the most efficient way. Planning establishes a level of performance and productivity—a standard which cannot be surpassed by execution. Also, people are motivated to pay attention and attempt to improve performance when it is planned and measured.

*Productivity* is a measure of performance estimated as a ratio of output to input over a fixed period of time:

$$\text{productivity} = \frac{\text{output}}{\text{input}}$$

*Output* consists of all goods and services produced over a period of time, and inputs consist of all resources consumed in producing these outputs—raw materials, labor, capital, and energy.

Productivity and efficiency should be planned in advance at the inception of a production plan. Say, for example, January output was 1,150 conveyor shafts. In February, your plan calls for the production of 1,200 conveyor shafts, an increase in productivity of 4.3 percent over the preceding month's production level provided input is constant. Planned output divided by your company's input will represent your planned productivity level. You can calculate your planned productivity by using the productivity equation as follows:

$$\text{planned productivity} = \frac{\text{planned output}}{\text{planned input}}$$

Productivity measure which compares the total output to just one of the inputs is known as *partial productivity.* Partial labor productivity is estimated based on units of output per direct labor-hour:

$$\text{labor productivity} = \frac{\text{output}}{\text{input (hours, days, or months)}} = \text{25 intermediate shafts per day}$$

Other examples of partial productivity are energy productivity, computed as units of output per unit of energy, (for example, per kilowatt hour or cubic foot of gas), or productivity estimated as the ratio of total output per dollar of input.

Productivity measure is used in examining trends over time: comparing the present productivity level to productivity at the previous time periods. Such analysis can show ways of productivity improvement—by increasing the numerator of the productivity increasing output or decreasing denominator, reducing resources for the same amount of output, or both, increasing output and decreasing input.

*Efficiency* is widely used to measure the labor performance. Efficiency is a measure that relates actual performance to the planned one:

$$\text{efficiency} = \frac{\text{actual units produced}}{\text{standard units scheduled}}$$

For example, 240 brake disks were produced per shift instead of the planned 250 disks. The efficiency is estimated as follows:

$$\text{efficiency} = \frac{240}{250} = 96\%$$

Efficiency also can be estimated in time units:

$$\text{efficiency} = \frac{\text{standard scheduled time}}{\text{actual time}}$$

Efficiency measures the degree to which resources are utilized. Measuring efficiency is a formidable tool for improving performance.

## MEASURING PRODUCTIVITY IN PROCESS INDUSTRIES

Process industries are characterized by homogeneous material flows consisting of standardized operations. These are capital-intensive processes featuring diminished labor contents. Estimating labor productivity in this situation is not a reflection of performance. Process industry features line production-type material flow where a stoppage of a single production unit abstracts the entire production line.

Maintenance becomes a major consideration in setting up a productivity level in process industry. Due to production lines being designed for a set amount of output per hour, the total output depends a lot on the hours the machine is in operation without stoppages or breakdowns. For example, a steel rolling mill has a capacity of 200 tons per hour. During an 8-hour shift it produces 200 tons × 8 hr. = 1,600 tons. If there is a breakdown taking 2 hours to repair, the production falls to 200 tons × (8 - 2) hr. = 1,200 tons. Production cannot be speeded up because the mill has been designed for 200 ton/hour capacity.

Utilization is a critical factor in process industries: utilization is expressed as a percentage ratio of the total productive time to the total available time:

$$\text{utilization} = \frac{T_p}{T_a}$$

where

$T_p$ = total productive time

$T_a$ = total available time

In process industry, improvement in maintenance services directly increases productivity in production, providing maintenance cost is kept under control.

Another factor influencing productivity in process industries is *setup time* due to the fact that many units of the production line must be reset for each work order.

In the foregoing example, a sheet steel manufacturing plant is in continuous production; nevertheless, the processing is done in various batch quantities starting from one or two coils—each weighing 8 to 12 tons—to large orders amounting to thousands of tons. In addition, adjustments must also be made for the grade of steel, its metallurgical composition and mechanical properties, and the sizes of the strip (thickness, width). Setup time reduction is an effective means for increasing productivity in the process industry.

## MEASURING PRODUCTIVITY IN JOB SHOPS

Job shop production is labor-intensive. The contents of labor constitute a significant part of total input. Job shops are characterized as having intermittent material flow and multiple products at various stages of product life cycle, queueing lines, and work-in-process (WIP). Job shop productivity can be improved by smoothing the *material flow* and reducing WIP when balancing production lines.

Another job shop factor is the variety of work orders and the need for resetting workstations for different jobs. Setups represent a significant content of job shop operations. Reduction of *setup time* is another means for improving productivity in job shops.

Productivity in job shops depends a lot on such performance indices as lead time and cycle time. Productivity level is also reflected in inventory turnover. An inventory turnover estimates how often the company sells its average inventory per year:

$$\text{inventory turnover} = \frac{\text{cost of goods sold}}{\text{value of average inventory}}$$

The measure shows how efficiently the money invested in inventory is used. Inventory turns increase when lead time and WIP are reduced.

## MAKING THE MOST OF LEAD TIME AND CYCLE TIME

Operation's *lead time* is the time elapsed from start to finish of an operation. Operations lead time consists of two segments: time related to performing the operation—*machine time*—and time in transit until the next operation—*transit time*. The division of operation lead time into machine time and transit time is illustrated in Figure 5-1.

Furthermore, machine time and transit time consist of a number of basic elements that are illustrated in Figure 5-2.

The elements of machine time are

1. *Queue time*—The time a job is waiting in a queue for an available capacity.
2. *Preparation time*—The time it takes to get ready for an operation. There are two elements in preparation time, *organization time*—the time spent on receiving an order, preparing drawings, specifications, tools, and materials—and *setup time*—the time spent preparing a machine for an operation

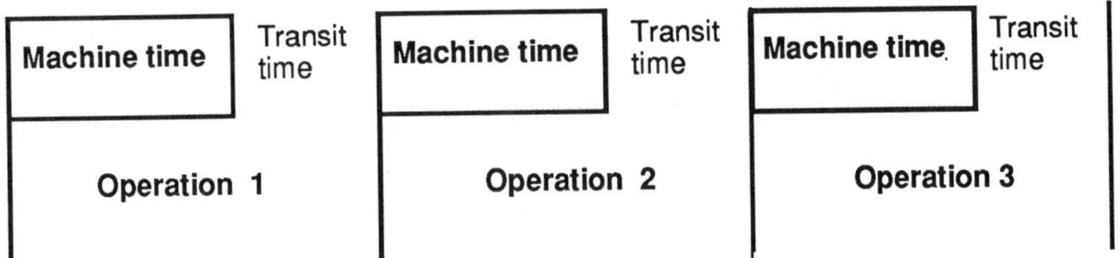


**Figure 5-1**
**The Elements of Operation Lead Time -- Machine Time and Transit Time**

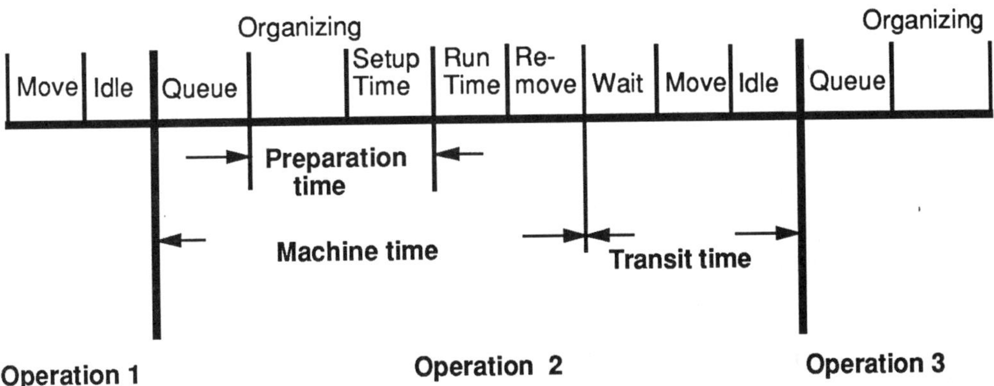


**Figure 5-2**
**The Elements of Operation Lead Time**

(for example, changing disks, fixing attachments and tools, and time spent working on the machine until the first quality part is produced). In general, organization time is spent outside the machine, and setup time is time spent on the machine.

3. *Run time*—Time spent on doing an operation.
4. *Remove time*—The time spent putting a completed job away and dismantling all the attachments and tools.

After a job is removed from the machine, a material handling decision should be made as to the next destination: where to move, how to move, and when to move.

The elements of the transit time are

1. *Wait time*—The waiting time after an operation is completed while the job is waiting to be moved.
2. *Move time*—The time when a job is in transit to the next operation or to a storage place.
3. *Idle time* or *interoperational time*—The time when a job is completed and moved away from the workstation but has not yet been claimed by the succeeding workstation and/or has not yet been accepted into the next workstation queue. Idle time is the most critical area in material flow because an abated authority over the job exists—the preceding authority regards the job as being completed, but the succeeding work center authority has not yet accepted the job. Idle time is a common source of overdue and "hot" jobs. Exercising control over idle time is the primary concern of a production manager.

*Cycle time* is the actual time of one operation—the time elapsed between the start of one and the beginning of the next operation. Cycle time includes operation time and transit time. Such a division of operational cycle time gives you the opportunity to keep track of various spheres of responsibility in material flow. This includes both the functional production responsibility and the interfunctional responsibility, when one production responsibility is relinquished, while the next production responsibility has not been assumed yet. Material handling a nonvalue-adding function is involved in the interfunctional responsibility stage.

The sum of setup time and run time is considered machine time—the time a job spends on a machine. The machine time is a productive, value-adding element of operation.

All other elements of lead time and cycle time are the time a job spends outside a machine. Queue time, wait time, and idle time are nonproductive elements of operation. In a job shop, such nonproductive tasks constitute up to 90 percent of lead time.

One of the main tasks in devising an efficient plan is to reduce lead time through the reduction or elimination of nonvalue-adding operation's elements. For example, intensifying workers' efforts and speeding up the work tempo may reduce the total operations lead time by about 10 percent, but eliminating some of the nonproductive operation's tasks can result in substantially larger reduction of lead time and cycle time.

### Assigning Responsibility During Operation Lead Time and Cycle Time

Control over lead time depends on the proper delegation of responsibility over the elements of operation lead time. Two segments of lead time correspond directly to two types of functional responsibility, namely, production responsibility and material handling responsibility. Areas of responsibility are illustrated in Figure 5-3. Functional responsibilities are obvious and easily traced.

Wait time and idle time, collectively termed slack time, have a decisive influence on operations lead time. Interfunctional responsibility takes place during slack time. Slack time is a decision-making time when the functional responsibility over jobs is relinquished, and the decision is made on how the job will be moved to next assignment. These are the areas of interfunctional responsibility. Interfunctional responsibility is the responsibility of production planning and control. In advanced manufacturing systems, programmed decision making addresses areas of interfunctional responsibility.

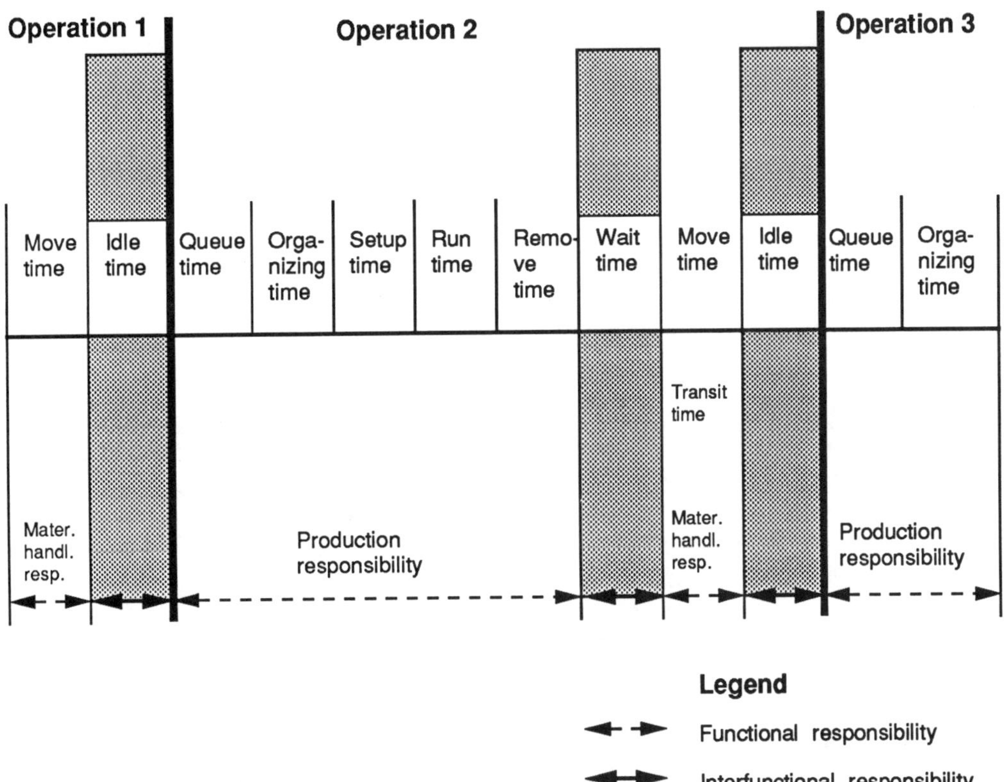


**Figure 5-3**
**The Operation Lead Time Responsibility**

## USING THE TECHNIQUES OF OPERATIONAL PRODUCTION PLANNING TO MAXIMIZE SHOP FLOOR PRODUCTIVITY

The *material requirements planning* (MRP) ordering system provides input to your shop floor execution stage where detailed operations scheduling and machine loading takes place. Previously, you have successfully laid out your production plans. Now it is time to put your plans into actions. The shop floor stage is where the actual product is produced. The viability of your plans is determined by your shop floor execution.

### Understanding the Stages of Production Planning

Planning can be divided into two stages: planning performed before your production takes place called *preproduction planning*, and planning performed at your execution stage, or *production planning*. Altogether there are three planning stages: *preproduction planning*, planning of logistics and integrated planning and control system and developing management information systems (MIS), *production planning*, aggregate planning, master production scheduling (MPS), and materials planning, and *material flow planning*, shop floor execution, or operations planning. In Figure 5-4, three stages of production planning are collectively termed as *relational planning* (RP).

#### PREPRODUCTION PLANNING

Preproduction planning involves decision making where you should determine your organizational goals and objectives. Along with engineering and process planning, this stage should include the development of strategic production plans (for example, you should identify your product lines, the capacity required, prices, distribution channels, and the markets to be served).

Preproduction planning also includes other business considerations, such as the availability of financial resources and your marketing strategy. Your basic strategic decisions on quantity and quality levels should be made at this stage. Preproduction planning also involves the design of an integrated production system at the onset of the company or when a new product or product line is introduced.

Preproduction planning also includes the determination of the production technology to be used in your manufacturing, time standards, operational routes, management information systems; the determination of your capacity requirements and logistics, including your material handling system; and the development of the means to manage the flow of materials and the accompanying flow of information and services. Preproduction planning or balancing is characterized by applying a planned alternative of adjusting your capacity in order to keep up with demand. Now is the time for the acquisition of production lines as

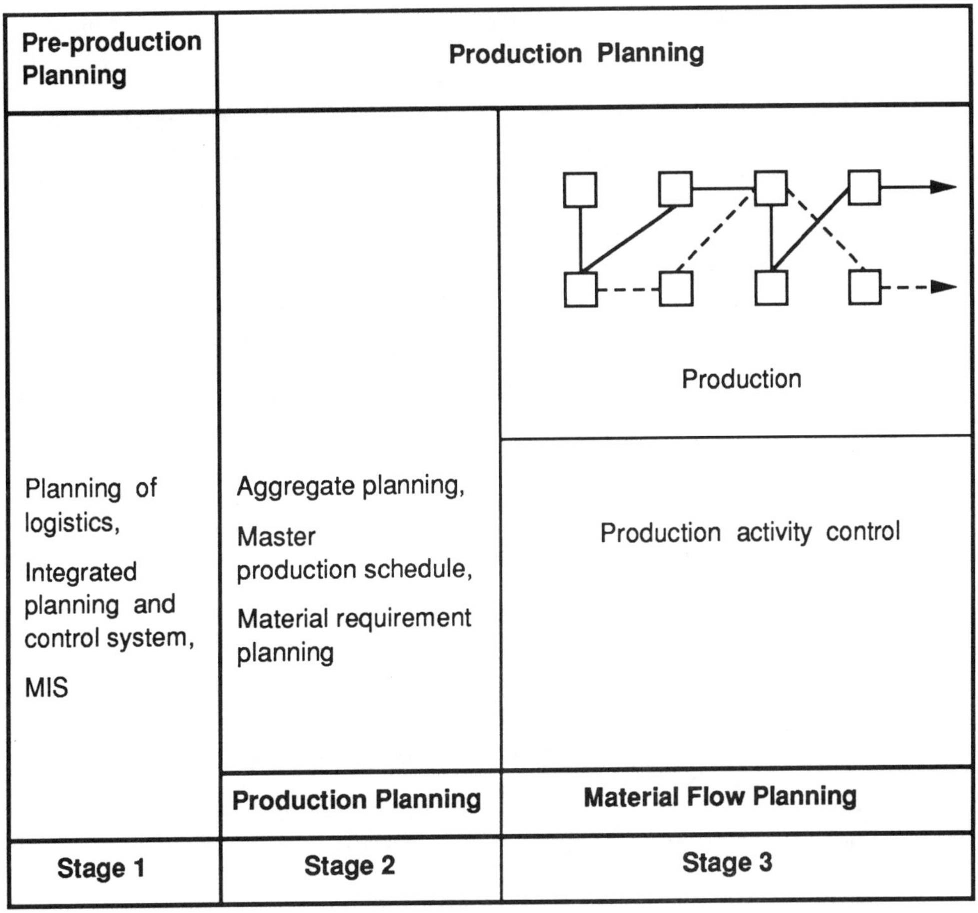

| Pre-production Planning | Production Planning | |
|---|---|---|
| | | Production |
| Planning of logistics,<br>Integrated planning and control system,<br>MIS | Aggregate planning,<br>Master production schedule,<br>Material requirement planning | Production activity control |
| | **Production Planning** | **Material Flow Planning** |
| **Stage 1** | **Stage 2** | **Stage 3** |

**Figure 5-4**
**Stages of Production Planning - Relational Planning (RP)**

called for by the increased demand or the contraction of other lines when demand declines.

PRODUCTION PLANNING

Production planning takes place after production lines are commissioned and your labor and time standards have been set, and when all the necessary product and process documentation is available and your resources are ready for production. Time restrictions apply if increased demand calls for expanding the capacity. Thus, production planning applies the second balancing alternative, namely, adjusting product requirements to correspond to the existing capacity level.

Two substages of production planning are stage 2, itemized production planning, and stage 3, operational production planning or material flow planning. In reality, material flow planning includes executional production control.

Preparatory planning stages, as is shown in stages 1 and 2 in Figure 5-4, should be completed before the flow of materials takes place. Manufacturing planning and control systems and procedures are developed and installed at the preproduction planning stage and are further utilized at the next production planning stage, the *itemized stage*, as well as at the material flow planning stage. This stage includes standards and procedures for operations planning and control as well as control over the material flow. Validated work orders are issued and production starts after production planning is accomplished. This includes the itemized production plan (stage 2) and the operational scheduling and machine loading production program plan or operations scheduling (stage 3).

Operations scheduling should be accomplished before production and production activity control (PAC) takes place and should not be done during the execution when the decentralized decision making is lacking an integrated overview of material flow. It is not possible to control something that has not been planned. Control means comparing the execution results with the performance standards, namely, production plans completed prior to production.

## The Division of Planning—Two Systems in Material Flow Planning and Control

Material flow is managed by two distinctly separate planning and control systems, which correspond directly to your dedicated and shared resources. A production control system over material flow controls your dedicated resources, supplying your workstations with raw materials and components and your operations scheduling. The supply of materials and components to workstations is controlled by inventory control planning when used with an independent demand inventory system.

A dependent demand inventory system, also known as product planning, which controls the supply of components to an assembly process, is a two-dimensional planning and control system answering two questions: "what" for example, 20 automatic distributor units (consideration is given to the component's position in the product structure), and "when" for example, 20 automatic distributor units should be available for an assembly process on April 20. Product planning and control are called *operations scheduling*. Operations scheduling applying a *Gantt chart* is shown in Figure 5-5. Production control over shared resources manages the utilization of such resources, namely machine loading.

*Operations scheduling* is a two-dimensional planning and control system answering the questions "what" and "when," while *machine loading* too is a two-dimensional planning and control system answering the questions "where" and "when." Machine loading, also known as process control, is shown in Figure 5-6. In machine loading, the priority is capacity utilization, that is, keeping machines running. In an example of machine loading, illustrated in Figure 5-6A, vertical milling machines are loaded through the beginning of May. In another example, shown in Figure 5-6B, machine 2 in the grinding

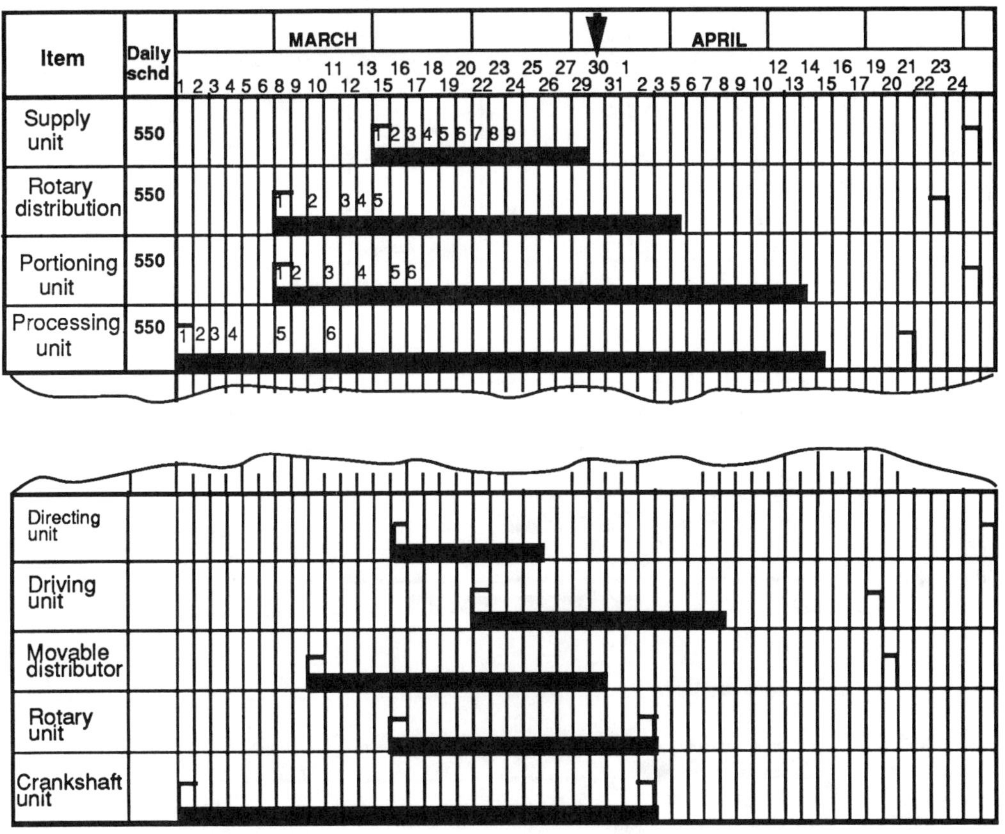


**Gantt Progress Chart for Production of a Dosing Machine**

**Figure 5-5**
**Product Planning**

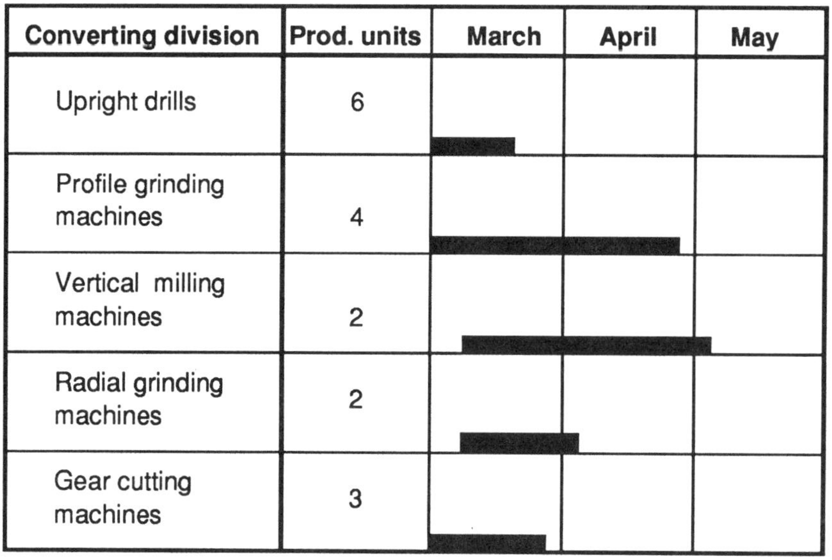

| Converting division | Prod. units | March | April | May |
|---|---|---|---|---|
| Upright drills | 6 | | | |
| Profile grinding machines | 4 | | | |
| Vertical milling machines | 2 | | | |
| Radial grinding machines | 2 | | | |
| Gear cutting machines | 3 | | | |

**A. Monthly Planning**

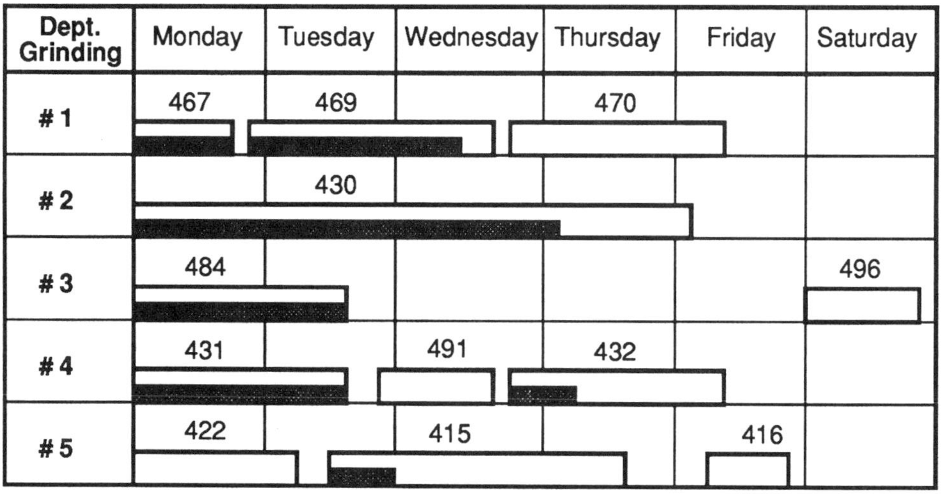

| Dept. Grinding | Monday | Tuesday | Wednesday | Thursday | Friday | Saturday |
|---|---|---|---|---|---|---|
| # 1 | 467 | 469 | | 470 | | |
| # 2 | | 430 | | | | |
| # 3 | 484 | | | | | 496 |
| # 4 | 431 | | 491 | 432 | | |
| # 5 | 422 | | 415 | | 416 | |

**B. Daily Planning**

**Figure 5-6**
**Machine Loading Applying Gantt Charts Process Planning**

department is loaded by job 430 from Monday through Friday morning, while machine 3 is available from Tuesday afternoon until Saturday.

An integrated production planning and control system includes both operations scheduling and machine loading. Integrated operations scheduling and machine loading is a three-dimensional production planning and control system providing the answer to three questions: "what," "when," and "where."

## AN ANALYSIS OF PRODUCTION STAGES—TWO DEGREES OF PLANNING

All planning stages—aggregate planning, MPS, MRP, and PAC—can be organized either as first-degree or second-degree planning.

### The First Degree of Planning: Rudimentary Planning

The first degree of planning is rudimentary planning which does not involve product and process balancing. It is centered on one concept only, either product planning or process planning.

Planning of raw materials or purchased components for the availability at a specific due date, or planning internal operations by identifying components' due dates based on BOM and route sheet information, could be cited as an example of the first-degree planning. First-degree planning is conducted successfully by applying, for example, the classic Gantt charts. Here, the objective of planning is to highlight the product priorities and scheduling of components' due dates or the MRP-based itemized operations schedule. Product-based first-degree planning is usually performed by material controllers and expeditors. Process planning is similar to first-degree planning where the objective is to plan and control the utilization of machines.

Such first-degree process planning is often performed at the shop floor, by the departmental or supervisory staff. The objective is to achieve maximum equipment utilization—machine loading. Machine loading is also readily planned on a Gantt chart. Machine loading is performed by both departmental planners and supervisory staff. Separately, scheduling and machine loading cannot be regarded as production planning since only one concept is involved, either product or process, and the balancing is not taking place. First-degree planning is a two-dimensional production planning system.

### The Second Degree of Planning: Integrated Operational Scheduling and Machine Loading

Second-degree planning is performed when more than one concept is considered, that is, when planning is conducted across product and process lines. Second-degree planning is an integrated operational scheduling and machine loading, where product requirements are expressed in the units of machine- and labor-hours per operation and process limitations are expressed in the congruent operational units. This operational optimization is an essential task in production control. The lack of well-developed operational optimization techniques has led to numerous failures in MRP installations and currently is preventing manufacturers from applying JIT.

Problems often occur when machine loading, performed as first-degree planning, is expected to fulfill the function of product and process balancing, which is basically second-degree planning. Initially, product planning, as well as process planning, is structured as first-degree planning. The master production schedule and MRP are first-degree planning because only the product priority is considered there. The next, second stage, integrated operations scheduling and machine loading, is a three-dimensional production planning and control system providing the answer to three questions: "what," "when," and "where." So you see, second-degree planning is a critical activity in any production planning and control system when productivity improvements and cost reduction are targeted.

## The Need for Material Flow Planning

Let's take another look at our Precision Mold & Tool Co. in Figure 5-6B. There are two scheduling options available in the example. *Option 1* is to look for any job to fill the gap on machine 3 in the grinding department (this is first-degree planning), or *option 2* would be to determine where jobs are assigned according to work order priorities (this is second-degree planning). Second-degree planning requires more comprehensive information than first-degree planning, namely, the information concerning both product and process.

Each step in the material flow is an individual operation requiring two distinctive production support tasks: supplying a workstation with raw materials or components (product control) and assigning a job to a workstation (process control). *Product control* is accomplished by material controllers managing both independent and dependent demand inventory systems. *Process control* is performed by foremen or departmental planners. The supply of components to workstations and the assembly processes through integrated product and process planning and control results from time-phased operational scheduling and machine loading. This is three-dimensional production planning.

In Figure 5-7, material flow planning (MFP) and control are shown as comprising two planning tasks: product control and process control. There the priority of each job is taken into consideration when assigning jobs to workstations (for example, a hot job is scheduled ahead of regular ones).

Both material controllers who are responsible for availability of components, and departmental supervisors, who are responsible for process control, are driven by their particular, often contradictory, objectives. When a compromise is reached,

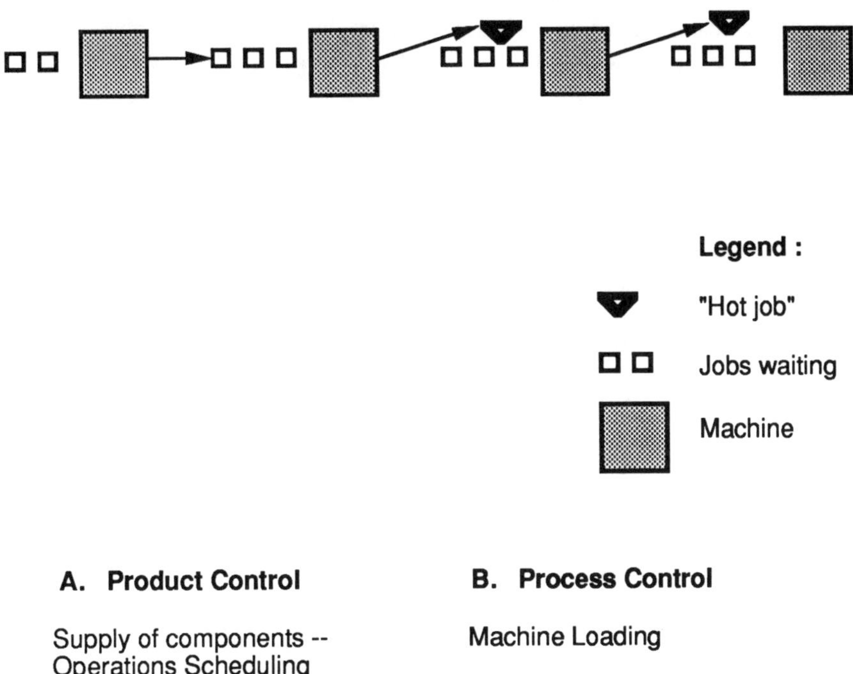


**Figure 5-7**
**Material Flow Planning and Control: Two Planning Tasks**

it is not always the optimum solution because the people involved have information related only to their particular tasks.

Multiple authorities obliterate responsibility, and this lack of allocated responsibility can be seen as one single reason for deficiency in production systems. Employees responsible for a product often blame the process staff for the late deliveries. The process staff, in turn, is unable to identify product priorities in the intermittent material flow when the intermediate operations' due dates are not identified by production planning prior to the execution.

You should have an allocated authority whose responsibilities include ensuring a smooth flow through the centralized and integrated product and process planning and control. Achieving this product and process priority is possible through proper operational planning and control. Decisions on assigning jobs to machines should rest with the departmental supervisory staff, within the constraints set up by centralized planning. Shop floor personnel assigning jobs to particular machines can perform two-dimensional process planning when they consider the utilization of capacity as a primary priority overriding other considerations, or they can perform three-dimensional production planning when the consideration is given to both product and process priorities.

## USING STRUCTURAL CONTROL TO ELIMINATE FOULUPS

Production planning and control that is directed at controlling components predominantly at their storage place is called *structural control* or *structural management*. Structural control focuses on the physical elements of the product structure—the elements of BOM, namely, parts and components. These are basically inventory-type manufacturing systems, with the emphasis at stores control rather than at shop floor material flow control.

The basic objective of structural control is to ensure a constant supply of components to your assembly processes. Often due dates verification takes place at the stores, thus failing to monitor the intermediate departments operational due dates.

MRP is a good example of structural control—a plan which oversees the availability of physical parts and assembly units. Structural control is associated with the practice of controlling in-process inventories and their expediting. Structural control is a direct result of the difficulties experienced in controlling numerous intermittent machining routes throughout the production stages. The greater the number of parts and work centers involved in your process, the more cumbersome it becomes to trace any particular item at any given time. Consequently, some companies' solution is to relieve the task of controlling numerous intermittent operational routes by exercising control in the terminus of all routes—the intermediate and assembly stores.

Structural control diminishes responsibility and accountability. When the stores detect that the components are missing, it is often very difficult to pinpoint the location of that item in the shop. When it is not coordinated, an intermittent material flow results in an increased level of in-process inventory. This increased amount of WIP makes it difficult to know the precise location of a specific job at any specific time.

Such deviations can be adjusted once a planning and control system is in place by checking the items as they proceed through the consecutive production stages. If no such tracking production procedure exists, production control over the material flow is a structural, store-based control. The control here is simply the assertion of the item being in the store at the time of enquiry, or the assertion of it being somewhere along the operational route.

Structural control does not assist the job shop staff in identifying job priorities and outlining operational schedules because it takes place when components should be completed. Such a controlling practice is dealing with past events and accomplished operations, if at all possible, often leading to a confusion, since it is usually too late to adjust a deviation from the plan when the items are already past due. As the result, structural control merely exposes overdue items, without any means for adjusting the material flow.

## THE SIGNIFICANCE OF A PRODUCT MIX WHEN COMPILING A PRODUCTION PROGRAM

Customer demand is the crucial factor in defining any good production program. Manufacturing companies widely diversify the range of manufactured products in order to provide better service and to become more competitive. Thus, a capacity profile becomes a multifaceted setup striving to accommodate a constellation of supported products.

In make-to-order companies, distinguished by a diversified capacity, it is not feasible to base production planning and control solely on product requirements, as it is with MRP and other inventory-control-type systems. Unbalanced machines and labor utilization increases the product cost, due to the fact that the production program was conceived not by the considerations of the capacity profile but by the customer order. Quite often, the product mix differs significantly from the capacity profile resulting in reduced productivity and efficiency.

One factory planner states: "We have a good planning system, whereby customer orders are lined up as they arrive, and in this sequence we release them to production one by one." This is based on the "first-come, first-serve" priority rule widely used due to its simplicity and perceived fairness to a customer. But there is a need to pay more attention to the productivity level and cost reduction by planning a better product mix at the master production scheduling stage. This can be achieved by balancing your product mix with capacity profile at MPS level by making use of rough-cut capacity planning.

Equipment underutilization, which is inevitable in the job shop environment, should be predetermined and planned. It should not be haphazard. In most modern high-performance manufacturing systems, underload situations are recognized in advance and the means are available to handle such situations without affecting the production program and without reducing the productivity. Flexible manufacturing systems demonstrate that underutilized equipment does not necessarily lead to an idle labor force. Flexible manufacturing systems are discussed further in Chapter 11.

## MAKING THE MOST OF PRODUCTION AND PLANNED OPERATIONS

There are two types of operations: production operations and planning operations. A *production operation* is a step in production for which a new tool and, consequently, setup time is required. Several production operations/tasks can be run in a sequence on the same machine. A *planned operation* includes one or several tasks performed in a row on the same machine. A planned operation is such an operation where the assignment to a machine should be conducted. For the purposes of planning, several production operations are regarded as a *single operation* if they run on the same machine because the assignment to this machine is done only once. For example, assembly-line production requires one planning operation as only one decision is made on assigning jobs to the first workstation in the assembly line.

### Using Planning Operations in a Process Industry or Assembly-Line Production

For the purpose of production planning and control, a production line or an assembly line can be regarded as a single workstation, despite the fact that it often is a major capital investment and is manned by a large labor force. This is illustrated in Figure 5-8. A production line or assembly-line production has been programmed or balanced at the preproduction stage when the line was designed. Thus the major task of a production line or assemblyl-ine production is to ensure a smooth uninterrupted supply of components to workstations. This is a dedicated resources control system.

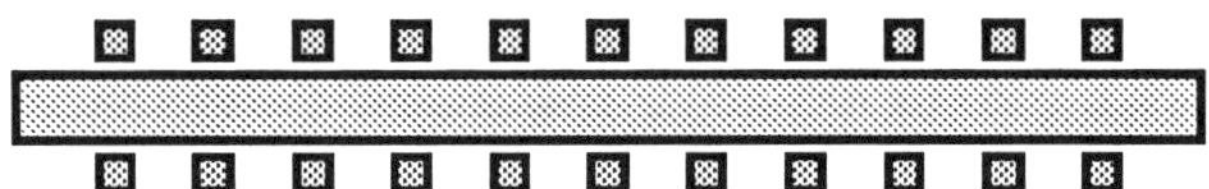

**Assembly Line**

**Figure 5-8**
**Assembly Line -- One Planned Operation**

## How Production Planning Relates to the Three Productivity Levels—$P_{max}$, $P_{pl}$, and $P_{act}$

The function of production planning is defined as setting the limits for manufacturing operations. Hence, the function of production control is to monitor production activities and to ensure they occur according to plan. It is difficult to separate production planning and control functions, and the best results are achieved by integrating planning and control into a unified production management control system. In an efficient and well-organized planning system, it should be possible to forecast the performance indices, such as the product cost, the productivity level, and the degree of plant utilization, while, at the same time, being able through operations scheduling to foresee the bottlenecks and to suggest the alternatives for "critical situations." In a production planning system, MRP itemized planning is followed by a scheduling of individual operations at work centers.

Performance limits, measured by such indices as product cost, profit, productivity, and lead time, are set up not during execution but by planning. Invariably, the execution is not able to surpass these planned productivity levels, and the task of production control is to minimize the deviation from the plan. These limits for product performance indices are planned when the production program is conceived and *cannot be exceeded* when the production program is put into effect, without a profound detriment to other orders and the entire program. One component completed ahead of the schedule does not mean that the entire order will be completed earlier than scheduled. Another component may be held up somewhere along the route, thus invalidating the progress achieved at other work centers. Hence, the significance and the role of production control are in close adherence to the standards laid down by planning. It is a function of production control to detect deviations from the established standards. Graphically, productivity levels in various planning and control systems are illustrated in Figure 5-9. As shown, productivity levels correlate directly with type of production: line production (planning type I) or job shop production (planning types II, III, and IV).

The main productivity rate levels are defined as follows:

$P_{max}$ is the maximum possible productivity, obtained by the dovetailing production facilities with product requirements. A balanced moving assembly line can serve as an example.

$P_{pl}$ is planned productivity, laid down by planning, within the framework of existing facilities and the customer orders load. $P_{pl}$ is an established productivity limit, which cannot be exceeded when the production program is being executed. For example, if the MPS plan envisages production of 12 units for product A, 190 units for product B, and 160 units for product C, then any other combination will result in a lower productivity.

$P_{act}$ is the actual productivity achieved. $P_{act}$ seldom exceeds $P_{pl}$. In a job shop, increasing $P_{act}$ can be accomplished at a workstation or a work

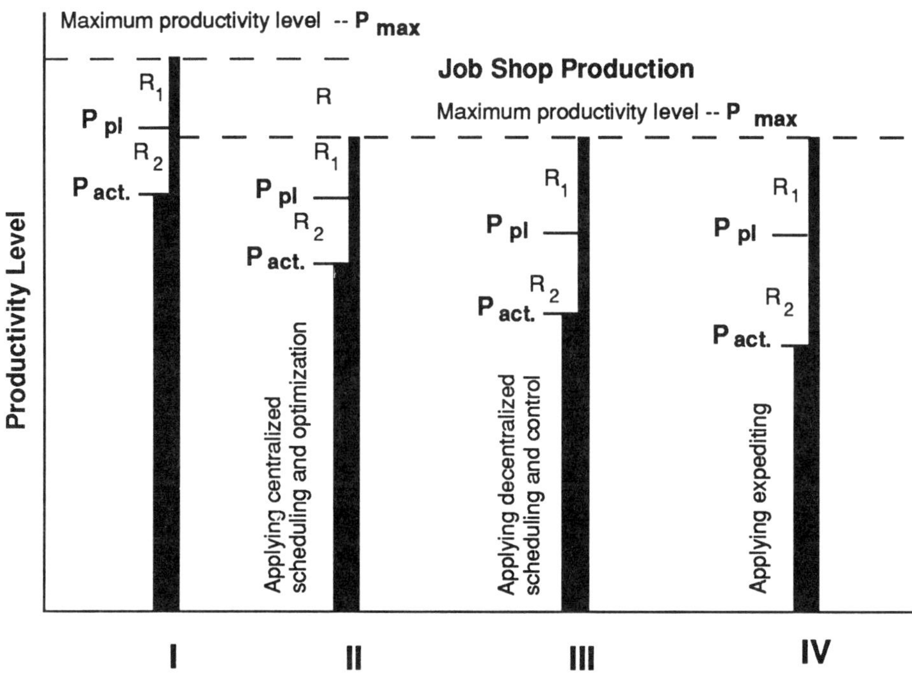


**Figure 5-9**
**How Various Planning and Control Approaches Affect the Productivity Level**

center, but increasing $P_{act}$ for the entire production program will require a concerted and coordinated effort of the entire set of facilities, namely, increasing the summarized orders output.

The deviations from the productivity rate levels are denoted as follows:

*Productivity reduction R* is the reflection of the line production being balanced so that there is no queue time, wait time, and idle time, distinguished from job shop production.

*Productivity reduction* $R_1$ is due to the disparity in order requirements and facilities. $R_1$ is the difference between $P_{max}$ and $P_{pl}$ or $R_1 = P_{max} - P_{pl}$.

$R_1$ is an indicator of the effectiveness of planning in selecting the product mix. Productivity reduction $R_1$ in line production occurs due to changing production from one order to another, and the need for resetting the production line.

*Productivity reduction* $R_2$ is the difference between $P_{pl}$ and $P_{act}$. $R_2$ is the result of production activities and the effectiveness of production control and is also affected by customer order changes and interferences requiring replanning. Productivity reduction $R_2$ in line production is the result of variations in production, largely due to equipment breakdowns.

The function of production is to ensure the minimum deviations from the established limit of productivity rate. Major efforts at present are directed toward improving $P_{act}$ through decreasing $R_2$ thereby improving production control. At the same time, however, a more significant factor, $P_{pl}$, does not receive the attention it deserves.

There is a need for establishing a production system applying more accurate product and process balancing techniques, an even material flow, standardized priority rules, and detailed scheduling and machine loading.

Often production planning is found to be concerned with larger issues of production programs, inadvertently omitting operations planning from the list of their priorities. The function of production control is to detect deviations from programs and to advise the planners who will then reschedule the operations. However, replanning affects the planned indices and should, therefore, be exercised with caution.

### INTERFUNCTIONAL CONTROL

Interfunctional control means rescheduled work orders and therewith reduced $P_{pl}$, which contributes to a reduction of $P_{act}$. This situation can be improved by applying preventive planning and execution production control.

### EXECUTIONAL CONTROL

Executional control is directed at adjusting the performance to the existing plans without changing $P_{pl}$. Execution control should not be confused with the corrective expediting type of shop control or management by crisis, where the itemized production plan and operational production plans are not established prior to production—planning type IV.

Production control systems monitor the adherence of execution to $P_{pl}$. In some instances, production control is associated with even more costly and not so effective methods of dispatching and expediting. The alternative to developing a dispatching and production control system is to increase the value of $P_{pl}$ via more effective planning techniques, particularly using detailed operational scheduling and machine loading.

This provides the execution with a valuable standard of performance. There are two consecutive steps to increase $P_{pl}$:

1. identifying the *optimum product mix* based on which the MPS is compiled
2. performing individual *operations scheduling, machine loading,* and *optimization*

The objective is to attain in a job shop the degree of efficiency, consistency, and control of operations and business decisions comparable to that of a well-balanced production-line facility. Examples of such production exist in Just-in-Time manufacturing systems.

## OPERATIONAL PLANNING AND CONTROL—GETTING DOWN TO THE NUTS AND BOLTS

Itemized production control identifies starting and finishing dates for building components. Operations scheduling and machine loading follow MRP itemized planning and involve establishing a timetable for performing individual operations and assigning these jobs to individual machines. Establishing intermediate operations due dates is essential for efficient material flow control. The most complex and responsible task in a hierarchical planning system, namely, operational planning and control and optimization of elementary intermittent operations, is assigned to shop departmental planners and the supervisory staff.

The job shop schedule is the result of decisions of the dispersed shop floor personnel. These decisions are made independently of one another on the basis of information available to each supervisor with the due consideration to departmental priorities concerned with the maximizing equipment utilization. The resulting shop schedules thus may deviate from the organizational objectives. Considering the significance of this task, it should not be abdicated and should be made an important part of production management commitments.

The best manufacturing planning and control systems are those in which a great deal of attention is paid to details (for example, planning of each single task in the material flow). A production planning and control system should not be disrupted by issuing MRP time-phased work orders, even if these orders are verified by capacity requirements planning.

*Production activity control* (PAC) should be an integral part of any production planning and control system, including operations planning and control. Job shop scheduling and control deal with many customized orders for which time and work standards are not immediately available. This causes an unpredictable material flow with some jobs running behind schedule. Further, it is difficult to identify these overdue jobs whenever operational due dates are not defined.

A large number of unstructured operational intermittent routes results in queueing lines because on some machines, there are more jobs than they can handle. Numerous random deviations such as machine breakdowns, absenteeism, and variations in material availability can make even the best optimized operational schedule obsolete when there is insufficient operational control of material flow.

Characteristics of material flow affect the planning and control procedure to a greater extent than previously has been assumed. For the purpose of planning and control, the majority of manufacturing companies, including many of high-volume manufacturing companies, should be treated as job shops due to the fact that at one stage or another, the material flow there has an intermittent pattern. Figure 5-10 illustrates an example of high-volume production so typical to many manufacturing companies. In the figure, five production and functional work centers (work centers 1, 2, 3, 4, and 5) each comprising of various number of workstations produce components for intermediate assembly lines (assembly lines 1 and 2) and the final assembly line. In Figure 5-10, these production units are exhibited in section 1—the actual production plant layout.

Section B of Figure 5-10 illustrates a plant layout used for production planning and control. There, each workstation in production and functional departments is a single planning object, as well as assembly lines, as the assembly lines are balanced at the preproduction stage, so that all its workstations produce a single output. Therefore, all these production units, individual workstations and the assembly lines require a single assignment decision as well as a single product and process balancing consideration. Continuous production applies to assembly lines, but the component fabrication is done in work centers where the intermittent material flow takes place. Although many problems discussed here are concerned with job shops, they are also relevant to other production organizations which find comfort in not being intermittent-type production in a scholarly sense of this term. Achieving an uninterrupted material flow is the main objective of all job shop planning. The task is to develop standard procedures outlining how decentralized material flow planning should comply with the organizational strategy. Developing planning standards and responsibilities for the job shop material flow should be concluded at the preproduction planning stage, along with operating procedures of how to coordinate departmental decisions when assigning jobs to workstations. The key issue is to make it all work together so that material flow is not interrupted. Operations scheduling, therefore, becomes extremely important in accomplishing smooth and balanced material flow.

## WHY IS THE OPERATIONAL SCHEDULING REQUIRED?

Some companies are reluctant to conduct detailed operational control due to its seemingly high cost and ineffectiveness in controlling intermittent operations. It is argued that it is not possible to predict the pattern of job completions and job arrivals in a job shop. But there are many reasons for job shop operations requiring detailed operational scheduling and control:

1. Plant and labor specialization requires a steady material flow, free of interferences and interruptions. Also, job shop activities involve a variety of interdependent jobs where intermittent routes become "interlocked," creating a complex multiproduct network of operations. A delay in a

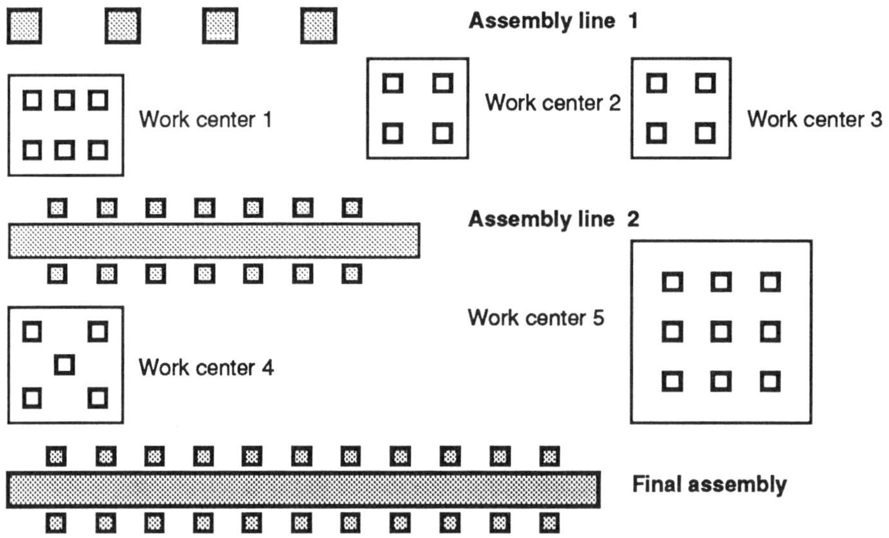

A. The Actual Production Plant Layout

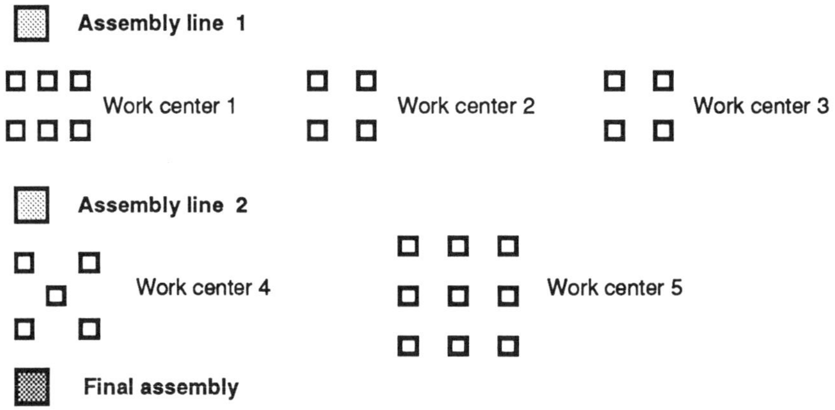

B. The Plant Layout Used for Production Planning and Control
(Assembly lines are treated as single workstations)

**Figure 5-10**
**An Example of High-Volume Production Applying Job Shop Planning and Control**

single operation of one product disrupts other work orders upon expedition. A productivity improvement through smoothing the material flow can be achieved only by the detailed scheduling, machine loading, and production control procedures. Job shop can continuously benefit from an operational production control procedure once set up.

2. Any departmental intermissions should be taken into account, since a production program is executed throughout the network of work centers. Centralized information about the material flow should be made available to the supervisory staff responsible for operational planning in order to enable them to perform their task efficiently.
3. In a job shop, overdue jobs are usually expedited by overtime, by subcontracting, or by postponing the less urgent orders. These measures seem to provide the solution. However, overtime affects quality, productivity, and production cost, while it not always brings the desired increased output. In fact, one fixture components manufacturer has reported a decline in the total output when the company chose overtime as the solution to increasing customer orders. The actual output per month has dropped to 28 tons since the 11- to 12-hour workday was introduced as compared with the standard rate of 32 tons with a regular 8-hour schedule.

Provided that the wage rate for overtime hours is usually 1.5 times the regular one, overtime is the least desired management decision among all the available alternatives. Productivity variations occur during overtime in these tasks which depend on a worker's physical efforts. Figure 5-11 shows that the workers' energy is highest during middle-shift hours and declines toward the end of the shift. In the overtime situation, workers tend to conserve energy for longer hours. In worker-paced operations, where productivity depends on a worker's physical and mental efforts, the physical and mental fatigue attributed to overtime reduces workers' energy and affects productivity. Overtime can be rational in a machine-paced operation where workers operate an automatic or semiautomatic machine set up for a fixed hourly rate.

4. So-called low-priority orders merely appear as such, while they are, in fact, of primary importance as far as the production program and process control are concerned. Although it is possible to postpone some work orders to meet obligations to another selected customer, this is unacceptable from the perspective of the production resource utilization program. Work orders are an integral part of the production program, and any changes in the program will reduce the $P_{max}$ productivity level.
5. Job shop capacities cannot be expanded in the short term, and thus they are accepted to be of a fixed value. An increase in the output and a reduction of the production cost can be achieved by ensuring an uninterrupted material flow and by optimizing the utilization of shared resources by performing operational scheduling and machine loading. Joe Spence of

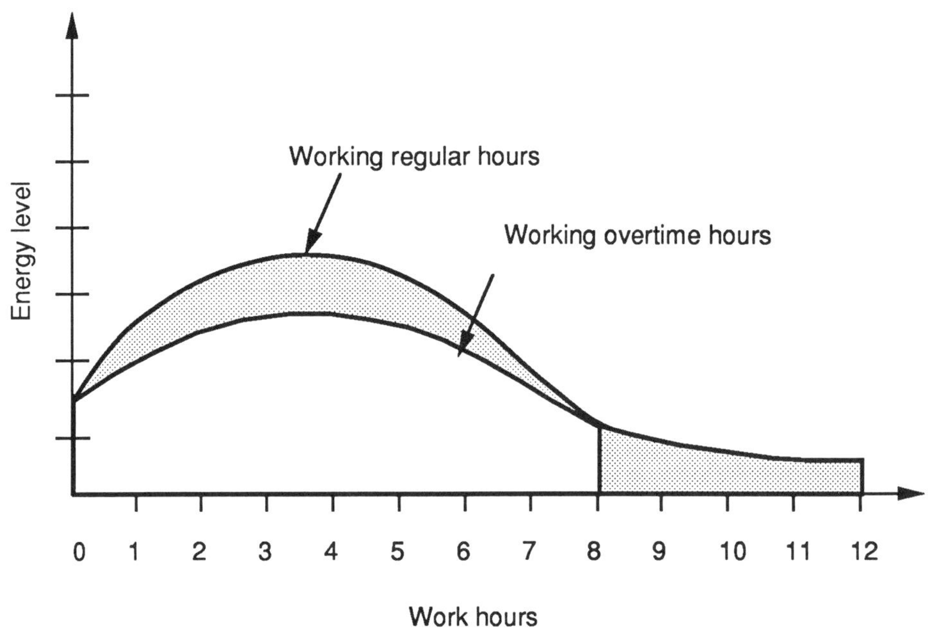


**Figure 5-11**
**The Distribution of Worker's Energy During Work**

T. D. Williamson, Inc., a piping equipment manufacturer, says in this regard that what many experts would have defined as an industry-acceptable MRP shop floor and capacity management solution proved inadequate in addressing many of the dynamic elements of the factory.

## WHAT'S YOUR CAPACITY? USING INFINITE AND FINITE MACHINE LOADING

Capacity refers to an ability to produce. According to *The Official Dictionary of American Production and Inventory Control Society*, capacity is "The highest reasonable output rate which can be achieved with the current product specifications, product mix, work force, plant, and equipment." Two approaches to capacity planning are backward scheduling using infinite loading and forward scheduling applying finite loading.

## Infinite Loading

Loading to infinite capacity means loading work centers without regard to their available capacity. Loading to infinite capacity is a product-focused production planning activity having components due dates as the main consideration. Loading to infinite capacity is the feature of many MRP-based production planning systems.

Infinite loading is applied in the frequent shifting of open-end orders to later or earlier due dates. In the instance where an order due date is shifted, there is a need to also move all the components' due dates to correspond to the final product due date. Open-end order due date changes are done within the specific flexible time fence. The reassignment should be accomplished as a single block of parts of the end item without changing the BOM-based time-phased linkage arrangement. Infinite loading assumes that production capacity limits can be overrun when it is required, and thus it creates overloading and underloading of capacity and causes many problems.

Infinite loading is usually done by applying operation-by-operation scheduling in the backward scheduling direction, starting with the final due date and assigning jobs to machines based on normal lead time in the reverse order of operational sequence. Infinite loading is first-degree structural planning because the priority is given to the product only. Infinite loading can achieve zero inventory production at the expense of the uniform plant loading. Infinite loading for a milling work center is illustrated in Figure 5-12. There, loading is done without regard to capacity level: time periods 2, 3, 5, 8, and 10 are overloaded while there is an excess of capacity at time periods 1, 4, 6, 7, and 9.

Infinite loading typical to backward scheduling is product focused in that it does not pay attention to overloading of facilities but merely indicates when each operation should take place. For a final balancing, backward scheduling is usually followed by operation-by-operation forward finite loading.

## Finite Loading

Finite loading means assigning jobs to work centers within a realistic capacity level, available in each time period. Jobs are not scheduled for the time periods when a work center's capacity is already assigned. Finite loading applies the operation-by-operation scheduling technique in a forward scheduling direction. Finite loading is illustrated in Figure 5-13. There, the capacity load does not exceed its maximum level.

Often, for the purpose of capacity balancing, finite loading is conducted as a second round of planning after the backward infinite loading. This is called *load leveling*. Production planning should take into consideration both product priorities (the timely completion of all the parts and components enforcing zero inventory) and process priorities (the maximum equipment and labor utilization).

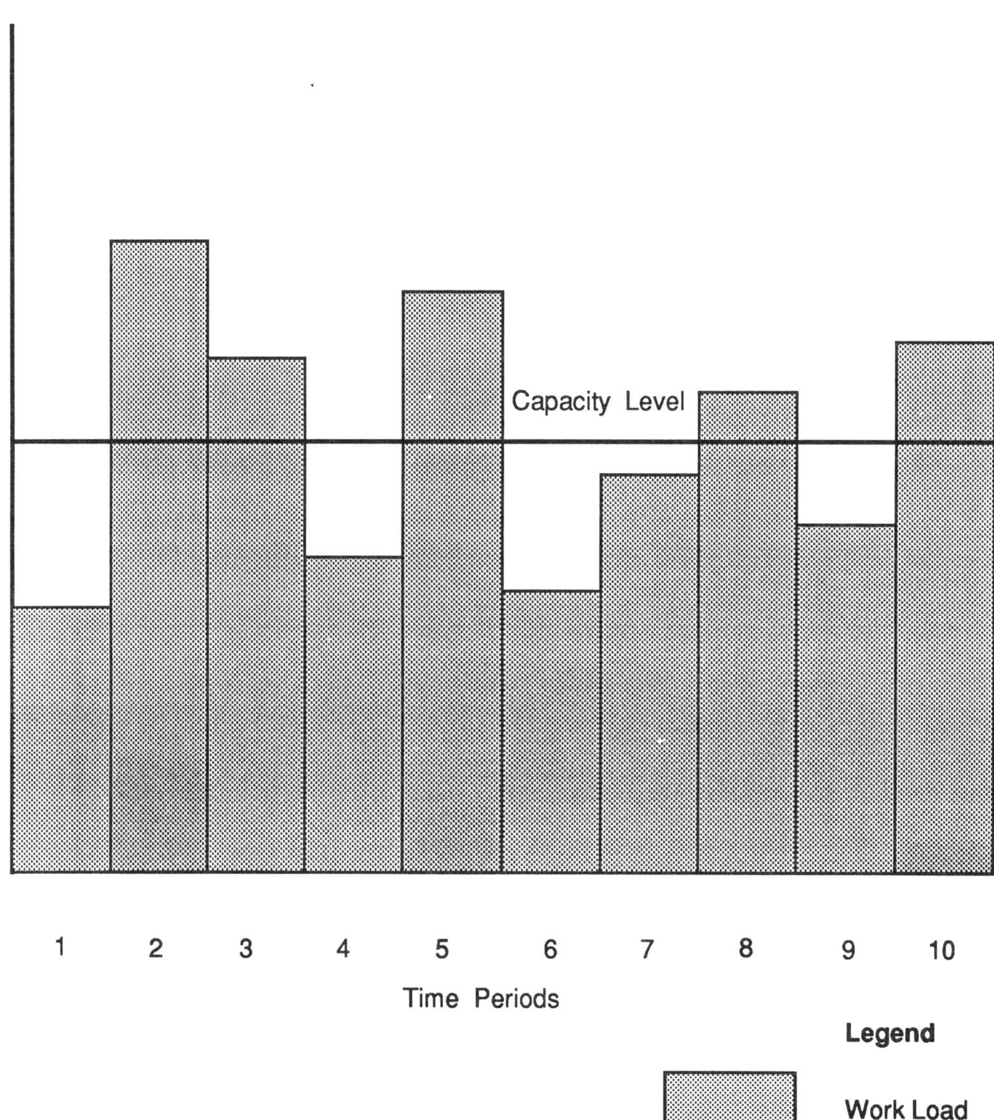


**Figure 5-12**
**Infinite Loading -- Milling Work Center**

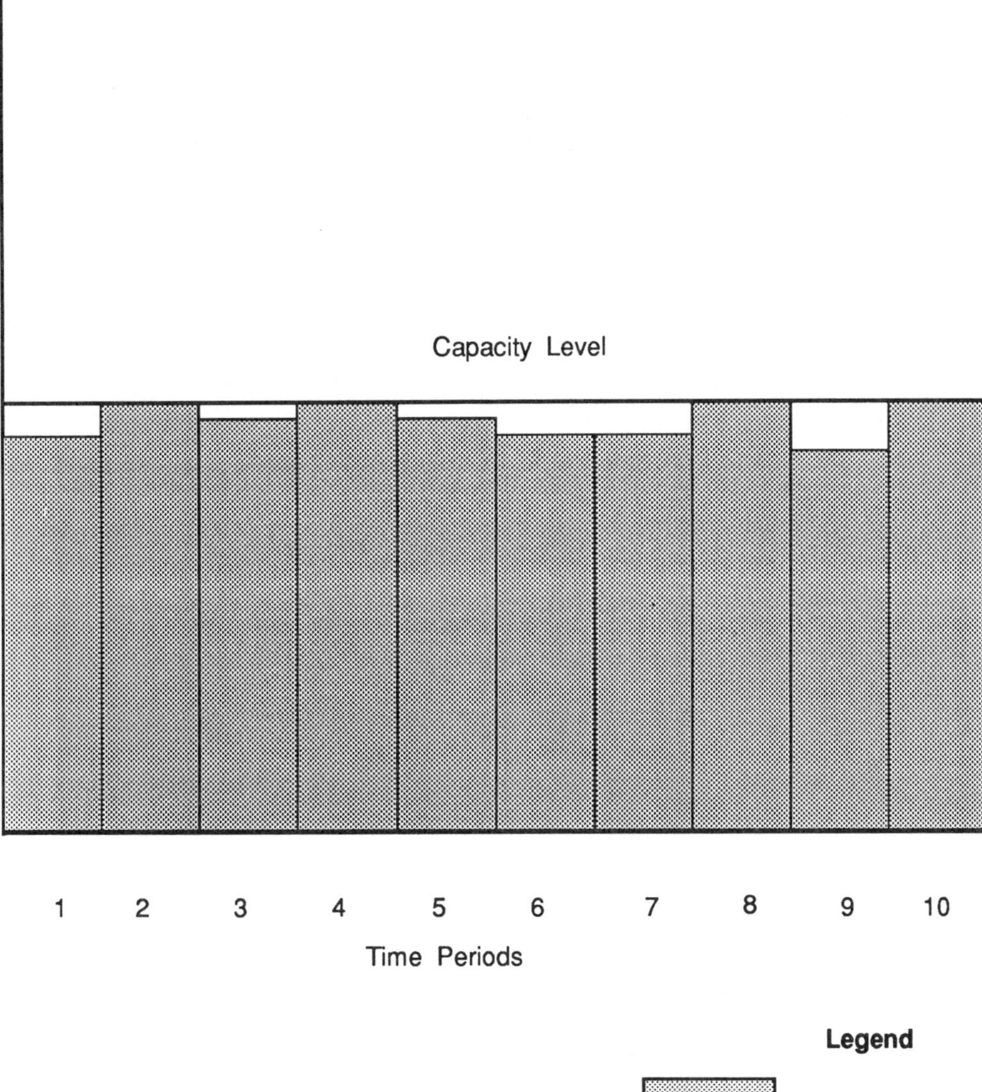


**Figure 5-13**
**Finite Loading -- Milling Work Center**

Finite loading appears to be second-degree planning which takes into consideration both product priority and equipment priority. This is true when finite loading is centralized throughout all departments. When finite loading is done for a single department, without considering the disposition in other departments affected by this loading, this is considered the first-degree planning. Machine loading is an activity which can integrate product requirements with process limitations and, therefore, should be approached as the second-degree planning.

Loading to finite capacity is easy in repetitive production where it is possible to plan a balanced load. In a well-organized planning system, to plan a balanced load means to load 15 to 20 percent below the capacity limit in order to make provision for any contingency or delay (for example, a machine breakdown or an unexpected "hot" job). As the schedule approaches the starting execution date, it requires constant reexamining of capacity and filling up reserves with job assignments. Finite forward scheduling results in a better, smoother material flow because it is process-focused operational planning.

Although loading to finite capacity does not always mean second-degree integrated product and process planning, it has many features and characteristics of this type of planning. Quite often the problem of a bottleneck capacity is resolved in a surprisingly simple way, namely, by having two to three times the capacity needed. This arrangement is possible in labor-limited flexible manufacturing systems.

So far, we've seen that in order to run efficient shop floor operations, you must make yourself aware of the various aspects of operations planning including the scheduling requirements and control. But what about your capacity? Just how much work can your shop floor handle?

## CAPACITY REQUIREMENTS PLANNING—A POSSIBLE SOLUTION?

MRP II is a two-dimensional product-focused planning system, while in a dynamic production environment, an integrated three-dimensional operational tasks planning and control is required. There is no substitute for operations scheduling. Many companies have found this out the hard way when they had attempted to run production based on *capacity requirements planning* (CRP) instead of short-term operations scheduling. CRP uses average queues and aggregate time phases, and this interferes with the job sequencing.

There are instances where CRP outlines the output needed to accomplish the master schedule for all work centers. However, some work centers are still overloaded and some are underloaded, and because each job takes a different route in the shop, it is impossible to predict the size of queues at all work centers in the future. There are hundreds of problems and several thousand jobs with which to contend. Consequently, some queues defer from the planned levels assumed by CRP, thus resulting in bottlenecks and late work orders.

The practice of expediting as a means of straightening out CRP plans also does not produce sufficiently successful results. Capacity requirements planning is back-scheduled for both planned and released orders applying infinite or finite back scheduling through routing, considering the order quantity, machine time, and queueing time. Nevertheless, computers are not able to foresee the disposition on a shop floor at the time of execution.

CRP is conducted in two stages: Primary CRP and Final CRP. Primary CRP generates an unleveled capacity plan based on the route sheet sequence of operations and does not take into consideration work center loads—the infinite loading.

Final CRP has a pattern of leveled capacity planning which takes into consideration the present capacity level—finite loading. Leveling capacity entails shifting operations to other time periods when the equipment is overloaded. Leveling of capacity is performed in two steps: backward infinite loading, *first pass*, followed by forward finite loading, *second pass*.

Figure 5-14 shows an example of the load-leveled capacity requirements planning performed at CAMCO Tool Co. The unleveled capacity requirements planning report for the same work center has been shown previously in Chapter 4, Figure 4-27.

As you can see in the figure, operations are assigned to specific machines against the time scale. The leveled capacity planning ensures that there is no overlap in the use of equipment. In the initial CRP report shown in Figure 4-27, there is an overloaded capacity through weeks 1, 2, and 3. This situation is rectified in the scheduled capacity report shown in Figure 5-14, where the capacity overload is eliminated. This CRP planning includes pegging up to end items and rescheduling the master production schedule.

## WHY YOU SHOULD CONSIDER ELAPSED TIME BETWEEN PLANNING AND EXECUTION

It seems that CRP-based operational schedules are sufficient for shop floor execution. In reality, leveled capacity planning is not able to resolve capacity problems because the plan takes into account only the *present* capacity—the capacity disposition at the time of planning. This can be quite different from what it will be at the time of execution due to variations in the queueing time, waiting time, idle time, and other interruptions such as breakdowns and "hot" jobs. CRP traditional weekly slotting is not sufficient for operations scheduling. Job shop is a dynamic environment experiencing daily and even hourly changes. The intervention of a planner is required at the time closer to execution, taking into consideration different production alternatives available at the time,

```
REPORT-ID    MA610B-A                                   C A M C O   I N C O R P O R A T E D          DATE 10/04/90                PAGE
SEQUENCE   DEPARTMENT/WORK CENTER                                 HOUSTON PLANT                          TIME 04.47
                                                          SCHEDULE LOAD/CAPACITY REPORT
                                                            REPORTED IN STANDARD HOURS
              DEPARTMENT 01          MACHINE SHOP
             WORK CENTER 0141        BRIDGEPORT MILL                                  E=  .92  U=  .91           MAX UNITS   6
                                      ********************** WEEK *********************  ************* CUMULATIVE *************
WEEK  START    WORK-PLAN     UNITS   CAP   LOAD    L/C  LOAD-TO-CAPACITY RATIO     OVER    CAP   LOAD   L/C    LOAD-TO-CAPACITY R
                S  D  H     1  2  3                    0         100      200   (UNDER)                        0         100
                                                       .    .    .    .    .                                   .    .    .    .

  1  10/04/90 2  2  7.7     5  4  0  116    116   100  .XXXXXXXXX.                        116    116  100    .XXXXXXXXX.
  2  10/08/90 2  5  7.7     5  4  0  290    286    98  .XXXXXXXXX.                 -4     406    402   99    .XXXXXXXXX.
  3  10/15/90 2  5  7.7     5  4  0  290    255    87  .XXXXXXXYY                 -35     696    657   94    .XXXXXXXXY
  4  10/22/90 2  5  7.7     5  4  0  290    255    87  .XXXXXXXYY                 -35     986    912   92    .XXXXXXXXY
  5  10/29/90 2  5  7.7     5  4  0  290    197    67  .XXXXYYY                   -93    1276   1109   86    .XXXXXXXXYY
  6  11/05/90 2  5  7.7     5  4  0  290    191    65  .XXYYYYY                   -99    1566   1300   83    .XXXXXXYY
  7  11/12/90 2  5  7.7     5  4  0  290    126    43  .XYYY                     -164    1856   1426   76    .XXXXXYYY
  8  11/19/90 2  3  7.7     5  4  0  174     40    22  .XY                       -134    2030   1466   72    .XXXXXYY
  9  11/26/90 2  5  7.7     5  4  0  290     60    20  .XY                       -230    2320   1526   65    .XXXXYYY
 10  12/03/90 2  5  7.7     5  4  0  290     29    10  .X                        -261    2610   1555   59    .XXXXYY
 11  12/10/90 2  5  7.7     5  4  0  290     48    16  .XY                       -242    2900   1603   55    .XXXXYY
 12  12/17/90 2  5  7.7     5  4  0  290     67    23  .XX                       -223    3190   1670   52    .XXXYY
 13  12/26/90 2  3  7.7     5  4  0  174     46    26  .YYY                      -128    3364   1716   51    .XXXYY
 14  01/02/91 2  3  7.7     5  4  0  174     41    23  .XX                       -133    3538   1757   49    .XXXYY
 15  01/07/91 2  5  7.7     5  4  0  290     50    17  .XY                       -240    3828   1807   47    .XXXYY
 16  01/14/91 2  5  7.7     5  4  0  290     58    20  .YY                       -232    4118   1865   45    .XXXYY
 17  01/21/91 2  5  7.7     5  4  0  290     73    25  .YYY                      -217    4408   1938   43    .XXXY
 18  01/28/91 2  5  7.7     5  4  0  290     87    30  .YYY                      -203    4698   2025   43    .XXXY
 19  02/04/91 2  5  7.7     5  4  0  290     23     7  .Y                        -267    4988   2048   41    .XXYY
 20  02/11/91 2  5  7.7     5  4  0  290     19     6  .Y                        -271    5278   2067   39    .XXYY

          READY LOAD       2 DAYS  AVAIL FOR WORK                         126     HOURS AVAIL FOR WORK
          TOTAL LOAD    3784 HOURS TODAY
          SCHD. LOAD    2067 HOURS WITH RESERVED CAPACITY
          SCHED CPTY     116 HOURS CURRENT OPERATIONS
          BASIC CPTY     290 HOURS SCHED MACHINES-NO OT
          FULL  CPTY     387 HOURS ALL MACHINES-NO OT
          CURRENT  Q       0 DAYS TODAY
          AVERAGE  Q       0 PAST 3 MONTHS                                .03     ALPHA FACTOR

          LONG TERM QUEUE

          PRIORITY 0-99       100       200       300       400       500       600       700       800       900
          NR JOBS   392        84        37        46        32        48        73       102        13        28
          QUEUE       0         0         0         0         0         0         0         0         0         0
          JOB HRS  1168       266        53        71        65       207       187       137        29        63
     NON-SCHEDULED HRS 1521     4         6

          SHORT TERM QUEUE - 2 WEEKS

          PRIORITY 0-99       100       200       300       400       500       600       700       800       900
          NR JOBS    44         6        15        12        17        19        43        98        13        27
          QUEUE       1         1         0         0         0         0         0         0         0         0
          JOB HRS    88        26        15        17        17        73       101       130        29        62
```

**Figure 5-14**

**A Final Capacity Requirements Planning (CRP)**

such as running the job on a different type of machine, lot splitting, overtime, or subcontracting. Figure 5-15 illustrates elapsed time between various planning stages and execution. Less elapsed time between planning and execution means fewer deviations. The duration of the elapsed time between planning and execution is one of the most important features of production planning and control system. In production systems where the elapsed time is too long, operations scheduling is necessary prior to execution, in order to update the plan with the present capacity level.

## SUMMARY

If to be effective, operational scheduling requires the latest information about product and process priorities. Some companies use expeditors to perform such up-to-date operational control. There is a difference in the productivity level,

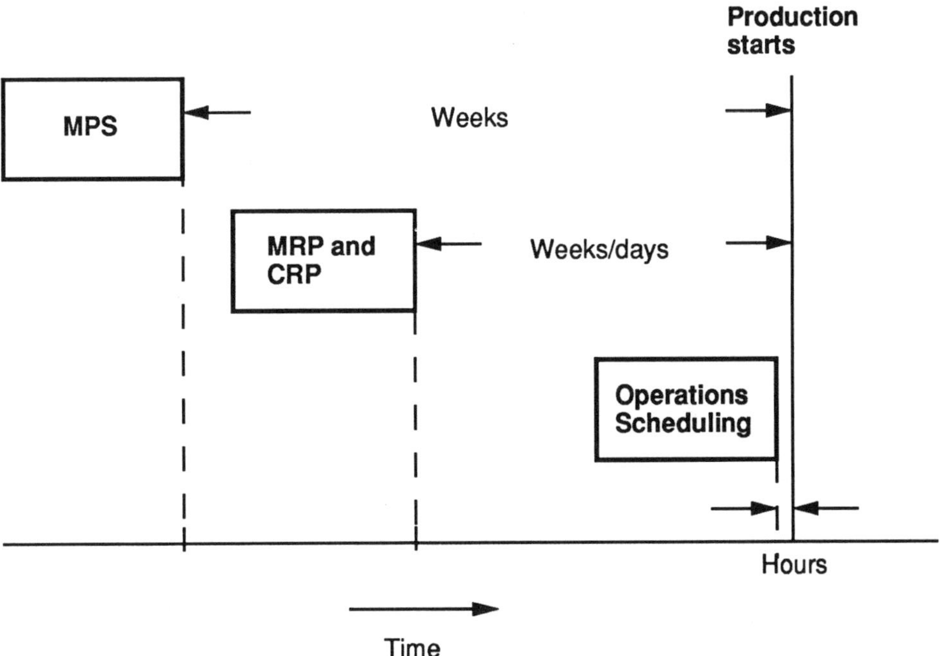


**Figure 5-15**
**Elapsed Time Between Various Planning Stages and Execution**

when production is controlled by CRP and that of operational scheduling and machine loading. Operations scheduling and machine loading is a single planning activity capable of drastically improving a material flow and reducing inventory and compressing lead time.

# 6

# Operations Scheduling and Machine Loading Techniques to Improve Job Shop Planning

A job shop consists of several production units arranged in a functional layout. Two essential features of a job shop are:

1. Production of nonstandard products in small quantities
2. Intermittent material flow

A job shop produces a large number of products comprising many parts and components, each one following a distinct operational route. An individual item may have to pass through several work centers before it is ready for assembly. In a job shop, the number of elementary operations performed at any given time can easily run into many thousands, with machine time ranging from 10 or 15 minutes to 6 or 8 hours or more. The issue of individual operations scheduling and machine loading is a complex one not only because of the great number of operations involved, but also because these operations compete for the same facilities. The problem can be formulated as the scheduling of multichannel waiting lines (consisting of individual intermittent operations) on an existing network of workstations.

Let's say that your material flow is being interrupted by pauses between operations due to restrictions imposed by your plant capacity. The material flow can be interrupted by waiting for production facilities or in waiting for manufactured or purchased items on order. Defining a job shop as an *intermittent production* is an accurate portrayal of this type of material flow.

In one way or another, any discrete type of manufacturing is organized as a job shop. The issue of job shop receives special attention in the present trend toward restructuring for production in smaller batches. Managing a job shop encompasses setting up an operational production planning and control system in order to control the points of intermission of the individual operations material flow. The productivity in job shop manufacturing can be substantially improved through more effective management of material flow. For reducing shop floor congestion, shop orders are verified and not automatically released to work centers.

Manufacturers report 20 to 25 percent increases in productivity when implementing operational planning and control.

In practice, when a scheduled job is not started on time, schedules at all the succeeding workstations will be disrupted and the job will be delayed by waiting in a queue. The interoperational time indefinitely delays and corrupts the material flow. In the example illustrated in Figure 6-1, Job 1, Part PKL-7023, is scheduled in week 1 in the Turning Department, in week 2 in the Milling Department, and in week 3 in the Grinding Department, and job 2, Part PKL-8315, is scheduled in week 1 in the Milling Department, in week 2 in the Grinding Department and in week 3 in the Turning Department. If Job 1 is delivered in the Milling Department in week 3 instead of week 2, it is further delayed as it missed its scheduled time both in the Milling Department and in the Grinding Department.

| Work Center | Week 1 | Week 2 | Week3 |
|---|---|---|---|
| Turning | Job1 | | Job 2 |
| Grinding . | | Job 2 | Job 1 |
| Milling | Job 2 | Job 1 | |

**Operations Route**

Job 1 -- part PKL - 7023 Week 1 Turning; Week 2 Milling; Week 3 Grinding

Job 2 - part PKL - 8315 Week 1 Milling; Week 2 Grinding; Week 3 Turning

**Figure 6-1**
**Scheduled Sequence of Operations**

The essence of job shop planning is to prepare your program for a steady progression of all jobs with a minimized total queueing time and idle time and making provision for any unexpected jobs and delays.

## HOW A JOB SHOP FUNCTIONAL LAYOUT AFFECTS PRODUCTION PLANNING

Due to its high productivity and flexibility in the make-to-order production environment, a functional layout is used in many manufacturing companies. The primary reasons for using a functional layout is in the possibility to build various products at the same time. But, the functional layout presents the job scheduler with a problem, that of controlling intermittent operations. This problem, in many instances, grows into a major production issue of turbulent material flow and a high level of work-in-process (WIP).

The first step in any problem-solving plan is acknowledging the problem. Many manufacturing companies overstocked with WIP inventories do not accept this as a problem. The opinion is that this is a normal situation attributed to the job shop intermittent material flow. Ignoring this problem in part comes as a result of difficulties in measuring productivity of functional production units. A problem of a job shop management is further compounded by a multilevel hierarchical structure of production planning and control.

## HOW TO ORGANIZE JOB SHOP HIERARCHICAL PRODUCTION PLANNING

Production planning is routinely performed at three levels as shown in Figure 6-2. These three levels are:

1. *Aggregate planning*—a broadly outlined production program
2. A *master production schedule* (MPS)—a production program with the time table for each individual product
3. *Materials planning*—a breakdown of MPS into the components and their shop ordering

Aggregate planning and MPS represent centralized planning where information concerning balancing product requirements (capacity required) with process limitations (capacity available) is at hand for those doing production planning. MRP itemized planning follows suit.

This situation is different at the operational planning level where the execution takes place. Planning and control at the operational planning level,

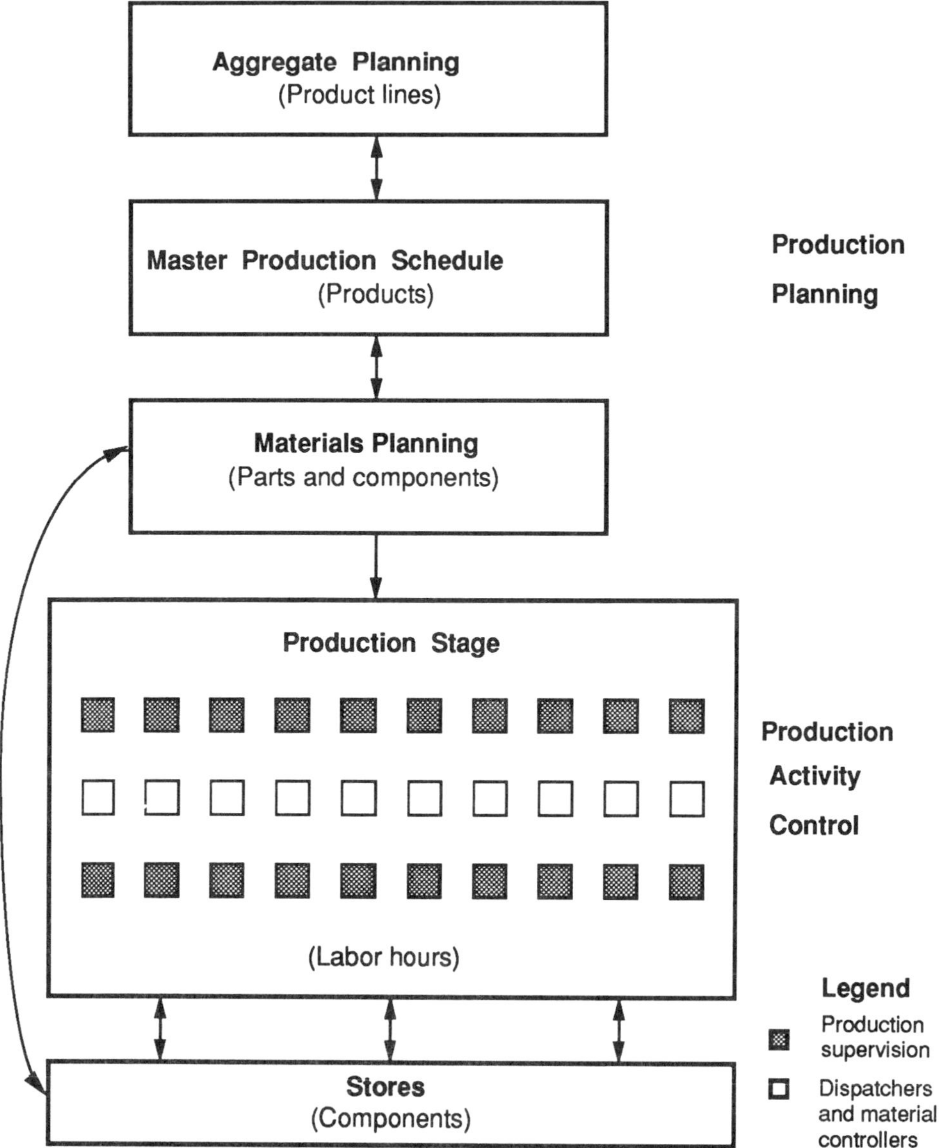


**Figure 6-2**
**Production Planning and Control System**

or *production activity control* (PAC), are decentralized. The objective of operational scheduling is fine balancing of product requirements with process limitations: both the concept of *product* (the processed part) and the concept of *process* (the processing machine) are observed in every operation. Even though this operational level is a part of production planning and control hierarchy, it is often ignored by production planners. The information flow is impaired between detailed planning and operational planning (shown in Figure 6-2 by an arrow passing over the area of production control).

Production systems are successful where master production scheduling, detailed planning (MRP), and shop floor control (operational planning) are integrated. Inadequate operational planning often imposes restrictions on aggregate plans and MPS either through holdups of the production program or simply by reduced productivity and the substandard performance.

Production control is regarded as part of the production planning system, whereas control standards and procedures are set up by planning. Operational planning is a key factor in the efforts to improve productivity through setting up higher performance standards.

## Assigning Job Priorities for Planning

Product priorities are set up within a framework of MRP followed by machine loading—job allocation to specific machines. Such machine loading takes into consideration the product priority and process priority. A number of existing solutions for job sequencing, machine utilization planning, and control rely on numerous assumptions and simplifications, and thus have a marginal practical value and significance.

Some scheduling techniques used in developing an optimal operational schedule are the second-degree integrated production planning. However, because of the scale of the task, it is possible to accomplish it only on larger computers. This fact severely restricts these applications because operational scheduling is a dynamic operational planning problem which must be continuously revised on a shop floor. At the production stage, an elaborate operational schedule is exposed to deviations—both subjective and objective—to such an extent that it often becomes a futile theoretical exercise. Above all, the computer-based operational optimization techniques do not find sufficient support at the shop floor; due to reasons associated with human factors: workers and the supervisory staff prefer to be involved in job sequencing and not blindly follow the computer's instructions.

Your shop floor personnel like to be involved in computer-based interactive scheduling, assigning job priorities, and job sequencing. The shop floor personnel should be given authority to sequence jobs and select operational task decisions from the set of computer-generated alternatives. There is a need for simple system solutions responsive to executional control and executional on-site schedule adjustments. One of such job allocation methods, block scheduling, which allows the shop floor personnel to sequence jobs within parameters set by centralized planning, is discussed further in Chapter 7.

## Determining Your Objectives for Operations Scheduling

*Operations scheduling* deals with the timing of operations subscribed by components' routes. *Machine loading*, which is short-term capacity planning, is aimed at maximizing the equipment and labor utilization. Machine loading involves sequencing jobs when assigning them to machines.

Operations scheduling and machine loading strategy is affected by what objective it seeks to achieve:

1. To reduce work in process
2. To facilitate production by combining several customer orders that require a similar set up and the same tooling
3. To maximize the equipment and labor utilization—a so-called "slot fitting technique" when jobs are selected to correspond to the time slot available
4. To enforce the uninterrupted JIT-*kanban* type of material flow aimed at zero inventory by applying the demand-pull approach
5. To reduce the production costs
6. To reduce the setup time

The methods of production control, namely, store-based itemized control, dispatching, expediting, feedbacked interfunctional planning, and control, are dependent on the operations scheduling. Operations scheduling and machine loading is a part of production activity control, the terminal point of production planning.

## Strategy for Deciding Your Operations Scheduling

Operations scheduling means that requirements are translated into operational time-phased work orders or time buckets. Scheduling strategies vary from company to company and can even be different in various departments of the same company. These scheduling strategies depend on the overall production planning strategy:

1. How far into the future is production planning projected and how long the elapsed time is between planning and execution.
2. Whether planning is based on a forecast or the customer orders on hand.
3. Whether there is a formal production planning and control system in place—strategic, tactical, or operational planning—or there is no formal planning and work orders are issued based on the outside orders as they arrive; whether scheduling is based on MPS or MRP itemized planning and operational scheduling.

4. Whether work orders are based on time-phased planning where material and capacity requirements planning are typically expressed in balanced weekly time buckets.
5. Whether there is a route sheet available with time standards prior to planning or this is jobbing-type production and the estimates are based on the actual time spent.

These are just several issues affecting the scheduling strategy.

## SETTING UP THE SHOP FLOOR CONTROL SYSTEM

### Using Static and Dynamic Scheduling

The function of any production planning and control system is to control the material flow by assigning jobs to workstations according to the allocated priorities. *Shop floor control* involves controlling the availability of capacity, labor, tools, materials, and services such as quality control, plant maintenance, and material handling. Shop floor control requires supervision, planning and control, providing the data, and ensuring the proper functioning of the information system.

An operational schedule, as a time-phased plan, is an ultimate result of a production planning and control system. There are two approaches to operations scheduling: static and dynamic. *Static scheduling* is job sequencing by identifying job priorities in a single work center. *Dynamic scheduling* considers the effect a scheduling decision will have on the material flow in successive work centers. It considers the minimum lead times, minimum WIP, and reduced queueing, along with the optimum work centers utilization. Due to the need for broad information, dynamic scheduling can be done centrally only. Static scheduling is first-degree planning, while dynamic scheduling is second-degree planning or integrated product and process planning.

Also, static scheduling assumes capacity disposition at time of planning, while dynamic scheduling attempts to predict availability of capacity in work centers at the time when operations take place.

### Using MRP and Shop Floor Controls

A priority-generated itemized requirements plan is translated into planned work orders. In case of an order cancellation, there is a postponement of order release, or alternatively, open orders can be expedited, lead time can be compressed, or new planned orders can be released. These MRP changes are translated further into changes of scheduled receipts' due dates.

Scheduled receipts and information on the open orders progress are continuously updated. The MRP flexibility can be used in balancing the load with the capacity (for example, releasing orders when a capacity is available). Alternatively, an open order can be delayed if there is a certainty that other components will not be supplied to assembly on time. Production control makes use of an MRP-generated job status report for each work center, with job priority identified and updated daily.

Other MRP reports such as exception reports, and status reports for customer order per work center are used in shop floor control. Changes in due dates are interpreted into actions helpful in controlling and adjusting the job shop material flow.

## OPERATIONS SCHEDULING AND MACHINE LOADING—HOW THE DIFFERENT TYPES OF OPERATIONS AFFECT PLANNING

Two types of shared resources are dealt with in operations scheduling and control: equipment and labor. Resources can be either machine limited or labor limited. This can be defined by identifying limitations at the bottleneck workstations: Are these limitations due to the insufficient labor force, or due to the insufficient equipment capacity? Figure 6-3 illustrates conditions attributed to labor limitations or equipment limitations.

### Is Yours a Machine-Limited Environment?

In a *machine-limited environment*, a piece of equipment is the major consideration when the limitations on capacity are examined. The breakdown of a machine can affect the material flow, especially in line-type production where a breakdown of one machine stops the entire line. Proper maintenance of equipment is a critical issue in a machine-limited environment.

### Using Labor-Limited Operations

*Labor-limited operations* are typical in the situation in which there are more machines than labor. If a machine breaks down, it does not affect production because the operator can then be shifted to another process. The labor assignment policy in worker-limited operations brings a flexibility in scheduling and can improve the material flow. Worker-limited operations are the features of flexible manufacturing systems (FMS).

## OPERATIONS SCHEDULING TECHNIQUES

Though applicable to any production environment, the described techniques are primarily oriented to the make-to-order and a job shop manufacturing environment, as particularly challenging ones. Studying scheduling techniques is essential

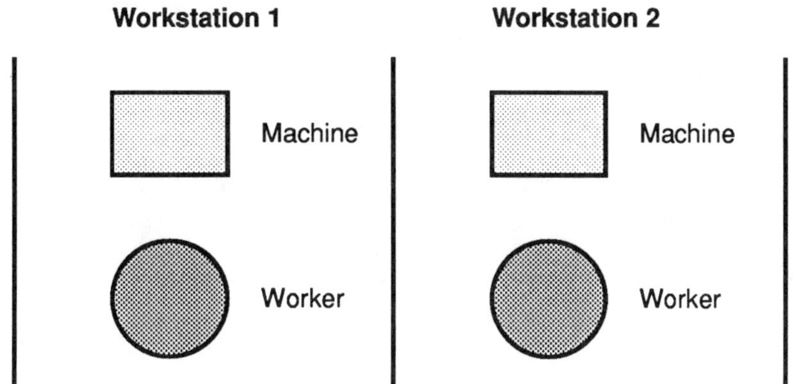


**A. Machine--Limited Production**

Worker and a single-machine workstation

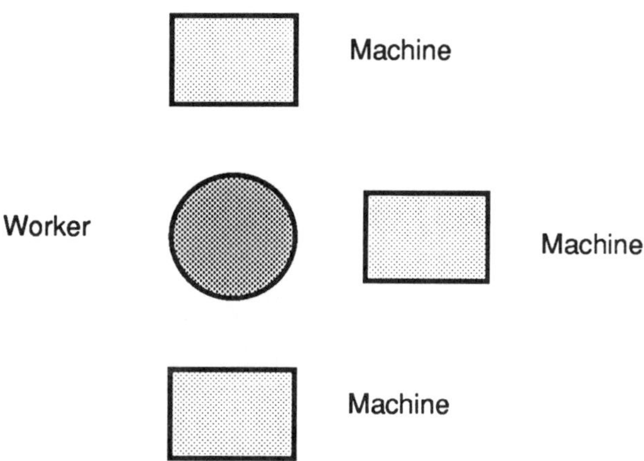


**B. Worker--Limited Production**

If one machine breaks, the operation continues

**Figure 6-3**
**Machine-Limited and Worker-Limited Production**

due to a pressing need to spearhead the efforts for reducing a queueing line, inventory, and lead time.

## Operation-By-Operation Scheduling

Operation-by-operation scheduling is a technique of breaking lead time into operation slots and scheduling the operations one by one. Operation-by-operation scheduling is a next step after MRP.

Components' lead time is broken down into the individual operations' starting and completion time, and these jobs are assigned to machines in a sequence one by one in such a way that the completion of the final operation corresponds to the item's due date.

Operation-by-operation scheduling can be conducted in two different ways having different results:

- Operation-by-operation scheduling can be conducted forward answering the question: "When can this item be completed?" or forward scheduling;
- It can be conducted backward, answering the question: "When should this item should be started?" or backward scheduling.

Two types of operation-by-operation scheduling are illustrated in Figure 6-4. An example of operation-by-operation forward scheduling applied at Tool and Implement Co. is shown in Figure 6-5. There weekly work release in each work center is shown along with standard capacity level. Job is scheduled whenever capacity is available. For example, the first operation requiring 26 hours in the shear-press work center is scheduled in week 1, as there are a total of 302 hours released against 400 hours of capacity level. The second operation requiring 32 hours in the lathe work center cannot be scheduled in week 2 as capacity there is fully loaded (800 hours released against 800 capacity available). Therefore, 32 machine hours required for the second operation are assigned to the lathe work center in week 3 as there are 640 machine-hours released against 800 standard capacity level. The remaining operations are scheduled at times when capacity in corresponding departments is available.

## Scheduling According to Priority Rules

The criteria for evaluating priority rules are:

1. Scheduling rules which take into account job's due dates and/or processing time
2. Least slack time priority rules
3. Priority rules which consider the sequence of the job arrival

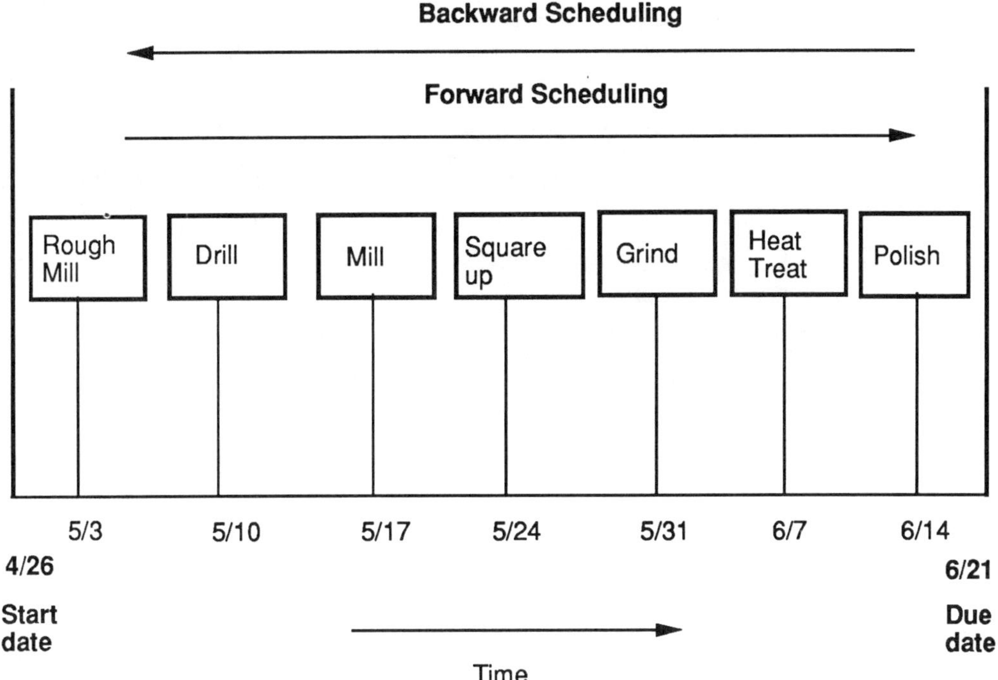


**Figure 6-4**
**Operation-by-Operation Scheduling**

| Work center | Week 1 | | Week 2 | | Week 3 | | Week 4 | | Week 5 | | Week 6 | | Week 7 | |
|---|---|---|---|---|---|---|---|---|---|---|---|---|---|---|
| | work | capac. | work | capac. | work | capac. | work | capac. | work | capac. | work | capac. | work | capac. |
| Shear/Press | 302 +26 | 400 | | | | | | | | | | | | |
| Lathes | | | 800 | 800 | 640 +32 | 800 | | | | | | | | |
| Milling | | | | | | | 360 +60 | 600 | | | | | | |
| Heat Treatment | | | | | | | | | 240 +16 | 320 | | | | |
| Grinding | | | | | | | | | | | 390 +38 | 480 | | |
| Assembly line | | | | | | | | | | | | | 220 +14 | 300 |

**Figure 6-5**
**Operation-by-Operation Forward Scheduling at Tool and Implement Co.**

4. Priority rules which take into account the inventory position, engineering considerations, or dynamics of the subsequent processes
5. Synthetic priority rules
6. Simulation scheduling techniques

The effectiveness of priority rules is measured by the degree of job lateness and average flow time.

1. The *degree of job lateness* (DJL) is tardiness—the amount of time by which job is late.
2. *Average flow time* is the time job spends in the shop.
3. The *average number of jobs in the system* is computed by dividing all jobs total flow time by the time assigned for these jobs.

Consideration is given to keeping all the jobs advancing in order to minimize lead time.

## Scheduling Rules That Take into Account Job Due Dates and/or Operation Time

1. *Due-date rules according to the operation due date or according to an assembly due date.* The earliest due date priority rule (EDD) is the following: jobs with earlier due date have the highest priority. According to EDD, jobs with earliest due dates are assigned a higher priority. In structural planning and control systems, due dates are given for finished components only. This obscures operations scheduling because intermediate operations due dates are not given.
2. *According to duration of machine time.*
   a. *Shortest processing time* (SPT). Orders with shortest processing time in a department are given the highest priority. This rule produces good results in reducing waiting lines, particularly when work must flow through several production units. However, some other jobs with long processing time can run late. Some companies applying SPT impose the limit on the time a job is allowed to wait in a single work center.
   b. *Longest processing time* (LPT). Jobs having longest processing time are given a higher priority. This rule is often used in order scheduling where larger jobs are selected first in cases where demand exceeds capacity. Again, this rule does not consider planning of the optimum product mix.
3. *Priority rules where final due date is considered.*
   a. *Earliest due date.* Operations having earliest due dates are scheduled first. This rule is intended to minimize the lateness of jobs.
   b. The *critical ratio (CR) scheduling* CR is calculated as the ratio between time remaining before the due-date and the workdays remaining.

$$CR = \frac{\text{(due date - today's date)}}{\text{lead time remaining}}$$

*Example*: A manufacturing facility has five jobs to be scheduled into production. Table 6-1 states the processing times and due dates for each job. Assume that today is April 3 and the jobs are due as shown:

**Table 6-1**
**Processing Times and Due Dates**

| Job | Total Time Required (days) | Date Job Due |
|---|---|---|
| 1 | 14 | April 30 |
| 2 | 13 | April 21 |
| 3 | 24 | April 28 |
| 4 | 16 | April 29 |
| 5 | 28 | April 27 |

$$CR\text{ job 1} = \frac{30 - 3}{14} = 1.93$$

$$CR\text{ job 2} = \frac{21 - 3}{13} = 1.38$$

$$CR\text{ job 3} = \frac{28 - 3}{24} = 1.04$$

$$CR\text{ job 4} = \frac{29 - 3}{16} = 1.62$$

$$CR\text{ job 5} = \frac{27 - 3}{28} = 0.85$$

According to CR priority rules, jobs having a *CR* of less than 1 are behind schedule, jobs with a *CR* equal to 1 are on schedule, and jobs with a *CR* of more than 1 are ahead of schedule. Jobs are scheduled in order of their priority, 5, 3, 2, 4, and 1, with job 5 at a *CR* = 0.85 being the most critical; all other jobs are ahead of schedule.

### Least Slack Time Priority Rules

1. *Slack time remaining* (STR) calculates the difference between the time remaining until the due date and the time required for processing.

slack = time until date item is required - lead time required for production.

2. *Slack time per remaining operations* (ST/RO) estimates the average slack time remaining per one operation.

### Scheduling Jobs According to the Sequence of Arrival

1. *First-come, first-served* (FCFS) orders are assigned to machines in the order of their arrival. This rule is the one most used in practice.
2. *Last-come, first-served* (LCFS) orders are scheduled in the sequence of latest arrival. There is a danger of the earlier arrived jobs waiting for too long before getting processed.

FCFS, LCFS, and SPT priority rules do not give any consideration to due dates of operations and can create an excessive WIP inventory.

*Example*: A manufacturing facility has six jobs to be scheduled into production. Their processing times and due dates are given in Table 6-2. Determine the sequence of jobs applying EDD, SPT, and FCFS priority rules. The jobs are shown in the order of their arrival:

**Table 6-2**
**Processing Time and Due Dates for EDD, SPT, or FCFS Priority Rules**

| Job | Total Time Required (days) | Due Date (days) |
|---|---|---|
| A | 9 | 28 |
| B | 3 | 11 |
| C | 7 | 12 |
| D | 6 | 26 |
| E | 4 | 8 |
| F | 7 | 29 |

1. *Earliest due date (EDD) priority rule.* According to the earliest due date rule, the job sequence is E, B, C, D, A, and F, with job E having the earliest due date. Job lateness is computed as shown in Table 6-3.

**Table 6-3**
**Estimating Job Lateness—EDD Priority Rule**

| Job Sequence | Time Required | Flow Time | Due Date | Job Lateness |
|---|---|---|---|---|
| E | 4 | 4 | 8 | |
| B | 3 | 7 | 11 | |
| C | 7 | 14 | 12 | |
| D | 6 | 20 | 26 | |
| A | 9 | 29 | 28 | 1 |
| F | 7 | 36 | 29 | 5 |
| Total | 36 | 110 | | 8 |

$$\text{average job lateness} = \frac{8}{6} = 1.33 \text{ days}$$

$$\text{average completion time} = \frac{110}{6} = 18.33 \text{ days}$$

$$\text{average number of jobs in the system} = \frac{110}{36} = 3.06$$

2. *Shortest processing time (SPT) priority rule.* The job sequence according to the SPT rule is B, E, D, C, F, and A.

   Job lateness is computed in Table 6-4.

**Table 6-4**
**Estimating Job Lateness—SPT Priority Rule**

| Job Sequence | Time Required | Flow Time | Due Date | Job Lateness |
|---|---|---|---|---|
| B | 3 | 3 | 11 | — |
| E | 4 | 7 | 8 | — |
| D | 6 | 13 | 26 | — |
| C | 7 | 20 | 12 | 8 |
| F | 7 | 27 | 29 | — |
| A | 9 | 36 | 28 | 8 |
| Total | 36 | 106 | | 16 |

$$\text{average job lateness} = \frac{16}{6} = 2.67 \text{ days}$$

$$\text{average completion time} = \frac{106}{6} = 17.67 \text{ days}$$

$$\text{average number of jobs in the system} = \frac{106}{36} = 2.95$$

3. *First come first served (FCFS) priority rule.* Job lateness is computed as shown in Table 6-5.

**Table 6-5**
**Estimating Job Lateness—FCFS Priorty Rule**

| Job Sequence | Time Required | Flow Time | Due Date | Job Lateness |
|---|---|---|---|---|
| A | 9 | 9 | 28 | — |
| B | 3 | 12 | 11 | 1 |
| C | 7 | 19 | 12 | 7 |
| D | 6 | 25 | 26 | — |
| E | 4 | 29 | 8 | 21 |
| F | 7 | 36 | 29 | 7 |
| Total | 36 | 130 | | 36 |

$$\text{average job lateness} = \frac{36}{6} = 6 \text{ days}$$

$$\text{average completion time} = \frac{130}{6} = 21.67 \text{ days}$$

$$\text{average number of jobs in the system} = \frac{130}{36} = 3.61$$

This example shows that priority rules which do not take into account production times and due dates result in a number of jobs being late: job lateness in FCFS is 6 days compared with 1.33 days in EDD and 2.67 days in SPT.

## Priority Rules

Priority rules take into account inventory position, engineering considerations, or dynamics of subsequent processes.

1. *Reducing the next queue.* The priority rule considers reducing a queue at the succeeding workstations. Jobs are selected in order of the smallest queue at the succeeding workstations.
2. *Reducing combined setup time.* The least setup time rule assigns priority jobs according to the duration of setup time. When applying this rule jobs are scheduled together in instances when similar setups are required.
3. *Sequencing operations.* Along with assigning jobs to specific machines, job schedulers should schedule downstream work centers as well.

Even job shop intermittent operations, to a certain degree, have an identifiable sequence of operations through the plant. The grinding operation must be preceded by the machining operation, and the forging operation must be completed before machining can start. Centralized operational scheduling is applied where a planner schedules several operations in a sequence trying to eliminate overloads on critical machines. See Table 6-6.

**Table 6-6**
**Scheduling Jobs in a Sequence for Eliminating Overloads**

| Sequence of Operations | Production Time (hours) |
|---|---|
| Shearpress | 26 |
| Lathes | 32 |
| Milling | 60 |
| Heat treatment | 12 |
| Grinding | 32 |
| Assembly | 14 |

A planner follows this above sequence, releasing a balanced time-phased load to ensure the minimum queueing time aiming at the smooth, uninterrupted material flow. The total hours of load released to the shop do not exceed the available capacity.

When scheduling, jobs in one department should be selected so as not to exceed the capacity of the subsequent departments when these jobs arrive there.

## Synthetic Priority Rules for Scheduling Jobs

*Even-flow scheduling* is a technique of applying uniform lead time for all the operations. No matter what is the duration of the operations, the lead time assigned to these operations is the same, usually one scheduled time period—one day, one-half week, or one week. Run time is only about 5 to 10 percent of the total lead time. Waiting and queueing times are the main components of the lead time. These components do not depend on the machining or run time. The queue time is an average for all the operations in a given work center.

Thus, it is prudent to accept the same lead time for all operations (for example, equal to the average queue time—one day, one-half week, or one week). This operations time can be increased in cases when machining time exceeds the average time period.

In cases when machine time is longer than one time period, it is rounded up to the next higher time period number. For example, in the daily scheduling there is run time of 9 hours while the workday is 8 hours, so the lead time is scheduled to be equal to 2 days.

The assumption of one operation, one time period substantially simplifies the scheduling, and, at the same time, it is a valuable incentive presenting work centers with an opportunity to sequence jobs they perform. An example of even-flow scheduling technique is illustrated in Figure 6-6.

### Using Simulation Probability for Job Shop Scheduling

Job shop scheduling in a multiproduct environment is a formidable task presenting substantial challenges for operations management professionals. Simulation proved to be one of the most effective, flexible, easy-to-use, scheduling techniques. *Simulation* is a statistical technique using the frequency distribution

| Work center \ Workdays | 162 | 163 | 164 | 165 | 166 | 167 |
|---|---|---|---|---|---|---|
| Shear/Press | 4.6 | | | | | |
| Lathes | | 3.5 | | | | |
| Milling | | | 7.8 | | | |
| Heat Treatment | | | | 6.4 | | |
| Grinding | | | | | 4.0 | |
| Assembly line | | | | | | 2.1 |

Work hours

**Figure 6-6**
**Even Flow Scheduling**

of events as a basis for predicting the future occurrences. Simulation consists of several steps which are examined on the following example.

*Example*: Two hundred machine breakdowns recorded in the maintenance log book occurred with the frequency shown in Table 6-7.

**Table 6-7**
**Frequency of Machine Breakdowns**

| Breakdowns per Day | Frequency | Probability | Cumulative Probability |
|---|---|---|---|
| 0 | 20 | 20/200=0.10 | 0.10 |
| 1 | 30 | 30/200=0.15 | 0.25 |
| 2 | 60 | 60/200=0.30 | 0.55 |
| 3 | 50 | 50/200=0.25 | 0.80 |
| 4 | 30 | 30/200=0.15 | 0.95 |
| 5 | 10 | 10/200=0.05 | 1.00 |
| Total | 200 | 1.00 | |

*The first step* is to establish the cumulative probability distribution from the relative frequency of each outcome of a breakdown. Initially, the probability is computed by dividing the frequency of breakdowns by the total number of breakdowns. *The second step* is to compute the cumulative probability distribution.

*The third step* is to assign a set of numbers or random number intervals representing the value of each outcome. Random number intervals should correspond to tables of random numbers used in simulation. These tables comprise either two- or three-digit numbers which are sequences of two or three digits randomly selected. In the example, two-digit number intervals are used starting from 00, 01, 02,...98, 99 or sometimes from 01, 02, 03,...98, 99, 00.

**Table 6-8**
**Assigning Random Number Intervals**

| Breakdowns per Day | Probability of Breakdown | Cumulative | Random |
|---|---|---|---|
| 0 | 0.10 | 0.10 | 00-09 |
| 1 | 0.15 | 0.25 | 10-24 |
| 2 | 0.30 | 0.30 | 25-54 |
| 3 | 0.25 | 0.80 | 55-79 |
| 4 | 0.15 | 0.95 | 80-94 |
| 5 | 0.05 | 1.00 | 95-99 |

*The last step* is to simulate the outcome of the experiment using random numbers. For example, a series of random numbers 27, 58, 92, 04, 36, and

12 will simulate the following expected pattern of breakdowns: 2, 3, 4, 0, 2, and 1 breakdowns per day.

Most simulation models are computerized systems, which makes them dynamic when the actual performance figures are applied in the real-time mode. Such a simulation model produces results which are quite sufficient for resources allocation and operational scheduling. One such simulation scheduling system used by CAMCO, Inc., is discussed in Chapter 7.

Scheduling techniques rely on prediction of operations lead time. Often such predictions are inaccurate due to uncertainty in queueing time, waiting time, and idle time. This makes it difficult to plan ahead. Some companies develop scheduling rules in which lead time relies on a number of operations, for example,

> lead time = 3 days + total machining time + allow 2 days for thermal treatment of components + 2 days for inspection

You do not need to adhere to one scheduling technique or one priority rule. Scheduling techniques and priority rules can be changed as conditions change.

## USING DISPATCHING SYSTEMS TO ORGANIZE MATERIAL FLOW

Some batch-type production companies develop interactive operational control systems or dispatching systems. The function of dispatching is to organize material flow control along material operational routes and to control each production stage by relating to end product's due dates. The system is viewed as an inventive solution to avoid integrated operational planning—detailed product and process planning—and still be in control of the material flow.

In line-type production, dispatching is simple because the material moves along the same path and there is no need to arrange and supervise intradepartmental communications because the machining routes are well known along with the interrelationship of production units. In the job shop intermittent material flow, dispatching attempts to sequence and to trace each operation.

Depending on the objectives of dispatching systems, there are two main categories of dispatching:

1. *Dispatching as means for job tracking.* In this category, dispatching does not serve as a material flow control. It affects the material flow through expediting, but this is not exactly the type of influence you would like to exert on the shop floor material flow.
2. *Dispatching as a means for operational planning and control.* In this category of dispatching, the due date for each operation is determined in

advance. Dispatching systems in this category seem to integrate product and process, resulting in issuing of operational work orders. However, it is still the first-degree product planning applying infinite loading techniques, where the priority is given to operational due dates without proper consideration to available capacity and to plant utilization factors.

The inherent contradiction here is that although dispatchers issue operational orders, they remain responsible for the product only, while the process responsibility rests with the departmental supervisory staff. The dispatching can be classified as centralized operational scheduling. A route sheet is the basis for compiling the elaborate dispatching documentation. Each operation on a route sheet is an object of control in dispatching.

A typical formal dispatching system, such as the one illustrated in Figure 6-7, maintains three files containing operational work tickets identical to that of three files used in job shop planning and control.

These files are an *order file*, compiled according to the machine center for the next operation; a *work file*, compiled by the part number; and a *due date file*, filed by the operational due dates. The departmental daily plans are prepared from orders in the order file. From the work file, job cards are issued to operators according to the daily plan. When a job is finished, the job card is returned to the dispatching, and the order is moved to the section in the order file for the next machine center. There exist to and from flows of operational cards between centralized dispatching, material handling, and tooling, and the respective work centers before and after each operation. In the due date file, jobs are checked regularly, and an overdue jobs list is compiled. It is the function of expeditors to ensure that these components are available for the next operation or assembly.

The systems just described are expensive, which often forces companies to abandon the system soon after its installation.

Despite such elaborate planning and control, dispatching still cannot be classified completely as a second-degree operational planning system. Dispatching falls into the category of job tracking systems. In most instances, dispatchers have no authority over assigning jobs to machines. This is the responsibility of the shop floor staff. The dispatching represents operational production control over the material flow and involves selecting and sequencing jobs according to the product priority. This also includes issuing operational job orders; issuing work orders to tool departments for tools, jigs, and fixtures for the operations; providing for material handling between the workstations; and providing for the quality control inspections.

Dispatchers attempt to influence decisions of the shop floor supervisory staff responsible for the process priority. This often leads to a conflict of authority. Dispatching systems are associated with expediting, the function created to resolve product and process conflicts.

Dispatching has the following shortcomings:

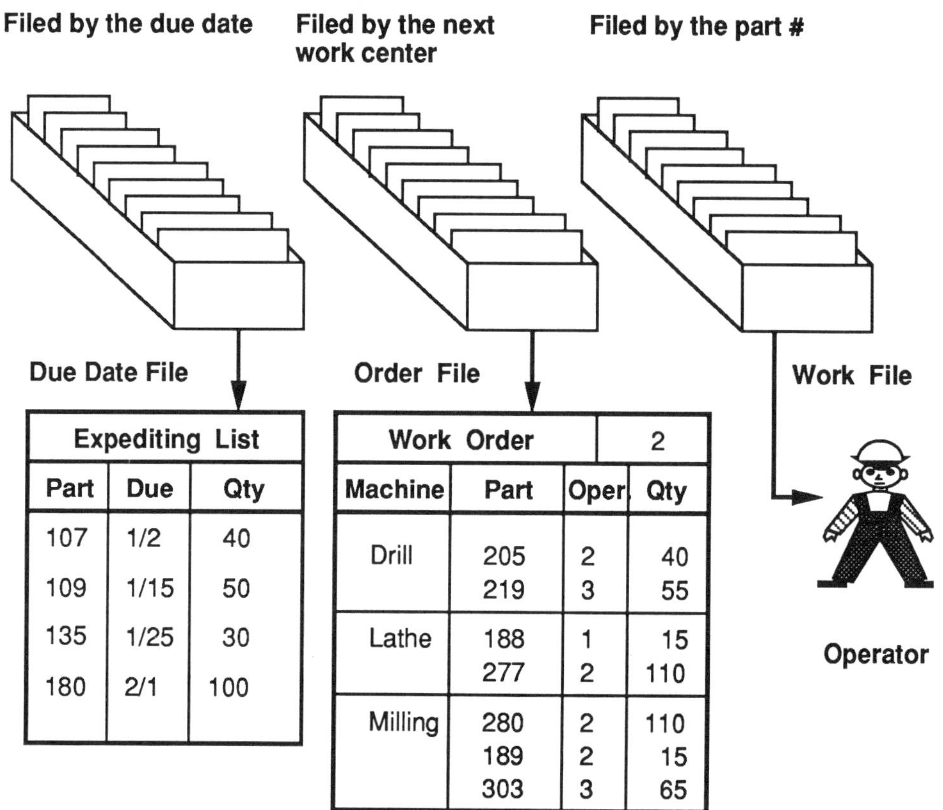


| Expediting List | | |
|---|---|---|
| Part | Due | Qty |
| 107 | 1/2 | 40 |
| 109 | 1/15 | 50 |
| 135 | 1/25 | 30 |
| 180 | 2/1 | 100 |

| Work Order | | | 2 |
|---|---|---|---|
| Machine | Part | Oper | Qty |
| Drill | 205 | 2 | 40 |
| | 219 | 3 | 55 |
| Lathe | 188 | 1 | 15 |
| | 277 | 2 | 110 |
| Milling | 280 | 2 | 110 |
| | 189 | 2 | 15 |
| | 303 | 3 | 65 |

**Figure 6-7**
**The Dispatching System**

- High cost
- Various degrees of authority but in most instances, dispatchers have no authority over the shop floor personnel

Some companies take shortcuts: a batch of parts accompanied with a route sheet having detachable operational coupons. These coupons are returned to the dispatching after each operation is completed. But in many manufacturing systems, route sheets accompanying a batch of parts highlight only the last operation's due date. Despite the shortcomings, dispatching systems respond most closely to the requirements for the design of an effective production planning and control system.

## USING ADVANCED SCHEDULING TECHNIQUES TO REDUCE LEAD TIME

### Overlapping Operations

Operation overlapping means starting the next operation before the previous operation is completed. Overlapping of operations reduces the total manufacturing lead time by reducing the size of the batch dispatched to succeeding operations. An example of operations overlapping is illustrated in Figure 6-8.

### Splitting Operations

Operation splitting means performing one job in parallel on two or more machines. Splitting operations reduces the total lead time by dividing production lots into smaller batches and at the same time, conducting operations on all these batches. An example of operations splitting is illustrated in Figure 6-9.

### Splitting Lots

Lot splitting means splitting the total quantity on order into smaller lots and to issue an order for the portion of the total order so as to satisfy immediate customer requirements. This technique is used in JIT manufacturing systems.

## SUMMARY

The operation scheduling and machine loading techniques discussed in this chapter are effective only when they are interactively applied in conjunction with other elements of an integrated production planning and control system such as MPS and MRP. This means that scheduling techniques covered should be used within a second-degree manufacturing system, namely, integrated product and process planning and control. Various examples of applying scheduling techniques within integrated manufacturing systems are discussed in the next chapter.

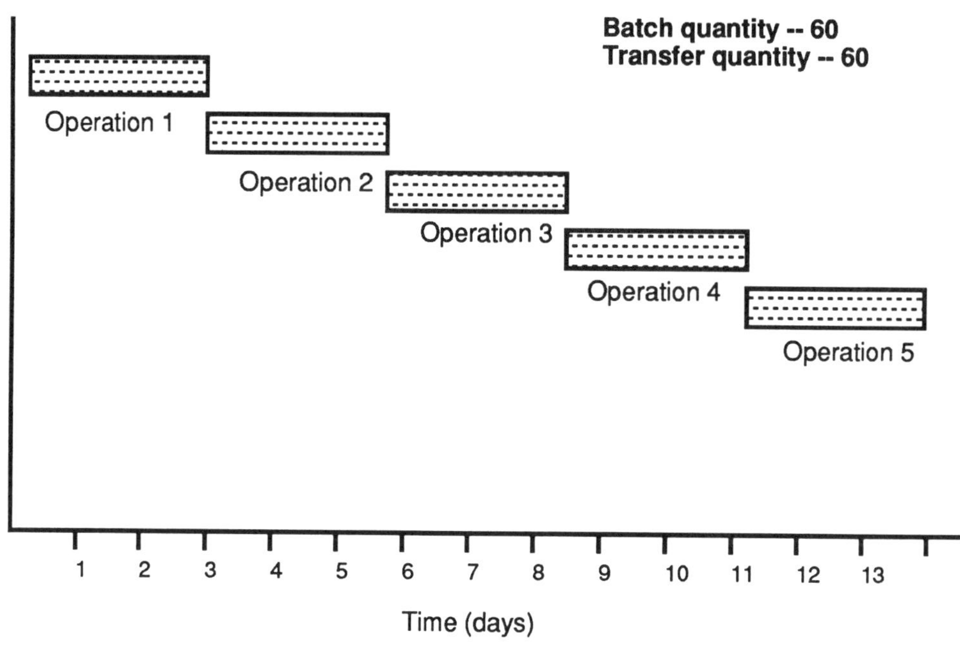


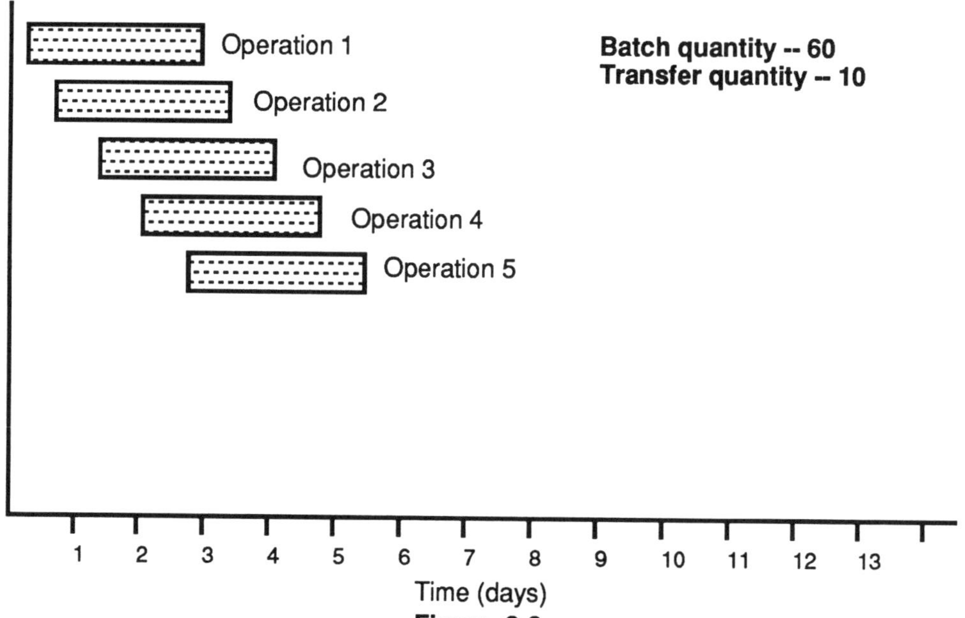


**Figure 6-8**
**Overlapping Operations**

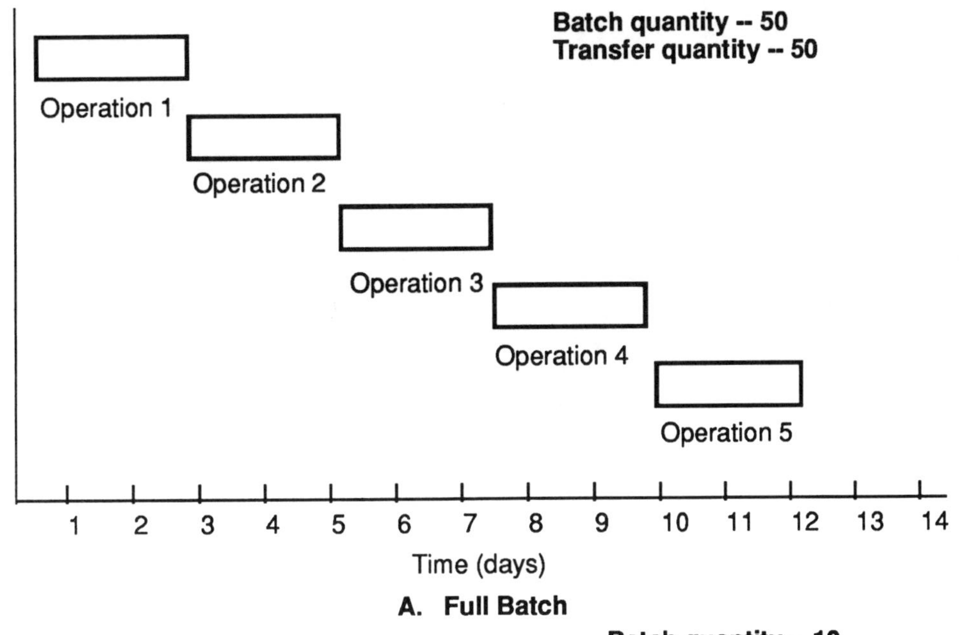


**A. Full Batch**

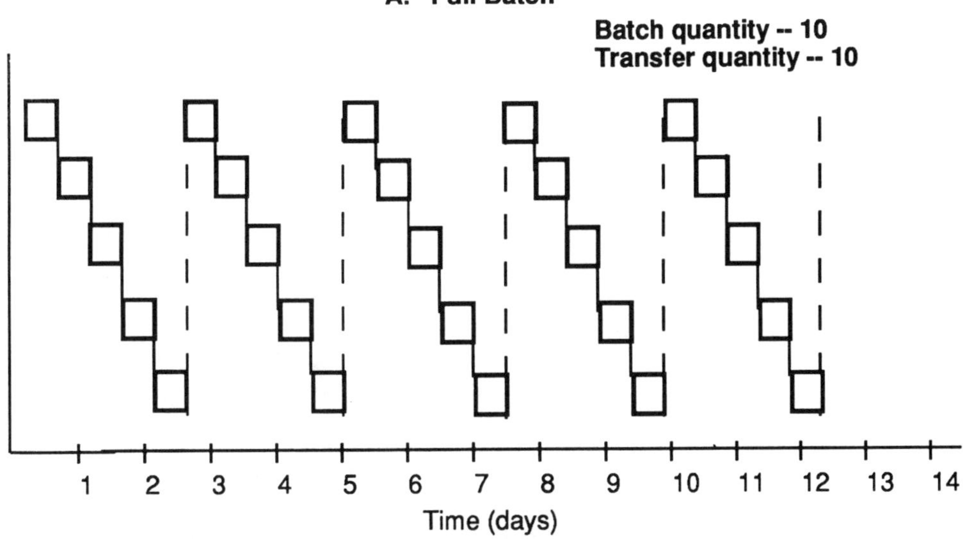


**B. Split Batch**

**Figure 6-9**
**Splitting Lots**

# 7

# Using Advanced Scheduling Systems to Organize an Operational Control and Reporting System

Material flow planning and control should be approached from the perspective of how the production is organized, that is, by continuous or intermittent material flow. In process industry and continuous production, production control of material flow is programmed in advance at the preproduction planning stage and, therefore, does not present the problems experienced in the job shop intermittent material flow.

The parameters used to characterize a material flow are as follows:

1. What type of operational planning and control over the material flow do you require? Do you need operational planning or planning based on the material requirements planning (MRP) schedule when the priority of intermediate operations is not stated on the work order?
2. Each stage of production has the characteristics of either intradepartmental or interdepartmental intermission. Which applies to your operation?
3. Who has the authority or "ownership" over the components along the flow path, and who has the responsibility to complete an operation on time—the centralized planning, dispatchers, departmental supervisory staff, or even workers?
4. Who orders material handling to move the components?

5. Who exercises control over the material flow—the centralized planning department, dispatching and expediting, the last department in line, or the store?
6. How are orders planned and sent to production—sequenced or as a product mix, balanced or nonbalanced, applying time fences or allowing hot orders, in full batches, split batches, or combined batches?
7. What is the timing in material flow? For the purpose of production flow control, elements of lead time are grouped into two categories—*productive time*, or work time, and *nonproductive time*. Work time is productive in that it includes preparation time, run time, and remove time. Nonproductive time includes *waiting time*, representing most of the total operation cycle time—queue time, wait time, and idle time. The material flow can be streamlined, when the attention is given to reducing nonproductive time through better operational product and process planning and control over idle time.
8. How does material flow relate to the cost centers? The order can be completed in one cost center, or several work centers in a sequence, or it can have an alternate forward/backward recurring flow pattern.

The characteristics of material flow just outlined ought to be considered if operational planning and control is to be effective.

## DEVELOPING A PRODUCTION PLANNING AND CONTROL SCHEDULING SYSTEM

In manufacturing systems, an obstacle to the development of an effective production planning and control system in job shop production is caused by certain deficiencies in the interdepartmental coordination, specifically in the following areas:

1. Company interdepartmental *process-coordinated* control: If a foreman delays one operation in his department, how will it affect queueing in the succeeding work centers? Or, on the contrary, if he expedites it, will it facilitate equipment loading in the succeeding processes? Figure 7-1 illustrates the situation when a job delayed in one department affects the waiting-line decisions, as when a delayed job must be treated with the higher priority in the succeeding departments.
2. Company *all-product coordinated* operational control: If one dispatcher decides to force the completion of his product, to what extend will it affect other products for which other dispatchers are responsible? Foremen and schedulers responsible for process control should coordinate their activities throughout the plant to the same degree as dispatchers and material

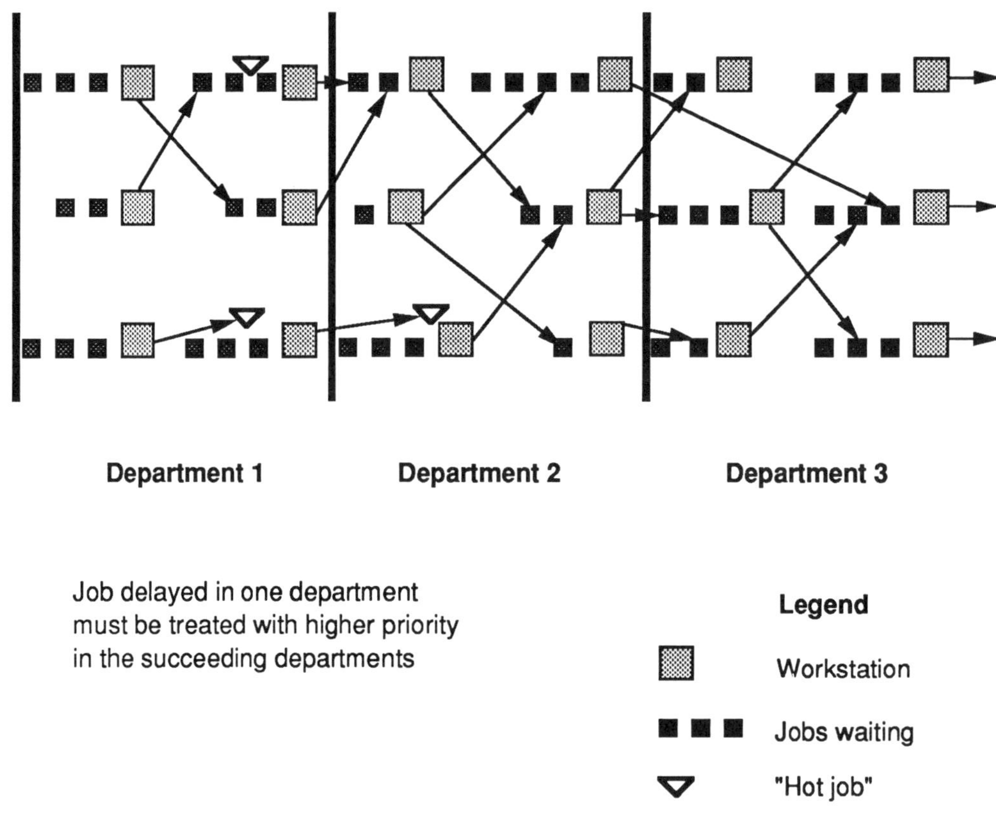


**Figure 7-1**
**The Effect of the Departmental Loading on the Disposition in the Succeeding Departments**

controllers require coordinate product control so that one-product expediting efforts do not affect other work orders

3. *Integration* of process planning and control with product planning and control—identifying job priorities: Production activity control (PAC) should be conducted according to the work order priority as well as the priority of individual capacities. This is a problem of creating a second-degree manufacturing system—integrated product and process planning.

Any improvements in these three areas of production control produce beneficial results in a manufacturing system by streamlining work orders and reducing mean flow time.

## TWO TYPES OF JOB SHOP INTERMITTENT OPERATIONS—INTRADEPARTMENTAL AND INTERDEPARTMENTAL

Most manufacture of parts and components is spread over a number of work centers. The major problem you face with production control, as far as intermittent operations are concerned, is the large number of processes and the crisscrossing of operations, many of these operations being of short duration only.

Intermittent production operations is a job shop reality, where the material flow is constantly being interrupted due to restrictions imposed by the plant capacity and other factors. There are two distinctive types of intermittent operations: intradepartmental intermittent operations and interdepartmental intermittent operations.

An *intradepartmental intermission* occurs between work centers of the same departmental administrative unit. An intradepartmental intermission occurs when the material flow is interrupted by a pause between the operations and parts are moved from one machine to another within a single department.

An *interdepartmental intermission* occurs when a job is completed in one department and is sent to the succeeding department. An interdepartmental intermission occurs when parts are moved from one department to another. Here, the supervision and responsibility are changing hands. Figure 7-2 illustrates intradepartmental and interdepartmental intermittent operations.

An intradepartmental intermission of material flow takes place within a single administrative unit, under the common supervision, planning, and control, while during an interdepartmental intermission jobs are moved from one administrative unit to another. It was found that changing the administrative and supervisory authority causes production control to relax, due to shifts in responsibility.

The interdepartmental intermission of material flow is an obstacle to production planning and control because the "ownership" of components is changing and the system should envisage an orderly and uninterrupted transfer from one ownership to another.

An interoperational intermission, the time after which one operation is completed but the next operation has not started yet, is the area where most of wait time and idle time delays occur.

### Dealing with Wait Time and Idle Time Delays

Wait time and idle time consist of interoperational delays when components are put away following an operation, and the succeeding operation has not yet

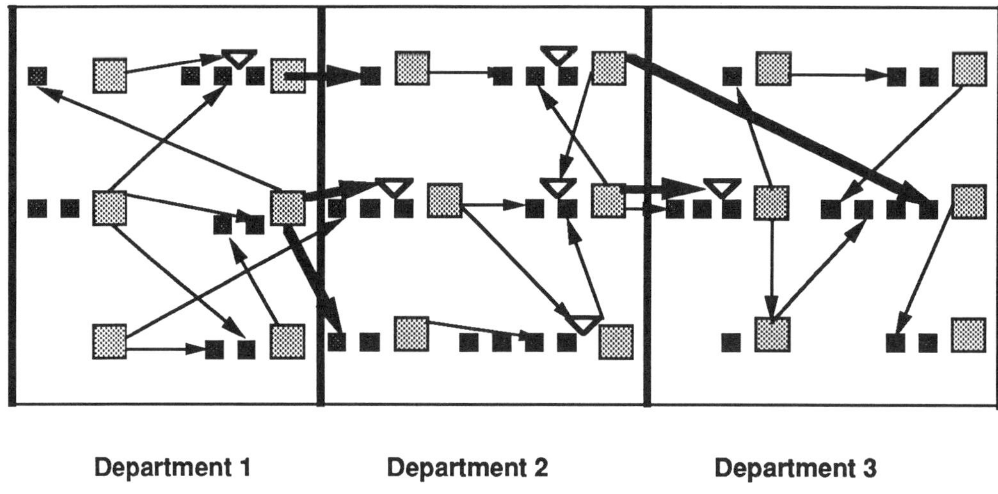


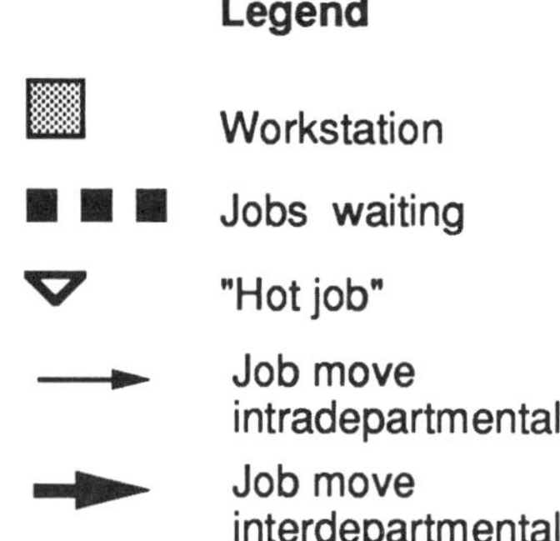


**Figure 7-2**
**Intradepartmental and Interdepartmental Intermittent Operations**

claimed them. Until they are claimed for the next operation, these components are often placed into temporary storage or even in a formal store. In some instances, the responsibility for product planning and control over these components has been relaxed and is reduced to the safekeeping function at best. Elements of operation lead time are illustrated in Figure 7-3.

Depending on type of production and production planning and control, wait time and idle time are responsible for a large part of lead time. Wait time and idle time are inactive, unplanned, nonvalue-producing operations elements still requiring decision making, information processing, and technical and man-

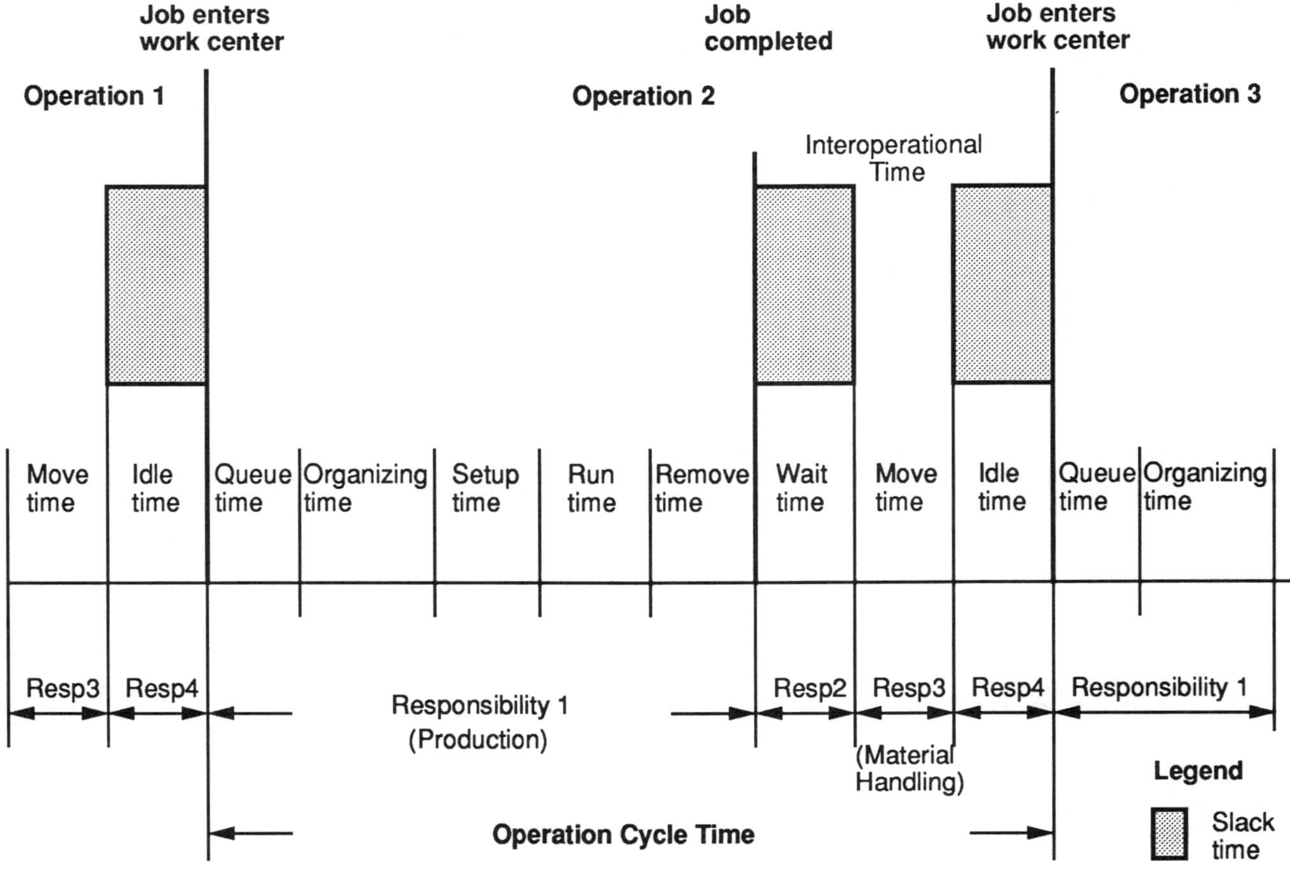


**Figure 7-3**
**The Elements of Operational Lead Time and Interfunctional Responsibility**

agerial services. Despite the seeming inactivity, they consume resources. "Hot" jobs and the subsequent expediting originate from wait time and idle time and not queueing time. Collectively, wait time and idle time can be called *slack time*. Wait time and idle time appear when there is no operations scheduling, a long elapsed time between planning and execution, or when there is slacked production control. The function of dispatching and expediting is to set up control over the slack time.

Your major task as production manager is to control material flow by controlling slack time. For the most part, control over the wait time and idle time produces a steady material flow. One of the main tasks of an integrated production planning and control system is to organize control over slack time by establishing a chain of responsibility. One such system which establishes control over the lead time is integrated task management (ITM), discussed later in this chapter.

## Optimizing Functional Responsibility Over Material Flow Routes

Operation lead time features two areas of responsibility: the *responsibility of the primary production function*, consisting of responsibility for queue time, preparation time, run time, and remove time, and the *responsibility of the secondary production function*, material handling or any other production services. A waiting delay and an idle delay occur between these two areas of responsibility, due to the functional responsibility changing hands. Areas of interfunctional responsibility are illustrated in Figure 7-3.

Changing responsibility from the production function to production services or conversely from production services to production function is an area of the *interfunctional responsibility*. Many manufacturing systems' loopholes occur when the preceding department regards its task accomplished, but the succeeding department has not yet assumed the responsibility. Changing the responsibility from one production department to the succeeding one is the area of the *interdepartmental responsibility*. These lapses are called "blank zones"—a source for much aggravation and many production problems.

Material handling is an important stage in material flow control since it holds an opportunity for improving the material flow and reducing lead time by eliminating the wait time and idle time delays. A synergy in material handling is realized when jobs are handled without a delay directly into the queue of the next operation. Dispatching systems, as cumbersome and expensive as they are, perform such a synergistic function of reducing wait time and idle time. Such is their primary mission. The primary function of any dispatching system is to provide a control over idle time in order to ensure that there are no "forgotten jobs" laying around. Remember, idle time can occur at any stage of material flow.

Changing responsibility from the production function to the material handling or any other production services can extend wait time into idle time. Often idle time can occur as a result of expediting and disruption of queue time, or even the interruption of run time in batch-type production when a "hot" job disrupts the material flow. Such interruptions can turn into idle time even within the same area of functional responsibility.

In a production planning and control system, procedures should be worked out for control of the stages at which the "changing hands" or "changing responsibility" is taking place. The advantage of JIT is in that the *kanban* exercises strict control over wait time and idle time. There, parts are actually handed over from one workstation to another thus eliminating wait time and idle time and significantly reducing move time. The JIT-*kanban* system is discussed in detail in Chapter 10.

## SEQUENCING OPERATIONS

Both MRP II and capacity requirements planning (CRP) have proven inadequate in addressing the dynamic job shop environment of a rapidly changing product mix, where parts are continuously competing for the scarce capacity at work centers throughout the plant.

*Example*: Dresser Industrial Tool Division (ITD), an assemble-to-order manufacturer, produces over 10,000 different component parts annually which are used in approximately 1,600 tool models. Manufactured parts average 12 different machining operations resulting in over 120,000 total operations. Over 50 percent of these manufactured parts are produced each month which presents a logistics problem of scheduling 60,000 operations monthly including turning, milling, drilling, grinding, debar, heat treat, assembly, and inspection.

Dresser ITD (Houston) assembles to order from components, but a few products are made-to-stock and others are engineered to customer specifications. Delivery requirements are very competitive, with the normal expected delivery within one to two weeks. This typical job shop production company is involved in three types of operations—make to stock, make to order, and make to customer specifications—despite the fact that the plant builds an established product line. In such a manufacturing application, organizing short-term shop floor schedule is really a formidable task. Here MRP and capacity requirements planning (CRP) are not particularly effective, unless supported by the operations scheduling and control.

CRP is an effective tool in intermediate time planning when demand is forecasted and is less effective in make-to-order shops, where jobs cannot be forecasted. In such job shops, dynamic realities require a fast response. One such system is *operations sequencing*. Operations sequencing is a scheduling technique applying simulation as a means of reproducing a real situation of what is likely to happen on the shop floor with the current production plan when it is executed within the existing staff and machine availability. This entails applying synthetic priority rules and simulation techniques in order to simulate the flow of jobs through all work centers. Scheduling technique applying simulation techniques proves to be effective in a number of manufacturing companies. These techniques are often regarded as a significant competitive advantage. Bill Pursell, vice president of manufacturing of CAMCO, Inc., writes: "Why did we spend three years in the development of an 'operation sequencing' system? Quite simply, we desired to improve our delivery performance in a very competitive market. As of July 1, 1984, there were 5,704 work orders in our MRP system. Of these, 3,137 were planned work orders. All work orders are manufactured in discrete steps. We could never confirm due dates to stock, nor could we promise customer deliveries with any accuracy without 'operation sequencing.'" (See W.U. Pursell, "Operation Sequencing: A New Technique for an Old Problem," *Readings in Production & Inventory Control and Planning*, APICS, 1986.)

CAMCO features even more dynamic operations than Dresser Tools as the former's significant jobs contents are design-to-order jobs. Steps in operations sequencing are discussed in the CAMCO example as CAMCO has utilized this simulation scheduling system successfully since 1982.

Operations sequencing is accomplished in several steps:

1. Identify the operation start and completion dates based on the standard routing times—setup time, run time, average work center queue time, transit time, and idle time. Determine all operations' start and finishing dates by applying backward operation-by-operation scheduling based on MRP-generated due dates. At this stage, jobs are scheduled without regard to the available capacity.

2. Perform load leveling by adjusting the planned capacity to the available capacity level in each time period. This step includes issuing a detailed load report listing the jobs that make up the load in each time period. This step also includes issuing the action plan—the outline for decisions in the weeks ahead—and a work schedule—hours per shift, planned overtime, number of shifts per day, holiday schedule, and routing to the alternative work centers.

   An adjusted planned capacity schedule is still not accurate enough and needs to be adjusted further for the purpose of short-term operations scheduling because it applies the average queue, wait time, and idle time which vary widely in the real world.

3. Generate order priorities. Initial priorities are generated from the need dates of the master production schedule. A slack time remaining (STR) scheduling priority rule is applied here in order to identify the job priority by evaluating slack time remaining—the difference between the time remaining between when the order is due and the time required to complete this order.

$$STR = \text{time remaining} - \text{work remaining}$$

4. Identify the so-called "management factor" according to customer needs and the job significance to the future business. This step is done in agreement with the marketing. Job priority is determined for both the slack time and management factor. Management factor refers to assigning job priority based on outcome of possible failure to produce job on time. The calculation for job priority applying management factor at CAMCO is shown in Figure 7-4. Their priority is computed based on the slack time and management factor. A CAMCO operational prioritized work orders feature three-digit job priority is assigned to all jobs. This is a dynamic job allocation where job priorities are changing daily depending on changes in slack time and variances in capacity.

5. A simulator builds the actual capacity profile for each work center. This is done by adjusting the available capacity by the utilization factor allowing for unproductive time on a machine, including down time, and taking into account the efficiency factor that reflects how a machine or an operator is performing compared to the established operational time standards.

   Actual capacity is calculated based on available capacity, utilization factor, and efficiency. The accuracy of utilization and efficiency indices is ensured by applying the moving average forecasting technique. The simulator can assign jobs to work centers after job priorities have been established.

6. Perform finite loading by applying horizontal loading technique where the highest-priority work order is loaded entirely throughout all work centers before any other work order is addressed. Horizontal loading is an example of preventive planning by ensuring that all the loaded work orders have an available capacity for completing jobs without interruptions.

Time-phased demand for the capacity is estimated for each work center, using among other measures, advanced operations scheduling techniques such as lot splitting and operations overlapping.

Two major reports of the system are the detailed planning analysis report and the scheduled load/capacity report. A *detailed planning analysis report* is sorted by equipment orders. It includes information about part number, description, part location, quantity information—on hand, quantity on order, requirement; due date, priority, and operation date. A *scheduled load/capacity report* is issued for each work center. In this report, jobs in a queue are grouped according to their priority for long-term queue and in the next 2 weeks. Jobs in report are sequenced according to their priority and according to the probability of their arrival to work center. This information assists when jobs at work centers are finally assigned to machines.

Among the advantages of operation sequencing are that all service departments including design department, product engineering, and tool room work to the same plan.

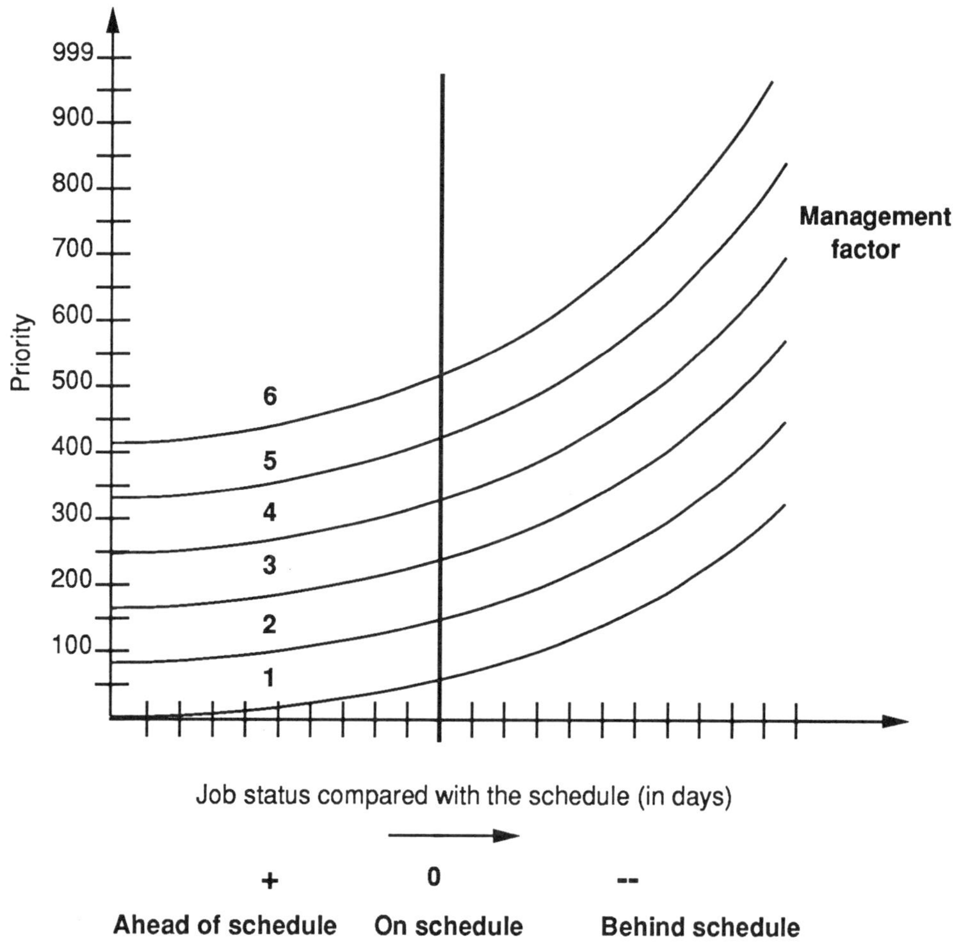


**Figure 7-4**
**Setting Job Priority Applying Management Factor at CAMCO, Inc.**

A fully integrated manufacturing system consists of several key elements: demand management based on forecasts and orders on hand; an inventory control system, including both dependent and independent demand; priority planning applying an MRP system; capacity management comprising capacity requirements planning and operations sequencing; and production activity control exercising control over the execution.

Operations sequencing is also available from ASK Computers as a part of its integrated manufacturing system which has been developed for Hewlett-Packard computers. The ASK integrated manufacturing system is illustrated in Figure 7-5.

## USING AN INTEGRATED TASKS MANAGEMENT SYSTEM FOR FUNCTIONAL CONTROL

Integrated task management (ITM) is a hierarchical time-phased manufacturing system which integrates production planning and control, quality control, plant maintenance, and product costing. Three production levels in the ITM are concerned with optimization: the MPS, where an optimum product mix is set up; the MRP and input/output control; and the shop floor operational control, operational scheduling, and machine loading.

### Monitoring Work Order Progress on a Shop Floor

Often seemingly minor decisions made on the shop floor affect overall performance. For example, a postponed job may result in too many jobs outstanding. If the entire program is thrown out of gear, the services of expediters have to be enlisted to put it right, often at the risk of delaying other jobs.

Even a single erroneous operational decision sometimes can have a profound effect on the overall job shop operational disposition. Priority given to one or more jobs of, say, product A, will not guarantee its final completion ahead of schedule, but due to the limitations imposed by production capacities, product B will definitely fall in arrears. An arbitrary postponement of one job will result in the increase of in-process inventories of both product A and product B.

Advancing the product's A job at the expense of the product's B job increases the inventory of product B. Moreover, such arbitrary changes in job priority will not correspondingly reduce the inventory of the product A; on the contrary, the inventory of the product A increases as well.

The main task in production control is to advance production of all jobs of all products evenly. This again stresses the importance of providing work centers with centralized information enabling them to perform integrated product and process planning-the second-degree production planning and control.

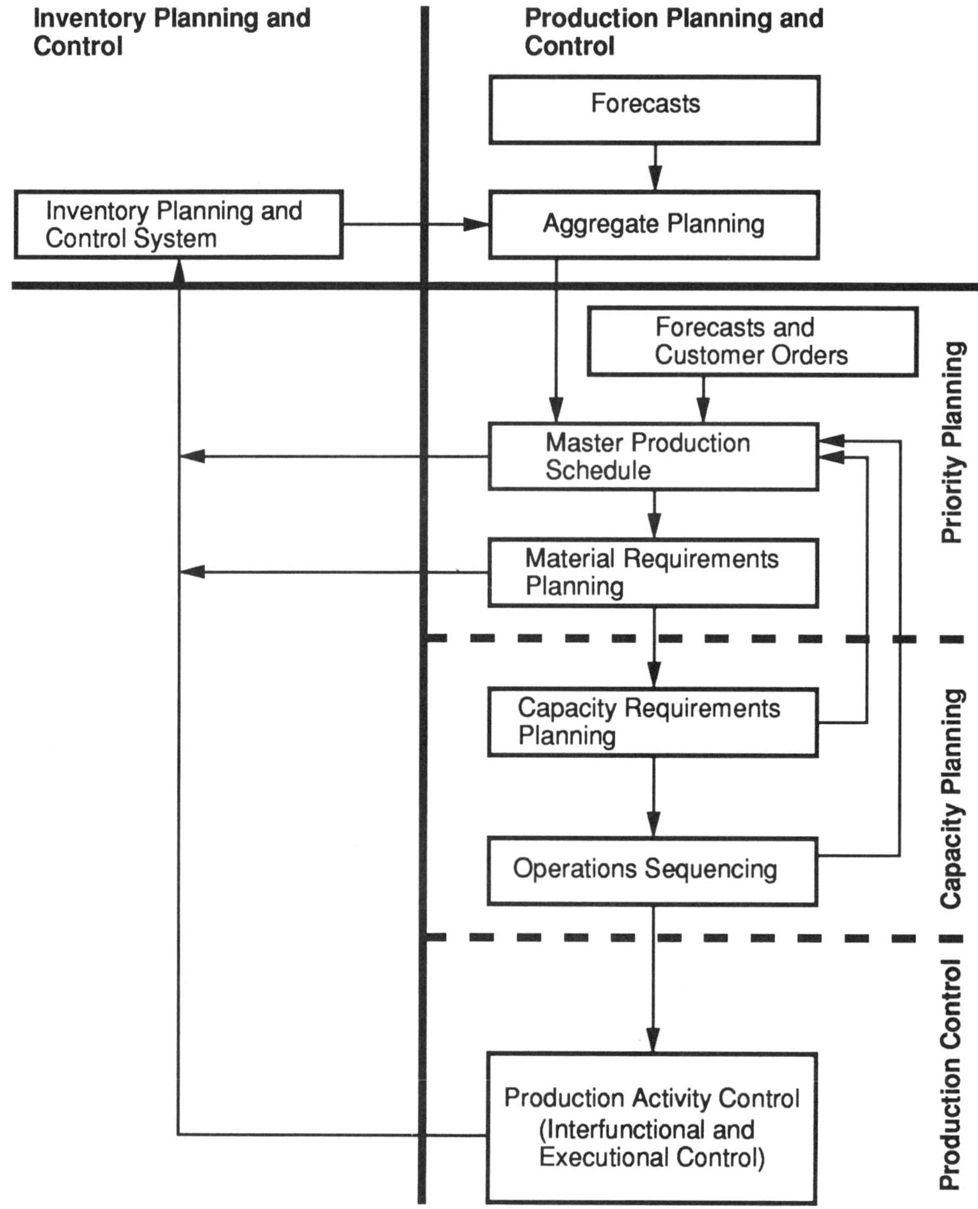


**Figure 7-5**
**The HP-Based ASK Integrated Manufacturing System**

A foreman's decision to assign or delay a job can directly affect production in successive departments. Most job allocations (machine loading in one department) are performed without consideration for the following stages of loading. Often machine loading is done relying only on departmental considerations and priorities. This is due to the fact that the loading disposition of successive departments is not always available. Also, it is impossible to foresee the changes which may occur at the time when the components arrive to the successive departments. The unpredictability of wait time and idle time and the irregular job arrival pattern adds twofold to the uncertainty. The essence of any effective job shop scheduling, within the constraints set by aggregate planning and master production scheduling (MPS), is to simulate a load throughout all operations, before the jobs are released to the shop floor. The final operational scheduling then takes place locally at work centers, having the latest load information just prior to jobs being assigned to workstations.

Recognizing the benefits of operational control, some companies have attempted to set up functional controls. In some instances, the task of job sequencing and scheduling is wrongfully left to the judgment of the supervisory staff—a task which cannot be accomplished without relevant product and process information, usually available to the centralized planning only.

*Example*: A military contractor producing electronic components was compelled to set up operational planning and control of material flow due to very rigid delivery requirements. Shop planning was based on a visual planning system comprised of three large planning boards equipped with rails for the sliding of job tickets containing operational information. A printing machine for operational work orders was part of the system. The initial investment in the system was equal to the cost of a comprehensive computer package, but the maintenance cost exceeded all expectations: 4 schedulers were busy full time updating the planning boards (this is for a company of 150 employees). Their job consisted of tracking and scheduling jobs in various work centers and issuing departmental operational work orders, as well as separate machine loading tickets, for every operation. The major problem was that a change in one operation led to numerous relocations of jobs on the boards. Finally, the company gave up the fight for operational optimization and reduced the task of the system simply to tracking the jobs based on the departmental reports.

This example stresses the complexity in solving the problem of the job shop intermittent material flow control due to the interrelationship of numerous operations. Experts studying job shop intermittent operations have come to the conclusion that job shop scheduling is a network of waiting lines with numerous interrelationships and constraints. In addition, the existence of a large number of operational deviations requiring continuous rescheduling adds to the uncertainty. The analytical results in queuing networks are limited because it is impossible to predict accurately when the parts will arrive, what unexpected jobs will intervene, what stoppages will occur, or how long the waiting time or idle time will be. But even a greater problem is encountered after the optimized or near-optimized schedules are compiled. This problem is operational control and reconciliation of various deviations, the task which the company in the foregoing example was not able to resolve.

Investigation of the best job shop production planning and control systems reveals similarities in this system which can be stated in five principles:

1. All investigated job shops, one way or another, have solutions for controlling the main issue of job shop, namely, intermittent material flow.
2. Investigated job shop systems differentiate between intradepartmental and interdepartmental intermittent operations by developing a different means for planning and controlling these two types of intermittent operations.
3. In most instances, there is centralized operations scheduling and machine loading approach to planning interdepartmental intermittent operations.
4. Shop floor is given authority for scheduling and sequencing intradepartmental intermittent operations.
5. All job shops exercise executional control with very little operational feedback: all stoppages and unexpected delays are adjusted on the floor.

Integrated task management is a job shop planning and control system which is developed by basing on these findings. All the listed five principles are cornerstones of ITM and are included in its planning and controlling methods. These are block scheduling methods—a centralized operations scheduling and machine loading—and operations group group (OGG)—departmental work order consisting of operations groups (OG). In general, ITM planning and control are characterized as *centralized/decentralized operations planning and control.*

### Using Operations Groups and Operations Group Groups—ITM Planning and Control Units

An *operation group* is one or more operations of a single part performed in the same work center. In practical terms, an OG underscores interdepartmental intermission and changes of authority and responsibility from one producing department to another. The OG is a basic construct of product operations/tasks, used in ITM's production planning and control and is a cornerstone of ITM. In ITM, OGs for one product are grouped into daily/weekly departmental work orders—*operations group groups* (OGG). The selection of daily, twice-weekly or weekly ordering procedures depends on lead time of produced products. The main attribute of an OGG is that it represents a weekly/daily operational departmental work order.

The advantage of OGG-type ordering is that all items in work order are from the same customer order or a single product, have the same due date, and are traced to the same work center.

OG and OGG are discussed on the example of a product (20–12) consisting of four assembly units produced by five functional departments. All operations performed in the same department are grouped into an operations group. For example, part 20-12171 undergoes 23 operations grouped into five operations groups:

1. OG-1, performed in deptartment 1, with the due date in week 5. This OG is included in the OGG D-1 week-5 operation work order for department 1 and comprises all the operations of product 20-12 that ought to be completed in department 1 in week 5.
2. The next operation group is OG-2 performed in department 3. This operation group is included in the work order with the due date in week 4.
3. The next operation group is OG-3 performed in department 2 and included in the work order with the due date in week 3.

4, 5. The remaining two operation groups for part 20-12171 are OG 4 and OG 5 processed in departments 6 and 4 correspondingly.

The ITM approach is to set up centralized production planning and control of interdepartmental intermittent operations while leaving intradepartmental intermittent control and decentralized operational scheduling to the departmental supervision and the workers themselves. An operations group is a synthetic operational planning and control unit with the operation's due date emphasized as a hallmark for production control.

The need for dispatchers to monitor each individual operation is eliminated. Also, the task of expediters, if there is a need for them at all, is made easier because they do not have to search for items along operational routes, since each item in a work order is allocated to a specific department, with the due dates in each department being highlighted.

An OGG is assigned to a single department under the same authority, with all the operations in the work order having the same due date. In other words, an OGG is a work order comprising jobs/operation having the same priority, a really unique feature for a functional department work order.

This makes it much easier to schedule and control OGGs. For example, OGG D-1 week 5 comprises OG-1 of part 20-12171, part 20-16726, and part 20-12763; OGG D-1 week 4 comprises OG-1 of part 20-12359 and part 20-12721.

An OGG represents both product and process priorities: while an OGG is indicative of a specific product (a product attribute), at the same time, it is allocated to a single departmental authority (a process attribute).

The *next unit* in the ITM product structure is the *product element* (PE), which consists of all work orders, OGGs, allocated to a single department throughout all the time periods of the order lead time. For example, PE D-1 comprises OGG-1, D-1; OGG-2, D-1; OGG-3, D-1 ... OGG-*n*, D-1, where PE, D-1 is a product element assigned to department D-1. OGG-1, D-1 is a work order for department 1 having a due date in week 1, and OGG-*n*, D-1 is a work order for department 1 having due date in week *n*.

All the levels on the ITM diagram (shown in Figure 7-6) consist of integrated product and process operational units—operations grouped into the OG, OGG, and PE constructs.

This structure is named *bill of integrated tasks* (BIT). BIT is a convenient tool for product and process balancing because an operation is a common structural unit in the product structure and process structure, expressed in labor- and machine-hours. Figure 7-6 illustrates the difference between bill of materials planning and ITM's bill of integrated tasks.

*Bill of materials planning* (BOMP) structure elements of BOM into three categories of components, assemblies, and final assembly corresponding to three stages of production (refer to Figure 1-4). Stage 1 features intermittent material flow and stages 2 and 3 usually have continuous material flow.

Three levels of BOMP representing physical components of product compared to three levels of BIT representing jobs measured in labor- and machine-hours are required for producing these components.

## Analyzing the Functional Control of Integrated Task Management

Functional control focuses its attention on those responsible for the development and implementation of production programs. Twenty-three operations of part 20-12171 are grouped into five groups, each included in a departmental work order—OGGs with the definite due date. It is the supervisory responsibility to complete an OGGs on time and to hand them over to another department. The approach is similar to that of JIT-*kanban*. The difference is that *kanban* represents a single operation, while an OGG is a unit which can be interpreted as an extended *kanban* tailored to job shop type material flow and structures.

Functional control shifts production control from the storeroom to the shop floor where most production problems originate. Planning and control is still directed to a product, but the emphasis is put on the process optimization and the elimination of wait time and idle time. The ITM functional control can be described as programmed planning and control system of allocated responsibilities. The integrated tasks, OGs and OGGs, make it possible to construct any order out of standard units corresponding to the company's process structure. OG and OGG are synthetic standards, the groups of operations/task compiled into operational time-phased departmental work orders.

Functional management shifts the emphasis from observing the availability of product components to a method of managing production units producing these components. Manufactured orders are integrated into operational constructs, OGGs, highlighting departmental responsibilities. Detailed operational control of OGGs is left to the care of departmental supervision.

Functional management centralized/decentralized production planning and control lead to realignment of material controller's and dispatcher's functions and the elimination of expediting. The majority of these functions can be assigned to the departmental staff and to the workers, thereby adding to the job enrichment.

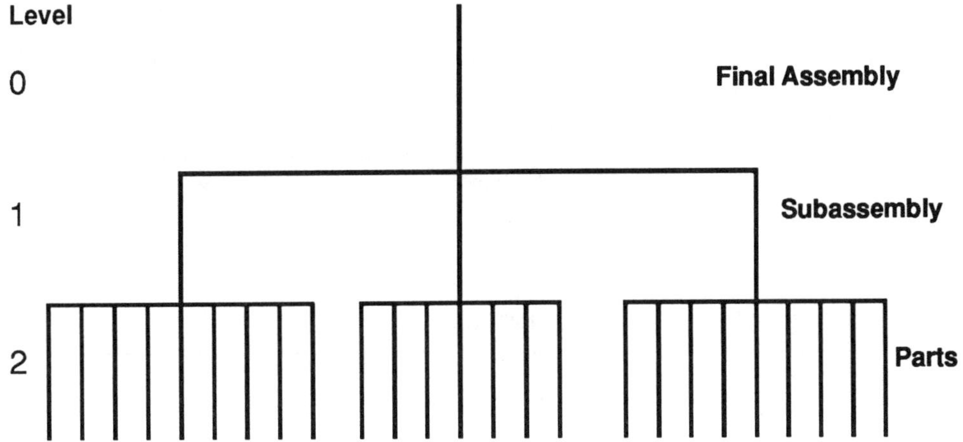


**A. Bill of Material Planning (BOMP)**

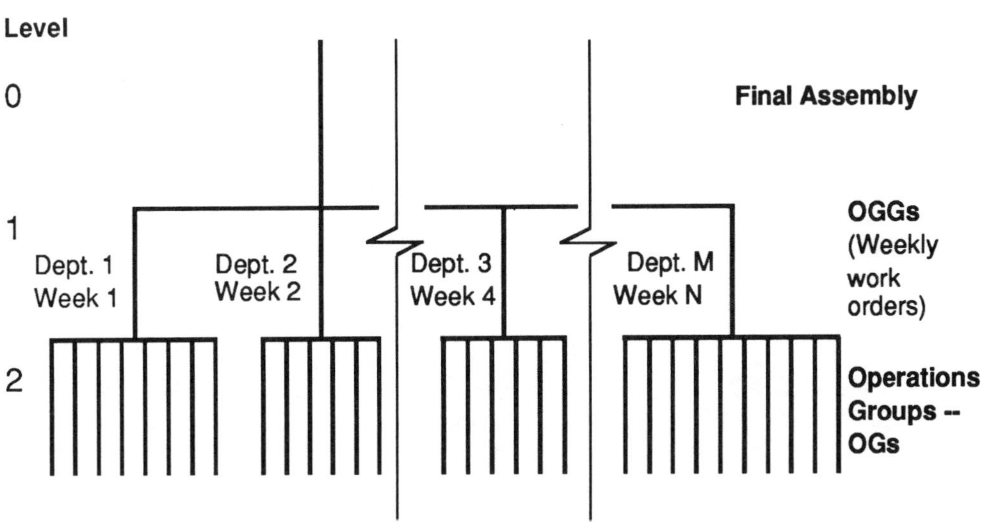


**B. Bill of Integrated Tasks (BIT)**

**Figure 7-6**
**Comparing BOMP with BIT Functional Control**

The benefit of ITM is in assigning the functions of operational production planning and control to a departmental staff. Morcovcr, the function of material controllers, dispatchers, and expediters can be reduced, while at the same time, the behavioral and motivation factors are enhanced. In this respect, ITM's OGG is a programmed decision-making tool contributing to involvement of shop floor staff into operational planning and control—preventive planning and executional production control.

## SCHEDULING WITH THE BILL OF INTEGRATED TASKS

*Bill of integrated tasks* (BIT) is a family tree interpreting MPS plans into departmental weekly/daily operational orders. BIT is an operational schedule relating both the product and process to production planning and control of material flow.

The critical interdepartmental intermissions of material flow arranged in BIT in such a way that the operational due dates are highlighted. Feedback information is meaningful and freely available because the planning units (individual operations expressed in labor- and machine-hours) are the same at all the ITM planning levels.

BIT is instrumental in improving communication and flow of information between all the stages of production planning and control and provides information for estimating their completion and production costs.

Product element (PE) can be cited as a management tool sufficiently adequate for functional managerial control and management control by exception. PE is a convenient planning unit for aggregate planning and MPS as it sets up aggregate capacity requirements for each functional department.

## USING INTEGRATED TASK MANAGEMENT TO AVOID SHORTCOMINGS IN TRADITIONAL SHOP FLOOR CONTROL

A traditional planning and control system is divided into two spheres distinguished by different planning and control units: *itemized planning* controlling finished products and components and *operational planning* where control unit is labor- and machine-hours per operation.

Different planning and control units restrict communication required for effective production planning and control. This leads to a division of production planning and control systems into two separate segments: itemized planning and control and operations planning and control. This leads to ambiguity in production management; that is, there are people responsible for planning and yet other people responsible for execution and control of these plans. Figure

7-7 shows that the communication between the itemized planning and the operational planning is disrupted, and the communication link exists mainly with stores.

In ITM, the communication between the levels in the planning and control system is not obstructed, since all levels of the BIT consist of the standard planning and control constructs, OGs, OGGs, and PEs composed of congruent measuring units, namely, labor- and machine-hours. Figure 7-8 shows an unobstructed flow of information between all the levels of the system hierarchy. Information on OGG compiled by the shop floor staff is used by all management levels with the various degree of integration: OGG or PE, single product, or groups of products. People producing plans are involved in the control of execution.

### Using Block Scheduling Techniques

What is required is a coordinated system where shop floor management takes active part in and is accountable for the overall control of material flow. Often, Lotus 1-2-3 computer programs are used to serve in establishing a data communication link between the shop floor and management.

In the ITM production planning and control system, an additional unit of planning is introduced, namely, centralized operational planning and control. The purpose of this unit is to interpret the MRP detailed plan into weekly departmental operational work orders, applying the technique of centralized scheduling defined as the *ITM block scheduling.*

Block scheduling is MRP-based operational backward scheduling, where product requirements are computed in a matrix format. The product matrix is compared with the available capacity matrix before the final work order is issued. This ensures that the capacities throughout work centers involved are assigned to a work order in corresponding time periods.

Block scheduling uses a horizontal sequencing method, where requirements for a single product are computed applying backward operation-by-operation scheduling. This represents one block in a matrix format. If it appears that the capacity in one or another time period is not available, the entire block is moved to another time period, thus trying to achieve zero-stock production by reducing queueing, wait time, and idle time. Detailed scheduling is done by comparing and adjusting the product and process matrix until the balance is reached.

## ADVANTAGES OF FUNCTIONAL CONTROL WITH INTEGRATED TASK MANAGEMENT

Structural production control is typical in a situation in which a number of expediters and material controllers rush about manufacturing departments and work centers chasing specific parts and components. Technical information and date searches involved in expediting activities are drawings, product specifications,

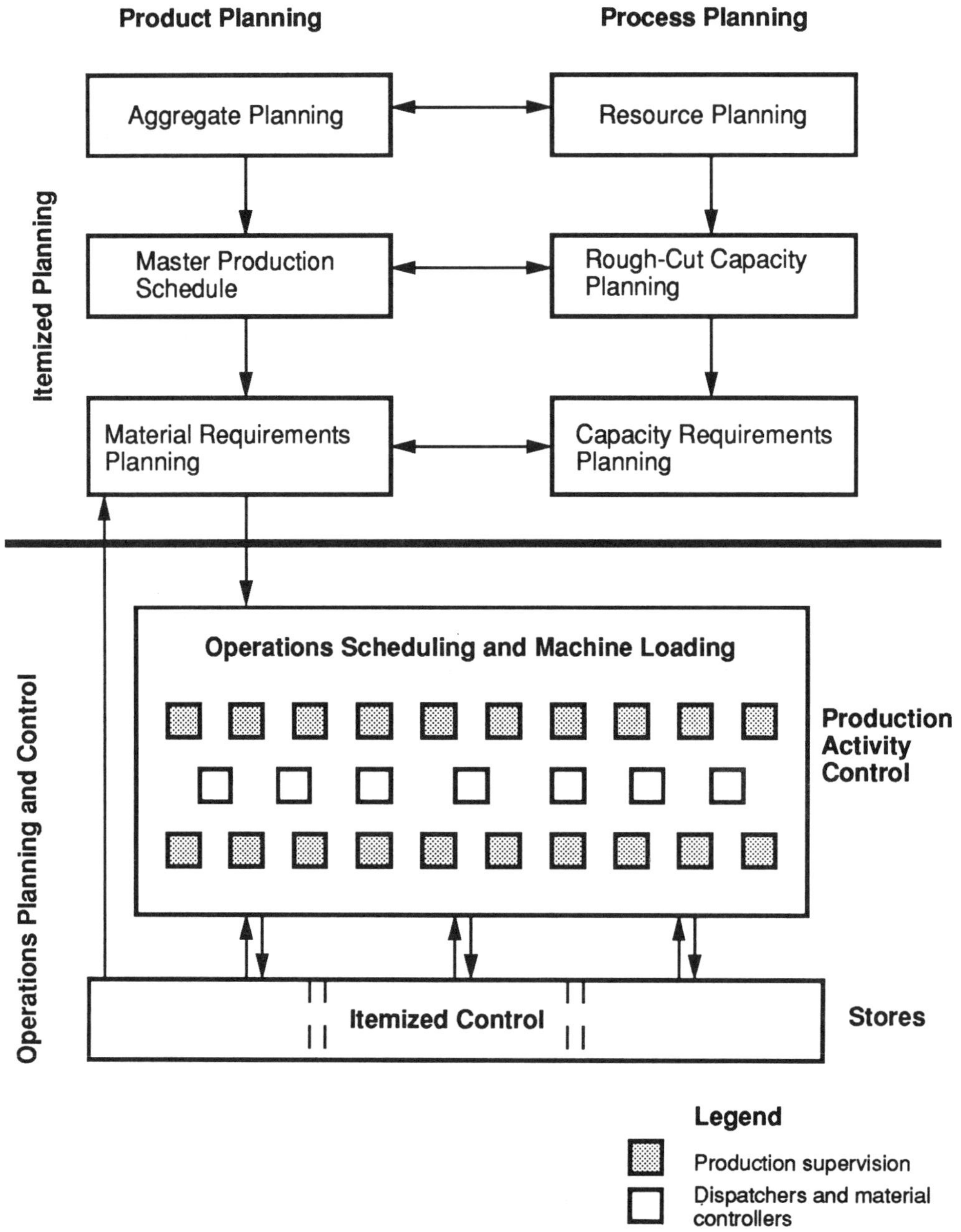


**Figure 7-7**
**Product and Process Planning and Control**

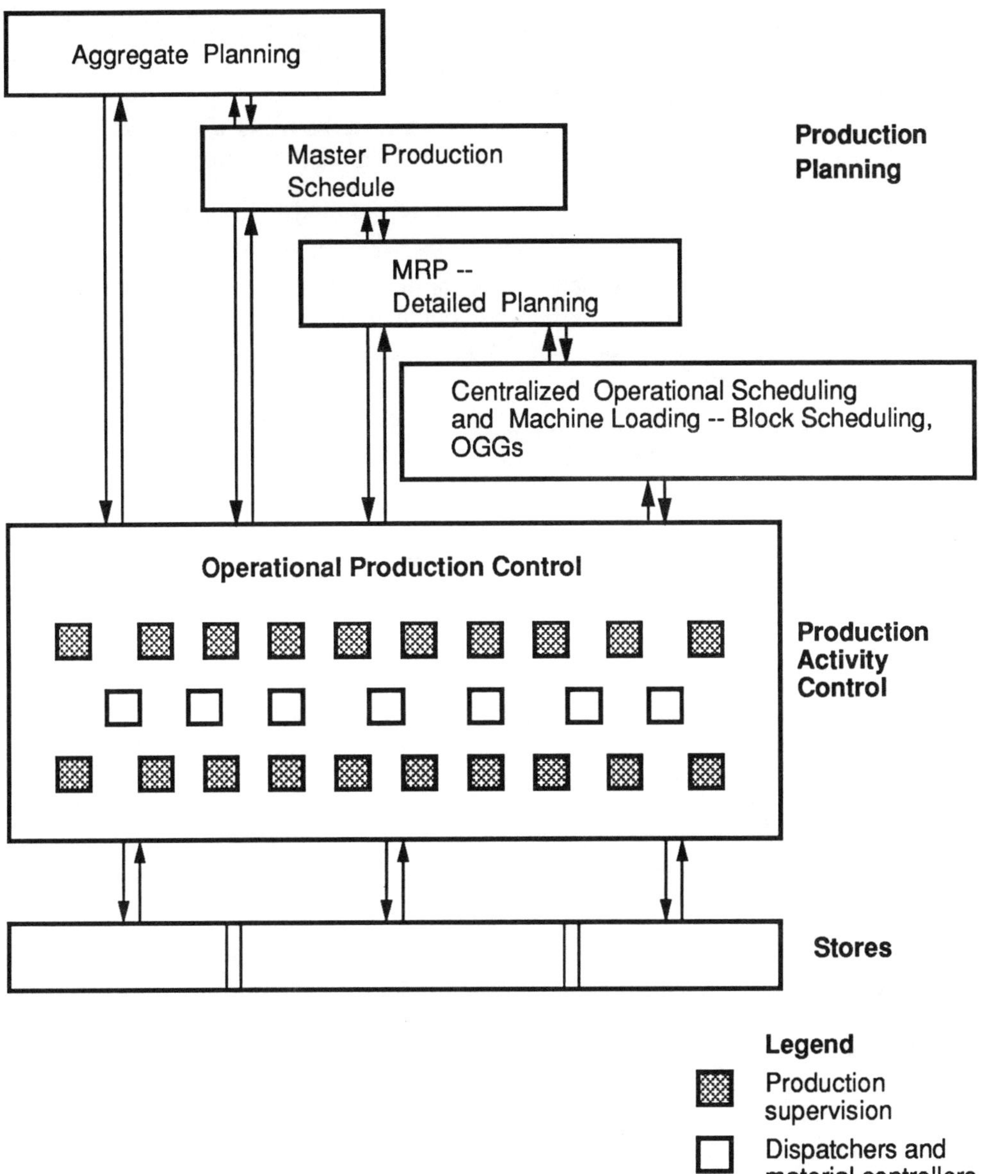


**Figure 7-8**
**The ITM Production Planning and Control System**

route sheets, assembly charts, and production schedules. Expediting is a cross-departmental activity. Expediters deal with several departments in order to facilitate the production of a single component.

In this context, functional control deals with the OGG work orders. Besides reduction in idle time, other advantages of the ITM functional control are

1. No specific knowledge of product is required. This point is especially valuable for multiproduct manufacturing companies.
2. All levels of management can be routinely involved in functional control. Production control is exercised continuously from the order launching through the final assembly. Thus, the possibility of "surprises" and "hot" jobs is significantly reduced.
3. A continuous reporting procedure and the responsibility for manufacturing departments are established for activities that went unreported in structural control.
4. A problem area can be tracked immediately to the specific work center in the company, and no chasing along operational component routes is required. Operational control over material flow is essential for efficient planning when dispatching does not present a feasible solution here.

Thus, ITM is a method for resolving the compound issue of dispatching intermittent operations by issuing work shop orders with defined operational due dates and priorities. These weekly work shop orders are OGGs, with such distinctive features as

1. Operational optimization planning
2. Functional and time phasing for departments, work centers, and single machines

The fact that the ITM does not exclude any existing inventory-type control methods (MRP included), but expands them and incorporates them into the ITM functional control operational optimization application, is an additional incentive, and is a solution to the existing structural control predicament.

(Additional information about an integrated task management system and assistance for implementation can be obtained from Integrated Management Systems—P.O. Box 741406 Houston, Texas. 77274-1406)

## USING COMPUTERIZED PRODUCTION PLANNING AND CONTROL TOOLS

At present, when manufacturing systems become synonymous to computerized manufacturing systems, computers are common tools for operational decision making and production control.

Due to operations management done through the media of computerized systems, it is essential for managers at all levels, and especially the shop floor personnel, to be conversant with the basics of the electronic data processing. Along with the word processing knowledge, which becomes a common expression and communication tool, the working knowledge of two other computer programs is essential for operations managers to be effective in dealing with the new set of functions expected of them in decision making, execution, and operations control. These programs are DBase III+™ or DBase IV™ and Lotus 1-2-3™.

It is known that in many manufacturing systems the amount of information required even for an elementary operation scheduling decision exceeds these systems' ability to provide such real-time operational data to various places in the organization. Moreover, centralized operational planning requires a significant computer power to ensure that the data are collected and interpreted and sent to production areas as work orders on time.

Dynamic features of manufacturing systems require a real-time access capability for decision makers, who at the operational decision level are shop floor personnel.

The presently observed shift from feedbacked control to executional control requires a shop floor to have multidimensional databases.

## Using DBase III+™ and DBase IV™

The second standard computer program, widely used in production planning and control, is a standard data base, such as Dbase III+™ or Dbase IV™, which can be used in structuring a large amount of production operational data necessary for operational planning and control.

DBase™ is regarded as data management or a computerized record-keeping system similar to an electronic filing cabinet containing a number of computerized data files. DBase™ helps to automate information processing and dissemination tasks: storing and retrieving data fast and easily, adding new files, inserting new data into existing files, deleting data from existing files, reporting, and above all, providing centralized control over the firm's operational data. The last feature is a valuable tool for decentralized dynamic material flow control in the environment where the operational data are widely dispersed.

DBase™ enables production units to share the data and to determine common priorities in a continuously changing environment, by being able to standardize their procedures and to balance the conflicting requirements.

In a relational database, data are arranged in the form of a matrix where rows represent individual records and columns represent fields of information contained in the records. In a computerized management system, where the number of records runs into many thousands, DBase™ makes it easy to extract and view information, manipulate selected records from the database, extract data from several files simultaneously, and produce a wide variety of reports.

DBase III+™ and DBase IV™ products are developed by Ashton-Tate, 20101 Hamilton Avenue, CA 90509-9972.

## Using Lotus 1-2-3™

A spreadsheet is a convenient tool for manipulating and estimating computerized data and for conducting the "what-if" analysis so essential to operations managers. Most production problems are complex issues consisting of simple components which can be resolved by using three universal tools—a calculator, a pencil, and a sheet of paper. Production planning problems are often resolved by applying these simple tools. Lotus 1-2-3™ or a spreadshet is a computer program which makes it convenient for a user to utilize the computer power, memory and electronic screen capability by easy means emulating the basic tools.

A spreadsheet is a large array of cells arranged in rows and columns in which the data are entered. In a spreadsheet, a computer screen is compared to a window that looks upon a large electronic worksheet comprising over 8,000 rows and approximately 250 columns. The intersections of rows and columns provide many thousands of entry positions. The data base is composed of records that are cells (entries in the spreadsheet). At times, you may wish to view the effect of a data entry on distant columns or rows. The spreadsheet provides such a tool by scrolling the window in four directions to look at any part of the worksheet or splitting the screen into two windows to see any other part of the worksheet at the same time.

Graphics and data management elements, among many features of Lotus 1-2-3™, make it a powerful production planning tool. These include the ability of the program to keep track of the formulas and calculations used in solving the problems.

The present decision making requires a real-time interaction of a management information system and the supporting data communication means. Lotus 1-2-3™ is an effective tool for such an interaction of a management information system (MIS) and floor data in management decision making. There are many examples of the use of Lotus 1-2-3™ in various modules of production planning and control, including forecasting, business strategic planning, aggregate planning, master production scheduling, material requirements planning, capacity requirements planning, and shop floor scheduling and machine loading.

Lotus 1-2-3™ templates incorporate user-written instructions consisting of macro programming commands. In production planning applications, the special functions of Lotus 1-2-3™, such as merging files and the data base capability, allow the user to evaluate alternative operating schedules. A spreadsheet is considered the best computer program that has ever been developed. Lotus 1-2-3™, and its latest release Lotus @ FACTORY™, developed by the Lotus Corp. are fast becoming the mainstays in many companies.

Recent changes in production systems make it imperative that manufacturing managers receive production data as near to real time as possible. That can't happen with older systems of factory scheduling and control that run on mainframe computers, work in a batch mode, and rely on data that is two to four weeks old. An alternative is to pick up production data directly from factory machine stations and feed it into a spreadsheet for an instant analysis.

## USING PCS ON THE FACTORY FLOOR

The link between the real-time performance and the people in the front office who must analyze it is critical. That link can be a system of automatic counting devices and communication paths or it can be a machine operator.

In either case, the spreadsheet is a natural vehicle for creating the link —with machines as rows and production counts as columns. Typically, production schedulers and manufacturing engineers in the front office are already using Lotus 1-2-3™ to analyze the production data.

It is an obvious step to capture the data in a spreadsheet to start with. The next obvious step is to link the operators and the office in a local area network so that the data won't have to be handled twice.

In the application described here, an operator logs in by selecting a machine from a list of machines, by selecting his or her own name from a list of operators, and by selecting the part to be processed from a list of parts. When that sequence is complete, the operator enters the total number of parts produced and the number of those parts that must be scrapped because of defects. The template calculates the net production.

The operator may then log off that machine and log on to another, or log off entirely. The template retains the production data and accepts new data from other operators on the list. It also maintains a running count of the total net parts production. When an operator or a supervisor selects "Quit," the production data are stored on a disk under a name that includes the current date.

The template features a vertical selection window. This allows the user (in this particular application) to specify an operator name or a part number by using the point-and-shoot method. A macro then enters that item into the correct cell. That avoids the need to retype information, obviates any need to learn the keyboard, and minimizes errors.

Such a macro might be designed also to log out shift operators automatically. Or you might decide you need more protection against the loss of data. You could cause a production record to be saved on a disk every time a new number was entered. You could also restrict an operator to entering data only in the row in the data chart on which his name was entered by the log-in procedure. You might also want to give the operator an option of processing a different part on the same machine.

As it stands, this template records only the departmental totals for each machine's output and scrap parts. Depending on the plant's production philosophy, it might be desirable to provide a separate worksheet for each machine or for each operator.

A Lotus 1-2-3™ template can consolidate factory data. The template can be used in two ways: where there is a manual input or it is retrieved automatically from many sources. It can read data from American Standard Code for Information Interchange (ASCII) files that are created by data collection servers. Or it can read data directly from a data collection board that is attached to the same PC on which Lotus 1-2-3™ is running. A board allows data to be collected, displayed, and updated in the 1-2-3™ worksheet in real time. Some of the useful features are

1. A report that shows how many parts were begun, finished, and released for each shift and for each machine, as well as how many hours each machine was busy. The program also allows you to see a graph of parts production and a graph of machine time instantaneously—a useful feature for product and process balancing.
2. Ability to retrieve a shift record as a worksheet and print it out or set up a worksheet to combine data from many shift records.
3. Production planning modules—aggregate planning, MPS, capacity planning, inventory control, operations, and scheduling, and statistical quality control are successfully resolved by using Lotus 1-2-3™. Practical examples of how to use Lotuse 1-2-3™ on the shop floor are explained by Nicholas J. Losole of Lotus Development Corp.*

The latest release from Lotus, Lotus 1-2-3 @ Factory™ supports integrated manufacturing applications and enables users to access directly a wide variety of external data sources from within their Lotus application. This is a software that provides a means of bringing real-time factory floor data into a spreadsheet by creating files readable by Lotus 1-2-3™. @Factory™ is completely integrated with Lotus 1-2-3™ and executes concurrently displaying real-time data, real-time data analysis, real-time reporting, and statistical process control.

With @ Factory™ you can make operating decisions based upon accurate, up-to-date information, becoming a communication gateway between the factory floor and corporate mainframe computers for data collection and reporting. Since Lotus 1-2-3™ is available for a number of different hardware platforms, data files can be easily shared among microcomputers, minicomputers, workstations, and mainframes.

Lotus 1-2-3™ is a development of Lotus Development Corporation, 55 Cambridge Parkway, Cambridge, MA 02142.

---

* Nicholas J. Losole "To Control Production, Point and Shoot," *Lotus* December 1989, and "Collecting Facory Data," *Lotus*, April 1990.

The spreadsheet can be applied in forecasting, capacity planning, inventory control, and quality assurance and can provide a single unique tool for MRP planning and shop floor control scheduling and machine loading.

For example, Lucia Peek and John Blackstone have developed a template using Lotus 1-2-3™ with a microcomputer for calculating a time-phased order point (TPOP) in inventory control systems. This includes a blank TPOP template and separate data files. In an interactive mode, the planner may retrieve the TPOP template and merge information from data file. This program calculates the projected available inventory and time-phased planned order releases (Lucia E. Peel and John H. Blackstone, Jr., "Developing a Time-Phased Order-Point Template Using a Spreadsheet," *Production and Inventory Management Journal*, Vol. 28, No. 4, 1987, pp. 6-10).

The problem of job shop scheduling for small companies is addressed by Norman Pendegraft. The program calculates the job finish times and displays alternative shop schedules. The author demonstrates the program on the example of a small shop with three machines and several jobs in queue. This program incorporates simple, user-written macros for generating operational schedules and their graphical display (Norman Pendegraft, "Job Shop Decision Support with a Microcomputer Spreadsheet," *Production and Inventory Management Journal*, Vol. 28, No. 4, 1987, pp. 11-14).

Jayavel Sounderpandian suggests a do-it-yourself MRP system on the spreadsheet that requires little knowledge of computer programming. (This article is entitled "MRP on Spreadsheets: A Do-It-Yourself Alternative for Small Firms" and it appeared in *Production and Inventory Management Journal* (Vol. 30, No. 2, 1989).

In the same publication (Vol. 31, No. 1, 1990), Rajen Parekh, in his article "Capacity/Inventory Planning Using a Spreadsheet," demonstrates the use of a spreadsheet for capacity/inventory planning.

## SUMMARY

Many companies achieve productivity improvement through streamlining the material flow by reducing interferences and interruptions. A delay in a single operation of one product disrupts other work orders upon expedition. Productivity improvement through smoothing the material flow can be achieved only by detailed scheduling, machine loading, and production control procedures.

Work centers should be provided with a detailed operational schedule, one that guides shop floor operating decisions. CRP-based operational schedules are not always a solution to operations scheduling problems, due to long time elapsed between planning and execution. Operations scheduling is most effective when it is conducted immediately prior to execution—by taking into consideration the latest capacity disposition. Studying scheduling techniques is essential, due to pressing needs for reducing a queueing lines, inventory, and lead time.

There are two approaches to operations scheduling: static and dynamic. Static scheduling is job sequencing by identifying job priorities in a single work center. Dynamic scheduling considers the effect a scheduling decision will have on the material flow in successive work centers. It considers the minimum lead times, minimum WIP, reduced queueing, and the optimum work center utilization.

Main operations scheduling techniques are as follows:

*Operation-by-operation scheduling*—a technique of breaking lead time into operation slots and scheduling the operations one by one. Operation-by-operation scheduling is a next step after MRP.

*Least slack priority rules*—slack time remaining and slack time per remaining operations.

*Scheduling jobs according to the sequence of arrival*—first-come, first-served, last-come, first-served.

*Scheduling rules which take into account job due dates and/or operation time*—due date rules according to the operation due date or according to the assembly due date, according to the duration of machine time, and priority rules where the final due date is considered.

*Priority rules which take into account an inventory position, engineering considerations, or dynamics of subsequent processes*—reducing the next queue priority rule, reducing combined setup time.

*Synthetic priority rules*—the even flow scheduling is a technique applying uniform lead time for all the operations.

*Simulation scheduling technique—operations sequencing* reproduces a real situation of what is likely to happen on a shop floor with the current production plan within the existing manpower and machine availability framework.

Advanced scheduling techniques for reducing lead time are operations overlapping, operations splitting, and lot splitting.

Integrated task management is an integrated planning and control system applying centralized/decentralized approach operations scheduling. ITM's OGG is a synthetic standard where groups of operations/tasks are combined into operational time-phased departmental work orders. An OGG is a programmed decision-making tool contributing to the involvement of the shop floor staff into operational planning and control—preventive planning and executional production control.

One of the computer programs essential to operations managers is a spreadsheet, convenient for manipulating and estimating these data and for conducting the "what-if" analysis. Lotus 1-2-3™ templates incorporate user-written instructions, consisting of macro programming commands.

Another standard computer program, widely used in production planning and control, is a standard data base, such as DBase III+™ or DBase IV™, which can be used in structuring a large amount of production operational data necessary for operational planning and control.

Applying these scheduling techniques will produce for you a competitive edge so essential in achieving a world-class performance.

# Part Three

## JUST-IN-TIME MANUFACTURING SYSTEMS

# 8

# Implementing Just-in-Time Systems*

Just-in-Time implies the timely completion as the essence of the system. Many people associate JIT with the *kanban*-type shop floor control or with inventory reduction efforts. To understand what JIT is, we must return to the fundamentals.

JIT developers have studied the Henry Ford's assembly line trying to find out how was it possible then, at the turn of the century, to achieve such efficiency in throughput time. History tells us that if his boats loaded with iron ore have docked their cargo at an unloading bay on Monday at 8:00 A.M., by noon Tuesday the ore has already been reduced to iron, and by 8:00 A.M. on Wednesday the car was rolling off the assembly line.

This exemplary integrated production pattern somehow faded into oblivion over the decades for most American industrial organizations. If the Ford assembly-line organization, with its resolute material flow, were applied to American discrete manufacturing today, and adjusted to present requirements of production in small quantities with a large variety of products, it could be an important measure for regaining our leading position in the world of manufacturing.

JIT applies the Henry Ford type of a work flow system in which manufactured parts are moved to assembly processes as soon as they are completed. Such manufacturing system features a *product-focused pattern* of material flow.

---

*Chapters 8 to 12 include information received from the recently conducted Just-in-Time survey of 4,000 American manufacturing companies in which author has taken part.

The Japanese, with their historical zeal, dedication, and national resolve, have selected the most rational American methods which produce the best results within the Japanese culture and its management-labor relationships. They have structured these methods into a system, integrating such elements as the workers' contribution to constant improvement, workers' involvement in services, employees' involvement in planning and control, and setup time reduction. They championed a quality standard as an undisputed code of conduct, not only at the fabrication stage, but also in services, engineering, and product design.

## THE PRINCIPLES OF JIT MATERIAL FLOW

The overriding consideration in any production system is its pattern of material flow. The JIT material flow resembles a pattern of assembly-line production. Two principles are essential to such an assembly-line operation: line balancing and line synchronization.

*Line balancing* means equalizing individual operations' lead times, similar to that of assembly-line balancing. The aim of productionl-ine balancing is to ensure that it takes the same time to perform each operation on the line. If one operation is accelerated, it should not lead to an increase of the line's output; rather, it should result in an increase in the interoperational inventory. Figure 8-1 illustrates four possible cases in production-line balancing and synchronization. Line balancing is achieved when output from all workstations of production line is the same. In case 1, there is a queue to machine 2 due to the fact that operation 1 requires only 6 minutes as compared to 8 minutes for operations 2, 3, and 4. All operations of the production line are balanced as shown in case 2, so there are no waiting lines.

*Line synchronization* means uniformity, like marching soldiers, where each soldier represents an operation, uniformly starting and stopping/freezing on command. In JIT, the commander is the next operation. The rational triggering of the command is the goal for reaching a uniformity in order to eliminate queues and achieve a zero inventory. This requires giving the commands to the work stations individually, due to the differences in production cycles and the inventory status. A line synchronization is based on the fact that operations are stopped when the succeeding operations do not need components. Cases in line synchronization are shown in Figure 8-1, cases 3 and 4. Case 3 illustrates a balanced but unsynchronized production line, due to the WIP inventory build-up. Despite the fact that the production line is balanced, there is a queue at operation 3.

In a dedicated production line, where jobs are balanced, synchronization means that all the processes start and finish at the same time. In essence,

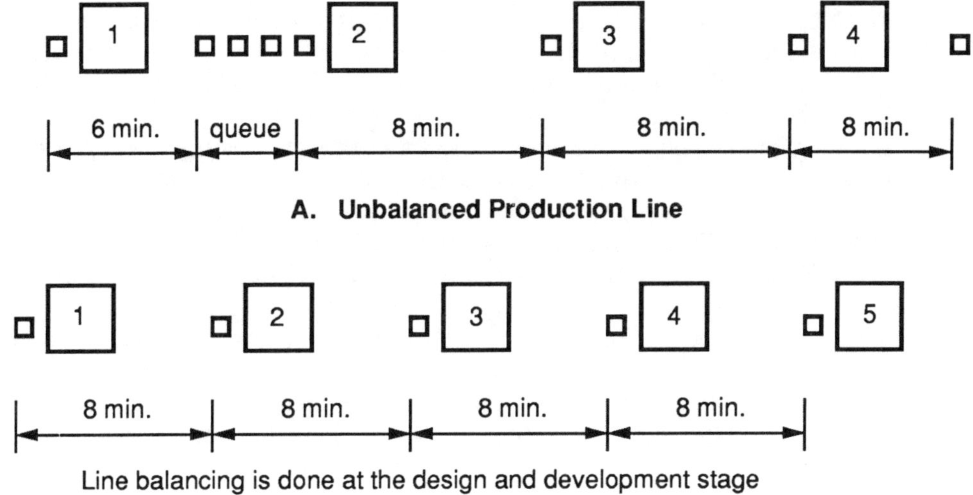


**A. Unbalanced Production Line**

Line balancing is done at the design and development stage

**B. Balanced Production Line**

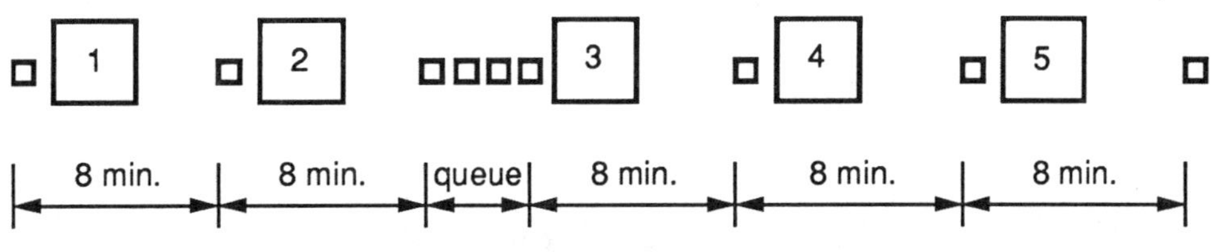


Operation 3 started late and there is WIP buildup

**C. Balanced Unsynchronized Production Line**

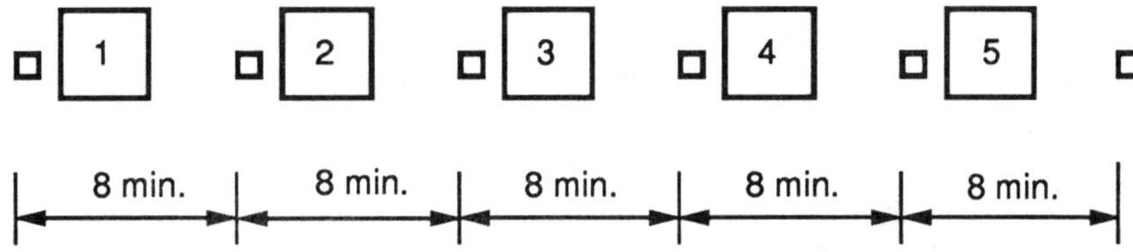


Line synchronization is done by production planning and control

**D. Balanced Synchronized Production Line**

**Figure 8-1**
**Production Line Balancing and Synchronization**

synchronization means to produce only what is needed now. The work flow system is designed so that the parts are fed into assembly on their completion.

In assembly-line production, operations scheduling is not required because the line has been balanced in advance at the project stage. However, in nondedicated job shop production, where jobs of various products compete for production facilities, operations have to be scheduled and assigned to machines at the shop floor. Seventy-five percent of all manufacturers are classified as job shops, including many batch type repetitive production systems.

JIT production control is aimed at attaining a balanced and synchronized material flow. When it comes to producing components, the distinction between repetitive and one-off job shop production is blurred because often these two production systems coexist and compete for the same machines. When considering such a productive system, JIT should be used for controlling not only repetitive products, but also other nonrepetitive orders. Nevertheless, some companies start JIT by selecting "favorable" product lines. Such an approach can be called fragmented JIT.

If JIT controls selective products only, it is classified as a product control-type production system, not as an integrated product and process control system. The fragmented JIT is comparable to a person who quits smoking at home but not at work. The benefits of such "partial" production planning and control are diminished due to selected JIT orders receiving priority at the expense of other jobs.

## THE EVOLUTION OF THE ASSEMBLY LINE AND JIT

Initially, before Frank and Lillian Gilbreths' time study efforts and scientific management, a shoemaker was able to produce a pair of shoes per day. This is the simplest possible scenario: one producer—one customer.

The revolutionized improvement in a production process comes with the division of labor. The shoemaking job was divided into several operations, with a person assigned to each operation. This change dramatically increased industrial productivity: instead of seven persons on the production line producing seven pairs of shoes according to the initial setup, the seven workers produced 20 pairs of shoes per day. But everything comes at a price:

- A supervisor is needed to supervise the team
- A quality control inspector is needed to control the quality of each operation preventing bad units proceeding through all the downstream operations
- Seven different pieces of equipment are required to perform these operations
- Semiproducts must be transported between the workstations (for example, conveyors)

- A plant maintenance worker must keep all this machinery in working order

But still it was a remarkable improvement, and the greatest excitement is that the further the process is divided into smaller operations, the greater increase in productivity is realized. An additional price paid for the improvement is what we collectively call manufacturing services (technical and clerical support of production):

- With further division of operations into smaller tasks comes an increase in the work force
- A second echelon of supervisors is needed to supervise the increasing number of quality control inspectors and maintenance people
- Managers are needed to supervise supervisors and to organize, plan, and control such multifunctional operations
- Clerical and housekeeping services are needed to support this staff

Productivity increase objectives have resulted in a large division of operations into smaller tasks with even greater proliferation of organizational infrastructure. There are mechanized shoe factories where a pair of shoes, before it is completed, passes through hundreds pairs of hands aligned at the conveyor, sometimes running over several floors of a factory building.

A further expansion of production lines and fracturing operations into smaller and smaller tasks leads to departmentalization, functionalization, specialization, and magnification of organizational structures, as for example, providing services to services and managing managers.

Fracturing operations into smaller and smaller tasks achieves a saturation point of diminished return when there is no more productivity gains from further division. At one point, a further work division has resulted in a mysterious productivity decline. The Hawthorne studies conducted in 1927 by Harvard University researchers and the findings of other research groups and individuals have identified a human factor and the lack of motivation as a cause for the productivity decline. Workers were depressed by continuously repeating one small operation, and they were dehumanized by seeing themselves as appendices to machines and conveyors relentlessly controlling the contents and the tempo of their work activities.

Modern advances in operations management, namely, job design, including job enlargement and job enrichment, call for return to integration of operations. We are witnessing a drastic turnaround in the job design. An example would be such cases as automobile manufacturers' organizing jobs so that a team of four workers assembles an entire car engine. Along with the restructuring of production lines, a fundamental restructuring of manufacturing support systems and organizational structures also takes place.

## PRODUCTION PLANNING USING JIT—THE JAPANESE ADVANTAGE

In discussing JIT, references are made to its original developers, namely, the Toyota car producer along with Japanese management techniques and management-labor relations in general. It is relevant to compare here American and Japanese management methods, since they have different approaches to manufacturing operations planning and control.

It is generally the opinion that Japanese manufacturers are known for their perfect execution of a plan, while Westerners are notorious for their fast reaction and replanning. The quick reaction and replanning practiced by American managers is due to the fact that they, distinct from Japanese managers, create "reactive" plans requiring a constant feedback and replanning. As previously discussed, a second updated plan is less efficient than the original plan, and the third one is even less efficient. The practice adopted by some management teams of vigorously patching the second- and third-choice plans is gradually changing.

Why are the Japanese better in preparing the plan?

It is often said that 90 percent of their lead time is spent on planning project activities. Thus, they are able to execute the plan in the remaining 10 percent of lead time. Japanese managers recognize the significance of the planning function in a manufacturing process, namely, the fact that planning outlines the limits for manufacturing operations.

The second reason is that the Japanese realize that they prepare a plan to be instrumental in producing a high-value product, while our planners view a plan as the final product of an individual managerial function: after the plan is compiled, the execution people are largely kept responsible for its outcome. Thus our planners do their best at preparing an impressive plan having nice figures instead of paying attention and envisaging, in operational terms, how these plans will be realized.

## ELIMINATING SOME ACTIVITIES OF PRODUCTION CONTROL —KEEP IT SIMPLE!

A major thrust in JIT is directed at simplifying the management function: supervision, planning, and controlling the material flow. It is often said that in real life, nothing happens as it was planned: deviations occur due to unforeseen delays and interruptions. To deal with this, the control function is invented. Control of a material flow by identifying job priority is often a deceptive approach because job priorities are constantly changing and what is of highest priority at a given time period, and consumes most of the material controllers attention and efforts, will be of lower priority at the consecutive production stages. In reality, job priorities are changing because the process priority (the capacity load) is constantly changing. Thus the job priority can be identified centrally only by considering the overall product and process priority.

The justification of production control can be compared with the justification of quality control inspections: if there is somebody down the line sorting out bad parts from good ones, then an operator can "relax" because this "somebody" is responsible for sorting out the operator's faults. The mere existence/presence of an inspector justifies making bad parts.

An analogous situation exists in production planning and control. In American manufacturing companies, employees are distinctively divided into product and process categories. If there is a cohort of dispatchers, expeditors, and material controllers running around chasing parts, such organization polarizes people into two groups of responsibility: product responsibility and process responsibility. The shop floor staff involved in scheduling and machine loading favors process priorities and the utilization of machines over the product priorities.

The process category employees feel free from the concern for the product priority, since there are dispatchers and expediters who should take care of product priorities. Thus, the process people (foremen and departmental planners) are concerned with the utmost labor and plant utilization. Process people feel that they execute their duty well if requests of dispatchers and expediters are satisfied in situations when there is anything behind the schedule. Process people, therefore, have the upper hand because they are in charge of machine loading, and they have the final say in controlling the material flow. This results in an increased WIP inventory such as splitting of product and process responsibilities.

The Japanese, especially the JIT-controlled companies, improve quality by *eliminating* the inspector and handing the responsibility to the person performing the operation, the same approach they apply to production control. They compile a production plan the same way as they design a product—for manufacturability. They ensure a one-way (only a good quality) operation, whether an assembly or a production process. Along with the quality control function, the Japanese effectively hand the production control function to the execution, thus applying execution production control in conjunction with the preventive-type planning.

As a result, a JIT production planning and control system is simplified in its critical area of operations planning and control. Programmed decision-making techniques are developed, assisting in identifying jobs priorities and interoperational and intraoperational planning and control and optimization decision rules. These programmed decision rules can be routinely managed and executed by a shop floor personnel.

Japanese planners know how their plans are executed, as there are programmed procedures for shop floor execution, such as the *kanban* system. If a job shop lacks such programmed procedures for operations scheduling and machine loading, the execution of tactical and operational plans is a difficult task to accomplish because there is a split in the product and process responsibility.

An ideal Japanese plan is submitted to the shop floor balanced to the point that it is managed by "juggling" two *kanbans*. No wonder that few JIT-based *kanbans* work in the United States: *kanbans* require preventive planning and executional control and not just a production line organization, as it is often simplistically presented. Our operational plans are not executable as they are. They require identification of "job priorities" at the shop floor and feedback information on variances. These plans are compiled for replanning and rereplanning and are known as the *"feedbacked" planning*. "Feedbacked" planning is contrary to the *kanban*.

For example, if there are feedback reports on a delay due to the unavailability of material, this component will be rescheduled, "feedbacked", and rescheduled again until the material is available and this component is produced. It means that the same job is scheduled and feedbacked several times. Such "feedbacked" planning is illustrated in Figure 8-2. In JIT, such planning and control activities are called a *waste,* and for a very good reason. JIT casts off old methods of production control with a new concept where the responsibility to a large degree is put in the hands of those conducting the execution. The waste of expediting staff is eliminated and the on-time production is emphasized.

## USING THE JIT INTEGRATED SYSTEM APPROACH

JIT features a steady and balanced material flow where there is no overloading of workers or machines. For JIT to work, we need to be able to produce a plan envisaging decisions that are largely programmed and which require minimum control. The solution to this problem is in executional control, in line with preventive planning, eliminating the need for the feedback and replanning.

When problems occur, such as the frequent machine breakdowns, the lack of tools and materials, or quality and productivity problems, we tend to deal with the symptoms by putting the blame on people directly related to these processes and functions. For example, when there is a quality problem, the first person who is expected to take the corrective actions is the machine operator, and it is common to blame the maintenance staff for frequent plant breakdowns and to blame the purchasing people for late deliveries.

One needs to search in a different place for one single cause of all of these problems, specifically, the inability of management to develop an integrated production management and production planning and control strategy which will synergistically structure the quality control system, the plant maintenance system, the JIT purchasing, and, eventually, the shop floor control system.

The top-echelon management cannot blame line managers for inefficiency in separate functions, unless there is an integrated production system in place, producing a reliable and objective production program. For example, if a cost accounting system exists as part of the integrated manufacturing system, it can

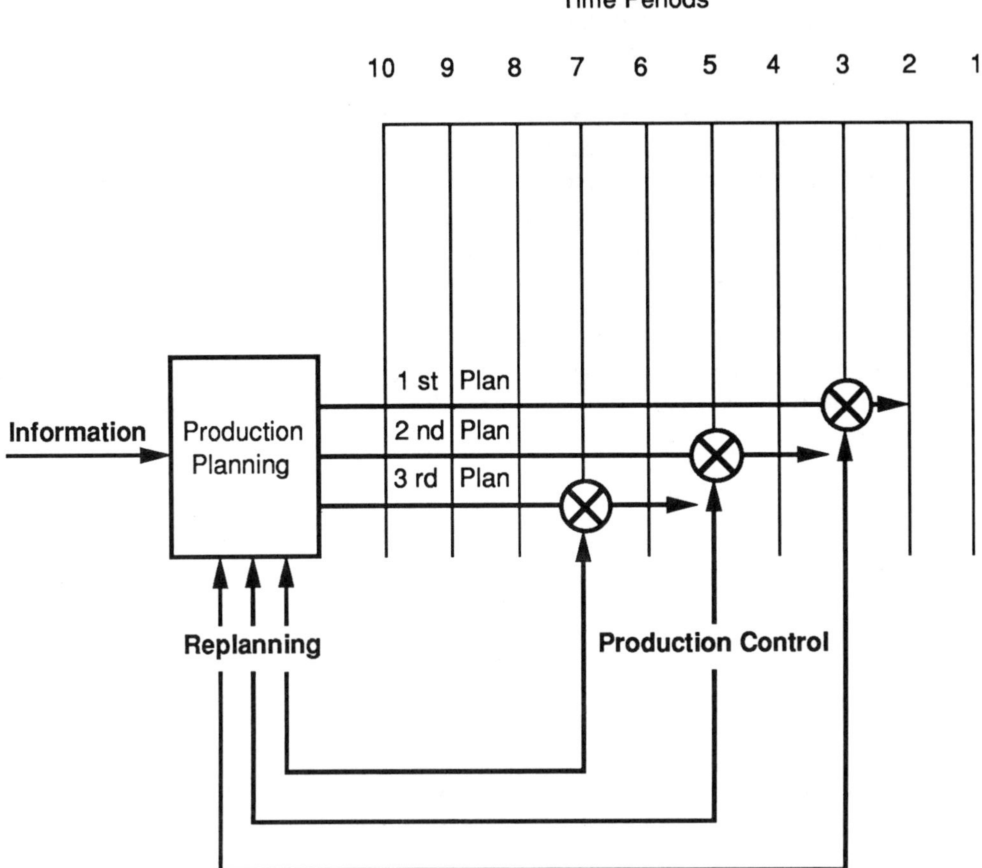


**Figure 8-2**
**Redundant Production Control**

assist line managers to expose their operations causing the greatest losses: expose equipment requiring replacement due to the fact that its further maintenance is not justified; or to focus attention on the process causing the greatest losses due to its quality problems; or to give a shop floor personnel data exposing an inflated production cost due to the increased inventory, long delays, and long lead times. Often, such information will not be news for line managers, but it will highlight the problem, emphasize the need for corrective actions, and above all, it will expose this particular problem as being part of the whole and causing problems in the system. Such exposure gives an incentive and a measurable standard for keeping this problem under control and even completely eliminating it.

An integrated production system focuses manager's attention at selected problems having the most effect on the company, singling them out from an array of issues they deal with. In the United States, we have achieved efficiency in labor and equipment utilization. Now, we must pay attention to the efficiency of a factory as a whole production unit. There are instances where parts of a "factory machine" (for example, individual workstations) are working efficiently at full speed, while the machine itself performs with reduced efficiency. It is not accompanied by a correspondingly higher output. This is equivalent to faulty machine design contributing to additional stresses on machine components and an excessive machine wear, which leads to "crisis situations" in an organization. And who is the "factory machine's" designer and operator? The *manager*—the factory machine designer—is responsible for the factory organization. His or her role is dedicated to organizing the firm's resources and making them productive.

### The Essence of JIT—Problem Solving

The many differences between the Japanese and Western management styles are reflected in JIT. But what is Just-in-Time manufacturing?

If several people are asked this question the answers will vary:

- JIT is a management philosophy aimed at reducing the inventory
- JIT is a manufacturing approach to produce everything on time
- JIT is associated with production of quality products
- JIT is a program comprising a number of techniques which are expected to produce beneficial results when shifting from a push system to a pull system of a material flow
- JIT is a waste reduction program
- JIT is a management philosophy ensuring the workers' motivation
- JIT is associated with cost reduction programs and continuous exposure of manufacturing problems.

Each of these answers projects only a partial image of JIT, since diversely organized companies attempt to obtain from JIT the benefits most essential for their particular operations. JIT is regarded as a problem-solving system rather than just a quality improvement or inventory reduction technique.

### JIT Principles—Elimination of Waste and Respect for People

JIT is a collection of principles classified into two groups: *elimination of waste* and *respect for people.*

JIT is a manufacturing system directed at improving the product value through the elimination of waste, through the systemized efforts of management and employees. The originators of JIT define *waste* as "anything other than a minimum amount of equipment, materials, parts, and working time absolutely essential to production."

The principle of continuous improvement conveys all the just-mentioned JIT features. A constant and persistent improvement brings the best results in enhancing the company's performance through the elimination of waste and detection and early prevention of problems.

### IDENTIFYING THE SOURCES OF WASTE

According to various sources in production, wastes are grouped into the following categories:

- Wastes due to organizational structures
- Wastes in management and supervision
- Wastes in planning
- Wastes in execution and control and in information systems
- Wastes in production processes and setup time
- Wastes in material handling and transportation
- Wastes in production services and communications
- Wastes in people efforts
- Wastes from the inventory and work-in-process (WIP)
- Wastes of overproduction
- Wastes of unproductive operations
- Waste of space
- Waste of queueing time and idle time
- Waste in terms of quality
- Wastes in human resources and talents
- Wastes of responsibility
- Waste in operating services
- Waste in startup of new products
- Waste in overcontrolling

*All wastes are the derivative of human wastes as a principal productive resource.*

### WASTES IN PRODUCTION OVERHEADS

Manufacturing operations are broken down into three categories corresponding to the three types of material flow:

1. Production
2. Decision making and information processing
3. Services to production, both technical and clerical

The cost of these accompanied operations is borne by the customer. In addition to the direct material and labor cost, manufacturing expenses include the costs of

- Product research and development
- Inventory
- Clerical processes, such as customer orders processing and order entry
- Requisitions and purchase orders in purchasing
- Standards in industrial engineering and specifications and blueprints in manufacturing engineering
- Invoices and receivables in accounting
- Processing the cost accounting data
- Programs development in data processing
- Preparing production programs—strategic, tactical, and operational
- Preparing quality programs and plant maintenance
- General administration, personnel, and clerical services vital to functioning of an organization

All these operations are an essential part of a manufacturing enterprise and constitute a substantial cost to a customer even before the first cut takes place in the machine shop. The accompanying costs are especially significant in production systems where batches are small and the cost of supporting operations is inflated compared with the production cost.

## MANUFACTURING WASTES

Manufacturing wastes fall into the following groups, according to the stages of production:

- Wastes due to preproduction planning—wastes attributed to the organization and human factors
- Wastes due to production planning, execution, and control
- Wastes due to technical reasons
- Wastes of redundant functions performed by people in an organization
- Wastes of unutilized human resources

How do we eliminate these wastes? JIT principles give an answer to this question.

## ORGANIZING A CONTINUOUS IMPROVEMENT SYSTEM

JIT principles are accomplished by applying the system approach. Creating a system requires identifying objectives and preparing a plan for the effective functioning of this system—the preproduction planning. Thus, every system comprises a plan, and every plan should be drawn within a framework of a system. If such a pattern is not followed, then the system is doomed to failure due to the deviations beyond the reasonable tolerances, notwithstanding the stepped-up control and replanning. A *system* is an order, a sequence, and a plan of action. A system joins together all its components justifying their purpose accomplished in association with other system components. Consequently, a system also is a sequence of events, an outline/plan of actions.

Because JIT has so many interpretations and different meanings, not without the reason, there is a reluctance to label JIT a "system." JIT is a collection of principles. In fact, JIT is an *unstructured manufacturing system* aimed at continuous, deliberate, planned, and systematic improvement of the product value.

JIT is quite different from other manufacturing systems, for it requires a greater management commitment and personal involvement at all its stages. JIT managers are working toward a company's becoming a harmoniously effective mechanism instead of being involved in the firefighting practice. Creating a JIT manufacturing system is a management function. The manager's task is to present JIT as a production system—a plan of action, a sequence of interrelated activities that recognizes responsibilities and operating procedures.

## A STRUCTURED APPROACH TO JIT IMPLEMENTATION

The essence of manufacturing is the creation and constant improvement of production systems. Any suggested improvement to a current manufacturing system is a system on its own comprising four consecutive steps/stages:

1. Initiation
2. Planning changes
3. Implementation
4. Utilization

Such integrated improvement system structure is relevant to any strategic, tactical, or operational function or activity in engineering, production, and services. In projects and improvement schemes, these four stages are regarded as systems.

The four stages of the JIT system are arbitrarily named as follows:

- Initiation—the management commitment stage

- Planning changes—the planning stage
- Implementation—the implementation stage
- Utilization—the continuous improvement stage

The introduction, planning, implementation, and improvement stages are collectively referred to as the JIT *continuous improvement system* (CIS).

An *introduction stage* is the essence/formulation of a suggested improvement of the system. Depending on the scope of improvement, it, to a degree, requires restructuring/changes to the existing production system and a program/plan of implementation in the existing production system. The principal issue at the implementation stage is a management commitment to the implementation of the JIT system.

The stages of continuous improvement system are illustrated in Figure 8-3. The system's introduction stage comprises proposals of what should be improved in the existing system, namely, the ground rules, and also includes the decision, in principle, on the JIT implementation. The introduction stage gives an answer to the question: "What is suggested to be improved?" Management makes a commitment to improvements if there is a justification for such proposals.

Planning improvements is the second stage of the project—the *planning stage.* It gives an answer to the question: "What should be done in order to accomplish an improvement?" The purpose of the JIT planning stage is to develop a step-by-step program for the JIT implementation. The existing system is not changed yet, but there is a plan of actions to be taken for its improvement.

The next, third step in the improvement program is the actual gradual implementation of the suggested improvement into the existing production system—the *implementation stage.*

The *implementation stage* includes the implementation of engineering and logistical changes in the existing production system. The planning stage produces a plan, while the implementation stage is the execution of this plan.

The fourth step in the improvement program—the *continuous improvement stage*—is the objective of the JIT system. An improved production system, CIS, is utilized for attaining the intended benefits, namely, improving on the product value and customer service.

## Introducing JIT—Obtaining Management Commitment

JIT's seemingly unrelated principles should be arranged into a structured framework before proceeding with the first JIT stage because nobody starts a project without a plan. JIT plan calls for all project events being scheduled in a sequence. The preliminary work involves

- Investigating and making an executive decision on JIT
- Management education and training
- Identifying what objectives and goals JIT is going to achieve

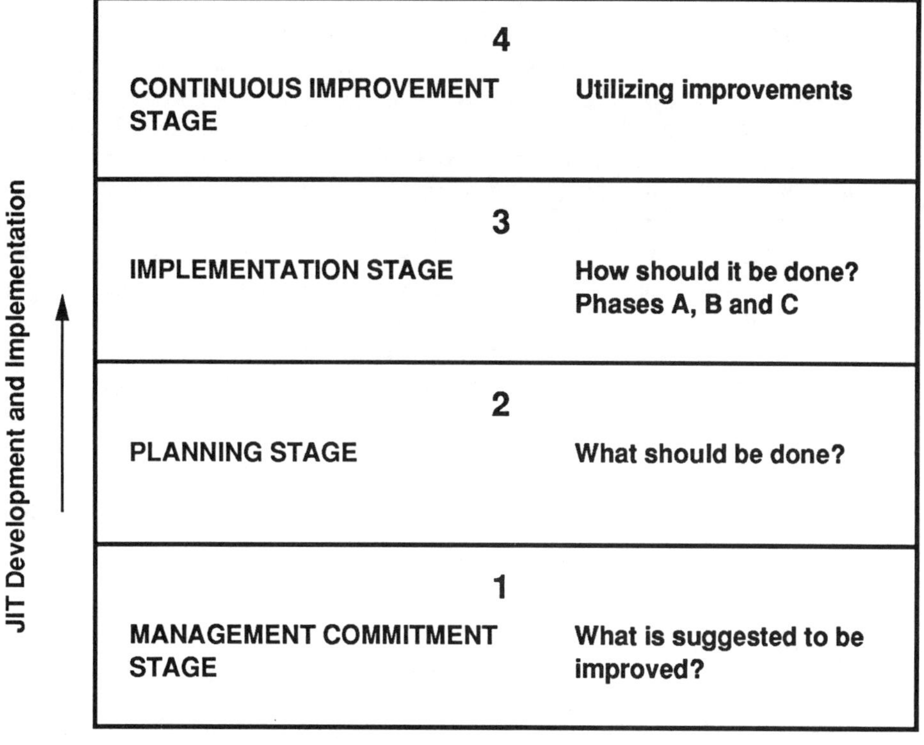


**Figure 8-3**
**The Four Stages of the Continuous Improvement System**

- Structuring the JIT project and identifying its major stages

At the initial stage, the duty of the senior management *steering committee* is to establish an overall policy and the strategy for achieving organizational objectives. The key personnel is provided with information about basics of the JIT program, outlining its philosophy, stages of implementation, as well as its expected cost and benefits.

The management indoctrination is the first important step because decisions about whether to proceed with JIT are made at this stage. After one year of the JIT development, a midwestern producer of electrical products indicates that the most difficult parts of changing an organization is

1. Getting management to realize that this should be a systemic change, if the full benefits are to be realized. The lack of management commitment is indicated by many companies as one of the causes in the JIT failure.

2. Retraining managers, all of them, or they cannot lead.

Some companies select their key staff to research JIT by attending various seminars and by visiting companies which are at the advanced stages of the JIT development. An energy products company from California writes: "The major problem in selling JIT to the user is their unbelief that JIT will work. We found that some supervisors could not understand or admit to as much until they saw it in operation." This manufacturer sends the management teams from three of their locations to familiarize themselves with the achievements of a successful JIT user. The management teams have returned as "believers in the JIT system" and now are successfully implementing JIT in their respective operations.

The assistance of a professional consultant with JIT experience often is sought at this stage. A short one- or two-day in-house seminar is sufficient to familiarize the top management with the JIT philosophy. The consultant should visit the company prior to the training session and get acquainted with its operations, future plans, and problems. Then the seminar should be tailored to the company's specific needs. Often companies implementing JIT make use of consultants on a two- to three-day-per-month basis. Objectives and goals are formalized at the initial stage. We will discuss them based on the example of the Dresser Industrial Tool Division.

*Example*: A JIT introduction stage signifies the purpose and objectives of JIT and the rationale behind its implementation. A sample objective is "To become a world class manufacturing company." This means producing a product supported by a consumer and which favorably compares with the competition. The Dresser objectives are

- Consistently achieve an acceptable high rate of return.
- Be recognized as the highest quality industrial tool manufacturer.

Objectives are long-term organizational targets. *Goals* are stages/milestones in achieving these objectives. The Dresser JIT goals are

- Develop a manufacturing concept based on manufacturing process cells—to improve quality, minimize setup time, and improve the material flow through the shop
- Apply simplicity and quality at every step of the production process
- Apply a holistic approach of letting workers solve the problems, solving as many problems as possible at the lowest level of the organization
- Consolidate and simplify manufacturing facilities
- Develop a two-shift operation with a flexible work force
- Simplify the product line and family groupings of component parts
- Simplify order entry and manufacturing paper flow

These policy statements formalize the executive decision aimed at improvement of present performance. This is a gradual program for enacting changes and improvements for achieving JIT organizational objectives.

It is critical that not a single condition essential for achieving these strategic objectives should be missed and not a single condition should be stated, unless it is absolutely essential for achieving these organizational objectives.

JIT objectives and goals should not be mere slogans and goodwill intentions, but should be an essential part of a deliberate JIT program. JIT preventive planning means that strategic and tactical planning envisage operational steps for the execution.

An excellent example is the Canon strategic plan: "In three years to become a leading corporation in Japan and in another three years to become a world leader in its field." A simple, bold, and daring plan, especially, when considering that the company, at that time, had experienced some financial problems.

Such plans in Japanese firms are not just expressed intentions of executive management, but a refinement of tactical and operational production programs. Such objective and goal setting has led to the Japanese advancing into becoming industrial giants and the champions of high-quality products, up from having a blemished reputation of producing poor-quality products.

The significance of the introduction stage is in understanding a compelling need for JIT, expressed in the executive management decision to commit the company to this improvement program. For some companies, few other alternatives exist. The importance of the JIT improvement stage is in that it outlines the direction and the final destination of the firm: if you do not know where you are going, you cannot get there.

Many manufacturers have voiced complaints about the lack of commitment and support from the top management as a major reason for the failure of JIT. Partly this is the result of misconceptions in defining Just-in-Time as the system pivoted around the almost mythical power of the *kanban*-type stockless material flow, where all operations run with the precision of a clock mechanism. There is no wonder that in these companies senior managements have reservations regarding the possibility of achieving such goals, and they adopt a wait-and-see attitude, expecting more convincing practical examples of JIT successes before they commit companies to such profound changes.

## Planning for JIT Manufacturing

The CIS *planning stage* involves outlining the steps for achieving JIT goals and objectives, identifying what should be done for implementing an efficient system, and estimating whether the benefits offset the expenses. The planning stage includes setting up ground rules and developing improvement techniques.

Improvement techniques encompass anything that contributes to reducing the waste and inefficiency present in a manufacturing system. This includes methods and operating procedures contributing to simplification and optimization of manufacturing processes and improved quality.

Before proceeding with JIT implementation, there are specific JIT requirements at this stage:

1. Ensure support from and involvement of all employees.
2. Develop a company-wide commitment to education and training, training a multiskilled work force.
3. Eliminate unproductive operations and functions, collectively known as a "waste," and reduce redundancy in the organization.
4. Identify and resolve fundamental problems within the framework of the JIT continuous improvement system. The JIT philosophy is a methodical search for problems and finding solutions to these problems. It is contrary to an attitude often seen in companies: "We do not have problems. We have worked this way for 20 years and are satisfied with results."
5. Strive for simplicity—simple systems, simple procedures, simple plans, and simple reporting.
6. Use a group technology to create part families.
7. Establish new cost justification methods for services and production support overheads. Such a cost accounting system is structured around the cost centers and is based on the cost drivers which use new overhead allocation procedures.

Answers to specific questions are provided at the planning stage:

- What means are to be applied?
- What wastes are to be eliminated?
- How much will this cost?
- How much will be gained?
- How should planning and control of the material flow be organized?

The planning stage involves an improvement in cooperation between departments, establishing a suggestion scheme and reward systems. For example, in some organizations, only supervisors are rewarded, although achievements are the result of an entire team's efforts. Such a reward system discourages employees from investing additional efforts in what they are doing.

JIT is a companywide multifunctional undertaking, including all business and manufacturing units—marketing and sales, finance, purchasing, engineering, quality control, R&D, and management information systems. Let's look at our example company, Dresser ITD and understand how they implement JIT ground rules.

*Example*: Management at Dresser has outlined these ground rules as to what should be done for achieving the JIT objectives:

- Complete a value analysis of all product lines to eliminate features and models that don't add value for the customer.
- Make excess machine tool capacity available to minimize setup times and the shop flow.
- Make specialized/single-purpose machine tools available for unique manufacturing processes.
- Move each component directly from operation to operation with minimum in-process time.
- Ensure 100 percent inspection of critical dimensions at each operation.
- Develop a multimachine-multitask flexible work force.
- Train each cell leader to perform and teach all operations.
- Lay out plant to facilitate manufacturing process cell concept.
- Complete a preventative maintenance and monitoring system.
- Standardize production planning and control procedures.

Ground rules outline the objectives for improving organizational performance and enumerating all the conditions required to be accomplished for achieving these objectives.

## Implementing JIT Manufacturing

The JIT *implementation stage* realizes the planned changes into the operational objectives. There is a determined sequence of steps which should be followed in the implementation stage. They are:

1. Ensuring the work force involvement in improvement schemes and quality circles activities by providing education and training and ensuring the employees motivation and elimination of waste in the organizational structure. This step is identified as the organized group involvement and activity.
2. Reducing setup time. The organized group involvement should be aimed at reducing setup time throughout all the processes. The setup time reduction is needed for all other JIT elements, such as uniform plant loading, production in small lots, zero inventory material flow, planning, and control.
3. Improving material flow planning and control. This involves straightening production routes, setting up a planning system of a balanced material flow, and establishing small-run batches, uniform plant loading, and pull production planning efforts as being a deliberate task in production of each component. Paying extra attention to detailed planning is the most

productive exercise to be undertaken for achieving the performance improvement.

4. Moving processes and operations closer together, for example, streamlining production lines; establishing a product-focused plant layout; and reducing material handling, automatization, and robotics.

The first step is by far most essential because the next three steps of the implementation stage are the consequence and the result of continuous employee involvement schemes.

Activities at the implementation stage fall into three levels of development:

- *Level 1*—employee empowerment
- *Level 2*—elimination of waste
- *Level 3*—technical improvements

The steps of the CIS implementation stage and their grouping into three levels are illustrated in Figure 8-4. The three phases of the implementation stage are followed by the continuous improvement stage—the very essence of a continuous improvement system.

## SUMMARY

The four concepts that are the cornerstones of JIT are (in order of their significance)

1. Employee involvement in continuous improvement schemes
2. Employee participation in service operations
3. Setup time reduction
4. Uniform plant loading

These conditions should be achieved at the implementation stage. Due to the critical role they play in the JIT development, these three levels of the implementation stage are further discussed in the next three chapters.

| | |
|---|---|
| | Automation<br>Improvement of plant layout |
| **Level 3** | **THE TECHNICAL IMPROVEMENTS** |
| **Level 2** | Straighten production routes<br>Small runs<br>Uniform plant loading<br>Pull production system<br>Setup time reduction |
| | **THE ELIMINATION OF WASTE** |
| **Level 1** | Team building<br>Work force involvement in planning<br>Motivation through education and training |
| | **EMPLOYEE EMPOWERMENT** |

**Figure 8-4**
**The Three Levels of the CIS Implementation Stage**

# 9

# Implementing JIT: Level 1—Empowering Employees

## MANAGEMENT'S ROLE IN WASTE ELIMINATION AND CONTINUOUS IMPROVEMENT

Management is the principal factor in ensuring efficient production. In JIT, management efforts are distributed among three areas of manufacturing, corresponding to the three interrelated management systems: product development, production and purchasing, and marketing. These three management functions are integrated into a single business system instrumental in achieving results through the elimination of waste. Eliminating waste in the manufacturing function refers to improving quality, reducting WIP, reducing direct and indirect labor, reducing start-up and trial costs of new products, and eliminating waste of talents and human efforts.

Just-in-Time is not what it sounds to be—to produce just in time and to eliminate an inventory. Some people may assume that if one decides to refrain from doing jobs in advance, then the inventory will be reduced and JIT will emerge. In reality, deliberate attempts to reduce inventory will produce temporary results. Successful JIT companies emphasize that their inventory reduction is not the result of deliberate actions but a by-product of some other improvements they have implemented, such as achieving a smooth, uninterrupted material flow, lead time reduction, and setup time reduction.

The degree of manager's success in the waste elimination and continuous improvement schemes depends on the ability and desire of all employees to contribute to these functions.

## Changes in Management and Supervision—Increasing the Span of Control

The function of management and supervision is changing to include the employee's involvement in decision making, delegating, and assigning more authority and responsibility. Such changes in industrial relations, reducing control over the work force, result in widening the span of control.

In some companies, there were areas where a supervisor-to-employee ratio was as low as 1 to 4. Currently, this ratio is changing to 1 to 15 and even more. Organizations peel off layers of organizational structures, starting with middle-management positions. Middle management is the first to undergo changes when companies search for the ways to cut expenses in order to be more competitive.

A well-developed corporate strategy is an integration in all work areas. Management functions are integrated at all levels: strategic management is integrated with operations management, production operations are integrated with service operations, there is a closer cooperation between line managers and staff managers, internal functions are integrated with the outside organizational activities, and above all, activities of employees are integrated into a single system poised to produce the highest value for a customer.

In a JIT organization, a manager performs a double function of the trainer and the team member; he or she is involved in interprocess communication and shares the collective responsibility for execution.

Improved communication encourages discussions and exchange of ideas and minimizes internal conflicts, which results in harmony. Managers facilitate work by offering their technical and administrative expertise and training and developing employees rather than directing them.

Constructive changes in management functions are reflected in new management titles which are changing into facilitators, counselors, and work consultants. These new management titles are a reflection of the new climate in organizations where the managers' paternalistic role is changing into one of partnership, support, and shared responsibility.

## Handling the Human Factors—Motivating Employees

People act as they do because they are trying to fulfill specific needs—the major one being to be useful. Long ago, it was discovered that productivity is directly related to the employees' motivation. Workers who are satisfied and challenged with what they are doing and see an opportunity to accomplish their goals are likely to be more productive. An emerging trend is known as *employee empowerment*—assigning a greater responsibility to the work force.

Various forms of motivation stem from the diversity of human needs: group activities, assuming a greater authority and responsibility, involvement in decision making, acquiring knowledge and on the job advancement, financial rewards, being given an opportunity to be productive, and being recognized.

## PRODUCTIVITY IS A FUNCTION OF WORK ENVIRONMENT

In the world of changing industrial relations, the emphasis is on the on-the-job satisfaction stemming from the increased work force involvement into basic decision making.

Where the work force is involved at the time a decision is being made and they see the plan as the best possible alternative, there is motivation to achieve what has been planned. The participation in decision making motivates employees to work harder toward attaining good results.

It has been found that the chances for success are better if work control, responsibility, and authority are moved downward. The job should be designed in such a manner that the whole job can be broken into several separate tasks allocated to people along with the defined responsibility and authority for detailed on-the-job planning and control and reporting procedures.

The move is toward minigroups with added responsibility, when it is common knowledge that a person or a group to whom a job is assigned bears the responsibility for it.

## APPLYING GROUP ACTIVITIES IN ORGANIZATIONS

Modern business is a team-oriented entity embracing everybody from the general manager to a worker on a shop floor. People want to be creative and wish that their contributions are recognized. They want to be identified with successful performance of their organizations.

As Donald Petersen, the CEO of Ford Motor Co., says in *Industry Week*: "Most important, we rediscovered that the critical factor in our success is people . . . people who continue to find innovative ways to work together for the common good" (February 19, 1990).

Managers, people responsible for the work of their subordinates, create an environment where the work force can be challenged and succeeds in their tasks.

The management task is to achieve the work force utilization through creating an environment conducive to motivation. Motivating line and staff people is the basic driving force in JIT programs, giving people an ownership of what they are doing, ensuring self-control and self-motivation of the work force. Motivation is an energetic behavior stemming from the desire to satisfy individual needs, and depending on the successful results of individual efforts. Motivation is not measured by the amount of these efforts, but depends on the results and quality of these efforts. Motivation depends on the environment created in an organization, that is, how it benefits employees' self-esteem and self-development, and on the individual recognition to a greater degree than financial rewards.

JIT means the elimination of waste, first and foremost, the elimination of waste of the major resource, namely, people, the elimination of waste of their time, their skills, their talents, and their desire to do a meaningful job and to help a company to succeed. Everybody wants to see good results of his or her work. Motivation comes with the advancement toward these objectives. Motivation is the satisfaction in achieving the desired results. Many companies have improved their production through a simple means of informing workers of results by posting daily figures and showing progressive day-by-day performance figures. This resulted in performance exceeding production goals.

## Tapping a Potential Resource—Restructuring Organizational Behavior

Employees are pleased with what they are doing and their work occupies a meaningful place in their personal lives when their work priorities are mingled together with family interests. Such an attitude goes beyond viewing the place of work only as a provider of livelihood and monetary rewards. Rather, the work is viewed as a source of satisfying one's individual and private interests—the need for educational enrichment, cultural improvements, and social association.

Monetary incentives are not the only objectives of employees when they attempt to perform better, but it is the punctuation of the good results achieved that makes people happy. It is a supervisor's choice whether to have a motivated or a defiant employee after the job is done: a pat on the back and you have a motivated person, or a "pass-by" and you have an unhappy person.

The function of managers is to ensure that needs of employees are fulfilled. The principal need and the purpose of employees is to perform a meaningful and a rational work. In the present work environment, a manager's task is to ensure that execution proceeds according to the plan—an important consideration in motivating employees. This condition requires good managerial planning and the elimination of waste, ensuring that everything is going to the customer, be it an end user or an intermediate product customer, or the next process, rather than to a storage place. Management planning ensures that the equipment performs well, without breakdowns (good maintenance), there is reduced inventory and material handling; quality is up to standard; and purchasing provides for reliability, on-time delivery, and reasonable cost.

JIT is based on the employees motivation. Do not start a JIT program without motivation factors in place. When this condition is met, the work itself is going to be a motivator. The JIT approach is to involve the work force into many business and production activities and functions. In doing so, you will nurture a greater sense of ownership of a process or a particular task, ownership of a part of a product, ownership of a place, and ability to communicate both horizontally and at higher vertical levels—T-organizational structures. The ownership comes with the responsibility for what you own and the desire to display it and preserve it.

There is a revision of a traditional opinion that only managers and an engineering and technical staff are able to resolve manufacturing problems and that the work force's only function is to do the job. The JIT approach is a systematic and consistent increase in the product value by improving everything that is possible to improve. Areas of JIT improvements spread over such wide areas of work activities and tasks that it is far beyond any supervisory and technical staff's ability to accomplish this assignment without involving the people who are constantly dealing with these tasks undergoing improvements.

The work force involvement in resolving engineering issues assists in further expansion of the engineering function, directly contributing to adding the value at the expense of administrative functions, communication, and control.

There is an opinion that in line production and in job shop intermittent operations, flow people are not motivated because they perform small tasks without being able to distinguish their work in the finished products. It is understood that people like to "own" what they do. The *anonymity* of job tasks in line production is one of the major reasons for the unsatisfactory performance of these lines in quality, productivity, and timely completion of jobs. Another major reason for the unsatisfactory performance of a production line is the lack of visibility and responsibility. What demotivates people is the realization that there is neither a reward nor a punishment regardless of what they do.

Identifying job priorities along production lines, as it is done in integrated task management (ITM) and operations group group (OGG), discussed in Chapter 7, introduces a motivational factor in the material flow as well as the desire to perform quality jobs on time and receive a recognition or an acknowledgment from the "customer," or at least not to be identified as the cause for the subsequent operations' delays. This is a sufficient incentive for the proper performance. What demoralizes and/or affects the work force is not so much a repetition of the same operation as the anonymity of what a worker is doing, a feeling that the worker's efforts are disregarded. A worker needs a self-assurance in the first place and the punctuation of his or her purpose and mission in an organization in general.

Operational scheduling and job sequencing performed on a shop floor produces a sense of ownership over these small jobs. In JIT, the ownership comes with the responsibility.

## AN OPEN-DOOR POLICY AND IMPROVED COMMUNICATION

An open-door policy (free access to management and cross-functional communications) has a beneficial effect on the work force morale and reduces the administrative claustrophobia. *Workplace claustrophobia* is reduced if workers have freedom to move about involving themselves in multistation operations and material handling (basically, extending their territory). *Communication claustrophobia* occurs when workers are assigned to their machines and cannot communicate with others during work hours. In JIT, communication is possible as part of the "producers'" and "customers'" relationships. In JIT, communication is improved due to organizational changes and improvements in the plant layout.

JIT restructuring involves simplifying and compacting plant layouts. This is known as "downsizing." It boils down to creating smaller work areas where employees are placed closer together. People who work closer together are exercising better communications, sharing problems, and helping each other with their resolution.

### HUMAN RELATIONS MANAGEMENT

Material resources are inactive and nonproductive, unlike human resources. Let's imagine for a moment that the entire factory resources are stored (materials, machinery, materials handling and other supporting equipment, and computers). Let's say, they all are unproductively sitting in the storage place, waiting for the humans to put them to use.

Engineers and managers are the people who plan how to distribute these resources on the factory floor, who will design logistical and management information systems, and who will put the work force in place to fulfill the planned manufacturing strategy.

This manufacturing system, as with any other system, has a hierarchical structure. Its lower level is a labor-machine unit, an essential basic unit triggering/moving an entire system. A manufacturing system is triggered by the management expertise, human resources dexterity, and work skills. Notwithstanding all other resources, the alliance between the management and the work force determines the output of the system.

A manufacturing system is only as good as its management-labor unit and labor-machine basic unit. A manufacturing system cannot be productive if its basic unit, a labor-machine unit, is not productive. On the other hand, a productive labor-machine basic unit does not necessarily signify a successive productive system. A productive manufacturing system requires both conditions to exist: a productive labor-machine basic unit and a productive management-labor unit.

With automation, we tend to downgrade the role of the human element in the labor-machine basic unit. The output of a production line is largely determined by the programmed capacity of the equipment. If a conveyor is programmed to run 100 pieces per hour, this is what it will do. If the output of 120 pieces per hour is required, then the speed of the conveyor's belt should be increased. At many conveyor lines, workers find that in the midshift, they are compelled to work faster than at the beginning of the day.

A deceptive factor in conveyorized production lines is that production capacity is considered mainly as the capacity of equipment, thus demeaning the role of the human element in the labor-machine basic unit. The emphasis in the labor-machine basic unit now is shifting so as to underline the undisputed significance of the human element of this basic system unit.

Contemporary manufacturing systems have proliferated into many manufacturing functions and activities, becoming complex interactive hierarchical structures. Due to the proliferation of manufacturing functions and activities, it is difficult to improve and carry out their execution without the assistance and cooperation of the work force.

Manufacturing systems are driven by the management knowledge. The basic unit of a manufacturing system is driven by the work force dexterity. In a JIT system, it is not enough for a worker to produce according to the plan 120 components per day; an operator is also expected to contribute to the system's improvement and maintenance. Such obligations are over and above the labor's functional role in an organization, and they take the form of voluntary employees' contributions.

This desire to contribute to the system is the result of motivation. Words that encourage motivation are "affection and respect," "compassion," "companionship," "friendship," "sharing knowledge", and "teamwork." Managers who are in agreement with this concept are able to motivate people and to invoke the desire to contribute to the continuous system improvement.

## ORGANIZING WORK GROUPS AND BUSINESS TEAMS

An emerging approach to job planning is mutually beneficial. Those companies where the goals of employees are congruent with those of the organization succeed, so that both the company and the employees benefit mutually. It was found that the work team and business team are strong work force motivators.

Teamwork enhances the quality of the work life—sociopsychological considerations to the work environment. Usually, a team organization changes process-focused functional production to product-focused production, enhancing the ownership of the employees' work. Workers are able to see the beginning and the end of the job in which they are involved and are able to trace their contribution to the product building. People are motivated when working on a problem together. Departmentalization by machine function is changed by the product-focused function where operations do not lose their identity with products or customers. In a JIT system, there is less need for traditional production scheduling activities, due to final operations scheduling being largely performed by the floor personnel. This also contributes to more meaningful measuring of results and a heightened sense of responsibility.

Such changes produce a more sensitive response to individual customer orders. Japanese management puts the emphasis on the group instead of the individual and on human relations rather than on functional relations. It was found that the workers' obligations to their teams take precedence over their responsibilities to superiors. Peer pressure is exerted, so as to reinforce the discipline. In Japanese organizations, decision making and problem solving are preceded by a direct exchanging of views and group discussions during which many alternatives are considered and understanding everybody's point of view is achieved before arriving at a consensus, as opposed to the Western approach of individual decision making. Decision making by consensus has a wider support of participants in executing these decisions.

People are content being team members. They have sense of association and feel secure as group members. One manufacturer in Connecticut has emphasized that the greatest gains from its JIT system have come from the team concept and employees' involvement in the improvement schemes.

In Japan, 70 percent of employees at all levels of organization are involved in problem solving and decision making, while in the United States, such sharing of responsibility and functional partnership is at its initial stages. In Japanese systems, employees are the driving force behind JIT. This is contrary to the practice when managers assume that it is their function to run JIT. Some JIT managers, in fact, are exhausted by lonely efforts to manage a JIT system on their own. In JIT, such individual attempts are condemned to die on the vine. JIT, unlike any other management system, requires total employee involvement.

A work group is a building block of Japanese production systems. The starting point in JIT all-out improvement is organizing working groups based on harmony, accord, cooperation, hard work, and on working relationships that value trust and support and share common results.

In JIT, a work force becomes actively involved in small-group activities, extending its functions both horizontally and vertically and contributing to the waste reduction through work improvement proposal systems. This stimulates motivation and builds morale and work force consciousness.

In addition to their regular duties, workers perform housekeeping and upkeep duties, maintain cleanliness and proper arrangement of tools and materials in its own places, and are involved in manufacturing services, such as quality control and plant maintenance.

The concept of a teamwork is an essential unifying force in an organization, promoting group activities and collective group responsibility for both planning and implementation. Employees feel motivated when they see that they are part of creating something useful, and that their individual work is channelled into a deliberate, systematic useful output.

Teams comprising 5 to 10 people, representing a cross section of functions and responsibilities, are formed at all levels of an organization. Work teams acquire a new purpose involving themselves in matters beyond their levels of responsibility and functional areas. Reflecting this, work teams, often designated as business teams, extend their span into the spectrum of other business activities, starting from the introduction of new products through the distribution stage, not only dealing with production matters.

For example, to improve productivity, Digital Equipment Corporation has adopted an approach that provides "a high quality human environment that values the goals of both business and people as interdependent and equally important. Using semi-autonomous work teams at DEC, have resulted in 30 to 50% productivity improvement." (Sam Tomas, "A Blueprint for Developing a Competitive Advantage" *International Conference Proceedings*, Vol. 32, APICS, 1989).

Cross-functional work teams are widely spreading and at the increasing rate are becoming the standards of job design, due to a remarkable result they produce. One major defense contractor, who took part in the JIT survey, reports: "Generally, the Plant has migrated from the classical quality circle to focused, empowered, cross-functional teams targeting unresponsive plant delivery systems. These teams are involved in work redesign, work flow, elimination of non-value-adding activities, and speed of throughput in both manufacturing and nonmanufacturing activities for entire targeted systems. The team improvement is system directed rather than locally directed. Ownership and enhanced system redesigns are achieved by involvement and empowerment of key performers, resource holders, and information holders regardless of organizational boundaries." (Martin Marietta Energy Systems, Inc.).

Small autonomous work groups are integrated so as to reinforce the final *triple business objective*—quality, cost, and timely completion—rather than merely perform functional tasks improvements.

***Improving the Quality of Work Life*** Workers identify themselves more closely with an organization and have a greater sense of commitment when management pays attention to quality of work life. Workers cannot assume a meaningful sense of responsibility for what they are doing if they believe they will be laid off when sales decline or as a result of the workers-suggested productivity improvement and cost reduction innovations. For example, in a plastic components manufacturing company, a staff employee suggested cutting costs by reducing overhead. The next month he was laid off as part of the self-initiated cost reduction program. The quality of work life and the desire to contribute to continuous improvement is contingent on basic job security rights. A quality of work life program is intended to give employees more control over their work activities, improved communication, and teamwork.

The JIT survey has shown that there is a good ground in the United States for JIT because manufacturers have succeeded in organizing work force-management teamwork—a primary requirement for starting and successfully accomplishing JIT. The need for JIT is recognized by the wide spectrum of employees, not only the top management.

Group activities and the collective group responsibility for both planning and implementation are essential unifying forces in an organization. Employees are motivated when they are involved in planning and when their individual work is channeled into a deliberate, systematic, useful output.

Experience has shown that when workers are trusted and they are given the responsibility for planning work for themselves, they plan more than managers will otherwise. Organizations thrive when there is a recognition that employees are a valuable resource.

## BROWNING-FERRIS INDUSTRIES: A CASE STUDY

Browning-Ferris Industries (BFI) is a nonmanufacturing company, the second-biggest company in the waste management business. This service organization has managed to develop its services into a high-quality product, thanks to the work force involvement in improvement schemes. BFI continuously draws on the work force contribution: truck drivers working on routes provide information and submit suggestions of how to improve the service and reduce the cost. This presents the most valuable input from people directly involved in running the operation, those who call the shots. All their suggestions are considered in planning and organizing the work and scheduling routes.

"We always work on quality improvement," says the BFI chief executive officer William D. Ruckelshaus. How does one define quality in the garbage industry? "We have defined quality as the degree of customer satisfaction—the number of complaints is the measure of quality."

Corporate improvements often start with a companywide campaign underlining the company's commitment to quality and customer service. BFI management uses a banner that says "Great Ideas Build Great Companies—Your Ideas Make BFI Great." This banner conveys the BFI's belief that the employees' motivation and involvement in improvement schemes are essential to the welfare of the organization. Such posters and banners containing company long-term objectives and short-term goals in quality improvement and cost reduction serve as a morale building tool.

Another such an example highlighting company objectives is a poster of *Camco, Inc.*, shown in Figure 9-1. The main theme of this poster is the flexibility and continuous improvement in producing at low cost and high quality in order to exceed customer expectations.

## USING REWARD SYSTEMS FOR POSITIVE REINFORCEMENT

People will perform better if their reward is contingent on their performance. The *expectancy theory of motivation* implies the probability that if one puts forth efforts, performance and the concomitant result will follow. In essence, a positive reinforcement is a primary mechanism that supports most organizational and managerial functions.

Workers who contribute to the product quality and continuous improvement can be motivated by a reward system, self-interest tied up to job security, promotion policy, and wage increases. In organizations where the reward system is tied to the number of skills, there is no resistance to change.

**THE CAMCO OBJECTIVE**

**THROUGH TEAMWORK WE WILL CONTINUOUSLY IMPROVE TO BE: THE LOW COST AND HIGH QUALITY PRODUCER, TECHNOLOGICAL LEADER AND HAVE THE FLEXIBILITY TO EXCEED CUSTOMER EXPECTATIONS.**

Figure 9-1
CAMCO's Poster Highlighting Company Objectives

Reprinted here by permission from CAMCO, Inc.

Flexibility in the work force can be achieved with on-the-job training, which is, in most cases, well accepted by employees. This is one of the initial commitments which an employer accepts at the onset of the JIT development. The "ownership" phenomenon increases workers' self-respect and confidence in their doing the right thing and directly links workers' activities to the profit of the organization. Besides, gains-sharing and stock ownership programs add to the employee participation in improvement programs, where piece-rate incentives are replaced by a gain-sharing plan.

Nonfinancial reward systems, such as reinforcing positive results (the most productive employees shown in company publications) encourage employee participation in improvement programs. Acknowledging employees' contributions is important, but it should be supported by expected rewards.

Companies implementing JIT indicate that short goals and appraisals have the utmost effect on performance and motivation, specifically short term (weekly) incentives immediately relating the employee's reward to the level of the employee's efforts.

## EDUCATING AND TRAINING EMPLOYEES

Management should recognize that the work force is a valuable resource in accomplishing JIT objectives. An average American worker is capable of performing any task if a basic training is provided. Invariably, when motivated, a worker is a keen participant in a variety of improvement projects, including the environmental protection projects. An American worker is resourceful and capable, having such important disposition traits as ingenuity and imagination, and like workers in many countries, he or she has appreciation for team work.

The difference between workers and management is not intellectual but circumstantial. A basic education and training enables a work force, along with performing their functions, to perform many tasks which otherwise require dedicated engineers and decision makers. Besides, the employees' professional advancement results in the work force motivation—willingness and the ability to contribute to improvement schemes. A trained work force takes over some planning and control functions thus reducing the need for nonvalue-adding activities, such as communication and information systems, otherwise required by dedicated decision makers.

With minimal attention, educating and training American workers can be instrumental for our companies to produce a competitive edge in the worldwide competition. To the contrary, if the work force is not actively involved from the beginning of the JIT implementation, the project loses esteem as it gradually subsides.

Education and training is a single cost-effective activity which, if properly organized, brings immediate benefits to the organization, and therefore it should not be waived aside regardless of the management's JIT considerations. Employee empowerment envisages that necessary on-the-job training has been provided.

## Conducting On-the-Job Training

Training results in a twofold gain: it contributes to the employees' motivation, and it provides them with the knowledge and skills necessary for improvement schemes. JIT includes employees' training in business and engineering subjects and multiskill training where workers cross-train each other to perform a number of diverse work tasks.

The aim of on-the-job training is to promote successful functioning of a production system by increasing the level of technical knowledge, individual responsibility, and involvement in improvement schemes. Training is the investment in work skills of employees, providing the means for the future growth, and work force revitalization. It is a known fact that employees are generally capable of much more than they do. Thus employee training is an activity of expanding human resources, leading to enhancing the utilization of material resources.

A supervisor who is involved in technical improvements planning should also be responsible for on-the-job training and for involving other functional and engineering specialists to diversify a company's training curriculum. Benefits, which can be obtained at a relatively low cost of employee education and training, are

- Employee participation schemes
- Job design and quality improvement programs
- Developing production planning and control systems
- Employee involvement in material flow control

On-the-job training builds up an employees' morale. Notwithstanding, machine operators find work more challenging and motivating when they serve multiple machines rather than perform few jobs on a single machine. Often, training operators enables them to produce simple solutions for automation and mechanization of their processes, which otherwise will require capital spending.

Nevertheless, some companies are more willing to spend their dollars on hard capital items, such as new equipment and other acquisitions, rather than on employees training. According to one JIT survey, 75 percent of the responding companies consider that less than 40 hours per year is sufficient for operators' education and training.

These organizations readily invest in an equipment because these investments are easily cost justifiable. However, equipment and machines are idle without people, while educated and well-trained employees often can make old equipment more productive than new machinery.

A company producing electronic products responding to a survey indicates that an unexpected problem they have encountered is the high level of worker stress that occurs when training is not provided.

Another manufacturer from Indiana states: "Essential to JIT is training . . . a lot of training. The employees have to believe in the philosophy and have all the resources to experiment and to build their understanding of JIT. JIT is not a quick fix. It is not an employee reduction program, where the *system* is the cure for all of the production problems that we experience. For JIT to begin to work—management commitment and resources are essential and training are the key starting point." Numerous indications point out that employees' training, as an important factor in JIT, should be intensified.

Avant-garde American companies recognize the benefits gained from employees' training. For example, Motorola spends 2 billion dollars on employee education and training which includes a basic school education, starting with literacy and math courses for those who need it.

Training is a challenging issue in JIT. Employees' involvement in improvement schemes requires on-the-job training. In JIT, the work force takes over the management initiative for improvement through the quality circles and suggestion schemes. People-oriented management combined with education and training enhances workers' involvement in management functions and reduces the need for supervisory control.

There is a changing role of the work force in a production process and the increased involvement in production services, taking over some supervisory and management planning tasks and contributing to the improvement in the organization.

In JIT, an insufficient work force training combined with the higher responsibility level inevitably leads to unsatisfactory performance.

## Implementing Specific JIT Training Programs

Education and training provided by Japanese companies to their employees comprises a comprehensive list of subjects, some of which follow:

- Quality control systems and statistical techniques
- Productivity and cost reduction techniques
- Product design and manufacturing processes
- Safety and hygiene
- Work improvement methods
- Group creativity and brainstorming
- Introduction to business and accounting
- Buildup of self-confidence
- Project-centered group activities

Training is organized by level and by function and includes problem identification and cross-functional communication problem solving. Employee training starts with basic business concepts of what business is, how a business operates, what major business functions are, and what an integrated business system means. It includes basic design techniques, a value analysis, and value engineering as well as skills in preventive maintenance.

Sometimes, depending on the type of production and the product, training requires refreshing the employees knowledge in trigonometry, calculus, and statistical operator control (SOC)—teaching a machine operator in the use of statistics in controlling processes and identifying the sources of problems, and how to reduce process variations and improve quality.

Often, a work force should be trained in basics of machine design, hydraulics and mechanical devices and attachments, as well as acquire basic knowledge in engineering disciplines, such as the details of machines and shop floor technology.

JIT-type leadership stands for trained and motivated work force which generates ideas and produces changes. JIT commences when there are such capable and determined people who carry on their duties through all the stages of this project.

Work force training is based on a sound business consideration and isn't just a social nicety and financial extremity as it is seen by some non-JIT-oriented organizations.

## JIT-BASED EMPLOYEE TRAINING PROGRAM AT DRESSER ITD

Dresser had a traditional functional plant layout that grouped identical or similar types of equipment into departments. This was instrumental in the development of "job classes" where an employee was hired and trained to operate one type of machine. Union rules quickly reinforced this "job class" division of labor with members zealously protecting "their" area of responsibility.

When forming JIT-type production centers, one goal was to have flexible employees, employees who could perform a wide variety of tasks required to produce a product. Those tasks included not only the setup and operation of all production center equipment but also support functions, such as inspection, material handling, minor repair and maintenance tasks, tool grinding, cleaning/sweeping, and any other task which was required. To develop flexible employees, a management commitment was essential to invest substantial time and energy to the task of training.

Initially, bidding lines were established from three classes:

1. CNC lathes
2. CNC machining centers
3. Grinding

Management reserved the right to select candidates from different work areas in order to achieve the balance of skills required to cross train. A "Pay for Skills" program was developed to ensure the proper training. "Pay for Skills" identified three major skill categories with three subcategories in each, with increased pay opportunities (in dollars per hour) as follows:

| | Setup | Operate |
|---|---|---|
| Turning | | |
| CNC lathes | 0.25 | 0.25 |
| Automatics | 0.25 | 0.25 |
| Manual lathes | 0.25 | 0.25 |
| Milling/Drilling | | |
| CNC machining centers | 0.25 | 0.25 |
| Milling machines | 0.25 | 0.25 |
| Drilling machines | 0.25 | 0.25 |
| Grinding | | |
| CNC grinding | 0.25 | 0.25 |
| ID grinding | 0.25 | 0.25 |
| OD grinding | 0.25 | 0.25 |

In order to certify as a production center technician, operators were given two years to learn how to set up and operate seven out of nine subcategories. A formal training program was developed to ensure training opportunities for all production center employees; however, the actual training was accomplished by the operators, teaching each other skills brought from their previous jobs. Certified skill achievements are recorded and maintained in employee records. Certified production center technicians are assigned to a given production center, but they may be moved to any work center to perform any task with no "temporary transfer" or other limitations, making the employees truly flexible.

## CHANGING THE ROLE OF THE WORK FORCE

We paid great attention to productivity at the expense of the job value. High productivity of a work force does not necessarily mean that a comparable value amount is added with each work task. The consensus is that at the lowest level of an organization, we must add more value to the job by reducing engineering, technical, and managerial services without reducing the output level.

In Japan, the work force takes over the management initiative in JIT constant improvement, through quality circles and suggestion schemes. A comparatively stable employment, and people-oriented management combined with education and training enable workers' involvement in management functions and reduces supervisory control. Here we observe a changing role of the work force in a production process and the increased involvement in production services, taking over some supervisory and management planning tasks and contributing to the embetterment of the organization.

A fundamental JIT requirement of employees involvement is channeled into JIT improvements wherever training is provided and the work force's basic needs are recognized. Human factors are not always governed by a quantitatively estimated logic. If, for example, one can save some dollars by laying off an employee, it can have far-reaching morale-damaging effects on all other employees. It is satisfying to see that about two-thirds of JIT respondents surveyed have already achieved these acceptable work life conditions and the remaining companies are considering implementing them.

All surveyed companies indicate that they have succeeded in motivating employees, the basic requirement on which all JIT programs hinge. In addition, to their regular duties, workers perform housekeeping and upkeep chores, maintain proper arrangement of tools and materials at their own places, and are involved in service operations, such as quality control and plant maintenance. A variety of additional functions performed by the work force within the JIT system is illustrated in Figure 9-2.

Some additional work functions performed by a work force, which can be utilized at the initial stages of JIT implementation, are quality circles, participation in plant maintenance and housekeeping.

**Figure 9-2**
**Work Force Involvement in Production Function within the Just-in-Time System**

## Obtaining the Participation of the Work Force in Quality Circles

*Quality circles*, an important part of JIT, contribute to continuous improvement projects. There is a little chance for JIT to succeed if companies do not see quality circles as a conduit for the work force suggestions. For example, at Toyota, 40 new improvement ideas are reported per one worker per year.

The task is to convert employees' suggestions into continuous improvements. Quality at source and zero defect are some of the outcomes of quality circles. According to the survey, the number of those companies achieving success in zero-defect programs is lower than the total number of responding companies maintaining quality circle programs. This indicates that quality circle schemes should be more effective. One way to accomplish this is by paying more attention to employees' training.

## Obtaining the Participation of the Work Force in Plant Maintenance

Maintenance by an operator is a nice benefit of JIT systems, capable of reducing the maintenance cost, improving the availability of equipment while simultaneously improving quality, with a minimal or no additional cost. Maintenance by an operator involves inspections and lubrication but excludes the repair work. According to the JIT survey, 53.1 percent of the responding companies are just now considering this option. This is an indication that these companies are hesitant to initiate the operators' training and involvement in maintaining their own machines.

## Housekeeping and Organizing the Workplace

Housekeeping refers to overall cleanliness and order of a facility and workplace organization. Order is enforced by removing the WIP inventory from the shop floor. Shops are kept tidy and clear of chips and debris, and everything is kept in its own place.

Housekeeping is an essential part of a JIT system. Disorder, such as a dirty floor and equipment surfaces, is incompatible with JIT. Dirt is the enemy of quality production. JIT is changing the old mentality that the manufacturing shop is a dirty place and does not need much time spent for cleaning it up, into adopting a positive attitude toward the cleanup. JIT daily production needs standardization and order, starting with the establishing order in the working area. Housekeeping is a yardstick for the workers' attitude and morale.

First-class housekeeping is reflected when everything is placed where it belongs, for instance, sorting, arranging all tools and materials in order, washing and cleaning, organizing the work area, and removing dust from machines reflect the level of morale and the degree to which the JIT involvement is taking place.

JIT is a system run by people having a positive attitude toward their workplace. JIT emphasizes a basic fundamental manufacturing practice: workers enjoy cleaning their machines and their working area because this is an indication of their image and an evidence of their craftsmanship, dexterity, and quality.

The visual state of a machine and the lubrication of its working surfaces often reflect a company mode of operation, for example, producing quality or substandard parts because cleaning a machine is one of the work tasks. The state of the machine and the organization of the workplace in general reflect the workers' attitude toward performing other work tasks.

The housekeeping discipline includes keeping everything clean enough for immediate use. Cleaning is the first action after use, to avoid visible problems, quality and safety problems, and maintenance problems. Cleanliness exhibits the standard by which the work is exercised at the workplace. Visitors to the production areas need to abide by the rules. Housekeeping eliminates stockrooms applying floor stockpoints materials, and tools and jigs are stored at the specified locations.

Housekeeping means removing the work-in-process inventory and removing things which currently are not used, for example, materials and supplies, gauges, and other measuring instruments. These are removed to fixed positions where they can be easily located by any team member when needed, eliminating the trash, which, when accumulated, affects the employees' morale and attitudes toward improvements and is contrary to the JIT philosophy.

A reduced space improves housekeeping, leads to better communication and feedback (reducing the need in data transfer), improves production planning and control, reduces material handling distances, and even reduces the need for material handling operations.

## SUMMARY

A majority of JIT companies are accomplishing significant gains already at the first level of the JIT implementation stage. This is ensured by employees' training—the cornerstone of JIT continuous improvement programs. Once the basic employees' motivational needs are fulfilled and on-the-job training is underway, JIT proceeds to the second level of the implementation stage, namely, the elimination of waste.

# 10

# Implementing JIT: Level 2—Eliminating Waste in Manufacturing Operations

Level 2 of JIT implementation involves the elimination of waste in product and process engineering and in organizational structures. JIT involves restructuring an organizational structure (that is, its engineering, production and management functions, and especially, its supervisory function). In management, an emphasis is placed on managing the technology and engineering at the expense of the managerial supervisory function.

Both product engineers and process engineers directly contribute to the product value. *Product engineers* contribute to the product value through improving product design, while *process engineers* improve the product value through improving productivity and reducing costs, and by enhancing production processes. In many instances, such a distinction is blurred, since a product engineer cannot design value products without envisaging the methods for producing these products. The JIT philosophy is to achieve a synergy between product engineering and manufacturing engineering through improved communication and coordination.

The engineering support in Japanese companies is an essential ingredient of their success in quality improvement and cost reduction. A high return on engineering efforts is utilized by Japanese manufacturing companies where the ratio of engineers to production workers is about 1 to 4; and in high-tech companies there are more engineers than production workers. It was estimated that an engineer increases productivity of each worker by roughly 5 percent, and each engineer generates savings far in excess of his or her cost to the company.

A high degree of engineering support in Japanese companies contrasts with the application of this human resource by American manufacturers, where the ratio of engineers to production workers is 1 to 10. This points to the source of enhancing the "output value"—increasing engineering support. A management technical function is closely related to engineering support and must be further expanded at the expense of management supervisory duties when flattening of organizational structures takes place.

Waste reduction starts with management: reevaluating its functions and reducing management redundancy and making use of programmed decision making. You should increase the management contribution to the engineering-based value-adding functions.

The distinction between traditional approaches and JIT is in that JIT permeates all units of an organization to achieve greater operating efficiency. There is evidence that companies implementing JIT systems reduce their operations management staff due to the reduction in operational control, replanning, and expediting.

The greatest waste is not readily detectable on the shop floor. Actually, it can be hidden in offices, in drawing cabinets, and in countless bits of data residing in a computer memory. For example, it can be a redundant reporting procedure not contributing to decision making. Such reporting procedures increase production costs while not adding to the product value either directly or indirectly.

There are wastes in organizational structures where there is one manager for every four workers and one secretary for every two managers. JIT organizational structures are flatter, partially because decisions are made at the lowest level of organizational structures and partially because preventive planning reduces the management controlling function and the need for information.

## ELIMINATING WASTES IN PRODUCTION

In JIT, a waste reduction is emphasized in the following areas of production:

1. Reduction of operations that do not add value to a product—for example, quality inspections, storage inventory transactions, and operations such as quantity count, material handling and transport, and setups—and the elimination of redundant operations, tasks, processes, and of productivity wastes
2. Reduction of nonvalue-adding unplanned operations, such as excessive material handling and moving components around from one storage place to another

Nonvalue-adding work tasks are the primary targets of the elimination of waste program. It can be found that value-adding operations, such as machining, welding, and painting, have many nonvalue-adding elements which often go unnoticed. Such nonproductive work elements should also be targeted in elimination of waste programs.

### Developing Work Improvement Schemes

Work improvements are accomplished by assessing operations manufacturing engineering; improving planning and control procedures; and improving organizational structures, engineering, and production services and the integrated manufacturing system as a whole. If something should be changed to achieve a planned improvement, such change should be considered.

For example, Precision Valve Co., a valve manufacturer in small lots, has found that production was hindered by a high rejection rate on one operation—the horizontal grinding of the valve housing. In order to uphold a quality standard, this operation would have taken 47 minutes instead of 33 minutes according to standard time. Still, rejects of 5.2 percent were interfering with a consistent material flow. Statistical quality control identified that the grinding machine is not capable of performing to a precision standard required by product specifications. The grinding machine was replaced by a newest high-precision grinder, and the bottleneck was eliminated. This is an example of a quality problem that occurs when equipment is not capable of performing to specifications. In such instances, the problem's typical resolution is seen in purchasing advanced equipment.

Upgrading equipment is not the only way to resolve production problems. As a rule, work improvements should be done before deciding to spend money on an equipment improvement. There are cases when time and money are spent on improving a process which is later eliminated, after the product design audit has been done. Often, an equipment improvement results in the unproportional increase of productivity and the buildup of an excessive inventory. Every decision to invest in an equipment must be based on the consideration of improving the material flow and reducing product's lead time. Productivity of all processes should be consistent with the velocity of material flow.

## ELIMINATING INVENTORY WASTES

Employees like to have buffers (an inventory and an excessive capacity) in case something happens in areas of their responsibility. Instead of building up a buffer stock, the Japanese force the shop floor people to confront such situations and eliminate them one by one.

Many companies start a JIT program by demanding frequent and small deliveries from their vendors and suppliers. Other companies do not care about their suppliers and rely on internally developed JIT methods and are not able or willing to extend this system to the suppliers network. The strategy which produces good results is to implement JIT internally and then show the suppliers how it works. One California computer equipment manufacturer taking part in JIT survey reports: "We are seeing very good results within our manufacturing organization and are beginning to see the results in our procurement group, but we still have a long way to go. We have to continue to minimize the 'adversarial relationships' of the past, and to build a team approach with a win/win relationship between our suppliers and ourselves . . . . We continue to encourage our designers to consider our suppliers as part of their team, as well." Your vendors and suppliers are the extension of your capacity. You should consider having them as productive as your own company. Reduce inventory not only internally but at your vendor factories as well. The lead time reduction, quality improvements, and cost reduction should be extended throughout an entire system, which includes your vendors and suppliers.

## ENSURING EMPLOYEE RESPONSIBILITY FOR THE SUCCESS OF JIT SYSTEMS

JIT is a system of the teamwork that exerts a collective responsibility on the part of the work force. In conventional systems, workers feel responsible for processes they perform, which puts them on the spot and makes them vulnerable to any blame for an unsatisfactory performance. In such a production environment, shop floor personnel are on the offensive to repudiate the blame for a problem which is often difficult to trace back in a fractured and departmentalized organization and a multiproduct functional-type material flow.

In JIT, an organization is structured around a product, and the employees' work can be traced to a specific element of the product. Such product-focused organization creates a climate of collaboration and mutual support within a team. This way, making visible the contribution of each team member, employees are not strained by individual responsibility, and they are more protected due to the collective team responsibility. JIT contributes to motivation, since the results of work are immediately visible and acknowledged and enforced by the established "producer-consumer" relationship. Even employees' motivation, which is a major management functional responsibility and concern in traditional production systems, is programmed in JIT so that it does not require management intervention and dedicated efforts of an ongoing reinforcement and incentives.

JIT restructures functional responsibilities and prevents the relinquishment of the responsibility and relegation so widely spread at all levels of a traditional organization. For example, although management is responsible for compiling production programs, the shop floor staff is responsible if these plans are not accomplished.

The key is to share the responsibility for work performance horizontally and to share the authority and responsibility vertically. In other words, an assertive job enlargement and job enrichment are combined to create a T-organization. Horizontally, a team responsibility now supersedes what was once the individual worker's responsibility. Vertically, managers involve themselves in the execution of the workers' plans. This positively affects the workers' morale by showing that managers are assisting in case of a need and share with them the responsibility within the framework of a functional partnership.

Moreover, the work force is involved in the process improvement and service operations, which until recently, have been the responsibility of manufacturing engineering. This includes working on improvements or adjustments, housekeeping (cleaning a machine and a work area), and conducting basic maintenance tasks and inspections.

The elimination of waste is ideally suited to small- and medium-sized manufacturing companies seeking to improve their performance. At level 2—elimination of waste—JIT implementation, a company should be able to obtain a financial clout and a technical expertise to proceed toward engineering improvements and automation envisaged at the subsequent Continuous Improvement System (CIS) stages.

## ACCOMPLISHING TOTAL QUALITY CONTROL

Total quality control begins with customer's requirements for a high-value product. These quality requirements are a critical issue in JIT (that is, the requirements for the high quality of incoming materials and internal production). A quality organization is an essential component of a JIT program. However, it is unreasonable to expect quality issues to resolve other production planning problems related to the material flow. The JIT approach to quality is known as *quality at the source*. Quality at the source is an approach of assigning the responsibility for quality control to people doing the work. It is true that it takes the same time to produce a good quality component as it takes to produce a faulty component. The difference is in that on completion, good components proceed to the subsequent production stages, while bad components delay production and still require an additional rework and inspection. It is easier to prevent a quality problem from happening than to rectify it after a fault has been discovered.

At the Precision Mold and Tool Co., quality controllers were inspecting all parts before they proceeded to assembly. According to the company's JIT program, the task of inspecting the quality has been assigned to operators performing the work. Quality is tested now only at the finished product test run. Such a change in the policy, considering a reduction in quality inspections, has resulted in quality improvements: the rate of molds returns for readjustment and surface polishing has dropped from 63 to 41 percent, not to mention the reduction in quality control inspections.

*Example*: Consider quality-at-the-source at the Dresser ITD. "Our approach at Dresser is that quality must be designed into products and the manufacturing process must be complementary to good design," says Bill Collins, manager of manufacturing at Dresser ITD.

Traditionally, engineering designed the component parts, while manufacturing engineering developed the process technology, including equipment requirements, tooling, and computer numerical control (CNC) computer programs. The machining operation involved three people:

1. A skilled setup worker who prepared the machine to produce a given part
2. An inspector who approved the setup piece and periodically returned to verify that parts were being produced to specifications
3. An operator whose primary task was to load and unload the machine

The responsibility for part quality was shared between the setup worker, the inspector, and the operator.

Dresser has adopted a policy that the part quality must be an inherent result of the machining process. While in production centers the operators were trained in the setup and operation of equipment, they were also trained in quality inspection, including the use of different measuring devices. A sole responsibility for part quality now rests with the operator who machines the part. There is no longer a "line inspector" to share the blame. An operator has the responsibility and duty to stop the job if it is not within the specified tolerance and make necessary adjustments or request assistance. All parts still go through the final inspection area as a measure to ensure that only quality parts proceed to assembly or stock.

## Improving Quality

Quality relates directly to the product value. A product manufacturing flow diagram superimposed on the shop floor plan helps in tracking parts' flow lines, reducing an interprocess inventory, reducing working spaces, shortening and eliminating material handling routes, exposing and eliminating future bottlenecks, improving a material flow and tooling flow paths, and examining the supplies of assembly processes.

Sources of quality problems are

- Design
- Production
- Vendors and suppliers

JIT attacks fundamental problems: if there is a persistent quality problem on a specific process, the reason should be identified first.

*Example*: Tin steel rolling at SKO Steel Company has experienced a daily problem of steel strip breaking. Every strip breakage requires about one and a half hours time to adjust a rolling mill. This problem has been persisting for many years until it was decided to investigate and expose its cause.

A production engineering laboratory technician was assigned for two weeks to collect data for the investigation, just by observing and recording the mill operator's performance. To everybody's surprise, there was not a single strip breakage during these two weeks' operations both in the morning and the afternoon shift. The result of observations has indicated that operators did not adhere to operating instructions. Since then this problem has disappeared without any further investigations or changes to process specifications or operating procedures.

It is logical to place the responsibility for quality of a production process on production, the same way as production is responsible for the quantity of produced components, say, producing 50 components as ordered, instead of, say, 48 or 46 components. It is justifiable to place the responsibility for detecting and correcting faults on the operator who sets up and monitors the process, and who should take corrective actions when deviations occur.

It is remarkable that the elimination of quality control inspectors results in improved quality. A word of caution should be said to those who assume that producing substandard quality components is purely the worker's fault, and thus quality is controlled at the source. It is a known fact that the majority of quality problems are management controllable and are attributed to process control. Examples are poor product design, equipment or tools not capable to produce to specifications, inability to adhere to precision standards, poor planning, and continuous changes in schedules. It so happens that these problems rise to the surface at the time of execution, although their causes go back to preproduction stages, such as product design and development, and to production planning and control system. Only a minority of quality control problems are worker controlled, as in the example with the steel mill operator.

The production manager's focal point is in integrating diverse and sometimes contradicting production support functions, such as product engineering, process engineering, industrial engineering, and other primary and support activities. Their essential task is to ensure that each workstation is capable of producing to specification and to ensure that the work force is provided with proper operating instructions, is motivated, and is sufficiently trained.

## REDUCING SETUP TIME TO ENSURE THE SUCCESS OF JIT MANUFACTURING

A *setup operation* is the time elapsed since the previous job was removed and until the first good part of a new job has been produced. The reduction of setup time makes economically feasible production in small lots, the cornerstone of JIT. The reduction of setup time facilitates small-lot production by reducing lead time and speeding up the material flow. JIT production in small runs calls for frequent changes in produced products, disregarding the rules of economic order quantity.

The Japanese found it possible to decrease batch sizes, due to their drastic reduction in setup times from hours to minutes. They sometimes eliminate entire setup operations and increase machine efficiency along with batch reductions. The setup reduction is aimed at reducing the preparation time and the machine time rather than reducing the setup cost.

Lot sizes is the function of setup time. It was found that the amount of work-in-process and finished-goods inventory, as well as the product lead time, are directly related to lot sizes. To maintain the productivity level in JIT production characterized by a reduction in lot sizes from the monthly requirements lot to such a small daily requirements lot production, calls for a 95 percent reduction in the setup time. It is fair to say that the setup time reduction is one single principal element which enables Japanese to come up with the JIT system as you know it now. You should pay attention to your setup time reduction at the onset of the JIT project and further on throughout the continuous improvement stage.

## HOW TO REDUCE SETUP TIME

The setup time reduction is approached as a teamwork project, not as an engineering one. A project team includes supervisors, setup people, operators, quality control, maintenance staff, technical support, process engineering, and tool designers. A particular machine or even a particular changeover is selected for the setup time reduction program.

The shop floor staff (foremen, operators, and setup people) are the driving force in teams working on solving the setup time reduction problems because people working on the equipment have firsthand experience and often have good ideas on how to achieve the setup time reduction. This gives them a sense of ownership in resolving the setup problems.

The engineering staff is supporting the setup reduction efforts and is involved in training the team members. The setup reduction is approached in the following sequence:

*Phase 1.* Setup operations are divided into internal and external tasks. *Internal tasks* are those which require the stoppage of a machine. The internal setup time is divided into the attachment time and the adjustment time and the first part production time. *External tasks* are those which can be done when the equipment is in the working condition, for example, obtaining and familiarizing with drawings and working instructions, collecting tools, materials, and setting the tools in toolholders. On the average, external tasks represent up to 50 percent of the setup time. Organizing a workplace to perform these operations while a machine is producing reduces the setup time by half. The elements of setup time are illustrated in Figure 10-1.

*Phase 2.* The timing of individual elements is recorded, both for internal and external setup tasks. The setup time reduction procedure can involve videotaping of actual setup tasks. This includes making a tape of setup activities by following the setup people throughout the plant while they perform their tasks. At this stage, setup elements are divided into internal or external, mounting, clamping, adjustments, and first-part production. It also includes examining internal events and trying to convert them into external events. Setup task charts are used when analyzing setup activities.

*Phase 3.* Setup time reduction includes reducing the time for each task, both internal and external, and trying to entirely eliminate the unnecessary tasks. Many setup operations can be reduced up to 40 percent, just by a better

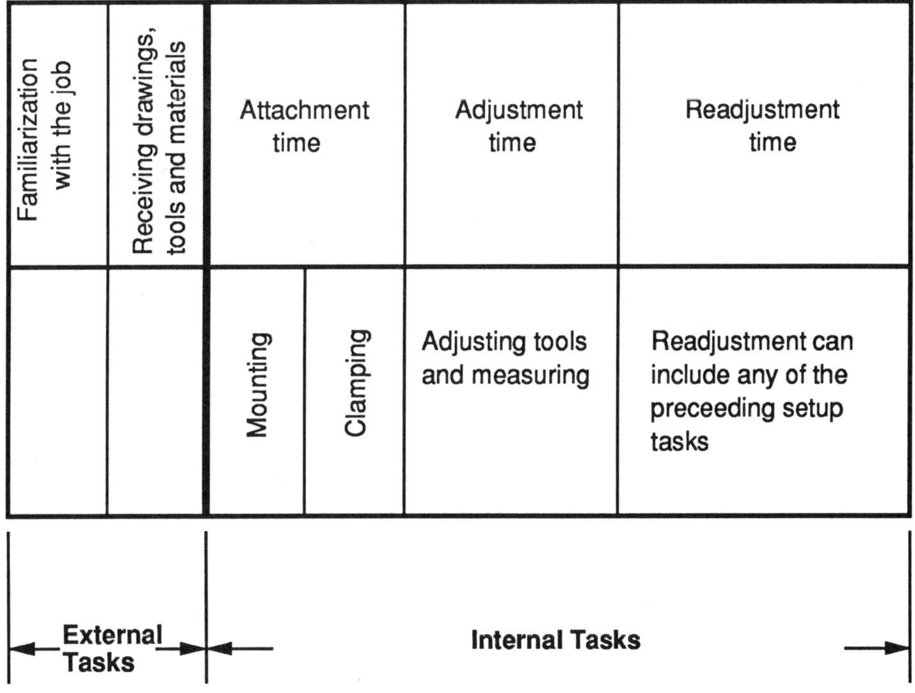


**Figure 10-1**
**The Elements of Setup Time**

workplace organization, by keeping tools in setup baskets in good working condition, and by applying dedicated toolholders.

Phase 3 includes eliminating adjustments—measuring and correct setting of tools and equipment; introducing time-saving devices, such as folding brackets and hinged bolts to avoid infinite adjustments; using special bolts and stops to apply preset ready-to-use tools; and scheduling a timely tool changeover to avoid breakdowns and eliminate faulty production. Adjustments are approached so that already the first part should be good. In most applications, current setup times can be reduced by 75 percent at a minimal cost, just by applying a setup time analysis after videotaping and documenting the setup tasks.

Setup time reduction is seen as a key to manufacturing in small lots, a leading issue when changing from the conventional material flow (the push system) to the JIT zero-stock pull system.

In general, a JIT setup time reduction program is conducted in two steps: In *Step 1*, the setup time reduction can be achieved in a short period of time by inexpensive means, such as converting internal setup tasks into work that can be performed externally; reducing or eliminating the adjustment process; applying time-saving devices, such as tools permanently placed in tool holders and roller platforms; and applying inexpensive tools and self-made attachments, such as ready setup baskets. At this stage setup time reduction is achieved by using standard hardware heads, shorter bolts, and standard quick disconnect clamping devices, and hydraulic line attachments.

This includes the elimination of an organizational task, ensuring that tools are sharp and in a good working condition and placing everything in its designated place (for example, an additional cabinet or a toolholding board placed next to the machine reduces the setup time), so that everything is easy to find.

Experience has shown that step 1 of the setup time reduction program can reduce setup time to an acceptable level without instituting major changes and spending a lot of material resources. In many operations, this is sufficient, unless the operation under review is a bottleneck process blocking the flow of materials and requiring further setup reduction.

*Step 2* requires greater efforts in time and money (for example, designing special fixtures which can be mounted quickly on standard plates or modifying equipment for quick execution of internal tasks). At this stage, a setup time reduction is achieved by producing special clamping devices, for example, using cam-action clamps rather than nuts and bolts; using special locating pins and slots, self-positioning dies, hydraulic and air pressure clamping devices, and rolling bolsters; modifying the machine and tools; or abolishing the setup tasks by making use of dedicated machines for each operation. For example, one manufacturer has refurbished four manual drilling presses and has used them for dedicated drilling and tapping operations by the operator supervising the work of two automated machines.

## Reducing the Setup Time at Stamping and Molding Jobs

Stamping and molding operations constitute a significant part of production processes and are the areas where an inventory builds up significantly, due to a great disparity between the long setup time and the negligible machine time. Stamping and molding operations require installation and adjustments of molds or dies on the press. Thus, the efforts of reducing the time needed for the exchange of a die or a mold (from hours to minutes), the single-minute exchange of dies (SMED), is an important factor in overall efforts of setup time reduction and elimination of inventories.

In many instances, this can be achieved through workers' efforts and creativity, after basic training is provided in product design and technology improvement techniques. Often, there is a possibility of reducing the time of internal tasks, such as clamping, unclamping, screwing, and measuring, by using molds and dies of the same height, reducing the number of bolts, making use of pins, wedges and stoppers, or applying ball lock systems and cam-action clamps.

A stamping and molding setup of these mostly heavy tools has a high content of external tasks, involving a withdrawal from the storage place and material handling procedures. External setup tasks include receiving a work order, searching for drawings and job instructions, searching for tools and materials, waiting for a fork-lift driver to deliver a new mold and to remove the used one, cleaning the workplace, heating the mold, and so on.

*Example*: At a furniture factory, one setup operation that usually takes 80 minutes has been selected for an experiment. The machine operator has been informed in advance that a time sample of this setup operation will be taken next week, as part of a JIT improvement program. To the supervisor's surprise, this setup operation was performed in 45 minutes. Nothing was discussed, or changed, or suggested as an improvement, but the reduction in setup time took place. Organizational tasks can take as much as 50 to 70 percent of the entire setup operation. In injection molding, the time required for adjustment, heating of molds, and trial processing of a mold or a die is often approaching 90 percent of the setup time. In the above example, the organizational tasks were considered by an operator in advance, so that the actual setup was conducted without interruptions.

Die setup time can be reduced when the mold is placed on an intermediate jig outside the press. Injection mold setup time is reduced when applying mold preheating by using heat available at the machine. You must learn to reduce the number and types of tools, eliminate some unnecessary bolts, and make some setups a one-touch operation.

More expensive means for setup time reduction use changes in the layout of tools and materials around the workstation by modifying the existing equipment.

You can design and build your own attachments or machines, designing not necessarily a high-productivity high-volume piece of equipment, but rather equipment that requires zero setup to reliably perform high quality operations. Additional bonuses can be gained by simplifying the equipment, performing maintenance inspections and encouraging simple maintenance by the operators, and using small sizes and low-cost equipment that you are able to reproduce and constantly improve.

*Example*: Consider tooling and setup reduction at Dresser ITD. The basic concepts of simplification, standardization, and organization for the product flow also apply to turning, milling, drilling, and grinding.

When JIT production centers were being established, tooling and its effect on the setup were considered. Bill Collins explains that for Dresser's machining centers, a traditional subplate with 360 precision drilled and tapped ports was being used to attach a part fixture to the machine. Of course, this design was universal and flexible from the designers' point of view. However, to set up an operation, the operator had to determine which ports would be used to attach the fixture, clean tightly packed chips and shavings out of those ports, find the proper length bolts to be used (or use washers, shims, etc.), and finally, establish the fixture's relationship with cutting tools on the machine. This was very time consuming. One design engineer had studied the process and designed a very simple subplate which eliminated those setup variables by having only one location utilizing standard ball lock devices: an Acroloc tool plate with four ball lock ports and a self-centered alignment slot, with a ball lock system (CP-4232) on the Acroloc tool plate. The holding force of up to 3,000 pounds is obtained with a locking torque of only 48 inches. The locking force of the ball lock is produced by the action of four 8.75-millimeter balls. Turning the ball screw clockwise forces a centrally located ball down into contact with three radially positioned balls lock shank, which in turn, makes contact with the angle in the ball lock socket mounted in the tooling plate. Turning the lock screw counterclockwise releases the ball lock. Lock screws screw in and out freely. The three balls in their bores move freely, and the ball lock fits freely in the ball lock socket of the tooling plate.

At Dresser, a 50 percent setup reduction was achieved simply by eliminating the central tool crib and organizing tooling within the production center where it is used. Of course, the quickest setup is achieved with no change, and this is being addressed by dedicating machines to producing part families. The setup improvement on *CNC lathes* is being achieved by standardizing CNC programs and dedicating toolholders to specific cutting tools. In CNC machining centers, standard processes and programs coupled with the fixture design reduce the complexities of the setup. In addition, combining multiple setups reduces setup time and reduces the number of exposures to mistakes, as well as improves dimensional relationships of the parts. In grinding, setup improvements have been achieved primarily by combining multiple grind operations on CNC grinders.

At this point, setups in production centers have been reduced approximately 75 percent overall, but the setup reduction continues to be a major area of concentration, to further reduce lot sizes.

## ELIMINATING WASTE IN PRODUCT DESIGN

In general, lead time is the time elapsed from the moment a customer has requested a product until the time the product is delivered. A new product's lead time is the time elapsed since the moment the customer demand is acknowledged until the time this demand is satisfied—the product has been developed and produced according to the requirements rate. Product design is the first stage in new product manufacturing and is considered to be a part of lead time. In design-to-order jobs, product design is an even more significant part of the order's lead time. Reducing the design time reduces new products' lead times, which means being the first on the market and securing a larger share of market sales. The same goes for modifications and improvements to the existing products and production of new models. For example, Japanese automakers reduce in half the development and design stage of their automobiles as compared with American car manufacturers. Consequently, they are able to put a new car model on the road every three to four years. American automakers begin to recognize the significance of the design stage in the product development. For example, Chrysler has constructed a billion-dollar center for designing and developing prototypes and for producing car models which are free of process and product quality problems. Product design means product planning, that is, planning a product of highest possible value. A product engineer should see his/her function as designing the product value (that is, to be able to provide a customer with the greatest value for money rather than merely designing the product). A design engineer is a person who among the first in the line deals with the customer need in a new product. He has a vision of the product itself, how this product will be created, how it will satisfy the customer need, and when it will be completed. The new product design stage includes not only designing the product but also planning production of the product. A present-day designer plans the product functions, performance, and quality level, along with planning how to produce this product so as to attain the greatest value. This includes the vendor part of production. Vendors are involved at the initial stages of product and specifications design, including developing the product structure, route sheets, material flow, and production planning, including daily rates. There must be assurance that vendors' resources are capable of producing to engineering specification and their manufacturing capacity is sufficient to satisfy demand.

Furthermore, the role a design engineer plays in an organization is the "maintenance of design." This function is changing toward assigning broader responsibilities not only for the design but also for the product value. If a product design is flawed, one can fight a losing battle in manufacturing. The initial task is to design the controllability into the product, ensuring that the engineering design will meet its specifications during the production.

Due to the ever-decreasing product life, a strategy adopted by avant-garde companies is to coordinate new products' design with manufacturing engineering. In one oil tool company, a 300-pound part is taken off the machine for inspection to a special control room having a reinforced foundation. If there is a need for additonal machining, the part is taken back to the machine. Along with designing a product consisting of components, subassemblies, and assemblies, a designer should envisage how these product elements are fabricated on the shop floor and then assembled together. At the design stage, along with materials, fits, and tolerances, a designer should foresee production concepts, such as designing the product for easy assembly, avoiding queues, reducing setup times, machine time, lead time, quality inspections, and material handling.

In our example, the designer should explore if there is any other way to measure parts while they are still on a machine? If not, then take a look back at the product design—is there a possibility to relieve tolerances without affecting the quality? This will reduce the production cost. However, in most instances, design is viewed as fixed. A designer should be engaged with a product throughout the entire product life. The JIT system requires product design adjustments to ensure the manufacturability, low setup time, and unrestricted access for inspection.

An evolving term that describes the quality of product design is *manufacturability.* This means that a product is designed in accord with engineering, suppliers, customers, and the production function so as to take advantage of the available resources, in order to ensure the highest quality level and, at the same time, take advantage of production processes for reducing the production cost.

It was found that Japanese products produced at American factories have the same quality as those produced in Japan. This means that these products are designed to ensure the quality of piece part and assembly processes regardless of the diverse manufacturing conditions. The Japanese have incorporated quality-enhancing features into the product design, so as to retain their quality advantages during manufacturing and assembly processes.

The common practice is to start manufacturing of a new product as soon as the drawings are available and the working prototypes function and are market tested. At this stage, the function of the design engineering group ends—it can be moved to the new product, and manufacturing engineering takes over the product. The perception of a designer should be altered from a person making drawings of a product to a person responsible for the manufacturability of the product.

In JIT-produced products, product structures are reviewed so as to flatten their bill of materials by eliminating subassembly, making it possible that the components are assembled at the highest assembly level.

The building parts process is organized close to the assembly line, in order to eliminate inventory and material handling operations. The material flow features a one-at-a-time component going directly into assembly. This way, production of the entire assembly and the components material flow are organized as a production line of one-off products. In job shop production, such a production line can be tailored for a variety of products.

Product design is reviewed for the possibility of reducing the number of parts, which leads to the reduction of the production cost, reduction of assembly time, and elimination of inventory of intermediate assemblies, not to mention the benefits of improved product quality (that is, fewer components, fewer causes for defects). For example, designers at Dresser ITD use a common motor in different products. This reduces the number of inventoried items, reduces inventory investments, standardizes the design, and reduces the design lead time. Such changes require teamwork of all people concerned—production, material control, product design, and industrial engineering. This is why cross-functional teams are an important feature of JIT systems.

Designers work in close coordination with internal production departments and services, as well as with the components supplier base, in order to ensure that the initial design can be supported by the current manufacturing system. The design should be adjusted to be compatible with the current production technology and range of resources on hand, and vice versa, resources should be adjusted to ensure an uninterrupted material flow, the reduction of waste, compliance with product specifications, and the controllability of parts fits and tolerance limits. Japanese JIT-type companies design quality into products by ensuring that the tolerance interval is not greater than 80 percent of six standard deviations. This condition requires that designers have an intimate knowledge of their company manufacturing processes.

Preparing each product for JIT includes reexamining and redesigning, involving people at all organizational levels rather than just a design engineer. A new function of design engineering is regarded as an interaction link between a potential customer and production processes. An integration of production, design, and marketing activities takes place here.

Often, production people assume the design is fixed, and they try hard to adhere to the existing tolerances and standards. Not in every company, a production foreman goes back to the design office to discuss with the product engineer possible changes or simply to be assured that there is a need for a tight tolerance, a surface finish, or a heat treatment procedure which currently presents problems to production or is a bottleneck operation in the material flow. In some cases, such intricate standards causing production problems are not essential and can be avoided after reviewing and making minor changes in the product design. This eliminates bottlenecks, streamlines material flow, and reduces product cost. In a JIT system, the communication of the product designer and shop floor is continuous and can be casually initiated by any party. For example, one oil tool company moved offices of design engineers from an administrative building to a shop floor, next to an assembly line.

In some Japanese companies, designers are required to work on the equipment they design, and many designers, as do most of Japanese and West German managers, have hands-on shop floor experience as machine operators. You should pay attention to how often product designers review the existing products. Start a design audit, and you will be surprised what changes you can initiate. Design is a function continuing throughout the product life. Product simplifications and improvements constantly update the design and take advantage of changes and improvements in production technology and processes. Design audits performed periodically are a good way to improve the manufacturability and product quality and to reduce product cost. An important point to emphasize is that such maintenance of the design extends the product life while making the product more acceptable throughout the entire product life.

Companies attempt to find synergy in design. Before starting an audit by a designer, solicit an input and suggestions from the processes. The result can be impressive. Synergy is an involvement and input of everybody in an organization.

You may ask: "What is the benefit of improving a process and eliminating a bottleneck by automating it, reducing setup time, improving quality, or buying an additional or high-performance piece of equipment, if after a design audit the designer finds it possible to change the product design so as to eliminate completely an entire assembly unit including this critical process/part?" In response, a Japanese manufacturer of home appliances in the United States has changed an assembly unit comprising four precision machined components that required an individual assembly and adjustments into a single component produced by a double-cavity plastic injection mold. This has effectively eliminated manual assembly and adjustments, not to mention the drastically reduced production cost, improved product quality, and reduced lead time.

Design should envisage the best material flow having the minimal WIP inventory. In other words, product design should correspond and be adjusted to specific manufacturing facilities.

At the design stage, along with the bill of materials (BOM), another document should be structured, namely, the bill of processes (BOP), comprising lead times for building components and assemblies, similar to that of the bill of integrated tasks (BIT).

Japanese manufacturers feel that if there is a production problem, it should be the problem of design because they view design as the way to satisfy customer needs. JIT design engineer's functions include:

1. Maintaining tolerances to ensure quality
2. Examining the work flow first before instituting any changes to a product
3. Flattening the product structure by reducing some intermediate assembly levels
4. Designing components requiring equal processing times amenable to the *kanban* material flow control
5. Designing for a convenient assembly and reduction in production costs

A designer is in a strategic position to plan the product building; production operations, including economic quantities; service operations, such as material handling, warehousing, and housekeeping; as well as operational planning and decision making, including the management information system and production control.

## The Significance of Preproduction Planning

The meanings of planning is to forecast future actions. It is important that a plan submitted to execution outlines the plan for actions, namely, how to conduct individual operations.

There are two types of production planning and control arrangements:

1. Quick planning and long execution
2. Long planning and speedy execution

Production planning should start at the design stage. It is the best place indeed to spend 90 percent of the project time. The key is to be able to execute in the remaining 10 percent of the time. Such an arrangement saves production time and reduces problems and production costs, especially when comparing resources involved in planning with the resources involved in execution. This is one of the reasons why Japanese products have a reputation of better value to customer. An investment in production resources is much costlier than that of planning resources.

The Japanese view planning as an operational task deserving the resources and time, akin to active production operations, such as cutting or drilling. There is one opinion that planning should prepare a pattern for production; in other words, it should be a testing ground for execution. Such preventive planning facilitates execution to the point of being fault free and requiring no control.

The difference between a low-performance company and a high-performance one is that the latter assigns more resources to planning. This includes all levels of planning, for example, executive management planning, line management planning, and operational planning. In such an organization, it is not essential how fast the execution of individual operations is performed, because the cycle and phases' pattern of the material flow for various products and production stages was established beforehand and reconciled by planners. The function of planning should include preparing such a pattern at the preproduction planning stage and at the planning stage. Such a pattern outlines productivity of the execution stage which cannot be exceeded. The production program should be deliberately and painstakingly prepared, and this requires more efforts and consideration than is customarily accepted.

A major JIT advantage is that it contains the instrument for producing such production patterns. Do not be misled by the opinion that JIT does not require detailed planning. Such an assumption leads to the complaisance that all the detailed planning and scheduling is done on shop floor. One manager has confessed that they consider abolishing the material requirements planning (MRP) and capacity requirements planning (CRP) system modules, in order to let the shop floor personnel to do JIT-type material flow scheduling and control. "It takes us three days to generate an MRP schedule. By that time this schedule is already outdated, and we have many disruptions on the shop floor." You should make sure that you have done your homework before embarking on such a drastic change in your production system. You should work out in detail how shop floor people will schedule and control operations before assigning them to such a task.

Here is one example of a simple, JIT-type production planning and control technique developed at Dresser ITD, which produces very good results. Dresser's planners have found that there is no priority technique, including the critical ratio scheduling, which differentiates between the factory backlog and forecast and which meets their business objectives for the customer service. Dresser wanted a production planning and control technique which would be consistent with company's objective of providing a quick response to customer needs. Consequently, they have developed a simple method of scheduling and controlling production work based on priorities, as determined by their customers themselves. Shop scheduling is accomplished by following a few basic rules:

1. *Minimize work in process inventory.* Higher levels of the WIP inventory result in longer average lead times, due to larger buffers in the queue. Lower levels of the WIP inventory result in faster throughput time by reducing queues and limiting the number of choices of work available for a given machine.
2. *Organize for production flow.* Standard processes in small production centers (machine cells) simplify scheduling. The starting operation is scheduled and the lot "flows" through the production center to completion.
3. *Control priorities.* Shop scheduling is driven by a report which contains the lot priority and all remaining operations to be performed. A Dresser production priority report is shown in Figure 10-2. Priority is determined by inventory control based on delivery promises first, followed by forecast requirements. A simple "X" scheme is used, up to five "X's" to indicate priority. "We are very satisfied with results of such simple priority rule procedures because they result in a steady material flow which proceeds exactly according to the plan," say Dresser planners and shop floor staff.

JIT presents an outstanding tool for detailed balancing and controlling of a material flow on the shop floor, managing flexible manufacturing system (FMS); however, it still requires centralized planning that involves preparing an optimum product mix beforehand, as well as input-output capacity balancing. JIT presents an outstanding execution control instrument able to be tuned up to precision with a high degree of accuracy. Planning is required to rise to

PRODUCTION PRIORITY REPORT
PRODUCTION CENTER 085 03/11/91 PAGE 2

| PRTY | PART | LOT | DESCRIPTION | OPERATION ROUTING | | | | | HRS | PROM DATE |
|---|---|---|---|---|---|---|---|---|---|---|
| | | | | BURR | PENT | INSP | ASSY | INSP | | |
| X | 8675007 | 21 | ANGLE HEAD | PENT | INSP | INSP | | | 14.0 | |
| XX | 867507 | 22 | ANGLE HEAD | HT | HT | INSP | SB | 03597 | 136.4 | |
| | | | | G3563 | PENT | | | | | |
| XX | 869030 | 17 | ANGLE HEAD | ASSY | INSP | | | | 0.5 | |
| XXXX | 869048 | 42 | ANGLE HEAD | 03476 | A3555 | M2637 | BURR | PENT | 42.2 | |
| X | 869372 | 40 | HANDLE | A3555 | BURR | BURR | BURR | BURR | 42.1 | |
| XX | 869611 | 39 | HANDLE | ASSY | ASSY | ASSY | INSP | | 5.4 | |
| X | 869972 | 29 | HANDLE | ASSY | BURR | BURR | INSP | | 28.5 | |

**Figure 10-2**
**Production Priority Report at Dresser LTD**

such an execution standard by producing a detailed, well-balanced and verifiable production program.

## INCREASING PRODUCTIVITY USING JUST-IN-TIME PRODUCTION SYSTEMS

Toyota Motor Corp. managers surprised their GM partners in a joint venture with the New United Motor Corp. (NUMMI) when they transformed a California assembly plant with outdated equipment into GM's most efficient factory performing at a productivity level twice that of the average in a GM factory.

What was the cause of such a spectacular result? In reality, what makes the difference is the ability to create efficient productive systems from the mosaic of individual diminutive operational elements, involving an array of diverse productive resources. The secret of Japanese managers is that, in designing manufacturing systems, they pay attention to details both at the planning and at the execution stage.

Do not leave anything without questioning if it is possible to improve it. Come in the morning to your plant as if you were going there for the first time. Do not get routinely used to things, standards, or procedures. Take a fresh look at everything as if you were there as an outsider/advisor. Standards and procedures make us complacent. We need to question all these established standards and constantly search for areas of improvement in productive systems.

Just-in-Time production means zero stock (that is, producing precisely the quantity required at the time it is needed). Such a practice can be regarded as a *time-phased, zero-deviation schedule.* Any deviation from the schedule, either delaying or getting ahead of it, leads to building up a WIP inventory.

Often inventory is portrayed as water covering underwater rocks (production problems such as lack of materials, lack of tools, machine breakdowns, and poor quality). When the level of water (the inventory buffer) covers the rocks, the problems are hidden. The JIT principle is to reduce the inventory and to expose and eliminate the hidden rocks, one by one.

Most often, an inventory is accumulated due to decentralized decisions aimed at improving productivity through production in economical batch quantities or due to assigning priority to the utilization of capacity, at the expense of product considerations. Traditionally, an economic order quantity has been seen as a measure by which to reduce lead times by building safety stocks, to make a provision for machine's breakdown, to accommodate a lack of materials or tools, or to buffer a chronic quality problem. This inventory buildup through production processes is often due to departmental, arbitrary, off-hand decisions to keep a large buffer stock between machines to ensure that downstream operations do not run short of work.

## MASTER PRODUCTION SCHEDULE PLANNING IN JIT

A master production schedule (MPS) is compiled in the final assembly configuration, having typically a two- to six-month planning horizon. Often, an MPS is compiled in 10-day blocks, which are finally broken down to daily schedules, roughly balanced for material and labor requirements. In such applications, a time fence of one month prior to production is frozen. MPS is planned on a monthly basis, but the minimum planning horizon is based on the products' lead time. Some manufacturers, producing short-lead time products, compile a 6- to 9-month MPS in weekly increments. Figure 10-3 illustrates an ASK MPS report compiled for 36 weeks in weekly increments.

An MPS is an initial schedule of deliveries exposing the relationship between the product quantity and time, in other words, representing time-phased product deliveries. In this capacity, the JIT short-term MPS program becomes an authority to production—production order. In conventional systems, entries in the MPS come from three sources: sales orders, inventory orders, and forecasts. In JIT, planning is done based on customer demand; thus the MPS depends on company orders on hand. In JIT, the MPS is congruent with the assembly schedule. Furthermore, sales and marketing are involved in preparing daily

```
RE,920,1.MDATABAS  ASKON CAMERA COMPANY -- MANUFACTURING          DISTRIBUTION: MANAGER - ASK COMPUTERS
MON, APR 15, 1991, 12:22 AM                      MASTER PRODUCTION SCHEDULE REPORT                         PAGE NO:   1
                                                 =================================

PART: 1001            REV : F  UOM: EA OPCODE: 4  FLTIME:    2   DEMDTF: 01/22/92  ACCATP: NO  MINQTY:   1.00 QOH:     10293.00
DESC: ASKON 10 CAMERA                  ABC    : C  ULTIME:  .0444 PLANTF: 01/21/92  RESCHD:  3 SAFETY:    .00 SHRINK:       .00
GROUPS:      0 -32767    SC: M  CC:      5 BC/PC : KB DTSTCK:    0   FCFDAT: NOT USED              HORIZ:      3 MULTPL:      1.00
DEMAND CALCULATION OPTION: MAXIMUM OF FORECASTS OR HARD DEMANDS
```

| | PAST DUE | 04/15/91 | 04/22/91 | 04/29/91 | 05/06/91 | 05/13/91 | 05/20/91 | 05/27/91 | 06/03/91 | 06/10/91 | 06/17/91 | 06/24/91 | 07/01/91 |
|---|---|---|---|---|---|---|---|---|---|---|---|---|---|
| FORECAST | 0 | 0 | 0 | 100 | 0 | 100 | 0 | 0 | 100 | 0 | 0 | 0 | 200 |
| PROD FOR | 0 | 0 | 0 | 0 | 0 | 0 | 0 | 0 | 0 | 0 | 0 | 0 | 0 |
| CUST ORD | 0 | 30 | 0 | 0 | 0 | 0 | 0 | 0 | 30 | 5 | 0 | 0 | 0 |
| OTHER | 0 | 0 | 0 | 0 | 0 | 0 | 0 | 0 | 0 | 0 | 0 | 0 | 0 |
| MPS ACTL | 0 | 0 | 0 | 0 | 0 | 0 | 0 | 0 | 0 | 0 | 0 | 0 | 0 |
| PLAN ORD | 0 | 0 | 0 | 0 | 0 | 0 | 0 | 0 | 0 | 0 | 0 | 0 | 0 |
| PROJ AVL | 10293 | 10263 | 10263 | 10263 | 10263 | 10263 | 10263 | 10263 | 10233 | 10228 | 10228 | 10228 | 10228 |
| AVL PROM | 6873 | 0 | 0 | 0 | 0 | 0 | 0 | 0 | 0 | 0 | 0 | 0 | 0 |

| | 07/08/91 | 07/15/91 | 07/22/91 | 07/29/91 | 08/05/91 | 08/12/91 | 08/19/91 | 08/26/91 | 09/02/91 | 09/09/91 | 09/16/91 | 09/23/91 | 09/30/91 |
|---|---|---|---|---|---|---|---|---|---|---|---|---|---|
| FORECAST | 0 | 0 | 0 | 5000 | 200 | 1200 | 0 | 0 | 5000 | 3500 | 0 | 0 | 2500 |
| PROD FOR | 0 | 0 | 0 | 0 | 0 | 0 | 0 | 0 | 0 | 0 | 0 | 0 | 0 |
| CUST ORD | 0 | 0 | 0 | 0 | 0 | 0 | 3475 | 0 | 0 | 5 | 0 | 0 | 20 |
| OTHER | 0 | 0 | 0 | 0 | 0 | 0 | 0 | 0 | 0 | 0 | 0 | 0 | 0 |
| MPS ACTL | 10 | 110 | 0 | 0 | 0 | 0 | 0 | 20 | 0 | 60 | 0 | 0 | 0 |
| PLAN ORD | 0 | 0 | 0 | 0 | 0 | 0 | 0 | 0 | 0 | 0 | 0 | 0 | 0 |
| PROJ AVL | 10238 | 10348 | 10348 | 10348 | 10348 | 10348 | 6873 | 6893 | 6893 | 6948 | 6948 | 6948 | 6928 |
| AVL PROM | 0 | 0 | 0 | 0 | 0 | 0 | 0 | 20 | 0 | 0 | 0 | 0 | 0 |

| | 10/07/91 | 10/14/91 | 10/21/91 | 10/28/91 | 11/04/91 | 11/11/91 | 11/18/91 | 11/25/91 | 12/02/91 | 12/09/91 | 12/16/91 | FUTURE | TOTAL |
|---|---|---|---|---|---|---|---|---|---|---|---|---|---|
| FORECAST | 0 | 1 | 0 | 0 | 5000 | 0 | 0 | 0 | 200 | 0 | 0 | 1000 | 24101 |
| PROD FOR | 0 | 0 | 0 | 0 | 0 | 0 | 0 | 0 | 0 | 0 | 0 | 0 | 0 |
| CUST ORD | 35 | 0 | 95 | 0 | 0 | 0 | 100 | 50 | 0 | 0 | 0 | 265 | 4110 |
| OTHER | 0 | 0 | 0 | 0 | 0 | 0 | 0 | 0 | 0 | 0 | 0 | 0 | 0 |
| MPS ACTL | 0 | 200 | 0 | 0 | 260 | 34 | 0 | 0 | 0 | 172 | 0 | 945 | 1811 |
| PLAN ORD | 0 | 0 | 0 | 0 | 0 | 0 | 0 | 0 | 0 | 0 | 0 | 0 | 0 |
| PROJ AVL | 6893 | 7093 | 6998 | 6998 | 7258 | 7292 | 7192 | 7142 | 7142 | 7314 | 7314 | 7459 | 0 |
| AVL PROM | 0 | 105 | 0 | 0 | 144 | 0 | 0 | 0 | 0 | 172 | 0 | 680 | 0 |

```
>>>>>>>>>>>>>>>>>>>>>>>>> D E M A N D <<<<<<<<<<<<<<<<<<<<<<<<    >>>>>>>>>>>>>>>>>>>>>>>>>>> S U P P L Y <<<<<<<<<<<<<<<<<<<<<<<<<<
ORDER NO.  DEMAND TYP WHERE REQUIRED        QUANTITY  DUE DATE    * ORDER NO.  STA WHERE REQUIRED         QUANTITY  DUE DATE NEED DAT
---------- ---------- ----------------- ---------- --------       - ---------- --- ------------------ ---------- -------- --------
10005      ORDER                                30.00 04/15/91
           FORECAST                            100.00 05/03/91
           FORECAST                            100.00 05/14/91
10001      ORDER                                30.00 06/04/91
           FORECAST                            100.00 06/07/91
10007      ORDER                                 5.00 06/10/91
           FORECAST                            200.00 07/06/91
           FORECAST                           5000.00 08/02/91    C IP-2001    IPO                           10.00 07/09/91 99/99/99
           FORECAST                            200.00 08/09/91    C WO-1112    WIP                           10.00 07/16/91 99/99/99
           FORECAST                           1200.00 08/15/91    C WO-1113    WIP                          100.00 07/21/91 99/99/99
10014      ORDER                              3475.00 08/20/91
           FORECAST                           5000.00 09/02/91    C WO-1007    WIP                           20.00 09/01/91 99/99/99
           FORECAST                           3500.00 09/09/91
10016      ORDER                                 5.00 09/09/91
           FORECAST                           2500.00 10/04/91    C IP-2001    IPO                           10.00 09/10/91 99/99/99
     ADDITIONAL ORDERS ON NEXT PAGES
ORDER RELEASE                              CANCELLATION                                              PART NO: 1001
```

**Figure 10-3**
**The Master Production Schedule Time-Phased Report**

schedules along with production departments, so as to ensure a daily load leveling.

In assemble-to-order applications, the final assembly scheduling is becoming increasingly popular, due to its response to order customization. Although the product is built to the forecast, the final assembly schedule is done after the customer order with its unique product configuration is received. The shift from "firm order" production to final assembly scheduling puts even more emphasis on master production scheduling.

The first stage of production planning is conducted under *planned orders*, while the second phase is known as *firm orders*. Firm orders are planned after the end-product configuration is finalized. In JIT, the MPS extends beyond its traditional function of providing information for budgetary decisions and long-term decisions regarding the acquisition of capacity. The MPS is a tool for short-term planning and the basis for short-term shop ordering. In JIT, an MPS is the production order, the authority to manufacture, the basis for the MRP itemized time-phased schedule. The major differences between the conventional and JIT-based MPS are as follows:

1. Due to a short increment of JIT planning, an MPS is based on firm customer orders and is a final production program tolerating a minimal interference and program changes;
2. MPS weekly increments are further broken down to daily requirements, which makes it a planning document accurate enough for detailed scheduling;
3. The time span between compiling an MPS and starting production is very short, often days, rather than months. This makes it a final preventive production schedule which requires no expediting and is easy to control.

These differences make the JIT-MPS a supreme production planning document.

## MRP—HOW TO ESTIMATE AND TO KEEP TRACK OF CAPACITY

An average-sized make-to-order manufacturer processes about 4,000 to 5,000 customer orders at the same time, and tens of thousands of components in batches. With the latest emphasis on operational scheduling and control, the amount of computation involved is a formidable task, even with the increased computer power. CRP detailed production planning sets a standard for production control, calling for the shop floor operational response to variances and for the further replanning.

A conventional MRP is a system where material requirements are derived from the master production schedule based on forecasted or estimated demand. MRP explodes demand for materials and parts applying lead time–offset scheduling and considering the level of an inventory. The JIT zero-inventory approach combined with shorter lead times makes the MRP task much easier.

MRP breaks down a master production schedule into specific raw materials and component requirements and identifies the quantities required and the dates when to place an internal or external order. In the unstable MPS environment, the capacity usage is dynamic because it arbitrarily changes from one period to another. A main reason for MRP failures occurs when MPS changes are interpreted into MRP updates, producing a rippling effect on the material flow. MRP requires a reliable and verified MPS—demand which corresponds to the accurate data on the available capacity. This stresses the significance of JIT-based capacity requirements planning, since work orders must be accurately balanced as a basis for the JIT-type material flow control.

### How to Write Off Jobs

Accurate capacity data depend on write-off methods applied, the frequency of computer runs, and the time elapsed between when the job is originated and the completion report is entered into the computer. Typical frequencies of the MRP computer data runs are weekend runs, twice a week runs, or even regular overnight runs. If the time between committing and recording a transaction is too long (for example, the computer data update takes place once per week), the computer output becomes unreliable.

More detailed planning requires a greater accuracy of data, which basically comes from more frequent computer records updating. The accuracy of the capacity data also depends on the frequency of completed jobs write-offs. For example, if a job takes 28 hours to complete, do you write this job off after its completion or write off a daily percentage of the job completed? For MRP, daily write-off will be sufficient, but for the operational scheduling this is not always good enough.

Some companies find that there is a need for a feedback, due to numerous deviations from the schedule. In such situations, write-offs are labor consuming and awkward to maintain. The on-line reporting discussed in Chapter 7 is the way to arrange write off jobs.

## THE ROLE OF MRP IN JIT-BASED MANUFACTURING SYSTEM

In one auto components manufacturing company, a confidence in the MRP system was undermined to such an extent that in order to ensure the accuracy of the plan, they ran two systems in parallel: a computer-based system and a manual system. Certainly, the computer system was largely to satisfy management and the primary system was still manual. This has happened at the initial stages of the MRP installation, not entirely due to the floats in MRP, but mainly due to the inability to overcome the resistance to change. A further investigation has indicated an insufficient staff training as the main reason for resistance to change. There is a limit for MRP detailed planning—a diminishing rate of return after reaching a certain degree of detailed scheduling.

The opinion is that in a JIT system, MRP can best perform global control of a factory, leaving detailed control over operations to JIT-type flexible material flow control.

MRP is a planning tool, while JIT is an execution tool. The MRP rationale is to make components available when they are needed, while in JIT, it is to produce components when they are needed. Few people address the issue of JIT from the operations management standpoint. This view is also shared by the Japanese experts indicating that American and European managers experimenting with JIT are flawed by a substantial system misunderstanding.

American companies rely on management and planning assuming that since a strategic decision was made, the execution will follow. In Japan, all decisions are made close to the execution line, by people who know in every detail how their decision will be implemented.

In JIT, components' throughput time is reduced to less than one day. Consequently, MRP is becoming significantly simpler. Requirements to the MPS become more stringent and detailed, due to the reduction in buffers, such as waiting lines and idle time and setup time. The buffers are designed so that they store only hours worth of parts. Conventional MRP is run on a weekly computer-run basis, while JIT requires daily or even hourly runs. In an accomplished JIT environment, production planning is conducted at the assembly level, while in MRP it is done at the component level. Table 10-1 compares the MRP and JIT time span—a conventional MRP deals with weekly runs while JIT controls daily runs.

**Table 10-1**
**Comparing MRP and JIT Planning and Control**

| | System Elements Controlled | Time Span |
|---|---|---|
| **MRP:** | Many items/components | Weekly runs |
| **JIT:** | Assembly units | Daily runs |

Often, there is a dual environment where production is planned and controlled partly by an MRP push system and partly by a JIT pull system (push and pull manufacturing approaches are discussed later in this chapter). The JIT reduction in lead time and in lot sizes combined with the uniform plant loading simplifies its interaction with MPS and MRP, since the plans sliced into short duration time phases are routinely verifiable on completion. For example, 50 items are produced over 10 days at a rate of 5 items per day. Such a plan is easy to control on a daily basis. Suppose you produced 5 items today; how much have you done since the start of this order? In contrast, with structural-type planning and control, in a functionally organized plant, you are able to verify such an order only at its completion. The reduction in setup time shortens lead time from weeks to days and makes it possible to produce in small lots based on the real (sometimes daily) consumption. Traditional MRP is designed for long-lead-time order-based production systems. Traditional MRP schedules the material requirements, while CRP identifies the capacity needs.

MRP is not intended to do detailed scheduling in a traditional environment or in an integrated MRP-JIT system. MRP and CRP produce a plan at the component level and ensure that sufficient capacity is available across the entire production area and purchased materials are ordered on time, so that the production cycle corresponds to the delivery cycle. MRP II–JIT operating plans relate to the financial function, marketing and forecasting, and accounting, and these operational plans are better translated into the product value. The JIT role is to ensure control over the shop floor execution. This task is easier due to the shorter lead time, but mainly because of the simplified product-focused material flow pattern—the components are produced in one place.

Changing plant layout reduces material handling and production control. The JIT production rate is adjusted through the variable cell manning. If the purchase lead time is short, then the supplier also can be incorporated into the JIT material flow system.

## RECOGNIZING THE PUSH AND PULL PATTERN OF MATERIAL FLOW

A producer-customer relationship in the material flow can be of two types—according to the "initiator" or the "respondent" in this relationship. The relationship, where a producer is the leader and a customer is the follower, is known as a *push pattern* of material flow because the relationship is cast by the producer's decision. The producer makes components and "pushes" them over to the customer, even if there is no immediate demand for them or a capacity is not available. In both instances, components build up a WIP inventory. Most of the conventional manufacturing systems discussed in Chapters 4 to 7 apply a push pattern of material flow.

A *pull pattern* of material flow takes place when a customer is the initiator of the relationship. A producer makes components on customer request, when they are needed. It means that there is immediate demand for components and they proceed into an operation as soon as they are completed. The pull pattern of a material flow is also known as *zero inventory* because an intercustomer-producer inventory is eliminated.

Establishing a pull system requires efficient production planning and control because customer requirements must be satisfied on demand and there is no buffer stock. In a pull system, production activities are initiated by customer demand. In JIT, a zero inventory should be enforced in both customer production and supplier-vendor production. Otherwise, the inventory burden is simply shifted from manufacturer to its suppliers and vendors. Such manufacturer-vendor relations often contradict the JIT philosophy and its spirit of goodwill.

The pull system is superior to the push system because customer demand is satisfied in the pull system, while producer considerations prevail in the push system. Furthermore, the pull system is a zero-stock system. Traditional MRP is considered a push system. There are the following possibilities:

1. A job is delayed at the "producer's" work center, resulting in a buildup of a WIP inventory.
2. A "customer" is not ready when the job is moved in, resulting in a buildup of WIP inventory.
3. A customer cancels the order while it is in process, resulting in a buildup of a WIP inventory, which often can become obsolete, due to product changes; also there is a chance of pilferage.

In JIT, a customer is doing the ordering. Customers, both internal and external, are ready and waiting for their orders. This results in elimination of queueing, waiting time, and idle time.

An obvious way for the inventory reduction is through improving planning, operational scheduling, reducing queueing lines, and avoiding the practice of producing that little extra in case something goes wrong. The way to reduce an inventory is by balancing the work flow and improving processes. Close attention is to be paid to the production process, everything from the market research, marketing, product design, production, through the product's delivery to the customer.

JIT means uniformity and standardization—improving processes, so that they invariably run according to the standards. Often, however, JIT is confused with the drive for a zero inventory. A complete elimination of waste is the condition for achieving a zero inventory. The JIT philosophy is to expose problems and work toward their elimination. The approach is to lower the "water" (inventory) level until the underwater rocks are visible and continue removing the impediments until the water flow is unobstructed. It is not necessary to remove all the rocks, but only those rocks that obstruct the flow. It is possible to redirect the flow to avoid the rocks and leave them if they are too difficult to move. Processes creating problems for one product can perform well on other products' jobs.

The rules are as follows:

- Make problems visible.
- Simplify everything.
- Achieve flexibility.
- Select problems for elimination.
- Eliminate these problems permanently.

In some companies, good housekeeping coupled with inventory control envisages storing WIP inventory in work areas especially at assembly line work stations. Production on demand reduces overcrowding of a workplace by making visible WIP inventory problems.

## Push and Pull Systems in Functional Planning and Control in a Process Industry and a Job Shop Environment

In both push and pull systems, only one active party is involved: in a push system, it is a producer producing items and pushing them to the consumer: in a pull system, it is a consumer who demands the item from the producer who is otherwise unattentive at the time.

Suppliers complying with JIT delivery requirements find themselves in a delicate position of an inventory holder for manufacturers. In such relationships, suppliers and vendors are confronted with increased production costs. The rule in JIT is: do not produce, do not buy, do not move, do not start anything, unless there is a customer who requires these items!

Not all pull systems are efficient. For example, there is demand for components, but the previous workstation is not available yet. Such a situation can be called a *late pull system* because the customer is delayed. A push pattern produces WIP, but a late pull pattern results in an idle "customer" capacity. Figure 10-4 graphically illustrates the push and pull material flow.

But what about assembly line? Is an assembly line a pull system or a push system? It is a push system because components are pushed to a customer, and it is a pull system because the customer requires these components. This situation can be expressed by the following model:

pull system = push system

This system is on the boundary where push and pull systems meet.

In this situation, there is a consent: the producer and the consumer meet at the boundary where the producer is ready to drop its produce which the consumer needs right away. Such a condition can be termed a *concur flow system* (CFS), where times of completing one operation and starting the next one (producers and consumers) are in full accord and agreement: the producer pushes when the consumer pulls.

In manufacturing, "producer-consumer relationships" start at the purchasing and raw material stage. Such relationships are triggered by the ultimate consumer pulling the needed product from the final assembly at the required rate. The assumption is that each process has a sufficient inventory to start up, basically, a standard container placed in the location where parts are made. This is probably why many regard JIT as the system which can function in repetitive production.

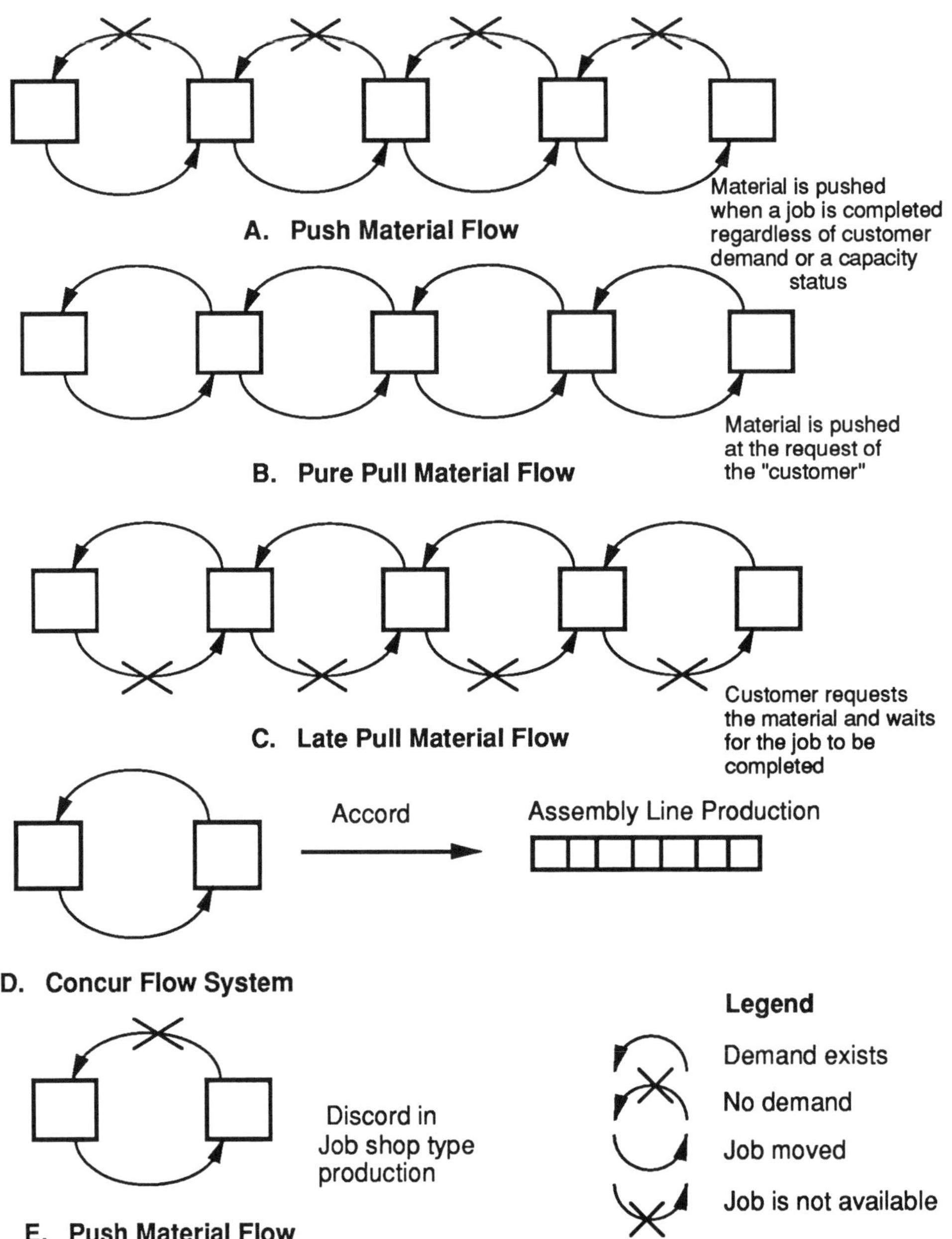
Material is pushed when a job is completed regardless of customer demand or a capacity status
A. Push Material Flow
Material is pushed at the request of the "customer"
B. Pure Pull Material Flow
Customer requests the material and waits for the job to be completed
C. Late Pull Material Flow
Accord
Assembly Line Production
D. Concur Flow System
Legend
Demand exists
No demand
Job moved
Job is not available
Discord in Job shop type production
E. Push Material Flow

**Figure 10-4**
**Push and Pull Material Flow Systems**

JIT is not a completely zero inventory: to start up, an inventory is required; otherwise, JIT is a late pull system. In a late pull system, workstations are waiting for upstream processes to supply them with components.

What about a job shop? Is JIT applicable to job shop production? A job shop is controlled by conventional means of a push system because there is no start-up inventory. This condition, combined with an intermittent material flow, makes a job shop a classic case of a push system.

A job shop can use JIT techniques as well in the situation where a push system equals to a pull system. If one is able to plan a material flow according to a concur flow system, it produces the best JIT results in the job shop environment. In a job shop, as in any other work environment, a pull system can work only if there is short response time (elapsed time between planning and execution).

Integrated task management (ITM) applies concur flow system techniques with JIT benefits of reduced inventory, reduced need for production control and rescheduling. Operations group group (OGG)-type work orders are designed for a concur flow system.

The second alternative in a job shop is to apply CFS with the elements of a late pull material flow system. CFS stresses centralized operational scheduling and optimization as the means for streamlining a material flow. In contrast, a late pull system is applicable to product-focused JIT-type systems with rough centralized planning. A final operational planning and control takes place on the shop floor. Such JIT systems make use of flexible manufacturing techniques.

## USING THE *KANBAN* PRODUCTION CONTROL SYSTEM TO CONTROL MATERIAL FLOW

The *kanban* is a JIT logistics system controlling a material flow by applying pull ordering techniques. A *kanban* is a card containing information about the part number, description, quantity per container, number of containers, and stock location, as well as information about previous and following processes, the total number of *kanban* cards per lot, material, and assembly unit.

The *kanban* is an information system applying a pull-type reorder system in which the authorization to produce or supply, serving as a work order, and a move order, comes from downstream operations. *Kanban* cards program the job priority. Workers just follow these simple withdrawing and ordering procedures. A *kanban*-type pull material flow links subassembly manufacture to a final assembly area, thus eliminating the need for a subassembly storage place. A JIT-*kanban* is the actual ordering by a "production line customer."

There exists a certain time period from the point when a finite CRP is compiled until the components are in process. This is the elapsed time period. Long elapsed time results in the situations where the jobs reach workstations when the capacity situation has changed. For a *kanban* to work, fine operations scheduling is still required after the capacity requirements planning. JIT-*kanban* ordering is more accurate than the conventional-type shop loading because the total lead time is short and there is less time for any changes and deviations.

## The *Kanban* Two-Card System

There are two types of *kanban*:

1. *Move kanban,* also known as the *receiving kanban*
2. *Production kanban* or *make kanban*

The two *kanbans* correspond to two areas of responsibility in a material flow, namely, production and material handling.

A move *kanban* contains the following information: part description, number of parts in a container, number of containers in use, previous work center, and next work center. One move card and one production card are issued for each container. Usually, a *kanban* system uses uniform dedicated movable containers which eliminate the need for material handling services, since the workers move the containers to and from the stockpoint. Containers are standard, containing the same quantity of parts. Figure 10-5 shows how a JIT-*kanban* system operates.

Containers with the designated quantity of components and with the attached production card are stationed in designated locations. These components are pulled to assembly processes when there is demand for them.

A *production card* is detached from the container at the time of withdrawal and is left behind as the authorization to the supplying workstation for production of another standard container. When withdrawing, a production card is replaced with a move card. A *move card* is attached to a full container at the time of its withdrawal from the storage place, as an authorization for the withdrawal.

In a repetitive production, the quantity in a container is approximately equal to the one-hour production needs. Sometimes, several containers are required to be available in place, for which several production and withdrawal *kanbans* are issued. This number depends on an order response time. JIT companies try to remove *kanbans* from the circulation one by one, in order to find the optimum number of *kanbans*, until the number of *kanbans* is equal to one.

A *kanban* is a planning tool: the number of *kanban* cards sets the rate of production. At present, *kanban* can work with balanced operations within the environment of a leveled production load. A *single-card pull system* uses only a move card permanently attached to containers. Returned empty containers are the signal to replenish them.

A *kanban* pull system is similar to the two-bin reorder point inventory system, and in itself, does not represent any new kind of a production planning and control and inventory control approach. For successful functioning, a pull

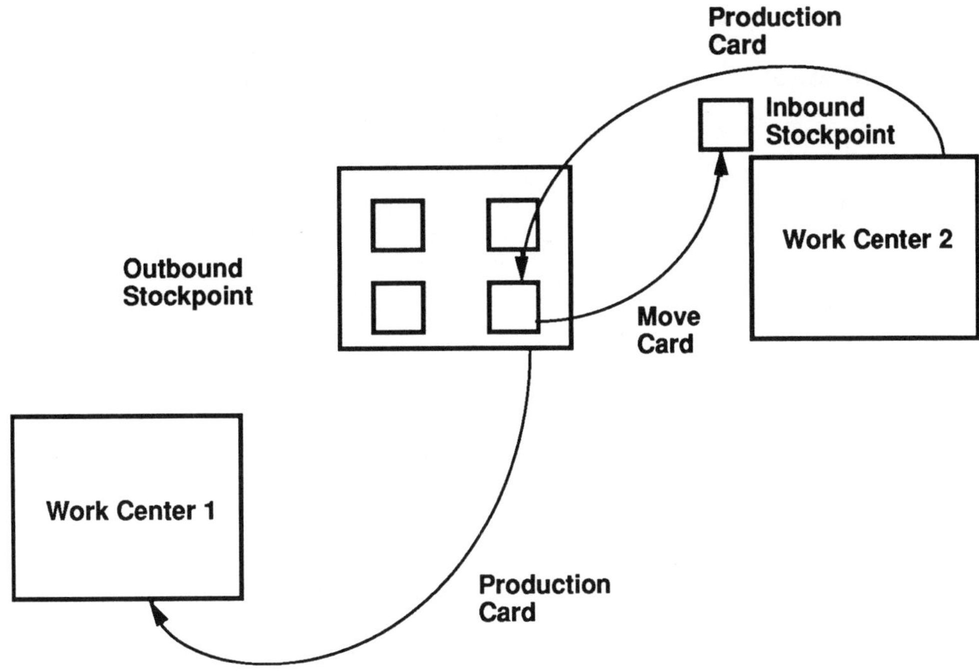


**Figure 10-5**
**JIT Kanban System in Operation**

system requires some specific conditions; that is, there should be a standardized flow of materials and an established interrelationship between the producer and the consumer—the producer knows where parts will go, and the consumer knows where to get them. In this respect, a *kanban* is the outbound queue control.

Many experts are of the opinion that a *kanban* system can work only in the repetitive type production having an established material flow. In reality there is a start-up minimal inventory required (at least one container), and a pull system requires balancing and synchronization of operations.

A *kanban* features the team mentality producing a positive reinforcement. In this respect, *kanban* helps to develop teamwork. *Kanban*-run execution is the last stage of a JIT process and is the punctuation of well-done production planning and control procedures and the JIT organization in general.

## MANAGING WORK FLOW IN PRODUCTION LINE

Two concepts are involved in a material flow: a *batch quantity* is a quantity of components produced at one setup, and a *transfer quantity* is a quantity of components produced at a workstation before they are moved to the next workstation.

In JIT, a batch can comprise hundreds of parts, but if all the jobs/operations are balanced, the work flow can be organized in a one-at-a-time flow line: as soon as one piece is completed, it is moved to the next operation; for example, finished components are moved to assembly processes in quantities of one as soon as they are completed. Correspondingly, subassemblies are moved to assembly and final assembly processes in single quantities, regardless of the total batch quantity. Figure 10-6 illustrates batch production and a JIT one-at-a-time flow production line. In conventional batch production lines, operations on batches are performed sequentially, while in the present JIT systems, these operations are overlapped. Such a JIT work flow arrangement reduces inventory in a pipeline.

There is an opinion that the assembly line, which is an example of one-at-a-time plan production line, is the most efficient way of production, and that concept should be applied not only to assembly processes but also to components manufacturing. Certainly, high productivity of conveyors and production lines is the result of a product-focused plant layout featuring specialized equipment and processes. The drawback is that capital expenditures are justified only by large-order-quantities production.

A JIT material flow resembles that of assembly-line production. The difference is that an assembly line, as we know it, is a production unit designed to produce specific products at the predetermined rate, while in JIT, a production line is a *flexible unit capable of constantly changing production rates and product types* so as to produce to immediate demand with a zero inventory.

Assembly lines and production lines can become obsolete when the product is discontinued. With decreasing order quantities and shorter product cycle times, such product-focused production lines are not feasible in many manufacturing companies. A JIT-focused factory is a flexible manufacturing system, which as its name suggests, brings flexibility into a production system. JIT flexibility allows to adjust the same facility to product-focused production of a variety of products. Focused factories and flexible manufacturing systems are further discussed in Chapter 11.

## JIT PRODUCTION PLANNING—USING UNIFORM PLANT LOADING TO ELIMINATE DISRUPTIONS

In JIT, planning level is the same as the accomplished result, due to the self-management on the shop floor. In a JIT production system, execution is

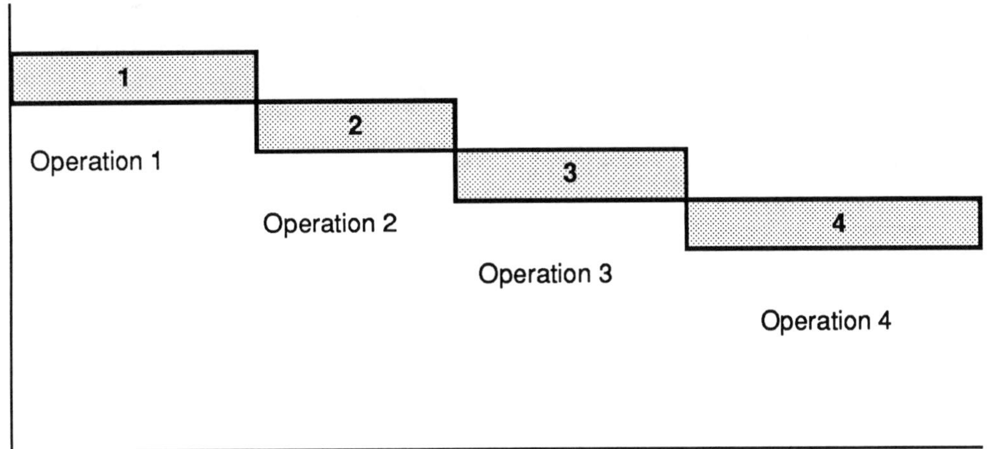


**A. Batch Production**

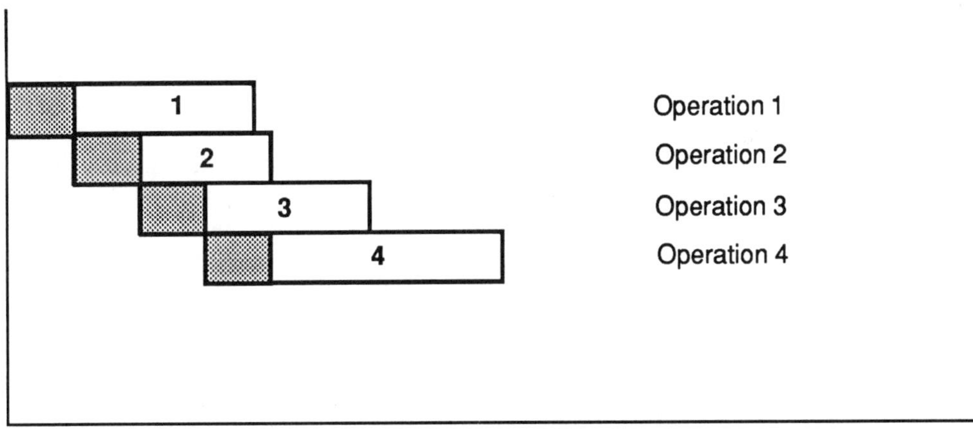


**B. JIT One-at-a-time Flow Production Line**

**Figure 10-6**
**Material Flow in Batch Production and Just-in-Time**

closer to planning, as waiting time is shorter and batches are smaller. Shorter waiting time between planning and execution improves communication and co-operation of employees, improves planning skills and morale, and brings people together. Figure 10-7 compares a traditional and a JIT production system.

JIT structures its production facilities and material flow in such a way that it is possible to balance them at the MPS-MRP level, prior to the execution, and then apply execution control at the shop floor, without keeping the records of deviations and without applying re-scheduling. One JIT tool contributing to this is the uniform plant loading.

### Uniform Plant Loading

The uniform plant loading means planning production in a manner which ensures a smooth uninterrupted material flow and an elimination of last-minute changes in the master production schedule.

Uniform plant loading prevents these disruptive shock waves by applying a firm production plan zone. Uniform plant loading features an established product mix of a large variety of products and daily production schedules in small lots. An overriding consideration in uniform plant loading is to correlate the production cycle with the ordering cycle. A *production cycle* is the time elapsed between any two units coming off the production line. A *production order cycle* is the time between the completion of any two successive production work orders. A customer *order cycle* is the time elapsed between the placing of two successive work orders with work centers. Production cycles and ordering cycles are illustrated in Figure 10-8. Often, a production order cycle corresponds to the customer order cycle, but this is not always the case, because in JIT customer orders can be split into several production orders.

For example, there is an order for 200 items, and 8 items will be scheduled for production daily. This daily lot is further intermixed on the assembly line with a variety of products. A uniform plant load depends on the demand rate. A traditional MRP is a time-phased system based on a *customer order*. JIT is a time-phased system based on a *customer time-phased demand.* The advantage in JIT is a WIP inventory and customer's inventory reduction, a greater flexibility in scheduling and in making changes.

If there is a change in one customer order, it will not produce violent waves because this order is executed in small lots. In JIT, cycle time is an important factor dealing with the rate of production, which is equal to the requirements rate. The concern is not to achieve a rated speed of an equipment but to structure the resources so as to correspond to the production program.

In a traditional manufacturing system, the reduction of inventory is focused at reducing a WIP interoperational inventory. JIT also attempts to reduce an inventory at manufacturing stages, namely, a purchasing, production, and customer inventory—an interfunctional inventory. This is achieved by planning the cycle time and ordering frequency to correspond to the production rate and customer

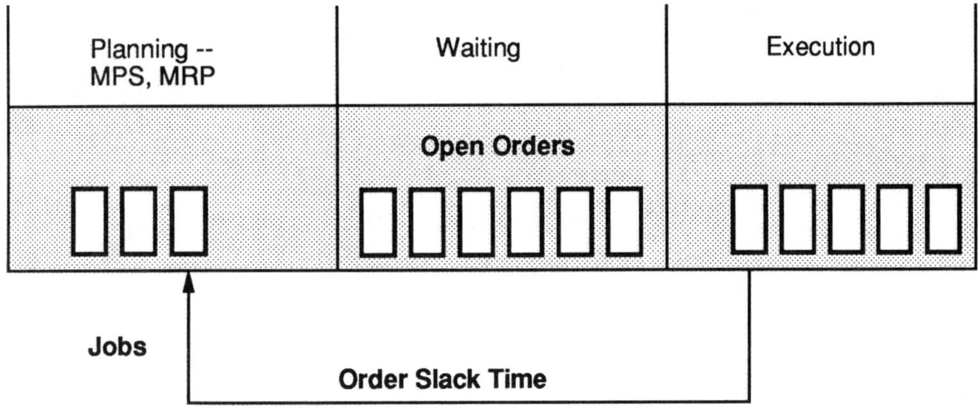


**A. Traditional Production System**

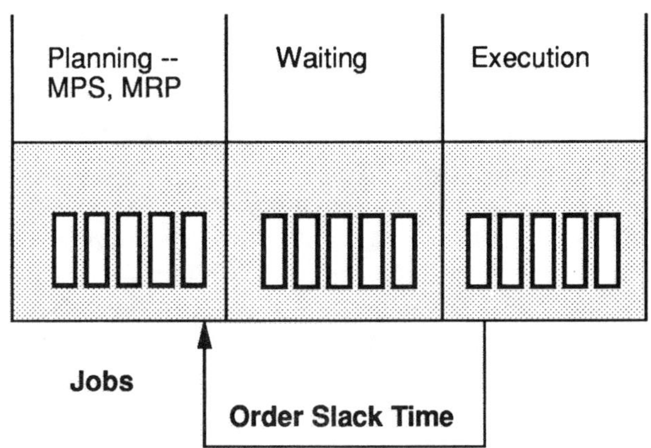


**B. JIT Production System**

Order Slack Time (OST) is time elapsed since planning was completed and the first units are ready for the customer

**Figure 10-7**
**Production Order Lead Time**

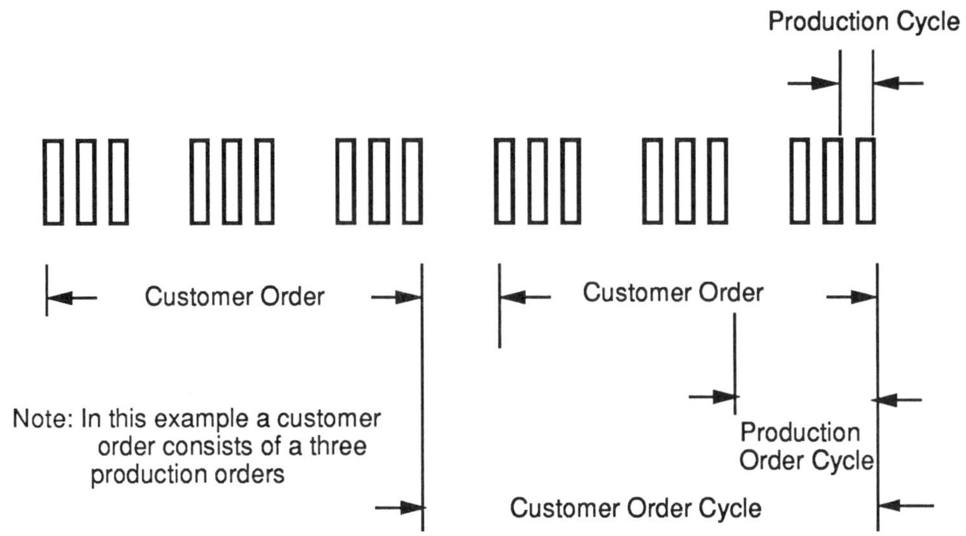


**Figure 10-8**
**Production Order Cycle and Customer Order Cycle**

consumption rate. This is the reason why in JIT systems both the interfunctional and interoperational inventories are reduced.

A major bonus in reducing lead time and inventory is not the reduction of investments, but the improvement in the material flow and in production planning and control, and an improvement in quality. Furthermore, just as time phasing introduced by MRP reduces a production inventory, JIT time phasing can reduce a customer's inventory and eliminate WIP inventory.

## HOW TO ESTIMATE PRODUCTION RATE AND ORDER QUANTITY

In repetitive production, a production rate is estimated per month based on a forecast for six or three months. One way or another, such a practice leads to the accumulation of inventories when orders on hand do not match the optimum product mix and the production rate.

In JIT, a production rate is estimated per day; thus it more accurately corresponds to the demand rate. What happens if demand is lower than estimated, or a customer decides to make changes in the order? It is easier to make changes to the production plan when one produces and dispatches daily 5 units rather than producing 100 units at once. As soon as these 100 units are completed or even started, no further changes to the plan are possible without production losses.

In conventional hierarchical production planning and control systems, production losses due to changes in the production plan occur even if production has not yet begun. This is due to changes to the production program, imposing restrictions to the product mix.

The advantage of JIT planning is in the possibility to adjust the machine rate to the requirements rate: daily production equals to daily demand. JIT planning begins with identifying customer demand. Customer requirements are estimated per daily time periods, and correspondingly, MPS and MRP are compiled in daily intervals.

In JIT, the level loading deals with the frequency of production. JIT planning is controlled by the final assembly schedule. JIT daily plans are flexible and can be changed easily when required. The intention is to reduce the inventory to a minimum by planning a daily output as close as possible to daily sales. For example, at Toyota, a daily plan is given to assembly lines, and from there it is fed to upstream operations. This situation is illustrated graphically in Figure 10-9.

Products at a conventional assembly line are assembled in batches: a batch of product X is completed before the batch of product Y has been started. Each product has different processes and requires a different capacity structure. Changes to the assembly processes are made each time new products are moving to the assembly process.

A JIT flexible system applies a mixed-model assembly instead of a batch assembly. This means that a number of product types and options are assembled at the same time rather than assembling only one product. An improvement in customer service is apparent because, first, production produces according to the daily customer consumption, relieving the customer from keeping a monthly or quarterly inventory requirement; second, lead time is reduced; third, quality is improved with production in small batches; and fourth, several customers (demand) can be satisfied at the same time.

An additional bonus is that there are great opportunities in selecting the best product mix. JIT production cycle time is estimated based on daily requirements for all products in the production program.

*Example:*

| Product | Monthly Plan |
|---|---|
| X | 2,400 |
| Y | 1,200 |
| Z | 3,600 |

The volume ratio of these three products is 2:1:3. The total production time is 200 labor-hours. The requirements per hour are as follows:

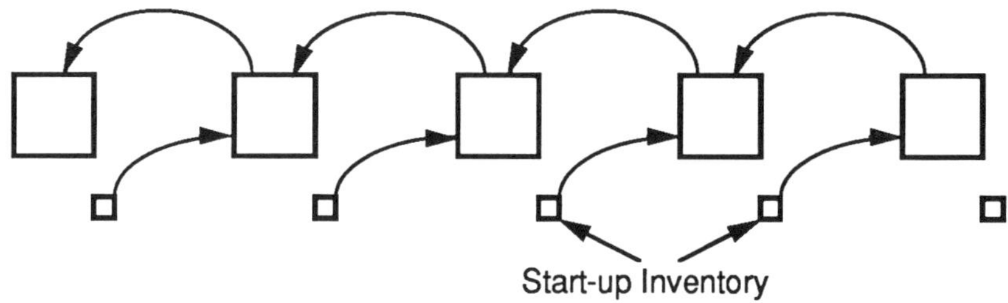


**A. Repetitive JIT Production at Toyota Plant**

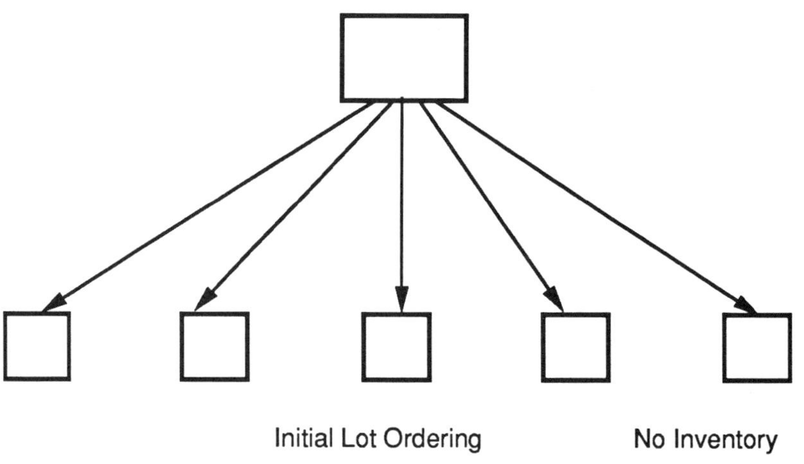


**B. JIT Job Shop Production**

**Figure 10-9**
**The Difference Between Kanban in Repetitive and Job Shop Production**

| Product | Hourly Production Rate |
|---|---|
| X | 12 |
| Y | 6 |
| Z | 18 |

Considering the volume ratio and the hourly production rate, an assembly pattern is selected: XYZZXZ × 6 times per hour or 10 minutes. One can regard 10 minutes as the cycle time and the "product" XYZZXZ is leaving the assembly line every 10 minutes (production cycle time). The "product" XYZZXZ will be changed every time the production plan is changing, which gives a remarkable flexibility to respond to customer demand and to effect any unexpected changes without the disruption to the production program.

The example shows how a monthly production program is planned. In JIT, attempts are made to keep the monthly plan fixed. In this instance, the "product" is produced for the duration of the entire month.

Not every company has a convenience of producing the same product for the duration of an entire month. Usually, "products" are changed weekly or even daily, and especially the options of individual products can be changed every second or third assembly-line cycle. Mixed models are applied mainly on final assembly lines.

It is understood that process and labor flexibility is essential in JIT line production, so that the labor cost per unit remains constant despite the changes in production rates. This is achieved mainly by moving the labor force in and out of the production line. One can also understand that changes on one production line should be coordinated with the changes in other production units of a company to keep the production cost fixed throughout the organization. This requires centralized planning and balancing applying MPS, MRP, and CRP and to a greater extent than in conventional production systems.

Because the feedback and rescheduling in JIT are not enforced as in conventional manufacturing systems, the submitted production plan is balanced (detailed product and process balancing) so that the rate of the labor cost for all products is constant. A flexible multiskilled work force is the result of cross-training provided by an employer and due to simplified work force grading that, in some instances, over a dozen grades are reduced to only one or two.

## DEVELOPING HOLISTIC MANUFACTURING SYSTEMS

A JIT approach is to simplify planning and simplify and reduce the need for detailed shop floor control. Conventionally, there is production of components (an intermittent job shop material flow, supplying an assembly line) organized as line production.

The idea of JIT is to organize an entire manufacturing process into a continuous production-line type of material flow. As one can understand, this requires balancing not only operations, but to a certain degree, components' lead times too. JIT production can be compared with a marathon where runners from various places arrive at the same time at the final destination, although they have covered different distances and have run at different speeds.

Likewise, the ordering of components by an assembly process requires a synchronous arrival to the start of assembly. JIT has a number of powerful tools to ensure balancing of components' lead times. These are techniques of uniform plant loading, planning cycle time and order frequency, and flexible manufacturing systems, capable of differentiating production rates without changing the capacity.

In Japanese JIT systems, a worker is not given a job unless there is a *kanban* (demand for this job). Also, there is a mechanism of flexibility in a system, allowing workers to contribute to the product value by producing on demand and utilizing their time to the best of their ability. Idle time is used to practice die exchange, making improvement tools and setup time devices, or cross-training coworkers. So, JIT flexibility stems from a multiskilled workforce being able to adjust to varying production rates. Variances in production rates are buffered when value adding production services and tasks are performed during production downtime.

## REDUCING LEAD TIME BY USING JIT SYSTEMS

Traditionally, long lead times and some restrictions imposed on ordering in minimal batch quantity compel customers to order in lots sufficient to satisfy a month or a quarter of demand. This leads to customers keeping an inventory to buffer extended lead time. A 95 percent reduction in lead time makes it possible to organize production in a daily requirements lot.

It is common that lead time is many times longer than the compounded machining time. Depending on the type of planning and control methods and order processing procedures used in an organization, a product requiring five or six hours of machining time can have lead time ranging from several weeks to several months. In some companies, it takes several months of waiting time before an order is even scheduled for production. Due to the uncontrolled waiting time and interoperational idle time, some products have 18 months and more of lead time. Such long lead times alienate customers and make the product more expensive.

An erosion of customer support due to the inadequate delivery time is partially to blame for the decline in support for the American tool industry. Quite often, American manufacturing companies lose their customers due to their inability to organize an efficient order processing and production planning and control system. Concerns over cost and quality arise as a consequence of such inefficiency. Unfortunately, it is the shop floor personnel who are often blamed for the turbulent material flow, long lead time, and late deliveries.

### Lead Time Reduction

Where does the production lead time reduction come from in JIT?

1. Uniform plant loading applying order splitting
2. Setup time reduction
3. *Kanban*-controlled material flow
4. Reduction in the operations waiting time and idle time and a general reduction of the elapsed time

The reduction or elimination of nonvalue-adding tasks assists in reducing an inventory. Reducing lead time helps to identify problem areas, to produce better, more accurate plans, and to improve control over the material flow.

### Variances in Lead Time

Variances in lead time are contrary to the JIT main principle of accomplishing everything in time for the next task. In JIT, the reduction of lead time goes along with making lead time accurate.

An analysis of lead time in a traditional production system shows that interoperational delays are the main cause for the inaccuracy of lead time. JIT is reducing the interoperational wait time and idle time, making lead time shorter and more predictable. Interoperational delays (idle time) are eliminated in JIT pull systems because there is an immediate downstream customer for each completed unit.

The reduction of an information flow in a JIT system due to execution control already eliminates a common area where the waiting time and idle time originate. The holistic nature of a JIT system is substantiated by a total onslaught on unproductive operations and tasks. This includes the reduction in dedicated production and service operations. This results in a dramatic reduction of operation lead time and production order lead time.

## USING JIT IN THE JOB SHOP

The two main features of a job shop are small quantities and nonrepetitive products. Considering existing marketing conditions, many manufacturing companies are effectively becoming job-shop-type production because they build products in small quantities and with a high variety of options.

Moreover, in most companies, only assembly processes are arranged as flow lines, while manufacturing of components is done with job-shop-type operations applying a functional layout and a group technology (GT). Some companies regard themselves as a job shop because they manufacture to order, even if they operate as a continuous production line. The ordering here is nonstandard with a significant content of a store-based inventory. Such production processes can fit into a JIT-type system.

JIT means flexibility; thus it should be able to deal with frequent, although planned-in-advance, product changes. Specialized make-to-order companies are also classified as job shops. There is no such a job shop company which produces such a wide range of products as, for example, home appliances and machine tool equipment.

Capacity constraints impose a limitation on the product selection. The capacity of a company producing commercial refrigerating equipment to customer specifications is not sufficient to produce automobile engines, despite the fact that it, according to its operations, is regarded as a job-shop-type production.

A job shop is engaged in building corresponding groups of products consisting of components that can be grouped further into families of components. Most job shops have much more repetitive business than they realize. By not taking advantage of this fact, they are losing the chance of improving their operations.

The main purpose of JIT is a means of solving the problems that prevent a company from achieving organizational objectives of higher efficiency and competitiveness. But which company does not have production problems?

Excluding a job shop from JIT restricts JIT applications to a few high-resource companies, featuring line production. Furthermore, control of a material flow, although essential, is not the only advantage of JIT. JIT flexibility assists in managing production of a wide variety of products in a job shop environment. Thus, we need JIT in any type organization: large or small, chemical processes, manufacturing, repetitive and nonrepetitive, and a job shop.

Moreover, excluding job shop applications from JIT restricts severely its usage. The opinion that JIT is applicable to repetitive-type production applying pure pull, near-zero inventory material flow control, is the result of viewing JIT as merely a *kanban* system controlling a material flow.

## SUMMARY

Richard Walleigh of Hewlett-Packard says: "Most production operations involve low volumes. The principles of JIT are just as applicable here as in high-volume operations. The emphasis on reducing setup times, building products in smaller batches, and making things only on demand will improve a small volume operation as much as a large one." (Richard Walleigh, "Getting Things Done:

What's Your Excuse For Not Using JIT:", *Harvard Business Review,* March-April 1986, pp. 38-54).

In fact, a small-volume operation may find it easier to convert to JIT because it may already be making products in small batches using simple equipment with short setup times. There are reports of small companies being more successful in implementing JIT, due to less red tape and due to already being more efficient and having less overheads.

JIT effectively deals with the first feature of a job shop, namely, production in small quantities. Organizing production in GT and especially in operational clusters and reducing setup times will make JIT an effective management program for all our industrial and business organizations, whether small, medium, or large ones. The flexibility of JIT planning and the material flow helps in handling the second condition of a job shop, namely, building certain products with a high variety of options.

# 11

# Implementing JIT Systems: Level 3—Making Capital Improvements

The term *focused factory* was coined by Wickham Skinner in 1974 in an article "The Focused Factory," *Harvard Business Review*, 52, 3, May-June 1974, pp. 113-121. The idea of a focused factory is to avoid multiproduct plants which try to do "everything." It is a fact that specialized plants are more productive than general ones; similarly, specialized machines are more productive than general-purpose equipment.

A focused factory is smaller and more specialized than a large manufacturing factory that produces everything. A focused factory is more economical than is a universal facility. The term "focused factory" suggests that in such a factory, everything, from production processes through the organizational structure, is tailored for production of a specific product or product line. This entails much less bureaucracy and avoids large overheads. Focused factories occupy less space and require a significantly lower level of investment than do multiproduct plants.

Production is seen as one "factory machine" in which each production unit and each piece of an equipment on the factory floor has a specific task to fulfil. Managing such a factory machine means coordinating and harmonizing actions of its individual production units as well as performance of many workstations—the labor-machine productive units.

Henry Fayol's teachings fit the description of a focused factory, where the waste of services and human resources is restricted because the activities follow a predetermined pattern. He suggested a system to determine the sequencing and timing of events so that they properly mesh and allocating the rightful proportions of resources, time, and priority to the things and actions. He indicated that each department must work in harmony with the others in a well-coordinated enterprise. The working schedules of various departments and their subdivisions should be constantly attuned to the circumstances.

Fayol stressed that all the forces in play must be kept in equilibrium and that management should not allow a department to take a narrowly conceived action that might create a sudden disturbance, thus threatening the running of the whole. Managers are designers, operators, and adjusters in a focused factory rather than just passive observers of its operations.

The designing function envisages design of a focused factory as an "automated machine" as compared with the mechanized one of a traditional factory. An "automated machine" features programmed decision making of production planning and production services—preventive executional control, distinct from a traditional factory featuring interfunctional production control, feedback, and replanning.

The operating function involves managers in the execution. They should not merely prepare production plans; they should share the responsibility for production line operations with the labor force.

The adjusting function puts managers at the firing line, requiring less communications and information flow, while adjustments of variances are done routinely as they occur. Do not confuse the adjusting function with the expediting activities which are contrary to the orderly preventive planning and executional control.

## THE PURPOSE OF FLEXIBLE MANUFACTURING SYSTEMS

*Flexible manufacturing systems* (FMS) refer to manufacturing strategies rather than to automation. Flexibility is the quintessence of JIT. Flexibility achieves economical production in small batches. This basically means flexibility in the planning and execution stages of production. An FMS is expected to ensure such flexibility in a manufacturing system. There are two basic types of FMS:

1. A traditional equipment that is structured into labor-served manufacturing cells. Such plant layout provides flexibility in planning because there is the possibility to produce at various production rates.
2. An automated flexible manufacturing system, such as an automated FMS using a specialized automated equipment, computerized process control, and robotics.

Usually, automated manufacturing systems are regarded as FMS, while labor-served flexible manufacturing systems are classified as *manual cells*.

## WHAT IS GROUP TECHNOLOGY?

*Group technology* (GT) was introduced and practiced in the United States after World War II as a type of a plant layout. The original idea was to avoid an intermittent material flow with its inefficiency in operations planning and control and losses in operational queueing time, waiting time, and idle time. Group technology is regarded as a product-focused plant layout where machines are assembled in one work center, so as to be able to produce a family of components that requires a similar equipment and processes. This is made possible due to the segregation of parts into families according to the product, shape, size, and sequence of operations. Sometimes, the group technology machine cells are organized so as to enable running parallel production lines. Such an arrangement offers more staffing options and flexibility in planning. One such arrangement is illustrated in Figure 11-1.

In the cell, operators are physically close together and are visually controlling the work flow. They receive immediate feedback on quality problems. They can easily assist each other because of their close proximity and their 360-degree mobility. There is flexibility in changing the production cycle by having different labor arrangements (that is, adding or reducing the number of workers in a line). Note, though, how a flexible JIT system differs from the approach of detailed (operations) balancing of a material flow. The paradox of JIT flexible production is that in JIT, a job shop is run as a continuous production line featuring a continuouslike material flow, while a continuous production line is run as a job shop because it is able to produce a variety of products in small lots and is able to deal with unexpected changes in production orders. Here we have the best of two worlds: make-to-order production and a continuous material flow.

The perception of the group technology in JIT is extended beyond being just a manufacturing unit for a family of components. Within a JIT flexible manufacturing system, GT represents machine cells capable of producing, not just a family of components, but the variety of components. The definition of a *machine cell* coincides with the wider perception of a product in JIT, and unlike GT, a machine cell is capable of producing a group of families of components and often is capable of producing components for an entire assembly unit.

In a machine shop, several types of machines are responsible for the majority of operations. There, a standard sequence of operations can be identified, depending on the type of a product produced. Such an often followed sequence of operations is known as an *operational cluster*. Due to the fact that machine

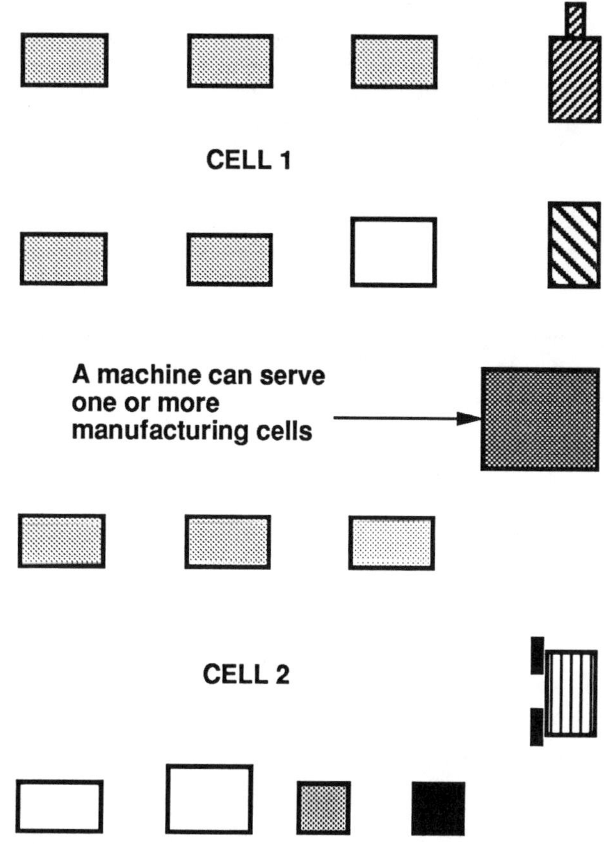


**Figure 11-1**
**Flexible Manufacturing Systems. Flexibility in Planning**

shops have a standardized equipment, operational clusters can be set up in all cases. An example of an FMS system at Dresser ITD is illustrated in Figure 11-2. There drilling is followed by the milling machine operations and, then the computerized numerical control (CNC) lathe and finishing lathe, after which the components proceed to the grinding processes. The flexibility of operational clusters is in that this is not a single product-focused arrangement of equipment but an arrangement that is capable of accommodating many products at the same time.

Along with the group technology, operational clusters can be identified in any company. In JIT, the group technology combined with flexibility has the following characteristics:

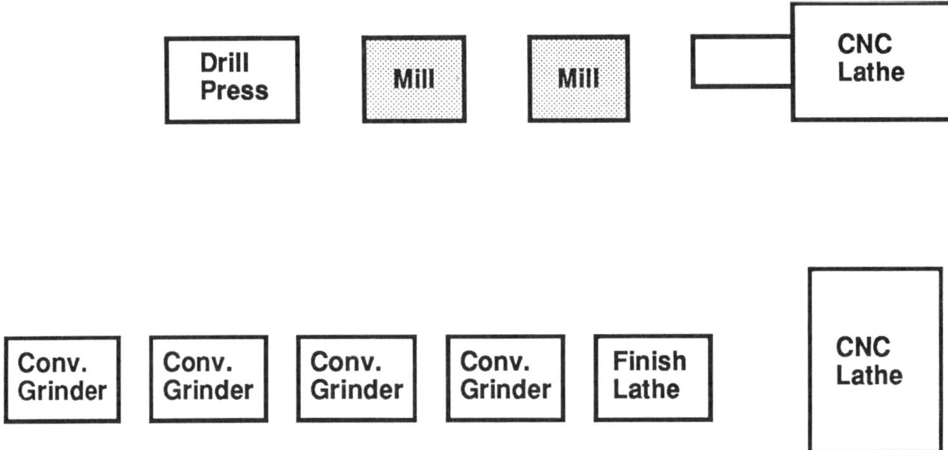


**Figure 11-2**
**Flexible Manufacturing Systems. Manufacturing Cell at Dresser Tools**

1. A convoluted routing intermittent material flow pattern is transformed into a focused material flow featuring short and direct lines, where visibility is promoted.
2. Material handling is reduced.
3. Number of job classifications is reduced.
4. Workers become multifunctional workers (the workers are rewarded by the number of jobs mastered).
5. Workers have a greater self-esteem and they are more alert.
6. Lead time is shortened.

## Setting Up a Group Technology Work Team

In a focused factory, a GT work team integrates a multiple-operation production function and multiservices—plant maintenance, quality, material handling, setting up machines and housekeeping, along with a planning and control function assigned to the shop floor. The work force develops quality improvement skills, changeover skills, and plant maintenance skills.

Workers assist and teach each other in mastering multi-station operations. Problem-solving skills are taught by an engineering personnel. Flexibility through line balancing, as we view it, is a function of industrial engineering. In JIT, shop floor people are involved in line balancing plus flexibility, so as to be able to shift the labor around in reaction to unforeseen changes and delays. A foreman is balancing the line by pulling workers off the line for other assignments or by assigning additional workers when it is required.

In GT, semidedicated machines can produce work for different cells or they can be scheduled independently. Such application of the group technology creates temporary machine cells with the ability to change their configuration for different products. Such an organization is especially beneficial in production systems consisting of small, movable machines.

JIT is an operator-limited system comprising semidedicated machines where one piece of equipment can run as a work cell only part of the day. There are instances where temporary work cells are arranged for a specific job and taken apart when this job is completed.

Manufacturing cells are beneficial for both operators' health and alertness and for their ability to move around within the work area. An operator is moving one item from one machine to another in a work cell. This eliminates material handling tasks, such as getting parts in and out of a container. Also, a quality control inspection is not required.

All these factors constitute a flexibility advantage in operations scheduling and balancing a material flow. Along with the possibility of producing families of components, and being able to perform operational clusters, the flexibility in operations scheduling presents an outstanding tool aiding operational control and balancing of a material flow. Until now, obstructed operational control and the inability to balance a material flow were unresolved stumbling blocks causing failures of so many manufacturing systems, including the failure of the material requirements planning (MRP) crusade.

The contribution of manufacturing to setup time reduction efforts cannot be overemphasized, but neither can the manufacturing cells' structure based on a multiskilled work force.. In simple terms, a manufacturing cell will not function as it is intended in the environments where the work force is neglected.

## DESIGNING PRODUCTS AND ORGANIZING PLANT LAYOUTS IN JIT

JIT calls for the redesigning of a plant layout in order to simplify the material flow. It often requires redesigning the product itself to facilitate the assembly lines. Organizing manufacturing cells requires changing the plant layout further. This leads to a changing queueing pattern, which essentially changes the move time, wait time, idle time, and setup time.

Establishing manufacturing cells involves defining product lines and families of components and operational clusters and ensuring the flexibility in products and production rates. The machine cell performs an important production function in simplifying production planning and control by reducing an intermittent material flow and by organizing a one-at-a-time flow line. This differs from GT batch type production. The machine cell is also superior for operations scheduling and machine loading.

Among other features, flexible manufacturing means flexible planning and flexible cycle time—being able to produce a variety of components at constantly altered output rates achieved by changing the crew sizes.

Manufacturing cell systems have several small simple machines, each producing a small range of operations, as opposed to having one complex universal machine capable of performing many operations. In this respect, multifunctional automatic machines cannot be regarded as true manufacturing cells. Manufacturing machines eliminate most of the intermittent operations because one piece can be fabricated at one setup, but these machines do not have the flexibility necessary for balancing the material flow. Flexibility in planning can be achieved in labor-limited production systems staffed by a flexible labor force.

Automated machine centers are machine-limited production systems which, for example, lose their efficiency when the work load is reduced. GT cell operators are positioned next to the persons performing the preceding and succeeding operations. At level 2 of JIT implementation, straightening of material flow lines should be approached without major changes in the plant layout. Settle on your product and, decide on your processes, automation, and planning systems before committing yourself to permanent changes in the layout for product-oriented production.

Families of parts requiring similar setups and manufacturing processes should be identified before the equipment is shifted to other locations in a plant. The objective is to reduce and simplify material flow lines for better planning.

The main features of machine cells that differ from the GT are machine cells are one-piece-at-a-time production systems where one multiskill operator serves multiple machines. This ensures flexible cycle time.

In a JIT-type structured one-at-a-time production, material handling and conveyor lines are eliminated, so that each component is handled manually to the next process. The proximate positioning of an equipment and the elimination of material handling operations makes the material handling equipment, including conveyors, unnecessary.

In traditional manufacturing systems, material handling operations are instrumental in collecting some extra inventory. Material handling performed by a worker-operated equipment, such as a forklift, is responsible for a large proportion of idle time and waiting time. Even conveyors carry an interoperational inventory. In addition, conveyors have a negative effect on the work force morale by imposing the work pace.

Workers' motivation and morale are affected when they are compelled to adopt a uniform work speed which they are not able to change individually or they are forced to perform small tasks requiring a few identical monotonous movements. Diversified motions, typical to multiskill flexible manufacturing cells, keep operators alert and reduce the fatigue and depressing effect of high-volume conveyorized flow-line production.

Manual cells comprise machine tools operated by a multiskilled labor force concurrently involved in material handling, manually passing components from one workstation to another, or some kind of power-and-free type or carry-and-free type of transportation systems also managed by operators, for heavier components. Such a combination of production and material handling tasks has an advantage of eliminating delays (wait time and idle time) while at the same time it improves communication and provides an immediate feedback on quality.

## PRODUCTION PLANNING AND CONTROL IN FLEXIBLE MANUFACTURING SYSTEMS

Flexible manufacturing systems centralize many operations at one station; apply fixed routing of standardized material flow where products follow the same machine line; decrease setup time and retooling time; reduce WIP and work space; reduce queueing time, waiting time, and idle time; and improve production planning and control. Benefits are derived from linking the machining, material handling, and quality and plant maintenance inspections.

Group technology changes a material flow pattern and restructures production planning and control. Thus, an integrated approach is important. You should involve the planning staff in your GT design and development. The reduction of the number of process steps, flattening of the BOM structure, reducing traveled distances and throughput time, and establishing dedicated setups all this presents an additional array of alternatives in capacity planning and material flow control. One manufacturer suggests that work force should be involved in planning JIT-type T cell so that workers have an "ownership" or workplace. They have found that workers were not sufficiently motivated to contribute to plant improvement because they were assigned to an already established GT cell.

Flexible manufacturing systems recognize flexibility in adapting to changes in work orders and changing the product mix. This stems from the flexibility in the use of equipment, the multiskilled work force, the flexible plant layout, the reduction of setup time, the flexibility in changing production line and support operations from production of one product to another, and from the ability to accommodate different volumes of production.

The capacity requirements planning (CRP) data base must be altered to reflect these changes. An accurate reflection of the capacity is vital in JIT because there is no interfunctional control and rescheduling, and there is a lower tolerance for errors.

MRP exploded requirements for intermediate components are not released because the material flow is controlled by *kanbans* rather than by intermediate work orders. The primary area of attention is the utilization of a worker rather than machines, which are considered a "sunk" cost—a cost that has been incurred and cannot be changed. Thus, a labor-limited manufacturing cell (having more machines than workers) is a real asset to your planning.

In production activity control (PAC), a material flow is intermittent, planning is done according to priority rules, waiting time and queueing lines are common, and balancing cannot be performed because there is no centralized information available about the downstream operations. A functional plant layout leads to production in batches and an intermittent material flow, while a JIT product-focused plant layout is characterized by the flexibility in material flow planning and control and a significant cost reduction.

When a company is in difficulty and the senior management is seeking immediate short-term benefits, JIT is a win-win arrangement for all the parties involved—the vendor, the manufacturer, and the customer—since it is based on trust and reduces the duplication of efforts. The reduction in cost is effected through the elimination of double checking, inspections, tracking, appraisal, and storage costs, double controlling by all parties involved: checking vendors, checking and controlling processes and individual employees, and through the reduction in production services and in production decision making. The JIT goal is to use a minimum amount of resources—raw materials, equipment, labor, and services—to perform the required functions.

## MINIMIZING CAPITAL EXPENDITURES AT LEVEL 3—JIT IMPLEMENTATION STAGE

Level 3 of JIT implementation stage consists of improvements requiring capital expenditures. Purchasing new equipment should be preceded by a careful analysis of the existing equipment. Often, the result of analysis is that the old equipment is sufficient, and what is required is an "orientation"—the focused use of pieces of equipment as an integral part of a focused factory.

However, when an improvement to the material flow (the straightening of material flow routes) requires major reshuffling of the equipment on the factory floor, this is done at the Level 3 of the JIT implementation. Rearrange your work centers into dedicated production lines according to the families of components or according to the operational clusters.

Figure 11-3 illustrates a rearrangement of a plant layout into U-shaped manufacturing cells in Precision Engineering Co.

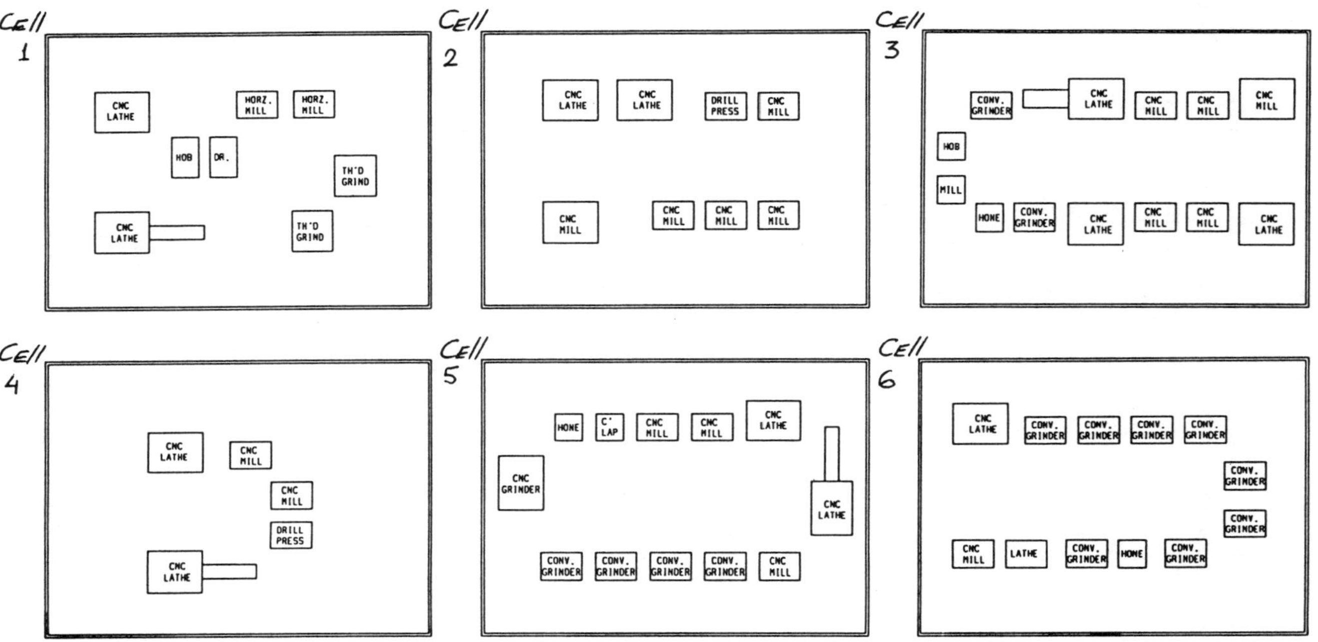


**Figure 11-3**
**Flexible Manufacturing Cells at Precision Engineering Co.**

## GLEANING THE BENEFITS OF AUTOMATION IN MANUFACTURING SYSTEMS

Automation is a technology dealing with the application of complex mechanical or electronic equipment used in production of large quantities of a single item, at a high production rate, without the human intervention in the production process. This is usually referred to as *fixed automation* because the sequence of production operations is fixed by the equipment configuration (for example, the first assembly lines). Here, the advantage of a high production rate is offset by the restriction of production for a single component or product.

The shift from mass production to production in smaller batches of frequently renewed products available in a variety of options has necessitated the need for a flexible automated equipment capable of being rearranged for new product situations. This gave way to a *numerical control* (NC) and later on to *computerized numerical control* equipment, allowing machine tools to be conveniently programmed for particular operations.

Along with improved quality, such automation gives a company manufacturing flexibility and a competitive advantage. Unless there is a high volume of homogeneous products, automation should be gradual and should be focused. A production cost reduction calls for low-cost automation to be considered first. For example, customized cam-operated automated devices can perform the same task as CNC machines at a fraction of the cost.

The JIT low-cost automation and machine improvement are approached in the context of continuous improvement schemes, often making use of homemade jigs and patterns as well as material feeding and removing devices.

### The Basic Objectives of Automation

*Automation* is a means of replacing human labor and human control by the mechanical labor and mechanical control. Historically, the division of labor and the separation of jobs into smaller tasks gave rise to *mechanization*—the use of machines to perform work previously performed by people. Mechanization is regarded as the catalyst of mass production. In a logical extension of mechanization, automation originated as a refinement of mass production techniques.

Further technical progress facilitated the application of complex mechanical, electronic, and computer-based systems in production. The attributes of automation evolved into the mass production of automobiles, featuring high production rates. This was fixed automation, that is, the automated equipment was inflexible, since it was designed to produce a high volume of a single item only. Lately, due to the shift in industry toward production in small batches, attempts have been made to design equipment that could be conventionally rearranged for new product situations. Today, production deals with smaller quantities of more complex products, with the heightened concern for quality and standards of precision.

The development of numerical control machines has allowed a conventional rearrangement of an equipment for new product situations. First, NC machines have controlled operations of a machine tool and the tool changes through the manufacturing instructions coded on punched paper tapes. Now, most industries are switching from hard-wired numerical control to computerized numerical control, in which a machine is controlled by a computer. CNC machines are controlled by detailed computer instructions, from machining to very rigid tolerances and inspection of individual components. The introduction of computers into automation has led to computer systems becoming a link between CNC machines and *computer-aided design* (CAD) and *computer-aided manufacturing* (CAM) systems.

The proliferation of automation had an immediate effect in the reduction of a direct labor input, largely the elimination of many tedious and routine operations, such as loading and unloading production machines. The by-product of automation is the elimination of routine, dull work tasks and the creation of new, more interesting jobs requiring a higher order of skills. In low-volume industries, like the aerospace industry and some industries that have contracts with the Department of Defense, the effect of automation is seen in consistency, quality, and accuracy.

The demand for higher flexibility, observed in virtually all industries, had resulted in the shift from *fixed automation* to *flexible automation* and to automated flexible manufacturing systems.

What is the final objective of automation? To replace people, to increase productivity, to improve quality, or to create a challenging work environment? In an organization, automation is a new element of a business system, which, like all others, should contribute to its main objective—satisfying a customer by producing a quality product, on time, at an acceptable cost.

Most automated systems consist of high-precision machines, which are inevitably contributing to quality improvements. Automation should be cost justified, and it should not result in an increased production cost. Automation should be planned for at least 85 percent time utilization, in order to be economically justifiable—the production cost is reduced when the high equipment cost is spread over a large number of units.

Although automation brings substantial advantages to production, it also has a number of pitfalls which you should consider when you make a decision on the viability of the project. To start with, you should consider the purpose of automation.

## Using Automation and Flexible Manufacturing Systems to Improve Material Flow and Reduce Inventory Levels

Like with any other production system, benefits from automation and FMS, particularly advantages in the form of the cost reduction, come from an improved, unobstructed material flow and a reduction in inventory. An underlying purpose of automation is to produce at lower cost with uniform quality and to replace people in high-volume monotonous and hazardous jobs and increase productivity. This objective can be accomplished through the improvement in an existing pattern of a material flow. The consideration here is that a high productivity rate of automation and the changing operation cycle do not lead to the buildup of an inventory.

Automation is tailored to two types of operations: *production operations* and *material handling operations*. The two types of operations in a production material flow are illustrated in Figure 11-4. Automation targets a production operation, a material handling operation, or both. Two basic types of modular units distinguished in automation are *production modules*, also known as *machining modules*, and *material handling modules*.

Your first consideration here should be the scope of automation. What to automate: one operation, a number of successive operations, or an entire production line (for example, stand-alone CNC milling and turning machines, boring machines, or an automated machining center capable of performing a whole range of machining operations in one setup)?

Machining time (metal cutting time) on automated machines does not greatly differ from that on conventional equipment, but all the service elements of lead time, such as queue time, organization time, setup time and delay time,

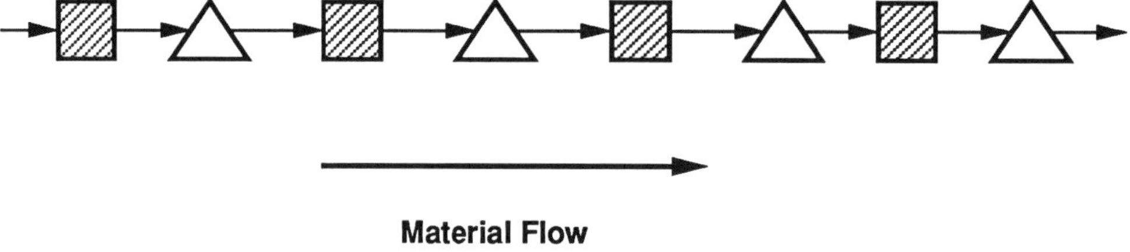


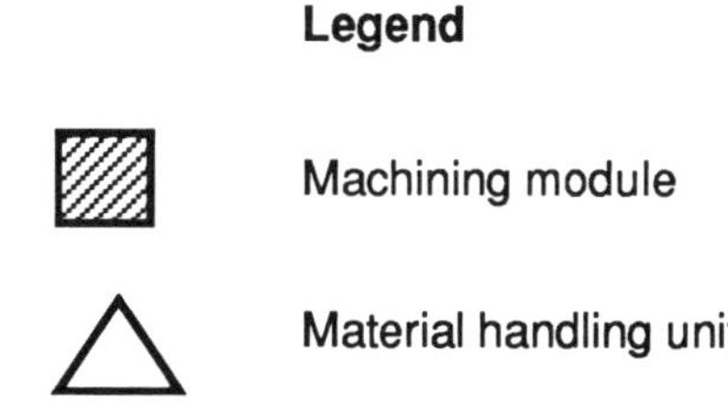


**Figure 11-4**
**Two Types of Operations in Production**

are significantly reduced. A special advantage of interpretational mechanization and automation is that along with replacing people in material handling jobs, it reduces and even eliminates wait time and idle time. Furthermore, an automatic machine center is capable of performing machining operations which otherwise require several kinds of machines. All these operations are conducted in a single fixing of a component, which eliminates the need for fixing and adjusting of components for each operation. This improves quality, along with the reduction in combined setup time and elimination of material handling operations. A significant result of automation is the elimination of WIP and substantially improved production planning and control, due to the reduction of intermittent operations.

Automation of a production operation should include automation of material handling, and delivery to the next workstation. Otherwise, the benefits of automation are diminished, since there is a danger of inventory buildup, as well as an increase in wait time and idle time. Some companies report good results from automation when applying a gradual/incremental approach to the modernization of their facilities (for example, when automation starts with a single stand-alone machining center).

In FMS, not all tasks are automated, and some require human intervention. Work tasks, such as loading and unloading the system, tool replacement, setup tasks, maintenance, and inspections still require a certain degree of human involvement. Installing a machine center is followed by establishing links between this automated unit and the adjoining production units, so as to achieve a harmony in the material flow. Thereafter, expanding automation to other production units can be considered.

In this regard, the latest research shows that you can expect about a 12 percent improvement in your capital recovery cost, if FMS is implemented on the incremental basis, as opposed to an all-out implementation. This is true, provided such a gradual FMS implementation is a part of an overall plan. Building on an experience in the incremental implementation opens the possibility of shorter intervals between further expansion steps.

## Applying Robotics in Automated Systems

The U.S. Labor Department has reported that injuries caused by repetitive motion disorders have accounted for most of the increase in the nation's job-related illness—a jump from 115,000 in 1988 to 147,000 in 1989. These disorders are often suffered by workers who are on an assembly line where they have to repeat the same motion of their arms and hands all day long. Human frailties can be a problem for any shop, but machines aren't perfect either. Automation often leads to overproduction when there is an attempt to achieve a 100 percent machine utilization. In JIT, the machine utilization rate is of secondary concern, and automation should be flexible so as to produce on demand. This is known as the *on-demand utilization factor*. Fixed automation is restricted in JIT, considering that the return on the investment automation standards require at least 15 to 18 percent of capital recovery per year at maximum utilization (usually about 80 to 85 percent). Also, automation aimed at replacing workers with machines contradicts the JIT principle of continuous improvement, since it removes the very means of this improvement—the work force.

The JIT approach to the machine improvement and automation is low-cost automation. This means automation of selective tedious movement tasks and those operations which present a health hazard instead of automating entire production lines. Eliminating these simple manual repetitive tasks is the most cost-effective means usually leading to productivity improvements of the remaining tasks. Furthermore, such automation leaves workers with interesting tasks, thereby creating a stimulating and challenging work environment required by JIT systems.

In automation, simple repetitive tasks are often replaced by robots. Robots have found a wide application on repetitive automotive assembly-line operations, such as spot welding and assembly of electronic products.

Industrial robots are an important part of automation. A robot consists of two major components: a manipulator handling the working tool and a control system guiding the manipulator.

A robot is a general-purpose reprogrammable multifunctional manipulator which can be adopted to low-volume production situations. Robots can perform a variety of tasks. Robots are often used to dispatch parts from one workstation to another within a working cell, to move materials, or to replace tools and specialized devices. Although industrial robots were first introduced in the United States in the 1950s, the Japanese are now the leading robot producer and user. They apply simply designed inexpensive robots that require minimal maintenance. In contrast, American companies apply universal, complex, and expensive robots which can be programmed for different tasks.

Most robots consist of a mechanical arm mounted on a base (a floor or a ceiling) with one or more articulated joints mimicking the behavior of a human shoulder, wrist, and elbow. At the end joint there is an *end-effector* which, depending on the task, can be a gripper, a welding gun, or a paint spray unit.

Mechanical complexity of robots range from an articulated arm capable of six degrees of freedom—three transitional and three rotational—to simple moving devices having only two axes of motion. Robots can have only a rigid arm which can be extended to pick up and replace a piece. Movements of the arm may be powered by electrical actuators capable of accuracy and repeatability, hydraulic ones which can lift a heavier load with a certain degree of accuracy, or pneumatic actuators used for light loads.

The movements of a robot are controlled by one of the two types of reprogrammable *microprocessor-based controllers:* a *servocontroller*, which senses and provides a feedback on the position of the arm, and a *nonservocontroller*, which provides no feedback. Usually, the cost of a robot is the function of their versatility (the number of various tasks performed).

Prices range from $20,000 for a simple task nonservocontrolled robot to in excess of $300,000 for more complicated models. Installation costs range from 15 percent to several times the amount of the purchase price. This includes the development of control software and start-up costs.

Japanese accept that it is a waste of resources to use a sophisticated electronic device that requires expensive maintenance to perform a single task which can be automated by a simpler, direct-purpose piece of equipment that often can be designed and produced internally. Along with the increased utilization of equipment, the purpose of robots is to eliminate the monotony in production by performing dull repetitive tasks, as well as replacing humans at jobs performed in a hazardous environment. When a company adopts such a strategy, there is no resistance to change and there is a motivated work force.

The Japanese have more robots than does the United States, but they are mostly an unsophisticated, simple task-performing variety. This is in line with their JIT philosophy of creating a work environment conducive to continuous improvement efforts of employees.

## DESIGNING FLEXIBLE MANUFACTURING SYSTEMS FOR MAXIMUM EFFICIENCY

There is a basic need for flexibility because JIT requires a faster reaction to changes in demand. Thus, an FMS is not just a mechanistic system composed of a multipurpose automated plant and robots able to produce a wide range of components; rather, it is a production management system that management must create. Depending on your management conceptual design of an FMS, the same equipment you have used for years can produce completely different results. Thus it is your input, the management factor, that substantiates, designs, develops, and maintains an FMS and makes it cost effective.

Some people argue that designing an FMS is a primary engineering function and that the management is in charge of maintaining and utilizing such a productive system. In real life, though, these functions overlap significantly, especially in the existing production systems where management, to a greater degree than before, exercises its technical functions. The difference between the engineering and management functions is blurred in most contemporary manufacturing systems. You, as a manager, should be a designer of an integrated manufacturing system and, at the same time, should be concerned with a product and a process engineering, and with designing, developing, and maintaining a synergistically reliable working system. This basic requirement for a management-engineering alliance cannot be overemphasized.

FMS can be built, and further expanded, around a single stand-alone machining center by adding other elements. An incremental FMS implementation known as the *modular expansion,* as opposed to the total implementation, saves initial capital costs and significantly reduces financial risks associated with costs of the FMS introduction.

An automated FMS should be able to restructure itself for producing a wide variety of components and automatically loading and unloading tools and work pieces on demand. An FMS is based on the group technology (that is, manufactured components should be sorted into well-defined groups according to the operations and equipment required).

## IMPLEMENTING A FLEXIBLE MANUFACTURING SYSTEM

An automated FMS can consist of one or several automated machine tools, NC or CNC, or a machine center. The material handling means, such as automated conveyors, automated guided vehicles, robots, or a computer-controlled unit instead of an operator-controlled one, will control the functioning of an automated equipment—tool changes and adjustments. An automated FMS can be served by an *automated storage and retrieval system* (ASRS) or an *automated guided vehicle system* (AGVS) operating on a defined route or a set of routes.

An FMS with its computerized communication of information and automated material handling (conveyors, robot-based operations, and automated guided vehicles) is an integrated system able to respond to constant changes in a manufacturing environment, such as a large variety of products and constant changes in the product mix.

It is clear that such a system is applicable to job shop production, and it is, in fact, tailored to this type of a production environment. In one computer manufacturing company, automated material handling units are linked by the computer-based shop floor data collection and data communication system and production planning in such a way that makes it possible to process families of components in the variety of quantity and product mixes.

With the advent of JIT, companies have realized the need for more flexible automation of their operations. Multipurpose machine centers are able to perform a variety of operations both on the cylindrical and prismatic shape components, reducing lead time. Automated machine centers run by an automated tool changer and pallet changers equipped with computerized control are the main features of an automated FMS. Such an FMS makes it possible to produce an entire component in one setup and to organize a dedicated one-piece-at-a-time zero stock production line.

The General Electric Erie, Pennsylvania plant that has implemented a JIT flexible manufacturing system reports improved quality, a decline in the number of machines required to produce these components from 29 to 9 with a corresponding reduction in the number of operators from 78 to 13, a 40 percent saving in the factory floor space, and a lead time reduction from 16 days to only 16 hours.

Often, an FMS results in the improved product value—better quality and competitively priced products and the concomitant increased demand, so that a reduction of the work force due to mechanization is avoided because of the expanding volume of production.

Many machine tool builders have considered a modular approach to FMS in order to make automation cost effective by reducing the cost through standardization. Here companies can install an FMS gradually, in stages, so that they can realize the benefits of the system before proceeding to the next stage. Your FMS conceptual design should be considered after a thorough product design audit and after identifying the alternatives for the group technology. When considering your FMS design options, parts are selected according to their production intensity (the difficulty of controling a sequence of processes), frequency of ordering, precision, and tolerances. In particular, an analysis should be done for complex parts absorbing a high degree of value-added costs during machining processes.

Some companies have reservations toward an automated FMS due to the uncertainty in future demand. Factors to consider in an FMS are equipment cost, operator training, auxiliary equipment and support systems, and maintenance.

## Financial Considerations in Implementing an FMS

A computer control system is a single, most expensive risk element within an FMS making up to 50 to 75 percent of the total risk involved in implementing an FMS. A computer-controlled FMS requires additional custom development in the form of programming which is extended through several years.

Although an investment in the FMS, in some instances, is returned within a short-term time period (often within one or two years from the installation), in general, it is regarded as a long-term investment carried out within the framework of a strategic business decision. Bill Pursell of CAMCO says: "In our analysis, even on the down side, the FMS investment had an acceptable internal rate of return." The long-term competitive advantages are flexibility and the possibility to expand the market share (not necessarily an immediate cost benefit).

A payback analysis defining the time required to recover a generated investment from the incremental profit and the return on investment are among the principal investment considerations. Other investment considerations are the improvement in work scheduling, which in many companies is seen as one of the most important tasks to be resolved, and the reduction of a degree of manual content of the work load, as well as the reduction of required support systems such as maintenance, quality control, and material handling. The reduction of labor cost may be offset by increased cost of maintaining more sophisticated systems.

## IMPLEMENTING COMPUTER-INTEGRATED MANUFACTURING

For most companies, the penetration of computers into all areas of manufacturing activities (such as engineering, production, sales and marketing, forecasting, and order processing) has reached a stage where it is desirable for computers in the different sectors of a company to communicate and exchange information with each other. *Computer-integrated manufacturing* (CIM) interprets customer orders into orders for component parts, while computer-controlled processes are producing, handling, and assembling the final product.

CIM uses data processing to integrate an entire spectrum of manufacturing activities—production operations, material handling and service operations, along with production planning and control. *Computer-aided design* (CAD) information is further converted into a process plan which, in conjunction with a *computer-aided manufacturing* (CAM) facility, effectively guides the execution process. Figure 11-5 is a flow chart of a CIM incorporating both CAD and CAM as the elements of a production planning and control system.

The first area of required improvement is an interaction of computer-aided design and computer-aided manufacturing operations, thus bridging the gap between the designer and the shop floor processes: the shop floor is constantly developing new ways for production planning and control, including shop floor material flow control.

### Using a CAD/CAM System

Computer-aided design includes mechanical drafting of a schematic drawing, design analysis, standards, and parts listing. CAD also provides an analysis of design and communicates information from the design office to the factory floor. Computer-aided manufacturing is a computerized information system generating manufacturing-oriented data, including process engineering, industrial engineering, machine control, and quality control. CAM specifies information concerning which tools are to be used, the cutting and feed rates that must be set, and the path which a job must follow.

In CIM, a central computer is supposed to integrate activities of all the automated production units. The same holds for the coordination of the production stage with the preproduction activities, such as design and prototype testing. CIM assists middle management in its day-to-day activities by providing accurate and timely information for decision making, which, to a great extent, can be programmed.

The purpose of CIM is to integrate various manufacturing and business functions into a single computer-driven comprehensive manufacturing system. It is understandable that such an ambiguous task requires a large communication

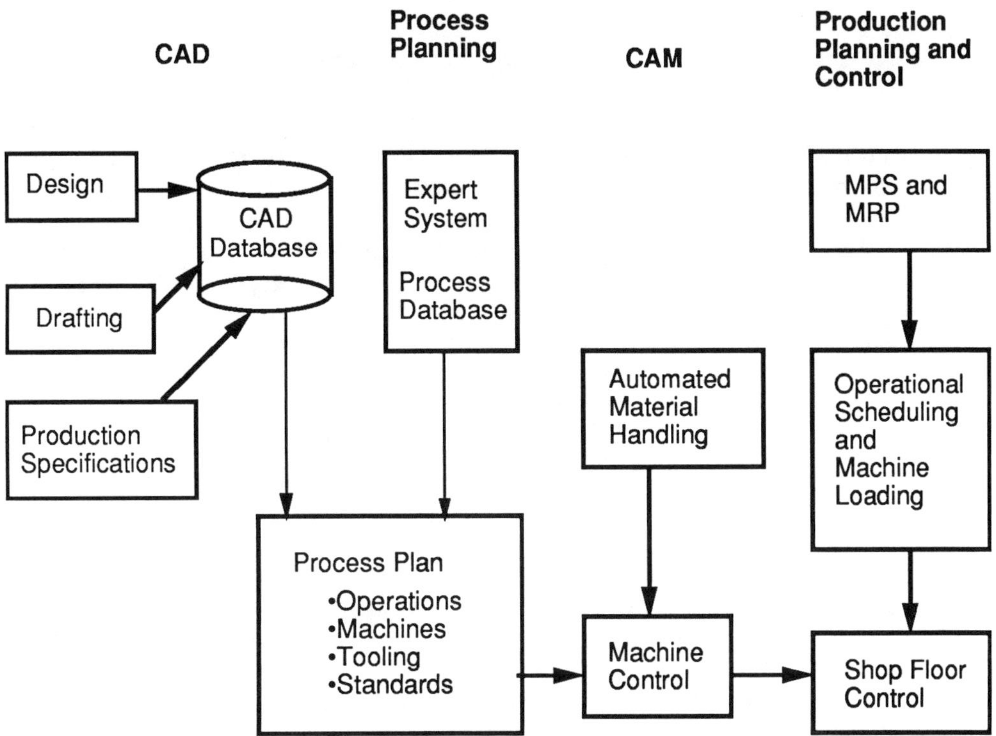


**Figure 11-5**
**The Elements of Computer Integrated Manufacturing**

system which cuts vertically across all the levels of an organization and horizontally through all the business and manufacturing functions.

For many automated companies which have realized the benefits of advanced technologies, CIM is the next logical step and the ultimate target of integrating their automated production units into a single unified computer-driven system. CIM is thought of as information management of a factory of the future—the strategy of linking technology, people, standards, and management to optimize manufacturing activities for greater profit, increased productivity, and improved customer deliveries. Automation and robotics should be selectively introduced to reduce pockets of inflated cost. For this, a detailed operational strategy must be developed.

## MRP AND JIT APPROACHES: DETERMINING WHICH IS BEST FOR YOUR COMPANY

JIT is not just another manufacturing system; it is a new manufacturing philosophy, new management, and new factory organization, along with the different arrangement of an equipment on a factory floor, different logistic systems, different functions assigned to the equipment, a different set of management functions and responsibilities, and different organizational structures.

Consequently, everything or almost everything is changed there, and this is exactly the task that managers are expected to do. The most difficult task is to change the human attitude and to ensure the cooperation of employees. As soon as the decision is made, you must decide what is going to be changed. With few or no exceptions, successful JIT companies follow the pattern of four stages of JIT implementation as described in the previous chapters.

Employees support JIT program and contribute to its success when they are involved in JIT planning. Prepare realistic plans which can be executed. The experience of CAMCO FMS has shown that for gaining benefits of JIT, FMS and CIM, it is most important to have a comprehensive plan for design and implementation of any or all of these systems.

The material requirements planning (MRP) features information feedback leading to substantial data processing. It requires further detailed planning process using work order control and input-output control. Under JIT, there is physical contact, an internal producer-consumer relationship; the material flow is highly structured with no intermission, and the capacity requirements are flexible and are regulated depending on the rates of production.

MRP is planned applying weekly time bucket units. Indeed, MRP and JIT have a commonality in the zero-stock philosophy, and MRP certainly should have a place in the JIT as a classical algorithm for manufacturing planning and control. Nonetheless, MRP should be restricted to the area of materials planning where its structural planning approach will not interfere with the execution.

JIT is a logical enhancement of MRP planning considering its weakest point—shop floor operational control. Do not change drastically planning and control without ensuring that it works and without testing it beforehand.

People are more receptive when they see that changes are improving a company's competitive position, when there is an ability to build products more frequently in smaller lots and provide a better service, serve more customers due to the lead time reduction and quality improvement, and reduce costs. This brings people more satisfaction through greater responsibility and job security. They develop a sense of a company ownership. Is this a challenge for you? Sometimes, it is easier to build a new company with a new set of equipment, staffed with a different work force specifically assigned to new tasks and functions. You provide the right training; change a job description; reduce the supervision;

assign a greater responsibility for quality, planning, and performing engineering and technical services; obtain the benefit of reduced overheads; and work with happy, motivated people eager to improve performance and the product value.

Make the best use of the existing conventional equipment before deciding to implement large-scale automation. One can enhance the existing equipment before spending money on automation.

For example, a sophisticated automatic material and work-in-process stacker and retrieval system was installed at one plant. One year later it was decided to decentralize stored material at places and at machining assembly lines in order to reduce handling and reduce an inventory through better visibility.

JIT envisages increasing the product value in every area of a company, not only on the factory floor. For example, it was found that the contribution of the corporate bureaucracy to the product value is declining over the years. At the same time, the return from engineering, product quality, labor productivity, and cost reduction is on the increase.

### Using JIT to Keep Up with Design Changes

Shorter product life cycles demand faster response to changes in design calling for improvement in design procedures by applying multifunctional team approach—a team consisting of design engineers, process engineers, production planners, and production engineers. It is common in Japan that there is no engineering specialization—the engineering function and the management function overlap. An engineer is seen as a professional, performing technical cross-functional assignments, which among others include making use of computerized shop floor control packages that also control processes and engineering design of new products.

## HOW TO IMPLEMENT FMS—FLEXIBLE MANUFACTURING SYSTEMS AT CAMCO PRODUCTS AND SERVICES: A CASE STUDY

### Reasons for Considering FMS

1. *To reduce setup time.* When small batch quantities are run, the product cost may increase. Each machine requires setup operations to get it ready for production. CAMCO has identified its operational cluster and has selected a Mazak's Slant-Turn 40 machine because it does both milling and turning and it has a chuck jaw changer, an automatic steady rest, an automatic tail stock, and an automatic tool changer. The setup has been reduced by more than 30 percent. A lot size of one part can be made cost effective.

2. *To reduce the amount of finished parts in stock due to a large number of different lots.* For example, a safety valve comprises 15 to 20 machined components and a number of small purchased piece parts. Each part was stocked separately. For an assembly, these parts are withdrawn in kits. It is thus necessary to wait for all parts to get to stock before a valve can be put together. Fifteen to 20 different parts for the safety valve are made by FMS at the same time and then put directly into assembly. This eliminates both work-in-process and finished-parts inventory.
3. *To reduce money tied up in finished goods.* Previously, a finished-goods inventory was built up for providing a better customer service. With JIT small-lot production, lead time is reduced and there is no need for finished-goods inventory.
4. *To reduce the labor content.* CAMCO has reduced some labor, but has had to hire others, such as software programmers. Once programs have been developed, the programmers are shifted to new jobs. CAMCO management emphasizes its experience with a continuous improvement of the operating system.

### Labor Fears Unfounded

CAMCO has not laid off anyone since it began an FMS. In fact, it has hired people since the introduction of the FMS. It has not had to hire from outside the shop and has found that people after about two months of working with the machines are capable of operating them. Everyone who has been put into the FMS system has made it. At CAMCO, people found that they can handlethis new technology.

## HOW CAMCO FMS AUTOMATED CELL IS ORGANIZED

CAMCO's shop is surprisingly quiet and clean. At the end of the building there is an upstairs office with a large computer that is the main control. Down the middle on the main floor there is a wide aisle for the automated guided vehicles and pallet changers to pass down. The FMS cells are on either side with seven on each side. Everything is well ordered. The shop feels busy, but you do not see a lot of people or movement. One operator runs two modules and is responsible for everything that happens in between those machines. A module consists of a Mazak Slant-Turn 40 machine with a robot. Figure 11-6 shows a CAMCO automated cell consisting of two machine centers and two robots.

AGVs pick up the parts and shuttle them to different areas of the shop. An AGV handles components between departments when needed. There are enough parts on the pallet to do a day's work. The FMS is designed for a

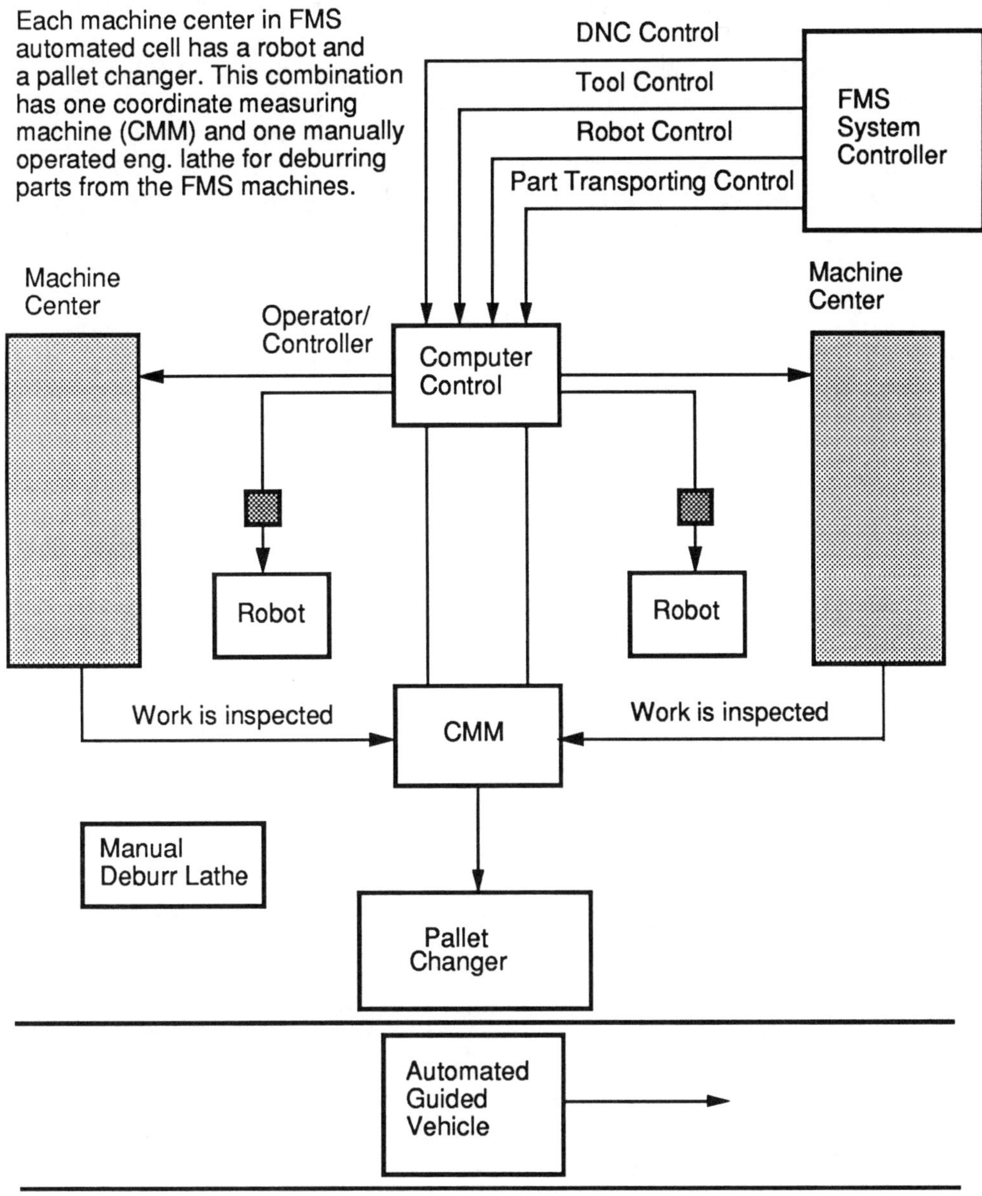


**Figure 11-6**
**CAMCO FMS Automated Cell**

Reprinted here with permission from CAMCO, Inc.

pallet system having capacity to hold different parts to make several assemblies at one machining session. Here both work-in-process and setup time are significantly reduced.

The cell controller runs the robot, pallet changer, the machines, and the coordinate measurement machine (CMM). The cell controller is an actual computer, and all movements of a major equipment within the cell are programmed. All the parts on the pallet are located within an 1/8th of an inch of the preplanned layout. Anything over that limit will cause the robot problems. Raw materials on the pallet must be within the prescribed dimensional tolerances. If the raw materials are too high up, too low, or too far to the side, this can cause problems.

Part of flexibility is being able to decide how many different parts to run today, how many to run tomorrow, so that a controller does not have to figure out all the spacing. All that is needed is to tell the computer what they want to run and the computer directs them where to put the parts on the pallet.

Preventative maintenance is also figured into this flexibility. CAMCO has an automatic tooling system. As an example, a certain insert on a certain boring bar has a lifespan of only a certain number of minutes. After these minutes have passed, there is a great chance that this insert will break down. Time standards are known, so a decision is made on how long to use that particular insert, say, 80 percent of the standard time. As an example, say, the insert is good for 20 minutes. If four parts have been cut taking 4 minutes each and the next part to cut will take 6 minutes, then it is known that the cutting of that last part will go over the allotted time for that insert. A tool change is called up in the program. A light will come on and the machine will stop. Since this tool change is scheduled ahead of time, tools are already set to go into the machine. To accomplish all this flexibility, CAMCO has developed the most sophisticated software programs found in the oil tools field.

## Management's Role in the CAMCO FMS Project—Looking Back at the Start of the Project

Many people have considered the aging equipment in American plants and the lack of resources spent on new high productivity automated machines and automated production lines as the major reason for American industry losing its ground to its overseas rivals. But increased investment in automation and FMS, at these times, was not rewarded by a comparable improvement in our competitive position, which could otherwise be expected. For example, American automakers have spent billions of dollars on automation, but were unable to detect any changes in productivity and the efficiency gap with their main Japanese rivals. The paradox is that a high-productivity equipment does not necessarily lead to high-productivity production.

We have not yet realized that throwing money on new high-productivity equipment is not going to solve our problems and that only an improvement in management systems is going to produce the desired results at a fraction of the cost.

One of these projects, an FMS at CAMCO, is claimed to be a remarkable success, largely due to the fact that it was accompanied by the development of an equally advanced production management system and the clear vision and leadership of its top management. "We have not met all our objectives," says Bill Pursell, vice president of manufacturing. "However, with support from the operators and inspectors we will meet our objectives."

#### MANAGEMENT'S OBJECTIVES

At the project planning stage, management tried to identify measures which would improve company performance. Among other measures, it targeted the reduction in lead time from 90 to 120 days to a 10-day cycle, the reduction of inventory (particularly WIP), and the reduction of scrap and obsolescence by reducing a lot size to a single unit.

It was estimated that $4 million would be saved on quality alone (CAMCO's quality depends largely on the precision of its equipment). Also, an increased production volume was planned, a condition to the 85 percent utilization factor. Further estimates indicated that simulation scheduling techniques (described in Chapter 7) and the calibration of automatic gauges on the machine would contribute to a 15 percent reduction in down time. In general, the reduction in the standard cost was thought to be about 10 to 15 percent.

#### MANAGEMENT'S DECISIONS

Before the decision on the FMS system has been made, CAMCO's top management conducted a study on how to bring an automation technique into a small-lot job shop production environment. It went into detail in selecting a specific equipment configuration for the higher efficiency and competitive cost.

Bill Pursell, has stressed an important factor in the success of these undertakings, namely, that the president of the company had supported a long-term manufacturing strategy which the management team had put together. Management has realized that it was going to be a costly renovation, due to the disruption of production when replacing the existing pieces of equipment by automated units. Such a delay of manufacturing processes was unacceptable. The decision was made to locate an FMS manufacturing facility in a new 33,000-square-foot plant.

### The FMS Project Organization

The FMS steering committee decided to form an implementation team composed of the

- vice president of manufacturing

- Senior vice president of operations
- Manager of manufacturing engineering
- Plant superintendent

Recognizing that software development is a critical function in the FMS implementation, it was decided to hire a senior software person having real-time experience. The FMS team had the task of evaluating a number of producers and selecting FMS equipment which is capable of producing economically in a lot size of one. This would require effective structural changes to machine tools: gauging tool changes, steady rests when machining long parts, and an automatic tool stock.

The approach that was taken was to buy a prototype machinery and to treat it as a research tool. The selected machine tool manufacturer has been explained process requirements and was presented with a detailed set of product specifications consisting of material grades, hardness, fits and tolerances, and machining conditions.

Bill Pursell indicates: "The FMS team should take time to specify the system configuration, the key requirements for software, and higher real-time data processing mode. Among other requirements, it should be conceivable to take a safety valve order, usually comprising about 15 to 20 components, and machine one set of parts in one work session (KIT—a set of components ready for asembly). These specifications were used when running the machine tool at the vendor location."

A CAMCO system analyst was sent to the vendor's facility for 9 months to ensure the adherence to the specifications. The machine tool manufacturer supplied two machines for development work at the CAMCO Belfast sister plant. This included two machines, pallet changer and a robot. The requirement was to produce a good part the very first time. Accuracy requirements were as important as the machine integrity: machine maintainability.

CAMCO found that it was possible to reduce the lead time to 10 days. However, the order entry, production planning and scheduling, and production of prints have extended significantly this time. Consequently, it was decided to add a paperless factory capability, receiving this information on line through the cathode ray tube (CRT) display. This decision was economically justified based on the reduction of the inventory and engineering support services.

Eventually it was decided to order four machine centers, after it was established that the prototype work meets the work specifications. Bill Pursell says: "Looking back, the success is due to us keeping the same group of managers from introduction to completion of the project. Early in the project, we sat down with foremen, assistant superintendents, finance, sales, engineering, discussing what will happen in the next 3 to 4 years." An employee's anxiety should be relieved, stressing that there are no layoffs expected due to automation. Although automation does replace workers, it requires people of higher qualification for supervising the FMS, programming, and maintaining the equipment.

The human resource department has announced a bid for FMS operators. At selection, workers were judged on creativity, willingness to learn the techniques and ideas, having a basic mathematical aptitude, interest in computers, quality production, attendance record, work record, and expressed interest in a job. The fundamental requirement for the success of the personnel is an in-house developed training program.

## Software Development Is Ongoing Project

Experience shows that a great number of failures of an automated FMS are attributed to inadequate software; the remainder are due to the inadequate management of the project. At CAMCO, software changes are still taking place, involving an operating and supporting staff, rather than just programmers.

The choice to make at the beginning of project is to purchase a software or to develop it in house. Altogether, an important condition is that the manufacturer holds the ownership over the computer programs, enabling him or her to institute software changes.

Pursell says: "If you are willing to pay for machines, you should envisage in a budget sufficient funds for developing and updating the software which makes it go."

Software development is the second largest expense item, after the FMS purchasing price. Almost all software changes are initiated by the users. Along with the operating personnel, the role of manufacturing engineering is crucial.

Here is an example of some software changes taking place at the initiative of production and engineering: It took a long time, up to 4 to 5 hours, to restart the pallet changer, robot, and machine tool operation after the equipment failure. Production has asked for updating the program featuring a more friendly restart.

Operating people are involved in developing and managing software changes and their detailed specifications bring a lot of discretion to the final software product. *For example,*

1. One production planner has been assigned to operations scheduling of all FMS cells.
2. A postcell operations equipment was moved next to the FMS cells. This includes milling machines, honing machines, engine lathes, the CNC turret lathe, and the centerless grinder.
3. One operator has the responsibility for two FMS cells and the deburring machine. His duty includes parts measurement. There are no quality inspectors. Dimensions are inspected and audited in the process. Here the function of the quality inspector is performed by the FMS operations. The automated system produces a part while the machine operator verifies the system performance.

4. Automatic guided vehicles were added to the FMS to move parts around to subsequent operations. All these changes have required changes in the software. All software changes were strictly centralized: no longer were operators able to alter a computer program to change feeds, speeds, depths of cuts, or tool path sequences. All programs are in the computer. Changes must be documented and can be executed only by manufacturing engineering. Very few changes are made to proven programs.

The discipline is a standard of conduct in production and support services, manufacturing engineering, and the inspection and programming group. The rule for programming is a consistency in the manufacturing methodology concerning tooling, cutting feeds, speeds, depths of cut, movements of the pallet changer and robot, and sequence of the coordinate measuring machine. Standardization leads to repeatability. For example, applying this methodology in the thread preparation simplifies computer programs, due to the application of modular programming. The same thread, used on two different components, is applied using the same modular program. Computer programs for new parts require proofing of machining parameters and tooling. The tool control system is important and includes

1. Preparing an accurate tooling bill of materials—a family tree structure corresponding to the bill of materials
2. An accurate tool inventory control system
3. Critical tools (for example, thread tools) undergo a 100 percent inspection on optical comparators prior to passing into inventory
4. A tool life data base used to prevent the tool breakage, which invariably leads to scrapping of expensive machined components

Statistical data on the tool life assist in preplanning the time when a tool is retired. In this instance, the tool is changed automatically, in advance, preventing its breakage. Also programs are compiled so that it is possible to plan the quantity of tools per job based on the number of parts in a kit.

An interesting feature of the CAMCO FMS is that the same technical person specifies the tooling and prepares the programs. Manufacturing engineering sees its function as facilitating a better way to manufacture parts. Engineers understand and assist with the shop floor problems.

A number of advanced features are successfully implemented in the CAMCO FMS system. For example, a customer can ask for an inspection of the records of any component, since all jobs are measured at coordinate measuring machines and the records are available at any time after that.

A paperless factory is tied to quality assurance (QA), and especially to nonconformance decisions which previously was taking from 5 to 10 days to resolve. Now an operator enters nonconformance parameters and receives the engineer's disposition on CRT in a matter of hours. In this regard, it is interesting to note a new system function, that of a QA engineer/programmer, who is responsible for designing CMM programs in the CAMCO FMS.

## CAMCO FMS Planning

CAMCO production is planned according to both KIT and conventional MRP systems. The system logic is quite different in these two systems. Lead time and inventory levels are different. These differences in the two systems affect the product cost. FMS KIT is further expedited by the fact that some jobs are partially performed in advance (for example, by preparing a series of blanks for components). Such pre-FMS operations are called *material preparation processes*. Component lead time is further reduced by conducting basic nonprecision operations concurrently with the automated FMS. This refers to hole drilling, gun drilling, rough boring, and turning operations. All parts there are bar coded, and all processes in routing are shown on the screen. Using KITs reduces lead time so that CAMCO can meet customer needs better, and this should lead to getting more business.

CAMCO's FMS system is dovetailed with the existing conventional shop floor system. The FMS foreman, in conjunction with production control, recommends the cells to run specific KITs to meet delivery requirements. In general, it takes 4 to 6 hours to compile a computer program and about 8 hours to prove its functionality. There is an increase in the customer confidence in product quality, which is resulted in the stronger customer support.

## Conclusions

Four stages of system development discussed in Chapter 8 are observed in the CAMCO FMS project.

1. The FMS *introduction stage* consists of making the decision in which a top-management team has decided to bring automation techniques into the small-lot batch-production environment of a job shop. Four stages of the FNS system development are shown in Figure 11-7.

   A management objective is to reduce lead time from 90 to 120 days to a 10-day cycle, reduce WIP, and reduce the lot size to 1 unit. These strategic management objectives were verified with operations. Additional benefits were estimated, such as a 15 percent increase in the utilization, and a 10 to 15 percent reduction in the standard cost.

   Bill Pursell says about long-term strategy: "The operations manager should have an input into the long-term strategy for the business unit of which he is a member. As part of this overall strategy, he must develop a strategy for the manufacturing operations. Issues for consideration are the size, type, and quantity of parts to be manufactured; the degree of automation;

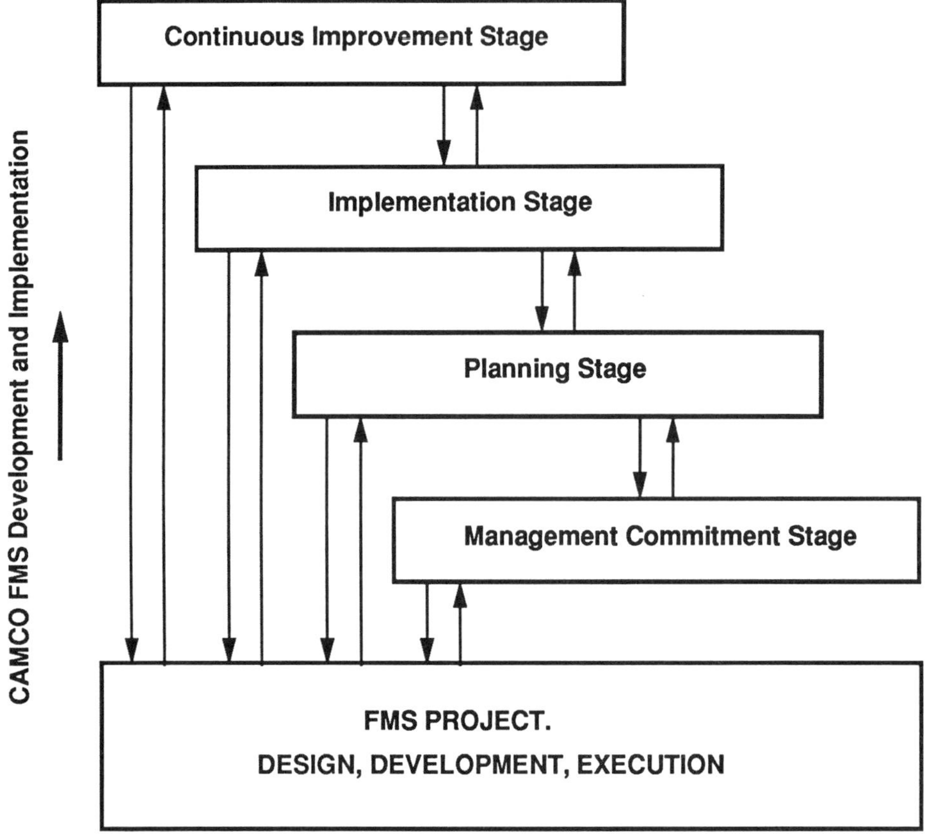


**Figure 11-7**
**Four Stages in Development of CAMCO FMS**

Reprinted here with permission from CAMCO, Inc.

and the type of equipment." The long-term strategy should be verified and derived from tactical and operational short-term programs.

2. The FMS *planning stage* consists of management's decision to locate an FMS manufacturing facility in a new plant of 33,000 feet square, selecting the machine tool manufacturer and identifying the details of effective structural changes to machine tools. All previous management decisions involve detailed specifications compiled jointly by the management team and operations people.

3. The FMS *implementation stage*, as with JIT, can be divided into several phases reflecting step-by-step FMS development, namely, supplying the tool manufacturer with the detailed set of product specifications and setting up experimental work in CAMCO's Belfast factory. Further on, it includes sending a CAMCO system analyst group to the vendor facility for nine months to ensure the adherence to the specifications.

   The CAMCO's FMS implementation stage includes selecting and training the operations personnel, as well as the software developers. The next stage is the software development involving production engineering and the computer personnel in developing software modules, such as cutting tool controls.

4. The FMS *continuous improvement stage,* as with JIT, includes an FMS continuous improvement done by joint efforts of the production, engineering, and computer personnel. This is further facilitated by the manufacturing engineering staff, which understands and assists in solving floor problems.

The reason for the success of the CAMCO's FMS project is due to its management's hands-on approach of relating its decisions with operations and the detailed knowledge of production. CAMCO's success is due to the superb planning of all four stages of the project and attention to details.

Stephen Smith, one of the top people behind the project, names three lessons learned during the planning and implementation of the FMS project as follows:

1. *Attend to details.* Only by replacing a machine operator with a piece of an automation equipment does one come to appreciate how well a human can deal with minor variations in the manufacturing process. In many cases, the only solution for a successful automation installation is to eliminate the variations.
2. *Make the system usable by ordinary people.* Create user-friendly operating instructions and procedures. It should be possible to train an existing operation personnel to operate a new automated system.
3. *Commit and train.* An FMS system cannot be effectively implemented without the commitment and dedication of many people within an organization because it will have either a direct or indirect effect on almost all.

Two specific features of the CAMCO FMS project should be emphasized once more:

1. The CAMCO FMS is the all-out automation of an entire factory division, which is essentially different from incremental automation of selected production tasks.

2. CAMCO had an advantage of being able to commit a substantial amount of resources to build a stand-alone automated division without interfering with the existing facility and existing production programs.

This has saved the project from many pitfalls and complications which any other company, lacking such resources, would have experienced during a total automation project.

## USING A JIT SYSTEM TO FULFILL ENVIRONMENTAL PROTECTION MISSION

Protecting the environment should be a major concern in the development of any production plan. An environmental protection, such as air pollution control and the elimination of the contamination to water supplies, is an important consideration in light of most recent limitation imposed on our manufacturing systems. Environment protection programs, although well intentioned and necessary, put an additional strain on our businesses in the already intense race with international competition.

Such severe restrictions on production systems cannot be resolved by management alone. In many companies, employee involvement in improvement schemes has produced solutions to environmental protection efforts, quality improvement, and cost reduction programs. A JIT system is an ideal vehicle in resolving environment protection problems, especially from the point of view that it is everybody's task and obligation, which is eminently compatible with the JIT philosophy of a broad employees involvement in an improvement scheme.

## JIT—THE CONTINUOUS IMPROVEMENT STAGE

The overall goal and philosophy of JIT is a continuous improvement. A continuous improvement is the last JIT stage, during which gains in production and services are reproduced and proliferated throughout the organization. One producer of medical products from South Dakota states: "We have been working in JIT for four years, and it's never ending. JIT is never completed. You can always do better. JIT is a challenge to constantly improve. In four years, we have achieved tremendous results. This is an opportunity that, if anyone turns it down, he/she will be missing being a competitive player."

For example, the objectives of a JIT continuous improvement program in various areas of operations at Long Reach, a forklift manufacturer, are stated in their company's policy as follows:

1. *Material handling*

a. Travel distances are reduced (there is less material handling equipment).
b. Expediting is reduced (expeditors eliminated).
c. Scheduling/coordinating is reduced (there is less inventory and production control).
d. Fewer material containers are required.
e. Less space is required for the material storage.

2. *Quality*
   a. Better overall control is improved.
      (1) Fewer operators are involved.
      (2) More jigs, go/no-go gauges for specific parts are made.
      (3) Correction for quality problems is faster.
      (4) Obsolescence is reduced due to a lower inventory.
      (5) Commitment to the outcome is enhanced.
3. *Lead time*
   a. Reaction to customer needs is faster.
   b. Response to last-minute changes is faster.
   c. Shipment is in days, not in weeks, from the order date.
4. *Labor*
   a. There is more flexibility in scheduling because all work cell operators are completely cross-trained, and work cell staffing can be scaled up or down as necessary to cover production needs.
5. *Floor space*
   a. Overall space required is reduced.
   b. Overall material required is reduced.
   c. Storage space is reduced.
6. *Inventory*
   a. Less is required with a lot size of one.
7. *Supervision*
   a. Less direction is required as the employees are running the show with little supervision.
   b. A work cell is easily defined as a team.

An overall synergistic effect cannot be discounted. There were performance improvements observed, after the initial stages of the JIT program:

1. *Group technology.* In Long Reach, some components traveled up to 1.5 miles before they arrived at an assembly process. Along with reduced travel distances, the group technology reduces the number of operations, dramatically reduces lead time, and virtually eliminates the need for the tracking of jobs. After the group technology was implemented, components

were requiring minimal material handling as they were produced in one work area.

2. *Space reduction.* In total, several thousand square feet of a manufacturing space has been made available for other purposes by tightening up work cells at both company's locations, Long Reach, Houston, Texas, and Rol-Lift in Little Rock, Arkansas. At Long Reach, 20 percent of the total shop floor space is targeted to be excess space by 1995. The Rol-Lift location will have 13 percent excess space by June 1993.
3. *Inventory reduction.* Inventory turnover has increased 31 percent in a matter of six months.
4. *Other areas of improvements at Long Reach:*
   a. Design simplification
   b. Drawings more consistent with the shop work
   c. Reduced shop lead time
   d. More relevant shop tracking of parts
   e. Faster assembly
   f. Opportunity for reduced warranty costs
   g. Opportunity for reduced shop rework
   h. Introduced standard tolerances on all new engineering design
   i. Suppliers are being certified
   j. Being able to indentify other areas of improvement

The incoming steel quality has improved, due to the tougher incoming quality checks instigated by the pallet truck quality improvement task force. Pump production has increased 82 percent thanks to employee involvement in improvement and the JIT (U-shaped) equipment relayout. Employee cross-training, with every employee trained to perform at least two tasks, has improved the overall plant productivity. Work cells continue to be tightened up, reducing space requirements and material handling distances. And, finally, parts are being organized in the work cells to allow an easier access, quick counting, and replacement visibility through *kanban* inventory control.

Another JIT system at work is at Dresser ITD.

## JUST-IN-TIME AT DRESSER INDUSTRIAL TOOL DIVISION: A CASE STUDY*

### History of JIT at Dresser ITD

Due to the nature of business, for production planning purposes, product sales are forecasted two years into the future, in order to provide for anticipated

*The material for this section is provided by Bob Collins, manager of manufacturing.

raw material requirements, such as bar stock, castings, and forgings. The assembly schedule is "fine tuned" each week with some changes on a daily basis.

Manufactured and purchased component orders are "launched" to a forecast and "pulled in" as incoming customer orders are received. Most manufactured parts have lead times of less than one month, excluding engineering and manufacturing engineering review for possible changes.

Manufacturing control systems including MRP, CRP, PAC, and purchasing were installed in the late 1960s and early 1970s to plan and schedule materials better. However, due to setup times, over 50 percent of the items were ordered in annual quantities which created a large investment in inventory and long lead times.

### PREPRODUCTION CENTERS

Before JIT-type production centers, the plant was functionally organized by the type of operation within departments (manual lathes, automatic lathes, CNC lathes, milling, drilling, grinding, and de-burring and heat treatment). Each department was headed by a foreman who reported to one of three areas superintendents. Problem solving often turned to fault finding, with each department blaming another for scrap parts or missed production schedules. The original organizational structure at Dresser ITD is illustrated in Figure 11-8.

Manufacturing engineering, likewise, was divided into three groups: process engineering, tool design, and CNC programming. New products and changes were most often routed to the newest machine for a cost reduction, resulting in an excessive scheduled load on some equipment and underutilization of others. Additionally, part routing varied according to the annual volume, with high-volume parts on newer machines and low-volume parts on manual machines. Improvement ideas for one part could not be implemented for other similar parts, due to the dissimilar processes and tooling.

A review of eight impact wrench anvils of slightly different sizes having similar machining requirements revealed six different processes at different work centers. To take advantage of the part similarities to reduce setup time and lot sizes, a group routing was developed and incorporated into the data base. By machining the required anvils as one lot, the setup changes would be avoided. This approach has reduced the time required to setup the anvils by over 83 percent, making smaller lots economically feasible.

## JIT PRODUCTION CENTERS

It was realized that in a focused production environment, to implement improvements effectively across a range of the like parts, standard controlled processes were required. Thus began the development of JIT production centers.

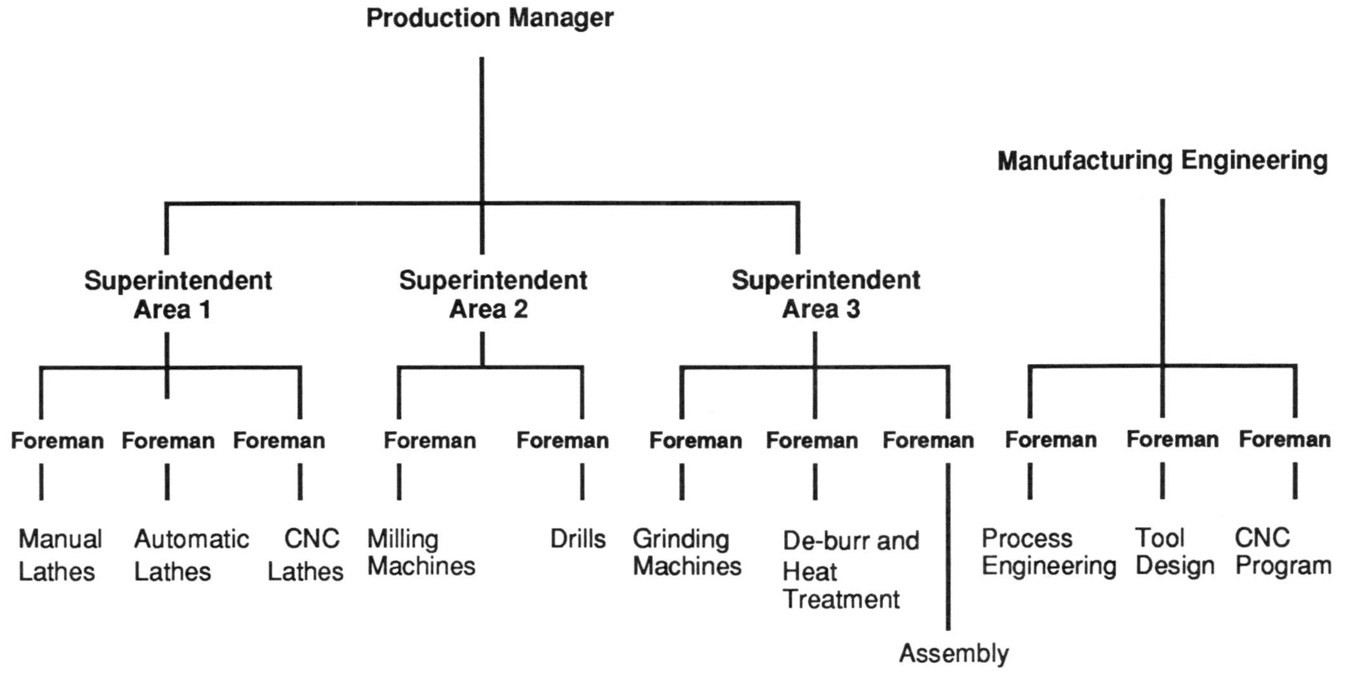


**Figure 11-8**
**The Original Organizational Structure at Dresser ITD**

Reprinted here with permission from Dresser ITD.

The development of JIT production centers included the following:

1. The identification of part families was accomplished by using the part description which encompassed approximately 60 percent of the machining requirements.
2. Standardization of the routing processes included defining "part groups" within a part family—parts which could be machined together with little or no change in the setup.
3. Selection of machines capable of performing virtually all the machining required to complete a part family. Machines were relocated to a small area and positioned in the classic "U" configuration to facilitate the production flow.
4. The standardization of tools and fixtures included redesign of fixtures for "quick change" and portability across several parts. Dedicated tooling was adapted on machine tool stations where practical.
5. Standardization of CNC programs was done to complete the presentation of work to be performed on like parts in a consistent manner.
6. The training personnel was most important, and a "pay-for-skills" program was adopted for production centers technicians. Unlike other machining departments, production centers have only one job class whose responsibilities include any task required to produce product. This includes the setup and operating all machines in production centers, inspection, cleaning and sweeping, part moving, and minor machine maintenance.

### MANUFACTURING ENGINEERING

Manufacturing engineering has been organized into three teams, each having responsibility for three functions: process engineering, working on process improvement; tool design, responsible for cutting tools and machine attachments, and CNC programming. An engineering team dealing with all 3 functions has been assigned to each production area. The improved organizational structure at Dresser ITD is illustrated in Figure 11-9.

### BENEFITS

With the reorganization of production services and the standardization of the production processes and tooling and programs into production centers, significant reductions in setup time were made possible. A setup reduction makes small-lot production economically feasible. Small lots, coupled with a standardized manufacturing approach for part families resulted in the following benefits.

***Quality*** Reject rates, particularly on extremely difficult, tight tolerance parts, were dramatically reduced. Small-lot production provided a quick feedback on the problem areas. The focused manufacturing of part families in small production centers made for a quick problem identification and problem solving across

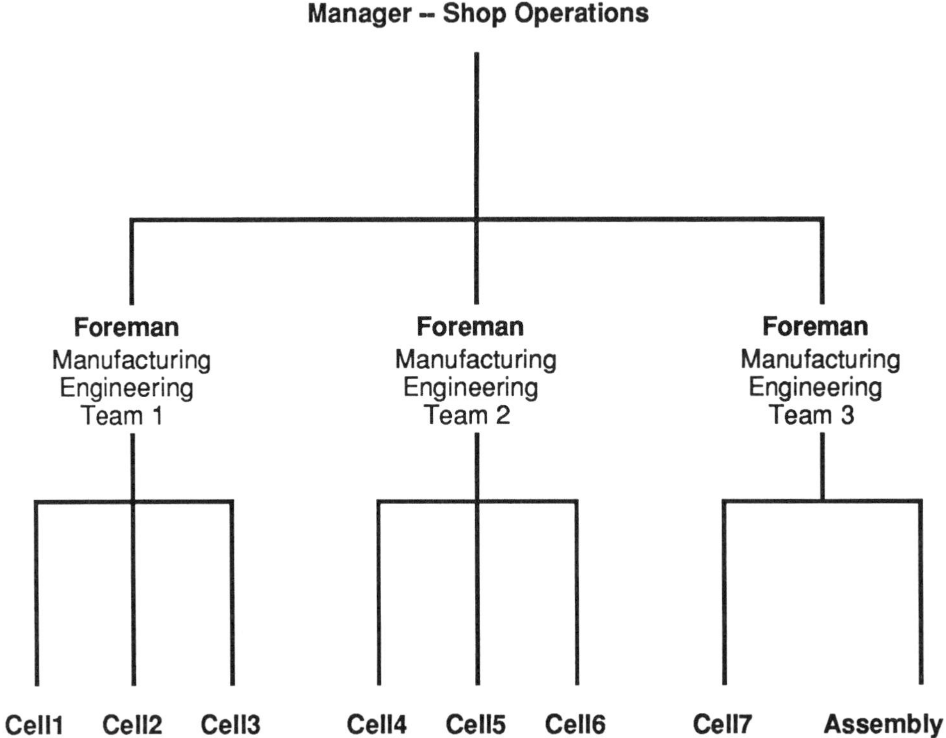


**Figure 11-9**
**The Improved Organizational Structure at Dresser ITD**

Reprinted here with permission from Dresser ITD.

the part family. Fixture improvements, including self-checking fixtures, resulted in consistent, high-quality parts that meet or exceed engineering specifications. One part family experienced a reject rate improvement from 30 to 40 percent to less than 1 percent. This was the result of the process analysis and development of standard tooling. At Dresser ITD, quality improvements are accomplished along with a reduction of the number of quality inspectors from 28 to only 2 inspectors left at a final product inspection.

***Setup Reduction*** An immediate setup reduction averaging 50 percent was realized when establishing JIT production centers, simply by having tooling in setup boxes in the center, eliminating lost time looking for and preparing setup tooling. With a standard, quick change tooling for part families, a total setup reduction of 70 to 95 percent was achieved.

***Reduced Inventories*** Overall inventories are most affected by a lot size reduction. Most parts are now made monthly instead of annual quantity runs due to setup time limitations. This has resulted in over a 50 percent reduction in inventories.

***Lead Time*** With production centers organized for the production flow, queue time, wait time, move time, and idle time are virtually eliminated. This, coupled with small-lot production, resulted in a substantial improvement in throughput time. Manufactured lead times have gone from months to days with an overall improvement averaging 80 percent in production centers.

***Quality of Life*** All production centers have just one job classification. Through the "pay-for-skills" program, operators have been developed into all-around machinists capable of setting up and operating a wide variety of machine tools. Employees no longer have to face the boredom of running the same machine day after day for months or years until an opportunity arises to learn another machine. Of course, the employees are more valuable since they have greater skills and flexibility and are compensated accordingly.

***Improvement Ideas/Problem Solving*** Perhaps the most important benefit of production centers is providing focused manufacturing processes in a small area which greatly simplifies the problem identification. Since family processes are standardized, problem solutions or manufacturing improvements can be quickly adopted for an entire part family instead of being isolated to one part/operation.

### OBJECTIVES FOR CONTINUOUS IMPROVEMENTS

Quality, service, and productivity are the major manufacturing objectives for the Dresser Industrial Tool Division. The world leadership in quality production must be maintained, while providing an outstanding service to support the ever-changing market demand. Most important, the ongoing productivity improvements to offset inflationary pressures must be achieved, in order to remain competitive in world markets. Production centers with standardized processes, tooling and programs, along with well-trained employees and modern machining technology provide the means of achieving these manufacturing objectives.

# Part Four

## PRODUCTION SUPPORT SYSTEMS

# 12

# Integrating Purchasing with Production Operations

Purchasing of material supplies, services, and equipment is an important business function that is increasingly seen as a mainline activity. Purchasing people say: "You can always sell it, if you buy it right." The mission of purchasing is to contribute to business profitability by adding value to a product. This refers not only to the price of purchased items, but also to the quality. Thus, in order to add value to a product, it should respond to the three value conditions: quality, quantity, and time. Purchasing is responsible for selecting a supplier which is capable of meeting these three objectives:

1. Supplying high-quality components in accordance with manufacturing specifications
2. Supplying these components at an acceptable price
3. Delivering these components on time when they are needed for production

As with the production function, purchasing has two concepts or spheres: product, which includes raw materials and component parts, and process, which includes equipment, tools and capital goods, spares and maintenance materials, and supplies. Product-focused purchasing is a major concern in production, due to the fact that, depending on the manufactured product, from 60 to 80 percent of the product contents is purchased from the outside sources.

The importance of purchasing for business profitability is stressed by the fact that the purchasing cost is seen as a variable cost while all the other costs, including the labor cost, are being increasingly regarded as fixed or semifixed costs. In this regard, purchasing professionals like to point out that one dollar saved on purchasing appears as one dollar of profit, while the contribution to the profit through savings in other functions is diminished by the overheads.

Purchasing is a strategically located business function providing vital services to production through a continuous relationship with outside sources or suppliers, as well as other internal functions and services. Purchasing interfaces with other business and production functions namely,

- Suppliers of raw materials and process items
- Vendors of parts and components
- Legal department
- Cost accounting
- Finance
- Marketing and sales
- Traffic
- Manufacturing engineering
- Manufacturing
- Material control
- Quality control
- Stores

Purchasing performs an interdisciplinary function.

Purchasing must have a detailed description of materials for the procurement of goods. This is known as *material specifications,* including engineering drawings, schemes, flow charts, recipes, and descriptions.

## THE ROLE OF PURCHASING IN MATERIALS MANAGEMENT

The purchasing function is concerned with a broad spectrum of activities aimed at achieving a greater coordination of a material flow within production processes. The relationship between purchasing and other production management activities, in traditional manufacturing systems, takes place in the following sequence: purchasing, stores, production, finished-goods inventory, and distribution. The sequence of business activities following purchasing is as follows:

1. Purchasing

2. Receiving and stores
3. Production
4. Finished goods inventory
5. Distribution and traffic

In general, purchasing is performed in three stages:

1. Preparation
2. Placing an order
3. Receiving and follow-up

All three stages substantially overlap with other functions in an organization: engineering, inventory control, stores and inspection, and production planning and control. Planning of purchasing proceeds concurrently with production planning stages of master production scheduling (MPS) and the material requirements planning (MRP). Figure 12-1 shows purchasing as being part of production planning and control.

It is important to realize that purchasing, as part of production planning and control, takes place before the execution. Purchasing should be accomplished before execution commences. The consolation is that vendor companies are usually smaller and thus have less red tape and shorter lead times. However, this is not always the case.

Purchasing people must make the time for the placement of a purchase order: planning time, production time, and receiving and inspection time. Figure 12-2 illustrates the elements of total procurement lead time.

The liaison of design engineering with production at the initial stages of product development may extend into purchasing when considering a make-or-buy decision for economical production. The interacting of purchasing and production takes place at production planning stages, specifically planning of production and assembly processes (MPS and MRP).

## HOW PURCHASING DECISIONS AFFECT PRODUCT VALUE

The purchasing department takes responsibility for the value of supplied items and their financial impact on company performance, and in maintaining a favorable competitive selling position. The value of vendor-supplied goods depends on purchasing people as follows:

- *Quality* depends on the vendor selection procedures and whether the vendor company has the know-how to produce quality components satisfying the product specifications.

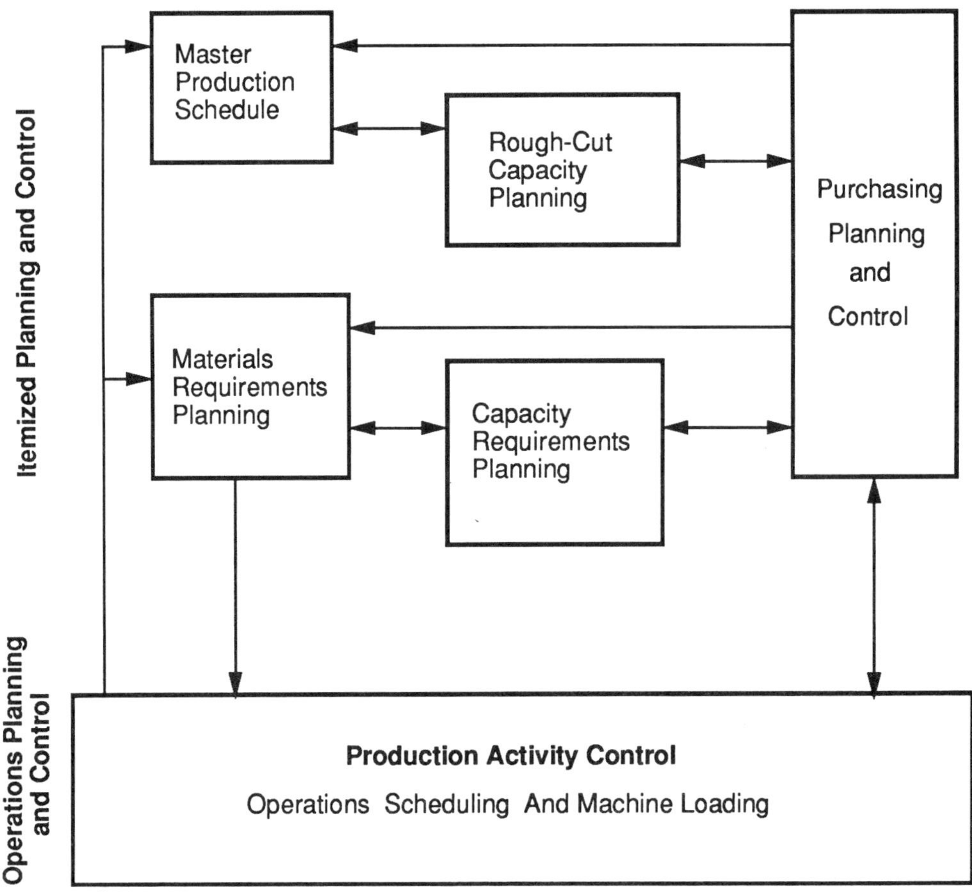


**Figure 12-1**
**Purchasing Is Part of Production Planning and Control**

- *Price of components* depends on the management system: how the company is organized, its planning and control procedures, and its managment information system (MIS). In manufacturing systems production costs are low when production is steady and the material flow progresses according to the plan, with the minimum amount of inventory.
- *A timely delivery* can be ensured, if the first two conditions are met, provided the orders are placed on time.

A variety of purchased items in an organization ranges from capital goods to component parts, varying from a quantity of one to large quantities. These

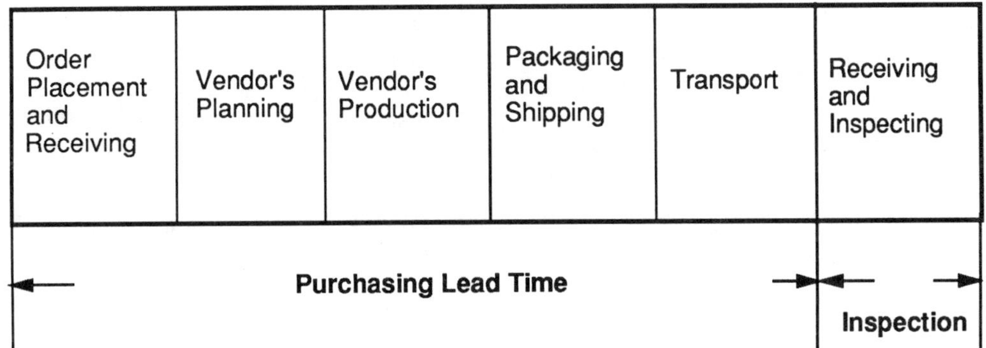


**Figure 12-2**
**Procurement Lead Time**

items may be bought for stock or for the immediate need. Purchasing decisions target the following criteria:

- Make-or-buy rationale
- Deciding which item to stock and which one to procure on demand
- Preventing shortages and overstocking
- Keeping storage cost to a minimum so that the total replenishment work does not overload the strength of a realistic personnel
- Deciding on the selection of reliable suppliers capable of responding to the three product value objectives
- Providing a reliable link between vendors and manufacturing departments
- Searching for new products, materials, and supplies that can further contribute to the final product value and profit

Purchasing decisions should be aimed at ensuring the balance between these sometimes conflicting inventory management and business objectives.

## SUSTAINING A GOOD RELATIONSHIP BETWEEN PURCHASING AND OTHER FUNCTIONS

The scope of your purchasing department's function depends on the size of your company. The purchasing function can be carried out by one or two buyers in small companies, or it can be exercised by a fully organized and specialized purchasing department comprising many buyers, each focusing on specific product lines. Such large purchasing departments often include assistant buyers, clerical assistants, and the supporting staff.

The purchasing function can be centralized or decentralized. *Centralized purchasing* means that purchasing for a company is the sole responsibility of a single person or a single department, reporting directly to the top management. The advantages are

- Better communication and coordination among management, engineering, production and other functions.
- People specializing in buying and negotiations, which means that better deals can be arranged.
- Standardized buying procedures, which creates better opportunities for the cost analysis. Buyers can cultivate new sources of supply along with research and development.
- Economical lots purchasing—where combined requirements result in larger orders and lower prices.

In a *decentralized organization,* purchasing is done by various departments or divisions of the company. In this type of organization, production units have a considerable degree of autonomy in their purchasing decisions.

In small companies, the purchasing staff is subordinate to the production function. The positioning of a purchasing department in the organizational structure varies widely. The purchasing function may report to the president, the vice president of manufacturing, the plant manager, the operations manager, or the materials manager. It depends on the size of a company, the type of a product manufactured, the volume of purchasing in its sales revenue, and the volume and type of inflow of purchased materials and components into the production process and production support services.

In larger, multiplant companies, purchasing is a centralized function headed by the purchasing manager or the director of purchasing who establishes and directs overall purchasing policies. Assistants to the director of purchasing are responsible for various geographical or product divisions and specialized purchasing functions, such as inventory control, planning and scheduling, cost and value analysis, research, and administration.

The most important development in the field of purchasing during recent years has been the evolvement of purchasing as a function of *materials management.* There are four functions involved in materials management:

1. Production planning and control
2. Purchasing
3. Inventory control
4. Shipping and traffic

The four functions of materials management are illustrated in Figure 12-3. The materials system controls all the material at various stages of the productive system between the supplier and the customer.

Materials management embraces production stages, starting from the raw materials through the finished-product state. The concept of material management, including the purchasing function, stems from the idea of *product-focused material flow control.* This includes warehousing and inventory control, material handling, production planning and control, dispatching and expediting. Material management improves a liaison of purchasing and production because both these functions report to the same superior.

*Physical distribution management* is considered part of the marketing function, including finished-goods inventory control, sales planning, order processing, traffic and transportation, and customer service.

Combined materials management and physical distribution management are known as the *logistics management.* Logistics management consolidates

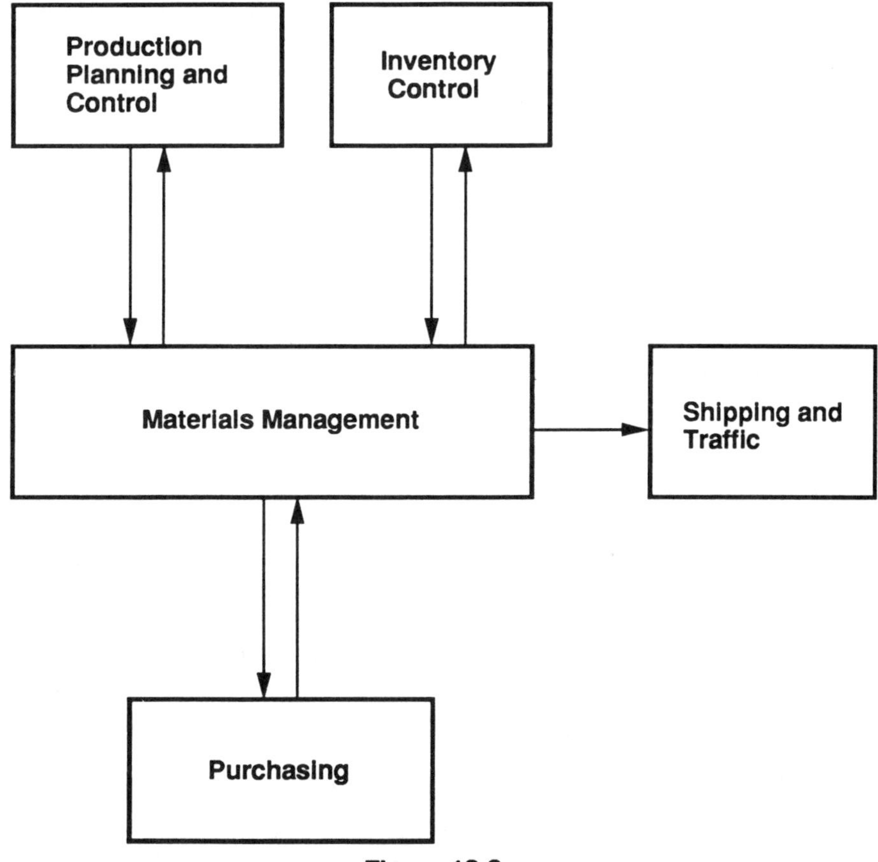


**Figure 12-3**
**The Four Functions of Materials Management**

activities involved in both materials management and physical distribution management, as shown in Figure 12-4. The concept of logistics management highlights the product value, as it oversees production activities, starting from the initial stages of product building until the finished product is delivered to a customer.

Customer service and after-sales technical service, also part of logistics management, enhance the product value by providing a customer response and after-sales information, assisting in the enhancement of the product value.

Some organizations divide logistics into *internal logistics* (comprising all the stages from receiving through the finished goods delivery to a customer) and *external logistics* (comprising outside company activities).

### Performing a Make-or-Buy Analysis

There are two alternatives available to any manufacturer in production, namely, to produce a component internally or to place an order for the component with an outside source. One scenario here occurs when the company is not able to produce an item, due to the lack of technology, expertise, or the lack of equipment due to a large capital outlay required. In this instance, the factor to consider is the selection of a right supplier-vendor from those available.

The second scenario occurs when the company is able to produce an item, but for a number of reasons is considering to subcontract the job. The reasons could be among the following:

- Cost consideration
- Quality
- Capacity factor
- Timely delivery
- Convenience in production planning and control over the material flow

The cost factor is not necessarily the most important, but usually one of the major considerations. Often, smaller focused factories produce at a lower production cost, due to the specialization and reduced overheads. Here, the item's price, shipping cost, cost of handling, as well as the inspection and storage costs, calculated on the annual basis, should be balanced against the production cost. The purchasing department must obtain information from engineering and manufacturing, in order to conduct a *make-or-buy analysis*. Usually, production control or inventory control initiate a make-or-buy analysis. A common reason is the shortage of capacity, due to variances in demand or due to the lack of technology or special-purpose equipment. A make-or-buy investigation may be triggered by a changing sales volume, either increased or decreased, especially when there is a freed capacity or an extensive work-in-process (WIP), due to the created bottlenecks. In the case of excessive capacity, you should consider producing the component internally rather than laying people off and spending money on retraining a newly hired work force later on.

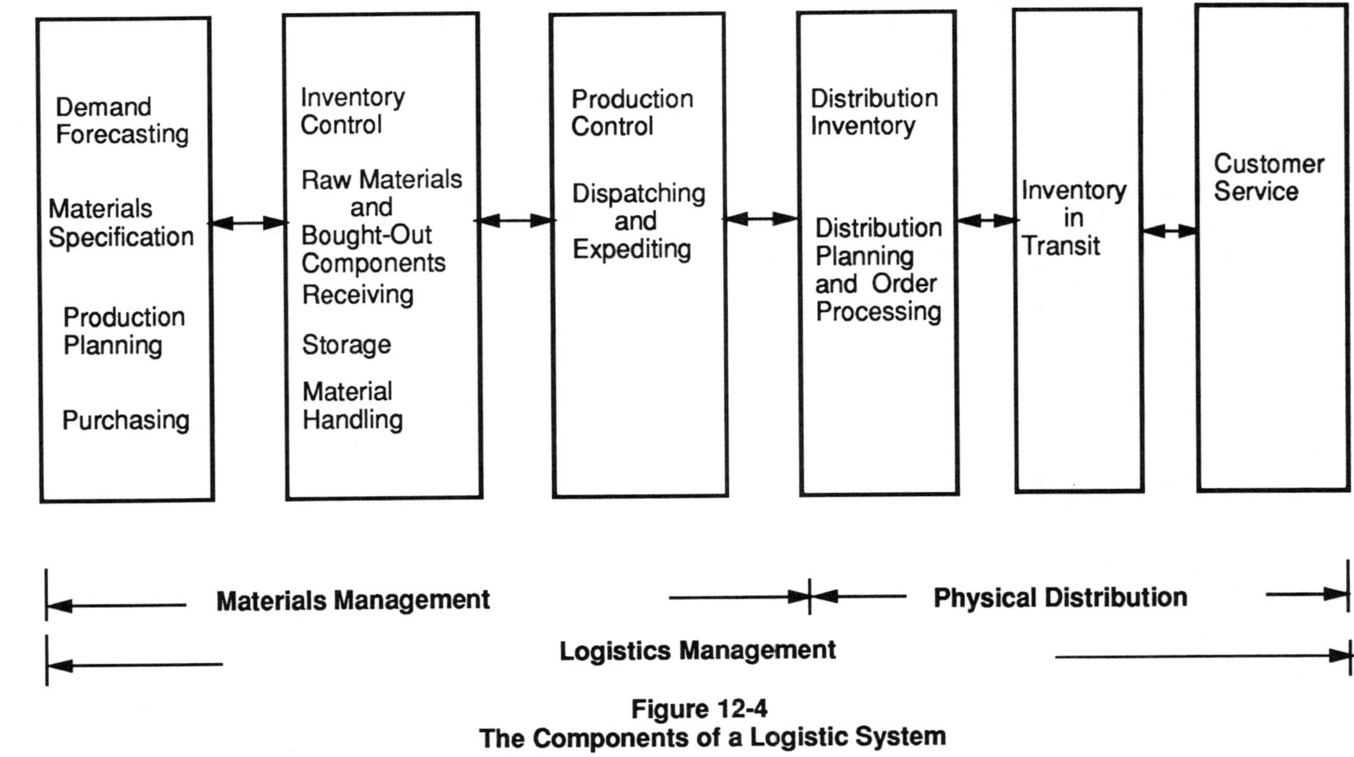


**Figure 12-4**
**The Components of a Logistic System**

Reprinted here with permission form CAMCO, Inc.

There are two types of information used in the make-or-buy analysis: production costing, or *make information,* and purchasing, or *buy information,* provided by a vendor or obtained by purchasing through negotiations. Make-or-buy is a multifunctional decision, which is often done by a committee or crossfunctional business team.

For any new product, every component should be studied for feasibility and cost effectiveness of its outside production. In other instances, unsatisfactory vendor performance can trigger a make-or-buy investigation. In other words, all components manufactured both internally and outside the company should undergo a periodic audit by production and purchasing as regards to their manufacturing status. A make-or-buy decision should be done with a broad companywide perspective and must be further reviewed and approved by management.

Making the right decision calls for an analysis of your equipment, tools, and labor force as well as your production support services. In this instance, a fixed overhead cost should be considered along with the resulting incremental cost (the fixed cost which occurs due to the make decision only). This topic, known as the *cost drivers*, dealing with overhead cost allocation is discussed further in the next chapter.

## HOW TO CONDUCT A MAKE-OR-BUY BREAK-EVEN ANALYSIS

A make-or-buy analysis uses the break-even graphical technique shown in Figure 12-5. If an item is produced in-house, fixed and total incremental costs are taken into account in addition to the variable cost of producing the item. The total *make cost* is compared with the *buy cost.*

*Example:* A machine manufacturing company needs to produce 1,200 helical gears for a conveyor gear box. To produce and grind, such a gear would cost $93 a piece. The fixed cost and overheads include the cost of a gear-cutting machine, a grinding machine, and tools for a total of $148,000. The incremental production cost and the cost of carrying inventory is $16,000. The buy cost for one gear is quoted as $165.

The total buy cost is calculated as follows:

$$C_b = n \times P = 1{,}200 \times 165.00 = 198{,}000$$

where:

$n$ = quantity on order
$P$ = price per one gear
$C_b$ = total buy cost

The total make cost is calculated as follows:

$$\begin{aligned} C_m &= (n \times P_1) + (C_f + C_i) \\ &= (1{,}200 \times 93.00) + (148{,}000 + 16{,}000) = 111{,}600 + 164{,}000 \\ &= 275{,}600 \end{aligned}$$

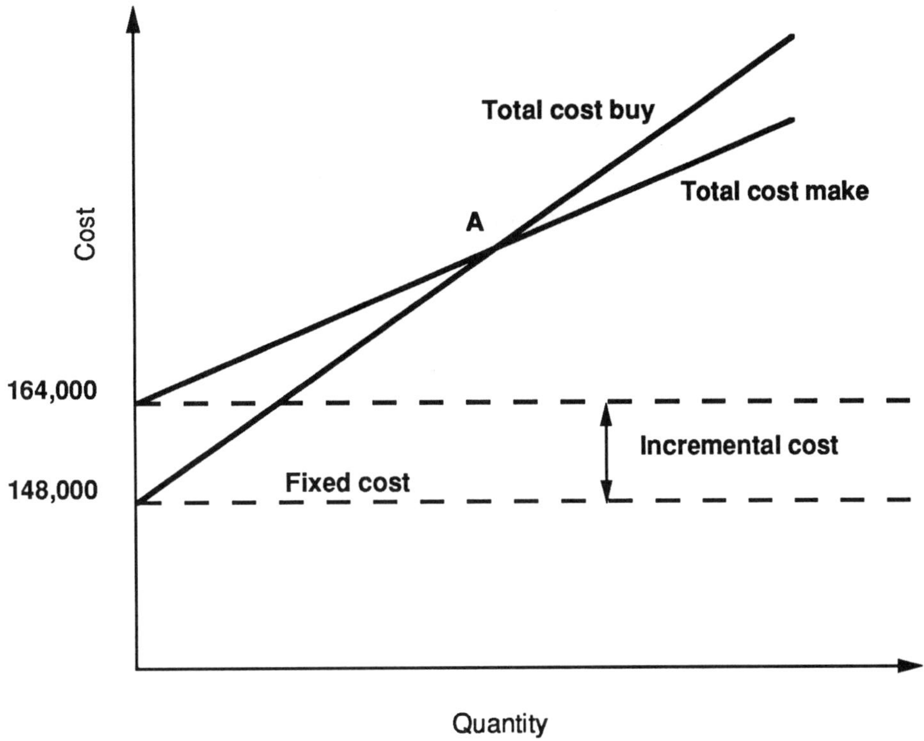


**Figure 12-5**
**The Make-or-Buy Break-Even Analysis**

where

$n$ = quantity on order
$P_1$ = production cost of one gear
$C_f$ = fixed cost
$C_i$ = incremental cost
$C_m$ = total make cost

Consequently, to buy the quantity of 1,200 is a more economical decision, producing the savings of

$275,600 - $198,000 = $77,600

The break-even point (point *A* in Figure 12-5) represents the condition when

$$C_b = C_m$$
$$n \times P = (n \times P_1) + (C_f + C_i)$$
$$C_f + C_i = (n \times P) - (n \times P_1)$$
$$C_f + C_i = n\,(P - P_1)$$
$$n = \frac{C_f + C_i}{P - P_1} = \frac{148{,}000 + 16{,}000}{165 - 93} = 2{,}278$$

The break-even point thus is 2,278 gears. The decision to buy should be made if there are no other considerations than the production cost. The make-or-buy decision can be substantiated by a desired quality level. The cost consideration is secondary to the quality, if the technology or know-how is not available in-house.

There are still a variety of other factors influencing the make-or-buy decisions, such as:

- Quantity on order
- JIT single-source policy (discussed further in this chapter)
- Labor-management relations
- National economic climate
- Long-term strategy and future developments
- Research and development of specialized technology and know-how

A basic purchasing management system is discussed in the following example, using the CAMCO Purchasing Department.

## A BASIC PURCHASING MANAGEMENT SYSTEM—CAMCO'S PURCHASING DEPARTMENT: A CASE STUDY

CAMCO's Purchasing Department is organized as a centralized purchasing department where buyers specialize in the following product lines:

1. Raw materials, casting, and forgings
2. Outside services
3. Elastomers (rubber and plastics)
4. Perishable tools (cutting tools)
5. Expandable purchases (standard fixtures and maintenance supplies)

At CAMCO, the document initiating any purchase is called a *traveling requisition.*

## Placing a Traveling Requisition

The *traveling requistion* is used for repetitive purchasing transactions of the same item and is issued by the department which recognizes the need for the purchase. The CAMCO traveling requisition is shown in Figure 12-6. This form contains an internal identification of the ordered item, its full description, the potential vendor or vendors, and the item's purchasing history.

Other information includes:

1. Buyers assigned to the item
2. Purchase order number and negotiated price
3. Quality requirements and quantity
4. Requested delivery date
5. Quality assurance approval (that is, the person who approved the order, the order date, and the supplier's compliance with CAMCO's specifications)

At CAMCO, all suppliers have to be quality assurance (QA) approved. The purchasing department, together with the QA, evaluates vendors at quality review meetings. Vendors who have fallen below quality requirements level are notified, and their status is further discussed at the joint QA committee.

CAMCO's traveling requisition is a double-sided form on which it is possible to accomplish about 30 to 40 purchases. All traveling requisitions proceed to a purchasing department clerk, who assigns the purchase order number and sends it to the buyer responsible.

## Cutting a Purchase Order

The *purchase order* is issued after the traveling requisition has been registered and the purchase order number has been assigned. The original of the issued purchase order is mailed to the vendor, and a copy is retained by the CAMCO Purchasing Department in the vendor's file. CAMCO's purchase order form is shown in Figure 12-7.

A special purchase order, illustrated in Figure 12-8, is issued to the Receiving Department. This form contains receiving information, such as the item number, quantity received, date, and the packing list, along with the signature of the person(s) receiving the ordered material. Purchase orders are monitored by buyers. Ten days prior to the due date, these data are compiled into an *expediting report*. This report, which also includes past due orders, is discussed at the weekly purchasing meeting.

When the item has been delivered, the Centralized Receiving Department generates a receiving report. One copy of this report goes to accounts payable, and another copy is sent to the Inventory Control. The CAMCO's order flow chart is shown in Figure 12-9. For a one-time purchase, a material requisition

FORWARD TR/PO TO:________ **TRAVELING REQUISITION** PART NO.________

| DESCRIPTION | | | QUALITY RQMTS |
|---|---|---|---|
| | ACC'T CODE | | |
| > | DWG REV NO LET DATE | | PSEUDO DATE |
| > | SPEC NO LET DATE | | |
| | | | |
| | WALL– | M/WT– | |
| | WT– | M/QTY– | |
| | U/M | | SPPE DATE |

| REQUISITIONER | | | | | | | QA APPROVAL | | PURCHASING | | | | | | | NOTES | |
|---|---|---|---|---|---|---|---|---|---|---|---|---|---|---|---|---|---|
| DATE | QTY | RQMT DATE | REQ'D BY | DWG REV | SPEC REV | DATE ON TR | APPROVED BY | DATE | DATE RECV'D | P.O. NUMBER | V | QTY | PRICE | DELIVERY DATE | BUYER | | |

| | VENDORS | CHANGES/NOTES | QUOTES |
|---|---|---|---|
| 1 | | | |
| 2 | | | |
| 3 | | | |
| 4 | | | |
| 5 | | | |
| 6 | | | |
| 7 | | | |

**Figure 12-6**
**Traveling Requisition**

Reprinted herre by permission from CAMCO, Inc.

#140622 (1) F

REQUISITION NUMBER | REQUISITIONER

CAMCO

Fax (713) 741-6719
Telex #: 775413
Cable Address: CAMCO
Phone 747-4000
Area Code 713

**CAMCO**
PRODUCTS AND SERVICES COMPANY
P.O. Box 14484
HOUSTON, TEXAS 77221

PURCHASE ORDER No. SAMPLE

THIS ORDER NUMBER MUST APPEAR ON ALL CORRESPONDENCE, INVOICES, BILLS OF LADING AND PACKAGES.

**INVOICE IN DUPLICATE**

VENDOR # DATE

REQUIRED AT CAMCO BEFORE

CONFIRMING ORDER ☐ YES ☐ NO | ORDER PLACED WITH

SHIP VIA | F.O.B. POINT ☐ DESTINATION ☐ SHIPPING POINT | FREIGHT CHARGES ☐ COLLECT ☐ FREIGHT ALLOWED ☐ PREPAID AND ADD

ISSUED TO

TAXABLE ☐
TAX EXEMPT ☐
TAX EXEMPTION
#1-133517570-6

SHIP TO CAMCO PRODUCTS AND SERVICES COMPANY
7030 Ardmore • Houston, Texas 77054

| ITEM No. | QUANTITY ORDERED | UNIT OF MEASURE | DESCRIPTION | CAMCO CODING | UNIT PRICE | CAMCO PART NUMBER |
|---|---|---|---|---|---|---|
| | | | | | | |

| QUALITY REQUIREMENTS | |
|---|---|
| COPY OF ALL MANUFACTURERS MATERIAL CERTIFICATIONS (INCLUDING THE ORIGINAL PRODUCING MILL). | ☐ YES ☐ NO |
| SUPPLIER MUST FURNISH STATEMENT OF COMPLIANCE TO REFERENCED CAMCO SPECIFICATION(S). | ☐ YES ☐ NO |
| SUPPLIER STATEMENT OF COMPLIANCE TO S.P.P.E.-1 (THE SUPPLIER MUST CERTIFY THAT THE MATERIAL, PART OR SERVICE WAS PRODUCED OR SUPPLIED IN ACCORDANCE WITH THEIR QUALITY PROGRAM REV.________DATE__________, OR A LATER REVISION LEVEL AND/OR DATE, APPROVED BY THE QUALITY ASSURANCE DEPARTMENT CAMCO) | ☐ YES ☐ NO |

CAMCO PRODUCTS AND SERVICES COMPANY

CAMCO AUTHORIZED SIGNATURE

VENDOR SHALL CARRY APPROPRIATE WORKER'S COMPENSATION AND PROPERTY INSURANCE TO COVER VENDOR'S EMPLOYEES AND VENDOR OWNED PROPERTY WHILE PERFORMING SERVICES ON CAMCO'S PREMISES. VENDOR SHALL PROVIDE CAMCO PROOF OF SUCH COVERAGE IN THE FORM OF INSURANCE CERTIFICATES UPON REQUEST.

**ACCEPTANCE OF THIS PURCHASE ORDER CONSTITUTES THE ACCEPTANCE OF ALL TERMS AND CONDITIONS CONTAINED ON THE REVERSE SIDE, WHICH ARE MADE A PART HEREOF FOR ALL PURPOSES.**

FORM NO. 1023-P (7/89)

ORIGINAL

**Figure 12-7**
**CAMCO Purchase Order Form**

Reprinted here with permission from CAMCO, Inc.

REQUISITION NUMBER | REQUISITIONER

CAMCO

Fax (713) 741-6719
Telex #: 775413
Cable Address: CAMCO
Phone 747-4000
Area Code 713

**CAMCO**
PRODUCTS AND SERVICES COMPANY
P.O. Box 14484
HOUSTON, TEXAS 77221

VENDOR # DATE

PURCHASE ORDER No. SAMPLE

THIS ORDER NUMBER MUST APPEAR ON ALL CORRESPONDENCE, INVOICES, BILLS OF LADING AND PACKAGES.

INVOICE IN DUPLICATE

REQUIRED AT CAMCO BEFORE | CONFIRMING ORDER ☐ YES ☐ NO | ORDER PLACED WITH

SHIP VIA | F.O.B. POINT ☐ DESTINATION ☐ SHIPPING POINT | FREIGHT CHARGES ☐ COLLECT ☐ FREIGHT ALLOWED ☐ PREPAID AND ADD

ISSUED TO

TAXABLE ☐
TAX EXEMPT ☐
TAX EXEMPTION
#1-74-1038310-7

SHIP TO
CAMCO PRODUCTS AND SERVICES COMPANY
7030 Ardmore • Houston, Texas 77054

| ITEM NO | QUANTITY ORDERED | UNIT OF MEASURE | DESCRIPTION | CAMCO CODING | UNIT PRICE | CAMCO PART NUMBER |
|---|---|---|---|---|---|---|
| | | | | | | |

QUALITY REQUIREMENTS

| | |
|---|---|
| COPY OF ALL MANUFACTURERS MATERIAL CERTIFICATIONS (INCLUDING THE ORIGINAL PRODUCING MILL). | ☐ YES ☐ NO |
| SUPPLIER MUST FURNISH STATEMENT OF COMPLIANCE TO REFERENCED CAMCO SPECIFICATION(S). | ☐ YES ☐ NO |
| SUPPLIER STATEMENT OF COMPLIANCE TO S.P.P.E.-1 (THE SUPPLIER MUST CERTIFY THAT THE MATERIAL, PART OR SERVICE WAS PRODUCED OR SUPPLIED IN ACCORDANCE WITH THEIR QUALITY PROGRAM REV.______ DATE_______, OR A LATER REVISION LEVEL AND/OR DATE, APPROVED BY THE QUALITY ASSURANCE DEPARTMENT CAMCO) | ☐ YES ☐ NO |

CAMCO PRODUCTS AND SERVICES COMPANY

CAMCO AUTHORIZED SIGNATURE

| ITEM NO | QUANTITY RECEIVED | BACK ORDERED | OVER SHIPMENT | REMARKS: | DATE REC'D | ITEM NO | QUANTITY RECEIVED | BACK ORDERED | OVER SHIPMENT | REMARKS: | DATE REC'D |
|---|---|---|---|---|---|---|---|---|---|---|---|
| | | | | | | | | | | | |
| | | | | | | | | | | | |
| | | | | | | | | | | | |
| | | | | | | | | | | | |

**RECEIVING DEPT.** RECEIVING CLERK

**Figure 12-8**
**CAMCO Special Purchase Order**

Reprinted here with permission from CAMCO, Inc.

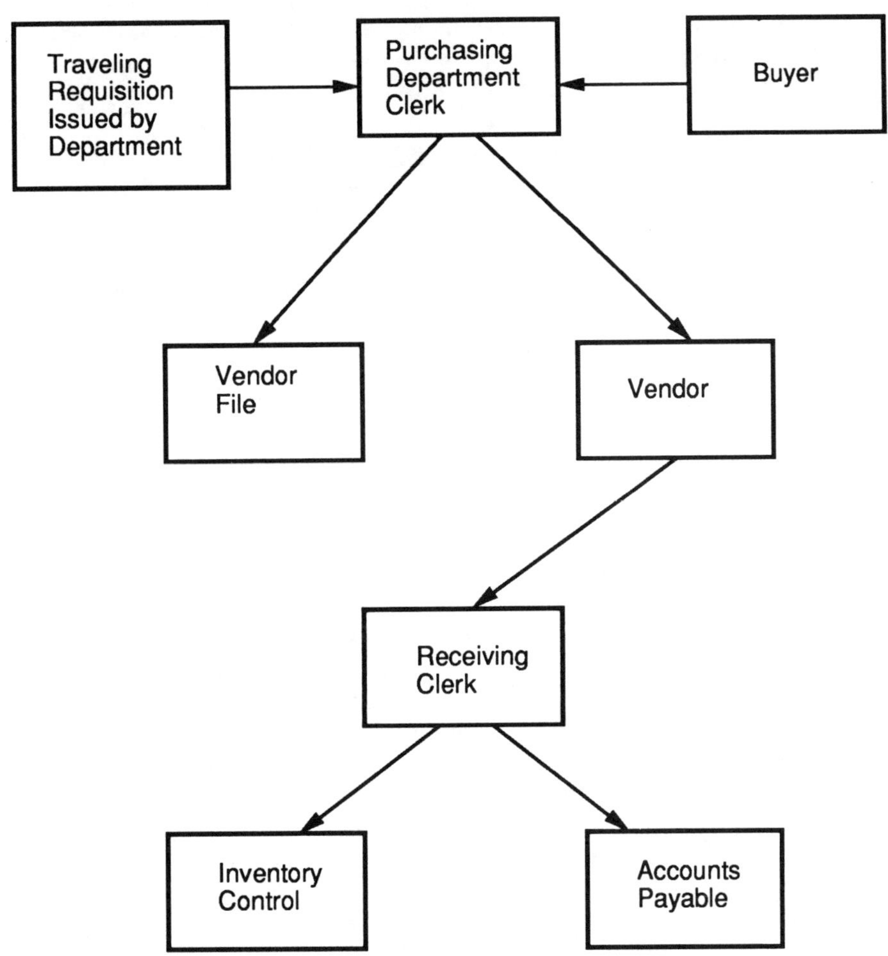


**Figure 12-9**
**CAMCO Purchase Order Flow Chart**

Reprinted here with permission from CAMCO, Inc.

form is filled out entirely by the requisitioner. The CAMCO's one-time requisition form is shown in Figure 12-10.

Some CAMCO vendors have on-line ordering systems. All delivery notes per month are summed up and one invoice per month is issued. This reduces the accounting transactions to one monthly payment instead of paying for each delivery separately.

## THE ADVANTAGES OF JUST-IN-TIME PURCHASING

In JIT purchasing, consideration is given to quality and cost, as well as frequent deliveries. Additionally, there are manufacturing considerations for simplifying the material flow, the assembly processes, and the inventory control and production planning and control considerations. For example, JIT companies prefer to assign a subassembly unit to one vendor who tests it and delivers it directly to the assembly line. This eliminates inventory control of components and their quality control because the subassembly unit is tested in the real-world working conditions.

Along with the inventory reductions, JIT purchasing systems also eliminate many service activities. A JIT relationship requires that a manufacturer has an ongoing JIT production program in place, particularly with regards to planning and control in small lots and a zero-inventory policy.

As with production manufacturing in small lots, zero-inventory in purchasing is accomplished through the producer-vendor accord, specifying frequent deliveries in small quantities, either daily or weekly, just in time for their use. Such frequent deliveries going directly to the producer's receiving dock or, sometimes, directly to the production line, become possible when applying *sole-source purchasing*. As in manufacturing, JIT purchasing is aimed at the continuous elimination of waste. Establishing trust between the producer and the vendor-supplier should be your first step in setting up a JIT relationship.

## A JIT PURCHASING PROGRAM—LONG REACH MANUFACTURING: A Case Study

Let's go back to our model company, Long Reach Manufacturing, to examine further a JIT purchasing program. The Long Reach JIT purchasing program contains typical objectives, the most significant of which are

1. Negotiate with vendors for value using the following criteria:

    a. *Quality*. Ensure that the vendor utilizes the necessary control techniques, including statistical process control, to supply the products meeting Long Reach/Rol-Lift quality standards.

REQUISITION NO.
A- 101541

7030 ARDMORE
HOUSTON, TEXAS 77054
P. O. BOX 14484
HOUSTON, TEXAS 77221
(713) 747-4000

CAMCO

**MATERIAL REQUISITION**
TAX EXEMPTION # 1-133517570-6

PURCHASE ORDER **No.** ______

☐ TAXABLE
☐ EXEMPT

DATE ______

| SUPPLIER | | | E.O. # ______ |
|---|---|---|---|
| | | | W.O. # ______ |
| REQUIRED AT CAMCO | SHIP VIA | FOB | CAMCO PART # ______ |

| QUANTITY | CODE | DESCRIPTION | PURCHASING DEPT. USE ONLY | |
|---|---|---|---|---|
| | | | | |
| | | | | |
| | | | | |
| | | | | |
| | | | | |
| | | | | |
| | | | | |
| | | | | |
| | | | | |
| | | | | |
| | | | | |

REQUISITIONED BY ______ APPROVED BY ______ RECEIVED BY VENDOR ______

Rev. 6/90 DATE REC.

**White - Purchasing**
**Green - Purchasing and/or Requisitioner**
**Yellow - Accounts Payable and/or Purchasing**
**Pink - Vendor**
**Gold - Requisitioner**

**Figure 12-10**
**CAMCO One-Time Requisition Form**

Reprinted herre by permission from CAMCO, Inc.

b. *Reliability*. A vendor should be able to meet all contractual delivery schedules.

c. *Price*. While the price is a factor in vendor selection, quality and reliability must be up to Long Reach/Rol-Lift standards, for a vendor to qualify as an approved supplier.

d. *Technical support*. Provide the necessary technical support to assist Long Reach/Rol-Lift in both product design development and problem solving.

2. Secure multiyear agreements using the following guidelines:

   a. Forecasted item usage will be shared with the vendor as required to meet each vendor's scheduling/planning needs.

   b. Longest price protection will be negotiated.

   c. Vendor will be encouraged to suggest alternative fabrication methods or dimensioning which might improve quality, save money, or increase value.

   d. Teaming relationship with the vendor will be developed, including a vendor involvement in the design process.

3. Certify vendors.

4. Increase the total number of blanket purchase items with control of releases at the point of use.

5. Reduce the total number of vendors by 50 percent.

## ASSUMING QUALITY WITH A JIT PURCHASING PROGRAM

Quality is a basic requirement in all JIT programs. Quality problems can build up an inventory and disrupt the material flow. JIT quality is achieved by considering two conditions:

1. Suitability (the correspondence to the technical specifications)
2. Price and availability

JIT vendors deliver components in time for assembly. At best, a fault can be detected during assembly, which will cause shutting down the line, with the resultant accumulation of WIP. At worst, the product will be assembled and will break down while being used by a customer. If out of 10 parts delivered 1 part is faulty, a customer order cannot be completed. Also, it means that the delivered components are not made according to the *order specification* (an order specification consists of technical specifications and the specified lot quantity). A lot quantity downsized below the specified amount due to quality problems will require an additional lot. Such a situation leads to additional production and service activities, storage and inventory control, production control, and inspection, as well as the involvement of supervisory staff and engineering.

## ACHIEVING INCREASED RELIABILITY IN JIT PROGRAMS THROUGH MANUFACTURER-VENDOR INTEGRATED PLANNING

Some vendors complain that producers push an inventory onto them, requiring frequent small-lot deliveries. In JIT, a vendor is an extension of the manufacturer's capacity, meaning that both the producer and the vendor are part of a single manufacturing system. The vendor's methods of production planning and control should correspond to that of the producer, so as to ensure the congruent cycle and the frequency of material flow.

JIT producers share their setup reduction techniques with vendors, in order to help them achieve economical production in small lots. The group technology is another ingredient which can be considered by vendors, along with the uniform plant loading.

Such sharing of JIT techniques and planning systems ensures that vendors are marching in-step with producers', which assists in keeping a uniform production tempo. Producers and vendors work as a team in accordance with the established common goals. A producer extends the JIT rule of planning executable plans into the vendor's operations. Vendors are provided with plans ahead of time to enable them to follow all planning steps of tactical and operational planning, and to develop an economical product mix. Ensuring the vendor's profitability is a cornerstone of the JIT producer-vendor relationship. A producer releases schedules to the vendor in time to process these jobs through the vendor's MPS and MRP systems. The vendor should be able to tune operations scheduling to the actual assembly line consumption rate.

A new business function, that can be referred to as the *buyer-planner,* merges these previously separated areas of buying and planning, thus strengthening the producer-vendor business relationship. Also, JIT purchasing transforms the role of shipping and receiving, since this function begins to work directly with the production department rather than with the stockroom.

In production, open work orders are delivered directly to the stockroom or the shop floor supervisor. In purchasing, there are additional tasks before these orders can reach the vendors' shop floor. There is a request for quotation, bidding procedures, negotiations, and credit approval at the beginning of the manufacturer-vendor relationship. In an already established manufacturer-vendor relationship, there are still requisition forms to be filled out and approved by the vendor's planning office and after the job is completed, there is the delivery and inbound inspection, as well as handling and storing operations, before the components will proceed to assembly. Thus, many JIT companies create a buyer-planner materials management position, in order to enhance the cooperation between their own and vendor planning departments. This contributes to an integration of the vendor's outbound logistic system with the manufacturer's inbound logistic system, through maintaining the centralized forecasting and production planning, ensuring data integrity, and highlighting the responsibility for the material planning procurement system.

## THE ADVANTAGES OF A LONG-TERM COMMITMENT TO A SINGLE-SOURCE SUPPLIER

A long-term commitment to a supplier (a one- to two-year agreement) ensures the stability of the producer-supplier relationship. A special producer-supplier relationship leads to better quality control, improved lead time, and a drastic reduction in the number of suppliers. The supplier who proves to be most reliable will eventually become a single-source supplier for the life of the product. These suppliers, who develop special producer-supplier relationships, are often certified.

The program of supplier certification often starts with the suppliers' product(s) being classified into A, B, and C groups according to the dollar value and according to the role they play in the production process. The certification is done for a single product or a product line. The main criteria is the reliability (quality and delivery) of the supplier and the supplier's desire to cooperate with the manufacturer.

The initial stage of certification includes

1. Identifying suppliers by commodity class
2. Documenting past quality and delivery achievements
   a. Percentage of defects reported (receiving audit)
   b. Percentage on time deliveries (delivery audit of performance analysis see Figure 12-11)
3. Holding a symposium for the communication of certificate benefits (long-term relationship, sole sourcing, and increased business)
4. Surveying the suppliers-vendors for process control through their organizations and informing them about the audit results
5. Consolidating the items with the qualified suppliers

At the beginning of the certification program, the number of suppliers may be significantly reduced, leaving an approved two or three suppliers for each of your commodities. These selected suppliers are candidates for a further certification. Your aim should be to select a single-source supplier with whom you can establish a special producer-supplier relationship, sometimes called *partnering*.

At Long Reach, a supplier becomes certified by meeting the minimum criteria in several important areas, such as quality, reliability, and technical support. They must also make 14 consecutive zero-defect shipments. Liz Tashakori,

## Performance Analysis for:

Part Number: ____________ Description: ____________

Supplier: ____________ Period: ____________

Type of Order: ____________

Method of Shipment: ____________

*Include date due and quantity received. One shipment per line.*

| | Early I | II | On-Time | Late I | II | III | IV |
|---|---|---|---|---|---|---|---|
| | Over 2.5 wks | 1–2.5 wks | 1 Wk to 1 Day | 2 Days–1 wk | 1–2 wk | 2–3 wk | 3 or more |
| | -18 or more | -8 to -17 | -7 to +3 | +4 to +10 | 11 to 17 | 18–24 | 25 or more |
| 1 | | | | | | | |
| 2 | | | | | | | |
| 3 | | | | | | | |
| 4 | | | | | | | |
| 5 | | | | | | | |
| 6 | | | | | | | |
| 7 | | | | | | | |
| 8 | | | | | | | |
| 9 | | | | | | | |
| 10 | | | | | | | |
| 11 | | | | | | | |
| 12 | | | | | | | |
| 13 | | | | | | | |
| 14 | | | | | | | |
| 15 | | | | | | | |

Comments: ____________

____________ Total Quantity Received: ____________

% On Time: ____________ No. of Defects: ____________ % Defects: ____________

Prepared by: ____________ Date: ____________

SCT 8/89

**Figure 12-11**
**The Supplier's Performance Analysis**

Reprinted here with permission from Long Reach Manufacturing Company.

the manager of purchasing, indicates that the company has established a multi-functional supplier certification team consisting of engineering, material control, production, quality control, plant maintenance, and other support groups. Periodic meetings are held with the suppliers (who are mostly distributors) and vendors to inform them about the certification program. Tashakori stresses: "Before the purchased components reach our factory, they can go through several stages of distribution—a distributor can purchase the components from another distributor. We attempt to bring a quality issue all the way down to those who produce the components. The distributors are expected to communicate to their vendors information regarding their progress in the certification program. We encourage the distributors to involve their vendors in our certification program, so that we can work with the producers and show them the benefits and ways how their products can be certified."

Long Reach puts an emphasis on the partnering for quality and on-time delivery rather than on the price. Management emphasizes that poor quality and late deliveries increase the initially quoted price. Conversely, a long-term relationship with a single-source supplier can bring overall costs down. The Long Reach policy is to pay for a value-added product and a value-added delivery, not for the inventory.

The next step is to write a multiyear agreement with each certified supplier. The provisions of a long-term agreement include the timely rolling forecasts and delivery schedules, lead time commitment, quality level, and price commitment. In turn, the supplier specifies his or her commitments to quality and on-time deliveries in accordance with JIT requirements. A long-term agreement includes the possibility of a disqualification of a vendor/supplier, if one or more conditions are not met. However, a probation program and help for the vendor-supplier to correct the problem also exists.

## USING BLANKET PURCHASE ORDERS

A *blanket order* is a special purchasing arrangement where the purchaser makes commitments to purchase a minimum to maximum quantity over a specified period of time. The usual term for a blanket order is about one year or until the prices are forced to change, or until changes to a product design occur. Under these circumstances, new order arrangements are negotiated. Multiyear agreements usually include blanket-type orders. The quantity can be further stated in a time-phased pattern. The negotiated prices can be either fixed or have a sliding scale, depending on the changing economic indices.

Blanket orders, also known as *open-end orders*, are a welcome feature of JIT purchasing because they reduce the cost of issuing and handling purchase orders. Subsequent deliveries are made against the order. Authorization for releases on blanket orders is done directly by production or inventory control without further involvement of the purchasing department. Figure 12-12 illustrates an annual contract blanket order. A blanket order is a general contract for quantities which will be required throughout a 12-month period—the note at the bottom of the contract states that all quantities on order represent an estimate of the annual usage—all material to be released as required by Long Reach. The same form is used as a *kanban*-type blanket order. Releases may be performed by workers through the media of *kanban* cards. Long Reach/Rol-Lift use a *kanban* card system with the *kanban* card as shown in Figure 12-12. The order quantity is standardized. When a bin is emptied, the card triggers order releases that are authorized by telephone or fax.

A *rolling schedule* is a more specific purchasing program stating a time-phased commitment to buy a specified product volume from the vendor. This type of program is not preferred by Long Reach/Rol-Lift, due to the fact that it places restrictions on the production program. In JIT purchasing, there should be fewer restrictions and more flexibility in quantities and delivery dates, although there is a general commitment to the vendor-supplier. Their involvement in planning goes back to the design and development stage of new products.

## HOW TO CONDUCT JIT PURCHASING NEGOTIATIONS

In purchasing, negotiations are the exchange of views and ideas on specific business issues, with the aim of coming to an acceptable agreement on delivery conditions and the price. Only issues where there is a disagreement are subject to questioning during the negotiations. JIT companies pursue different negotiating objectives, since JIT significantly changes the equation of the total cost structure. Unlike a bidding system, where an order is usually awarded to the lowest bidder, in JIT negotiations, the cost is not the major criterion. The total cost does not include the purchasing price only; rather it involves a contribution to the product value, and it targets the elimination of waste. Selecting a single supplier contributes to the elimination of waste, since many ordering and controlling procedures can be either simplified or entirely eliminated. It should be noted, however, that the cost of delivery will often increase, due to frequent deliveries in small lots.

Quality affects the product value to a greater degree than the purchasing price. Thus, quality is an undisputed factor and is not subject for negotiation. The JIT quality approach, JIT-total quality control (TQC), is known as a *zero-defect program.* Remarkably so, a zero-defect program eliminates the quality inspection, since there are no defects to inspect. The support services, such as warehousing and materials handling, are also reduced, due to the delivery in small lots at a higher frequency. Such substantial waste elimination provides negotiations with a wide scope of mutually beneficial prices. A buyer-planner negotiator is in a better position to negotiate ordering and delivering procedures. In addition,

**PURCHASE ORDER**

12300 AMELIA DRIVE • P.O. BOX 45069 • HOUSTON, TEXAS 77245-5069
(713) 433-9861 • FAX (713) 433-9710

| IMPORTANT |
|---|
| PURCHASE ORDER NO. |
| **MUST APPEAR ON ALL PAPERS, INVOICES AND PACKAGES.** |

TO

PLEASE SHIP TO

| DATE | VENDOR CODE | TERMS | QUOTATION | BUYER |
|---|---|---|---|---|
| DUE DATE | | F.O.B. | SHIP VIA | |
| PURCHASE AUTHORITY | | | | |

| [illegible] | QUAN. | STOCK NUMBER | DESCRIPTION | UNIT COST | EXTENDED COST |
|---|---|---|---|---|---|
| | | | | | |

☐ CONFIRMING - DO NOT DUPLICATE ☐ NON-CONFIRMING ☐ TAXABLE ☐ TAX EXEMPT - PERMIT NUMBER 1-36-3474825-8

**IMPORTANT: ACCEPTANCE OF THIS PURCHASE ORDER ASSENTS TO ALL INSTRUCTIONS, TERMS AND PROVISIONS ON FACE AND REVERSE SIDE HEREOF.**

| ORDER REMARKS |
|---|
| |

LONG REACH MANUFACTURING CO.

PURCHASING AGENT

ORIGINAL

**Figure 12-12**
**Long Reach Purchase Order Form Used for Blanket Order**

Reprinted here with permission from Long Reach Manufacturing Company.

HOUSTON, TEXAS

LITTLE ROCK, ARKANSAS

**COMPONENT PURCHASE CARD**

| | |
|---|---|
| PART NUMBER | |
| PART DESCRIPTION | |
| COMSUMPTION LOCATION | DELIVER TO: |
| USED FOR | |
| NUMBER OF CARDS | ____ OF ____ |

| | |
|---|---|
| VENDOR | |
| RELEASE QUANTITY | LEAD TIME |
| PURCHASE ORDER NUMBER | |
| PHONE NUMBER | |
| ACCOUNTING CODE | |
| VENDOR CONTACT | |
| VENDOR ADDRESS | |

FORM 56505

**Figure 12-13**
**Long Reach Kanban Purchase Card**

the negotiators deal with technical information, such as specifications and standards describing the purchased components and their functions in the product.

The buyer's-planner's function has been extended into a buyer-planner-cost estimator, which puts more emphasis on the product value during the negotiations. A significant feature of JIT purchasing negotiations is that it formulates a producer-supplier partnering arrangement widely recognized as a win-win situation. There are a number of techniques used by negotiating parties in order to arrive to a consensus on the debated issues. Here are some of them:

1. Negotiations are not just a discussion of various business issues—you must do your homework. Plan ahead. Develop objectives which you will try to achieve through negotiations. Predict main points of disagreements and prepare a strategy for possible arguments.
2. Stress the need for both parties to arrive to an agreement through concessions and compromises. You need to determine beforehand the extent of possible concessions essential to the other party, in order to ensure gains on the specific issues which are important to you.
3. Hold on and do not rush with your demand and concessions. Try to make your opponent do most of the talking. Experienced negotiators say that those who talk the most give up the most. Maneuver so that the other party asks for concessions. Then you can show that you are doing the best for your opponent. Consequently, you can expect the reciprocal concessions on the issues important to you.
4. In JIT-type negotiations, you should attempt to recognize the needs of the other party. Try to understand your opponent and be fair if you want a long-standing relationship. You, as a JIT manufacturer, have a better idea about your JIT requirements which must be complied to by the vendor (namely, frequent and timely deliveries in small lots, the elimination of an inbound inspection, and simplified purchasing procedures). Price is not the main issue. A price which may be fair in a conventional manufacturer-vendor relationship can put your vendor out of business in a JIT-type relationship. Thus, a single-source supplier is not the one who quotes the lowest price but the one who has a better technology and management systems to respond to your JIT needs. In JIT negotiations, you negotiate as if you were sitting at both sides of the negotiating table. In JIT-type negotiations, an adversarial attitude, so common in the business world, is replaced with the long-term commitments of both parties: the *vendor-supplier*, to deliver high-quality components in small quantities, frequently and on time, and the *manufacturer*, to provide a long- and medium-term reliable forecast, firm production schedules, and engineering and manufacturing systems support.

## USING AN IN-PLANT STOCKROOM TO SAVE THE TIME AND MONEY

Frequent JIT deliveries call for deliberate planning, close communication and other additional activities because of such a close relationship between the vendor-supplier and the manufacturer. This problem is partially resolved when selecting the suppliers that are in a close proximity to the manufacturer's plant. For example, in Japan, vendors are selected within a radius of 25 to 30 miles from the manufacturer's location.

Some companies try to avoid an additional transportation and receiving cost by establishing in-plant stockrooms. Such stores become popular for stocking raw materials and long lead time items, especially in situations where the supplier's production cycle is difficult to adjust to the producer's cycle. In this instance, the inventory acts as a buffer against the failure to deliver materials on time.

In-plant dedicated stores are located at the point of materials use. This way, materials are available when you require them, thus eliminating further purchasing and ordering procedures. You withdraw the quantity you require and just inform your supplier by a notification form. Planning is coordinated by you and the supplier. In-plant stockrooms are also known as *inventory on consignment*. In most instances, these are locked stores which you may enter when the materials are required for your production. In this case, the supplier does not carry the expenses for managing the store. An *in-plant stockroom agreement* may include a provision for recovery of additional overhead expenses, such as the inventory cost and store management.

In other cases, the supplier provides the staff to manage the stockroom and take delivery, as well as communicate to the supplier's plant the required production information, such as MPS and MRP schedules, and track purchase orders and inventory. Also, the agreements expect that you, the producer, will provide mid- and short-term rolling forecasts, updated monthly based on performance.

In the MRP environment, an in-plant store makes it easier to perform itemized scheduling: items' lead time is practically eliminated because most items are available on request and components are withdrawn in kits and paid for on the same invoice. Because purchase orders are eliminated, your accounting is simplified, and it is easier for you to keep track of and to provide a fast response to engineering changes. Your production department can plan and place orders without involving the purchasing department.

In-plant stores are also ideal for JIT-*kanban* material control, since it is your opportunity to stock start-up containers with components.

## USING AN AUTOMATED ORDER ENTRY TO INTEGRATE MANUFACTURER AND VENDOR PRODUCTION SYSTEMS

With an *automated order entry system*, your purchasing department has an immediate access to all vendors' inventory records. The advantage of this computer system is its timeliness: *on-line ordering* from an on-site terminal. This system allows the customer to enter a new order or add items to previously placed orders instantaneously without further paperwork. The customer can have access to item information regarding the available stock, for instance, quantity on order, back orders, orders in transit, bin location, item price, and the discount structure.

In some automated order entry systems, the customer enters the date and a computer generates a purchase order number. Summary billing may be included in the system (that is, bi-weekly billing). The automated order entry system eliminates many purchasing activities, including a significant reduction in paperwork and is a valuable feature of JIT elimination of waste programs.

The purchasing function becomes an effective weapon in business competition, due to constantly increasing purchasing contents in the final product, which often reaches 70 percent of the total costs. Today's purchasing people, with sophisticated management skills, lead the way in complex interfaces between manufacturers and suppliers.

Due to the fact that purchasing is part of the materials management system, it is in a strategic position to facilitate an uninterrupted material flow. The most important role of purchasing is to reduce nonvalue-adding operations, and to ensure a timely and uninterrupted supply of materials and components to all three stages of production with minimal inventory outlay. (The role of the purchasing function in a JIT-type material flow is illustrated in Figure 12-14).

## SUMMARY

Computer-based purchasing system at CAMCO, Inc. is shown in Figure 12-15. Integration is the prevailing mode of operations in contemporary business structures—an integration of planning levels, as well as the integration of business functions. In such organizations, the integration of purchasing into the overall business system (the integration of purchasing with other business and production functions, such as engineering, materials control, quality, inventory control, marketing, and finance) leads to purchasing departments becoming individual profit centers. There is a variety of business factors by which the purchasing function

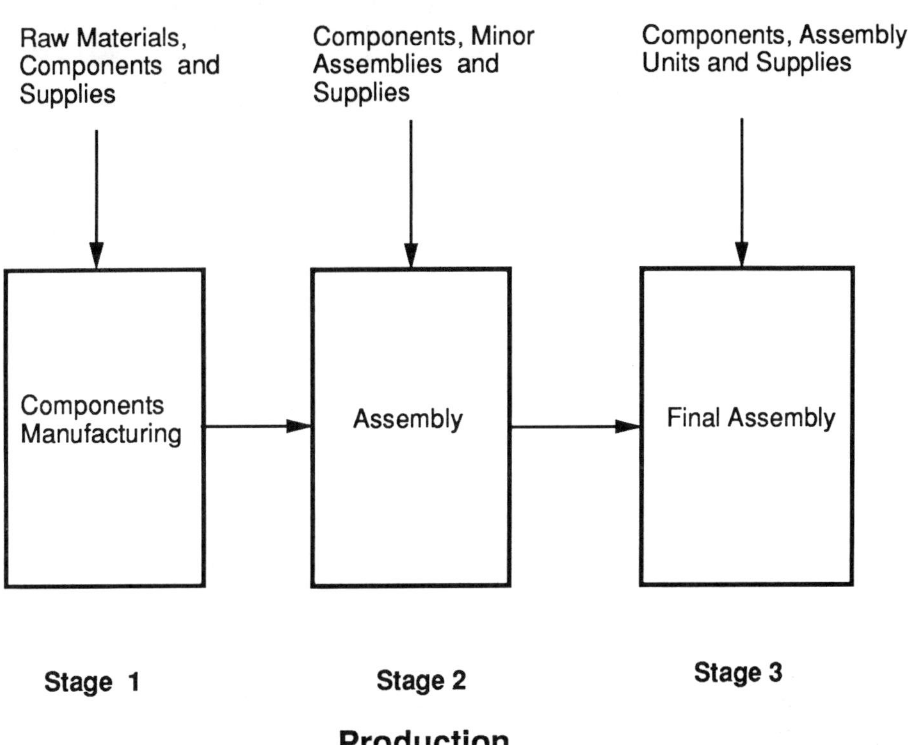


**Figure 12-14**
**How Purchasing Integrates with Three Stages of Production**

is judged, such as vendor quality, reliability, and timely delivery, rather than just the negotiated price. The bottom line is how effectively the purchasing function contributes to the organizational objectives of increased profit and improved return on the investment ratio (return on investment) through quality improvement and cost reduction. Purchasing cost centers are part of the total business cost accounting structure, which is discussed in the next chapter.

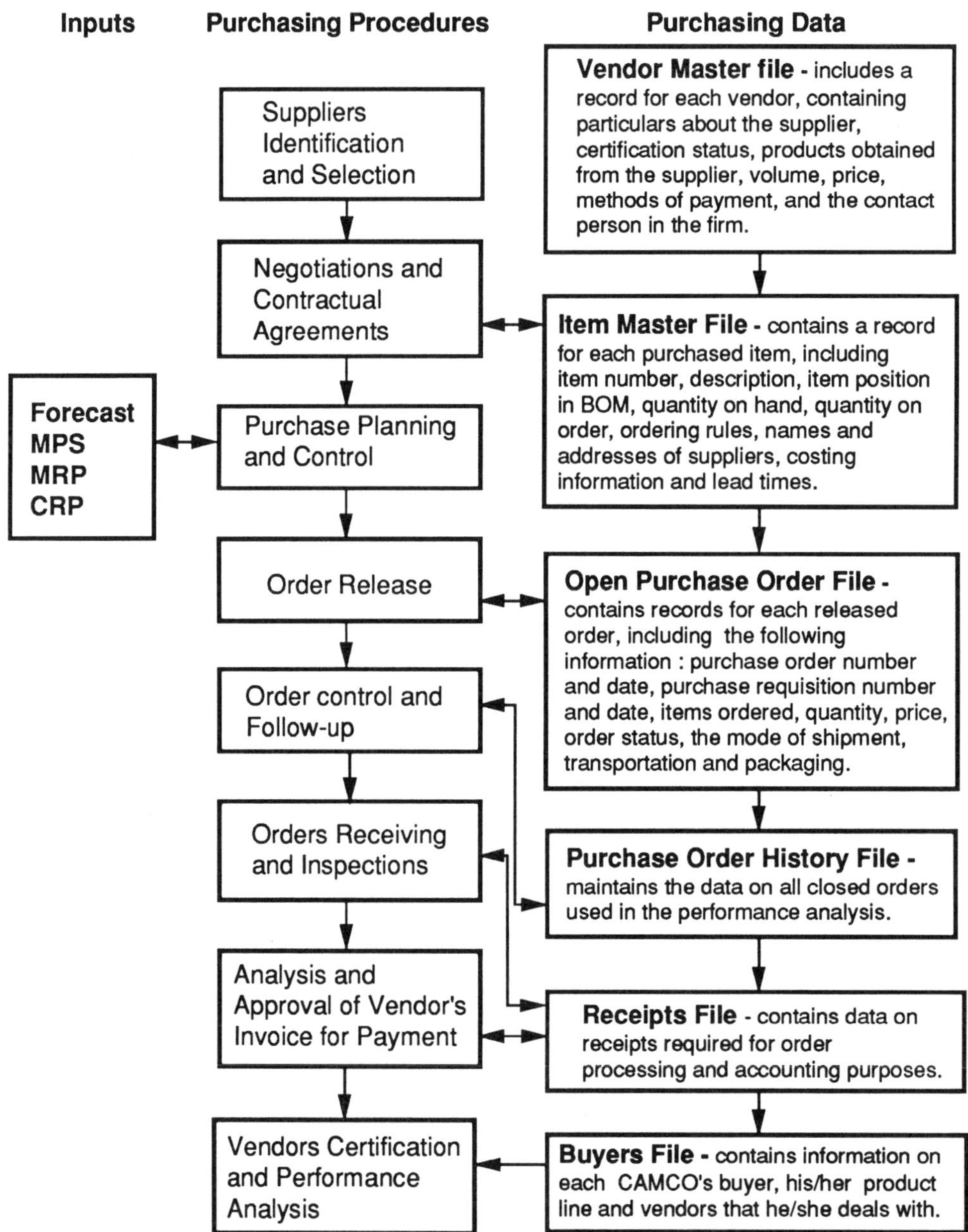


**Figure 12-15**
**Purchasing System at CAMCO, Inc. Inputs, Procedures and Data Files**

# 13

# Improving Cost Accounting Systems for Integrated Operations Management

Accounting, particularly cost accounting, applies discrete quantitative standards which can outline the direction in which an entire production-operation discipline can develop.

The significance of cost accounting in any good production plan is in that it influences the product value through an analysis of product costs. In an organization, a cost accountant possesses unique information based in cost analysis and internal performance evaluation, which, in a constructive way, can assist production managers in identifying problem areas and improving performance. Despite this need, not all cost accounting systems reflect the latest development in production management. It has been claimed that our cost accounting methods are outdated and that there is a need for integrating cost accounting systems into a basic production system, so that they become a useful management tool.

Traditionally, cost accounting has been seen as part of general accounting, which provides information for financial reporting on inventory status, along with general production cost information. In the past few years, however, the perception of cost accounting has dramatically changed from being a reactive financial reporting business function to becoming an active production management tool. Cost accounting establishes its rightful place as an important production management function for the tactical and operational production analysis and decision making at all levels of production planning and control. Essential functions served by the cost accounting are providing information in support of three types of activities:

1. Inventory valuation
2. Cost analysis
3. Internal performance evaluation

*Inventory valuation* requires that the cost of production is allocated to all the items produced. The total cost of direct material, direct labor, and overheads is applied to work-in-process, finished goods in stock, and goods sold.

Until recently, the focus of cost accounting was on an inventory valuation, which is also the basis for compiling information for cost analysis and an internal performance evaluation. Back in 1988, in the *Harvard Business Review,* Robert Kaplan stated that cost accounting systems designed mainly to value an inventory for financial and tax statements are not giving managers the accurate and timely information they need to promote operating efficiencies and measure product costs.* However, this situation is rapidly changing, due to companies conducting an intensive search for new ways to control their production activities, which recognize an opportunity the cost accounting presents for accomplishing this management function.

Effective management decision making requires information concerning the acquisition and usage of business resources. Cost accounting, which is identified as a part of managerial accounting, is aimed at assisting management in choosing the right course of actions from among the set of alternatives and providing the accumulated cost structures and analysis of organization's products and services. Thus, cost accounting is also known as *product costing.*

Cost accounting, or internal accounting, achieves its objectives through identifying, selecting, accumulating, measuring, interpreting, analyzing, and communicating information vital for internal and external decisions and performance reporting. You, as a manager, need information for evaluating the performance of individual production units. When production departments are structured as cost centers, you can control them as autonomous economic entities.

Often, one department comprises several cost centers reporting to one administrative authority. The purpose of a cost accounting system is to trace all production costs to cost centers for evaluation performance of parts of organization and their viability as an economic investment.

---

*"One Cost System Isn't Enough." *Harvard Business Review*, Jan-Feb, 1988, #66 pp. 61-66.

## UNDERSTANDING COST CLASSIFICATION

In cost accounting, business resources are represented in two forms: a cost or an expense. A *cost* is the value of assets used in acquiring another asset. An *expense* is the value of an asset given up to generate revenue. In production resources, an accumulated cost is the production cost, while resources directly assisting the sales force become expenses.

Cost accounting assembles and interprets information on stages where an asset is transformed partially or completely from one form into another. Two types of cost are identified: variable cost and fixed cost.

*Variable cost* is a cost that changes proportionally to the volume of an activity or its qualitative level. Figure 13-1 illustrates the cost classification used in cost accounting. *Fixed cost* is a cost which remains unchanged regardless of the volume of an activity or its qualitative level. There are two categories of cost, identified according to how the cost can be traced to the cost objective, which is an activity under examination. These are direct cost and indirect cost. *Direct cost* is a cost which can be easily traced to a cost object activity, whereas *indirect cost* is a cost which is not easily traced to a cost object.

Direct costs are direct material cost and direct labor cost. A cost is direct if it can be physically identified with a cost object and measured in terms of the quantity of input. Direct material and direct labor are also known as the *price cost.*

Indirect cost includes all costs other than direct material and direct labor costs. It includes indirect labor and indirect materials and overheads. There is a separate cost category known as the *manufacturing cost*, identified as a type of cost comprising direct materials, direct labor, and manufacturing overhead costs.

manufacturing cost = direct labor + direct materials + manufacturing overhead

Figure 13-2 illustrates elements of the product manufacturing cost.

*Manufacturing overhead costs* sometimes called factory burden or plant overhead, consists of the variable factory overhead and fixed factory overhead, or common cost.

*Common costs* are those costs which provide benefits for all company products, but do not vary with small changes in the volume of production (for example, land and buildings).

The sum of direct labor and overhead is known as the *conversion cost* or the *processing cost*. The conversion cost is calculated as follows:

conversion cost = direct labor cost + factory overhead cost

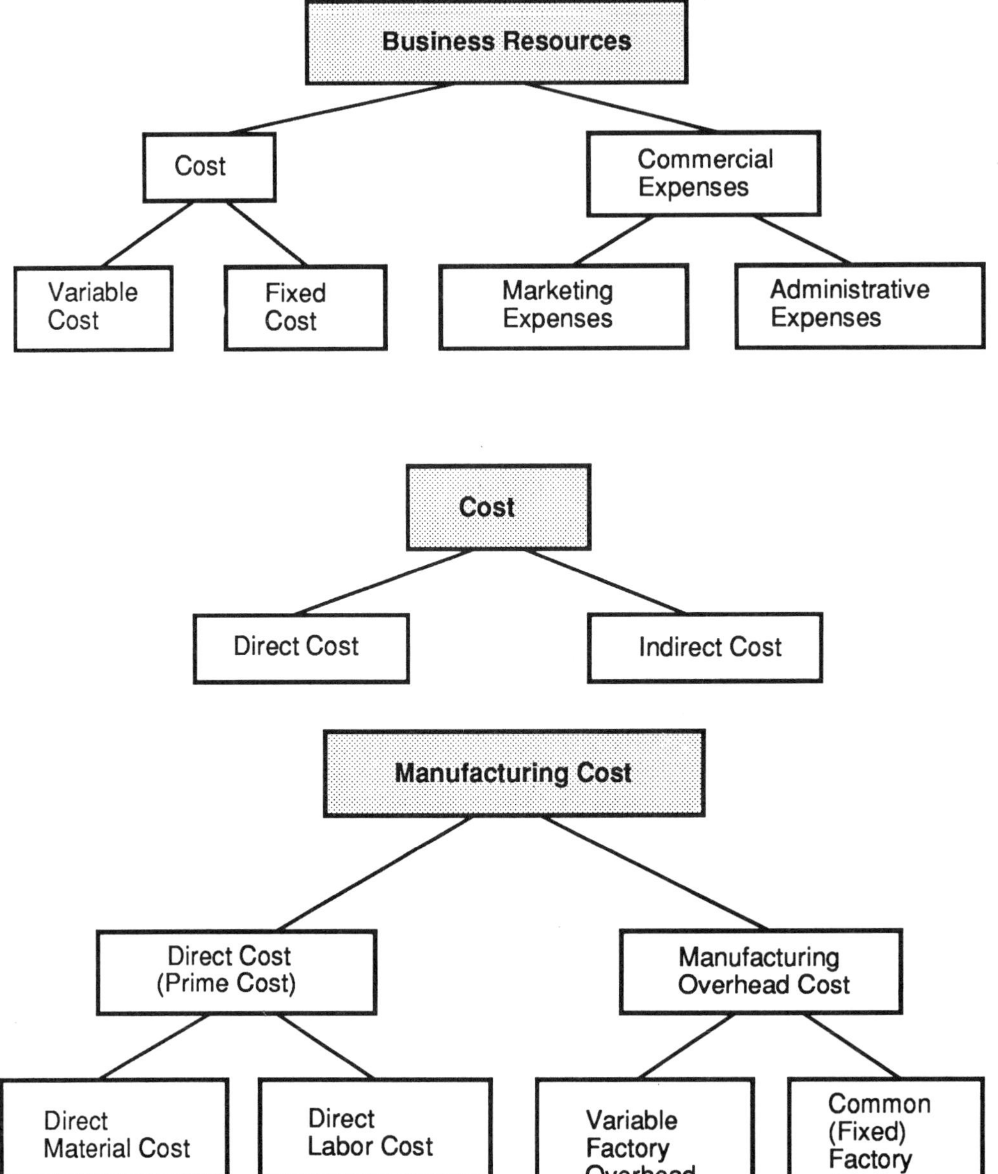


**Figure 13-1**
**Cost Classification**

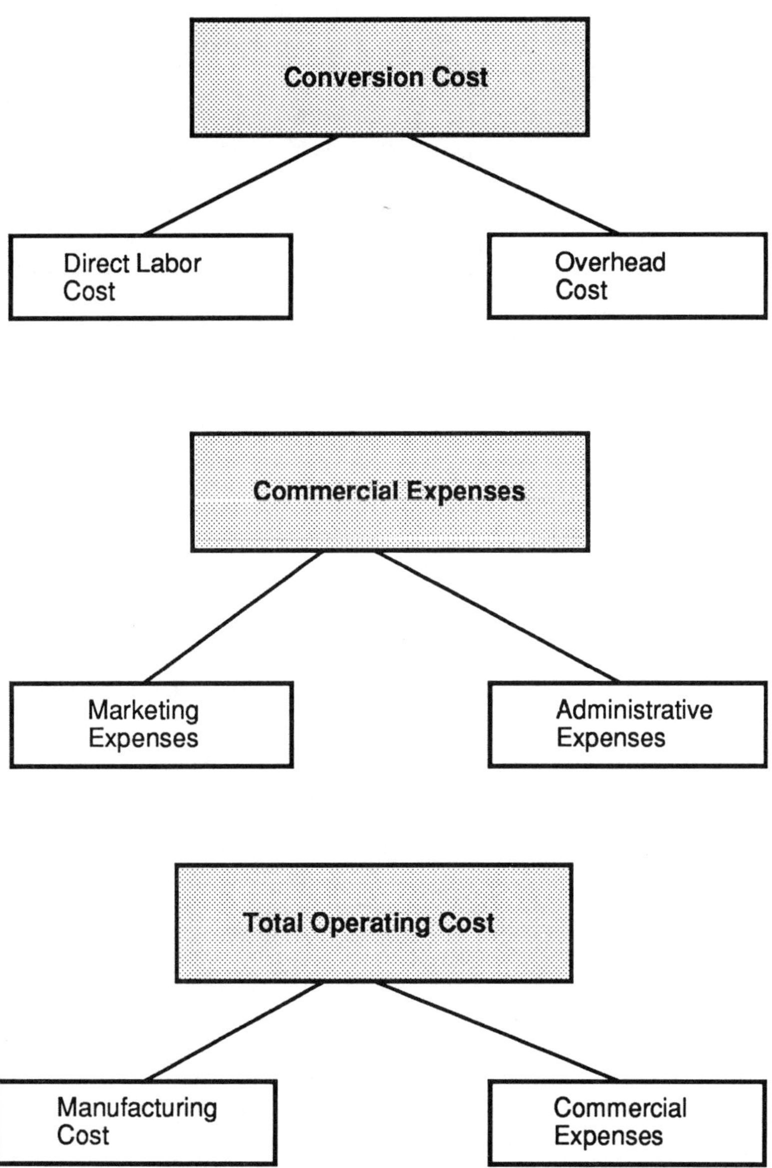


**Figure 13-1** (continued)

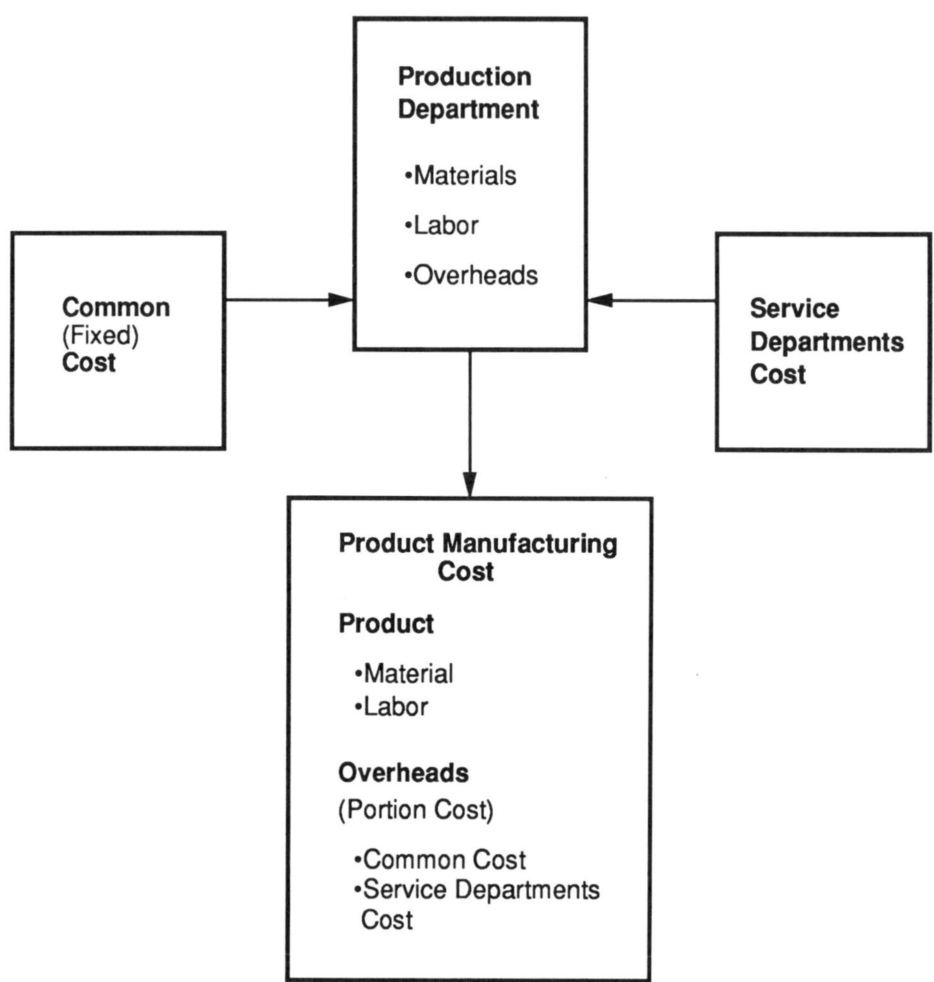


**Figure 13-2**
**The Elements of Product Manufacturing Cost**

*Commercial expenses* consist of marketing expenses and administrative expenses. Total operating cost consists of manufacturing costs and commercial expenses. How cost categories are reflected in business revenue is shown in Figure 13-3.

*Marketing expenses* include sales and delivery expenses, starting from the point of the product completion. *Administrative expenses* include administrative and office salaries, rent, legal expenses, and auditing expenses. Commercial expenses are calculated as follows:

commercial expenses = marketing expenses + administrative expenses

total operating cost = manufacturing cost + commercial expenses

Elements of total operating costs are shown in Figure 13-4. Initially, cost accounting was applied to the inventory valuation and income determination. Now, cost accounting is seen also as a powerful tool in strategic, tactical, and operational decision making and analysis.

## ALLOCATING COMMON COSTS TO ENSURE PROFITABLE PRODUCT LINES

In contemporary manufacturing systems, the principal mission of cost accounting is to collect information which assists you in estimating the cost and viability of production of individual products and product lines. Realistic cost estimates can uncover unprofitable products, making them subject to a further management analysis. Without cost accounting, these unprofitable products are often concealed under average efficiency figures. In most instances, high production costs can be improved through combined efforts of manufacturing engineering and production management.

The mission of cost accounting in a JIT system is to highlight those activities where the cost can be reduced and to select an activity that can be a subject for the elimination of waste. The cost of a product consists of all the cost directly traceable to it—direct labor and direct materials plus its proportional share of common costs or factory overheads.

The assignment of direct manufacturing costs to different jobs is a straightforward task since the material can be traced to different jobs via material requirements and direct labor cost (via a labor reporting system).

A major concern of cost accounting is to ensure that a fair share of the factory overheads, including departmental overheads and service departments costs, is assigned to the finished goods. This is known as the cost allocation. *Cost allocation* is a proportional assignment of a cost or a group of costs to multiple cost objectives. *Cost allocation* in a costing system is illustrated in Figure 13-5.

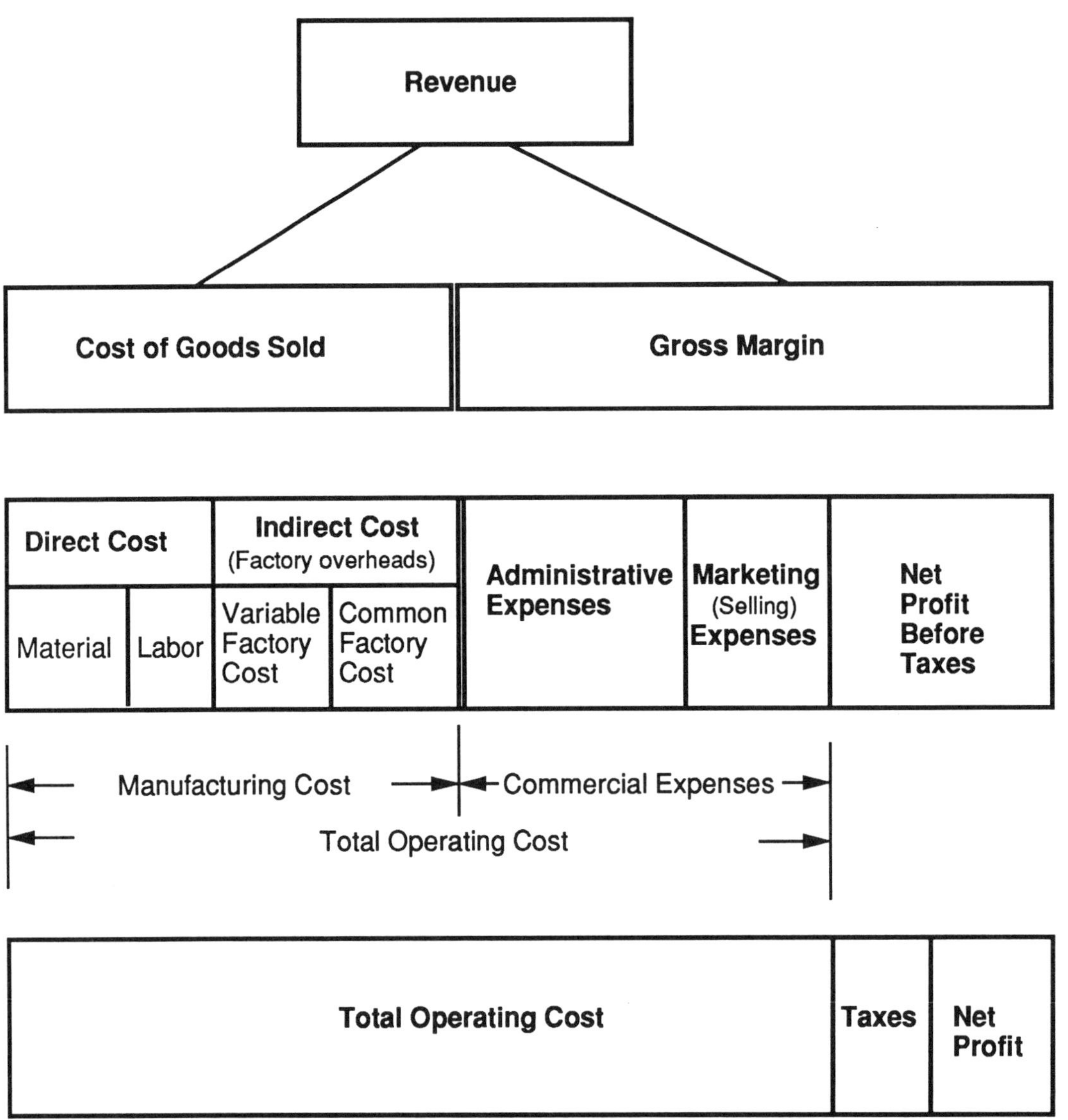


**Figure 13-3**
**The Cost Categories**

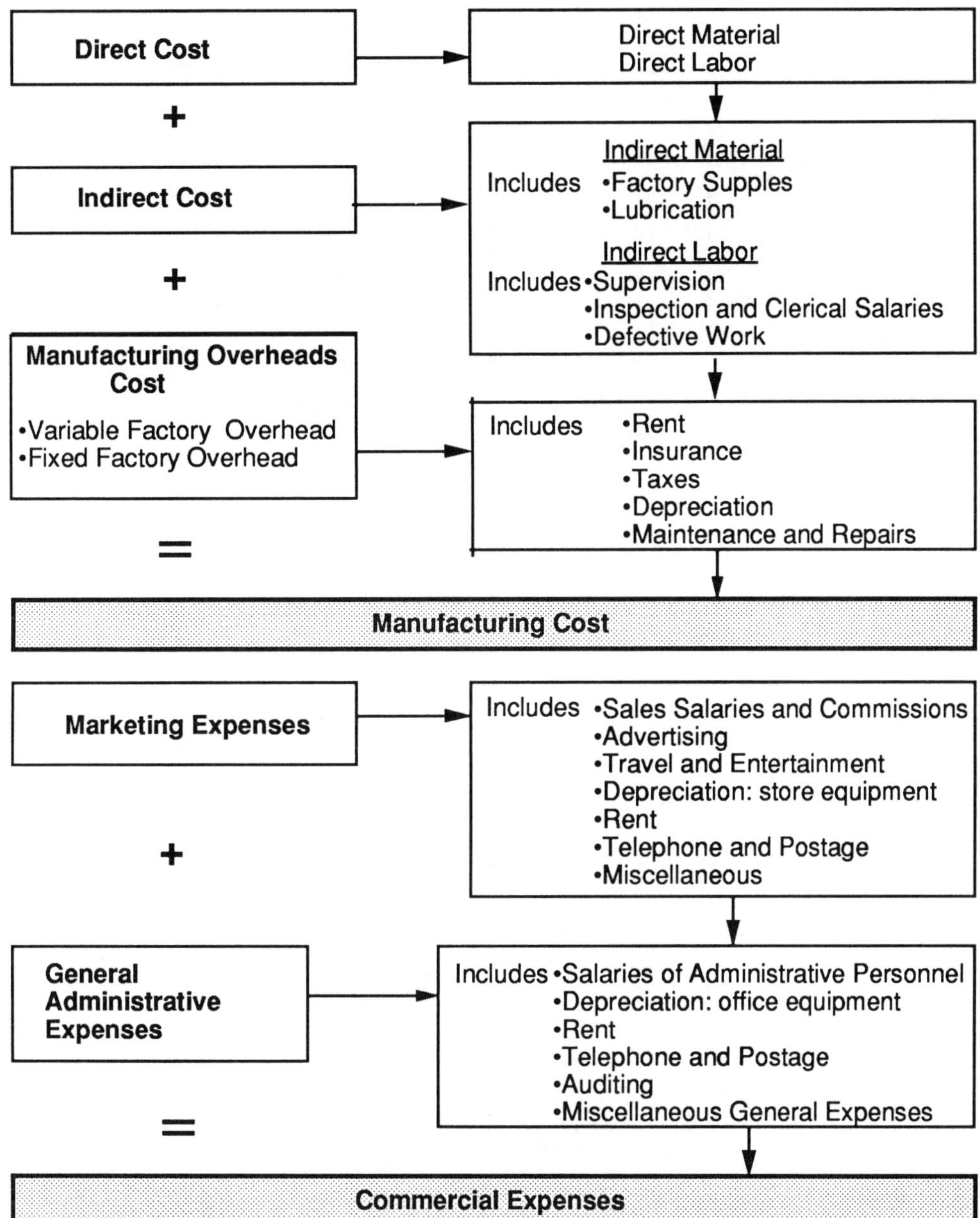


**Figure 13-4**
**Classification of Operating Cost Components**

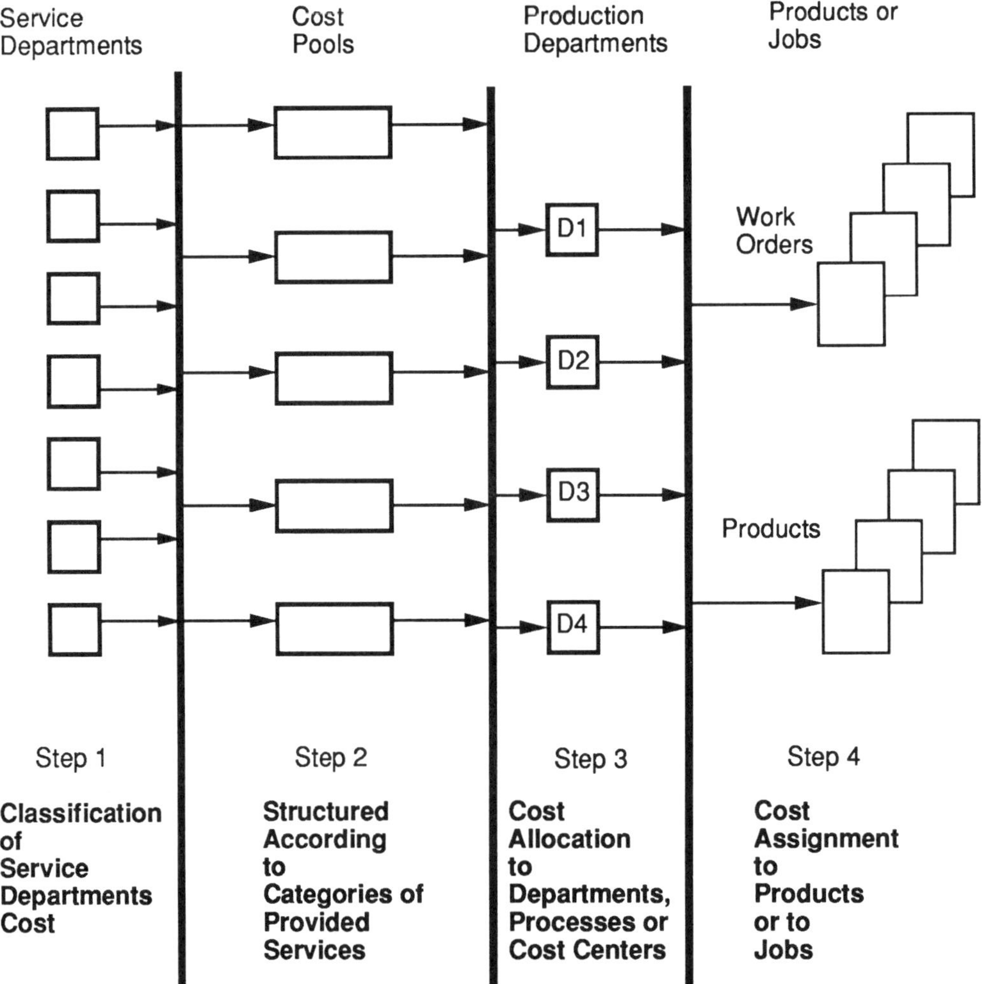


**Figure 13-5**
**Cost Allocation Applying Cost Pools**

Allocated costs consist of direct material and direct labor plus overheads, which are calculated as a proportion of common fixed costs and service departments costs.

Allocation of service department costs refers to the distribution of the costs of facilities and resources, which are not directly involved in the production of goods but which provide service to production departments. For example, housekeeping is a service department because it provides cleaning and janitorial services to manufacturing departments.

Cost allocation is an important cost accounting consideration in any organization. For example, how should a computer cost be allocated to various departments? How should the administration cost, cost of sales, and advertising and services departments costs be split? It is commonly accepted that the cost allocation is conducted mainly for external reporting, not for an internal use. Such an opinion is changing, due to the fact that cost accounting is being seen as a powerful tool for the production analysis. For example, in one company, the foreman in charge of a conveyor line for painting and drying of kitchen trays has indicated that the cost of the paint alone is higher than the price of the tray in a retail store. One possible explanation for this is that the company had multiproduct lines ranging from an office equipment to kitchen appliances and hardware and that the cost structures of individual products were not controlled.

Some companies use their accounting systems to generate a product line income statement assisting in the detection of unprofitable products. After such analysis, management can make a decision on the continuation of such a product or product line. In many cases, a design audit coupled with a Just-in-Time continuous improvement program converts products previously produced at a loss into profitable product lines.

The selection of the basis for your cost objective, your cost pool, and for the assignment of a single cost to multiple objects is the essence of cost accumulation and cost allocation. A *cost objective* is an independent variable representing an action to which an accumulated cost is allocated. An example of a cost objective is a product or a service, a functional department recipient of such a service, or individual processes of building a product. The cost is usually traced to responsibility centers—divisions or departments where the cost objects originating the cost are located.

A *cost pool* is a grouping of indirect costs allocated to the cost objective. An example of a cost pool is the grouping of costs according to direct or indirect labor costs, direct material costs, and overheads.

The best reflection of the cause and effect of costs and activities takes place in homogeneous pools. It is said that a cost pool is homogeneous if each activity whose cost is included in the pool has a cause and effect relationship to the cost objective identical to other activities contributing their cost to this cost pool.

Homogeneous cost pools call for departmental cost pool structures rather than the plantwide cost pool. Departmental cost pools can result in a representative relationship or overhead costs with specific jobs. For example, a ratio of direct labor-hours to indirect labor-hours is different in labor-intensive versus machine-intensive processes. In such instances, production labor and machine-hours are not representative as a basis for the cost pool structure. Also, departments can differ in the cost of tooling purchasing and maintenance costs. In this instance, indirect costs lose their individual identity when making use of a single plantwide cost pool having a single labor- and machine-hour base.

A *cost allocation base* is a unit of a measure relating a cost pool to the cost objective. For example, if we are trying to allocate such a cost pool as the factory overhead to a job order cost objective, we can use such cost allocation base as direct machine-hours, direct labor-hours, direct labor cost, or direct material cost. An allocation base is used in cost allocation for establishing a relationship between the overhead cost and the cost object. Two or more allocation bases might be used within each department for different categories of overhead costs.

## Procedures for Allocating Service Departments Operating Costs

A significant issue in cost accounting is how to allocate the cost of service departments—service to production and service to central administration. Usually, companies allocate their central service cost to profit centers—either divisions or departments.

Service departments benefit manufacturing departments, despite the fact that they are not directly involved in producing products. A service department's operating cost is a sizable part of the total operating cost, though. The storeroom, the purchasing department, the computer center, and the planning and control department—all render a needed service to production departments.

The total expenses for operating service departments are considered overheads, which should be equally distributed among the production departments. These expenses can be ascertained by direct accounting of wages and salaries, heat and light, power and supplies. Service department expenses are usually apportioned among production departments as shown in Figure 13-6.

Mechanization and automation of production processes have resulted in numerous changes in cost structures of manufacturing companies—namely, the direct labor cost is a decreasing percentage of the total manufacturing costs, while factory overhead costs are correspondingly on the increase. In manufacturing companies, total factory overhead costs—from corporate services and service departments through production departments—usually range from 26 percent to 55 percent of the product cost. Increasing overhead costs reveal the importance of the manner in which these costs are allocated to individual products. The effectiveness of any allocation method depends upon the selection of a proper relationship between the manufacturing overheads and the production activities which have caused the overheads. The selection of a correct method can reveal the underlying causes and problem areas in unprofitable products, thus targeting these products for continuous improvement programs.

### TWO APPROACHES TO CLASSIFYING SERVICE DEPARTMENT COSTS

There are two approaches to classifying service department costs:

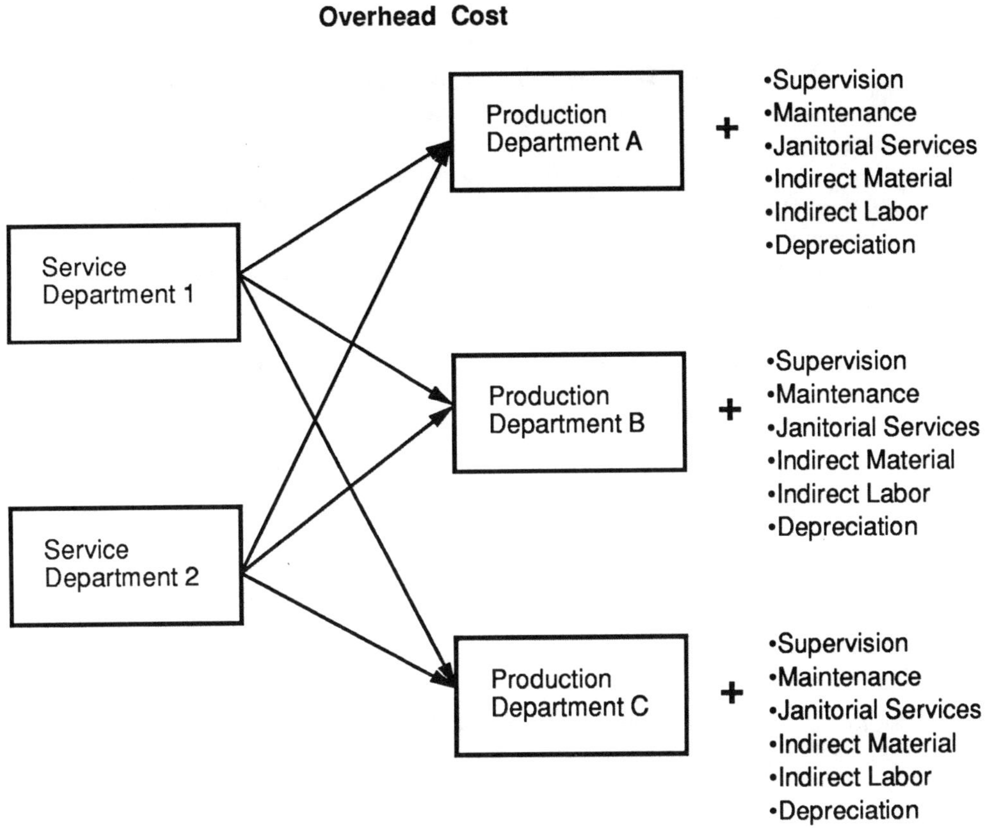


**Figure 13-6**

**Overhead Cost. How the Expenses of Service Departments are Allocated to Production Departments**

1. The *single-cost method*—collecting service department costs into a single-cost pool. This method does not make a distinction between a fixed cost and a variable cost.
2. The *dual-cost method*—collecting service department costs into two or more cost pools. Under this method, service department cost items are classified into either a fixed or a variable category.

## Allocating Service Department Costs and Common Costs

Cost allocation is the distribution of the service department cost and common cost to the production departments. Various allocation bases can be applied to fixed and variable costs, thus providing better information for the performance analysis. In Figure 13-6, service departments' cost allocation is accomplished by a single-cost method, without the differentiation into a fixed or a variable cost.

The total factory expense for a production department is estimated as a sum of the direct cost for this department plus a proportion of operational costs of each service department that provides services to production departments. For the example shown in Figure 13-6, the factory expense is calculated as follows:

$$P_A = D_C + aS_1 + bS_2$$

where

$P_A$ = factory expense of production department A

$D_C$ = the direct cost of operating a production department

$S_1$, $S_2$ = total expenses of operating service departments 1 and 2, respectively

$a$ = the proportion of total expenses of operating service departmen $S_1$, incurred by department A

$b$ = the proportion of total expenses of operating service department $S_2$, incurred by department A

There are several methods to apportion the total operating expenses of service departments to production departments. The *relative cost method* is used quite often. Using this method, the costs are apportioned according to the volume of work done by the production departments or according to the total labor or machine-hours performed during the preceding time period.

*Example*: Let's allocate your service department's total cost of $480,000 to four production departments with the following capacity:

| Production Department | Total Machine-Hours | Proportion of Total Hours | Allocated Service Cost |
|---|---|---|---|
| D1 | 5,000 | 10/100 | $ 48,000 |
| D2 | 6,000 | 12/100 | 57,600 |
| D3 | 17,000 | 34/100 | 163,200 |
| D4 | 22,000 | 44/100 | 211,200 |
| Total | 50,000 | | $480,000 |

The allocated service cost is added to the production department cost to find the total operating cost for this production department.

In the example, the allocation base is a machine-hour of capacity. However, depending on department, the base can also be a maintenanceh-our or the number of maintenance calls for a maintenance department. The allocation base for allocation of the personnel department cost can be the number of new hires, while for computer services it can be the number of hours of central processing time devoted to each user. This allocation is estimated applying a single-cost method.

In a dual-cost method, the total service department cost of $480,000 (in the example) is separated into a fixed cost and a variable cost. Consequently, the fixed cost will be allocated according to the *actual capacity* of departments, while the variable cost will be allocated according to the *utilized capacity.*

## USING THE ONE-STEP AND TWO-STEP DIRECT ALLOCATION METHOD

The allocation of a service department cost only to final users, ignoring the services rendered by one service department to another, is known as the one-step *direct allocation method.* Another method of allocating cost to production departments is accomplished by taking into account the cost of services provided by one service department to another. The allocation of a service department's cost to the end user, taking into account the interaction of service departments, is a *two-step direct method* of cost allocation.

To illustrate this method, let us consider an example of an interactive cost allocation for three service departments and three production departments. Here, the allocation of cost is performed in two steps.

The first step is to allocate each service department cost to all other production and service departments using the direct proportion method explained in example 1.

| Service Department | Cost Traced to Service Department | Cost Allocated to Service Department | | | Cost Allocated to Production Department | | |
|---|---|---|---|---|---|---|---|
| | | M | J | EL | D1 | D2 | D3 |
| Maintenance | 180,000 | — | 14,000 | 8,000 | 44,000 | 86,000 | 28,000 |
| Janitorial | 42,000 | 4,000 | — | 2,000 | 10,000 | 14,000 | 12,000 |
| Electrical | 90,000 | 3,000 | 1,000 | — | 26,000 | 22,000 | 38,000 |

Here, the cost of service departments has been divided among all the users of these services. The next step is to find the total cost for each service department by combining the cost traced to service departments with the cost allocated to each service department from other service departments.

total cost = cost traced + cost allocated

Maintenance department: 180,000 + (4,000 + 3,000) = 187,000
Janitorial department: 42,000 + (14,000 + 1,000) = 57,000
Electrical department: 90,000 + (8,000 + 2,000) = 100,000

Now we can allocate the total service departments cost to final users, applying the direct proportion method.

The proportional user of services is estimated in such a way, as if the services of service departments were provided only to production departments. For example, the maintenance department cost allocated to production departments is calculated as follows:

Maintenance cost allocated = Dl + D2 + D3 = 100%

44,000 + 86,000 + 28,000 = 158,000 = 100%

The proportions in our example are then as follows:

D1 = 27,85%, D2 = 54,43%, D3 = 17,72%

| Service Department | Total Cost | Cost Allocated to Production Department D1 | D2 | D3 |
|---|---|---|---|---|
| Maintenance | 187,000 | 52,080 | 101,784 | 33,136 |
| Janitorial | 57,000 | 15,835 | 22,167 | 18,998 |
| Electrical | 100,000 | 30,230 | 25,580 | 44,190 |

Figure 13-7 and 13-8 show the allocation factor and the direct burden rate allocation to production departments. This is a one-step allocation method used at CAMCO. Cost allocation should be a tool that you make use of for the total cost reduction. Since managers of production departments are responsible for the costs allocated to their departments, they should be able to control these costs as part of continuous improvement.

In previous examples, we have discussed the direct cost allocation method, where the allocation of a service department cost is proportional to the utilization of its services by production departments. An argument against the direct proportional cost allocation is that user departments do not have real control over the cost per unit of service, which depends entirely on how efficiently service departments are managed and controlled. In proportional cost allocation, production departments do not know the actual cost of services until after the services have been rendered. This prevents them from reacting to changes in the cost per unit of service.

## USING THE STANDARD ALLOCATION METHOD

An allocation method, using standard prices per unit of service and standard quantities allowed, helps production managers to make a decision on the volume of a service to request. A standard service cost and standard quantities motivate service departments to improve their efficiency. For example, if the cost per unit of service is too high, there will be less demand for these services from production departments. Consequently, service departments will be forced to

CAMCO, INC. JANUARY 1, 1991
BURDEN FACTOR ALLOCATION TABLE*

| MACHINE NUMBER | MACHINE CENTER DESCRIPTION | ALLOCAT. FACTOR | ADJUSTED DIRECT LABOR HOURS | BUDGETED DIRECT LABOR HOURS |
|---|---|---|---|---|
| | WORK CENTER 01 | | | |
| 01-01 | TURRET LATHE | | | |
| 01-02 | ENGINE LATHE | | | |
| 01-05 | TURRET LATHE | | | |
| 01-06 | L&S 7/8 SPINDLE | | | |
| 01-07 | B&S LATHE | | | |
| 01-09 | DRILL D&L | | | |
| 01-11 | 1-AB AUTO LATHE | | | |
| 01-12 | TURRET LATHE (LARGE) | | | |
| 01-13 | 1-AC AUTO LATHE | | | |
| 01-15 | 2-AB AUTO LATHE | | | |
| 01-17 | 2-AC AUTO LATHE | | | |
| 01-20 | NC J&L 4515 | | | |
| 01-21 | NC 4515 COMBI | | | |
| 01-23 | MAZAK M-5 | | | |
| 01-24 | NC MAZAK PM | | | |
| 01-25 | MAZAK-FMS | | | |
| 01-26 | SLANT 15 CNC | | | |
| 01-27 | ENGINE LATHE LARGE | | | |
| 01-28 | DRILL STANLEY | | | |
| 01-29 | L&S 10 5/8 SPINDLE | | | |
| 01-35 | ENGINE LATHE MED. | | | |
| 01-36 | RWK ENGINE LATHE SMALL | | | |
| 01-37 | REWORK MILLS | | | |
| 01-38 | RWK ENGINE LATHE LARGE | | | |
| 01-39 | NC K&T 180 MILL | | | |
| 01-40 | NC K&T EA MILL | | | |
| 01-41 | BRIDGEPORT MILL | | | |
| 01-42 | S-15 UNIVERSAL MILL | | | |
| 01-44 | 5 H VERTICAL MILL | | | |
| 01-45 | CINCINNATI MILL | | | |
| 01-46 | GUN FRILL | | | |
| 01-47 | BALLIZER | | | |
| 01-48 | POST CELL - FMS | | | |
| 01-51 | REDA - FMS | | | |
| 01-55 | GRINDER 12X36" | | | |
| 01-57 | SHAPER | | | |
| 01-60 | DEBURR | | | |
| 01-61 | MARKING | | | |
| 01-65 | SAW | | | |
| 01-69 | HAND OR VIBR. FINISH | | | |
| 01-99 | WIP DATA CONTROL | | | |
| | TOTAL | | | |
| | WORK CENTER O2 | | | |
| 02-80 | SAFETY VALVE ASSY. | | | |
| 02-81 | ASSY. THIRD PARTY REQ. | | | |
| 02-82 | TOCCO INDUCTION WELD | | | |
| 02-84 | SMALL GL & WL | | | |
| 02-86 | LARGE PACKERS & ORIF. | | | |
| 02-89 | PAINT | | | |
| 02-99 | PROBLEM SAFETY VALVE | | | |
| | TOTAL | | | |

*Note: The allocation factor is used to allocate budgeted expenses from departments to machine centers.

**Figure 13-7**
**The Allocation Factor at CAMCO, Inc.**

Reprinted here with permission from CAMCO, Inc.

CAMCO, INC. JANUARY 1, 1991
BURDEN RATE ALLOCATION TABLE

| | | DIRECT DEPARTMENTS | | | | | |
|---|---|---|---|---|---|---|---|
| EXPENSE CODE | DESCRIPTION | SHOP 550-A2 | FMS 550-C2 | ASSEMBLY 550-A3 | FABR 55-A5 | FABRICAT 550-A4 | TOTAL |
| 101 | SALARIES-OFFICERS | | | | | | |
| 102 | SALRIES-MANAGERS | | | | | | |
| 103 | SALARIES-EXEMPT | | | | | | |
| 104 | SALARIES-MONTHLY NON-EX. | | | | | | |
| 105 | SALARIES-HOURLY NON-EX. | | | | | | |
| 106 | MG SALARIES-FOREMEN | | | | | | |
| 107 | MFG WAGES-DIRECT LABOR | | | | | | |
| 108 | MFG WAGES-INDIRECT LABOR | | | | | | |
| 109 | PREMIUM PAY-OVERTIME | | | | | | |
| 122 | EMPLOYEE-BENEFIT | | | | | | |
| 138 | PAYROLL TAXES | | | | | | |
| 140 | TEMPORARY HELP | | | | | | |
| 199 | INNER-DEPT LABOR TRANSF | | | | | | |
| 201 | SECURITY SERVICES | | | | | | |
| 202 | DISPOSAL SERVICE | | | | | | |
| 203 | JANITOR &GROUNDS MAINT | | | | | | |
| 230 | UTILITIES | | | | | | |
| 231 | COMMUNICATION | | | | | | |
| 233 | OFFICE OPERATING | | | | | | |
| 234 | OFFICE EQUIPMENT | | | | | | |
| 236 | COMPUTER HARDWARE & SOFT | | | | | | |
| 237 | FACILITIES MAINTENANCE | | | | | | |
| 301 | SHOP OPERATING | | | | | | |
| 304 | SHOP SUPPLIES | | | | | | |
| 306 | OUTSIDE MACHINE WORK | | | | | | |
| 308 | SCRAP | | | | | | |
| 309 | INVENTORY EXPENSED | | | | | | |
| 310 | INDIRECT EVALUATION EXPENSE | | | | | | |
| 330 | MECHANICAL TESTING | | | | | | |
| 338 | WELDING GAS CYLINDERS | | | | | | |
| 340 | TOOLING REVISIONS | | | | | | |
| 358 | PATTERNS, DIES & TOOLING | | | | | | |
| 360 | WAREHOUSING | | | | | | |
| 400 | AUTO - LEASING | | | | | | |
| 401 | AUTO - OPERATING | | | | | | |
| 402 | AUTO - REPAIRS | | | | | | |
| 704 | ENTERTAINMENT | | | | | | |
| 715 | TRAVEL EXPENSE 0 AUTO RENTAL | | | | | | |
| 717 | TRAVEL EXPENSE | | | | | | |
| 718 | AIR TRAVEL FARES | | | | | | |
| 908 | EMPLOYEE TRAINING DEVELOPM | | | | | | |
| 909 | EMPLOYEE RELATIONS | | | | | | |
| 913 | MISCELLANEOUS EXPENSES | | | | | | |
| 930 | DEPRECIATION | | | | | | |
| 950 | LIABILITY INSURANCE | | | | | | |
| 951 | WORKMENS COMPENSATION INS | | | | | | |
| 999 | EXPENSE TRANSFERS | | | | | | |
| | TOTAL DIRECT DEPARTMENTS | | | | | | |
| | TOTAL SUPPORT DEPARTMENTS | | | | | | |
| | TOTAL | | | | | | |
| | DIRECT LABOR HOURS (BUDGETED) | | | | | | |
| | DIRECT LABOR HOURS (FULL CAPACITY) | | | | | | |
| | BURDEN PER HOUR | | | | | | |

**Figure 13-8**
**The Burden Rate Allocation at CAMCO, Inc.**

Reprinted here with permission from CAMCO, Inc.

improve efficiency and to reduce the cost, in order to sustain demand for their services. Another alternative is the downsizing of a service department.

From the cost allocation, a service departments' cost report is compiled and the variances are controlled. At CAMCO cost of services is allocated directly to production departments. Cost variances are controlled as is shown in Figure 13-9, where actual performance is compared with the budget.

Standard cost allocation is used in allocating budgeted overheads to machine centers or individual machines. Standard costing, applied to machine centers and individual machines, makes it possible to estimate efficiency at these basic production units' level as shown in Figure 13-10.

## HOW TO MAKE THE RIGHT PRODUCT COST ASSIGNMENT

After all production costs are allocated to production departments, the next step is to assign the production cost to individual product units. This is known as the *cost absorption.* The major accounting systems used for cost assignment are

- Job costing
- Process costing

Depending on the nature of production units, many organizations employ two or more cost accounting systems combined into a hybrid accounting system.

### THE JOB COSTING SYSTEM

In a job costing accounting system, a production cost is assigned to individual customer orders. Job shop is a typical environment for a job costing cost assignment.

Job cost accounting starts with preparing a job cost sheet, listing a product quantity on order, material, labor categories, equipment and tools required. A job cost sheet is similar to a route sheet except that the job cost sheet's primary purpose is to present cost information related to production activities. Thus a job cost sheet is combined with a route sheet, physically following a job route. Each department on this route records on the cost sheet the cost of material used and labor, along with the cost basis for overhead costs. A job cost sheet is shown in Figure 13-11. In companies where a centralized cost accounting department maintains job cost sheets, costing information is collected from each work center via work tickets. Job costing accounting involves a considerable amount of paperwork, which often makes this system expensive.

CAMCO PRODUCTS AND SERVICES
PRODUCTION SUMMARY
FEBRUARY 1992
($000)

PAGE 6

| | DIRECT HOURS | BUDGET HOURS | HOUR VARIANCE | TOTAL APPLIED | ACTUAL EXPENSES | BUDGET EXPENSES | UNPLANNED CAPACITY VARIANCE | PLANNED CAPACITY VARIANCE | SPENDING VARIANCE | ABSORPTION VARIANCE | ACTUAL RATE |
|---|---|---|---|---|---|---|---|---|---|---|---|
| **YEAR–TO–DATE 1991** | | | | | | | | | | | |
| MACHINE SHOP | | | | | | | | | | | |
| ASSEMBLY | | | | | | | | | | | |
| FABRICATION | | | | | | | | | | | |
| HEAT TREAT | | | | | | | | | | | |
| W/L FABRICATION | | | | | | | | | | | |
| FMS | | | | | | | | | | | |
| MANDREL PKT CELL | | | | | | | | | | | |
| MANDREL BORE/THD | | | | | | | | | | | |
| TOTAL | | | | | | | | | | | |
| **JANUARY** | | | | | | | | | | | |
| MACHINE SHOP | | | | | | | | | | | |
| ASSEMBLY | | | | | | | | | | | |
| FABRICATION | | | | | | | | | | | |
| HEAT TREAT | | | | | | | | | | | |
| W/L FABRICATION | | | | | | | | | | | |
| FMS | | | | | | | | | | | |
| MANDREL PKT CELL | | | | | | | | | | | |
| MANDREL BORE/THD | | | | | | | | | | | |
| TOTAL | | | | | | | | | | | |
| **FEBRUARY** | | | | | | | | | | | |
| MACHINE SHOP | | | | | | | | | | | |
| ASSEMBLY | | | | | | | | | | | |
| FABRICATION | | | | | | | | | | | |
| HEAT TREAT | | | | | | | | | | | |
| W/L FABRICATION | | | | | | | | | | | |
| FMS | | | | | | | | | | | |
| MANDREL PKT CELL | | | | | | | | | | | |
| MANDREL BORE/THD | | | | | | | | | | | |
| TOTAL | | | | | | | | | | | |
| **YEAR–TO–DATE 1992** | | | | | | | | | | | |
| MACHINE SHOP | | | | | | | | | | | |
| ASSEMBLY | | | | | | | | | | | |
| FABRICATION | | | | | | | | | | | |
| HEAT TREAT | | | | | | | | | | | |
| W/L FABRICATION | | | | | | | | | | | |
| FMS | | | | | | | | | | | |
| MANDREL PKT CELL | | | | | | | | | | | |
| MANDREL BORE/THD | | | | | | | | | | | |
| TOTAL | | | | | | | | | | | |

**Figure 13-9**
**The Monthly Variances Report at CAMCO, Inc.**

CAMCO INC
MFG -PRODUCTION
MACHINE GROUP FILE

SEQUENCE - DEPT, M/C

03/03/90
PAGE 3

| AREA CODE | DEPT NO | MACH NO | DESCRIPTION | EST WAIT | EST MOVE | AVL HRS | SHIFT | M.C. TYPE | LABOR RATE | BURD FACT | EFF FACT |
|---|---|---|---|---|---|---|---|---|---|---|---|
| 103 | 01 | 14 | TOSHIBA MILL | | | | | | | | |
| 102 | 01 | 15 | 2-AB AUTO LATHE | | | | | | | | |
| 102 | 01 | 17 | A-AC AUTO LATHE | | | | | | | | |
| 103 | 01 | 18 | NC 818 COMBI | | | | | | | | |
| 104 | 01 | 19 | MANDREL LATHE | | | | | | | | |
| 103 | 01 | 20 | N/C J&L 4515 | | | | | | | | |
| 103 | 01 | 21 | NC 4515 COMBI | | | | | | | | |
| 103 | 01 | 22 | N/C P&W | | | | | | | | |
| 103 | 01 | 23 | MAZAK M-5 | | | | | | | | |
| 103 | 01 | 24 | MC MAZAK PM | | | | | | | | |
| 103 | 01 | 25 | MAZAK-FMS | | | | | | | | |
| 103 | 01 | 26 | SLANT 15 CNC | | | | | | | | |
| 104 | 01 | 27 | ENGINE LATHE LR | | | | | | | | |
| 101 | 01 | 28 | DRILL STAMLEY | | | | | | | | |
| 104 | 01 | 29 | L&S 10 5/8 SPND | | | | | | | | |
| 103 | 01 | 30 | 4515 SW BORE | | | | | | | | |
| 103 | 01 | 31 | 1036 J&L CNC | | | | | | | | |
| 103 | 01 | 39 | N/C K&T 180 MILL | | | | | | | | |
| 104 | 01 | 41 | BRIDGEPORT MILL | | | | | | | | |

**Figure 13-10**
**Standard Cost Allocation**



## THE PROCESS COSTING SYSTEM

Process costing is used for costing in an environment where the volume production of the like units is organized mainly as the flow-type production. In process costing, the production cost for each department, accumulated for a period of time, is divided by the number of units produced during this period, estimating the average unit cost.

A process costing system is less expensive and is simpler to maintain than a job costing system. This is because in a process costing system there is only one cost object per department to control, while in a job costing system, each job is a cost object, which requires considerable clerical efforts for cost assignment.

## JOB COST SHEET

CUSTOMER NAME ______________
DATE REQUESTED ______________
DATE STARTED ______________
DATE COMPLETED ______________

JOB NUMBER ______________
PRODUCT ______________
NUMBER OF UNITS ______________

### DIRECT MATERIALS

| DATE | DEPARTMENT | REQUISITION NUMBER | TOTAL |
|---|---|---|---|
| | | | |
| | | | |
| | | | |
| | | | |

### DIRECT LABOR

| DATE | DEPARTMENT | LABOR TIME TICKET # | TOTAL |
|---|---|---|---|
| | | | |
| | | | |
| | | | |
| | | | |

### APPLIED OVERHEAD

| DATE | DEPARTMENT | BASIS FOR OVERH APPLICATION | UNIT OF RATE BASE | TOTAL |
|---|---|---|---|---|
| | | | | |
| | | | | |
| | | | | |
| | | | | |

TOTAL MANUFACTURING COST ______________
UNITS PRODUCED ______________
UNIT COST ______________

**Figure 13-11**
**Job Cost Sheet at CAMCO, Inc.**

In both cost systems, the direct labor, direct materials, and manufacturing overheads must be traced to specific products or jobs. In a homogeneous production environment, these costs are standard, while in a job shop environment typical to job costing, each job requires additional time study and cost estimates. The cost flow in process costing is illustrated in Figure 13-12. Job costing and process costing systems are compared in Figure 13-13.

## ABSORPTION COSTING AND VARIABLE COSTING

There are two ways to assign a fixed manufacturing overhead, namely, absorption costing and variable costing also known as direct costing. In an *absorption product costing* system, fixed manufacturing overhead is absorbed by the product's inventory costs.

In a *variable product costing* system, fixed manufacturing overhead is excluded from the inventory costs. In such a system, only the variable cost of product is considered the product cost. The fixed cost is written off as an expense for the period, along with the administrative cost and fixed selling expenses rather than becoming an integral part of inventory costs. Here, only the direct cost of materials, direct labor, and variable overheads are absorbed by individual products. Absorption costing and direct costing are illustrated in Figure 13-14.

Job costing and process costing systems apply absorption costing. In a traditional income statement applying absorption costing, expenses are classified by management functions, namely, manufacturing, selling, and administrative.

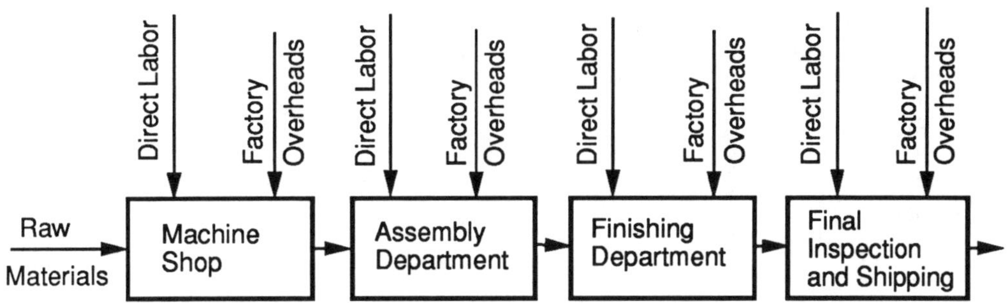


**Figure 13-12**
**Cost Flow in Process Costing**

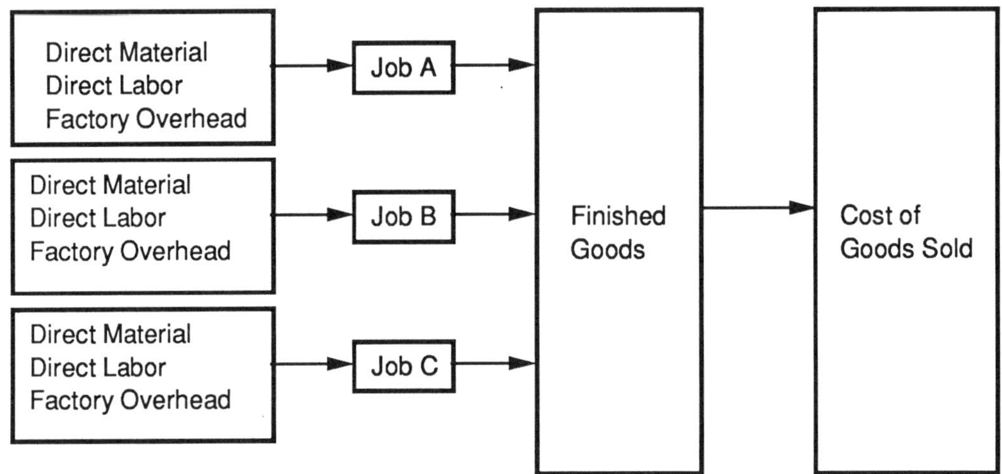


**A. Job Costing System**

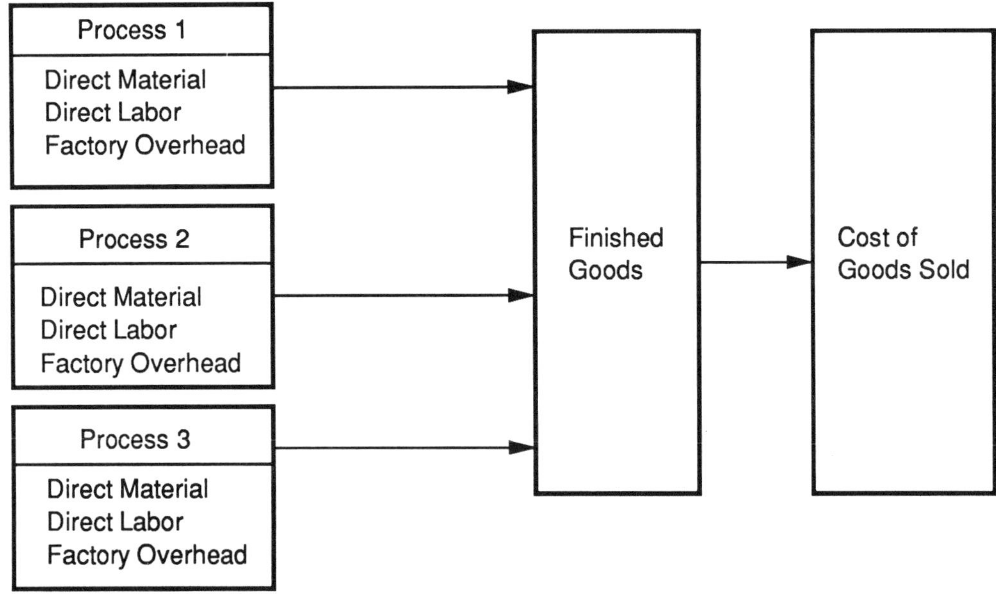


**B. Process Costing System**

**Figure 13-13**
**Job Costing System and Process Costing System**

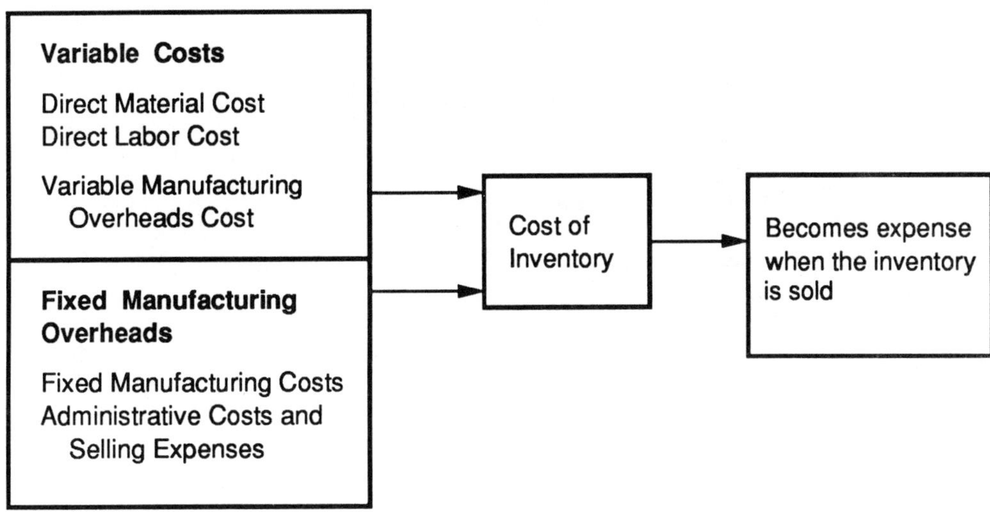


**A. Absorption Costing**

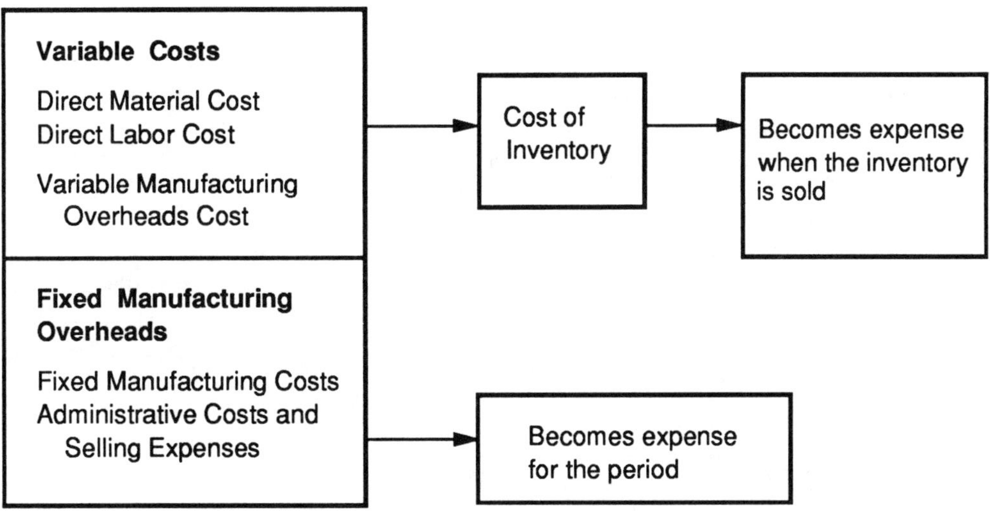


**B. Variable (Direct) Costing**

**Figure 13-14**
**Expense on the Income Statement**

*Example:*

| *Absorption costing method* | | | |
|---|---|---|---|
| Sales | $300,000 | | |
| Less: Cost of goods sold | 190,000 | | |
| Manufacturing margin | $110,000 | | |
| Less: Administrative and selling expenses | | $ 90,000 | |
| Net profit before taxes | | $ 20,000 | |

| *Variable costing method* | | | |
|---|---|---|---|
| Sales | | $300,000 | |
| Less: Variable expenses | | | |
| Manufacturing expenses | $110,000 | | |
| Selling expenses | $ 30,000 | | |
| Administrative expenses | $ 20,000 | | |
| Total variable expenses | | $160,000 | |
| Contribution margin | | | $140,000 |
| Less: Fixed expenses | | | |
| Manufacturing expenses | $ 80,000 | | |
| Selling expenses | 30,000 | | |
| Administrative expenses | 10,000 | | |
| Total fixed expenses | | | $120,000 |
| Net profit before taxes | | | $ 20,000 |

The variable costing method eliminates unit costs variations due to production volume. It is used primarily as a basis for managerial decisions on pricing and reengineering product lines. This method appeals more to small-lot production situations.

In the variable costing income statement format, net income is a function of sales. There is a separation of variable and fixed costs, focused on the contribution margin, sales revenue less all the variable costs of goods sold, instead of manufacturing margin, as with the absorption costing. Variable costing is not accepted for external financial and IRS reporting and is used as an internal cost control tool for short-term decision making. For external reporting, many companies transform the variable cost format into absorption cost reports.

## HOW JUST-IN-TIME COST ACCOUNTING REVEALS WASTE

The original function of cost accounting was to evaluate inventory production costs by keeping track of the actual cost of products in manufacturing. A drastic inventory reduction in JIT systems, as well as a reduction in lead time, reduces as much expenses for collecting and analyzing costing information. The basic JIT principle of waste reduction finds its embodiment in the reduction of many JIT cost accounting tasks. For example, many JIT-type companies have eliminated work-in-process inventory accounts typical of job order costing systems. The elimination of waste in JIT is accomplished through labor and materials resource aggregation.

### Saving Labor Resources

With the reduction of the contents of labor in the total production cost, some companies find it beneficial to include direct labor costs in the manufacturing overheads. In a JIT environment, labor hours are not a representative unit as a cost allocation base. Also, with the diversification of labor activities into multiskill and multifunctional areas of production activities, it is becoming increasingly difficult to differentiate between the direct labor cost and the indirect labor cost.

Machine operators involve themselves in auxiliary activities, such as plant maintenance, inspections, housekeeping, and improvement schemes, which could not be traced to individual products but which are included into the factory overhead costs.

### Saving Material Resources

JIT-controlled companies use combined accounts of raw materials and work-in-process. A joint *raw and in-process inventory account* (RIP) further reduces the accounting required for JIT systems. The cost of raw materials and in-process inventory is transformed from the RIP account to the finished-goods account and thereafter to the cost of goods sold account. The conversion costs (the total of direct labor cost and manufacturing overhead cost) are charged *directly to the cost of goods sold.* Figure 13-15 illustrates cost accounting approaches in traditional batch production and JIT production.

JIT accounting eliminates the need to transfer the cost from one department's account to the next one throughout the material flow route because the accumulated departmental costs are charged directly to the cost of goods sold.

## USING ACTIVITY-BASED OVERHEAD COSTING TECHNIQUES

The increasing level of automation and the changing role of the work force in computer-controlled production systems have been forcing many managers to critically evaluate traditional cost bases for the overhead allocation and overhead assignment. Allocation bases, such as direct labor-hours used in the allocation of an overhead, are increasingly coming under criticism due to the deminishing labor contents in production costs.

It was found that the cost effectiveness is best influenced at its source, namely, at the activity level where people identify the need for a cost incurring activity and where the resources are actually consumed. The philosophy of

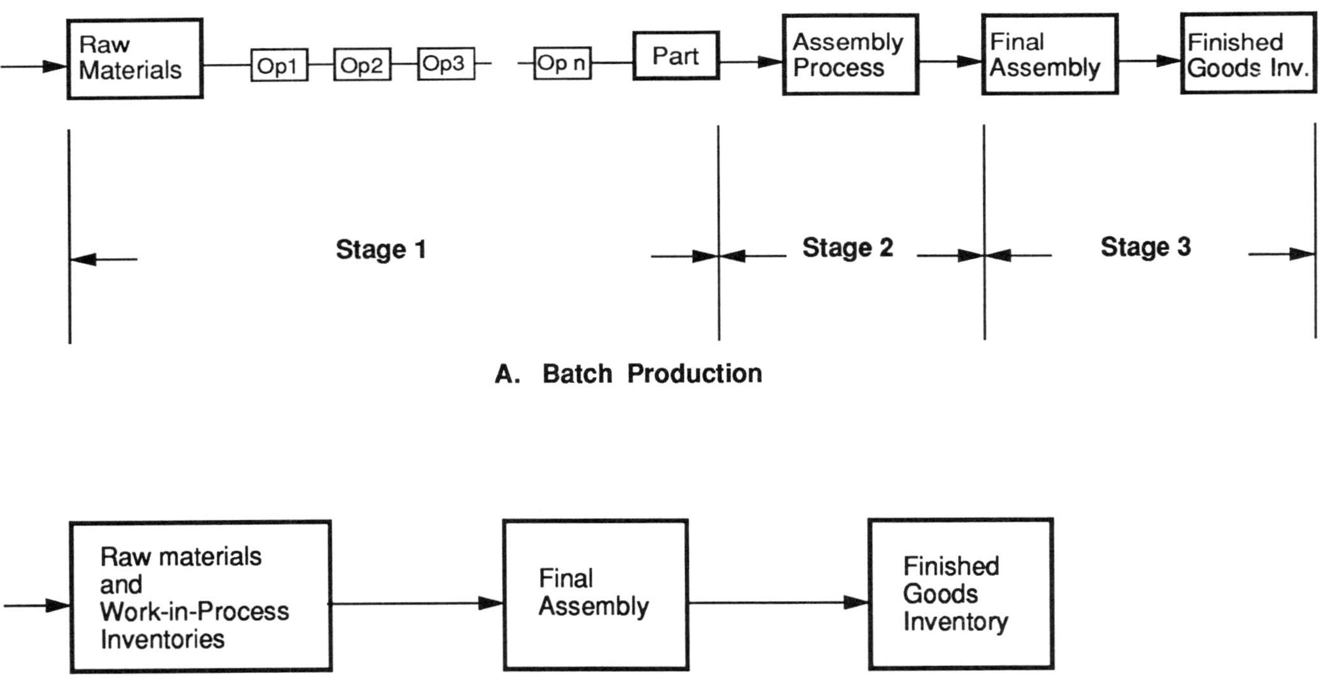


**Figure 13-15**
**Cost Accounting in Traditional Batch Production and in JIT Production**

activity-based product costing is that activities consume resources while products consume activities.

The contemporary accounting pays greater attention to the sources of costs, analyzing the reason and the rationale for activities, rather than just plainly performing a postevent cost allocation. The inquest of what drives a cost leads to a new concept of a cost driver. A *cost driver* is a measure of a business activity that causes an overhead to be incurred. An analysis of cost drivers can help companies realize the actual causes for overheads instead of just trying to distribute these overhead costs evenly.

The following are examples of cost drivers:

- Number of deliveries
- Number of labor transactions
- Number of options
- Number of breakdowns
- Number of vendors
- Number of engineering changes
- Number of schedule changes
- Number of material moves

It often happens in cost accounting that the cost allocation base linking the cost pool with the cost objective is confused with the cost driver which can be defined as the reason for the activity taking place. This list can explain the distinction between using an allocation base and cost drivers, namely, that an allocation base derives from a production standard, while a cost driver is the measure of performance.

The rule of effective cost accounting is that all the costs should be charged directly to products. This is accomplished easily with variable resources, such as direct labor and direct materials. However, the assignment of overheads to end products cannot be accomplished as easily. Since products consume activities, the overhead-causing activities can be reduced through analyzing the drivers originating these overhead activities. The emphasis is on the cost reduction. The reduction and elimination of activities starts at the preproduction stage, when dealing with the product design and the process selection—preproduction and production planning.

How many bottlenecks are eliminated, how much inventory is reduced, how many queues are reduced, how many quality problems are eliminated, and how far is lead time shrunk when simplifications to the product design are made are just some of the questions answered by using this ABCS method. Sometimes it is called *reverse engineering*, which means that the changes to the product design were initiated by production to reduce the cost by smoothing out the material flow or eliminating a specific problem. Reverse engineering often starts with establishing a target cost for a business and also for individual production and functional departments. A target cost can also relate to a product and to its component parts.

## COST ACCOUNTING SYSTEM AT COMMUNICATION EQUIPMENT MANUFACTURING CEM, INC.: A CASE STUDY

CEM is a medium- to large-sized company manufacturing a communication equipment for the oil exploration industry. CEM's accounting system applies a single-cost method in classifying service department costs—warehouse and purchasing, support procurement, shipping, and manufacturing. Figure 13-16 illustrates the CEM's cost accounting model.

The relative cost method is used for the allocation of the service department cost to the production departments. A one-step direct cost allocation method is used where service department costs are allocated directly to the final user. The percentages of the procurement and shipping cost are used to calculate directly a division procurement and shipping percentage. (See section I in Figure 13-16.)

The calculation in section II in Figure 13-16 is done by adding the support overhead cost for a particular manufacturing area to the direct manufacturing overhead of that area. In the manufacturing system, each part has a standard number of hours necessary to build it, and the total overhead dollars divided by the total capacity hours of each area have provided a cost per hour.

Estimated overhead costs in the truck shop amount to $19.67 per hour and in the machine shop to $18.38 per hour. The manufacturing cost is calculated as a standard cost equal to the direct cost of material plus the cost of labor at overhead standard rate.

## AN ACTIVITY-BASED COSTING SYSTEM (ABCS) AT SIECOR, INC.: A CASE STUDY

Siecor is a leading supplier of telecommunication products, including fiber optic cables, hardware, connectors, network interface devices, and copper-based hardware. The management accounting system used is a product line (P&L) management accounting system. This system, described here, belongs to Siecor's equipment division located in Keller, Texas. This system incorporates both a traditional cost accounting system for direct costs and an activity-based costing system for fixed and administrative costs. The purpose of this management accounting system is to provide management with information that can impact decision making.

MANUFACTURING COST MODEL

| I. SUPPORT DEPT. | TOTAL | PROCUR | SHIPPING | MFG | MFG COSTS TRUCK SHOP | MACHINE SHOP |
|---|---|---|---|---|---|---|
| WAREHSE | 100% | 30% | 25% | 45% | 60% | 40% |
| | $100,000 | $30,000 | $25,000 | $45,000 | $27,000 | $18,000 |
| PURCH | 100% | 100% | 0% | 0% | 0% | 0% |
| | $75,000 | $75,000 | | | | |
| PURCH | 100% | 60% | 0% | 40% | 30% | 70% |
| | $50,000 | $30,000 | | $20,000 | $6,000 | $14,000 |
| TOTAL | 100% | 60% | 11% | 29% | 51% | 49% |
| | $225,000 | $135,000 | $25,000 | $65,000 | $33,000 | $32,000 |

II

$$\text{PROCUREMENT \%} = \frac{\text{PROCUREMENT COST}}{\text{PURCHASES}} = \frac{\$135{,}000}{\$2{,}700{,}000} = 5\%$$

$$\text{SHIPPING \%} = \frac{\text{PROCUREMENT COST}}{\text{PURCHASES}} = \frac{\$25{,}000}{\$1{,}250{,}000} = 2\%$$

III

<u>TRUCK SHOP</u>

| | |
|---|---|
| SUPPORT COST OVHD | $33,000 |
| DIRECT MFG OVHD | $85,000 |
| TOTAL OVHD COST | $118,000 |
| TOTAL CAPACITY STD HOURS | 6,000 |
| OVHD COST/HR | $19.67 |

<u>MACHINE SHOP</u>

| | |
|---|---|
| SUPPORT COST OVHD | $32,000 |
| DIRECT MFG OVHD | $115,000 |
| TOTAL OVHD COST | $147,000 |
| TOTAL CAPACITY STD HOURS | 8,000 |
| OVHD COST/HR | $18,38 |

IV STD COST OF PART A123 ( TRUCK SHOP) =

= DIRECT MATERIAL @STD + (STD LABOR HOURS x HOURLY RATE) =
= $100,000 +2,000 HRS @ 18,38 =
= $100,000 +$36,760 =
= $136,760

**Figure 13-16**
**The Cost Accounting System at Communication Equipment Manufacturing Co.**

The Keller plant is segregated into eight different product lines. They include

1. Network interface devices (NIDs)
2. Cross-connect boxes
3. Station apparatus
4. Cable stubs (these are the traditional copper products)

The fiber optic products include

5. Interconnect hardware
6. Splice hardware
7. Connectors and mechanical splices

The electronic products include

8. Automatic meter reading (AMR)

The manufacturing processes include injection molding, sheet metal fabrication and assembly. The manufacturing centers are

1. Molding
2. Metal fabrication
3. Cable preparation
4. NID assembly
5. Cross-connect assembly
6. Electronic assembly

Manufacturing is done in medium-volume batches, using shop orders, and every product is processed by at least one of these cost centers. Siecor-Keller also uses several outside subcontractors, including *maquilidoras* in Mexico.

## The Organization of Activity-Based Costing System

The end result of any accounting system is a series of reports that help to analyze the business. This includes the summary and the product line profit and loss statements that compare actual results to the budget projection. Siecor's current and year-to-date budget report is shown in Figure 13-17. The cost accounting system at Siecor-Keller is illustrated in a flow chart shown in Figure 13-18. Although fixed spending is about 40 percent of total spending, this includes all spending that does not directly vary with volume. This was not traditionally emphasized in the cost accounting system. Fixed spending also includes expenses at the manufacturing plant—engineering, purchasing, shipping, accounting, data processing, R&D, sales, and marketing.

KELLER PLANT BUDGET REPORT

| | CURRENT | | | | YEAR TO DATE | | | |
|---|---|---|---|---|---|---|---|---|
| | ACTIAL | BUDGET | VARIANCE | PCNT. | ACTIAL | BUDGET | VARIANCE | PCNT. |
| GROSS SALES | | | | | | | | |
| SALES DEDUCTIONS | | | | | | | | |
| FREIGHT ON SALES LINE | | | | | | | | |
| NET SALES | | | | | | | | |
| STANDARD COST - MATERIAL | | | | | | | | |
| STANDARD COST - DIRECT LABOR | | | | | | | | |
| STANDARD COST - VARIABLE OVHD | | | | | | | | |
| COST OF GOODS SOLD (STD) | | | | | | | | |
| SCRAP | | | | | | | | |
| LABOR USAGE VARIANCE | | | | | | | | |
| MATERIAL PRICE VARIANCE | | | | | | | | |
| STANDARD TO ACTUAL - VARIABLE | | | | | | | | |
| COST OF GOODS SOLD (ACT) | | | | | | | | |
| VARIABLE MARGIN | | | | | | | | |
| FIXED ADMIN EXPENCES | | | | | | | | |
| OTHER | | | | | | | | |
| TOTAL FIXED ADMINISTRATIVE | | | | | | | | |
| GROSS MARGIN | | | | | | | | |
| SELLING | | | | | | | | |
| MARKETING | | | | | | | | |
| TECHNOLOGY | | | | | | | | |
| CORPORATE SVCS TRANSFER | | | | | | | | |
| CORPORATE ALLOCATION | | | | | | | | |
| COST OF ASSETS EMPLOYED | | | | | | | | |
| BUSINESS OPER MARGIN | | | | | | | | |

**Figure 13-17**
**Siecor-Keller Current and Year-to-Day Budget Report**

This material is used with permission of Siecor Corporation, Keller, Texas plant.

In 1989, the Keller plant's fixed spending began to be analyzed and allocated, using an ABCS costing system. An ABCS analysis segregates fixed spending into cost pools. These pools are of expense type and are usually either cost centers (shipping, maintenance, and materials) or expense categories (depreciation and sales aids).

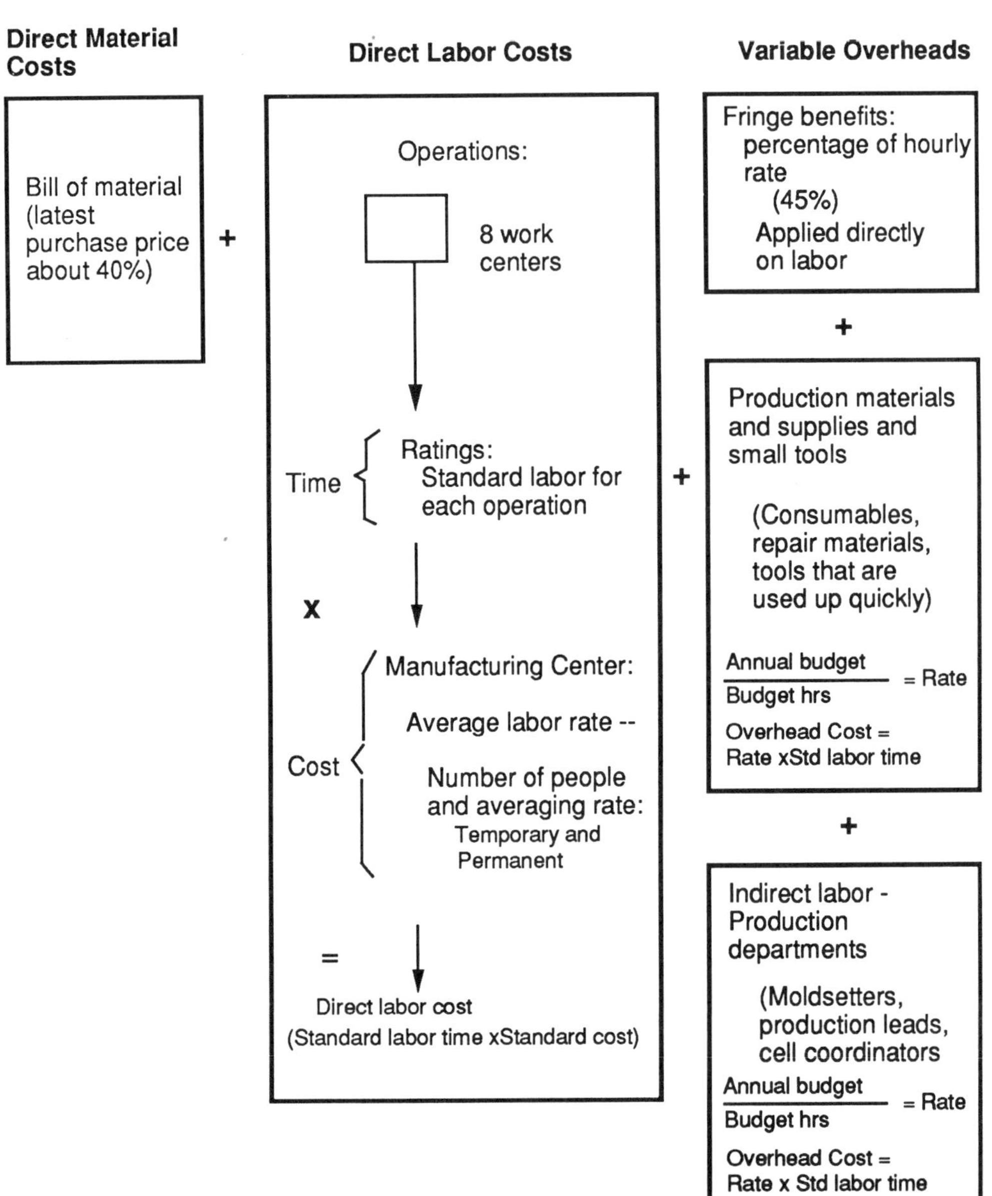


**Figure 13-18**
**Cost Accounting System at Siecor-Keller Plant**

**Fixed Manufacturing Costs**

Service centers:
Shipping, Receiving, Maintenance, Toolmakers, Quality Inspectors
Indirect Labor + Other Expenses
(materials, shipping supplies, repairs and tools)

+

Administrative centers:
Accounting, Management, Data Processing, Purchasing, Scheduling -
Salary + Other expenses
(travel, office supplies, etc.)

+

Depreciation:
Directly to manufacturing centers
(molds, mold makers, sheet metal fabrication)
Indirect cost centers
(tool making equipment, building, office furniture)

+

Other manufacturing expenses:
(insurance, property tax, warranty, obsolesce, etc.)

+

+

**Administrative/ Corporate Costs**

Technology
Marketing
Sales
Corporate costs

+

Allocated same as fixed manufacturing -- ABCS

<u>Activity-Based Costing System (ABCS)</u>

Each cost center determines what "drives the cost" or what percent of total services is spent on each product line. This is known as cost drivers.

Cost drivers are used as follows:

**Fixed cost associated with each product line =**
**Actual service cost x Allocation rate**
The depreciation cost is allocated directly to cost centers and is further split by the product line. For example, molding work center splits depreciation into 5 product lines by the following arrangement: the largest product line is responsible for 50% while the second largest product line absorbs 20% of the depreciation cost. This is an Allocation rate used in estimating services cost.

**Figure 13-18** (continued)

The next step is to determine what activities cause these costs to be incurred. These activities are cost drivers. An example of a cost driver is the number of individual shipments for shipping costs. The next step is to allocate the cost pools based on the activities that cause the spending. The final step is to use these data to find ways to reduce the spending or to ensure a proper return on the spending.

Siecor segregates manufacturing plant expenses into approximately 30 cost pools and corporate spending into 6 cost pools. For each cost pool, the activities that drive these costs are analyzed (e.g., the number of specialists needed for marketing). The cost driver data are collected quarterly and are used to allocate the total spending to various product lines. More important, it is also used to analyze the spending with an emphasis on reducing or improving the utilization of that particular type of spending.

The following is a summary of how this works and how some lines in the P&L are generated, along with a description of other information that is generated by the accounting system for analysis and control. A product line P&L report is shown in Figure 13-19 is an allocation of cost pool overheads.

### Sales

Sales reports are generated by the order processing system, based on the shipments to the customer. Any returns or freight paid by Siecor is deducted from the gross sales. These reports are sorted and summarized by product.

### Direct Costs

The direct costs are generated using the cost accounting computer system, based on the bill of materials (BOM) and labor routings. The bills and routings do not include any scrap or efficiency factors. All costing is done with standard variances. Direct costs are 60% of Keller's total costs.

### Standard Costs—Material

A standard cost is loaded for each part in the inventory system. These costs are adjusted periodically, as they change significantly (a monthly impact is greater than $20,000). The standard costs are exploded through the BOM to arrive at the total material cost for each product. These data are included in the sales reports.

### Material Usage Variance

When the actual usage of materials differs from the standard usage, a material usage variance is reported. At Keller, the primary causes of material usage variances are metal drop (unusable metal after fabrication), manufacturing

Siecor-Keller Product Line P/L--1991 DECEMBER YTD--ALLOCATION %

| Category | Product Lines | | | | | | | |
|---|---|---|---|---|---|---|---|---|
| (Cost Pools) | NIDs | X-Conn | St App | Stubs | Conn/M | Splinter Hdw | SpHdwe | Total |
| Depreciation--Direct | | | | | | | | |
| Depreciation--Space | | | | | | | | |
| Depreciation--Manning | | | | | | | | |
| Information Systems | | | | | | | | |
| Personnel | | | | | | | | |
| Accounting | | | | | | | | |
| Property Tax/Insurance | | | | | | | | |
| Utilities | | | | | | | | |
| General Plant Expense | | | | | | | | |
| General Administration | | | | | | | | |
| Materials | | | | | | | | |
| Maintenance | | | | | | | | |
| QC | | | | | | | | |
| Receiving/Stockroom | | | | | | | | |
| Shipping | | | | | | | | |
| Mold Making | | | | | | | | |
| Other Fixed: 936 | | | | | | | | |
| Warranty | | | | | | | | |
| Obsolescence | | | | | | | | |
| Other | | | | | | | | |
| Total Plant Fixed | | | | | | | | |
| PLANT GROSS MARGIN | | | | | | | | |
| PERCENT OF SALES | | | | | | | | |

**Figure 13-19**
**Siecor-Keller Product Line P/L Report**

scrap (bad parts manufactured), outside processing scrap, cycle count adjustments, and marketing aids. Since material makes up more than 80 percent of the direct product cost, this is where a lot of the management analysis is done. After identifying each cause of the material usage variance, it is summarized by the type and by the product line.

### Standard Cost—Labor

For each operation in the manufacturing process, a standard labor time study is generated. This represents the number of labor minutes to generate the part at 100% productivity. The time study is loaded into the inventory system and extended by the average labor rate in a particular cost center, in order to arrive at the total labor cost for each product. This data are included in the sales reports.

### Labor Usage Variance

When the actual labor spending differs from the standard, a labor usage variance is reported. This can be caused by employees not working on products at all times (utilization), by performance below the accepted standard (efficiency), or by the labor rate changes within a department (rate). Since the labor makes up less than 10 percent of the direct product cost, there is less emphasis on the management analysis. This is a change instituted during the last five years, and it can be seen in the fact that a part-time employee now does time studies. After identifying the primary causes of the labor usage variance, it is summarized by the cost center and by the product line.

The labor variance is reported weekly by the cost center, using the productivity report. The Siecor's weekly productivity report is shown in Figure 13-20. Efficiency is a measure of hours spent versus the standard hours. Since the deemphasis is on the labor reporting, this report is no longer a representative measure of absolute productivity, but it is good for measuring the trends. Total productivity is compared to the budget. Additionally, each cost center is measured for its ratio of temporary employees to the total employee base (since keeping the ratio in line is essential for meeting the average labor rate) and for the percentage of overtime worked. Finally, the total labor usage variance is compared to the budget in absolute dollars.

### Standard Variable Overhead Costs

At Siecor-Keller, a *variable overhead* (VOH) is made up of

1. Indirect labor in the direct cost centers (for example, leads, molds setters, material handlers—18 percent of total VOH)
2. Fringe benefits on direct and indirect labor (51 percent of total VOH)

WEEKLY PRODUCTIVITY

WEEK ENDING: 01-JUL-90

DEPARTMENT: PLANT

| | WEEK 26 | MTD 6 | QTD 2 | Y.T.D. 90 | Y.T.D. 89 |
|---|---|---|---|---|---|
| DIR. LABOR HOURS | 8695 | 49648 | 126099 | 241590 | |
| EARNED HOURS | 6863 | 40104 | 105875 | 206109 | |
| REAL TIME HOURS | 791 | 4113 | 10177 | 17572 | |
| VARIATION | -1041 | -5432 | -10047 | -17910 | |
| EFFICIENCY | 88% | 89% | 92% | 93% | 92% |
| WAITING HOURS | 0 | 12 | 51 | 105 | |
| MAINT. DOWN HOURS | 106 | 549 | 1579 | 2865 | |
| REWORK/REPAIR HOURS | 77 | 857 | 1965 | 3342 | |
| TOTAL LOST HRS. | 183 | 1418 | 3596 | 6311 | |
| UTILIZATION | 98% | 97% | 97% | 97% | 98% |
| COMMUNICATION HOURS | 30 | 307 | 1156 | 2120 | |
| TRAINING HOURS | 18 | 84 | 733 | 1141 | |
| INDIRECT HOURS | 1011 | 5111 | 13226 | 26998 | |
| TOTAL VAR. OH HRS. | 1059 | 5502 | 15116 | 30259 | |
| TOTAL HOURS | 9937 | 56568 | 144810 | 278161 | |
| TOTAL PRODUCTIVITY | 77% | 78% | 80% | 80% | 80% |
| OVERTIME HRS | 375 | 3176 | 7393 | 12318 | |
| TRANSFER HOURS | 52 | 489 | 1477 | 2818 | |
| ENG/MKTG SUPPORT HRS | 261 | 664 | 1427 | 2768 | |
| SCRAP | -43500 | $12,045 | $25,715 | $32,031 | |
| % REAL/EARNED + REAL | 10.3% | 9.3% | 8.8% | 7.9% | 4.1% |
| % WAIT/EARNED + REAL | 0.0% | 0.0% | 0.0% | 0.0% | 1.0% |
| % MAINT/EARNED + REAL | 1.4% | 1.2% | 1.4% | 1.3% | 1.2% |
| % REWORK/EARNED + REAL | 1.0% | 1.9% | 1.7% | 1.5% | 0.8% |
| % COMM/TOTAL | 0.3% | 0.5% | 0.8% | 0.8% | 0.9% |
| % TRAIN/TOTAL | 0.2% | 0.1% | 0.5% | 0.4% | 0.7% |
| % INDIRECT/TOTAL | 10.2% | 9.0% | 9.1% | 9.7% | 10.1% |
| % OVERTIME/TOTAL | 3.8% | 5.6% | 5.1% | 4.4% | 10.5% |
| DIRECT LABOR VARIANCE | -13187 | ($72,830) | ($157,577) | ($279,218) | |

**Figure 13-20**
**The Weekly Production Report**

3. Operating materials and supplies in the direct cost centers (21 percent of total VOH)
4. Repairs on and maintenance of production equipment (6 percent of total VOH)
5. Overtime premium (4 percent of total VOH) see Figure 13-21A.

Annually, a rate that compares the VOH to labor, by cost center, is further adjusted by the productivity factor as shown in Figure 13-21B. This rate is extended by the labor time study to arrive at the total VOH cost for each product using adjusted variable cost (VC) per hour and per minute rate. Since 73 percent of the total VOH is directly labor driven, this system is adequate. An improvement would be to apply the operating materials and repairs to some other basis than labor.

## Variable Overhead Usage Variance

When the actual spending on a variable overhead differs from the standard, a VOH usage variance is reported. At Keller, this is primarily caused by

1. Labor usage variance (since fringe benefits are tied directly to labor costs)
2. Overtime
3. Spending on supplies and repairs at a different rate than the VOH rate

Since VOH makes up less than 10 percent of the direct product cost, there is less emphasis on the management analysis. After identifying the primary causes of the variable overhead usage variances, it is summarized by cost center and product line.

VOH is reported monthly, using the cost center responsibility report. This report compares the actual spending on a variable overhead to the budget. Differences in fringes and overtime are explained using the labor reports. Significant differences in other items are explained in the monthly reporting package.

At Keller, all variances are compared to the annual budget, which assumes that actual production levels are the same as the budgeted levels. If they differ by more than 20 percent, the reports are less useful. Additionally, the total VOH usage variance is compared to the budget in absolute dollars.

## Fixed Overhead Costs

Fixed overheads include all other expenses at the manufacturing plant (e.g., engineering, purchasing, shipping, accounting, and data processing). Traditionally, these costs were allocated to product lines, based on their labor content. This assumes that labor is an activity that drives the size of the fixed overhead. Prior to the current high level of automation, this was probably true. However, at Siecor, this is not the case. Consequently, the current management accounting system measures *activities that cause resources to be needed* and allocates these overheads accordingly. Fixed costs are 15 percent of Keller's total expenses.

Within the fixed overhead pool, there are costs referred to as *variable-fixed* (they change as a product line changes) and *fixed-fixed* (they do not change as dramatically as a product changes). The fixed-fixed costs are also referred

1990 KELLER PLANT BUDGET: PRODUCTION RATES

| CC | DESCRIPTION | HOURS | STD DL | VOH: DL FRINGES | VOH: WKMN COMP | OTHER DIRECT VOH | ALLOCATED VOH | TOTAL VOH | TOTAL VC |
|---|---|---|---|---|---|---|---|---|---|
| 910 | Stubs | 23,477 | $ 189,284 | 37,523 | 7,289 | 47,124 | 18.800 | 110,736 | 300,020 |
| 920 | Cross Connect Assm | 62,240 | $ 591,601 | 209,663 | 40,730 | 65,010 | 60,634 | 376,037 | 967,638 |
| 923 | Crating | 8,429 | $ 66,476 | 20,784 | 4,038 | 16,325 | 7,195 | 48,342 | 114,818 |
| 924 | Fiber Optic Hrdw | 17,616 | $ 140,567 | 51,412 | 9,987 | 41,723 | 16,291 | 119,413 | 259,980 |
| 931 | PCB Assembly | | | | | 0 | 0 | 0 | 0 |
| 932 | Electronic Assembly | | | | | 0 | 0 | 0 | 0 |
| 933 | Connectors | 69,756 | $ 543,678 | 171,098 | 33,238 | 76,952 | 55,149 | 336,437 | 880,115 |
| 936 | Nid Assembly | 195,528 | $1,480,501 | 484,555 | 94,131 | 243,622 | 153,943 | 976,251 | 2,456,752 |
| 945 | Fab Shop | 66,813 | $ 691,081 | 258,338 | 50,186 | 376,556 | 91,997 | 777,077 | 1,468,158 |
| 960 | Molding | 78,473 | $ 585,039 | 182,233 | 35,401 | 498,600 | 86,991 | 803,225 | 1,388,264 |
| | Total Keller Plant | 522,332 | $4,288,227 | 1,415,606 | 275,000 | 1,365,912 | 491,000 | 3,547,518 | 7,835,745 |

| COST CENTERS | | VOH TO BE ALLOCATED |
|---|---|---|
| 068 | General Plant Expense | $ 230,000 |
| 095 | Maintenance | 135,000 |
| 096 | Model Shop | 0 |
| 097 | Quality Control | 0 |
| 098 | Receiving/Stockroom | 0 |
| 099 | Shipping | 102,000 |
| 930 | Mexico Assembly | 24,000 |
| | Total Allocations | $ 491,000 |

> VOH allocation based on direct variable cost dollars

**Figure 13-21A**
**Siecor-Keller Variable Overhead Rates**

1990 KELLER PLANT BUDGET: PRODUCTION RATES

| CC | DESCRIPTION | DL Rate | Prod Factor | Adj DL Rate | VOH Factor | Adj VOH Rate | Adj Var Hr Rate | VC Rate /Min |
|---|---|---|---|---|---|---|---|---|
| 910 | Stubs | $ 8.06 | 90% | $ 8.96 | 0.585 | $ 5.24 | $14.19 | $ 0.237 |
| 920 | Cross Connect Assm | $ 9.51 | 90% | $10.57 | 0.636 | $ 6.72 | $17.28 | $ 0.288 |
| 923 | Crating | $ 7.89 | 85% | $ 9.28 | 0.727 | $ 6.75 | $16.03 | $ 0.267 |
| 924 | Fiber Optic Hrdw | $ 7.98 | 85% | $ 9.39 | 0.850 | $ 7.98 | $17.36 | $ 0.289 |
| 931 | PCB Assembly | | | | | | | |
| 932 | Electronic Assembly | | | | | | | |
| 933 | Connectors | $ 7.79 | 85% | $ 9.16 | 0.619 | $ 5.67 | $14.84 | $ 0.247 |
| 936 | Nid Assembly | $ 7.57 | 85% | $ 8.91 | 0.850 | $ 5.87 | $14.78 | $ 0.246 |
| 945 | Fab Shop | $10.34 | 85% | $12.16 | 1.124 | $13.68 | $25.84 | $ 0.431 |
| 960 | Molding | $ 7.46 | 90% | $ 8.29 | 1.373 | $11.38 | $19.67 | $ 0.328 |
| | Total Keller Plant | $ 8.21 | 87% | $ 9.49 | 0.827 | $ 7.85 | $17.34 | $ 0.289 |

**Figure 13-21B**
**The Variable Cost (VC) Rate by the Cost Center**
**(Hourly and Minute Rate)**

to as an *administrative overhead.* Whether the fixed-fixed costs are allocated to specific product lines depends on the management exercise. The goal is to provide an as accurate as possible allocation of all the expenses associated with a product line. To measure the overall profitability of the product lines, fixed-fixed costs are allocated to each product line according to the format illustrated in Figure 13-22. To determine whether to abandon a product line, or go on with production, fixed-fixed costs are considered in a separate product category. Following is the methodology used in this activity-based costing system.

### DEPRECIATION

Depreciation is the cost of the capital equipment in the business (30 percent of total fixed costs). Some of this equipment is machines used in direct manufacturing cost centers (75 percent of total depreciation). Quarterly studies are done to determine how much each product line uses of this equipment and the percentage is used to allocate the appreciation. The remaining 25 percent of depreciation is considered to be fixed-fixed and is allocated based on the

1. Number of people employed by each product line
2. Amount of space used by each product line

PRODUCT LINE F&LS W/FIXED/FIXED

| 1991 BUDGET | Product Lines | | | | | | | |
|---|---|---|---|---|---|---|---|---|
| | **NIDs** | **X-Conn** | **Stubs** | **Conn/M Spl** | **Inter Hdwe** | **Sp Hdwe** | **Fixed/Fixed** | **Total** |
| NET SALES | | | | | | | | |
| VARIABLE MARGIN | | | | | | | | |
| PERCENT OF SALES | | | | | | | | |
| TOTAL--# INDIRECTS(F) | | | | | | | | |
| TOTAL--# EXEMPTS & A&TS | | | | | | | | |
| TOTAL FIXED SPENDING | | | | | | | | |
| PERCENT OF SALES | | | | | | | | |
| PLANT GROSS MARGIN | | | | | | | | |
| PERCENT OF SALES | | | | | | | | |
| EXEMPT MARKETING--# | | | | | | | | |
| TOTAL MARKETING | | | | | | | | |
| PERCENT OF SALES | | | | | | | | |
| EXEMPT TECHNOLOGY--# | | | | | | | | |
| TOTAL TECHNOLOGY | | | | | | | | |
| PERCENT OF SALES | | | | | | | | |
| SELLING | | | | | | | | |
| PERCENT OF SALES | | | | | | | | |
| TOTAL CORPORATE | | | | | | | | |
| PERCENT OF SALES | | | | | | | | |
| BUSINESS PROFIT | | | | | | | | |
| PERCENT OF SALES | | | | | | | | |

**Figure 13-22**
**Siecor-Keller Report Assigning Costs and Expenses to Product Lines and Fixed/Fixed "Product Category"**

There is little that can be done to control this expense after the equipment is purchased. However, understanding the cost drivers is improving the prepurchase analysis of appropriation requests.

### THE PEOPLE EXPENSE

Approximately 55 percent of total fixed costs, which constitutes 30 percent of the total spending, are associated with people. This includes both their wages and fringes as well as the related expenses to support them in their jobs (for example, operating supplies, travel, outside contractors). These expenses are grouped into specific cost pools, and a cost driver is identified for each pool. This cost driver is used for both allocating and controlling the spending in that cost pool.

For example, in the stockroom, the cost driver is the number of parts picked, as shown in Figure 13-23. Quarterly, they track one week of parts picking. Accounting uses these figures to allocate the stockroom spending. This drives the total stockroom spending down.

| PRODUCT | # PARTS PICKED BEFORE JIT & KANBAN | # PARTS PICKED NOW | % PARTS PICKED NOW VS BEFORE |
|---|---|---|---|
| SAC 3600 | 7 | 1 | 14.3% |
| 3600 WIRE TRAY | 41 | 4 | 9.8% |
| 3600 FINAL ASSY | 120 | 24 | 20.0% |
| FDC-001 | 56 | 2 | 3.6% |
| WIC-001 | 24 | 1 | 4,2% |
| C-MIC-012 | 30 | 0 | 0.0% |
| C-MIC-024 | 32 | 1 | 3.1% |
| BH 1800 | 97 | 16 | 16.5% |
| HEAD ASSY 1800 | 17 | 2 | 11.8% |
| FSC-03D | 35 | 0 | 0.0% |
| CPC-D24 | 40 | 5 | 12.5% |
| TOTAL | 499 | 56 | 11.2% |

**Figure 13-23**
**Controlling Stockroom Spending by Applying Cost Drivers**

Also, quarterly, studies are done to determine on which product lines each cost center spends their time, and the percentage is used to allocate their costs, as shown in the Keller product line report. Management also uses this data to decide where to set up Just-in-Time programs. Thus, the ABCS costing system is used for both analyzing and controlling the fixed spending.

Another example of ABCS use is configuration control. This is the department that maintains product structures on the computer system. Quarterly, they track where they spend their time. This information is used to allocate the configuration control spending and, more important, to determine the ways to streamline their jobs. Once again, we see the ways of analyzing and controlling the fixed spending—says Tony Tripeny of Siecor-Keller plant.

A final example is the technology spending. This is what R&D spends on the business. Weekly, everyone completes a time card showing where he or she spent his or her time. Quarterly, these data are analyzed by the type of spending (e.g., development project, marketing support, manufacturing support). The product line data are the cost driver used for allocating the technology spending. Both analyses are used for determining changes in manning and priorities. Thus, this is not only used to control the fixed spending, but also to ensure a proper return on the spending.

#### OTHER EXPENSES

The remaining 15 percent of the fixed costs and 5 percent of the spending are made up of the building expenses (e.g., property tax, insurance, utilities) and other business expenses (e.g., warranty, royalties, obsolescence). Quarterly, each of these costs is reviewed, based on the primary activity that generates them (e.g., investment levels for property tax, machine utilization for utilities), and they are then allocated to each product line. The product line analysis is the cost driver used for allocating the sales aids spending. Both analyses are reviewed to ensure a proper return for this spending.

#### CONTROLS

The primary control for fixed expenses is the cost center responsibility report. This compares the actual spending to the budget projections. Any significant variances are analyzed as part of the monthly reporting package. Additionally, fixed costs are compared to the budget both by the product line and totals.

### Selling, Marketing, and Technology

Selling, marketing, and technology overheads include all the expenses associated with these three activities. Traditionally, these expenses were not allocated to product lines, but were assumed to be a nonproduct expense. This assumes that these costs have no relationship to the profitability of the product line. Obviously, this is not the case. Consequently, the current management accounting system measures activities that cause these resources to be needed and allocates them accordingly.

Selling, marketing, and technology constitute 15 percent of Keller's total costs. The same methodology used for fixed costs is used for allocating and controlling the selling, marketing, and technology expenses. Also, the same distinction between fixed-variable and fixed-fixed expenses applies. Quarterly, studies are done to determine on which product line each cost center spends its time and the percentage used to allocate these expenses.

### Corporate Allocation

Corporate allocation costs are a portion of total corporate expenses that are allocated to the Keller's business. Traditionally, these costs were not allocated to product lines, but were assumed to be nonproduct expenses. In a lot of ways this is still the case, since there are few activities within the product lines that cause corporate resources to be allocated. Thus a simplified method of allocating is used, whereby half the corporate costs are allocated based on sales and the other half are allocated based on assets. This is not 100 percent accurate, but it is reasonably close. Corporate costs constitute 10 percent of the Keller's total costs.

### Inventory and Fixed Assets Investment

In addition to the profit and loss data, the accounting system is used to manage the assets. Inventory reports generated by the costing system are sorted by the product line. These reports are used monthly to calculate inventory turns, which are compared to budget. They are used to identify problem inventory areas. Fixed assets are allocated by the product line using the same methodology as the depreciation allocation (direct use, floor space, and staffing).

### Return on Net Assets

At this point, BOM is divided into inventory and fixed asset investment to generate a modified *return on net assets* (RONA). RONA differs from the traditional financial measurement, since it doesn't include taxes in income or cash, receivables, or payables in the investment base. However, it is good for measuring all the variables the Keller business can control and is used for comparing product line performance, as shown in Figure 13-24.

### Benefits

The Siecor cost accounting system is similar to the traditional standard cost accounting, good at measuring the direct cost associated with building a product. Since direct costs constitute 60 percent of the total expenses at Keller,

OPERATING RESULTS
KELLER HARDWARE BUSINESS
1989 ACTUALS

| CATEGORY | NIDS | STAT-APP | STUBS | CONN/MECH | AMR | X-CONN | IC- HDWE | SPLICE | TOTAL |
|---|---|---|---|---|---|---|---|---|---|
| SALES | | | | | | | | | |
| DIRECT COGS | | | | | | | | | |
| VARIABLE MARGIN | | | | | | | | | |
| PLANT FIXED | | | | | | | | | |
| GROSS MARGIN | | | | | | | | | |
| TECHNOLOGY | | | | | | | | | |
| SELLING | | | | | | | | | |
| MARKETING | | | | | | | | | |
| CORPORATE CHARGE | | | | | | | | | |
| BUSINESS PROFIT | | | | | | | | | |
| INVESTMENT | | | | | | | | | |
| DIRECT ASSETS | | | | | | | | | |
| INDIRECT ASSETS | | | | | | | | | |
| INVENTORY | | | | | | | | | |
| TOTAL | | | | | | | | | |
| RONA | | | | | | | | | |

**Figure 13-24**
**Estimating RONA for the Keller Hardware Product Line**

This material is used with permission of Siecor Corporation, Keller, Texas plant.

it is important to report, analyze, and control these costs. However, if the management accounting system stops here, relying on inaccurate allocations for fixed costs, 40 percent of the remaining controllable costs are missed. Fixed spending is ignored by most traditional standard cost accounting systems. They are controlled by some method (e.g., last year's spending plus inflation), but they will not be accurately integrated into product costs. Thus, they are not used in many decisions that require a good understanding of a product cost structure (e.g., pricing, resource allocation, capital expenditures). Using a system that allocates the fixed expenses based on the activities that generate these costs provides a more accurate measure of product costs.

An activity-based costing system addresses fixed spending. An ABCS system improves control by analyzing a critical item—what drives the expenses. This is used to reduce the total spending or to ensure a proper return on that spending. An ABCS costing system also improves control by accurately integrating the fixed spending into the product costs.

At Siecor-Keller, moving to the product line P&L management accounting system provides a number of benefits says R. Tony Tripeny, controller, one of the principal architects of the Siecor-Keller plant's activity-based costing system. Based on this system, all product lines were reviewed, those that were not profitable were addressed with specific action items, the total amount of overhead was reduced, and the annual profitability was greatly improved. This system truly meets the requirements of providing management with information that impacts decision making.

# 14

# Getting the Most Out of Quality Control Systems

*Quality* is defined as fitness for use. The consumer expects a product to look attractive, to function as it was intended, and to last for a reasonable amount of time. Such expectations correspond to what we'll call the *three product attributes*: appearance, function, and reliability. Quality and production cost are the main factors in a production system which influencing the product's inert value. Quality control, then, is a single function dealing with two variables of the product value: its quality and its cost. The cost of maintaining quality in American industry sometimes can reach up to as much as 20 to 25 percent of the total production costs.

The objective of quality control is to build an effective system for integrating the efforts of those in an organization responsible for designing and maintaining quality standards and for taking corrective actions.

Two factors are considered when measuring quality:

1. Quality of product's design
2. Quality of product's performance

## THE IMPORTANCE OF DESIGN IN QUALITY CONTROL TO INCREASE PRODUCT VALUE

Design is the first step in the production process, during which a designer conceptualizes the product and develops its adequate form and pattern. Up to this stage, a customer has had a general idea of what his or her needs are. A designer formalizes this idea into a concrete product.

There are basically two parties in any business relationship—a customer who has a need and a production facility with the capacity to satisfy that need. A designer provides the link between the customer and the producer by formalizing the customer's need into the designed product. This relationship is illustrated in Figure 14-1. A designer exerts an influence on both the customer and the producer, since there are many ways to attain the result the customer wants. Design is a stage of selecting quality attributes and establishing product specifications, along with planning manufacturing processes, while the product characteristics are being selected.

If a designer is familiar with the available production capacities, he or she designs a product that can be quality produced with the existing production resources. For example, the same assembly housing can be produced by forging, machining, stamping, or sometimes injection molding. Thus, a designer should

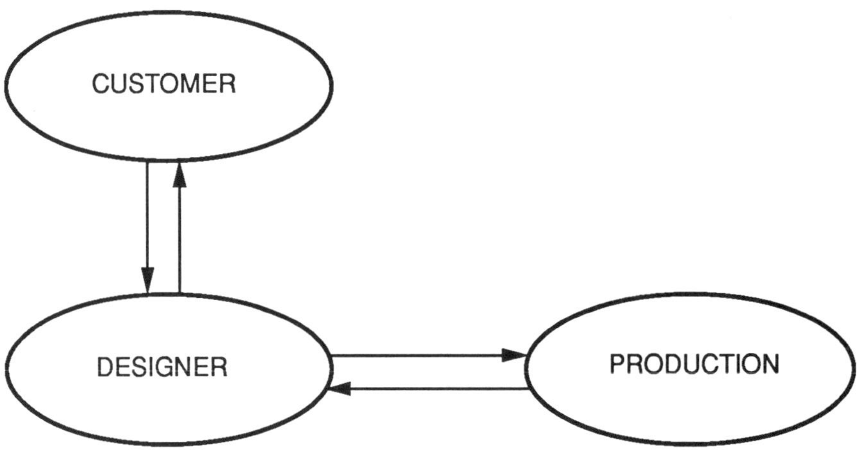


**Figure 14-1**
**A Designer Is a Link Between the Customer and Production**

also be a manufacturing engineer, in order to make the most out of the available resources. This role of a designer-process engineer is a recently emerging function because a designer should be able to envision how each of the designed components is going to be produced. The emerging function of a designer-process engineer is illustrated in Figure 14-2.

The Japanese say that 40 percent of quality problems is attributed to the unsatisfactory design. Another 40 percent of quality problems is attributed to poor production management. Managers are the designers of the production systems and, as such, are responsible for putting adequate production and business resources in place. The equipment should be capable of producing components according to the product specifications, fits, and tolerances specified in the drawings. The operators should be competent, well trained, and motivated to do the job correctly. In other words, the manager's responsibility is to create a reliable industrial environment where people and machines can adequately perform according to a quality standard. Both design and management functions take place at the preproduction stage. The remaining 20 percent of quality problems occur at the production stage, with many of these faults being attributed to the execution function.

Figure 14-3 illustrates the distribution of responsibility for quality problems between production and support functions. It is just accidental that quality

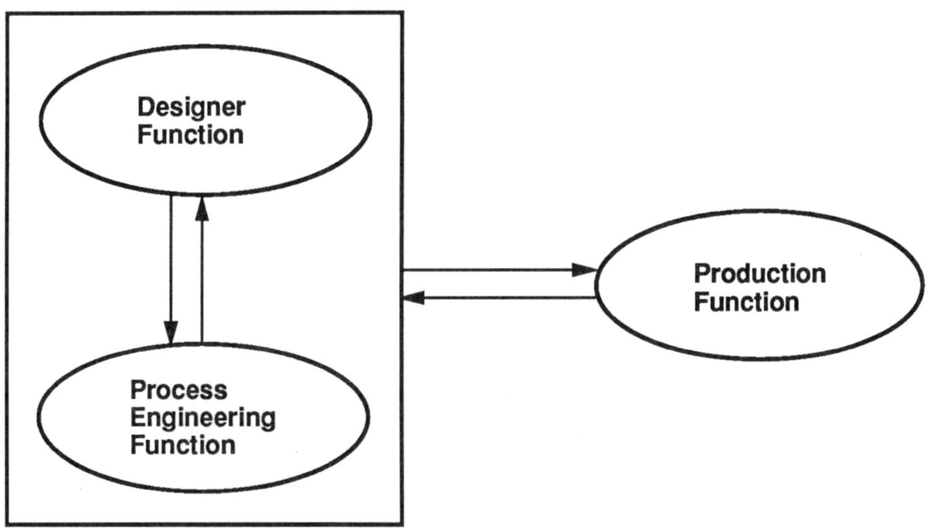


**Figure 14-2**
**The Emerging Function of Designer/Manufacturing Engineer**

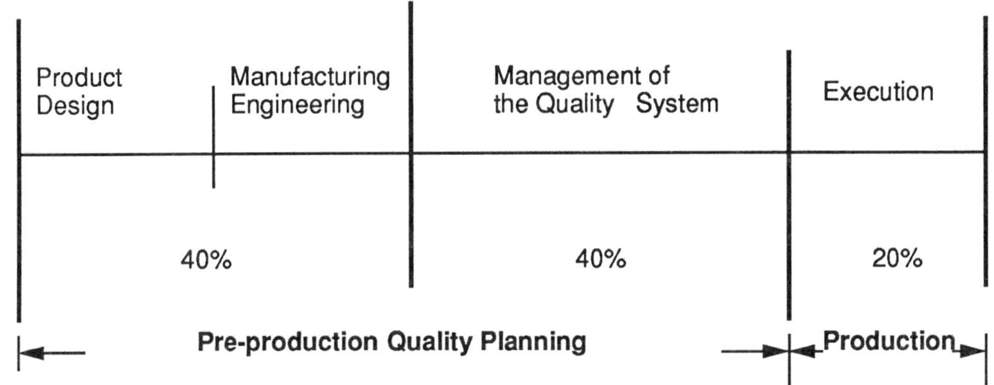


**Figure 14-3**
**The Distribution of Responsibility for Quality Problems between Production and Support Functions**

faults come to the surface during execution. Nevertheless, many causes of these faults can be traced back to the preproduction stage.

## HOW QUALITY OF CONFORMANCE INCREASES PRODUCT VALUE

Quality of conformance refers to the degree to which products conform to design. Conformance can be attained by either sorting the products into good and bad after production or by taking preventive measures to guard against any deviation from the established standard.

Until recently, quality was regarded as the function of cost—quality can be improved, but it costs money. Now quality is considered in relation to the product value. A quality improvement that increases production costs often does not increase the product value, and in the some instances quality improvements increase the production cost to a such an extent that the product value is reduced.

In production, quality is a function of attitude and morale, not a function of increased cost. If the attitude is wrong, then a costly quality improvement does not last long. Quality enhancement, based on such a condition as employees' motivation, is compatible with the JIT principles of continuous improvement programs. Now, this is considered a standard for the quality improvement.

A constant attention to quality issues and a concerted effort by designers and engineers, production managers, and shop floor personnel highlight quality as an acknowledged mode of conduct. Classifying the production planning function into product and process concepts is also useful in quality control.

Quality issues dealing with product design, specifications, and quality standards are known as *product control.* This is the first factor required for adequate product quality. The process capability to perform according to the product specifications is known as *process control.* There are two factors in process control: the technical factor and the human factor. The *technical factor* is attributed to the technical side of operation (that is, the capability of an equipment to adhere to quality standards). The *human factor* is attributed to the operation and management of equipment, to the operators' skill level, as well as to how well they are trained and their degree of alertness and motivation. The three factors affecting quality are illustrated in Figure 14-4. All quality control problems can be traced to one or more of these factors, since for an adequate quality level, all three factors must be present.

| **Product control** | **Process control** | |
|---|---|---|
| | Technical factor | Human factor |
| Quality of design, specifications and standards | Capability of equipment | Work force motivation and morale |

**Figure 14-4**
**The Three Factors Affecting Quality**

## GETTING A HANDLE ON THE QUALITY COST SYSTEM

Cost is becoming a common measure of performance for functional production units and services. Thus, cost can be used as a common denominator for evaluating performance of diverse production and service activities. Consequently, the cost of quality becomes a measure of efficiency of the quality control system. A quality cost evaluation within the framework of a quality control system lists procedures for identifying and quantifying all costs associated with quality losses. These three quality cost categories correspond directly to the three stages of product development:

1. Costs accrued at the preproduction stage
2. Costs accrued at the production stage, including delivery
3. Costs accrued at the post-production stage

### Cost Prevention at the Preproduction Stage

Quality costs incurred at the preproduction stage are known as *prevention costs*. Prevention costs include the cost of activities taking place after design and manufacturing engineering specialists have prepared their specifications and quality standards.

Execution is preceded by planning. The quality function is no exception: a satisfactory quality performance requires preliminary planning known as *quality planning*. Quality planning is a management function which involves

- Developing a quality strategy
- Creating a quality control system, as well as an overall quality plan, a reliability plan and an inspection plan
- Compiling operating instructions, manuals, and procedures for installation and compliance with quality standards

Prevention costs include the cost of preparing and conducting quality programs. Training is an ongoing process. Individual training programs are determined by the actual needs of employees for increasing their technical knowledge, job skills, or changing attitudes. Quality training programs include training in statistical quality control. The emphasis should be on the prevention of poor quality, while inspection is deemphasized.

### Minimizing Quality Control Costs at the Production Stage

Quality costs at the production stage include the cost of inspections, known as *appraisal costs*, and the cost of defects, known as *failure costs*. Appraisal costs include the cost of measuring, evaluating, or auditing products, components, and purchased materials to assure the conformance with the quality standards for both internally produced components and incoming materials. The appraisal cost also includes the cost of maintaining the test equipment in proper working condition.

An *internal failure cost* refers to two major quality cost categories: *scrap* and *rework*. Quality losses, incurred from the net loss in capacity and material due to defects, cannot be economically rectified. Each scrap case usually involves rework of the defect-causing operation. Rework includes correcting defective components so as to make them fit for use. Such rework often requires special operations, along with devising new temporary work standards.

The internal failure cost includes hidden losses due to the interruption of the production program and material flow as well as the inevitable buildup of inventories and postponed delivery dates.

### Eliminating Quality Costs at the Postproduction Stage

The postproduction quality cost arises from product failure at the customer's site. It includes the cost of a returned material and complaints adjustment, warranty costs, and sometimes even litigation costs. Postproduction quality cost improvements accomplished through quality assurance projects and product and process control establish final product inspection procedures, employees training, and on-site service support and customer training.

An efficient way to effect postproduction cost improvements is to standardize and intensify the final product inspection procedure. This produces a twofold advantage, namely, reducing the number of faulty products sent to a customer and enabling the identification of elements in product design and operations or production processes responsible for quality defects.

## HOW TO ORGANIZE A QUALITY COST REPORTING SYSTEM

The effectiveness of any quality control system can be measured in the monetary value by the total quality cost computed as the sum of four cost categories. The four quality cost categories are internal failure cost, external failure cost, appraisal cost, and prevention cost. The total quality cost is strongly influenced by an interplay between these cost categories. In well-developed quality control systems, cost estimates are reported in monthly, quarterly, and annual quality reports. Often it becomes a formal quality cost reporting system. An example of an annual quality cost statement is illustrated in Figure 14-5.

There are three steps in establishing a quality cost reporting system:

1. First is to draw a list of four cost categories and their constituent costs.

| | Cost Description | Amount (in dollars) | | |
|---|---|---|---|---|
| | **Internal Defectives in the Mill** | | | |
| 1 | Scraped components | | 18,510 | |
| 2 | Start-up cost | | 33,155 | |
| 3 | Machine efficiency losses | | 59,290 | |
| | | **Total** | | 110,955 |
| | **External Defectives in the Field** | | | |
| 1 | Returned goods by customers | | 19,200 | |
| 2 | Warranty cost | | 8,650 | |
| 3 | Consequential loss claims | | 10,780 | |
| 4 | Customer complaints | | 7,000 | |
| | | **Total** | | 45,630 |
| | **Inspection Costs Appraisal** | | | |
| 1 | Incoming material control | | 29,800 | |
| 2 | Rejects | | 3,860 | |
| 3 | Rework | | 10,300 | |
| 4 | Testing at machines | | 38,760 | |
| 5 | Final assembly testing | | 11,900 | |
| 6 | Maintenance of testing equipment | | 2,010 | |
| | | **Total** | | 96,630 |
| | **Quality Improvement Costs** | | | |
| 1 | Quality assurance project | | 15,880 | |
| 2 | Process improvement | | 8,500 | |
| 3 | Employees training | | 3,000 | |
| | | **Total** | | 27,380 |
| | **Total Quality Costs** | | | 280,595 |
| | **Percentage Of Total Sales** | | | 4% |

**Figure 14-5**
**An Annual Quality Cost Statement**

2. Second is to collect quality cost data, using quality reports, scrap and rework reports, inspection and tests records (including the salary of the quality control personnel), quality budgets, and the cost of quality improvement schemes.
3. Third is to analyze quality cost categories and draw up a course of action to reduce the total quality cost.

Investments in the prevention and appraisal are considered inputs, while the internal and external failure costs are considered outputs.

Figure 14-6 illustrates four steps for the quality cost reduction at the Precision Mold and Tool Company. An initial analysis (shown in step 1) indicates a high content of external failure costs. The target of any quality improvement program, therefore, is to eliminate external failure costs by imposing inspections, in order to detect defects and to prevent the faulty components from being assembled. Such a tactic increases the appraisal cost but, at the same time, drives down external failure costs. Increased inspections prevent defective products

| **Quality Cost Category** | **Steps in Quality Cost Reduction** ($0,000.00) | | | |
|---|---|---|---|---|
| | Step 1 | Step 2 | Step 3 | Step 4 |
| External failures | 40 | 12 | 7 | 2 |
| Internal failures | 8 | 15 | 8 | 3 |
| Sorting | 1 | 4 | 2 | 1 |
| Process control | 1 | 1 | 2 | 2 |
| Prevention | 1 | 1 | 1 | 2 |
| **Total** | 51 | 33 | 20 | 10 |

**Figure 14-6**
**The Model of Interplay Among Quality Cost Categories**

from being delivered to customers and hence reduce the external failure cost. Initially, this measure for the cost reduction (shown in step 2) increases the internal failure cost. In our example, internal failure cost rises from $8,000 to $15,000, since the defects revealed by inspections are then addressed within the company. However, the total quality cost is reduced from $51,000 to $33,000.

In batch production, statistical quality control performed by operators can reduce such defects. Statistical quality control reduces the internal failure cost and the appraisal cost (the cost of inspections and process control shown in step 3), while the external failure cost continues to decrease. The total quality cost is reduced at this stage from $33,000 to $20,000.

The next stage in this quality cost reduction program (step 4) is setting up a defect prevention program, including the education and training of operators. At Precision Mold and Tool Company, this includes the training of operators in the basics of trigonometry, drafting, and computerized numerical control (CNC) programming as well as the high-precision machining and finishing operations typical for injection moulds production.

Raising the prevention cost has resulted in further reduction of the total quality cost from $20,000 in step 3 to $10,000 in step 4 of the quality cost improvement program. A further decrease of the total quality cost is achieved within the framework of the Just-in-Time system, widely known as JIT-total quality control (JIT-TQC).

## USING STATISTICAL METHODS IN QUALITY CONTROL

Statistical quality control was introduced in 1924 by Walter Shewhart of Bell Laboratories as a method for tracking quality control in the mass production environment. In this method, two quality control techniques have been identified for verifying the degree to which a product meets its quality standards:

1. An acceptance sampling plan
2. Quality control charts

### Using Acceptance Sampling

An *acceptance sampling quality control method* is used when a decision must be made on accepting or rejecting a lot of components, based on the established percentage of defective quality standards. The sure way to adhere to the quality standards is by means of a 100 percent inspection and by replacing or repairing all the faulty components. However, this is not always feasible, due to human error, inaccuracy in measuring tools when inspecting large lots, or situations that require a destructive test, not to mention the high cost of a 100 percent inspection. Go no-go or pass-fail inspections are known as the *sampling by attributes*. Inspections of qualities which are measured in figures (e.g., an amount of deviation from the set standard) are known as the *sampling by variables*.

An acceptance sampling or, as it is often called, random sampling, is used to determine the acceptability of the lot, based on how many defects are found in a sample.

The following quality standards established as part of a sampling plan:

- An acceptable quality level (AQL)
- A lot tolerance percentage defective (LTPD)

An *acceptable quality level* is the quality level of a lot which is considered good. For example, if the agreed quality level is 2 defects in a lot of 100 items, then the AQL is 2/100, or 2 percent defective. A *lot tolerance percentage defective* is the agreed quality level of a lot which should be rejected. For example, if the agreed unacceptable quality level is 7 defects in a lot of 100 items, then the LTPD is 7/100, or 7 percent defective.

The risk in the acceptance sampling is attributed to two types of errors:

1. *Producer's risk* (type 1 error). This is the probability that a lot will be rejected when it, in fact, meets the specifications. Producer's risk is designated by $\alpha$ and is typically set at $\alpha = 0.05$, or 5 percent.
2. *Consumer's risk* (type 2 error). This is the probability that a lot will be accepted when it, in fact, does not meet the specifications. Consumer's risk is designated by $\beta$ and is typically set at $\beta = 0.10$, or 10 percent.

The possible outcomes of an acceptance sampling plan due to two types of errors are illustrated in Figure 14-7.

After selecting the values for AQL, LTPD, $\alpha$, and $\beta$, a sampling plan can be structured. The following types of such plan are distinguished:

1. A single sampling plan
2. A double sampling plan
3. A multiple sampling plan

In a *single sampling plan,* each component in a random sample is examined. There $n$ denotes the sample's size, while $c$ denotes the allowed number of defective in a sample. A lot is accepted, if the number of defective in a random sample does not exceed $c$. A lot is rejected, if the the number of defective in a random sample is greater than $c$.

In a *double sampling plan,* a second sample is drawn from the lot, if the results of the first sample are inconclusive. A double sampling plan specifies the sample size, according to the lot size, the acceptable quality level $c_1$, the number of defective found in a sample, and the rejection level $c_2$. Samples containing the number of defectives over $c_2$ call for rejection of the lot. Samples containing the number of defectives between $c_1$ and $c_2$ call for a second sample

| Quality Level | Outcome of Inspection | |
|---|---|---|
| | Lot Is Accepted | Lot Is Rejected |
| A Good Lot -- AQL | Correct Judgment | Incorrect Judgment: Producer's Risk **Type 1 Error** |
| A Bad Lot -- LTPD | Incorrect Judgment: Consumer's Risk **Type 2 Error** | Correct Judgment |

**Figure 14-7**
**The Outcome of the Acceptance Sampling Plan**

to be taken. The second sample in a double sampling plan considers $c_3$, a single cumulative acceptance number which, if exceeded in a sample, requires the rejection of the lot.

An example of a double sampling plan, if we had a sample of 20, would be

$n = 20;\ c_1 = 2;\ c_2 = 4;\ c_3 = 5$

Where:

$n$ = sample size
$c_1$ = allowed number of defectives in sample
$c_2$ = number of defectives in sample calling for rejection of the lot
$c_3$ = the second sample—a cumulative number of defectives in two samples calling for rejection of the lot

A lot is rejected if the cumulative number of defective in two samples is greater than 5.

Using a sampling plan, an *operating characteristic* (OC) curve can be developed. An operating characteristic curve shows the characteristics of the acceptance sampling plan devised, as well as the accuracy with which the plan discriminates between good and bad lots. The OC shows the probability of acceptance of the sample. For each combination of $n$ and $c$, there is a unique OC curve.

Figure 14-8 shows an ideal case with the acceptance rate of 2 percent, where all lots less than 2 percent defective are accepted (a shaded area on a graph) and lots of more than 2 percent defective are rejected.

The relationship among α, β, AQL, and LTPD is shown in Figure 14-9. According to this curve, there is a 5 percent chance that lots of 2 percent defective will be accepted—producer's risk. There is a 50 percent probability of lots being accepted with 5 defective and a 10 percent probability of lots being accepted with 7 percent defective. But the actual number of accepted 5-percent defective lots and 7-percent defective lots is small, considering that there are few such lots submitted for inspection in 2 percent defective acceptance

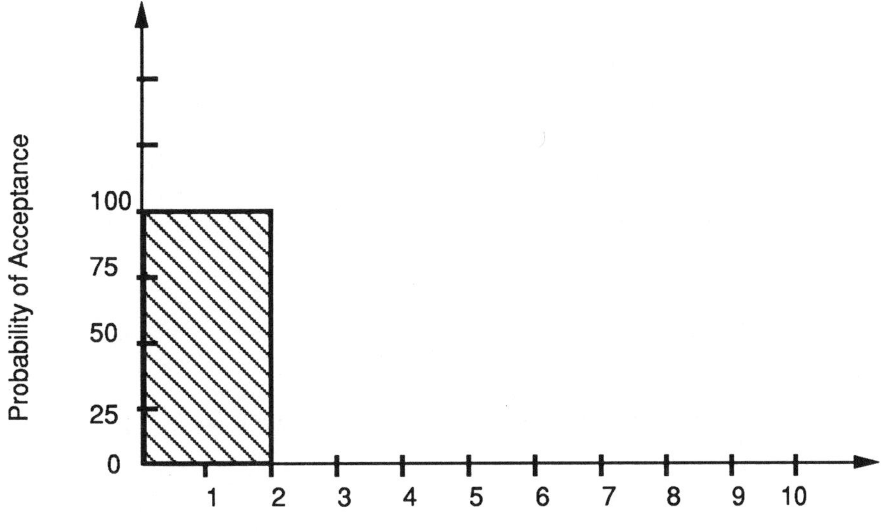


**Figure 14-8**
**Ideal Sampling Plan Performance**

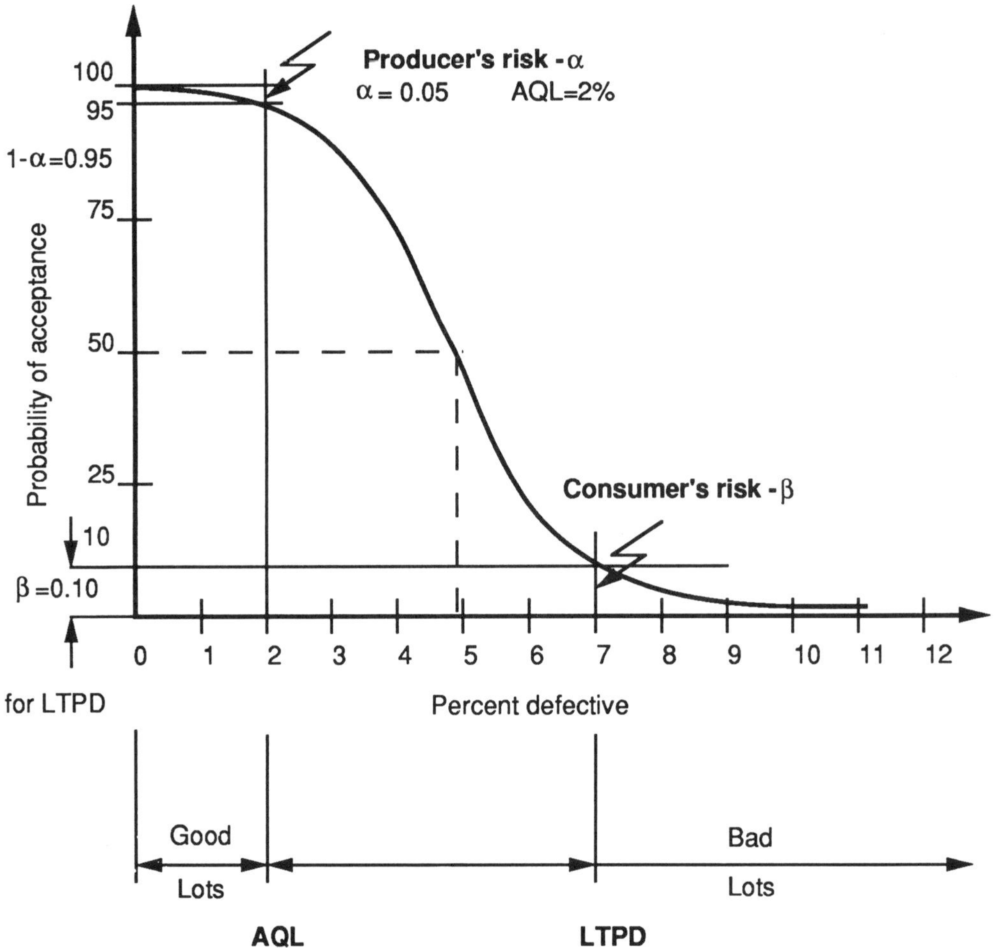


**Figure 14-9**
**The Operating Characteristic -- OC Curve**
**Showing Producer's and Consumer's Risk**

plan situations. Producer's risk $\alpha$ at AQL level and consumer's risk $\beta$ at LTPD level, from which the sample size $n$ and the acceptance number $c$ are determined, are set by a mutual agreement between the manufacturer and the supplier.

*Example:* Identify a sampling plan ($n$, $c$, $\alpha$, and $\beta$) for a lot of 1,000 semiconductors with AQL = 1% and LTPD = 3.4%.

*Solution:* The first step is to identify $n$ and $c$. Usually, these parameters of a sample are determined through military standard sampling procedures. The

U.S. Department of Defense has published tables for identifying the sample size according to the inspection level: *Military Standard Sampling Procedures and Tables for Inspection by Attributes* (MIL-STD-105E) (Washington, D.C.: U.S. Government Printing Office, 1989). The MIL-STD-105E tables present the coordinates of the OC curve and the sample size, based on information on the batch size, AQL, and level of inspection (level I, II, or III). In most cases, an inspection level II is selected.

To resolve this problem, we will use a general inspection level II, according to the Table 14-1. A general inspection level II for a lot size of 1,000 units corresponds to letter "J." In Table 14-2, the sample size for "J" is 80 units (shown in the second column). The acceptable number of defects $c$ for AQL = 1% is **2,** and the rejection number *Re* is 3 defectives per sample. The values of $\alpha$ and $\beta$ are found from the Table 14-3 in the column of the acceptable quality level AQL = 1%. In this column, the percentage defective $p$ for AQL = 1% is 1.03, which corresponds to the probability $P_o$ = 95% or 0.95 (see column 1). Then $\alpha = 1.0 - 0.95 = 0.05$.

In the same column, we find the value closest to the LTPD = 3%, which is 3.33, having the probability of acceptance of 50 percent or 0.5: So $\beta = 1.0 - 0.5 = 0.5$

The OC curve, illustrated in Figure 14-10, is drawn by joining the intersections of percentage defective $P$ with the probability of the acceptance $P$ presented in Table 14-3.

## SAMPLING PROCEDURES AT RUSKA INSTRUMENT CORP.: A CASE STUDY

Ruska Instrument Corporation is a 50-year-old instrument manufacturer located in Houston, Texas. The company designs and manufactures a variety of pressure measurement, control, and pressure, volume, and temperature (PVT) analysis instrumentation for use in industrial, government, military, and scientific applications. Ruska's Quality Department is headed by Greg Stocker, who over the past 10 years has also held positions in materials management. He has a background in materials and logistics management and in business management at the MBA level. He recognizes the significance of a wide spectrum of quality issues in business, especially statistical quality control, which he helped to develop at Ruska. Ruska Sampling Procedure for Dimensional Characteristics, shown in Exhibit 14-1, describes the sampling procedure used by the Inspection Department. This procedure is based upon MIL-STD-105E General Inspection Level II Sampling Plan, according to a lot size and dimensional characteristics (refer to page 6 of Exhibit 14-1). These statistical quality standards are successfully used by Ruska Instruments since 1984.

| Lot or batch size | | | Special inspection levels | | | | General inspection levels | | |
|---|---|---|---|---|---|---|---|---|---|
| | | | S-1 | S-2 | S-3 | S-4 | I | II | III |
| 2 | to | 8 | A | A | A | A | A | A | B |
| 9 | to | 15 | A | A | A | A | A | B | C |
| 16 | to | 25 | A | A | B | B | B | C | D |
| 26 | to | 50 | A | B | B | C | C | D | E |
| 51 | to | 90 | B | B | C | C | C | E | F |
| 91 | to | 150 | B | B | C | D | D | F | G |
| 151 | to | 280 | B | C | D | E | E | G | H |
| 281 | to | 500 | B | C | D | E | F | H | J |
| 501 | to | 1200 | C | C | E | F | G | J | K |
| 1201 | to | 3200 | C | D | E | G | H | K | L |
| 3201 | to | 10000 | C | D | F | G | J | L | M |
| 10001 | to | 35000 | C | D | F | H | K | M | N |
| 35001 | to | 150000 | D | E | G | J | L | N | P |
| 150001 | to | 500000 | D | E | G | J | M | P | Q |
| 500001 | and | over | D | E | H | K | N | Q | R |

**Table 14-1**
**Source: MIL-STD-105E, Department of Defense, 10 May, 1989**

| Sample size code letter | Sample size | Acceptable Quality Levels (normal inspection) | | | | | | | | | | | | | | | | | | | | | | | | | |
|---|---|---|---|---|---|---|---|---|---|---|---|---|---|---|---|---|---|---|---|---|---|---|---|---|---|---|---|
| | | 0.010 | 0.015 | 0.025 | 0.040 | 0.065 | 0.10 | 0.15 | 0.25 | 0.40 | 0.65 | 1.0 | 1.5 | 2.5 | 4.0 | 6.5 | 10 | 15 | 25 | 40 | 65 | 100 | 150 | 250 | 400 | 650 | 1000 |
| | | Ac Re | Ac Re | Ac Re | Ac Re | Ac Re | Ac Re | Ac Re | Ac Re | Ac Re | Ac Re | Ac Re | Ac Re | Ac Re | Ac Re | Ac Re | Ac Re | Ac Re | Ac Re | Ac Re | Ac Re | Ac Re | Ac Re | Ac Re | Ac Re | Ac Re | Ac Re |
| A | 2 | ↓ | ↓ | ↓ | ↓ | ↓ | ↓ | ↓ | ↓ | ↓ | ↓ | ↓ | ↓ | ↓ | ↓ | 0 1 | ↓ | ↓ | 1 2 | 2 3 | 3 4 | 5 6 | 7 8 | 10 11 | 14 15 | 21 22 | 30 31 |
| B | 3 | ↓ | ↓ | ↓ | ↓ | ↓ | ↓ | ↓ | ↓ | ↓ | ↓ | ↓ | ↓ | ↓ | 0 1 | ↑ | ↓ | 1 2 | 2 3 | 3 4 | 5 6 | 7 8 | 10 11 | 14 15 | 21 22 | 30 31 | 44 45 |
| C | 5 | ↓ | ↓ | ↓ | ↓ | ↓ | ↓ | ↓ | ↓ | ↓ | ↓ | ↓ | ↓ | 0 1 | ↑ | ↓ | 1 2 | 2 3 | 3 4 | 5 6 | 7 8 | 10 11 | 14 15 | 21 22 | 30 31 | 44 45 | ↑ |
| D | 8 | ↓ | ↓ | ↓ | ↓ | ↓ | ↓ | ↓ | ↓ | ↓ | ↓ | ↓ | 0 1 | ↑ | ↓ | 1 2 | 2 3 | 3 4 | 5 6 | 7 8 | 10 11 | 14 15 | 21 22 | 30 31 | 44 45 | ↑ | ↑ |
| E | 13 | ↓ | ↓ | ↓ | ↓ | ↓ | ↓ | ↓ | ↓ | ↓ | ↓ | 0 1 | ↑ | ↓ | 1 2 | 2 3 | 3 4 | 5 6 | 7 8 | 10 11 | 14 15 | 21 22 | 30 31 | 44 45 | ↑ | ↑ | ↑ |
| F | 20 | ↓ | ↓ | ↓ | ↓ | ↓ | ↓ | ↓ | ↓ | ↓ | 0 1 | ↑ | ↓ | 1 2 | 2 3 | 3 4 | 5 6 | 7 8 | 10 11 | 14 15 | 21 22 | ↑ | ↑ | ↑ | ↑ | ↑ | ↑ |
| G | 32 | ↓ | ↓ | ↓ | ↓ | ↓ | ↓ | ↓ | ↓ | 0 1 | ↑ | ↓ | 1 2 | 2 3 | 3 4 | 5 6 | 7 8 | 10 11 | 14 15 | 21 22 | ↑ | ↑ | ↑ | ↑ | ↑ | ↑ | ↑ |
| H | 50 | ↓ | ↓ | ↓ | ↓ | ↓ | ↓ | ↓ | 0 1 | ↑ | ↓ | 1 2 | 2 3 | 3 4 | 5 6 | 7 8 | 10 11 | 14 15 | 21 22 | ↑ | ↑ | ↑ | ↑ | ↑ | ↑ | ↑ | ↑ |
| J | 80 | ↓ | ↓ | ↓ | ↓ | ↓ | ↓ | 0 1 | ↑ | ↓ | 1 2 | 2 3 | 3 4 | 5 6 | 7 8 | 10 11 | 14 15 | 21 22 | ↑ | ↑ | ↑ | ↑ | ↑ | ↑ | ↑ | ↑ | ↑ |
| K | 125 | ↓ | ↓ | ↓ | ↓ | ↓ | 0 1 | ↑ | ↓ | 1 2 | 2 3 | 3 4 | 5 6 | 7 8 | 10 11 | 14 15 | 21 22 | ↑ | ↑ | ↑ | ↑ | ↑ | ↑ | ↑ | ↑ | ↑ | ↑ |
| L | 200 | ↓ | ↓ | ↓ | ↓ | 0 1 | ↑ | ↓ | 1 2 | 2 3 | 3 4 | 5 6 | 7 8 | 10 11 | 14 15 | 21 22 | ↑ | ↑ | ↑ | ↑ | ↑ | ↑ | ↑ | ↑ | ↑ | ↑ | ↑ |
| M | 315 | ↓ | ↓ | ↓ | 0 1 | ↑ | ↓ | 1 2 | 2 3 | 3 4 | 5 6 | 7 8 | 10 11 | 14 15 | 21 22 | ↑ | ↑ | ↑ | ↑ | ↑ | ↑ | ↑ | ↑ | ↑ | ↑ | ↑ | ↑ |
| N | 500 | ↓ | ↓ | 0 1 | ↑ | ↓ | 1 2 | 2 3 | 3 4 | 5 6 | 7 8 | 10 11 | 14 15 | 21 22 | ↑ | ↑ | ↑ | ↑ | ↑ | ↑ | ↑ | ↑ | ↑ | ↑ | ↑ | ↑ | ↑ |
| P | 800 | ↓ | 0 1 | ↑ | ↓ | 1 2 | 2 3 | 3 4 | 5 6 | 7 8 | 10 11 | 14 15 | 21 22 | ↑ | ↑ | ↑ | ↑ | ↑ | ↑ | ↑ | ↑ | ↑ | ↑ | ↑ | ↑ | ↑ | ↑ |
| Q | 1250 | 0 1 | ↑ | ↓ | 1 2 | 2 3 | 3 4 | 5 6 | 7 8 | 10 11 | 14 15 | 21 22 | ↑ | ↑ | ↑ | ↑ | ↑ | ↑ | ↑ | ↑ | ↑ | ↑ | ↑ | ↑ | ↑ | ↑ | ↑ |
| R | 2000 | ↑ | ↑ | 1 2 | 2 3 | 3 4 | 5 6 | 7 8 | 10 11 | 14 15 | 21 22 | ↑ | ↑ | ↑ | ↑ | ↑ | ↑ | ↑ | ↑ | ↑ | ↑ | ↑ | ↑ | ↑ | ↑ | ↑ | ↑ |

Table 14-2
Source: MIL-STD-105E, Department of Defense, 10 May, 1989

TABLE X-J-1 - TABULATED VALUES FOR OPERATING CHARACTERISTIC CURVES FOR SINGLE SAMPLING PLANS

| $P_a$ | Acceptable Quality Levels (normal inspection) | | | | | | | | | | | | | | | | | | | | | |
|---|---|---|---|---|---|---|---|---|---|---|---|---|---|---|---|---|---|---|---|---|---|---|
| | 0.15 | 0.65 | 1.0 | 1.5 | 2.5 | 4.0 | X | 6.5 | X | 10 | 0.15 | 0.65 | 1.0 | 1.5 | 2.5 | 4.0 | X | 6.5 | X | 10 | X | 15 |
| | p (in percent defective) | | | | | | | | | | p (in defects per hundred units) | | | | | | | | | | | |
| 99.0 | 0.0126 | 0.187 | 0.550 | 1.04 | 2.28 | 3.73 | 4.51 | 6.17 | 7.88 | 9.76 | 0.0126 | 0.186 | 0.545 | 1.03 | 2.23 | 3.63 | 4.38 | 5.96 | 7.62 | 9.35 | 12.9 | 15.7 |
| 95.0 | 0.0641 | 0.446 | 1.03 | 1.73 | 3.32 | 5.07 | 6.00 | 7.93 | 9.89 | 11.9 | 0.0641 | 0.444 | 1.02 | 1.71 | 3.27 | 4.98 | 5.87 | 7.71 | 9.61 | 11.6 | 15.6 | 18.6 |
| 90.0 | 0.132 | 0.667 | 1.39 | 2.20 | 3.99 | 5.91 | 6.90 | 8.95 | 11.0 | 13.2 | 0.132 | 0.665 | 1.38 | 2.18 | 3.94 | 5.82 | 6.79 | 8.78 | 10.8 | 12.9 | 17.1 | 20.3 |
| 75.0 | 0.359 | 1.201 | 2.16 | 3.18 | 5.30 | 7.50 | 8.61 | 10.9 | 13.2 | 15.5 | 0.360 | 1.20 | 2.16 | 3.17 | 5.27 | 7.45 | 8.55 | 10.8 | 13.0 | 15.3 | 19.9 | 23.4 |
| 50.0 | 0.863 | 2.09 | 3.33 | 4.57 | 7.06 | 9.55 | 10.8 | 13.3 | 15.8 | 18.3 | 0.866 | 2.10 | 3.34 | 4.59 | 7.09 | 9.59 | 10.8 | 13.3 | 15.8 | 18.3 | 23.3 | 27.1 |
| 25.0 | 1.72 | 3.33 | 4.84 | 6.30 | 9.14 | 11.9 | 13.3 | 16.0 | 18.6 | 21.3 | 1.73 | 3.37 | 4.90 | 6.39 | 9.28 | 12.1 | 13.5 | 16.3 | 19.0 | 21.7 | 27.2 | 31.2 |
| 10.0 | 2.84 | 4.78 | 6.52 | 8.16 | 11.3 | 14.3 | 15.7 | 18.6 | 21.4 | 24.2 | 2.88 | 4.86 | 6.65 | 8.35 | 11.6 | 14.7 | 16.2 | 19.3 | 22.2 | 25.2 | 30.9 | 35.2 |
| 5.0 | 3.68 | 5.79 | 7.66 | 9.41 | 12.7 | 15.8 | 17.3 | 20.3 | 23.2 | 26.0 | 3.74 | 5.93 | 7.87 | 9.69 | 13.1 | 16.4 | 18.0 | 21.2 | 24.3 | 27.4 | 33.4 | 37.8 |
| 1.0 | 5.59 | 8.01 | 10.1 | 12.0 | 15.6 | 18.9 | 20.5 | 23.6 | 26.6 | 29.5 | 5.76 | 8.30 | 10.5 | 12.6 | 16.4 | 20.0 | 21.8 | 25.2 | 28.5 | 31.8 | 38.2 | 42.9 |
| | 0.25 | 1.0 | 1.5 | 2.5 | 4.0 | X | 6.5 | X | 10 | X | 0.25 | 1.0 | 1.5 | 2.5 | 4.0 | X | 6.5 | X | 10 | X | 15 | X |
| | Acceptable Quality Levels (tightened inspection) | | | | | | | | | | | | | | | | | | | | | |

Table 14-3

Source: MIL-STD-105E, Department of Defense, 10 May, 1989

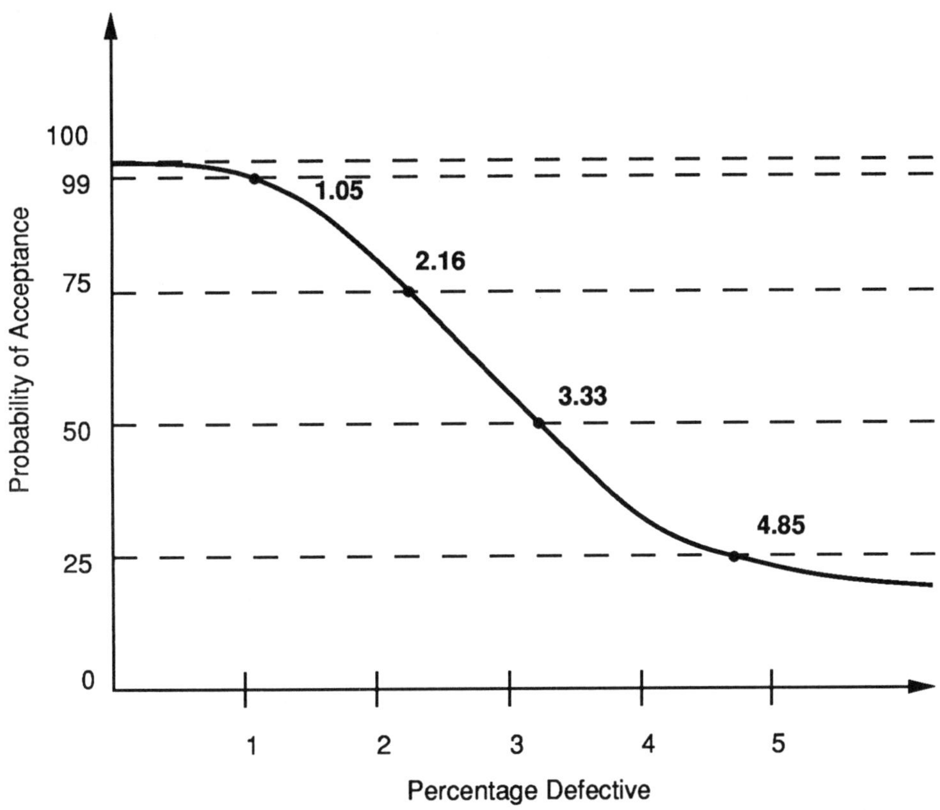


**Figure 14-10**
**The OC Curve for the Example**

## Using Quality Control Charts

Quality control charts are used to ensure that a process is performing according to specifications. The application of statistical quality control charts is also known as process control because it controls quality during production. The advantage of using quality control charts is that a process can be adjusted as soon as deviations from the standards are detected. In contrast, an acceptance

| Prep<br>Date 0?-18-84 | RUSKA INSTRUMENT CORPORATION HOUSTON, TEXAS | Effective Date | Number<br>QAI 06001 |
|---|---|---|---|
| Ckd<br>Date | | Page 1 of 6 | Revision<br>B |
| App<br>Date 10-22-84 | SUBJECT: SAMPLING PROCEDURE FOR DIMENSIONAL CHARACTERISTICS | | |

1.0 PURPOSE

The purpose of this document is to standardize the procedure used by Ruska Instrument Corporation (RIC) Inspection Department for statistical sampling of dimensional characteristics.

2.0 SCOPE

Applicable to all characteristics machined by or for RIC, and which have not been specified by engineering as critical.

3.0 GENERAL

The Quality of a lot may be verified by either one hundred percent or sampling inspection procedures. This document describes the single sampling procedure to be used by the Inspection Department. The procedure used here is based upon the General Inspection Level II detailed in MIL-STD-105, Table I.

4.0 SUPPORTING DOCUMENTS

4.1 MIL-STD-105, Sampling Procedures and Tables for Inspection by Attributes.

4.2 HANDBOOK H53, Guide for Sampling Inspection.

5.0 DEFINITIONS

5.1 ACCEPTANCE NUMBER (Ac)- The maximum allowable number of defects per sample size.

**REVISION RECORD**

| Para No | Ltr | Description | By | Date | App |
|---|---|---|---|---|---|
| 6.1.3/6.7 Pg. 6 | A | Changed AQL's based on 1984 yeilds, removed limit dimension from characteristics | TK | 3/11/85 | [illegible] |
| | B | Changed No. From INS-5.7001 | DEF | 11/6/87 | [illegible] |
| | | | | | |
| | | | | | |
| | | | | | |

Q-282-1 Rev A

**Exhibit 14-1**
**Ruska Sampling Procedures for Dimensional Characteristics**

Reprinted here with permission from Ruska Instrument Corporation, Houston, Texas

| RUSKA INSTRUMENT CORPORATION HOUSTON, TEXAS | Page 2 of 6 | Revision B | Number QAI 06001 |
|---|---|---|---|
| | Subject: SAMPLING PROCEDURE | | |

5.2 ACCEPTABLE QUALITY LEVEL (AQL)- A nominal value expressing the maximum percent of defects per lot, which for sampling purposes is considered an acceptable approximation of the Process Average.

5.3 CLASSIFICATION OF CHARACTERISTICS (CC)- The various characteristcs of a component classified according to their importance.

5.4 CRITICAL CHARACTERISTICS- A characteristic which if defective could result in either hazardous or unsafe conditions for personnel using or maintaining the end item.

5.5 DEFECT- A single characteristic which fails to meet engineering specifications.

5.6 DIMENSIONAL MEASUREMENT- The process used to determine the linear and angular magnitudes of specific features possessed by a component.

5.7 HOMOGENEITY- Means that a series of components should be alike or similar in nature.

5.8 LOT SIZE (N)- The number of homogenious components submitted for inspection, from which a sample will be taken.

5.9 MAJOR CHARACTERISTIC- A characteristic which if defective is likely to result in failure, or to reduce materially the usability of the unit of product for its intended purpose.

5.10 MINOR CHARACTERISTICS- A characteristic which if defective will not materially reduce the usability of the component for its' intended purpose.

5.11 NORMAL INSPECTION- A severity of inspection which is used when there is no evidence that the quality of the components submitted for inspection is better or poorer than the specified quality level.

5.12 RANDOM- One or more individual components selected by chance from a lot, without regard to their quality.

5.13 SAMPLE- A group of components randomally selected from a lot, for the purpose of verifing the level of quality.

5.14 SAMPLE SIZE (n)- The number of components which are drawn from a lot.

Q-282-1/2

**Exhibit 14-1**
**(Continued)**

| RUSKA INSTRUMENT CORPORATION HOUSTON, TEXAS | Page 3 of 6 | Revision B | Number QAI 06001 |
|---|---|---|---|
| | Subject: SAMPLING PROCEDURE | | |

6.0 SAMPLING INSTRUCTIONS

6.1 CLASSIFICATION OF CHARACTERISTICS

6.1.1 Classification of characteristics are summarized in Table One, Sampling Plan.

6.1.2 CRITICAL characteristics will be specified by Engineering on appropriate documents.

6.1.3 MAJOR A characteristics are those having an angular tolerance of less than or equal to ± 14 minutes and linear tolerance of less than or equal to ± .001 inches on the engineering document. Class III threads will be classified as Major A.

6.1.4 MAJOR B characteristics are those having an angular tolerance of ± 15 to ± 29 minutes and a linear tolerance of ± .0011 to ± .005 inches. Class II threads will be classified as Major B.

6.1.5 MINOR A characteristics are those having an angular tolerance of ± 30 to ± 59 minutes and a linear tolerance of ± .0051 to ± .01 inches.

6.1.6 MINOR B characteristics are those having an angular tolerance of greater than or equal to ±1 degree and a linear tolerance of greater than or equal to ±.011 inches. Hardness measurements will be classified as Minor B.

6.2 DETERMINING THE REQUIRED SAMPLE SIZE

6.2.1 The sample size (n) required by a lot size (N) will be deterimined by the appropriate classification of characteristics listed in Table One, Sampling Plan.

6.2.2 When a lot possesses more than one characteristic, draw the largest sample size required.

Q-282-1/2

Exhibit 14-1
(Continued)

| RUSKA INSTRUMENT CORPORATION HOUSTON, TEXAS | Page 4 of 6 | Revision B | Number QAI 06001 |
|---|---|---|---|
| | Subject: SAMPLING PROCEDURE | | |

6.2.3 Once this characteristic has been inspected, select a sample from this original sample, to meet the required (n) of the next largest classification.

6.2.4 Repeat step 6.1.3 for all required characteristics.

6.3 SELECTING THE SAMPLE

6.3.1 All samples must be selected at Random to assure a representative sample for determination of the lot's quality status.

6.3.2 Select the components for sampling from various areas of the container, shelf, box, carton, or package.

6.3.3 DO NOT search for, or attempt to avoid, apparent defective components.

6.3.4 When more than one container constitutes a lot , a proportional number of components will be selected from each container as outlined in section 6.3 .

6.4 ACCEPTANCE CRITERIA

6.4.1 Accept the lot per characteristic being inspected, if the number of defects found does not exceed the Acceptance number (Ac), listed in Table One for the appropiate characteristic.

6.4.2 Reject the lot per characteristic being inspected, if the number of defects found does exceed the Ac listed in Table One.

6.5 DISCREPANT COMPONENTS

6.5.1 All defective components, whether the the lot is accepted or not, must be processed as discrepant material in accordance with the appropiate procedure for discrepant material.

Q-282-1/2

Exhibit 14-1
(Continued)

INSTRUMENT CORPORATION
HOUSTON, TEXAS

| Page 5 of 6 | Revision B | Number QAI 06001 |
|---|---|---|
| Subject: SAMPLING PROCEDURE | | |

6.6 NORMAL, TIGHTENED, AND REDUCED INSPECTION

6.6.1 No provision is made in this procedure for switching to, or from Normal, Tightened and Reduced inspection.

6.7 ACCEPTABLE QUALITY LEVEL (AQL)

6.7.1 The AQL used for particular classification of characteristics, when not specified by Engineering documents, will be as designated in this document.

6.7.2 The procedure described here is based upon the following AQL's:

6.7.2.1 MAJOR A, uses an AQL of 1.0

6.7.2.2 MAJOR B, uses an AQL of 1.5

6.7.2.3 MINOR A, uses an AQL of 2.5

6.7.2.4 MINOR B, uses an AQL of 4.0

Q-282-1/2

**Exhibit 14-1**
**(Continued)**

| RUSKA INSTRUMENT CORPORATION HOUSTON, TEXAS | Page 6 of 6 | Revision B | Number QAI 06001 |
|---|---|---|---|
| | Subject: SAMPLING PROCEDURE | | |

TABLE ONE: SAMPLING PLAN

| ANGULAR TOLERANCE | +/- 14' or LESS | | +/- 15' to +/- 29' | | +/- 30' to +/- 1° | | +/- 1°1' or GREATER | |
|---|---|---|---|---|---|---|---|---|
| LINEAR TOLERANCE | +/- .001" or LESS | | +/- .0011" to +/- .005" | | +/- .0051" to +/- .0100" | | +/- .0110" or greater | |
| CLASSIFICATION | MAJOR A (1.0 AQL) | | MAJOR B (1.5 AQL) | | MINOR A (2.5 AQL) | | MINOR B (4.0 AQL) | |
| LOT SIZE (N) | n | Ac | n | Ac | n | Ac | n | Ac |
| 2-8 | * | * | * | * | 5 | 0 | 3 | 0 |
| 9-15 | 13 | 0 | 8 | 0 | 5 | 0 | 3 | 0 |
| 16-25 | 13 | 0 | 8 | 0 | 5 | 0 | 3 | 0 |
| 26-50 | 13 | 0 | 8 | 0 | 5 | 0 | 13 | 1 |
| 51-90 | 13 | 0 | 8 | 0 | 20 | 1 | 13 | 1 |
| 91-150 | 13 | 0 | 32 | 1 | 20 | 1 | 20 | 2 |
| 151-280 | 50 | 1 | 32 | 1 | 32 | 2 | 32 | 3 |
| 281-500 | 50 | 1 | 50 | 2 | 32 | 3 | 50 | 5 |
| 501-1200 | 80 | 2 | 80 | 3 | 80 | 5 | 80 | 7 |
| 1201-3200 | 125 | 3 | 125 | 5 | 125 | 7 | 125 | 10 |
| 3201-10000 | 200 | 5 | 200 | 7 | 200 | 10 | 200 | 14 |

WHERE:

* = one hundred precent inspection

n = sample size drawn randomally from lot

Ac = maximum number of defects allowed per sample

N = lot size

Q-282-1/2

**Exhibit 14-1**
**(Continued)**

sampling cannot change quality because the job has been completed and what has already been done can only be accepted or rejected. Basically, establishing process control means to find statistical limits (upper and lower control limits) within which process is allowed to continue. As soon as limits are identified, a machine operator is capable of effectively controlling quality as he or she proceeds with production.

## HOW TO ESTIMATE UPPER AND LOWER CONTROL LIMITS IN PROCESS CONTROL

Process control is used to monitor product quality when production is in progress. Process variances are revealed as they occur and the corrective actions are taken before the job is completed. As with acceptance sampling, a random sample is taken periodically as parts are being produced. The measurements should be within the boundaries of the *upper control limit* (UCL) and the *lower control limit* (LCL).

The commonly used quality control charts are

1. $\bar{p}$ charts
2. $\bar{\bar{X}}$ and $\bar{R}$ charts

***How to Set Up $\bar{p}$ Charts*** Control charts are used to control either the attributes data or the variable data.

***How to calculate UCLp and LCLp.*** A $\bar{p}$ chart is used to control the fraction of defective products when the attribute data is controlled. The sample size for a $\bar{p}$ chart should be large enough to detect at least one defective item on the average. For example, a control limit of 4 defective out of 1,000 will require at least 250 samples to be measured.

The overall procedure for setting up a $\bar{p}$ chart is as follows:

1. Take $m$ number of samples, each of the size $n$. The samples are taken periodically within the short interval of time in the span of a shift or a day.
2. The number of defectives, $k$, is recorded and the fraction of defective $p$ is calculated for each sample as follows:

$$p = \frac{k}{n}$$

3. The average of $p$ - $\bar{p}$ over all $m$ samples is calculated as follows:

$$\bar{p} = \frac{p1 + p2 + p3 + \dots + pm}{m}$$

and the standard deviation $S_p$ is calculated as follows:

$$Sp = \sqrt{\frac{\bar{p}(1-\bar{p})}{n}}$$

Now the upper and the lower control limits for a $\overline{\overline{P}}$ chart can be calculated as follows

$$UCLp = \bar{P} + k \sqrt{\frac{\bar{p}(1-\bar{p})}{n}} = \bar{p} + kSp$$

$$LCLp = \bar{P} - k \sqrt{\frac{\bar{p}(1-\bar{p})}{n}} = \bar{p} - kSp$$

where $k$ is the number of standard deviations from the process average.

Typically, $k$ is accepted at +3 ÷ (- 3) standard deviations, which corresponds to 99.72 percent of the variations falling within the control limits.

4. The result of each sample is plotted on the $\bar{p}$ control chart showing the central value $p$ as well as $UCLp$ and $LCLp$. The fraction defective is under control, if all the values are between the upper and lower control limits. One or more samples outside the limits are the cause for investigating and correcting the problem. An example of a $\bar{p}$ control chart is shown in Figure 14-11.

***How to Set Up $\overline{\overline{X}}$ and $\overline{R}$ Charts*** X and R charts are used together when monitoring variables:

- An $\overline{\overline{X}}$ chart shows whether changes have occurred in the central tendency of a process.
- An $\overline{R}$ chart shows the process variability—the average of the range of each sample.

An $\overline{\overline{X}}$ chart is a plot of means of at least 25 to 30 samples, *m*, taken each consisting of 4 to 5 components, *n*, produced close together. The mean of a sample *X* is computed as follows:

$$\bar{X} = \frac{X_1 + X_2 + X_3 + \cdots + X_n}{n}$$

Then the average of the averages is computed;

$$\overline{\overline{X}} = \frac{\sum_{j=1}^{m} \bar{X}_j}{m}$$

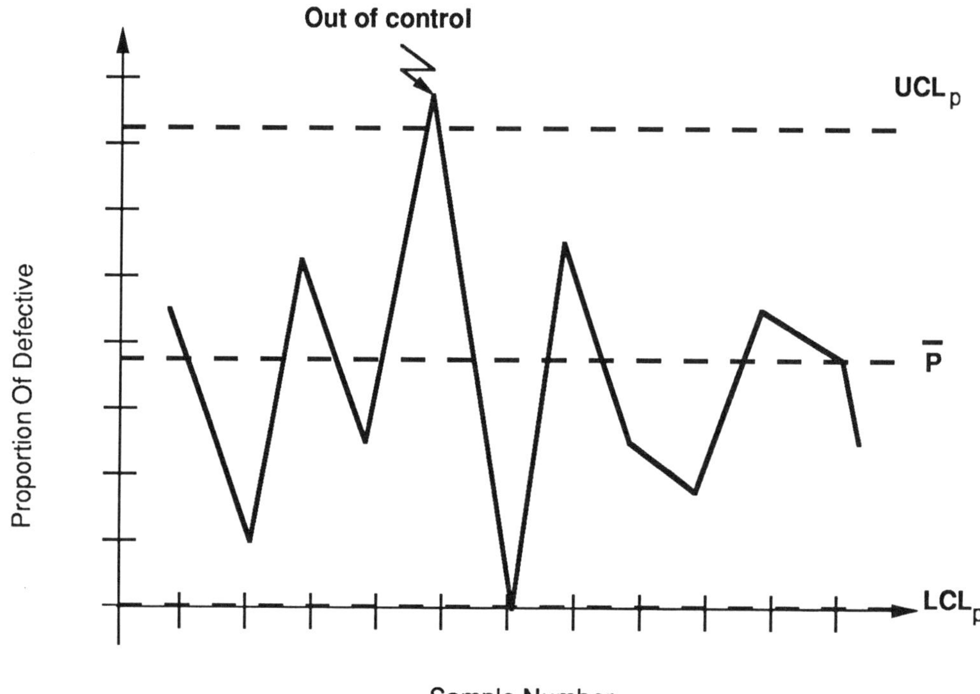


**Figure 14-11**
**$\bar{p}$ Control Chart**

where
$\bar{\bar{X}}$ = the average of the means of a sample
$j$ = a sample member
$m$ = the total number of samples

The value of the range in each sample is the difference between the highest and the lowest measurement in the sample: $R = X_{largest} - X_{smallest}$, and

$$\bar{R} = \frac{\sum_{j=1}^{m} R_j}{m}$$

where
$\bar{R}$ = the average of the ranges $R$ for all the samples

The upper and lower control limits for $X$ are computed as follows:

$$UCL_X = \bar{\bar{X}} + ZS_{\bar{X}}$$

$$LCL_X = \bar{\bar{X}} - ZS_{\bar{X}}$$

where

$\bar{\bar{X}}$ = the means of the sample means

$Z$ = the number of normal standard deviations

$S_{\bar{X}}$ = a standard deviation of the sample means

Samples which are out of control should be further investigated. The causes for variations should be rectified. Additional samples are collected when the process is resumed, and, if necessary, the control limits are revalidated based on new data. An example of revision of $\bar{p}$ chart control limits is illustrated in Figure 14-12.

Sometimes, a process can be out of control but it is not reflected in the $\bar{\bar{X}}$ chart, due to the average being within the upper and lower limits of samples averages. This is the reason why $\bar{\bar{X}}$ control charts are used in conjunction with $\bar{R}$ charts, where samples ranges show the dispersion of sample readings. An example of $\bar{\bar{X}}$ chart and $\bar{R}$ chart is illustrated in Figure 14-13.

A widely used method for estimating the $X$ limits is to use the sample range as a measure of the process variability:

$$UCL_X = \bar{\bar{X}} + A_2R$$

$$LCL_X = \bar{\bar{X}} - A_2R$$

Values of $A_2$ are obtained from Table 14-4.

Control limits for range charts are used applying the following formulas:

$$UCL_{\bar{R}} = \bar{D}_4\bar{R}$$

$$LCL_{\bar{R}} = \bar{D}_3\bar{R}$$

Values of $D_3$ and $D_4$ are also obtained from Table 14-4.

## USING CAUSE AND EFFECT DIAGRAMS

Statistical methods of quality control deal with detection of problems. This is followed by problem-resolving efforts. One of the most commonly used tools for problem solving is the cause and effect diagram (sometimes referred to as the fishbone or Ishikawa diagram).* Kaoru Ishikawa has developed this visual

---

* Diagram was developed in 1950 by Prof. Kaoru Ishikawa of Tokyo University. For further information, see Inoue, Michael S. and James L. Riggs, "Describe your System with Cause and Effect Diagram." *Industrial Engineering,* April 1971, pp 26-31.

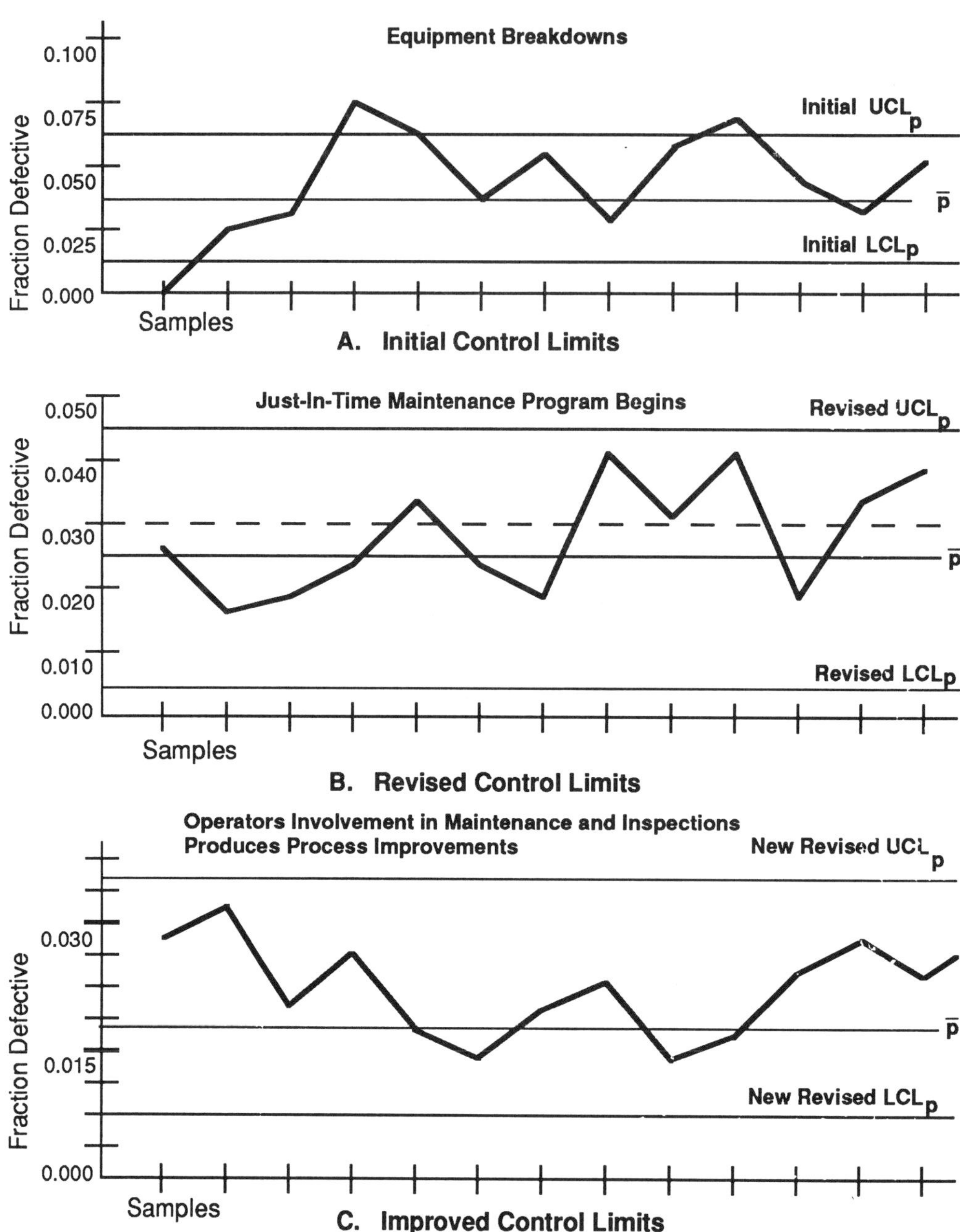


Figure 14-12
$\bar{p}$ Chart to Control Fraction Defective

UCL$_{\bar{X}}$
0.396
0.392
.3880
0.384
0.380
$\bar{\bar{X}}$
0.376
0.372
0.368
0.364
LCL$_{\bar{X}}$
0.360
Average
1 2 3 4 5 6 7 8 9 10 11
Sample number

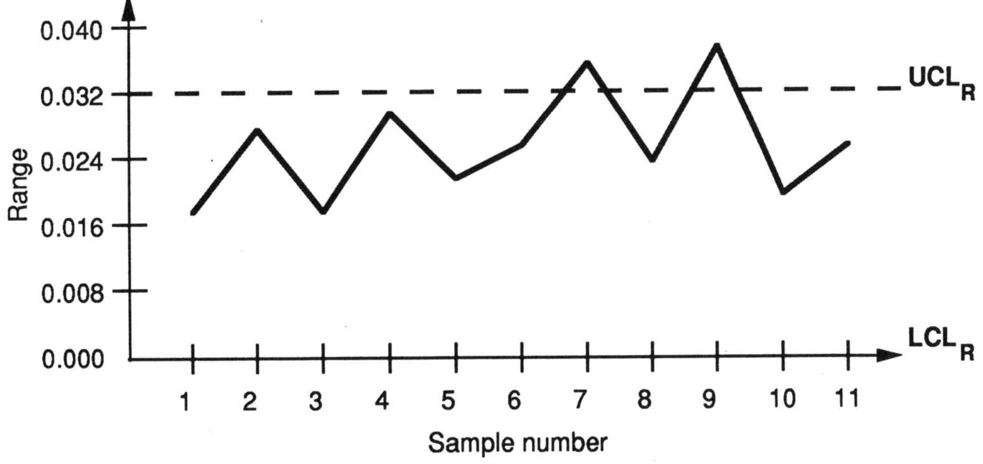

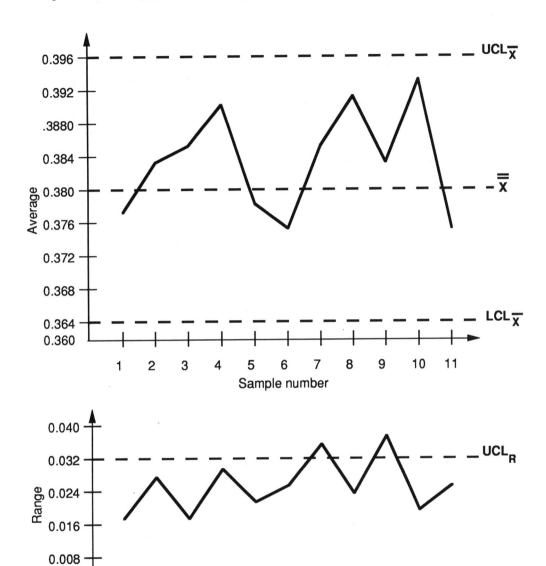


**Figure 14-13**
**Control Charts: Mean, $\bar{\bar{X}}$ and Range $\bar{R}$**

| Number of observations in subgroup n | Factor for $\bar{\bar{X}}$ chart $A_2$ | Factors for $\bar{R}$ chart | |
|---|---|---|---|
| | | Lower control limit $D_3$ | Upper control limit $D_4$ |
| 2 | 1.88 | 0 | 3.27 |
| 3 | 1.02 | 0 | 2.57 |
| 4 | 0.73 | 0 | 2.28 |
| 5 | 0.58 | 0 | 2.11 |
| 6 | 0.48 | 0 | 2.00 |
| 7 | 0.42 | 0.08 | 1.92 |
| 8 | 0.37 | 0.14 | 1.86 |
| 9 | 0.34 | 0.18 | 1.82 |
| 10 | 0.31 | 0.22 | 1.78 |
| 11 | 0.29 | 0.26 | 1.74 |
| 12 | 0.27 | 0.28 | 1.72 |
| 13 | 0.25 | 0.31 | 1.69 |
| 14 | 0.24 | 0.33 | 1.67 |
| 15 | 0.22 | 0.35 | 1.65 |
| 16 | 0.21 | 0.36 | 1.64 |
| 17 | 0.20 | 0.38 | 1.62 |
| 18 | 0.19 | 0.39 | 1.61 |
| 19 | 0.19 | 0.40 | 1.60 |
| 20 | 0.18 | 0.41 | 1.59 |

Upper Control Limit for $\bar{X} = UCL_{\bar{X}} = \bar{\bar{X}} + A_2 \bar{R}$

Lower Control Limit for $\bar{X} = UCL_{\bar{X}} = \bar{\bar{X}} + A_2 \bar{R}$

(If aimed-at or standard value $\bar{X}'$ is used rather than $\bar{\bar{X}}$ as the central line on the control chart, $\bar{X}'$ should be substituted for $\bar{\bar{X}}$ in the preceding formulas.)

Upper Control Limit for R= $UCL_R = D_4 \bar{R}$

Lower Control Limit for R= $UCL_R = D_3 \bar{R}$

All factors in Table C are based on the normal distribution.

**Table 14-4**
**Factors for Computing Control Chart Limits for $\bar{\bar{X}}$ and $\bar{R}$ Charts.**

Source: E. L. Grant and R. S. Leavenworth, *Statistics and Quality Control*, New York: McGrawH-ill, Inc. 1979. Reprinted here with permission form McGaw-Hill, Inc.

technique as a part of quality control training program for Japanese foremen. The cause and effect (C-E) diagram, which entails dissecting a quality problem into its elements and highlighting possible causes and their effects, has proven to be of considerable versatility and is now used in numerous applications.

Two basic types of C-E diagrams are dispersion analysis and process classification. *Dispersion analysis,* the most commonly used type of C-E diagram, involves several steps:

1. A statement is made of the problem and its specific effect.
2. The effect becomes the "head" of the fish.
3. During the brainstorming session possible causes of the problem are enumerated and main groups of the effect are identified according to categories of their origin. These groups of causes become a backbone of the fish. Further, each of the listed causes should be placed under the appropriate bone of the fish. Figure 14-14 illustrates a dispersion analysis C-E diagram, where all possible problems are grouped according to major production categories, namely, labor, process methods, material, and measurement.
4. The reason for each of the causes is analyzed in order to identify the root cause of the effect of the entire group. Each cause is to be studied further and selected for elimination is then identified.

Examples demonstrating the effectiveness of a dispersion analysis applied at Ruska Instrument Company are shown in Figures 14-15 and 14-16.

The difference between the dispersion analysis and process classification type of C-E diagram is in the way of grouping all possible causes of the problem into the fish backbone. In the dispersion analysis, all possible causes of a problem are grouped according to categories of their origin or according to main categories of productive resources, while in the process classification, these causes are grouped according to the sequence of production tasks. In a *process classification analysis,* the problem is traced to a specific location in a production area or to a specific operation or task(s). Figure 14-17 illustrates a process classification C-E diagram, where all possible problems are grouped according to major steps in production process.

There are the following steps in drawing a process classification C-E diagram:

1. The process is divided into smaller tasks and placed in a sequential order or steps. Each step then becomes a major bone in a backbone of the fish.

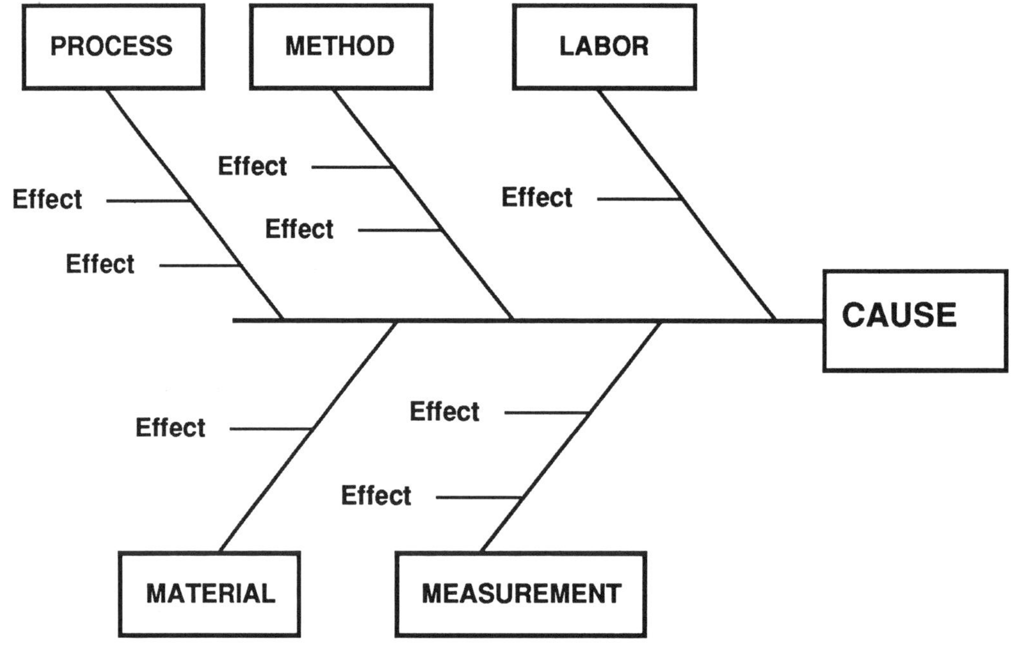


**Figure 14-14**
**The Dispersion Analysis C-E Diagram**

2. Each step is analyzed and any possible cause that prevents it from operating smoothly is identified. These possible causes become branches of the process steps.
3. The reason for each of the causes is identified and analyzed, and the cause to be studied further and selected for elimination is identified.

The following examples demonstrate the process classification technique applied at Ruska Instrument Company (see Figure 14-17).

## HOW DEMING'S 14 PRINCIPLES RELATE TO JUST-IN-TIME-BASED QUALITY CONTROL

The Japanese attribute their success in JIT quality control to the fact that they have recognized the value of the teachings of J. M. Juran and Edwards Deming,

A Ruska Instrument Corporation design team working on the development of a new electronic pressure gauge determined through interviews with customers that a "good display" was a very important attribute for the new product. In an effort to organize their thought patterns in determining the characteristics of a "good display," the team members decided to use the dispersion analysis cause and effect diagram.

After listing "good display" as the effect, the team began to develop the list of all attributes that contribute to a "good display." The list included color, operator vision, variable light, content capacity, character size, distance, and others.

After constructing the diagram, they analyzed the causes to determine if any other items needed to be addressed. Under the category of "Operator Vision," the team decided to list "Safety Glasses" to ensure that the display was readable through safety glasses. The final chart looked as follows:

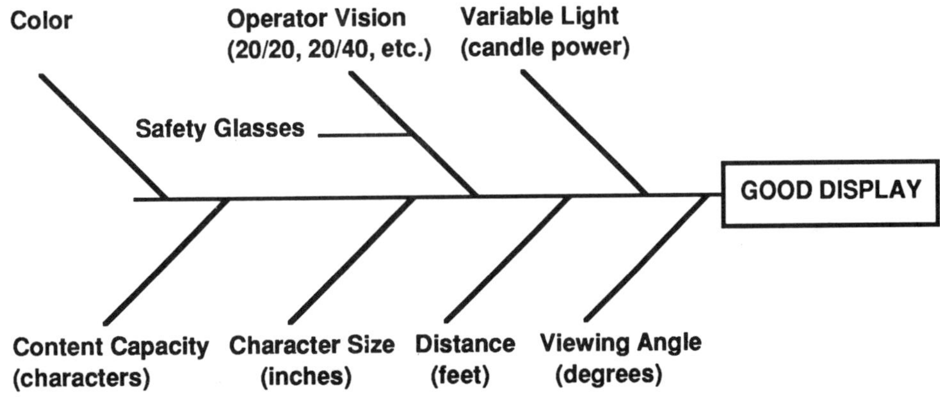


After completing the diagram, the team voted on the extent of the relationship between "good display" and the identified causes (none, weak, medium, or strong). The team determined that "distance" and "character size" had a strong relationship; "viewing angle," "operator vision," and "variable light" had a medium relationship; and "color" and "content capacity" had a weak relationship.

Through the development of the C-E diagram, the team was able to concentrate most of its efforts on the most important causes identified (distance and character size).

**Figure 14-15**
**Applying the C-E diagram based on process classification at Ruska Instrument Corp.**

Diagrams in figures 14-15 to 14-17 reprinted with permission from Ruska Instruments Corporation.

Several people within the company formed a team to address the problem of the high scrap rate for machined threads in valve bodies. The team brainstormed a list of possible causes to the problem, using the 5 resource types as the category heading. The resulting C-E diagram is presented here.

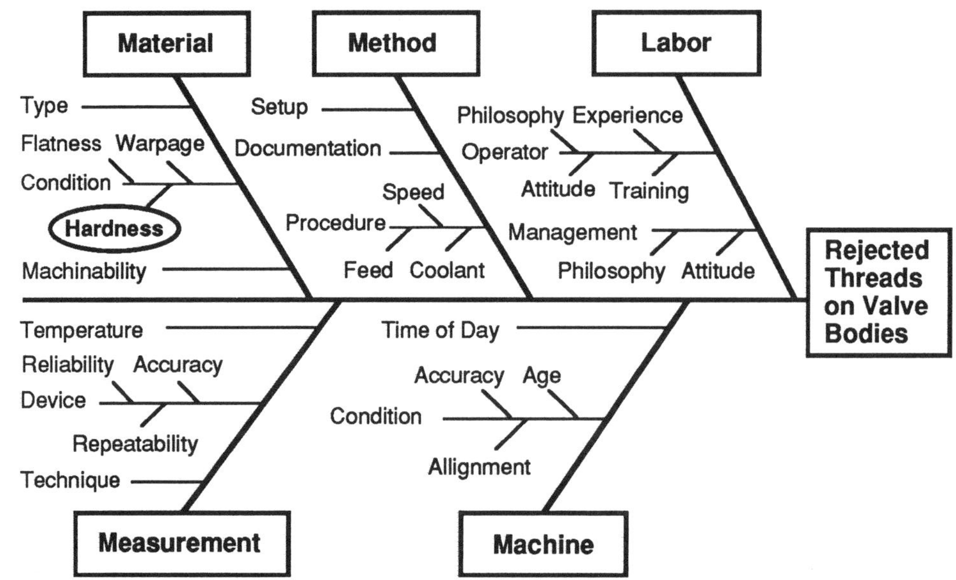


The team voted on the possible causes and determined that the softness of the raw material is the major contributor to the high reject rate in the threading process. The decision was made to verify this cause by checking the relationship between the reject rate and material hardness. Once the suspected cause was proven, the raw material hardness specifications were modified and the reject rate due to defective threads was eliminated.

**Figure 14-16**
**Applying the C-E diagram based on resource classification at Ruska Instrument Corp.**

whom they refer to as "the father of the third wave of the industrial revolution." They consider the first revolution to have been the factory mechanization started by Eli Whitney and the second revolution to have started with the mass production introduced by Henry Ford. The third industrial revolution (started by Edwards Deming) that has included statistical techniques in quality control has heralded the transformation of the Japanese national industry, notorious for its low-quality products, into the internationally recognized leaders in production of quality products.

The Ruska inspection department was concerned at the lengthy cycle time associated with the final instrument acceptance operation. After deciding to use the process classification cause and effect diagram, the team listed the exact process steps that are required to accept a completed instrument:

After agreeing on the process description, the team began to brainstorm all the factors that prevent the operation from running smoothly. As a result, the following branches were added to the chart.

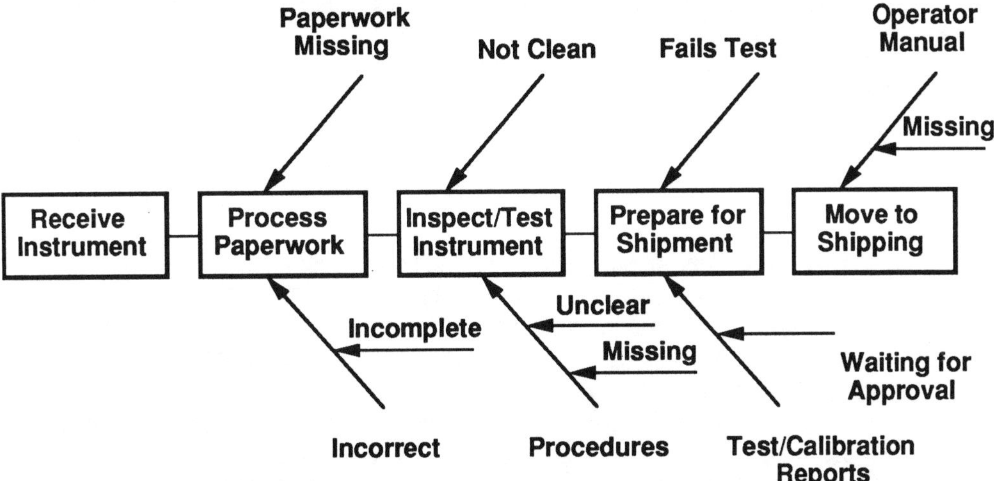


The team agreed that the cause making the biggest impact on the process cycle time was waiting for test and calibration reports during the "prepare for shipment" step. The manufacturing process was modified to have the test and calibration reports submitted for approval at the same time the instrument is moved to the acceptance area. This allowed the reports to be processed in at the same time the instrument was being inspected.

As a result, the final acceptance cycle time was reduced by several hours for every instrument shipped.

**Figure 14-17**
**Applying the C-E diagram based on production stages at Ruska Instrument Corporation**

The success of quality control is based on the blend of statistical methods with the human aspects of production, clearly stated in the famous Deming's 14 principles for quality control known as "Deming's Guide to Quality and Competitive Position." These 14 principles are the underlying standards for successful quality control programs known as quality circles, zero defect, JIT-TQC, and quality at source, as well as the Just-in-Time philosophy as a whole.

The philosophies of Deming and Juran have heralded a new era in production, since quality control is now considered an integral part of the production system. Improvement in quality is achieved through across-the-board improvement of other production functions and activities. Since the teachings of Deming and Juran have laid down the foundation for the development of the Just-in-Time system, it is prudent to examine them in detail.

Here is how Deming's 14 principles coinsides with contemporary management approaches:

1. *Become competitive.* This means developing a long-term strategy for achieving organizational objectives through continuous improvement. A plan to become competitive and stay in business is implemented by creating a meaningful organizational structure—a production system capable of producing a value product that satisfies customer needs.

2. *Eliminate waste.* A new world reality calls for elimination of waste. Delays lead to the buildup of inventory, which, one way or another, affects the quality level. Deviations from planning standards eventually lead to lowering quality standards. Quality is the state of consciousness, the state of mind, the standard of conduct throughout the organization. Mistakes persisting in management, engineering, and planning eventually extend onto the processes. Constant delays and schedule changes by managers and planners affect the work force morale, resulting in lower-quality standards. Philip Crosby estimates that only 20 percent of quality problems can be attributed to the work force, while the remainder of the quality problems are in the offices of white collar workers.

3. *Do not depend on a mass inspection.* Inspections cannot impose quality. They are, essentially, just sorting out faulty components from the good ones. Inspections do not improve the process, because the job is already done, but they increase the production cost and thereby reduce the product value. The Japanese say that inspectors are extra employees who lower productivity. A new approach to quality is to enforce quality at the source rather than rely on inspections as a means for quality improvements. This quality-at-source plan places a greater significance on what people are doing.

4. *Do not define the product value or any part thereof by price alone.* A purchasing price is meaningless without considering the quality level, timely delivery, and reliability of a supplier. Purchasing agents should select suppliers who provide the highest value of products or services rather than buy from the lower bidder.

Deming advocates that the total quality cost indicative of the product value should take precedence over considering a short-term price advantage. He stresses the need to eliminate multiple sources of supply to ensure a long term special relationship between the buyer and the supplier. This is the principle of JIT purchasing—dealing with a single-source supplier, who, in conjunction with the purchaser, is capable of responding to the need for continuous elimination of waste.

5. *Make continuous improvements in the production system.* One of the factors of managing a production system is ensuring its continuous improvement by extracting synergy in the interfunctional relationship of production system components, such as design, inspections, incoming materials and internal process control and improvements, machine maintenance, and work force motivation and training. A continuous improvement is a management responsibility which is presently considered the main management mission in an organization.

6. *Undertake on-the-job training.* Deming stresses that employees are the most important asset in an organization. Their contribution to the efficient functioning of an organization can be enhanced by providing an adequate education and training. Quality, however, is one factor directly related to other parts of a production system. Providing a general knowledge and educating employees results in quality improvement as much as the job training and skill training. Work force multiskill training and performing several consecutive operations by a single employee improves quality since one person is the producer and the consumer at the same time. In general, providing training motivates employees and improves quality by boosting employees' morale. Deming's position on on-the-job training is in line with the JIT employees training and motivation principles.

7. *Change the role of supervision.* The role of a supervisor is changing in that the emphasis is put on the technical assistance. It starts with the implementation and work force training in statistical quality control. A supervisor is perceived as a person who organizes and directly involves himself or herself into work force training and promoting the teamwork.

8. *Eliminate fear.* One military aircraft components contractor has complained that the JIT implementation exerts an excessive stress on its employees. A truly JIT environment should have the directly opposite effect: it should alleviate the tension attributed to a sole responsibility by replacing it with the collective team responsibility. JIT preventive planning eliminates causes for interruptions and ensures smooth and on-time completion of jobs. In JIT, people are involved in planning production activities that they perform. People have a say in what they are doing. They feel more secure and confident in results, due to the fact that they participate in the decisions over jobs they do.

9. *Eliminate functional barriers.* Communication problems are alleviated when interfunctional barriers are reduced. Team building at the shop floor and decision-making levels and team spirit improve the cooperation and unity. The elimination of waste in communication and in conferences is due to removing

interdepartmental and crossfunctional barriers at the administrative levels in the hierarchy (vertical communications). Companies reduce the number of work force grades from 30 to 2 or just to a single grade. Japanese companies reduce interfunctional barriers in engineering supporting staff by permitting a single engineer to perform functions previously defined as design engineer, industrial engineer, and manufacturing engineer. Decision making closer to the execution line further reduces the need for vertical communication. The elimination of all organizational barriers results in people identifying themselves with organizational objectives, instead of working for the individual gains of functional departments.

10. *Eliminate numerical goals and slogans.* Numerical goals should have a direct relevance to what people are doing. Such slogans and posters in a shop as "zero defect" and "increase productivity by 20%" are meaningless to workers because these are organizational goals that can be achieved only through the efforts of many specialized departments, not a single functional unit. Workers should not be blamed for faults in the production system, which are beyond their control. A production system's design and maintenance are a management responsibility. Posters such as "Please bring your monthly suggestions on how to improve quality" will have a better response because people can relate such a request to the tasks they perform, as well as to what personally prevents them from eliminating quality problems.

11. *Restrict work standards and quotas.* Quantitative work standards measuring a day's work and piecework have had a negative effect on performance, due to the fact that these standards disregard quality and other factors affecting the product value by putting an emphasis on numerical figures of production output. Deming stresses the importance of the product value over dealing with quality as an isolated factor in production. Product quality is measured by technological standards, while the product value is a measure of efficiency of the entire integrated business system.

12. *Design meaningful tasks for workers.* In a well-organized production system, workers perform meaningful tasks distinctly recognized as part of an extended production process. Teamwork, rather than an operation of an individual worker, can readily be recognized in the final product. Workers take pride in contributing to recognizable work efforts rather than work for individual gains. Every individual contribution to team efforts is followed by an instant "recognition" and "reward" by the team members. This motivates individuals to perform better and improve quality.

13. *Institute a program for education and training.* Deming recognizes education and training as essential ingredients for a quality improvement program. These are regarded as a cornerstone of a JIT system. If there are quality problems in an organization, people should be trained to find the reasons and improve performance. Statistical education of the work force is essential for quality improvement programs.

14. *Create a structure in top management.* Organizing for quality requires creating an organizational structure. By this, Deming means that management is in charge of developing and maintaining an integrated production system which is capable of ensuring synergistic fulfillment of all the earlier principles.

Deming states that it is not enough if everyone does his or her best, unless their tasks are a fundamental part of the total organizational scenario. The significance of Deming's principles is in that he views quality as a constituent ingredient of the product value and one of many interrelated factors in an integrated business system. Consequently, quality improvement is accomplished through the general improvement of the productive system.

## SETTING UP A QUALITY CONTROL MANUAL

A quality control manual is a collection of policies and procedures, which serves as a legitimate way to conduct company activities aimed at achieving the highest product value. Most quality control manuals contain interdepartmental quality plans and procedures, the information necessary to assure the compliance with company's quality objectives. This includes an entire spectrum of organizational production and business activities.

Excerpts from CAMCO's quality control manual are illustrated here as an example. The manual has been compiled in compliance with the quality system requirements of the American Petroleum Institute (API) and International Organization for Standards (ISO).

CAMCO's quality control manual contains company policies and controls for organizational functions, such as the quality assurance program, design control, procurement, maintenance, material handling and shipping, and quality assurance audit procedures. The table of contents of CAMCO's quality assurance manual is shown in Exhibit 14-2.

CAMCO's quality control manual begins with the statement of the company's quality policy, emphasizing the commitment to quality of products for customers and to quality of work life for company's associates. For example, the section on the quality assurance program explains the scope of the manual, the responsibility of the QA personnel and management for the quality assurance program, including employees training. CAMCO's quality policy is stated in Exhibit 14-3. The main points of CAMCO's quality assurance program are explained in Exhibit 14-4.

Further on, each section of the manual makes reference to Operations Manual procedures that provide the details for the performance of activities affecting quality. For example, Section 14.0, Quality Assurance Records, includes such items as QA Records, Storage, and Retrievability, as shown in Exhibit 14-5.

# QUALITY ASSURANCE MANUAL

SECTION: i
REVISION: "B"
PAGE: 1 OF 1

SUBJECT: TABLE OF CONTENTS

| | | REVISION | DATE |
|---|---|---|---|
| i. | Table of Contents | "B" | 06/01/90 |
| ii. | Statement of Policy | "A" | 01/01/89 |
| iii. | Approvals of Quality Assurance (QA) Manual | "B" | 06/01/90 |
| iv. | Approvals, Delegation and Rights of Access | "B" | 06/01/90 |
| v. | Terms and Definitions | "B" | 06/01/90 |
| vi. | Appendices | "B" | 06/01/90 |
| 1.0 | ORGANIZATION | "B" | 06/01/90 |
| 2.0 | QUALITY ASSURANCE PROGRAM | "B" | 06/01/90 |
| 3.0 | QUALITY ASSURANCE MANUAL | "B" | 06/01/90 |
| 4.0 | DESIGN CONTROL | "A" | 01/01/89 |
| 5.0 | DRAWINGS, PROCEDURES, AND SPECIFICATIONS | "B" | 06/01/90 |
| 6.0 | PROCUREMENT CONTROL | "B" | 06/01/90 |
| 7.0 | MANUFACTURING CONTROL | "B" | 06/01/90 |
| 8.0 | INSPECTION PROGRAM | "B" | 06/01/90 |
| 9.0 | FUNCTIONAL TEST CONTROL | "B" | 06/01/90 |
| 10.0 | EQUIPMENT FAILURE | "A" | 01/01/89 |
| 11.0 | HANDLING, STORAGE, AND SHIPPING | "A" | 01/01/89 |
| 12.0 | CONTROL OF MEASURING AND TEST EQUIPMENT | "A" | 06/01/90 |
| 13.0 | NONCONFORMANCE CONTROL | "B" | 06/01/90 |
| 14.0 | QUALITY ASSURANCE RECORDS | "B" | 06/01/90 |
| 15.0 | QUALITY ASSURANCE AUDITS | "B" | 06/01/90 |

APPROVED BY: [illegible] DATE: 17 Sept 90
DIRECTOR OF QUALITY ASSURANCE

**Exhibit 14-2**
**CAMCO's quality Assurance Manual Table of Contents**

SECTION: ii
DATE: 01-30-89

OFFICE OF THE PRESIDENT

INCORPORATED

**QUALITY POLICY**

**Camco** is a company dedicated to the pursuit of excellence in the products and the services that it provides to its customers. To achieve this excellence, we are committed to Quality; both in the quality of products for our customers and in the quality of work-life for our associates.

We have two basic goals:

1. To provide the Oil and Gas Industry with products at a level of quality that exceeds our customers expectation and at a fair price; through innovation and creativity in product design and manufacture.

2. To provide quality service to our industry before, during and after the sale by constantly improving our service technology and personnel.

We will pursue our goal of excellence with the highest regard and concern for:

**OUR CUSTOMERS** who are our reason for being. Our customer's problems are our opportunities and the fulfillment of their needs is our goal.

**OUR ASSOCIATES** who comprise this company. We respect the rights, dignity and have a genuine concern for the development of the individual. We are committed to provide meaningful work, a safe, clean and pleasant work environment with fair treatment, competitive compensation and good benefits.

**OUR SUPPLIERS** who supply us with goods and services which enable us to perform our tasks. We pledge to them fair consideration of their products and services and require of them high quality standards and on-time performance.

This Quality Assurance Manual sets forth the requirements for establishing and maintaining programs for the quality of work performed under the above stated requirements.

**G. H. TAUSCH**
**PRESIDENT**

7030 ARDMORE ZIP 77054 • P.O. BOX 14484 ZIP 77221 • HOUSTON, TEXAS • PHONE (713) 747-4000

**Exhibit 14-3**
**CAMCO's Quality Assurance Manual Quality Policy Statement**

Reprinted here with permission from CAMCO, Inc.

## QUALITY ASSURANCE MANUAL

SECTION: 2.0
REVISION: "B"
PAGE: 1 OF 4

SUBJECT: QUALITY ASSURANCE PROGRAM

2.1 SCOPE: This Quality Assurance program has been established to comply with requirements set forth by industry standards, product application, and customers. This program applies to all products and complies with ISO-9001. For SPPE parts and assemblies, this program complies with the requirements of SPPE-1, API-14A, API Q-1, License Agreements, and referenced standards.

2.1.1 There are two groups of products:
SPPE
Non SPPE

All requirements of this program apply to all products, unless specific reference is made to include or exclude a requirement for a particular group of products.

2.1.2 This program is planned, implemented and maintained in accordance with specified requirements. In addition, it is applicable to all spare and replacement parts.

2.2 DOCUMENTATION: This Quality Assurance Manual documents the Quality Assurance program. The supporting Operations Manual provides the procedures and specifications for implementation.

2.3 PERSONNEL: Management shall ensure that the Quality Assurance department has the authority to maintain and enforce the requirements of the Quality Assurance program. Management shall provide an adequate staff for the Quality Assurance department to attain those goals.



**Exhibit 14-4**
**CAMCO's Quality Assurance Manual Quality Assurance Program**

# QUALITY ASSURANCE MANUAL

CAMCO

SECTION: 2.0
REVISION: "B"
PAGE: 2 OF 4

SUBJECT: QUALITY ASSURANCE PROGRAM

2.3.1 <u>Quality Assurance</u>: Personnel are given the responsibility to:

A. Identify problems affecting product quality.
B. Initiate, recommend or provide solutions to quality related problems.
C. Verify the implementation of solutions to quality related problems.
D. Control further processing, assembly and delivery of any nonconforming product or unsatisfactory condition until the proper final disposition is completed.

2.3.2 <u>Indoctrination and Training</u>: Indoctrination and training shall be conducted for new employees prior to their performing activities affecting quality. Quality Assurance shall develop yearly indoctrination sessions to provide an employee oriented overview of the current commitments and requirements of the Quality Assurance program. Indoctrination sessions are presented to managers, supervisors and other key employees responsible for or performing functions which affect product quality. Applicable sections of the Quality Assurance Manual and other appropriate requirements are reviewed and discussed at these sessions. These sessions will be documented on an Indoctrination and Training form (Appendix 2.0).

A. Managers and supervisors shall then develop and present training sessions to familiarize their personnel with the requirements of the Quality



**Exhibit 14-4**
**(Continued)**

# QUALITY ASSURANCE MANUAL

SECTION: 2.0
REVISION: "B"
PAGE: 3 OF 4

SUBJECT: QUALITY ASSURANCE PROGRAM

Assurance program as it pertains to their job functions. These sessions will be documented on an Indoctrination and Training form.

2.4 **MANAGEMENT RESPONSIBILITY**: The President is responsible for ascertaining the adequacy and effectiveness of the Quality Assurance program by management audit (Section 15.0). The management officials responsible for engineering and manufacturing shall ensure that their personnel comply with the requirements of the Quality Assurance program.

2.5 **AREAS OF CONTROL**: All activities and services including those of subcontractors which affect the quality of CAMCO products shall comply with the requirements of the Quality Assurance program.

2.6 **AUTHORIZED REPAIR LOCATIONS**: These are additional CAMCO locations approved by Quality Assurance to receive, disassemble, replace parts, reassemble and functionally test CAMCO SPPE products. Authorized Repair Locations may not heat treat, weld or monogram products. To become authorized and to remain approved, each location must:

A. Have a Quality Assurance Manual approved by CAMCO Quality Assurance.
B. Be audited for compliance with the approved Quality Assurance Manual by CAMCO or CAMCO, LTD. Quality Assurance at least once every three years.



**Exhibit 14-4 (Continued)**

# QUALITY ASSURANCE MANUAL

CAMCO

SECTION: 2.0
REVISION: "B"
PAGE: 4 OF 4

SUBJECT: QUALITY ASSURANCE PROGRAM

C. Ensure that repairs and tests are performed in accordance with the CAMCO Operations Manual procedures and specifications (Section 5.0 of this manual) and API Specification 14A.

D. Ensure that all personnel involved in the repair and test of SPPE are certified to perform the specific activity by CAMCO Quality Assurance.

E. Ensure that traceability data is transmitted to the original CAMCO manufacturing plant using the Camco Equipment Order and Shipping Ticket (Appendix 2.1).

F. Ensure that all SPPE assemblies failing while in service have a failure analysis performed in accordance with the operator's instructions. Should the operator want CAMCO to perform the failure analysis, the SPPE must be returned to CAMCO for processing in accordance with Section 10.0 of this manual.

2.7 PROCEDURES: Operations Manual procedures exist for the control and maintenance of the Quality Assurance program. Procedures shall include, but are not limited to indoctrination and training of personnel.



**Exhibit 14-4 (Continued)**

## QUALITY ASSURANCE MANUAL

SECTION: 14.0
REVISION: "B"
PAGE: 1 of 3

SUBJECT: QUALITY ASSURANCE RECORDS



14.1 **RECORDS, STORAGE, SECURITY AND RETRIEVABILITY**: Quality Assurance shall determine the adequacy of storage,security and retrievability of records required by the Quality Assurance program. The department responsible for the maintenance and storage of records shall also be responsible for their completeness, legibility, and retrievability.

14.2 **STORAGE**: Storage in designated areas shall provide adequate protection from damage, deterioration or loss and may be accomplished using files, computer storage, and/or microfilm. Those records required for traceability and failure analysis shall be retained for a minimum of 5 years from the product shipment date. Records of SPPE Design Verification Tests and associated files shall be maintained in accordance with API-14A. The following documents shall be retained for a minimum of five years from product shipment date:

14.2.1 Quality Assurance Manual and API License.
14.2.2 Drawings, specifications, standards and procedures.
14.2.3 Quality control reports.
14.2.4 Failure reports and corrective action records.
14.2.5 Verification and functional test files.
14.2.6 Mill and other test reports.

14.3 Documents shall be in written form and/or electronic data.

A. Electronic forms shall be initiated, controlled, and revised by procedures approved by the Directors of

**Exhibit 14-5**
**CAMCO's Quality Assurance Manual Quality Assurance Records**

Reprinted here with permission from CAMCO, Inc.

**QUALITY ASSURANCE MANUAL**

SECTION: 14.0
REVISION: "B"
PAGE: 2 of 3

SUBJECT: QUALITY ASSURANCE RECORDS



Information Services and Quality Assurance. These procedures shall be controlled and revised in accordance with Section 5.0. Procedures shall include:

A. Minimum data required on electronic forms which shall be the same as written forms.

B. Processing, storage, security and retrievability requirements.

C. Requirements for electronic signatures secured by unique password access (for approvals of restricted data).

D. Methods used to secure access for authorized signatures. Quality Assurance shall provide the Director of Information Services with a documented list of personnel authorized to electronically approve those portions of forms that are restricted. This list shall exhibit the persons electronic signature as it will appear on electronic forms. Approval tables shall be initiated by the Director of Information Services which lists these individuals and provides security against unauthorized individuals approving (entering) restricted portions of forms. Revisions to these tables shall only be made by Information Services personnel after receipt of a documented change request from Quality Assurance. Those portions of forms that are unrestricted shall be identified and individuals completing these portions shall enter their employee number for identification.

**Exhibit 14-5**
**(Continued)**

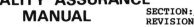

## QUALITY ASSURANCE MANUAL

SECTION: 14.0
REVISION: "B"
PAGE: 3 of 3

SUBJECT: QUALITY ASSURANCE RECORDS

14.4 **PROCEDURES**: Procedures exist for the control of Quality Assurance records. Procedures shall include, but are not restricted to the following:

A. A list of Quality Assurance records, their storage locations, and the department responsible for maintenance and retrievability.

B. The systems for transmittal, distribution, retention and disposition of Quality Assurance records.



**Exhibit 14-5**
**(Continued)**

## SUMMARY

The quality concept receives special attention at the time when American companies attempt to regain their lost local and international markets. In a quest for economic leadership, the struggle for quality improvement is a dominant one because, as many say, the Japanese have become leading industrial competitors, currently producing high-quality products. Consequently, many American companies start their improvement programs with quality improvement measures. Will it produce the desired effect? In reality, what has helped the Japanese to establish themselves in such a position of distinction in a world economy is not just improved quality of their products as such, but rather their coordinated national economic policy and integrated business strategy. It started with establishing the Ministry of International Trade and Industry (MITI). In general, MITI has developed and introduced a global national policy in purchasing, marketing, and sales.

The Massachussetts Institute of Technology (MIT) Commission on Industrial Productivity indicates that the Japanese success is based on a macroeconomics policy coordinated by the MITI involving such measures as standardization of industrial products and directing firms to specialize in one or two products as well as support of R&D and development of flexible manufacturing systems. At the microeconomics company level, efforts were directed toward all areas of production and services, with the purpose of not just quality improvements, but also a product costs reduction and improvements in the customer service. The Japanese coordinated national policy existed long before their Just-in-Time system was acknowledged.

Deming's teachings recognized by the Japanese include fundamentals of what later became known as the JIT system. For example, his 14 quality principles include such goals as becoming competitive, eliminating waste, and seeking continuing improvements. These are the cornerstones of JIT, which is aimed at elimination of waste throughout a spectrum of business activities, not just a product quality. The emerging term "quality at source" means enforcing quality of daily tasks of everyone in an organization, so that all jobs are performed at the best of the employees' ability and that output does not require further quality inspections. These provisions are aimed not just at production, but at the entire spectrum of business activities, production services, engineering, product design, and development of improved produceability, which is correlated with manufacturing engineering, planning and control systems, MIS, and management control systems. The ultimate objective of the quality control function is to contribute to quality improvement, along with cost reduction and better customer service. The term total quality control, or more recently total quality management, came as a recognition that quality improvements start with improvements in management systems and spreads to all processes and functions, down to the execution. Total quality improvements stress an integrated business approach.

# 15

# How to Organize and Control Plant Maintenance Systems

Maintenance is a production function consisting of activities designed to keep facilities and resources in good working condition and restore them to their operating status in order to prevent disruptions in production. Maintenance is a service to production. However, due to the effect of maintenance on the product value—namely, on the product cost, product quality, and product timely completion—it has increasingly been viewed as part of production, partially performed by the production people.

Maintenance "produces" the availability of productive resources at a specific cost, which in some organizations constitutes a substantial part of the total production cost, ranging from 8 to 33 percent depending on the equipment and the type of product. Also, maintenance affects product quality, since the equipment's ability to perform to engineering standards depends to a large degree on how well it is maintained.

Moreover, the availability of equipment, along with production planning, is an important condition for an uninterrupted material flow, low inventory, and timely completion of jobs. Since maintenance is a part of an integrated production system, its main purpose is to maximize contributions to the product value by ensuring regular equipment availability at minimum cost.

Maintenance does not need to provide a 100 percent equipment availability; it is sufficient to make production resources available when they are needed according to the production plan. This is achieved by a comprehensive maintenance planning and control system. Maintenance planning and control are reminiscent of job shop planning and control, requiring maintenance system flexibility when responding to unforeseen breakdowns and unexpected "hot" jobs.

## THE ROLE OF THE MAINTENANCE DEPARTMENT

The organization of a maintenance department depends on the size of a company, the type and sophistication of equipment, the type of production, the labor utilization skills available, and management's attitude toward the maintenance of the facility.

The functions of a maintenance department can be segregated into two main groups:

1. Restoration of equipment to an acceptable standard
2. Physical plant maintenance, including installation and alteration of a plant, equipment, and services

The maintenance function thus covers the plant, equipment, buildings, and services (steam, gas, water, ventilation, electricity). Plant or production equipment involves all machinery and tools necessary for production. Common maintenance jobs done on production equipment include

- Installing machinery, and aligning and securing it to the foundation and testing
- Checking equipment alignment and vibration, clearances, functioning of control devices, and safety
- Replacing or repairing worn bearings, bushings, packings, and gaskets
- Inspecting general conditions and reporting on the work to be done, including cost estimates

Physical plant maintenance includes maintenance of buildings (walls, roofs, foundations, floors), elevators, heating and ventilation equipment, air-conditioning, sanitation, and lighting. Services involve electrical, plumbing, roofing, masonry, carpentry, and other trades—quite often done by outside contractors.

There are three approaches in organizing plant maintenance:

1. Centralization by trade
2. Maintenance coverage by area
3. Combination of the centralization by trade and maintenance coverage by area approaches

The combined form is quite popular in industry today.

## THE TWO BASIC FORMS OF MAINTENANCE

There are two general categories of maintenance: planned maintenance and unplanned maintenance. *Planned maintenance* is a deliberate maintenance activity carried out within the framework of the maintenance system. Planned maintenance can be either preventive maintenance or corrective maintenance. *Prreventive maintenance* is essential in continuous or process-type production, and where the failure of equipment can cause a hazard. Preventive maintenance is of two types:

1. Running maintenance
2. Shutdown maintenance

Various forms of maintenance are shown in Figure 15-1.

*Corrective maintenance,* also known as *planned corrective maintenance,* consists of the work undertaken to restore a facility to an acceptable standard after an equipment failure has occurred. Corrective maintenance is of one type, namely, breakdown maintenance.

*Unplanned maintenance* consists of maintenance activities which are reactive to the occurred emergency situations. Such maintenance is also known as the *emergency maintenance.* Emergency maintenance refers to the maintenance work necessitated by a breakdown or damage without a prior knowledge. This is an unplanned maintenance work carried out without a prior arrangement for maintenance resources, such as materials, spare parts, and work instructions. Everything should be supplied in the emergency order.

To start with, a maintenance inspection should be organized to find the cause for the breakdown, as well as the nature and the extent of the damage, to decide what should be done and what kind of materials and work force is required. If spare parts or materials are out of stock, they will have to be purchased at a premium price, since there is no time to shop around. The same goes for the work force: people are taken off other jobs when an emergency breakdown occurs, since these unexpected jobs are not included in the maintenance plan. In many instances, the work force will require supervision and special instructions on how to do the job because the work specifications have not been studied in advance.

In general, emergency maintenance is the most expensive way of doing the plant maintenance, since emergency breakdowns are more frequent and last longer than when maintenance work is planned.

Breakdown maintenance refers to planned maintenance work which is carried out after a failure. How do we get a prior knowledge of a breakdown? By conducting regular inspections of the equipment. Breakdown maintenance is applied in cases where equipment failure would not immediately affect the overall production or constitute a safety hazard.

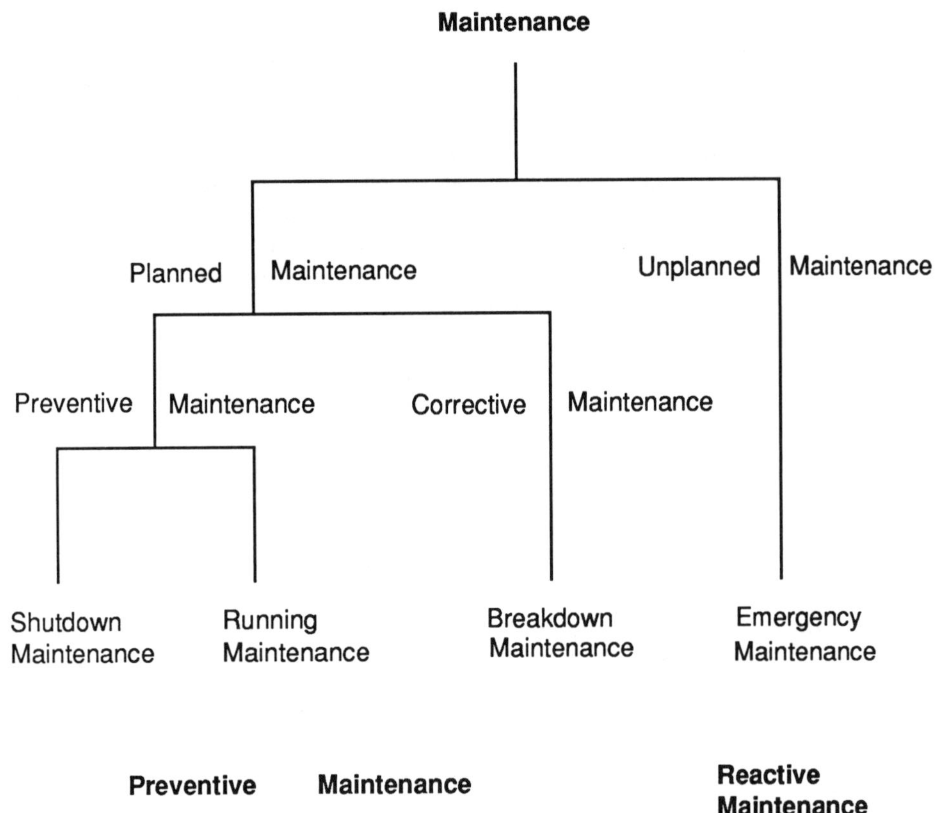


**Figure 15-1**
**Various Forms of Maintenance**

Breakdown maintenance differs from emergency maintenance in that the former is carried out within the framework of a maintenance system, while emergency maintenance is not planned for. A maintenance system requires regular scheduled inspections and makes a provision for the potential breakdown work in the form of spare parts, materials, labor, and equipment as well as all the required documentation and job instructions. Under breakdown maintenance, those components that will be expected to fail sometime in the future are not replaced immediately, in order to reduce labor and spare parts costs. But in the meantime, all the necessary preparations are made for the eventual replacement of the component: ensuring the availability of this item in stock or ordering it if it is out of stock, planning labor for the replacement job in the expected failure time period, and ensuring that everybody involved has access to the job instructions.

For example, if a component with 15,000 running hours projected lifetime is approaching its 13,000th hour, it is left working until it wears out. The projected lifetime curve for this example is illustrated in Figure 15-2. Such an extension of a component's life, which can be substantial due to the continuing functioning of some components far beyond their average life expectation, is acceptable if the machine units in question do not directly or indirectly lower the quality of a process and if their failure or breakdown will not cause a major breakdown or present danger to people. With such arrangement, a breakdown job is performed in an orderly manner.

*Running maintenance* refers to the work carried out without a scheduled stoppage of the facility. Running maintenance does not interrupt production, since the work can be conducted outside the working hours—lunchtime, evening time, or nighttime in a one- or two-shift operation or during holidays when the facility is not in operation. The repair is done without an interruption to the production program.

*Shutdown maintenance* refers to work which is carried out while the facility is out of service. In breakdown maintenance and emergency maintenance, the facility is also out of service, but it is due to the breakdown, while with shutdown maintenance, the stoppage is planned in advance, usually in coordination with the production program. Major repairs and revamps are planned as a shutdown maintenance.

## CALCULATING THE RELIABILITY OF EQUIPMENT

The goal of any maintenance plan is to ensure well-maintained items—equipment, plant, and factory buildings— to sustain production activities and reliability for a reasonable length of time. The reliability of equipment, as is in any other system, is the probability that all its parts and interrelated components, each performing a specific task, function properly. Failure of one of these components can lead to a failure of the entire system. Thus reliability of equipment depends on the reliability and on the number of its components.

The reliability of a system is computed as a product of the reliabilities of its individual components:

$$R_s = R_1 * R_2 * R_3 * \cdots * R_n$$

where

$R_s$ = the reliability of the system

$R_1, \ldots, R_n$ = the reliability of components 1 through $n$

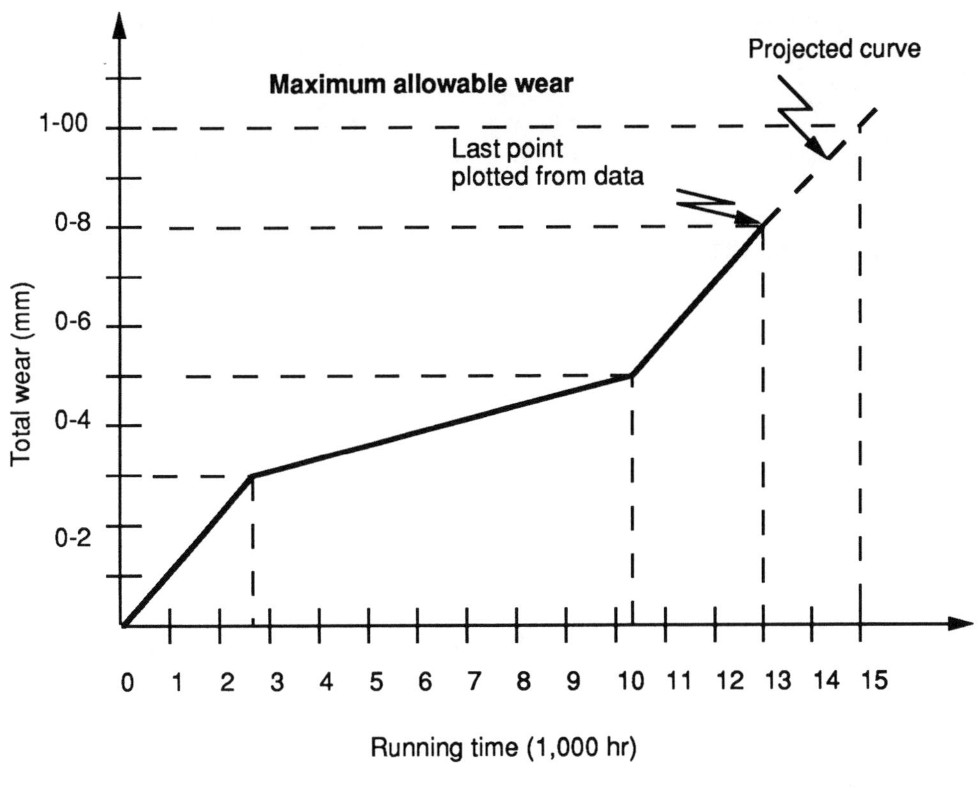


**Figure 15-2**
**The Projected Life-Time Curve**

For example, the reliability of an assembly unit comprising four components with the reliabilities of 0.92, 0.85, 0.90, and 0.88 is computed as follows:

$$R_s = R_1 * R_2 * R_3 * R_4$$
$$= 0.92 * 0.85 * 0.90 * 0.88 = 61.93\%$$

Thus, the fewer the parts used, the higher the reliability of an equipment.

The reliability equation assumes that the reliability of an individual component does not depend on the reliability of other components. The reliability of individual components is computed as a statistical probability, based on historical data. Thus, for a component with 92 percent reliability, there is a 99.74 percent probability (if the calculation assumes $\pm$ 3*S*) that this component will perform as expected 92 percent of the time, and it will fail 8 percent of the time (100% - 92% = 8%).

A graph of equipment failure rates against time throughout the equipment life shows three distinct time periods:

1. Early failure rate
2. Constant failure rate
3. Wear out-failure rate

Graphically, three time periods in the equipment life are illustrated in Figure 15-3.

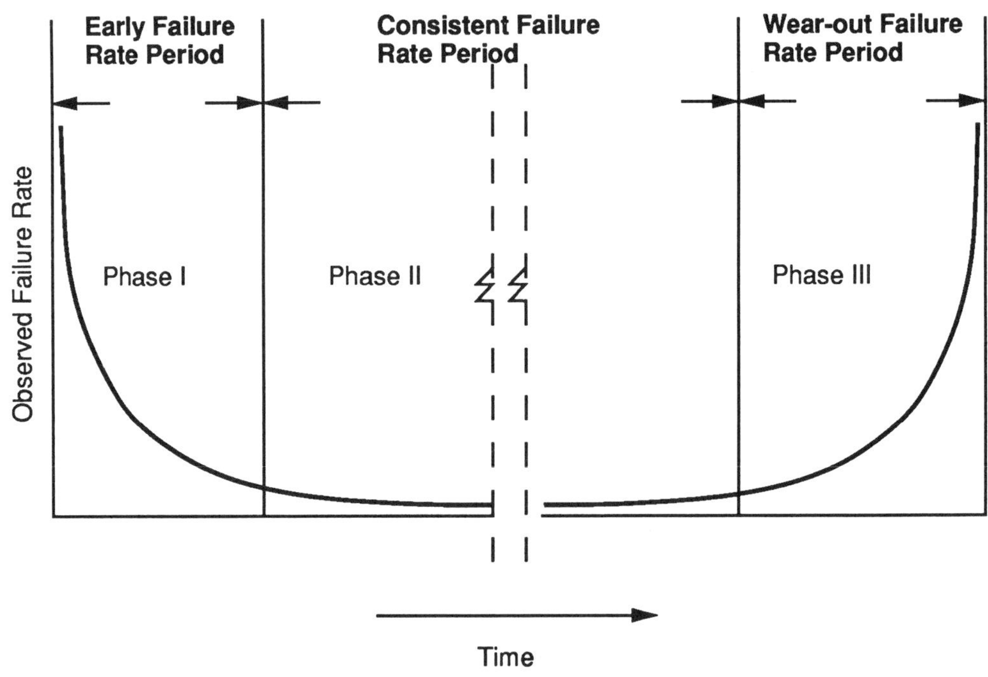


**Figure 15-3**
**The Bathtub Curve**

The lifetime curve, also known as the bathtub curve, shows that failures occur at different rates during the life of equipment or any of its components. Phase I, the early failure rate period, takes place at the first stage of the equipment use and is attributed to the following reasons:

- Manufacturing faults which are not detected at the production stage (external failures)
- Design faults
- Start-up problems due to the misuse or lack of experience in operating the equipment

At this stage, the initial faults in an equipment are rectified through adjustments or replacements. This is an increased maintenance activity time period.

During phase II, the constant failure rate period, the failure rate settles down to a reduced level for a considerable time. The functioning of the equipment stabilizes and it requires less maintenance.

During phase III, the wear-out period, the failure rate rises again, due to the wearing out and aging of the equipment. This is the time of an ever-increasing maintenance activity during which the combined maintenance cost and production losses due to equipment failures may exceed the cost of new equipment. The plant maintenance system should be able to forecast and to plan for a timely replacement of the plant and equipment.

## CALCULATING THE COST OF THE VARIOUS CATEGORIES OF MAINTENANCE

The objective of maintenance is to keep the building facilities, plants, and equipment in good condition and in working order at a minimal cost. The cost is considered when selecting one or another type of maintenance. For example, breakdown maintenance is used when the cost of preventing equipment failures may be greater than the cost of a breakdown. Another option is to prevent breakdown through a program of scheduled maintenance inspections, cleaning, adjustment, lubrication, and replacement of parts and assembly units. This option seems to be the best way to organize the maintenance work because it excludes surprise breakdowns and production delays, due to maintenance work being conducted according to the plan. While this is true, there also is a reservation for using preventive maintenance because of its high cost. The elements of the total maintenance cost are illustrated in Figure 15-4.

The difference between preventive maintenance and emergency maintenance lies in maintenance inspections. Preventive maintenance is organized maintenance work conducted for rectifying the faults detected by regular scheduled inspections of an equipment.

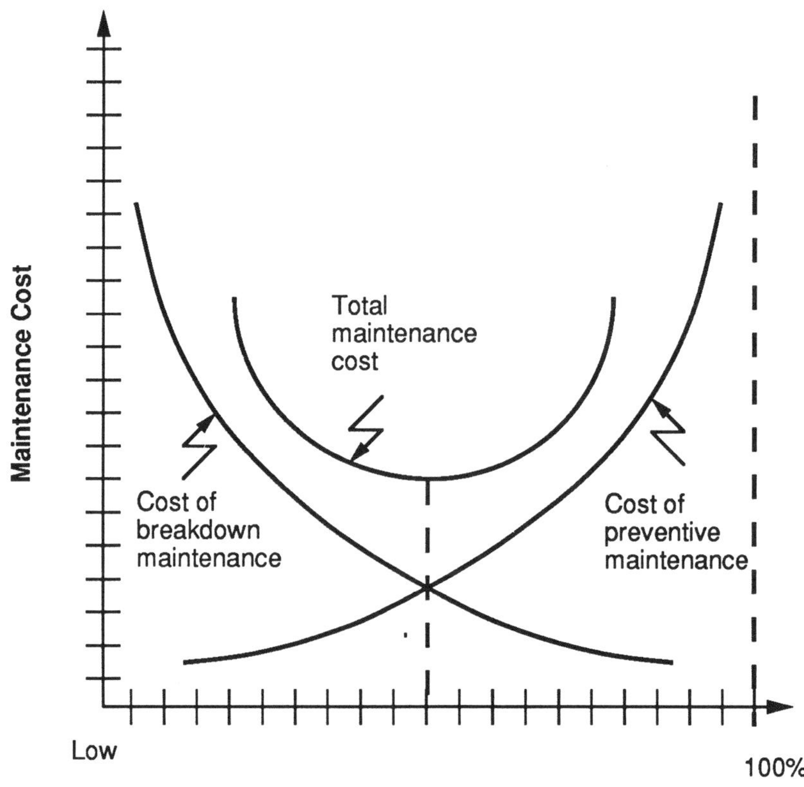


**Figure 15-4**
**Total Maintenance Cost as a Trade-off Between Preventive Maintenance and Maintenance of Breakdowns**

The *cost of inspections* is a significant part of the preventive maintenance cost. The difference between preventive maintenance and breakdown maintenance is in the timing of repairs. In preventive maintenance, the replacement or repair of the equipment and parts is scheduled at the earliest convenience after the fault has been detected by an inspection. In breakdown maintenance, the equipment is allowed to operate until a breakdown. This saves spare parts and labor costs. More frequent maintenance repairs is another factor to consider in the inflated cost of preventive maintenance.

The task of maintenance management is to make a trade-off between the maintenance of breakdowns and the preventive maintenance, in order to arrive at the lowest total maintenance cost. Depending on the type of an equipment and its age, each company has its individual operating characteristics affecting the ratio of breakdown and preventive maintenance. For example, one company with a continuous production cycle has identified its lowest total maintenance cost as consisting of 72 percent preventive maintenance, 22 percent corrective maintenance, and 6 percent emergency maintenance. A maintenance planning and control system assists in organizing and controlling maintenance operations in order to obtain the 72:22:6 ratio.

## SETTING UP A PLANT MAINTENANCE PLANNING AND CONTROL SYSTEM

The main objectives of maintenance planning and control are

1. *To acheive a greater plant availability with fewer breakdowns by planning maintenance work when it is most convenient and will cause a minimal loss of production.* Regularly scheduled maintenance results in lower downtime than does infrequent and more expensive ad hoc maintenance. Planned servicing and adjustments maintain a consistently high level of the plant output, quality, and performance.
2. *To acheive a greater and more effective labor utilization.* Maintenance is a labor-intensive type of production, where the labor cost is a significant part of the total maintenance cost. The labor cost is reduced, and its allocation can be controlled effectively, if a weekly work load is known in advance and the provision is made for breakdowns and other unexpected jobs so typical in maintenance operations.
3. *To acheive a maintenance cost reduction.* The next goal of the maintenance planning and control is to reduce the maintenance cost. Regular simple planned servicing is cheaper than the sudden expensive repairs. A maintenance cost reduction is a direct contribution of maintenance operations to the product value. This also refers to the improved budgetary control—realistic budgets can be formulated and subsequently controlled, if a maintenance planning and control system is in place. The foregoing goals of maintenance present major maintenance cost categories.
4. *To accomplish through advanced planning a reduction in the cost of spare parts inventory and the maintenance equipment, without affecting orderly maintenance operations.* Realistic quantities of spares are stocked when demand is predictable.
5. *To provide a source of information upon which management can make realistic forecasts and operating decisions, by focusing attention at frequently*

*recurring jobs and types of defects, as well as the type, frequency, and cost of individual repairs.*

As with production planning, *maintenance planning* requires standards for balancing the "requirements" with the "limitations."

Requirements standards refer to the plant and equipment identification, equipment priority rating, maintenance schedule, and specification of jobs. Limitations refer to the capacity limitations—labor, equipment, tools, supplies, and the spare parts inventory.

## Setting Up Your Maintenance Standards

Maintenance control, budgeting, and cost control require maintenance standards and information for a history analysis. Elements of a plant maintenance system are illustrated in Figure 15-5.

### PLANT REGISTER

A plant register gives an answer to the question: "What must be maintained?" Sometimes, it is called an inventory of the facility and includes a listing of all company facilities, plant, equipment, and buildings. A plant register includes the following information about each inventory item:

- Item identification number
- Description of a facility
- Administrative units in the company, such as a division or a section
- Location
- Cost center
- Priority rating
- Special remarks

A sample inventory sheet is shown in Figure 15-6.

### ITEM IDENTIFICATION NUMBER

A unique symbol must be assigned to each item of the plant and equipment for a clear identification and for a reference to the relevant documents and the whereabouts of each piece of equipment within the plant. The equipment identification number is coded differently in different companies. A coding system can use letters in combination with numbers or use numbers only, for example, K-67, where the prefix "K" is the identification of a department and "67" is an item number within the department. The identification number can also can contain costing information—the item's identification and the cost center.

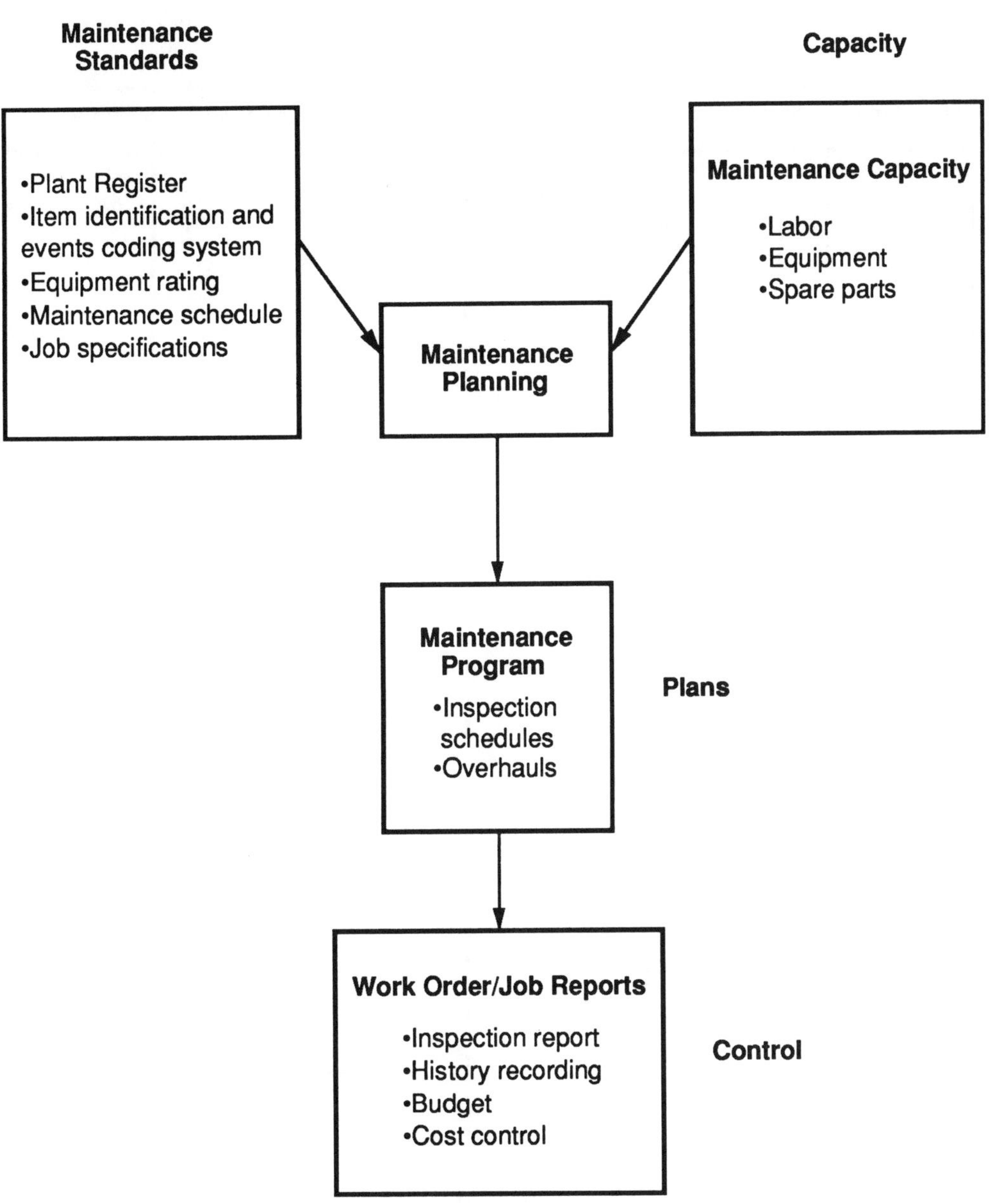


**Figure 15-5**
**The Plant Maintenance System**

| Plant Inventory | | | | Page______ | |
|---|---|---|---|---|---|
| Item Code | Description | Type | Priority Rating | Location | Remarks |
| | | | | | |

**Figure 15-6**
**Sample Inventory Sheet**

Here's an example of a C-G-P-M numbering system used in one steel manufacturing company:

C = cost code number. This three-digit number represents a cost area or a cost function (e.g., C-148 denotes the hot strip mill area of the plant).

G = number or group number. This four-digit number is always coupled with a C-number and is used to indicate a specific machine or a piece of equipment within the particular area (e.g., G-0189 indicates a casting mold at the continuous casting plant).

P = number of position number. This four-digit number is used to identify the position of an assembly unit on a drawing. A P-number is used in conjunction with the G-number, GP (e.g., 0189-2620 is a roller bearing unit in a continuous casting mill).

M = number of item numbers. This three-digit number is used to identify individual parts of an assembly or subassembly. Each part has a unique P-M number combination, assisting in exercising control over the spare parts inventory.

F = a unique number allocated to parts that are economically reconditionable. An F-number is physically attached to a unit when it is sent to the machine shop for repairs. An F-number assists in tracing a history of this part or the assembly unit.

Functions and advantages of the numbering system are the following:

- A cryptic and concise machine description decreasing the volume of paperwork
- Accurate maintenance planning and control improving communication
- A unique identification and coding of elements of the plant and equipment
- A convenient reference to use in other plant maintenance subsystems

### PRIORITY RATING

Priority rating codes differ in various organizations. However, usually these ratings are 1 to 5, 1 to 8, or 0 to 9 in descending order of the item's importance in production. For example, the 0-9 coding is applied as follows:

A 0, 1, and 2 rating is assigned to all the items whose availability is vital to the production process. A failure of an equipment in this priority category can hold production or create a safety hazard.

A 3, 4, and 5 rating is assigned to all the items whose failure will not immediately affect production, although it can do so soon.

A 6 and 7 rating is assigned to all the items which are not directly involved into production. These are items whose failure affects service operations to production, which are not immediately required or may be postponed for the time being.

An 8 and 9 rating is assigned to all nonproductive items whose failure will not directly or indirectly affect production or create a safety hazard.

Priority of maintained items assists in the long- and short-term maintenance planning, scheduling, and job sequencing in breakdown and emergency maintenance situations.

## MAINTENANCE EVENTS NUMBERING SYSTEM

For effective maintenance planning and control, it is necessary to convert data related to maintenance events and faults into an acceptable numerical code. This information is converted into a code consisting of a series of digits, where each digit or a group of digits represents a particular aspect of the maintenance function or a fault. The following is a very simple example to illustrate the application:

The first digit or group represents the field of activity involved.

1 Mechanical
2 Electrical
3 Electronic
4 Lubrication
5 Instrumentation
6 Hydraulic

The second digit or group represents the form of maintenance.

1. Planned preventive running maintenance
2. Planned preventive shutdown maintenance
3. Planned corrective shutdown maintenance
4. Planned corrective breakdown maintenance
5. Emergency maintenance

The third digit or group represents the type of the specific component involved. The fourth digit or group represents the type of the fault, failure, service, or adjustment carried out.

Other information presented in a code number can be

Drawing number

Assembly

Sub-assembly area

Cost area

Cost function

A code number can be numeric or alphanumeric. A code number is physically attached to a unit when it is sent to the machine workshop for repairs or reconditioning.

## USING A MAINTENANCE SCHEDULE

A maintenance schedule is a comprehensive list of maintenance works with the aim of maintaining the physical characteristics of the equipment. The frequency of maintenance tasks depends on the type of equipment, its functions, and its priority rating. A maintenance schedule includes individual maintenance tasks: lubrication, inspections, components and assembly units adjustments, replacements, and overhauls. A maintenance schedule also contains a detailed list of tasks performed during maintenance, time required, labor, tools and equipment, materials, and spare parts. Frequency of inspections and repairs is often recommended by the equipment manufacturer. An example of a maintenance schedule form is shown in Figure 15-7.

This schedule sets the frequency for each maintenance job and lists everything required for this job: tools and equipment, spare parts, and supplies. For each machine, the maintenance schedule represents the maintenance labor load. This is coordinated with production, so that the maintenance work is scheduled when the facility is available, and thus the production program is not affected.

Quite often, parts are changed in sets, in order to get a longer life span from each part and to reduce the labor cost. In this instance, the maintenance schedule indicates the phases of a replacement and the associated equipment or facilities, which should be serviced simultaneously.

## PLANNED EQUIPMENT LUBRICATION: NOT JUST THE SQUEAKY WHEEL GETTING THE GREASE

Equipment lubrication is an important part of planned maintenance. Insufficient lubrication results in an excessive friction between the parts and their premature deterioration. This is one of the major reasons for breakdowns during the maturity stage of the equipment life (the normal failure rate period).

Lubrication points and frequency of lubrication are specified by the manufacturer in service instructions and are divided into daily, weekly, and monthly lubrication tasks and oil changes. Based on these recommendations, a lubrication card is compiled for each piece of equipment, along with the lubrication schedule. An example of a lubrication schedule form is shown in Figure 15-8.

In centralized maintenance departments, lubrication is performed by specialized oilers/greasers, according to the prepared lubrication route cards. This ensures that the lubrication specification is followed through: correct grades of lubricant are applied, the right amount is used, and all the aspects of safety are adhered to.

Lately, maintenance planners frequently ask if the lubrication can be done by the operating personnel rather than the maintenance department. In JIT

| Equipment Maintenance Schedule________________________ | | | | | | I.D.No.______ |
|---|---|---|---|---|---|---|
| Drawing No. ________________ Modifications____________ | | | | | | Location______ |
| Schedule Reference .No.________ Service Manual_____ | | | | | | Date________ |
| Item Code | Job Description | Job Specification | Trade | Time | Avail. for Maint. | Remarks |
| | | | | | | |

**Figure 15-7**
**Sample Maintenance Schedule Form**

| Company name: | | | LUBRICATION CARD | | | | | |
|---|---|---|---|---|---|---|---|---|
| Plant: | | | Identification: | | | | | |
| Cost code: | | | Priority code: | | | | | |
| Ref. | Description of lubrication point | Location of lubrication point | Freq. | Lub. | Oper. | Time | Related activity | Remarks |
| | | | | | | | | |
| | | | | | | | | |
| | | | | | | | | |
| | | | | | | | | |
| | | | | | | | | |
| | | | | | | | | |
| | | | | | | | | |
| | | | | | | | | |
| | | | | | | | | |
| | | | | | | | | |
| | | | | | | | | |
| | | | | | | | | |
| Date completed: | | | Completed by: | | | | | |

**Figure 15-8**
**The Lubrication Schedule**

systems, the scheduled daily and weekly lubrication is done by machine operators themselves, but monthly lubrication tasks and oil changes also involve the maintenance personnel.

Equipment lubrication by machine operators familiarizes them with the equipment, improves the utilization, and reduces breakdown possibilities. It also reduces the need for inspections, due to operators reporting to the maintenance people any variations in performance, such as an abnormal noise, vibration, oil leaks, or temperature increases. These occurrences are recorded by the machine operators in various reports.

## JOB SPECIFICATIONS: ORGANIZING MAINTENANCE TASKS FOR INCREASED EFFICIENCY

A job specification includes a complete list of work tasks, their sequence, and detailed instructions on how to perform these tasks effectively. It is a document which provides a communicating link among the maintenance team, supervisors, and those who are in charge of maintenance planning.

Each task listed in the maintenance schedule (an inspection, servicing, an adjustment, or a replacement) requires a job specification. Furthermore, a job specification is compiled for each trade involved—mechanical, electrical, lubrication, and instrumentation. A job specification is a document containing the following information: name and type of an equipment, identification number, location, a reference to the maintenance schedule which this job is part of, the trades required to perform each operation, the description of the elements of the tasks (such as tests, inspections, and adjustments, including limits and tolerances, as well as any required parts changes and replacements), and the frequency of each task.

Instructions for changes and component replacement describe the ways and means of doing maintenance jobs so as to ensure that they are carried out in a uniform manner. These descriptions should include reference drawings and safety procedures.

Service instructions are issued on separate sheets for each service or function. For instance, there should be a separate instruction to the spare parts store, describing which spare parts and supplies should be made available for each maintenance job. These should also include instructions for various tasks and elements, ranging from the replacement of individual units to the notification of the supervisor in case of an accident.

Job specifications are kept in the foreman's office in file folders, grouped according to the type of maintenance jobs. This information, readily available to the maintenance people and artisans, is a programmed instruction eliminating the need for a supervisor personally to instruct each maintenance crew. A complete set of job specifications should be available for the reference by all members of the maintenance department and should be on hand when a maintenance work order is initiated.

Such use of job specifications saves time and reduces the need for supervision. Maintenance work can be done in many different ways achieving different results. Such maintenance tasks as individual inspections, breakdowns, dismantling machines, replacing parts, salvaging, and reconditioning should not be left to the sole initiative of individuals and to decisions made on the spur of the moment. Job specifications standardize the maintenance work, often widely open to an individual interpretation based on previous experience, skills, and attitudes.

It is advantageous to observe specified standard prescriptions for performing certain jobs, specifically as they relate to regular repetitive operations that should be carried out during the lifetime of the equipment. Categories for which job specifications and the standard set of instructions are compiled include

- Jobs typical to an entire plant
- Jobs related to groups of machines and a service plant, such as a heating and air conditioning system, a water plant, electrical generators, and so on.

Job specifications are also compiled for common and administrative procedures, such as reporting breakdowns and accidents, requests for shutdowns, cleaning, painting, wiring, lubrication, color coding, and so on. These standard procedures, common to many production units and departments, are usually called service instructions.

## THE IMPORTANCE OF GOOD MAINTENANCE SUPERVISION, ANALYSIS, AND CONTROL

Maintenance supervision involves activities relating to job assignments, planning and controlling of maintenance services, conducting an analysis by comparing the actual performance against the maintenance plan, and compiling regular reports to management. Supervision in maintenance plays a greater role than in production, due to a greater proportion of unscheduled and urgent jobs, wider cost variances, and increased interfunctional and administrative communications with production and services, especially during emergency situations. These features of maintenance operations lead to centralization of maintenance planning and control and feature a significant amount of clerical work.

Maintenance control involves control of unscheduled repair work and breakdowns. Good maintenance practice calls for an unscheduled maintenance work being performed only with a written request that has been put through the proper authorization channels. A maintenance request, or a work requisition, can be originated by production or by maintenance as a result of an inspection. An example of a maintenance request form is shown in Figure 15-9. A request for maintenance should have the following information:

- Name of the person requesting the service
- Reason for the request
- Description of the fault
- Job priority
- Date the service is required
- Name of the person authorizing the repair
- Cost center

| SERVICE REQUEST | | | Date: |
|---|---|---|---|
| From: | Department: | Machine No.: | Cost code: |
| To: | Department: | Factory No.: | Priority code |

| Job# | Material | Description of work/service required | Drawing |
|---|---|---|---|
| | | | |
| | | | |
| | | | |
| | | | |
| | | | |
| | | | |
| | | | |
| | | | |
| | | | |
| | | | |

| Cost | | | | Remarks |
|---|---|---|---|---|
| Materials | Labor | Misc. | Total | |
| | | | | |

Signature (Cost clerk) — — — — — — — — Signature (Supervisor) — — — — — — — —

**Figure 15-9**
**The Service Request Form**

The next step is to conduct a maintenance inspection to identify the extent of the damage and the type of work and resources required for repair. Based on the maintenance request and the inspection report, the job is scheduled by the foreman's office, and a job card is issued to this effect.

## USING JOB CARDS WITH THE PLANT MAINTENANCE SYSTEM

A maintenance work order form, know as a *job card,* is a source document for all the maintenance labor and supply charges. A work order is a key maintenance document initiating the maintenance work; it is a basis for maintenance cost control.

Maintenance work has two major categories:

1. Regular maintenance tasks
2. Irregular maintenance tasks

Regular maintenance tasks are scheduled inspections; lubrications; and general maintenance tasks, such as making specific tools and accessories, working with drawings, studying service instruction, and labor cross-training. Irregular maintenance tasks refer to all the emergency work, repairs, and breakdowns, both planned and unplanned.

An analysis of the maintenance cost shows that most of the maintenance expenses occur during irregular maintenance tasks. Three reasons can be attributed to the increased cost of maintenance of irregular jobs:

1. Irregular maintenance tasks are taking place when production is at standstill. Consequently, the maintenance cost also includes the cost of lost production.
2. When a piece of equipment is idle, an entire maintenance capacity is mobilized, in order to repair the breakdown and return the facility to operation. Overtime is a frequent occurrence during an irregular job. This adds to the maintenance cost, since overtime is less productive and more expensive.
3. Irregular maintenance tasks are usually accomplished by repairing or replacing components and assembly units. The cost of reconditioning and spare parts adds even more to the cost of irregular maintenance jobs. An example of a maintenance cost histogram is illustrated in Figure 15-10.

### The Format of the Job Card

Some companies attempt to reduce clerical work in issuing job cards, especially in the light of the recent drive to eliminate waste. In many maintenance systems, job cards are issued for irregular jobs and the jobs whose duration

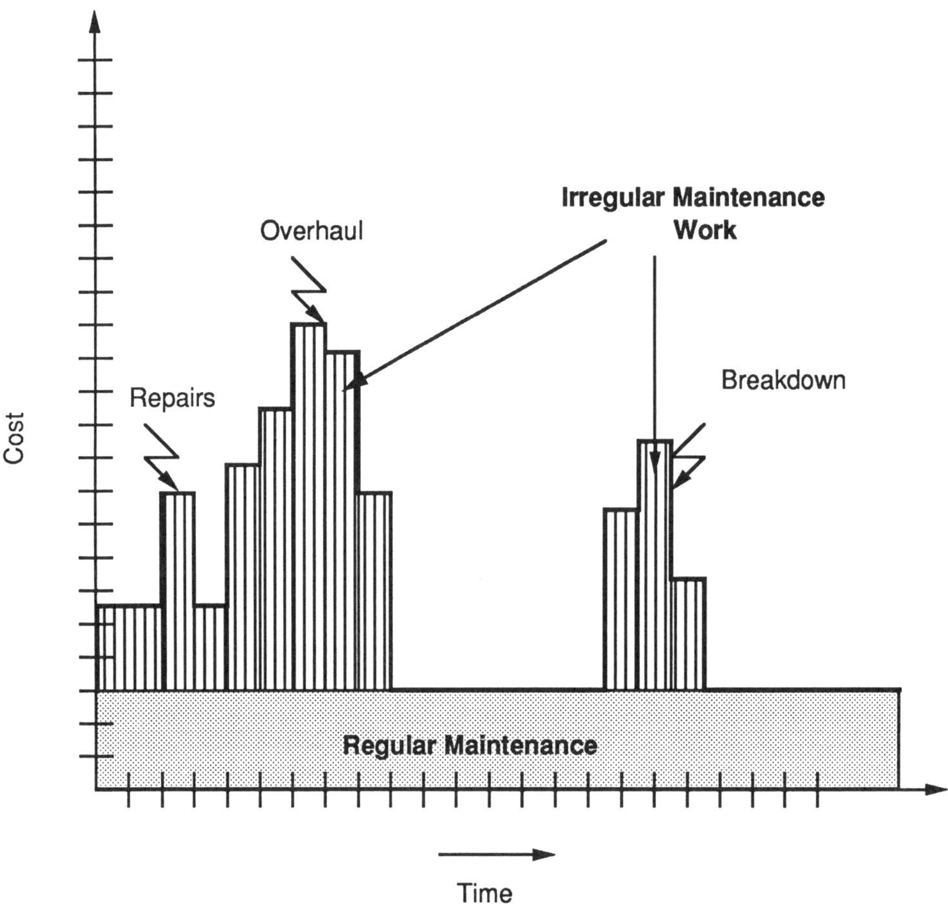


**Figure 15-10**
**The Histogram of the Maintenance Cost**

exceeds 15 minutes. Smaller jobs, scheduled inspections, and lubrication are controlled by marking their completion on a checklist. For example, if there is a standby order for a certain maintenance job to be done at regular intervals, these jobs do not require a work order. Jobs lasting less than 15 minutes can be jointly recorded in a weekly card. These work orders written on preprinted forms require only a checkmark indicating their completion.

The job card serves as a written instruction to execute a task within the specified time frame and within the available resources. It serves as an authorization document for an artisan to do the job, as well as a control and reporting document for data processing, history recording, and operational and budgetary maintenance planning. The job card is a document assisting in control and an analysis of periods of a higher maintenance cost.

The date, the time estimate, and the requested completion date, as well as the required spares and supplies, allow a certain degree of planning. This information helps to activate effectively a repair service and provide data regarding expenses for a cost center or a charge account. Companies report an increase in the personnel utilization by 60 to 70 percent after implementing job card procedures, as a result of improved maintenance procedures.

A general format of information contained in a job card is segregated into four categories:

1. Identification of the equipment, department, location of the problem, the person initiating the request, and urgency;
2. Actions required—the identification of a problem, trade involved, and work instructions;
3. Actions taken—the description of work done, standard and actual time, spare parts and materials involved, and remarks concerning the future maintenance needs;
4. Cost estimates and cost center identification—the cost is estimated according to maintenance categories.

For jobs where the total cost exceeds a certain limit, an additional authorization has to be obtained and recorded. Often a job card contains information about the stoppage time and start-up time, recorded by the production personnel. Space also should be provided for an additional unplanned cost of spares and supplies, and manpower, when the supervisor has to recheck and diagnose the fault on the spot and issue instructions accordingly.

### The Flow Sequence of a Job Card

The number of copies of a work order vary from three to five in different maintenance systems. The following is an example of a flow chart of a three-copy job card. Flow diagram of the job card is shown in Figure 15-11.

The *planning office* issuing a job card retains the original copy and forwards the remaining two copies to the head of plant Maintenance for approval, whereupon these are handed over to the foreman concerned. The original copy retained by the planning office is routed to data processing on completion of a job. A duplicate copy is issued to the foreman and retained there while the task is being executed.

The *foreman* completes both copies, filling in the artisan's name, grade, and employee number. A pasteboard copy is issued to the artisan by the foreman.

The *artisan* fills in the job card with the following information, during the task and after it has been completed: time worked, report on the work

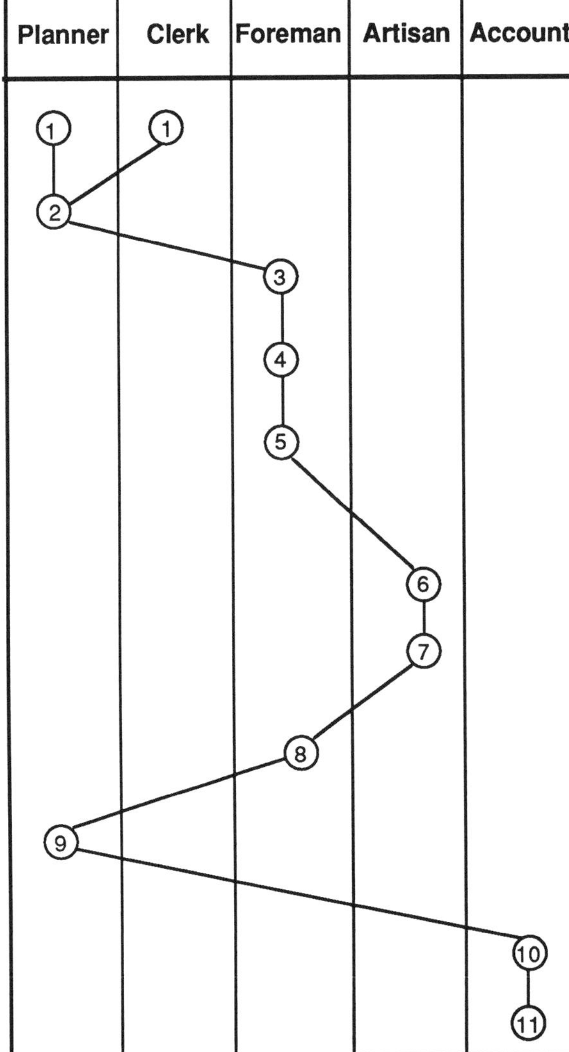


1. Make out a job card (triplicate).

2. Describe the task and work out target time.

3. Send through the foreman.

4. Allocate an artisan and fill in (duplicate).

5. Discuss the task and issue a job card to the artisan, along with the job specifications and service instructions.

6. Receive the job card and carry out the task.

7. Complete the job card, enter deviations and sign the card.

8. Control all entries by the artisan and sign the job card.

9. Take note of work done and mark out for history recording and/or replanning.

10. Do the necessary recording.

11. Codify deviations and complete white flimsies.

**Figure 15-11**
**A Flow Diagram of the Job Card**

done, deviations, equipment used, and parts replaced. He or she signs the job card and returns it to the foreman immediately.

The foreman then checks all the entries made by the artisan, signs the card, and returns it to the planning office immediately.

The *planning office* enters the completion date into the original copy, along with the employee number, time worked, a short description of the work done and the foreman's authorization number.

The next destination of the job card is the accounting office, where the total cost of the job is computed and posted against the appropriate cost center account. After the necessary recording is performed, the white copy is forwarded to data processing, where it is filed for about six months.

Distinct from a production system, in a maintenance system, records are kept in many different ways, ranging from card files to a computer storage. This information is used for history recording, cost accounting, and maintenance financial control. The job card system is a well-planned procedure that ensures that all the parties concerned comply with the instructions.

## USING A JOB REPORT AS FEEDBACK

Sometimes, a *job report* is compiled in addition to a job card. It has informative value for the future maintenance work and cost analysis. A job report is feedback from the person who performed the work to the person responsible for planning, representing a recording of the condition of the facility and the maintenance work done. The front side of a job report is shown in Figure 15-12. More information can be written on the back side of the form.

Any fault diagnosed during the inspection, which cannot be rectified at that time, should be reported; for example, faults such as the following:

- Faults that, if continued running, would cause damage to the plant, product, or would constitute a safety hazard
- Work that can be planned for later

A job report should be brief and concise and should not include what was found to be satisfactory.

## USING A HISTORY RECORDING SYSTEM TO COLLECT VITAL INFORMATION

In maintenance, the most appropriate action can be initiated if there exist up-to-date records and information. Collecting maintenance information is a function of a *history recording system.*

| JOB REPORT | Date: | Report No.: |
|---|---|---|
| Name of artisan: | Trade: | |
| Facility: | | |
| Identification No.: | | |
| Location: | | |
| Defect: | | |
| Cause: | | |
| Corrective action: | | |
| Spares/materials used: | | |
| Measurements/ observations: | | |
| Replacements: | | |
| Standard time: | | |
| Actual time: | | |

**Figure 15-12**
**The Job Report**

History recording contains information about the maintenance work done at a particular facility. A subsequent analysis and interpretation of the recorded data assess the effectiveness of the maintenance function and highlight shortcomings in the maintenance system. An example of a history recording card is shown in Figure 15-13. The following information is logged in chronological order:

- Inspections, repairs, servicing and adjustments carried out
- Breakdowns and failures, their effect, their causes, and corrective actions taken
- Work done at the facility; components required or replaced
- Conditions of wear, tear, erosion, and corrosion
- Measurements of readings taken, clearance, results of tests and inspection

| HISTORY CARD | | |
|---|---|---|
| Equipment: | | Cost center No.: |
| Priority code: | | |
| Function performed: | | |
| Related equipment: | | |
| Date | Work description | Work order |
| | | |
| | | |
| | | |
| | | |
| | | |
| | | |
| | | |
| | | |
| | | |
| | | |
| | | |

**Figure 15-13**
**The History Card**

- Time and cost to carry out the maintenance or repair work

History recording of maintenance operations are further classified into three categories:

1. Production equipment
2. Physical plant
3. Service facilities

### Production Equipment

Production equipment includes all machinery and tools necessary for production. Practice shows that the best method for keeping production equipment records is a unit log. In the unit log, each piece of production equipment has its own daily record, where all information relevant to the operation of equipment is entered. This information includes work time, shutdown time, the reason for the shutdown, and the action necessary to restore the equipment to working conditions as well as the actual production output of the equipment. A unit log book contains information which helps to determine the effects of overloading and underloading of the equipment on its performance.

### Physical Plant Maintenance

Physical plant maintenance involves electrical services, plumbing, roofing, masonry, carpentry, and other trades. Physical plant maintenance jobs are often conducted by outside contractors.

### Service Facilities Maintenance

Service facilities maintenance includes lubrication, greasing, and inspections. Data for this form are taken from job orders issued according to the plant lubrication program. In JIT systems, lubrication work and its record keeping are also performed by the operating personnel.

### Benefiting from the Many Advantages of the History Recording System

A history recording system has the following advantages:

1. Parts are ordered on time because the life span of parts is known.
2. Planning can be carried out to the extent that parts are replaced simultaneously in an economical manner.
3. Technical modifications are evaluated by comparing the life spans and costs before and after such a modification.
4. The life span of components can be used to adjust inspection schedules.
5. An unnecessary equipment replacement can be avoided, and spare parts from various suppliers can be compared.
6. Based on facts and information available, the system provides an input for the acquisition of a new equipment.
7. A more accurate and realistic budget can be drawn up.
8. Improved cash flow control results from planning of maintenance repairs and replacements.

## HOW TO DEVELOP A LONG-TERM AND SHORT-TERM MAINTENANCE PROGRAM

A maintenance program allocates specific maintenance to a specific period. The program is prepared in agreement with production and takes into consideration production schedules. There are two stages in a maintenance program:

1. Compiling long-range schedules
2. Compiling short-term programs and daily schedule adjustments

Planned maintenance does not guarantee the elimination of breakdowns. Thus, the program must make provision for performing emergency jobs. Maintenance time schedules must be flexible because of the nature of short routine operations of maintenance services, more flexible than production planning and control systems.

The main purposes of a maintenance program are

1. To set up a maintenance plan:
   a. To spread the maintenance work load evenly over the year
   b. To ensure that the required maintenance is carried out with the specified frequency
   c. To coordinate maintenance of associated facilities
   d. To coordinate maintenance with production requirements.
2. To present an overall picture of the maintenance work, present and future commitments (on the short- and long-term basis):
   a. To assist the forward planning, ordering of spares, future labor requirements, and to present a basis for budgetary control.
3. To formulate a short-term maintenance plan:
   a. To formulate weekly work plans (for immediate future)
   b. To arrange for the availability of a production plant
   c. To ensure the availability of labor, spares, auxiliary materials, and sub-contractors.

Steps in compiling a maintenance program include

1. Identifying maintenance resources and capacity requirements:
   a. Estimating production volumes based on productivity rates
   b. Planning equipment replacements, installation, alteration, and removal work
   c. Analyzing the existing plant condition (major overhauls, etc.)
   d. Compiling maintenance standards and maintenance methods
   e. Compiling the summary of normal maintenance work required by each craft
   f. Making an allowance for emergency work, based on past experience

   g. Leveling peak work loads (e.g., long and major shutdowns, labor economics, and more sophisticated tools/equipment)
2. Develop long-term and short-range plans, including
   a. An even distribution of all maintenance jobs
   b. A yearly program for routine maintenance (e.g., inspection and lubrication)
   c. Scheduling each piece of an equipment for an inspection and overhaul within safe limits of an uninterrupted service, based on the manufacturer's schedule and recommendations, and the history recording
3. Develop capacity plans, including
   a. Estimating the required labor force
   b. Making use of the operating personnel
   c. Estimating the use of the contract labor during peak loads
   d. Planning for the size of a crew needed to complete the work during the shutdown hours
4. Control and correct the variances, taking into account that a maintenance program is not static. A maintenance program is a dynamic plan undergoing continuous revisions and adjustments.

### Using an Annual Maintenance Program

A maintenance program is usually compiled for one year, in collaboration with the production department, specifying when machines are to be inspected or repaired. Provisions must be made for the following:

- Annual leave and statutory holidays
- Annual shutdown
- Statutory regulations concerning the inspection and testing of a lifting equipment, pressure vessels, power presses, and so on

As far as possible, the annual maintenance program should be performed during normal working hours. A maintenance program is not static, but should be in a continuous process of improvement. An annual review is a useful guide in directing efforts to the steps promising the best results. The following are examples of inadequate planning:

- A lack of cooperation with production (maintenance work can interfere with the production plan if machines are not released on time)
- Persistent emergency maintenance, a sign of insufficient or incorrect maintenance or inadequate maintenance standards
- An increase in the number of major overhauls that must be performed during the annual shutdown (this indicates insufficient maintenance throughout the year)

The next step is to group the work load into work categories, such as emergency work, work to overhaul major pieces of equipment, routine maintenance work, and preventive maintenance work, and to compile a labor-hour summary of normal maintenance work performed by each craft. A long-term maintenance program is compiled based on major maintenance work, such as construction and major overhaul of an equipment, and general requirements for routine and prophylactic maintenance.

## How to Reduce Peak Work Loads

Peak loads of required maintenance work can be reduced considerably both by planning ahead and by improved organization of the job itself. Plant operating personnel should be considered as a possible source for additional labor during an equipment shutdown. Where a shutdown will be of long duration, this source should be drawn upon in any case, in order to reduce the shutdown time when planning annual shutdown. Consideration should be also given to the use of a contract labor for maintenance.

In short-term maintenance planning, the work load should be arranged in some kind of a priority sequence. Work orders are ranked on a basis of

- Accident hazards
- Repairs of breakdowns
- Repairs, the need for which was determined by an inspection
- Routine requests from operating executives

In planning for maintenance, management can give priority to such work, as may be necessary to keep the downtime of the equipment at a minimum. Besides the ranking, the beginning and completion dates for each work assignment should be indicated in the maintenance program. A useful technique in maintenance planning is to plan to 75 percent of capacity level, leaving reserve 25 percent for breakdowns and emergency repairs.

In addition to the major maintenance work included in a long-term maintenance program, a short-term maintenance program contains a detailed plan (daily and weekly) for routine tasks, such as inspections and minor repairs. Planning and scheduling of any kind of work permit an orderly and efficient procedure. Although excessive paperwork should be avoided, the scheduling of the maintenance work should allow adequate preparations for instructions to the personnel, obtaining parts, tools, and materials. Forward planning permits workers to make detailed plans of their own. Maintenance people should have some assurance that they can complete any task they start without being shifted back and forth from one place to another.

## USING A LABOR UTILIZATION SYSTEM TO COORDINATE STAFFING INFORMATION

A labor utilization system allows planning and control of maintenance and an effective labor utilization by means of labor standards. It furnishes maintenance management with coordinated information on all maintenance activities and with control over the maintenance staff. The information is presented as weekly or monthly reports and reflects the following details:

1. Utilization of staff work force
2. Effectiveness of a maintenance team
3. Recorded deviations (in percent)
4. Hours worked on standard time (in percent)
5. The labor analysis per work category

Labor utilization is reported according to maintenance work categories, for example,

- Routine preventive maintenance
- Planned corrective maintenance
- Breakdown due to the failure or malfunctioning of an equipment
- Breakdown beyond control of maintenance

Further, each work category is subdivided into trades, for example,

- Scheduled mechanical inspections
- Scheduled electrical inspections
- Nonscheduled mechanical inspections
- Nonscheduled electrical inspections
- Scheduled lubrication

## USING AN EQUIPMENT UTILIZATION SYSTEM TO COORDINATE EQUIPMENT INFORMATION

An equipment utilization system provides management with information about the availability of an equipment and its maximum utilization. Common inputs into an equipment utilization system include such primary documents as

- *A history reporting system.* Information is obtained from the history system, in order to determine the trend of improvement or deterioration of an equipment.

- *Shift reports.* A shift report is the most important source of information to the equipment utilization system and must be accurate, especially where it concerns the identification of an equipment and time recording.
- *Job cards.* A job card provides information on causes of breakdowns.
- *Defect reports.* A defect report is compiled by the production staff. It describes the specific causes of equipment delays.

Equipment utilization time categories include

*Unutilized time.* Unutilized available time is the time when no workers are at the plant for the purpose of production, maintenance, or plant preparation. It includes statutory holidays and the scheduled time off determined by the management. Categories of production time identified in one steel factory (24 hour opertion) are illustrated in Figure 15-14.

*Order preparation time.* Order preparation time is the time scheduled in advance for certain tasks (e.g., scheduled maintenance). Delays as a result of product changes fall within this category.

*External delay time.* External delay time includes all delays over which the plant personnel (production and maintenance) has little influence with regard to their occurrence and duration (e.g., external power failure).

*Internal delay time.* Internal delay time includes recorded delay times over which the plant personnel has control.

*Unidentified delay time.* Unidentified delay time includes gap time, ineffectual process time (tempo deviation), and unidentified delays.

*Setup time.* Setup time is the period of time required to refit a separate machine or production line and prepare it for the next job.

*Utilized production time.* Utilized production time is the time during which production takes place.

Some benefits of an equipment utilization system are

- The utilization of an equipment can be measured.
- The reason for the nonutilization of an equipment can be determined.
- The information is released which enables management to increase the utilization of an equipment.
- The results of the management action taken to increase the utilization of an equipment can be measured.
- By computing costs incurred due to the lost production time, it can be determined whether the equipment should be replaced as a result of excessive breakdowns.

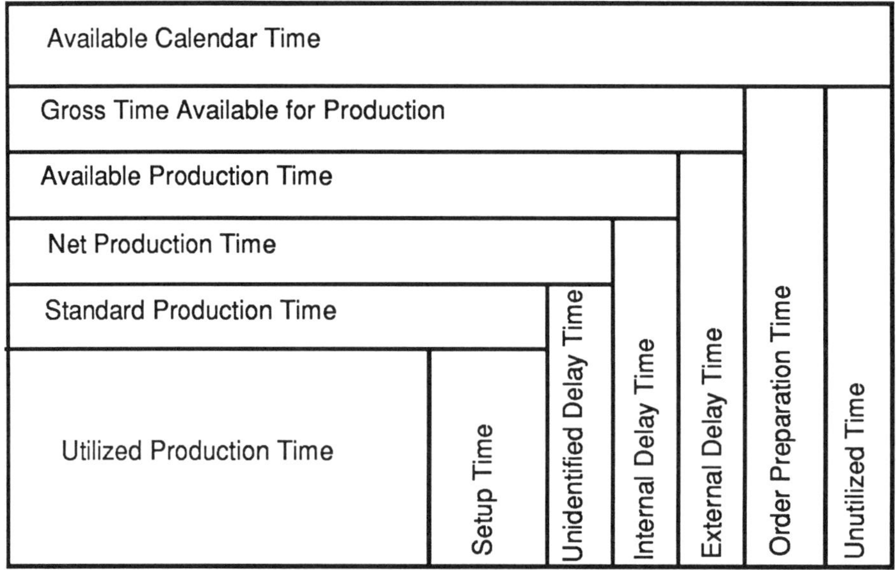


**Figure 15-14**
**The Elements of Production Time**

## MEASURING PERFORMANCE BY USING A MAINTENANCE BUDGET

Budgetary control is a means to plan and measure the maintenance department's performance. Due to the cost of maintenance being a considerable component of the manufacturing cost, it cannot be left uncontrolled. Nevertheless, it is sometimes argued that no matter what the budget limits are, when a facility breaks down, it has to be repaired. Such an attitude toward maintenance control can lead to wide variations in a maintenance budget.

A maintenance budget can be of several types, such as expenditures budget, operations budget, or overhaul budget. Maintenance budgets can be prepared

- As a percentage of total factory cost
- Based on the last year total expenditures

In process industry, a maintenance budget is often computed in proportion to the production cost per unit of production, per ton or per barrel of oil, for example. More accurate maintenance budgeting is based on a systematic assessment of all the expected work to be done on all the factory units within the budgeted time period, such as projects, construction and commissioning, shutdowns, and reconditioning of the premises.

The maintenance budget is specified as an operating plan which coordinates and summarizes individual estimates for future periods. Distinct from production budgets, a maintenance budget is built in a reverse sequence, from the bottom up, starting with the budgeting of basic plant units. Budgeting starts with identifying the services to be provided to all recipients within the budgeted period.

The next step is to identify the price tag for these services for each plant unit. The cost categories in the operations budget are coded and often preprinted on job cards, so the expenditures can be accounted for through the collection of data by the account number and the budget.

Projected expenditures are structured according to major cost categories, such as labor cost, including the projected overtime cost, materials and supplies cost, and overhead standard costs.

Budget fluctuations according to the variances in service demand are reflected in subsequent performance reports where both projected costs and actual cost variances are shown. These variances are further investigated, and preventive measures are taken. An example of a budget variance report is shown in Figure 15-15.

Establishing a maintenance budget offers the following advantages:

1. A maintenance budget allows to plan for future periods.
2. A maintenance budget is a set of standards which enables management to measure performance and exercise control over maintenance operations.
3. A maintenance budget defines centers of authority and responsibilities for budget control and cost control at various levels of an organization.
4. A maintenance budget provides cost information for decision making while, at the same time, allowing some latitude to act at present and in the immediate future.

## VIEWING MAINTENANCE COST AS PART OF PRODUCTION COST

Maintenance cost control is part of an overall company cost control system. The cost of maintenance, including expenditures and the overhead cost, is charged to production departments which use the maintenance services. In maintenance systems, a job card is adopted as a medium for gathering costing data, according to the operating account expense number or according to the capital appropriation number to which the cost of work is to be charged.

An account number for the maintenance cost allocation is usually identified on or before the request for maintenance is authorized. The costs are posted

| BUDGET VARIANCE REPORT | | | | | Date:____________ | | |
|---|---|---|---|---|---|---|---|
| Monthly Maintenance Costs | | | | | Cumulative Costs | | |
| Dept. | Cost Code | Budget | Actual | Variance | Budget | Actual | Variance |
| | | | | | | | |
| | | | | | | | |
| | | | | | | | |
| | | | | | | | |
| | | | | | | | |
| | | | | | | | |
| | | | | | | | |
| | | | | | | | |

**Figure 15-15**
**The Budget Variance Report**

from job cards, time cards, downtime cards, and material requisition forms to the appropriate account numbers. Also, a complete cost analysis can be performed based on the maintenance records—the history of inspections, repairs, and revamps—to reveal the cost history of each plant unit. This analysis enables management to make qualified decisions on budgeting, identifying high-cost areas of the plant, and to predict accurately the feasibility of replacement of an equipment.

### Maintenance Analysis and Reports

Every week, all completed maintenance requests and inspection reports are passed on to the maintenance planning office by the maintenance foremen. These include all uncompleted maintenance requests and inspection reports for which work orders will be issued for the following week.

It has been found that weekly maintenance programs are the most appropriate form of maintenance planning, with corresponding weekly control in the form of a weekly analysis, including the following information:

- Total labor hours
- Total repair hours
- Emergency hours
- Downtime hours
- The percentage of planned work as compared to the unplanned work
- The ratio of preventive work to corrective work
- Overtime hours worked as a ratio to regular hours
- The consumption of spare parts

A weekly analysis is summarized every four weeks in the form of monthly management reports by a plant group and the total per maintenance department. Management reports are presented both in numerical and graphical form, the latter being a convenient visual aid for daily and weekly maintenance meetings. An example of graphical maintenance reporting is illustrated in Figure 15-16.

The top 10 report produces good results. It contains the following information:

- Machines with the highest maintenance cost
- Machines with the highest breakdown hours and breakdown cost
- Machines with the highest breakdown hours and breakdown cost beyond maintenance control

An example of a top 10 report listing machines with highest maintenance cost is shown in Figure 15-17. An example of a report on machines with highest total breakdown hours is shown in Figure 15-18.

The top 10 report exposes critical plant units where maintenance efforts should be reinforced. Usually, after five to six months, these plant units become less expensive to maintain due to improved maintenance planning and control, and other items move into the top 10 list. The top 10 report is a class A in the ABC classification of plant maintenance cost items.

## Breakdown Analysis

A breakdown analysis is especially significant, due to breakdown times being the periods of an intensified maintenance cost which is difficult to control. An analysis of breakdown data provides the following information:

- A ratio of downtime to working time
- Shortcomings in design or installation
- The need to replace a particular machine
- Inadequate maintenance or the need for additional services
- Poor utilization practices or the need for training for machine operators
- The quality of replacement parts

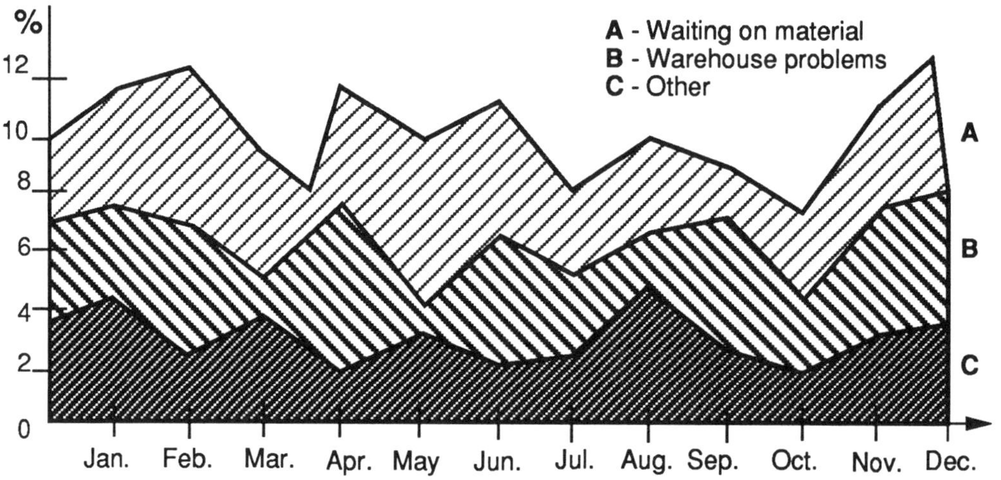


**A. Production Delays**

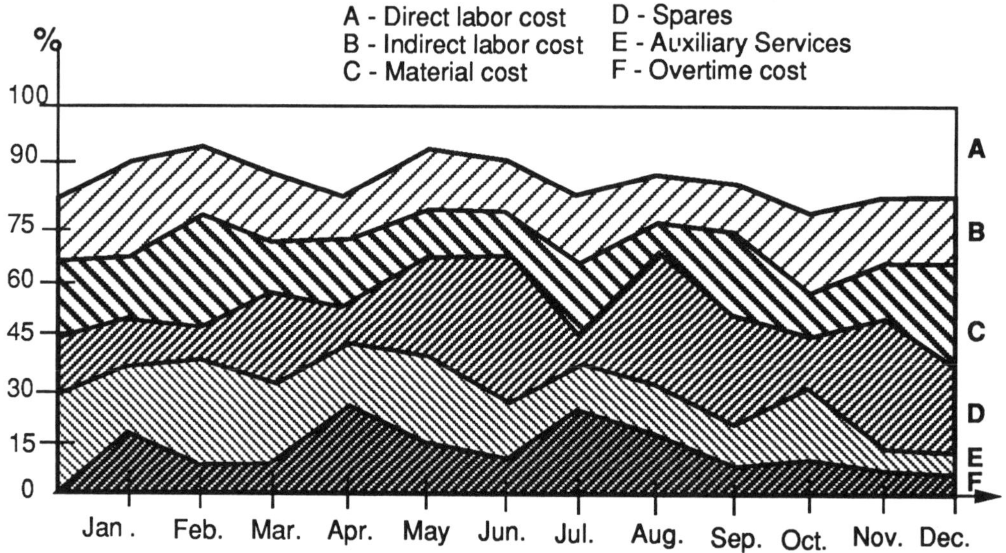


**B. Maintenance Cost**

**Figure 15-16**
**Graphical Maintenance Reports**

MAINTENANCE ACTIVITY REPORTING
SECTION 02 RUN DATE O4/12/91

MACHINES WITH HIGHEST TOTAL MAINTENANCE COST

| MACHINE COST CODE | DESCRIPTION | TOTAL MAINT. | TOTAL LABOR | TOTAL MATER. | TOTAL WORKORD. |
|---|---|---|---|---|---|
| 69-04-00 | LIGHTING-L.D.FURNACE | 4587.16 | 2074.24 | 2241.92 | 31.00 |
| 59-04-00 | SLUDGE FILTER NO.6 | 4587.19 | 177.12 | 2499.07 | 1911.00 |
| 14-54-00 | FINE EXTRACTION LADLE | 26209.95 | 1957.95 | 510.00 | 24642.00 |
| 04-08-00 | CONVERTOR NO.4 | 5578.78 | 0.00 | 5578.78 | 0.00 |
| 85-98-00 | SKIRT ASSEMBLY | 4040.06 | 35.85 | 4004.21 | 0.00 |
| 47-72-00 | SLAG POT TRANSF CAR 4 | 4134.36 | 271.56 | 3862.80 | 0.00 |
| 47-70-00 | SLAG POT TRANSF CAR 2 | 6045.59 | 299.19 | 3746.40 | 2000.00 |
| 47-14-00 | CONVERTOR NO.4 | 22493.58 | 21.58 | 22472.00 | 0.00 |
| 47-05-00 | CONVERTOR NO.2 | 5408.63 | 906.74 | 4133.89 | 358.00 |

**Figure 15-17**
**Report on Machines with Highest Maintenance Cost**

MAINTENANCE ACTIVITY REPORTING
SECTION 04 RUN DATE O4/12/91

MACHINES WITH HIGHEST TOTAL BREAKDOWN COST

| MACHINE COST CODE | DESCRIPTION | TOTAL MACHINE-HOURS |
|---|---|---|
| 148-08-00 | FUME EXTRACTION AT DESULPHIRIZATION PLLANT | 86 |
| M07-05-00 | SLAG POT TRANSFER CAR NO.2 | 78 |
| 147-11-00 | SKIRT LIFTING HYDRAULIC SYSTEM | 76 |
| 147-71-00 | SLAG POT TRANSFER CAR NO.5 | 70 |
| 174-70-00 | SLAG POT TRANSFER CAR NO.2 | 64 |
| 147-21-00 | OXYGEN LANCES - L.O. FURNACE NO.2 | 62 |
| 147-04-00 | CONVERTOR NO1 | 60 |
| 147-08-00 | CONVERTOR NO3 | 56 |
| 145-05-00 | HOT METAL LADLE TRANSFER CAR NO. 2 | 48 |

**Figure 15-18**
**Report on Machines with Highest Total Breakdown Hours**

- A gap in responsibility or an oversight in service instructions

The costing of each breakdown repair should include the repair costs (labor and materials) and the lost production time. A log book should be kept to facilitate the breakdown analysis. A log book is compiled in a chronological date sequence for all breakdowns for critical units. A periodic analysis of breakdown causes and costs can indicate the need for spare parts and materials, intensified operator training, or the need to spend more resources on preventive maintenance. Examples of a breakdown log book and a breakdown record sheet are shown in Figure 15-19 and Figure 15-20 respectively.

## Economic Analysis of Maintenance Operations

In general, a plant maintenance system should provide information for the following analysis of maintenance operations, including the efficiency of resources (the ratios):

| BREAKDOWN LOG BOOK | | | | | | | |
|---|---|---|---|---|---|---|---|
| Date of Breakdn. | Plant Unit | Dept. | Work Order | Reason for Breakdown | Total Repair Cost | Total Down Time | Corrective Actions Taken |
| | | | | | | | |
| | | | | | | | |
| | | | | | | | |
| | | | | | | | |
| | | | | | | | |
| | | | | | | | |

**Figure 15-19**
**The Log Book for Chronological Recording of Breakdowns**

| BREAKDOWN RECORD SHEET | | |
|---|---|---|
| Plant equipment name and description: | Plant # | Location: |
| | | Period covered: |

| Parts affected: | | Dates: | | | | | | | | | Repeated events: |
|---|---|---|---|---|---|---|---|---|---|---|---|
| | | 1/15 | 2/19 | 4/20 | 5/12 | | | | | | |
| Mechanical parts | Shaft | * | | | | | | | | | |
| | Reduction gear | | * | | | | | | | | |
| | Power transmission | * | | | | | | | | | |
| | Housing | | * | | | | | | | | |
| | Bearings | | | * | | | | | | | |
| | | | | | | | | | | | |
| | | | | | | | | | | | |
| Electrical parts | Motor | | * | | | | | | | | |
| | Starter | | | * | | | | | | | |
| | Brushes | * | | | | | | | | | |
| | Instruments | | | | * | | | | | | |
| | | | | | | | | | | | |

**Figure 15-20**
**A Breakdown Record Sheet for One Machine**

1. Labor efficiency

   a. $\dfrac{\text{Total hours worked (including overtime)}}{\text{total standard hours (estimated hours ) for all tasks}}$

   b. $\dfrac{\text{Number of reported defects}}{\text{total number of repair jobs}}$

   c. Turnover of maintenance employees

2. Machine efficiency

   a. $\dfrac{\text{Total machine hours (including overtime)}}{\text{total standard hours (estimated hours) for all tasks}}$

3. Workshop efficiency

   a. $\dfrac{\text{Total hours worked (including overtime)}}{\text{total standard hours (estimated hours) for all tasks}}$

4. Cost efficiency

   a. $\dfrac{\text{Actual cost}}{\text{budgeted cost}}$

## SUMMARY

Maintenance is not a haphazard service function of repairing what breaks down: rather, it is a deliberate production service system, having its logical sequence of activities, being an essential part of an integrated production management system. The sequence of maintenance procedures is shown in Figure 15-21. Plant maintenance information flow and the sequence of activities of elements are shown in Figure 15.22.

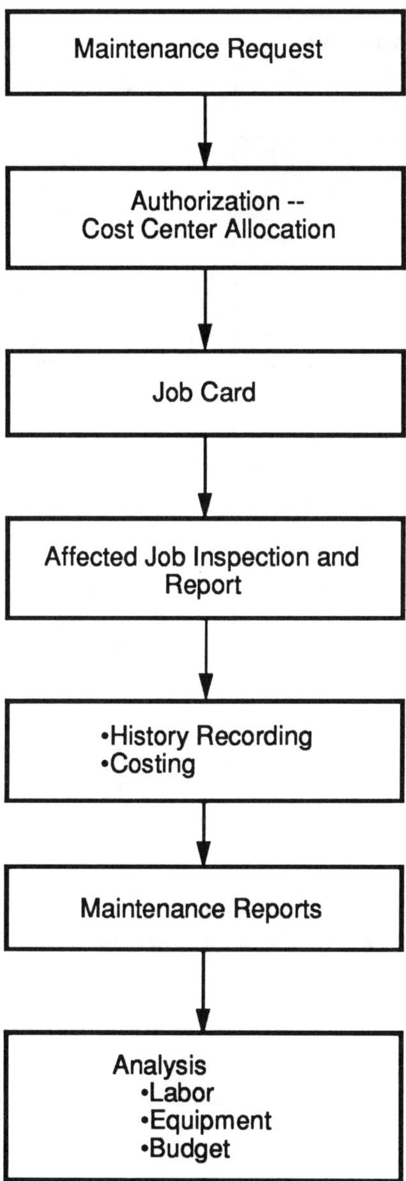


**Figure 15-21**
**Maintenance Procedures**

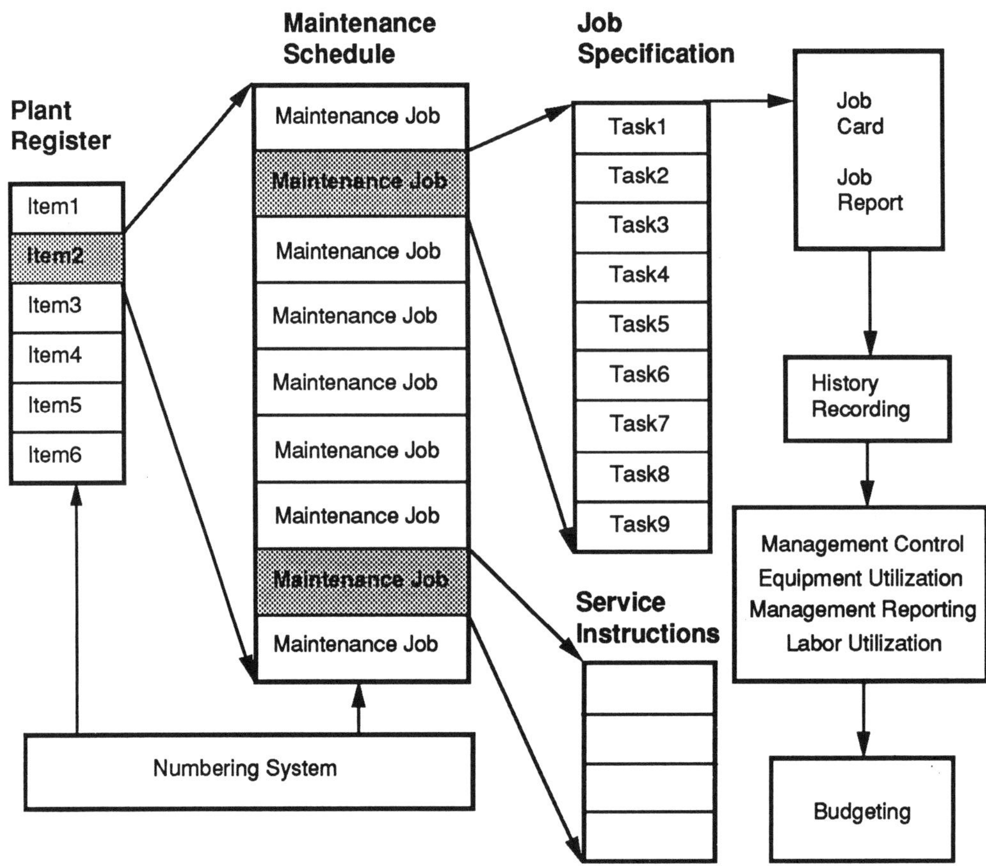


**Figure 15-22**
**The Plant Maintenance System**

# 16

# Using Project Management to Maintain Schedules and Costs

## THE DEFINITION OF PROJECT MANAGEMENT

*Project managment* is a form of production management because, as with production, the objective of a project is to transform material resources into useful output. However, projects cannot be controlled like production, due to the irregular pattern of their activities.

A *project* is a set of nonroutine activities directed at accomplishing some nonstandard major output. A project is a one-time undertaking featuring a diverse resource structure and organizational constraints. Each project will differ essentially from other projects and will require a different set of material resources and a different task force to gather information from the diverse disciplines.

In most cases, material and human resources are moved to the project location and are utilized on site, for example, when erecting a building or an industrial complex, installing an air-conditioning system, or changing the equipment layout on the shop floor. Installing a computer-based production planning and control system is an excellent example of a management project. Such a project planning and control system can be installed using the existing organizational human resources within the stipulated time frame so as to avoid directly affecting production during the conversion to the new system.

In other applications, the production of a prototype of the first 10 items of a new product is approached as a "project." After prototype is approved, the subsequent manufacture is viewed as regular production. Thus, projects can relate to construction, production, and services, as well as to research and development in, for example, space- and defense-related industries.

In general, projects can be seen as the "production" of a nonroutine output, which must be completed within the set time frame by applying a one-time organizational structure of both material and human resources.

## HOW TO USE PERT AND CPM NETWORK STRUCTURES

Project managers use special *operations research techniques* for planning and controlling these activities. These techniques are known as *network analysis techniques,* including PERT and CPM.

The *program evaluation and review technique* (PERT) was developed in 1958 by consultants of Booz, Allen & Hamilton and the Special Projects Office of the U.S. Navy for managing the Polaris missile project, one of this country's largest research and development projects, involving about 3,500 subcontractors and agencies. The *critical path method* (CPM) was developed in 1957 by the Catalytic Construction Company at the time of the construction of a chemical plant for Du Pont. Both PERT and CPM have become standard project planning and control methods widely used since then. Both methods utilize network analysis techniques to optimize the use of project resources.

The essence of project planning and control is to split an entire project into its constituent elements—activities. These activities scheduled on a basic time scale form a project network. A *project network* is a graphic flow diagram describing a sequential relationship between the project's activities. The network is constructed out of two basic elements: activities and events.

### Network Conventions

In the critical path method, each activity is represented by an arrow as shown in Figure 16-1*a*. *Activities* are project elements consuming time as well as human and material resources. An activity represents an action in the network. In a network, a project is presented as a list of activities or a sequence of arrows.

Project activities are marked by circles or nodes at the beginning and end of each activity. Nodes separating the activities are known as events. An *event* does not consume time or resources. It is simply a statement of the beginning or the end of an activity. Due to an uninterrupted project work flow, a finishing event of one activity is also the starting event of the succeeding activity, as shown in Figure 16-1*b*. Each event serves two purposes: marking

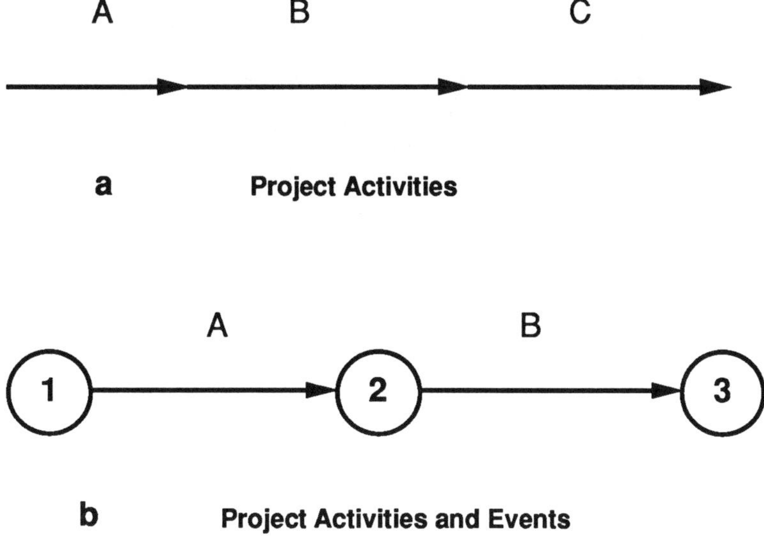


**Figure 16-1**
**Project Elements: Activities and Events**

the completion of one activity and the beginning of another activity. The exception is the project's starting event, denoting only the start of activities, while the finishing event denotes only the end of activities and the entire project. The network convention is that an event's succeeding activity may not start until its preceding activity has been completed.

In a CPM project network, you may encounter the situation where one activity has been completed but the event's succeeding activity has been delayed due to a lack of labor or material resources. Such an event has been partially completed as shown in Figure 16-2.

In this instance, an event has two parts: E (early completed part) and L (late part). Such an event has a time duration and can consume resources. The time elapsed between the early part and late part of an event is known as the *slack time*. Such unplanned delays of activities need to be avoided in all projects.

The possible productive relationships of events and activities are

1. One starting event and one finishing event for an activity (refer to Figure 16-2)
2. One starting event for two or more activities
3. One finishing event for two or more activities

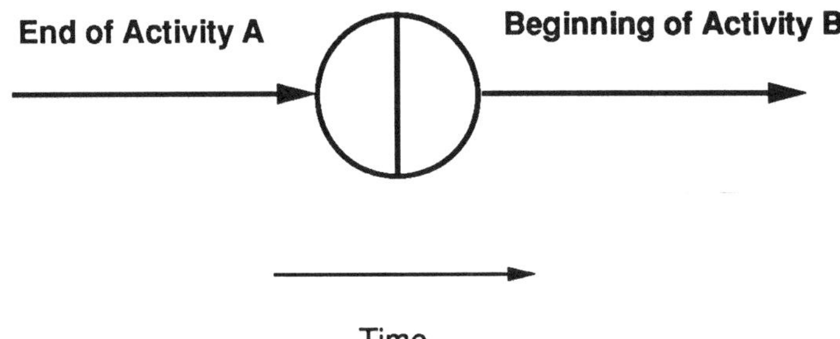


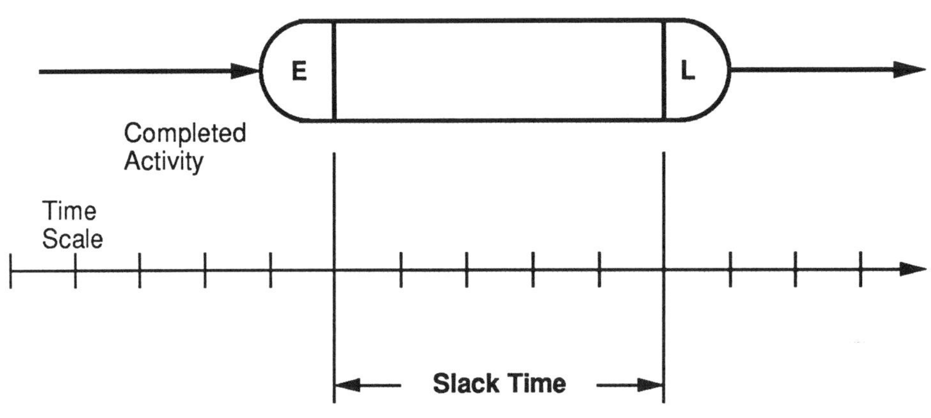


**Figure 16-2**
**Analysis of the Elements of a Project Event**

Figure 16-3 illustrates the relationship between activities and events in the critical path method. In Figure 16-3*b*, activities A and B can run concurrently, but both must be completed before activity C can begin. Sometimes, it is necessary to establish a firm relationship between two events running concurrently. For example, in a network A, B, C, D, E, (see Figure 16-4) there is a need to constrain the start of activity E before activities B and C are completed. This can be resolved by inserting a *dummy activity*. Figure 16-4 illustrates a dummy activity. The feature of a dummy activity is that it does not require

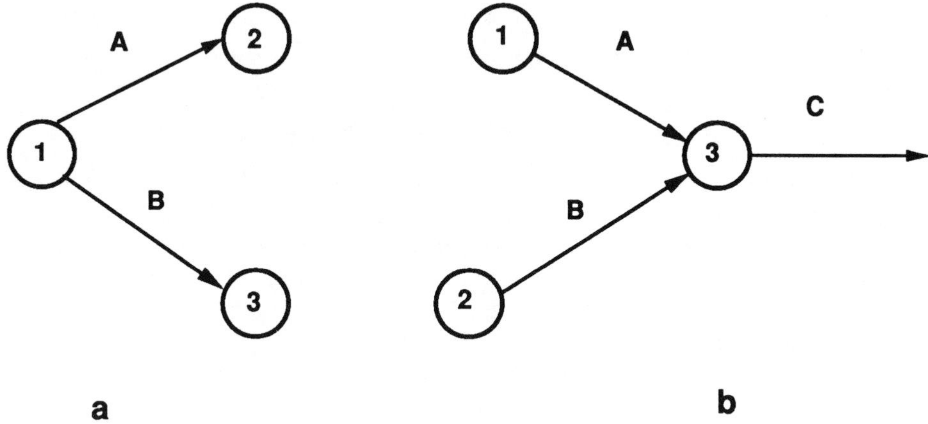


**Figure 16-3**
**Activities and Events**

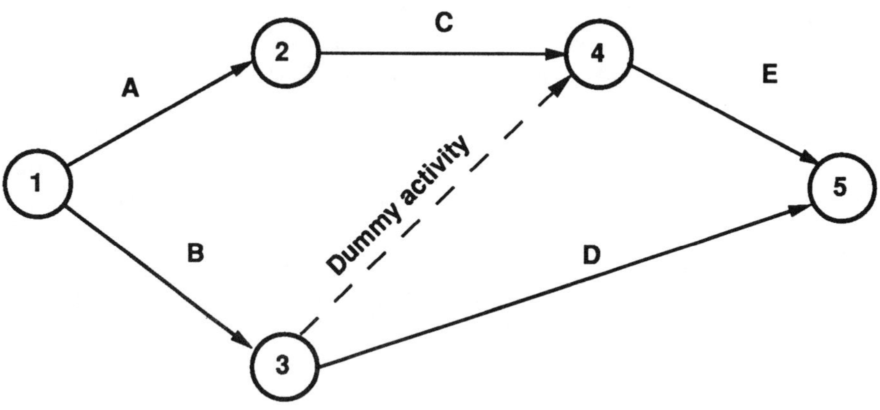


**Figure 16-4**
**Dummy Activity**

any resources and it takes no time. It just establishes a constraint; in this case, it shows that activity E cannot commence until two preceding activities, activity C and the dummy activity, are completed. In this instance, a dummy activity acts as an extension of activity B.

## How to Estimate Project Time Using Network Analyses

The construction of a project network starts with compiling a list of all project activities and their immediate predecessors. See Figure 16-5. A network always begins with the starting event, event 1, for those activities that do not have predecessors. In this example, this is activity A. A network is ending with the finishing event for the last project activity or activities. In our example, activity M is the last activity in the project, see Figure 16-6.

The next task in the network procedure is to estimate the duration of the project and to identify the critical path. This is accomplished in three stages:

1. Etimating the earliest completion time
2. Estimating the latest completion time for each event
3. Identifying the critical path.

The estimate of the earliest event time begins from the project's first event, starting as a zero time and adding up the activities durations one by one. The calculation of the *earliest event time* (ET) is known as a *forward pass* calculation. The rule to follow when calculating ET is to find the longest path. For example, where two or more activities are ended by a common event, the longest path is chosen. In Figure 16-6, activities D and H are both ended by event 6. Event 6 can take place in 32 days, if the path through activity H is selected (20 days + 12 days). However, if activity D is considered, event 6 takes place in 42 days (14 days + 28 days). The earliest time of the event 6 is the longest one of 42 days. The earliest time the project can be completed is 89 days from the start of the project.

The next step is to estimate the *latest time of each event* (LT) or time each event can be extended without delaying the completion of the project. This procedure is known as the *backward pass* and consists essentially of subtracting the duration of activities from the total project duration. The latest time of the last event is the same as its earliest time, due to the longest path having been selected during the "forward pass."

A basic rule to follow is the same as that in the "forward pass," only in reverse order: select the longest path backward when multiple activities start with the same event. In our example, the backward pass to event 7 has two paths (activities L, K, and J, in one path and activity F in the second path). Event 7 will take place in 52 days, if the first path (activities L, K, and J) is considered (79 days - 9 days - 10 days - 8 days), or it will take place in

| Activity ID | Activity Duration (in days) | Immediate Predecessor of Activity |
|---|---|---|
| A | 5 | None |
| B | 6 | A |
| C | 3 | B |
| D | 28 | C |
| E | 10 | D |
| F | 11 | E |
| G | 6 | C |
| H | 12 | G |
| I | 22 | D, H |
| J | 8 | E |
| K | 10 | J |
| L | 9 | K |
| M | 10 | F, I, L |

**Figure 16-5**
**Estimating Project Time**

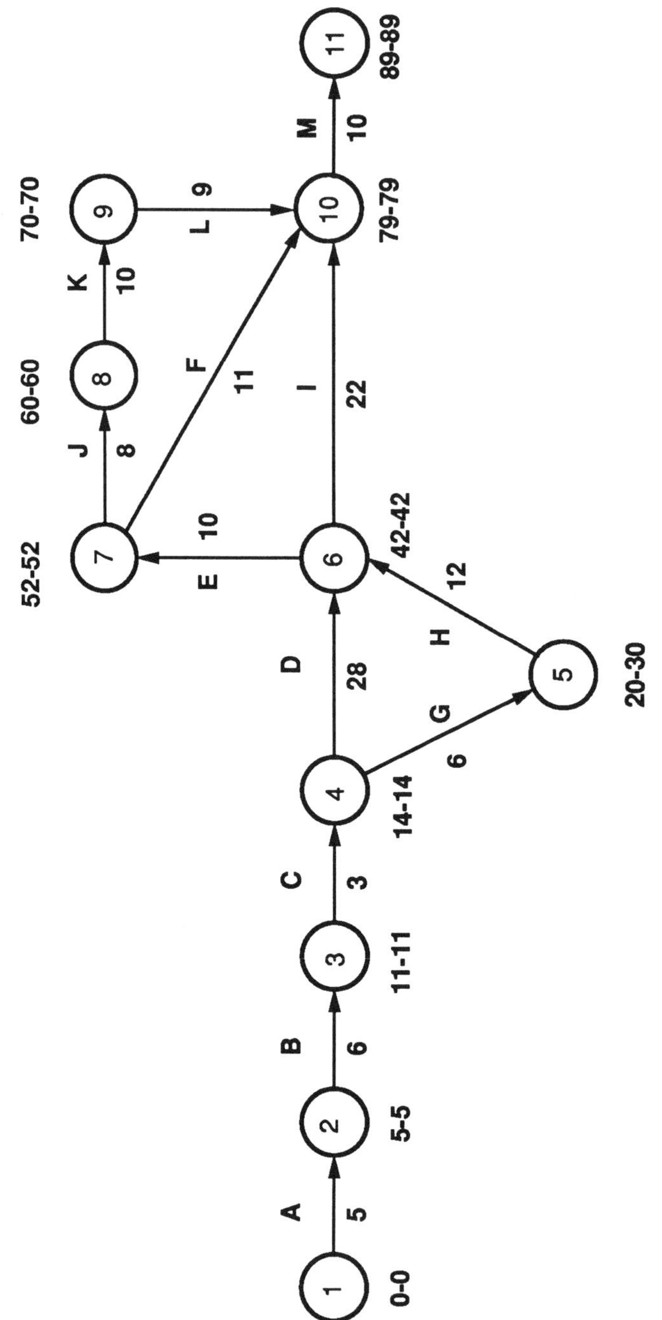


Figure 16-6
Project Network Time Estimates

68 days, if the second path (activity F) is considered (79 days - 11 days). The longest path is considered here (activities L, K, and J). Thus, the latest event 7 time is 79 - 9 - 10 - 8 = 52 days.

Having estimated ET and LT for all events, the next step is to identify the *critical path* (the longest time chain of activities through the network). In our example, it is the path which has the duration of 89 days. All the activities on this path are critical: delaying any activity will delay an entire project. Considering that there are starting and finishing events for each activity, an activity is critical if the slack time for both its events is equal to zero. After the project activities times are calculated and the critical path is identified, a project activities worksheet can be compiled, as shown in Figure 16-7.

| Activity ID | Activity Description | Activity Duration | Starting Time | | Finishing Time | | Slack Time | Critical Activity Y/N |
|---|---|---|---|---|---|---|---|---|
| | | | Early ES | Late LS | Early EF | Late LF | LS-ES or LF-EF | |
| A | | 5 | 0 | 0 | 5 | 5 | 0 | Y |
| B | | 6 | 5 | 5 | 11 | 11 | 0 | Y |
| C | | 3 | 11 | 11 | 14 | 14 | 0 | Y |
| D | | 28 | 14 | 14 | 42 | 42 | 0 | Y |
| E | | 10 | 42 | 42 | 52 | 52 | 0 | Y |
| F | | 11 | 52 | 68 | 63 | 79 | 16 | N |
| G | | 6 | 14 | 24 | 20 | 30 | 10 | N |
| H | | 12 | 20 | 30 | 32 | 42 | 10 | N |
| I | | 22 | 42 | 57 | 64 | 79 | 15 | N |
| J | | 8 | 52 | 52 | 60 | 60 | 0 | Y |
| K | | 10 | 60 | 60 | 70 | 70 | 0 | Y |
| L | | 9 | 70 | 70 | 79 | 79 | 0 | Y |
| M | | 10 | 79 | 79 | 89 | 89 | 0 | Y |

**Figure 16-7**
**The Project Activities Work Sheet**

## How to Estimate Activity Time in the PERT Network

Our example of a network analysis uses predetermined of activity times. In contrast, the program evaluation and review technique uses a probabilistic approach where activity times are subject to variations. In PERT, there are three time estimates for each activity rather than only one as is in our example. These time estimates are as follows:

1. *Optimistic time (a)* is the best time that could be expected, if everything goes well. There is a small probability, only about 1 percent, that this can be achieved.
2. *Most likely time (m)* is the most realistic time estimate for completing an activity.
3. *Pessimistic time (b)* is the worst time that could be expected, if everything went wrong. There should also be a small probability, only about 1 percent, that the activity will take that long to complete.

The expected weighted average time for an activity is computed as follows:

$$t_e = \frac{a + 4m + b}{6}$$

where:

$a$ = optimistic time estimate
$m$ = most likely time estimate
$b$ = pessimistic time estimate
$te$ = expected weighted average time for an activity completion

Three time estimates in the equation above are averaged in the following proportion: four most likely times and one of each pessimistic time and optimistic time. This is based on the concept that there is 6 standard deviations in a bell curve of a frequency distribution (± 3 standard deviations from the mean) at a 99.72 percent confidence level of the statistical probability.

The variance Σ2 of the expected time estimate is as follows:

$$\text{Variance} = \left(\frac{b-a}{b}\right)^2$$

An example of a PERT estimate of the activity time is shown in Figure 16-8.

| Activity | Activity time | | | Expected time | Variance | Predecessor |
|---|---|---|---|---|---|---|
| | Optimistic a | Most Probable m | Pessimistic b | $t_e = [(a+4m+b)/6]$ | $[(b-a)/6]^2$ | |
| A | 2 | 3 | 4 | 3 | $\left(\frac{4-2}{6}\right)^2 = \frac{4}{36}$ | None |
| B | 4 | 6 | 8 | 6 | $\left(\frac{8-4}{6}\right)^2 = \frac{16}{36}$ | None |
| C | 1 | 2 | 3 | 2 | $\left(\frac{3-1}{6}\right)^2 = \frac{4}{36}$ | B |
| D | 5 | 8 | 17 | 9 | $\left(\frac{17-5}{6}\right)^2 = \frac{144}{36}$ | A |
| E | 3 | 7 | 11 | 7 | $\left(\frac{11-3}{6}\right)^2 = \frac{64}{36}$ | D |
| F | 6 | 13 | 20 | 13 | $\left(\frac{20-6}{6}\right)^2 = \frac{196}{36}$ | C |
| G | 2 | 4 | 6 | 4 | $\left(\frac{6-2}{6}\right)^2 = \frac{16}{36}$ | C |
| H | 3 | 6 | 9 | 6 | $\left(\frac{9-3}{6}\right)^2 = \frac{36}{36}$ | G |
| I | 4 | 7 | 10 | 7 | $\left(\frac{10-4}{6}\right)^2 = \frac{36}{36}$ | E, F |

**Figure 16-8**
**Estimating PERT Activity Time**

## HOW TO PLAN AND CONTROL A PROJECT NETWORK

The network analysis system is a standard project control method widely used since its inception in 1958. It is so effective in project control that many companies attempt to emulate it for their planning and control of regular manufacturing operations. It is interesting to note, however, that efforts of software manufacturing systems developers to have network analysis techniques as basis for controlling manufacturing operations had either limited success or no success at all.

There are several reasons why network analysis systems are not suitable for the control of manufacturing operations. The major reason is that PERT and CPM are intended to control amalgamated project activities made up of many such operations/tasks rather than to control individual operations/tasks. What would happen if a manufacturer worked according to the master production schedule (MPS) for (planning at the level of products and assembly units) without further converting the plan into the operating timetable (i.e., without accounting for operations scheduling)? We know that the company would show a lower productivity, a reduced output, and increased production costs. This is exactly what can happen with projects. They can incur an exorbitant project cost. The consolation is that a project is a one-time affair. A project cost has no existing standard to compare against, and a particular project will not be repeated. Thus an excessive project cost is absorbed by a customer whose only means to measure the cost are different bid estimates, which are not always indicative of the project value.

At execution, project activities should be further converted into operating more detailed schedules to reduce the project cost. The *major deficiencies* of network analysis techniques are in the areas of intricate control and resource utilization. This is because the network analysis represents product-focused project management.

The difficulty in resource management leads to the *second problem* area of a network analysis systems, namely, control over the project's completion time. Similar to production, project activities are interrelated through the use of the same set of material and labor resources. Delaying one activity leads to delaying other activities, due to the fact that the resources are moved around and there is no overlapping. Lot splitting is not possible as with production.

A chain reaction of activities' delays is the major problem in any network analysis control. Delays produce continuous changes in the critical path. Initial critical activities become less critical as compared with the delayed activities. Control over the critical path becomes a full-time job in some projects where activities are interlocked by sharing the same, often scarce, resources.

*Computer System News* writes that a common denominator linking troubled projects is management rather than technical issues: most projects do not fail for technical reasons. Such issues as scheduling and project planning are central to the project success (*Computer System News*, November 26, 1990). These problems in project control are the main reasons for inadequate control over project costs. It is very common to hear that projects run over their budgets because of delays.

Deficiencies in project control are aggravated by the sometimes intricate integration of activities into network systems. Many project managers could avoid quality, time, and cost problems if they paid attention to the integration of project activities through more extensive use of dummy activities. The function of the dummy activity, in this case, is the integration of sometimes diverse activities which nevertheless share common material and human resources.

Effective project management should address all the foregoing problems, in order to produce the best product value for a customer (i.e., completing the project on time, within the budget constraints, subject to all quality standards).

## HOW TO COMPILE A PROJECT NETWORK

As with production management, effective project management starts with design of a detailed project plan as the standard for the project's execution and control. As in production planning, the 90/10 rule (90 percent of the time is spent on planning and 10 percent on execution) is an imposing factor in project management. With the practical use of the network analysis systems, several advanced practical techniques have emerged, enhancing project planning and control.

The first such technique deals with project work packages. A work package is a group of consecutive project activities which collectively reflect a recognizable step toward the completion of a project. *Work packages* are set up based on the similarity of the constituent activities location, (e.g., a the interior finishing of the northwest ballroom of the building), or a functional area of the project (e.g., the air-conditioning and boiler system of the building), or a test run and adjustments of a number of production units on the production line. Work packages can be viewed as miniature projects, usually with a starting event and a terminating event. Figure 16-9 illustrates how project activities can be grouped into work packages convenient for planning and control.

Grouping project activities into work packages depends on your type of industry and the size of your projects. The grouping can be done according to time periods (for example, setting up packages on the basis of the eight weeks ground rule) or according to work package dollar value, ranging from $20,000 to $100,000. It is obvious that, in the first instance, the emphasis is on time control, while in the second one, the cost is regarded as a deciding factor.

In project management, the advantage of work packages is in that these work packages integrate individual activities into recognizable groups which can be distinguished by those in authority. A work package is a convenient standard for the aggregated project time and cost control.

## DON'T OVERLOOK THE DETAILS IN PROJECT PLANNING

Many project failures are attributed to project plans that have been laid out in too general terms, neglecting details when designing a network structure.

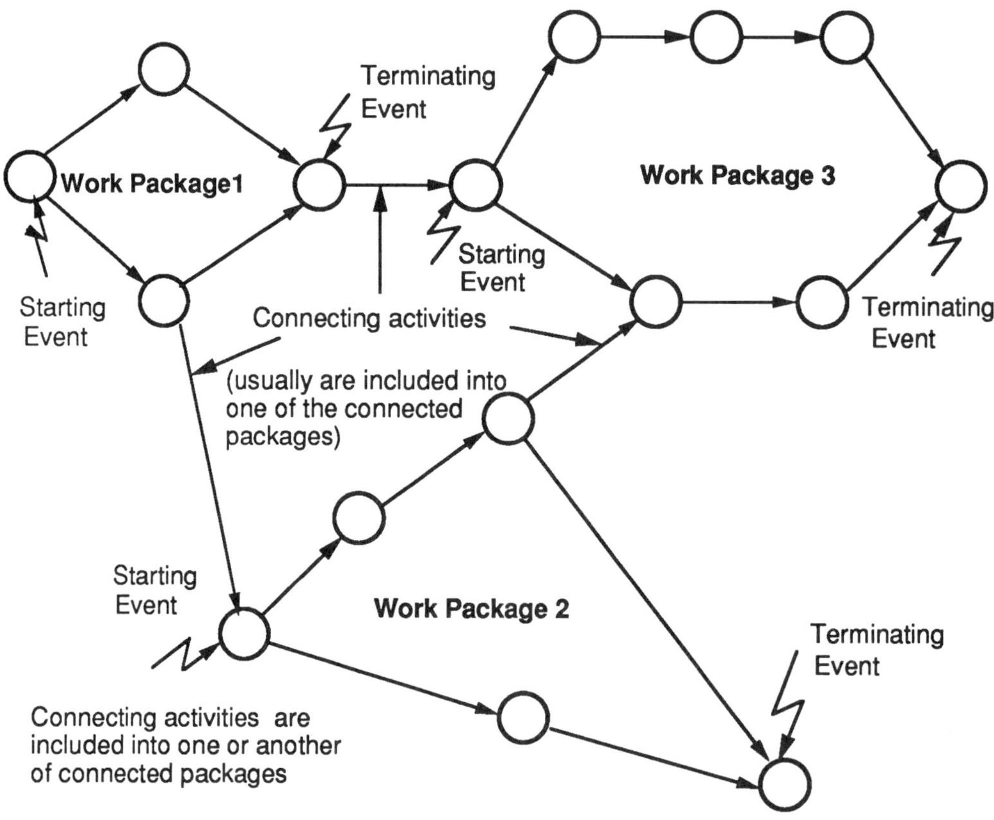


**Figure 16-9**
**Grouping of Project Activities into Work Packages**

Take, for example, a network activity producing 10 prototype samples of office furniture sets. Figure 16-10 illustrates that producing the first 10 samples is, in fact, a project consisting of a sequence of at least five activities involving different units of production and services. Thus many network activities can be further exploded into their constituent subactivities. They can often be structured as miniature networks or work packages.

Another cause for project failures is attributed to the fact that planning of a network analysis system assumes that resources are unlimited. Project planning should take into account that each activity requires different resources and labor skills and can involve several organizational functional units and responsibility levels.

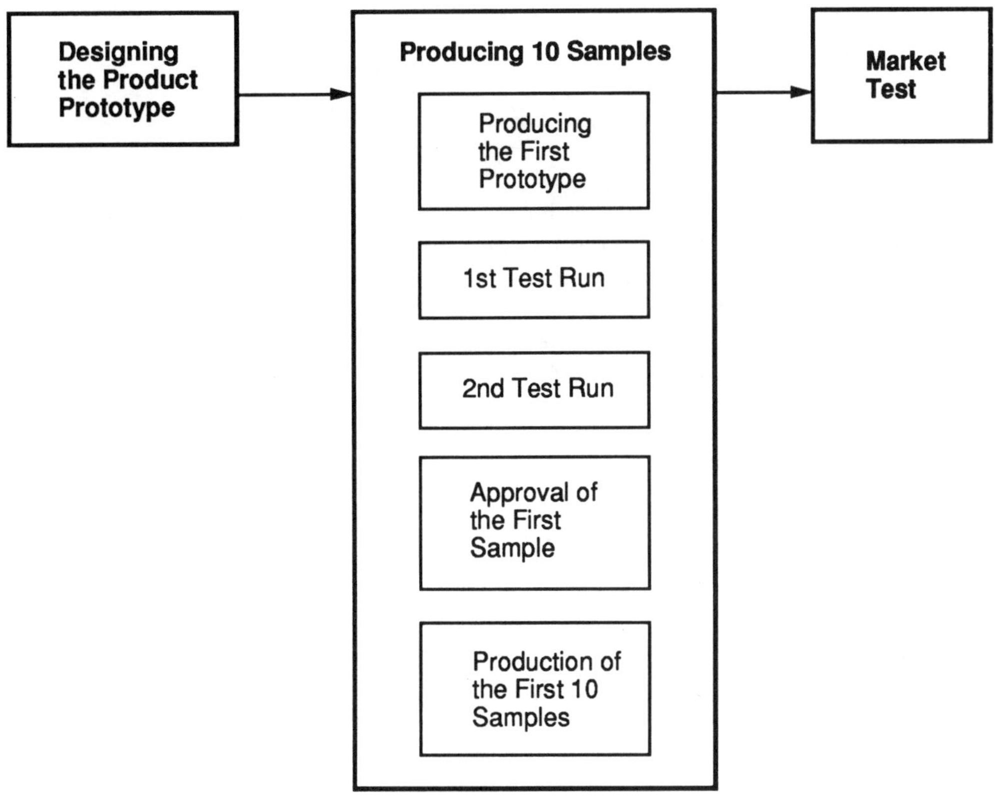


**Figure 16-10**
**Dividing Activities Into Tasks**

The following steps are recommended for project planning and designing networks:

1. Design network activities so that each corresponds to only one production unit resource and only one responsibility.
2. Each arrow (an activity in a network) should be indicative of the completion date and should stand for only one production function or labor skill.

Of course, such detailed planning is not always possible at the preexecution stage, especially in large projects. Like operations scheduling in production, detailed explosion of activities into functional project tasks is essential for an accurate resource allocation and for improving the utilization rate. Ensuring the availability of resources reduces time variances and project cost. Such network planning establishes a meaningful standard for idiosyncratic project time and cost control.

## HOW TO CONTROL PROJECT COSTS

Total project cost can be estimated as the sum of direct and indirect costs. Figure 16-11 illustrates project's cost-time relationship. An *indirect project cost* consists of overhead charges that cannot be associated with individual activities. This cost continues for the life of the project, due to indirect administrative expenses, supervision, and assigning and charging a general-purpose equipment to a specific project. An indirect cost varies in proportion to the project duration.

A *direct cost* is directly tied to a particular activity. This includes direct labor, direct materials, and the cost of equipment used directly in project tasks. A direct cost varies inversely with time, which means that it costs more to complete an activity in a shorter period of time. Time crashing decreases the efficiency of resources, since the normal time assigned to an activity, by definition, is most efficient.

A direct cost for a project is the sum of direct costs of *all* the project activities. Project cost reduction efforts are directed mainly at project time management (i.e., sticking to the timetable and keeping under control fixed and overhead administrative and supervisory expenses and other indirect costs that vary with the length of the project). As with production planning, a planned project network is an optimum program which seldom can be expedited without the detriment to other jobs.

## HOW TO SCHEDULE PROJECT RESOURCES

A project is classified as a production situation, which means that basic production management considerations are valid in project management as well, especially in project planning and control and project scheduling. The production management principle of detailed planning and the need for interpreting a production program into operational schedules is as important in projects as in production. Since the network analysis is a product-focused planning technique which assumes that the resources are unlimited, it is important to integrate the project activities plan with the resource utilization plan to ensure that everything needed is available for the timely completion of activities.

A project cost reduction plan calls for product and process balancing, which means ensuring the timely completion of project activities, along with the maximum utilization of human and material resources. As in production, project integration of product and process can be done at the operational level,

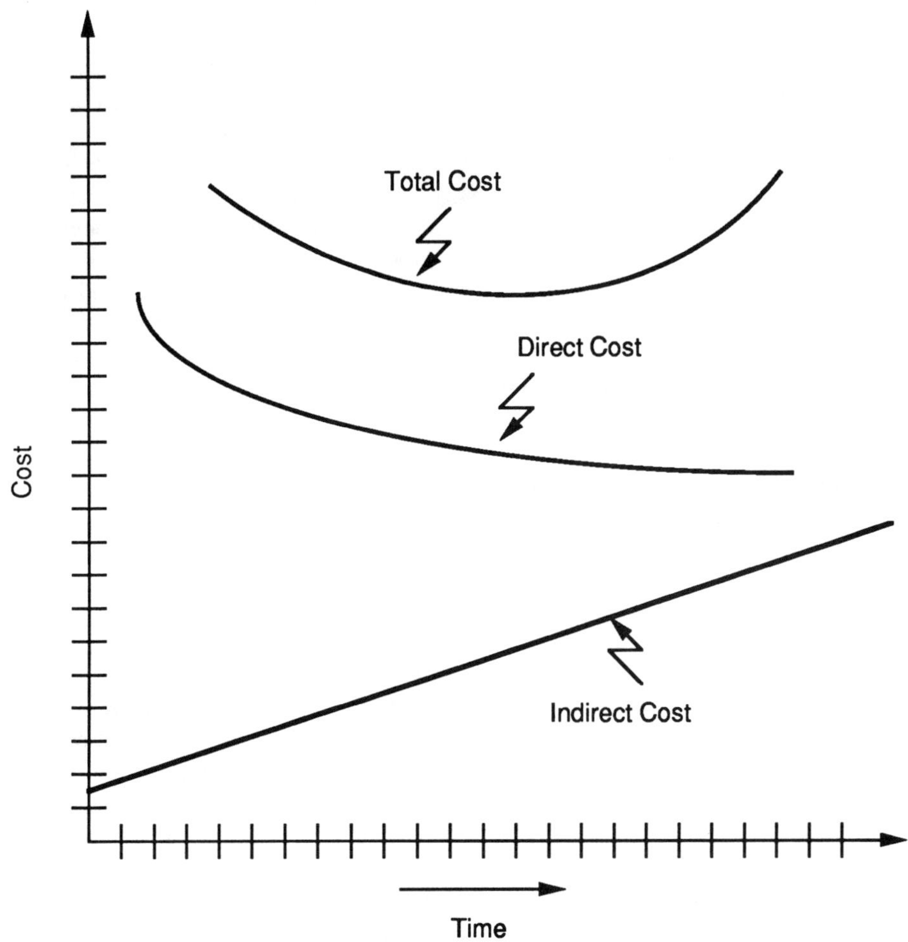


**Figure 16-11**
**Project Cost-Time Relationship**

where project requirements are balanced with the project resources. Project requirements and project resource balancing calls for project activities to be structured around a single type of resource. Due to the fact that many project activities are amalgamated production elements using a range of resources, it is necessary for project resource scheduling to split these activities into the constituent tasks, each requiring a single type of limited resource, various labor skills, or equipment type.

Project resource utilization and resource leveling is one of the most contentious issues in the network analysis, directly affecting the project cost and completion date. A project activities worksheet is compiled along with a project input data form, which is showing the project resource requirements and direct cost estimates. A project input data form stipulates the resources required for each activity, along with the estimated direct labor and material cost.

Activity resource requirements are grouped by labor categories and the types of equipment and materials. In a project input data form, these resource types are shown according to the time periods when they are needed, along with the total cost estimated per period of time. Further, this information is entered into two types of forms: project financial requirements and a resource requirements schedule.

A project financial requirement form, illustrated in Figure 16-12, presents absolute and cumulative financial requirements for each period of the project. This is initial financial information which will be updated after resource leveling is done. A project financial budget is drawn based on the final form of project financial requirements.

A resource requirements schedule is compiled separately for each labor skill or equipment type, by time periods throughout the duration of the project. In a resource requirements schedule, information is displayed in a numerical and graphical format. The bottom part of the form displays resource requirement on a bar chart. The rule for scheduling is to compile initial resource requirements so that all the activities start at the earliest start date. This project scheduling stage can be compared to the infinite loading technique in production scheduling.

Fluctuations throughout given time periods necessitate further resource smoothing, a planning procedure comparable to finite loading in production. *Float times* are an adequate initial tool for resource leveling because shifting an activity within the float limits does not affect the project completion date. Caution should be exercised when making use of float time, due to the fact that it is usually being shared by several network activities.

For example, in Figure 16-13, activities A, D, and E have two weeks of float time. In fact, these two weeks are shared by all three activities. If, say, activity A will take up all the float time, it will leave activities D and E without the float, thereby making them critical, in addition to the existing critical path activities.

The use of float time, to various degrees, resolves resource leveling problems. Otherwise, additional means are used, such as subcontracting, overtime, hiring temporary work force, or utilizing labor in multiproject applications, so as to keep overloads and underloads to a minimum.

The objectives of project management could be defined as follows: to *develop an original network that is instrumental in producing a realisitic and sufficiently low-cost estimate, as well as reduced lead time, thus providing a competitive advantage.* While the technique of the network analysis is relatively simple, project execution can show significant variations, unless project control

| Activity | Duration | Scheduled Start | 0 | 1 | 2 | 3 | 4 | 5 | 6 | 7 | 8 | 9 | 10 | 11 | 12 | Activity Cost Budget |
|---|---|---|---|---|---|---|---|---|---|---|---|---|---|---|---|---|
| **A 1-2** | 3 | 0 | 3 | 3 | 3 | | | | | | | | | | | 9 |
| **B 1-3** | 2 | 0 | 5 | 5 | | | | | | | | | | | | 10 |
| **C 1-4** | 4 | 1 | | 4 | 4 | 4 | 4 | | | | | | | | | 16 |
| **D 2-5** | 4 | 1 | | 5 | 5 | 5 | 5 | | | | | | | | | 20 |
| **E 3-5** | 6 | 2 | | | 5 | 5 | 5 | 5 | 5 | 5 | | | | | | 30 |
| **F 3-6** | 3 | 5 | | | | | | 3 | 3 | 3 | | | | | | 9 |
| **G 4-6** | 5 | 7 | | | | | | | | 4 | 4 | 4 | 4 | 4 | | 20 |
| **H 5-7** | 4 | 8 | | | | | | | | | 6 | 6 | 6 | 6 | 6 | 30 |
| **E 6-7** | 3 | 10 | | | | | | | | | | | 5 | 5 | 5 | 15 |
| **Total** | | | 8 | 17 | 17 | 14 | 14 | 8 | 8 | 12 | 10 | 10 | 15 | 15 | 11 | 159 |
| **Cumulative Total** | | | 8 | 25 | 42 | 56 | 70 | 78 | 86 | 98 | 108 | 118 | 133 | 148 | 159 | |

**Figure 16-12**
**The Financial Requirements Schedule**

is not effectively enforced. Often, project control is conducted as cost control, controlling the expenditures over time periods.

Figure 16-14 illustrates the status on July 1 of a steel factory project of commissioning an annealing line. Thin vertical lines represents the budgeted cumulative project cost, while heavy lines show the actual cost. Figure 16-14 shows eight project activities (A, B, C, D, E, F, G, H) and their progress on the reported date. The cumulative project cost at the specified period of time is compared against the actual cost reported. In the network, the first three activities (A, B, C) are completed and other activities are in progress. It should be noted that such a procedure is aimed at project cost control and does not

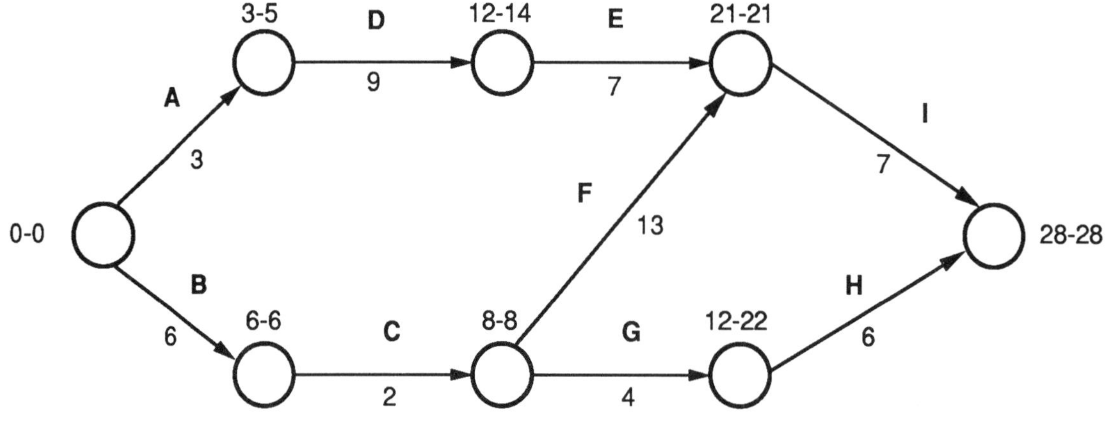


**Figure 16-13**
**Project Network**

have a verifiable means to control other performance figures, such as the resources utilization or project progress.

Since the actual cost on July 1 is within the budget, and the three activities were completed on time, the project appears to be under control. It should be noted that the Gantt chart, often the choice for project activities control, can better serve your purpose when these activities are further broken down into their constituent tasks. However, the Gantt chart can become cumbersome to use, if there are many tasks to be controlled.

The table in Figure 16-15 shows that activities A, B, and C are completed but their budgets have been expanded to a various degree, ranging from $15,000 to $25,000 to a total amount of $60,000. A detailed project analysis shows that each project activity comprises different tasks corresponding to different functions and labor skills:

- Task 1—incoming inspection
- Task 2—mechanical
- Task 3—electrical
- Task 4—automation
- Task 5—inspection and testing
- Task 6—first test production run

According to the detailed project plan activities, D, E, and F are behind the schedule: task 2, mechanical, and task 3, electrical. Mechanical and electrical project functions are responsible for the budget overrun and should be placed

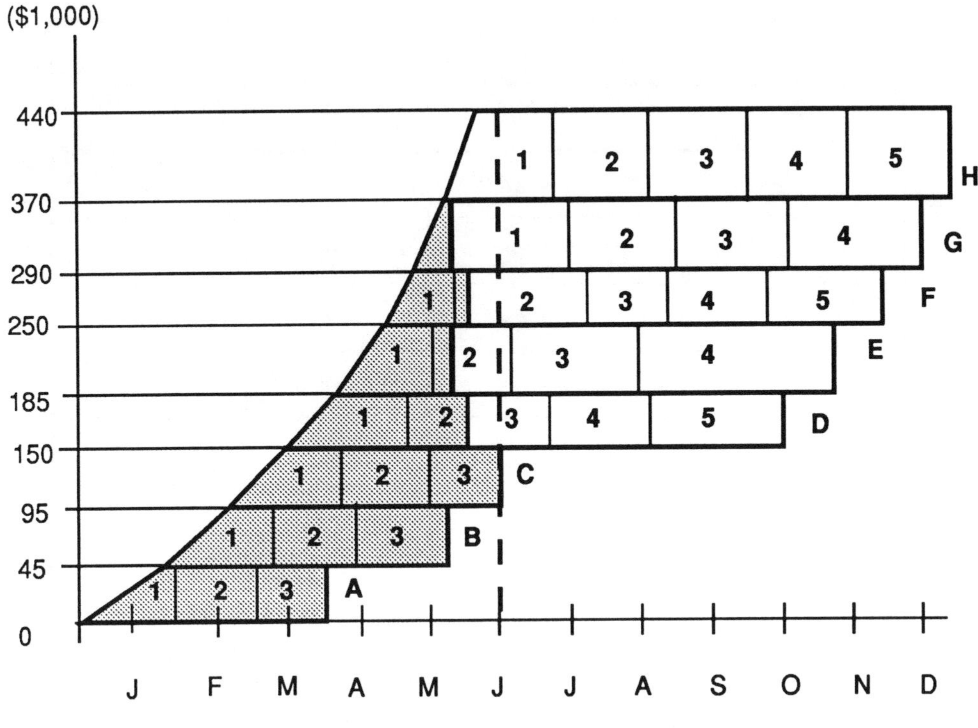


**Figure 16-14**
**The Project Performance Chart**

under control before it is too late. These two functions are included in other project activities and can cause project delays and total cost overrun if not set under control.

## HOW TO EXPEDITE PROJECTS

Often, conditions imposed on projects warrant accelerating some project activities aimed at expediting the entire project and reducing total project cost. A project time reduction targets expediting of critical path activities, the time crashing. The *crash time* is the shortest time for an activity that could be achieved, if everything possible was done, such as if all the required resources were made available for this activity. For example, three bricklayers can erect building walls in 28 working days. By adding two more bricklayers, this job could be completed in 18 working days. Adding more direct resources aimed at activity

| Project Status on July 1, 1990 ($1,000) | | | |
|---|---|---|---|
| Activity | Budget | Actual | Variance |
| A | 45 | 60 | +15 |
| B | 50 | 75 | +25 |
| C | 55 | 75 | +20 |
| D | 35 | 25 | -10 |
| E | 65 | 20 | -45 |
| F | 40 | 15 | -25 |
| G | 80 | 10 | -70 |
| H | 70 | -- | -70 |
| **Total** | 440 | 280 | -160 |

**Figure 16-15**
**The Project Status by Date Report**

time reduction leads to an increase of the direct cost and a decrease of the indirect cost.

A project cost reduction is achieved by reducing project time, so that the savings in indirect project costs will offset the increases in direct activity costs. The lowest project cost is found by computing the least sum of direct cost and indirect cost for several project durations.

An activity cost-time trade-off graph, shown in Figure 16-16, is a linear programming technique that assists in identifying the best project crashing schedule by analyzing the direct crashing cost for each targeted activity. The normal activity time and cost are shown at point *A*, while the crash activity time and cost are shown at point *B*. A straight line connecting points *A* and *B* indicates that a linear cost-time relationship is assumed. In this example, it means that the cost of reducing an activity duration for three weeks is

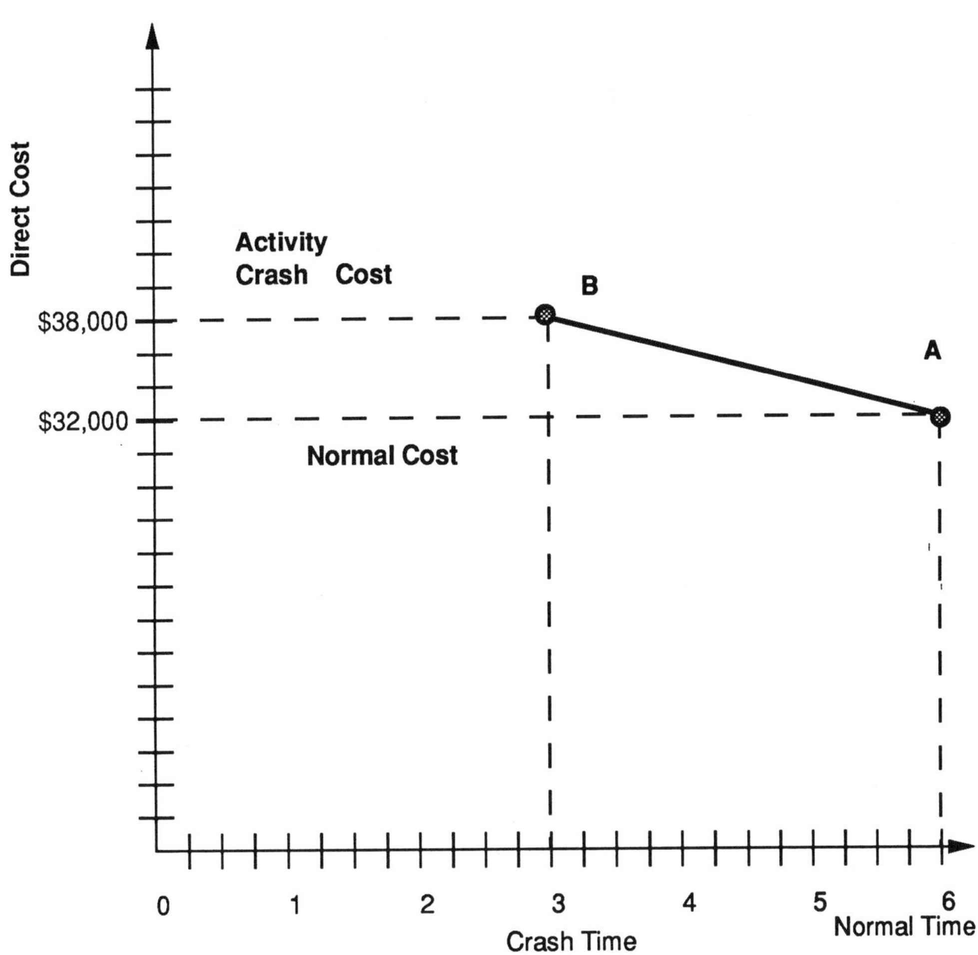


**Figure 16-16**
**Activity Cost-Time Trade-off**

$$\$38,000 - \$32,000 = \$6,000$$

and the cost of one week is

$$\$6,000 \;/\; 3 = \$2,000$$

The slope of the line *AB* represents the crashing cost, also known as the *cost slope.* The cost slope is an incremental cost of reducing activity time and is estimated as follows:

$$\text{cost slope} = \frac{\text{crash cost} - \text{normal cost}}{\text{normal time} - \text{crash time}}$$

Minimizing the total project cost by expediting project activities includes five steps which are illustrated in the example of a network work package shown in Figure 16-17.

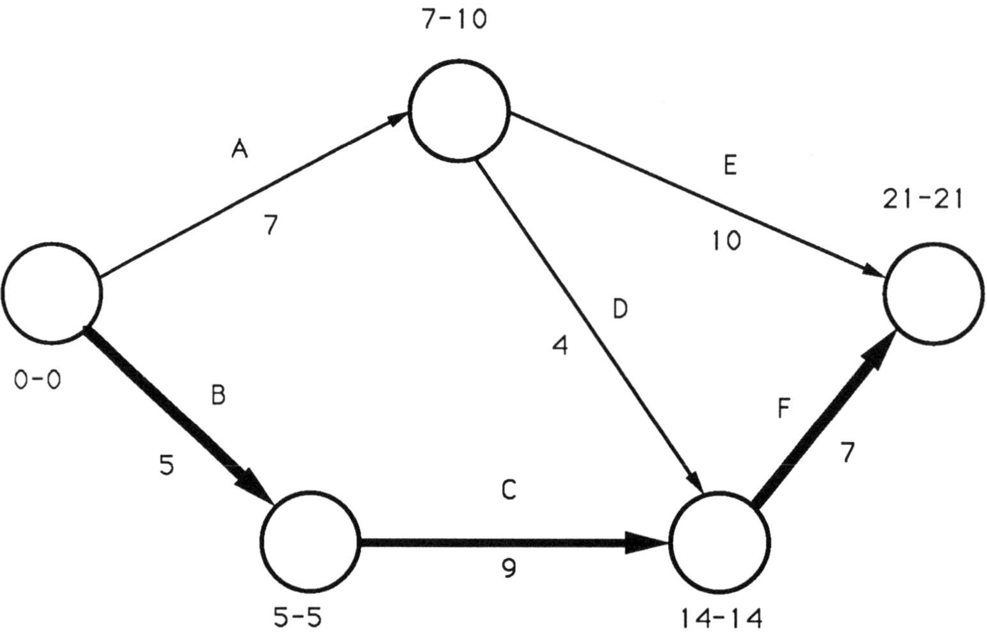


**Figure 16-17**
**Project Network**

The five steps of identifying a project duration that will minimize the total project cost include computing dates for the selected project activities by correlating the normal time and crash time costs. Information from the project input data form is used for collecting normal and crash time and costs. This form provides information used in the first four columns in the project crashing data form illustrated in Figure 16-18.

| Activity | Normal Time | Float | Normal Direct Cost | Crash Time | Expediting Cost per One Unit of Time | Crash Cost | Total Time Reduct. | Indirect Project Cost per Unit of Time |
|---|---|---|---|---|---|---|---|---|
| 1 | 2 | 3 | 4 | 5 | 6 | 7 | 8 | 9 |
| **A** | 7 | 3 | 8,000 | 1 | 2,200 | | | |
| **B** | 5 | 0 | 13,000 | 2 | 5,800 | | | |
| **C** | 9 | 0 | 18,000 | 2 | 2,900 | | | |
| **D** | 4 | 3 | 15,000 | 1 | 5,200 | | | |
| **E** | 10 | 4 | 21,000 | 4 | 3,400 | | | |
| **F** | 7 | 0 | 16,000 | 1 | 5,300 | | | |

| | | Direct Cost | | Indirect Cost | | |
|---|---|---|---|---|---|---|
| **Total Cost:** | 21weeks | 91,000 | + | 131,000 | = | 222,000 |
| **1st iteration** | 20 weeks | 93,900 | + | 119,000 | = | 212,000 |
| **2nd iteration** | 19 weeks | 96,800 | + | 110,000 | = | 196,800 |
| **3rd iteration** | 18 weeks | 102,100 | + | 101,000 | = | 203,000 |
| **4th iteration** | 17 weeks | 107,900 | + | 94,000 | = | 201,900 |
| **5th iteration** | 16 weeks | 115,400 | + | 87,000 | = | 202,400 |

**Figure 16-18**
**The Project Crashing Data Form**

The network's critical path consists of activities B, C, and F for the total of 12 weeks' duration. The following are the five steps of the project time crashing procedure:

***Step 1.*** Define crash time, crash direct cost, and the cost slope using the equation on page 610. This information is for columns 5, 6, and 7. Compute the total direct cost at normal time. In the example, it is equal to $91,000. Refer to Figure 16-18.

***Step 2.*** The project time crashing starts with critical activities which have the least expediting cost per unit of time. The least expediting cost is for activity A and is equal to $2,200, but this activity is not on a critical path, which means that expediting this activity will not reduce the total project time. The critical activity which has the least expediting cost is an activity C, having a $2,900 expediting cost per one unit of time. The crashing is done in several iterations one week at a time:

- *Twenty-week schedule.* This schedule is a 1-week improvement over the normal project time. The project direct cost is $93,900.

| Project | | | Charge No. | | | Due Date | | | | Report Date | | |
|---|---|---|---|---|---|---|---|---|---|---|---|---|
| Activity | Resource Code | Earliest Date | Critical (Y/N) | Resource Estimate | | | | | | | Total | Earned | Variance |
| | | | | Months | | | | | | | | | |
| | | | | Feb. | Mar. | Apr. | May | Jun. | Jul. | Aug. | | | |
| | | | | | | | | | | | | | |
| | | | | | | | | | | | | | |
| | | | | | | | | | | | | | |
| | | | | | | | | | | | | | |
| | | | | | | | | | | | | | |

**Figure 16-19**
**The Project Activity Report**

- *Nineteen-week schedule.* A further 1-week reduction of the time for activity C results in the direct project cost of $96,800. Activity C cannot be crashed further.
- *Eighteen-week schedule.* The critical activity with the least expediting cost now is activity F. A 1-week crashing of this activity increases the total project direct cost to $102,100.
- *Seventeen-week schedule.* Activity B is shortened for 1 week to the total project direct cost of $107,900.
- *Sixteen-week schedule.* A further project time reduction requires expediting two activities (A and F) because both paths now are critical, having a 17-week duration. Here, the combined expediting cost is $7,500. This increases the project direct cost to $115,400.

***Step 3.*** Collect accounting data and estimate an indirect project cost for different project durations.

***Step 4.*** Compute the total project cost, direct and indirect, for each project duration. The lowest-cost project schedule in our example is 19 weeks.

***Step 5.*** Project time crashing assumes that you have unlimited resources. This is not always possible. Thus the last step is to compile a new resource allocation schedule. A project schedule incorporating the lowest total project cost can be selected after the availability of resources is verified.

## USING PROJECT MANAGEMENT REPORTS FOR BETTER CONTROL

Project reporting procedures are an essential part of project management and control. If information is provided on time, a decision can be made to improve performance before it is too late. The following are typical project management reports:

- Project activity report
- Project cost report
- Project status report
- Activity costing report
- Labor utilization report
- Project cost status report
- Project cost summary report

### The Project Activity Report

This is a weekly or monthly report on project activities, given in dollar value per time period, together with the percentage of the cumulative completion.

The total activity cost is stated against the budgeted cost. A project activity report is shown in Figure 16-19. Starting and finishing dates of an activity are included in the report, and critical activities are highlighted. In larger projects, project activity reports are structured around work packages.

### The Project Cost Report

This is an activity cost-based report, showing information on the earned cost against the actual cost, as well as the cost variances. The project cost report is shown in Figure 16-20. The project cost report includes a cost analysis showing the projected activity cost and its variances against the planned activity cost. This report can include a graphical part where the completion rate of activities is illustrated on a bar chart.

### The Project Status Report

This report shows the time status of activities with the cost of work performed to date as well as variances and the projected overruns-underrun cost. This report is similar to the project cost report, except that, in this report, a time analysis (i.e., the computation of the early start, early finish, late start, late finish, and critical slack time) can be conducted in conjunction with the cost analysis. The project status report is illustrated in Figure 16-21. The project status report is also used for an analysis of work packages.

### The Activity Costing Report

This report contains cost accounting information of the direct cost as well as applied overheads. Costing information includes the latest revised figures, according to the scheduled time and the actual completion time. The activity costing report is shown in Figure 16-22. This report is compiled for activities and work packages.

### The Resource Utilization Report

A resource utilization report shows the resource utilization by time periods for both labor and equipment. The planned and the actual figures are compared, and the latest revised estimated figures are computed based on variances. A resource utilization report is shown in Figure 16-23. A resource utilization report can contain a graphical section where the resource utilization is shown on a bar chart.

### The Project Cost Status Report

This report shows the project cost history by periods. The cost of project activities is reported by periods, concerning the planned cost, the actual cost, and the earned cost. The value of work completed is estimated in proportion

| Project | | | | Charge No. | | | Due Date | | Report Date | | | | | |
|---|---|---|---|---|---|---|---|---|---|---|---|---|---|---|
| | | Cost of Work | | | | | | | Schedule | | | | | |
| | | Work Completed | | | Projected Completion | | | | | | | | | |
| Activity | Cost Code | Value | Actual Cost | Variance | Planned Cost | Latest Revision | Projected Variance | Completion Date | (months) | | | | | |
| | | | | | | | | | | | | | | |
| | | | | | | | | | | | | | | |
| | | | | | | | | | | | | | | |
| | | | | | | | | | | | | | | |
| | | | | | | | | | | | | | | |
| | | | | | | | | | | | | | | |
| | | | | | | | | | | | | | | |
| | | | | | | | | | | | | | | |
| | | | | | | | | | | | | | | |
| | | | | | | | | | | | | | | |

**Figure 16-20**
**The Project Cost Report**

to the original budget. The earned budget per activity is computed based on the original budget, revised budget, and actual cumulative cost, as follows:

$$EB = OB\left(\frac{CC}{RB}\right)$$

fig 16.21

| Project | | | Charge No. | | Due Date | | | | Report Date | | |
|---|---|---|---|---|---|---|---|---|---|---|---|
| | | Time Status | | | Cost | | | | | | |
| | | | | | Work Performed | | | | Projected Completion | | |
| Activity | Charge | Scheduled Date | Completion Date | Critical Slack | Actual | Planned | Earned | Variance | Planned | Revised Estimate | Projected Variance |
| | | | | | | | | | | | |
| | | | | | | | | | | | |
| | | | | | | | | | | | |
| | | | | | | | | | | | |
| | | | | | | | | | | | |
| | | | | | | | | | | | |
| | | | | | | | | | | | |

**Figure 16-21**
**The Project Status Report**

where

$EB$ = earned budget
$OB$ = original budget
$CC$ = cumulative cost
$RB$ = revised budget

A project earned budget is computed as a sum of the individual activities' earned budgets. An example of a project cost status report is shown in Figure 16-24.

The total budget per activity is shown in a separate column as well as the total cost to date. A project cost status report includes the revised activities budget updated per period as well as the total actual budget and cumulative actual budget, earned budget, and cumulative earned budget per activity per time period. This report contains valuable financial planning information, namely, the history per activity per time period. For the project's top management, a

| Project | | | Activity | | | | | Due Date | | Report Date | |
|---|---|---|---|---|---|---|---|---|---|---|---|
| Identification | | | Labor Hours | | | | Direct Cost | | | | |
| Charge No. | Organizat. Unit | Cost Code | Plan | Actual | Earned | Projected Variance | Plan | Actual | Latest Revised | Projected Variance | |
| | | | | | | | | | | | |
| | | | | | | | | | | | |
| | | | | | | | | | | | |
| | | | | | | | | | | | |
| | | | | | | | | | | | |
| | | | | | | | | | | | |
| | | | | | | | | | | | |
| | | | | | | | | | | | |
| | | | | | | | | | | | |
| | | | | | | | | | | | |
| | | | | | | | | | | | |
| | | | | | | | | | | | |

**Figure 16-22**
**The Activity Costing Report**

project cost status report is compiled showing a summary of project information presented in the project cost report.

## SUMMARY

Project management is a form of production management because, as with production, the objective of a project is to transform material resources into useful output.

| Project Charge No. | | | Due Date: | | Report Date: | |
|---|---|---|---|---|---|---|
| Labor Identification | | | Labor Hours | | | |
| Time Period | Skill Code | Charge No. | Planned | Actual | Earned | Projected Variance |
| | | | | | | |
| | | | | | | |
| | | | | | | |
| | | | | | | |
| | | | | | | |
| | | | | | | |

**Figure 16-23**
**The Resource Utilization Report**

Although a project is a one-time affair, project activities are encountered throughout all production and services functions. Many products and customer orders are approached as projects. All newly developed products and modifications to existing products are planned and controlled as projects. New product development equipment installation and commissioning are individual projects taking place prior to the start of production constitute 90 to 95 percent of the total product life expenses. Furthermore, management systems development (i.e., MPS, MRP, MRP II, CRP, and JIT) and installation are projects which often stretch over a long period of time. These projects' activities are run concurrently with regular production and, thus, should be integrated with the existing production planning and control systems. You can understand how important it is for a production manager to manage projects effectively, along with regular production functions, as projects exert such an influence on product quality and costs.

Network analysis systems (PERT and CPM) are standard project control methods widely used in project planning and control. When applying a network analysis to project management, you should pay attention to the resource utilization and costs control as the critical areas in the present project management.

| Activity ID | Description | Duration | Total Budget | Costs Reported by Period | | | | | | | | | | | | | | Actual Cost to Date | | Revised Cost by Period | | | | | | | | | | | | | | Estimated Complet. Cost |
| --- | --- | --- | --- | --- | --- | --- | --- | --- | --- | --- | --- | --- | --- | --- | --- | --- | --- | --- | --- | --- | --- | --- | --- | --- | --- | --- | --- | --- | --- | --- | --- | --- | --- | --- |
| | | | | 1 | | 2 | | 3 | | 4 | | 5 | | 6 | | 7 | | | | 8 | | 9 | | 10 | | 11 | | 12 | | 13 | | 14 | | |
| | | | | A | E | A | E | A | E | A | E | A | E | A | E | A | E | A | E | A | E | A | E | A | E | A | E | A | E | A | E | A | E | |
| | | | | | | | | | | | | | | | | | | | | | | | | | | | | | | | | | | |
| | | | | | | | | | | | | | | | | | | | | | | | | | | | | | | | | | | |
| | | | | | | | | | | | | | | | | | | | | | | | | | | | | | | | | | | |
| | | | | | | | | | | | | | | | | | | | | | | | | | | | | | | | | | | |
| | | | | | | | | | | | | | | | | | | | | | | | | | | | | | | | | | | |
| | | | | | | | | | | | | | | | | | | | | | | | | | | | | | | | | | | |
| | | | | | | | | | | | | | | | | | | | | | | | | | | | | | | | | | | |
| | | | | | | | | | | | | | | | | | | | | | | | | | | | | | | | | | | |
| | | | | | | | | | | | | | | | | | | | | | | | | | | | | | | | | | | |
| | | | | | | | | | | | | | | | | | | | | | | | | | | | | | | | | | | |
| | | | | | | | | | | | | | | | | | | | | | | | | | | | | | | | | | | |
| | | | | | | | | | | | | | | | | | | | | | | | | | | | | | | | | | | |
| Total | | | | | | | | | | | | | | | | | | | | | | | | | | | | | | | | | | |

**A** - Actual Cost

**E** - Earned Cost

**Figure 16-24**
**The Project Cost Status Report**

Effective project management starts with developing a detailed plan that is the standard for continuous (functional) project control. This is done by grouping project activities into work packages, based on the similarity of the constituent activities. Another effective way of the project time and costs reduction is the technique of time and cost crashing, consisting of the five consecutive steps.

An effective way of project control is a management reporting system which includes project cost control and resources scheduling and control.

# Appendix

## JEC STRATEGIC PLAN OVERVIEW as of June 7, 1991

### WHERE WE ARE NOW...Fiscal 1991, Third Quarter

- Sales: $68.7 million
- Earnings before taxes (EBT): $7.3 million
- Return on investment (ROI): 26.4%

Who buys our products: major industrial companies (perceived product value: productivity, safety, quality, service, *technical support*)

Our products are:

- Energy related, 40%
- Motor vehicle, 30%
- Aircraft, 12%
- General industry, 18%

## Sales by Market

| | Sales (millions) | Sales as a % of Total |
|---|---|---|
| United States | $40.2 | 59% |
| Export | 4.0 | 6 |
| Mexico | 3.6 | 5 |
| Germany | 10.6 | 15 |
| Netherlands | 6.3 | 9 |
| Canada | 4.0 | 6 |
| Total | $68.7 | 100% |

## Sales by product

| Code | Sales (millions) | Sales as a % of Total | EBT (millions) | ROI |
|---|---|---|---|---|
| 1-2025 | $38.9 | 57% | $4.5 | 30.2% |
| 1-2036 | 15.9 | 22 | 1.3 | 37.1 |
| 1-2039 | 6.0 | 9 | 2.1 | 39.6 |
| 1-2042 | 5.9 | 9 | (0.7) | — |
| 1-2061 | 2.0 | 3 | 0.1 | 4.3 |
| Total | $68.7 | 100% | $7.3 | 26.4 |

### Current Organization (Sales)

- 17 employees (12/5)
- Additional technical salesperson required in 1992 and 1993
- Additional productive personnel as sales grow
- 10 employees (8/2)
- 1992 level (11/3)
- 1993 and 1994 levels (11/4)

### Market Status

Key point is customer base has grown and market share has increased.

| | |
|---|---|
| Repeat 1990 customer activity in 1991 (in thousands) | |
| Chrysler Chassis (all four product lines) | $1,000 |
| CPC Flint Engine (electrics) | 1,050 |
| Detroit Diesel (electrics/arms) | 200 |
| Significant new customers in 1991 (in thousands) | |
| Cadillac Chassis (electrics/arms) | $500 |
| Caterpillar Mossville Engine (electrics/arms) | 65 |

| | |
|---|---|
| CPC Tonawanda Engine (electrics) | 105 |
| Boeing Seattle (arms) | 35 |
| BOC Wilmington Chassis (electronics) | 180 |

### Product Line/Engineering Development

Product development phase is now in maintenance mode. Projects/products completed include

- Arms
  - — Zero-gravity balancer
  - — High-torque/high-load-torque tube
  - — 75-ft-lb articulated arm
- Pneumatic tooling
  - — Assistance in Houston development of fixtured solenoid control tools (critical to Chrysler account)
- DC/RAN
  - — 335/355 tools
- Electronics
  - — Finalization of DL1 and DL2 systems.
  - — Development of X and $\overline{R}$ charts for DL3 statistical software package (customer financed)
- 1992 new product development projects will be based solely on customer sponsorship (i.e., GM Wilmington)

### Market/Product Strategy

Key factors for future market expansion are

- Arms (tools and material handling)
- Continued growth of electric wheelnut multiples and oil-less pneumatic multiples
- Replacement at GM Chassis plants of obsolete existing electronic systems with DL3 electronics
  - — BOC Wilmington (line tracking)—$500,000 in 1992
  - — Cadillac Hamtramk (SPC)—$200,000 in 1992
- Third quarter 1991 introduction of DC/RAN

*Product line and business in place. Profitability with continued growth is key priority.*

### Major Economic/Planning Assumptions

1992 flat; 1993, 1 to 2 percent; 1994, 2 to 3 percent

- Moderate inflation, 4 to 6 percent range
- U.S. dollar remaining at April 1991 level
- A 4 to 6 percent increase in material costs, wages and salaries; fringes will be 35 to 40 percent of salaries and wages.

### Competitive Environment

- Atlas Copco—CP/Renault/DeSoutter—movement, direct sales
- Ingersoll Rand—ARO—changing distributors
- Cooper—Rockwell/Dotco
- Cooper/Rockwell
- Dolar
- Recoules—France/Germany
- Elliott, Wilson—United States
- Maus—Italy
- Sugino—Japan
- Ingersoll-Rand
- Atlas Copco-CP
- Deutsch Gardner Denver

### Key Business Objectives

- Quality—people, products, service
- Statistical quality control
  - ISO 9000 certification
  - Manufacturing, marketing, engineering, administration
  - Malcolm Baldrige Award
- Market-driven—quality, higher-margined products requiring field technical support
- Improved plant performance—world-class competitor
- Sales increase
  - 15 to 20 percent over three years (without acquisitions)
  - Minimum 25 percent ROI
- 35 percent ROI
- Minimum $6 million per year positive cash flow

## WHERE WE ARE GOING...

| | 1991 | 1992 | 1993 | 1994 |
|---|---|---|---|---|
| Sales (millions) | $68.7 | $72.8 | $77.0 | $81.3 |
| EBT (millions) | 7.3 | 7.8 | 9.0 | 10.0 |
| ROI | 26% | 28% | 32% | 36% |
| Cash flow (millions) | 5.1 | 8.6 | 8.5 | 8.8 |

### Concerns/Changes

- Aircraft market changes. 1990 versus 1991—sales increase: $9 million; margin increase: $6.0 million
- Fringe benefit costs
  - — Medical, $600,000
  - — Pension, $400,000—Houston
  - — Less total depreciation, $50,000—Springfield
- Legal costs, $300,000 per year

### SHIFT IN KEY MARKETS, 1990–1991

| | 1990 | 1991 |
|---|---|---|
| Aircraft | 25% | 12% |
| Motor vehicle | 25 | 30 |
| Energy | 35 | 40 |
| General industry | 15 | 18 |

Change from 1990 in aircraft products was substantial; large aircraft orders from Boeing, McDonnell Douglas, and General Dynamics, did not repeat.

### KEY MARKET SALES OUTLOOK, 1991–1994 (thousands)

| | 1991 | 1992 | 1993 | 1994 |
|---|---|---|---|---|
| Aircraft | $8,240 | $8,013 | $10,015 | $12,188 |
| | 12% | 11% | 13% | 15% |
| Motor vehicle | 20,600 | 22,582 | 24,654 | 26,000 |
| | 30% | 31% | 32% | 32% |
| Energy | 27,464 | 29,867 | 30,816 | 30,875 |
| | 40% | 41% | 40% | 38% |
| General industry | 12,359 | 12,384 | 11,556 | 12,188 |
| | 18% | 17% | 15% | 15% |
| Total | $68,663 | $72,846 | $77,041 | $81,251 |

Emphasis has shifted to other key markets:

- Additional sales to motor vehicle
- Ford certification program in progress
- Energy market sales up
  - Additional sales
  - Increased maintenance requirements
- General industry
  - Up in 1991 and 1992—returning to more normal levels in 1993 and 1994
    - New impact wrench introduction
    - Fabrication and maintenance promotions

## STRATEGY: QUALITY, SERVICE, AND TECHNICAL SUPPORT

- Aircraft
  - Military
  - Commercial
- Motor Vehicle
  - General Motors
  - Chrysler Corp.
  - Ford Motor Corp.
  - Foreign manufacturers
- Energy
  - Downstream
  - Upstream
- General industry
  - Electronic assembly
  - Maintenance and fabrication
- U.S. government
  - GSA contract
- In all product lines, we will continue to
  - Stay with the basics
  - Be strong end-user presence
  - Maintain pricing integrity
  - Maintain key account selling
  - Use mobile sales van

  - — Support training school/seminars
  - — Support catalogs/advertising
  - — Support trade shows
  - — Utilize audio/visual aids
- Monitor channels to the market
  - — Distribution (50 percent)
    - Specialty
    - Full line
    - MRO systems contracts
  - — Direct (50 percent)
- Selective accounts/segments
- Service sales
  - — Offset cost of branch operations
- New product introduction
  - — New impact wrench
  - — Fixturized pneumatic tooling
  - — Air feed peck drill
  - — DC/RAN
  - — DL1 and DL2 electronic control
  - — Consolidation
  - — Electric rolling control systems
- Generic arm distributor package
- Manpower utilization

## 1991 STRATEGIC PLAN

### Projected Sales

INTERNATIONAL (millions)

| 1991 Plan | 1991 | 1992 | 1993 | 1994 |
|---|---|---|---|---|
| $23,898 | $24,385 | $26,713 | $28,483 | $30,236 |

INTERNATIONAL OPERATIONS (SALES)*

- Germany (31 employees)

* See more detailed forcast (Germany) on next page.

  - — Hamburg
  - — Eltville
  - — Remscheid
  - — Munich
  - — Hanover
- Netherlands (12 employees)
  - — Capelle
- Mexico (14 employees)*
- Houston (3 employees)
- Total international (60 employees: 16 administration, 3 engineering, 1 manufacturing, 40 customer service/sales, includes 20 salespeople)

  Average revenue per salesperson is $1,219,250.

GERMANY, 1991–1994 (millions)

| 1991 Plan | 1991 Actual | 1992 | 1993 | 1994 |
|---|---|---|---|---|
| $9,578 | $10,076 | $12,365 | $13,135 | $13,933 |

- Outlook
  - — Stable
  - — Weaker Deutsche Mark
- Markets
  - — Motor vehicle
    - Control tools, electric and pneumatic

      Product sales manager
      DL-I and DL-II
    - Ford Motor Co.
  - — Aircraft
- Smaller operations
- Buy packages (engineering firm)
- Product specialist from United States
  - — Energy
    - New route to the market
    - Fabrication tools
    - Tools

---

* See Mexico on page 629.

- — General Industry
    - Distribution
    - Eastern Germany
    - Build export

MEXICO, 1991–1994 (millions)

| 1991 Plan | 1991 Actual | 1992 | 1993 | 1994 |
|---|---|---|---|---|
| $3,504 | $3,622 | $3,720 | $3,887 | $4,062 |

- Market outlook
  - — Increased automobile production
  - — Increased spending in energy market
  - — General industry
- Motor vehicle
  - — Direct sales
- Energy
  - — Pemex
    - More maintenance
    - More contracts
- General industry
  - — Free trade
  - — *Maquiladora*

## AVERAGE INVESTMENT, 1991–1994

| | 1991 | 1992 | 1993 | 1994 |
|---|---|---|---|---|
| Accounts receivable | $11,059 | $12,100 | $12,900 | $13,200 |
| Inventory | 16,202 | 15,700 | 14,750 | 14,100 |
| Property, plant, and equipment | 10,072 | 9,900 | 9,700 | 9,600 |
| Other | (9,833) | (9,700) | (9,350) | (8,900) |
| Total | $27,500 | 28,000 | 28,000 | 28,000 |
| Capital spending | 3,519 | 2,500 | 2,500 | 2,500 |
| Depreciation | 2,589 | 2,850 | 2,850 | 2,850 |
| Investment turnover | 2.5% | 2.6% | 2.8% | 2.9% |
| ROI | 26.4% | 27.8% | 32.0% | 35.9% |

## INVENTORY TREND SCHEDULE, October 1991–1994

| Responsibility/Location | 1991 3RD QTR | 1992 | 1993 | 1994 |
|---|---|---|---|---|
| Troy | $600 | $625 | $650 | $700 |
| Domestic Sales Branches | | | | |
| | 1,400 | 1,400 | 1,500 | 1,500 |
| | 300 | 300 | 300 | 300 |
| Total branches | 1,700 | 1,700 | 1,800 | 1,850 |
| Germany | | | | |
| Eltville | 400 | 425 | 450 | 500 |
| Remschied | 650 | 450 | 300 | 300 |
| Hamburg | 1,100 | 1,000 | 1,000 | 1,000 |
| Total Germany | 2,150 | 1,875 | 1,750 | 1,800 |
| Mexico | 400 | 400 | 400 | 400 |
| Canada | 650 | 650 | 650 | 650 |
| Netherlands | 600 | 600 | 625 | 650 |
| Eliminations | (200) | (200) | (185) | (190) |
| Total McDonnell Douglas | $5,900 | $5,650 | $5,690 | $5,860 |
| Houston | | | | |
| Production | 8,400 | 7,600 | 6,900 | 6,300 |
| Other | 100 | 100 | 100 | 100 |
| Total | $8,500 | $7,700 | $7,000 | $6,400 |
| Springfield production | $1,600 | $1,650 | $1,650 | $1,650 |
| Division Total | $16,000 | $15,000 | $14,340 | $13,910 |
| Inventory turn | 2.8 | 3.0 | 3.3 | 3.7 |

## HEADCOUNT AND SALARY, 1991–1994

| TOTAL DIVISION | 1991 | | 1992 | | 1993 | | 1994 | |
|---|---|---|---|---|---|---|---|---|
| Responsibility/Location | Headcount | Amount | Headcount | Amount | Headcount | Amount | Headcount | Amount |
| Germany | | 0.61925 | | 0.592 | | 0.592 | | 0.592 |
| Hamburg | | | | | | | | |
| Selling (+1, 6/91) | 15 | 813 | 16 | 857 | 17 | 922 | 17 | 954 |
| Administrative | 5 | 168 | 6 | 191 | 6 | 198 | 6 | 205 |
| Total | 20 | 981 | 22 | 1,048 | 23 | 1,120 | 23 | 1,159 |
| Reimscheid | | | | | | | | |
| Selling | 5 | 142 | 5 | 140 | 5 | 145 | 5 | 150 |
| Administrative | 1 | 14 | 1 | 14 | 1 | 14 | 1 | 14 |
| Total | 6 | 156 | 6 | 154 | 6 | 159 | 6 | 164 |
| Eltville | | | | | | | | |
| Manufacturing | 1 | 31 | 2 | 63 | 3 | 97 | 3 | 101 |
| Selling | 0 | 0 | 1 | 35 | 1 | 36 | 1 | 37 |
| Administrative (+1, 6/91) | 2 | 48 | 3 | 72 | 3 | 75 | 3 | 78 |
| Engineering (+2, 6/91) | 7 | 300 | 8 | 342 | 8 | 354 | 8 | 366 |
| Total | 10 | 379 | 14 | 512 | 15 | 562 | 15 | 582 |
| Total Germany | 36 | 1,516 | 42 | 1,714 | 44 | 1,841 | 44 | 1,905 |
| | | 0.5494 | | 0.5225 | | 0.5225 | | 0.5225 |
| Netherlands | | | | | | | | |
| Manufacturing | 1 | 34 | 1 | 33 | 1 | 34 | 1 | 35 |
| Selling (+1, 6/91) | 7 | 409 | 7 | 403 | 7 | 417 | 7 | 432 |
| Administrative | 3 | 119 | 3 | 117 | 4 | 146 | 4 | 151 |
| Total | 11 | 562 | 11 | 553 | 12 | 597 | 12 | 618 |
| Mexico | | | | | | | | |
| Selling | 6 | 159 | 6 | 165 | 6 | 171 | 6 | 177 |
| Administrative | 5 | 41 | 5 | 42 | 5 | 43 | 5 | 45 |
| Total | 11 | 200 | 11 | 207 | 11 | 214 | 11 | 222 |
| Canada | | | | | | | | |
| Selling | 11 | 372 | 11 | 385 | 11 | 398 | 11 | 412 |
| Administrative | | 0 | | | | | | |
| Total | 11 | 372 | 11 | 385 | 11 | 398 | 11 | 412 |
| Troy | | | | | | | | |
| Manufacturing | 1 | 53 | 1 | 55 | 1 | 57 | 1 | 59 |
| Selling | 3 | 168 | 3 | 174 | 4 | 230 | 4 | 238 |
| Administrative | 2 | 88 | 3 | 116 | 4 | 145 | 4 | 150 |
| Engineering | 6 | 259 | 6 | 268 | 7 | 302 | 7 | 313 |
| Total | 12 | 568 | 13 | 613 | 16 | 734 | 16 | 760 |
| Domestic marketing | | | | | | | | |
| Houston | | | | | | | | |
| Branches | 31 | 861 | 31 | 891 | 31 | 922 | 31 | 954 |
| Field Sales | 59 | 2,673 | 59 | 2,767 | 59 | 2,864 | 59 | 2,964 |
| Houston | 10 | 480 | 10 | 497 | 10 | 514 | 10 | 532 |
| Total | 100 | 4,014 | 100 | 4,155 | 100 | 4,300 | 100 | 4,450 |
| Springfield, Customer Service | 4 | 138 | 4 | 143 | 4 | 148 | 4 | 153 |
| Total | 185 | 7,370 | 192 | 7,770 | 198 | 8,232 | 198 | 8,520 |

## Total Capacity Costs
## ($ 000)

### TOTAL DIVISION

| Description | 1991 3QFC | Cost % Incr | 1992 | Cost % Incr | 1993 | Cost % Incr | 1994 |
|---|---|---|---|---|---|---|---|
| Wages | 12866 | 5.9% | 13627 | 5.5% | 14373 | 4.4% | 15006 |
| Incentive | 1139 | 1.1% | 1152 | 3.6% | 1193 | 2.8% | 1226 |
| Fringes | 3129 | 21.2% | 3792 | 5.3% | 3994 | 4.5% | 4173 |
| Travel & Entertainment | 1911 | 3.3% | 1975 | 3.9% | 2053 | 3.9% | 2134 |
| Automotive Expense | 859 | 3.0% | 885 | 3.7% | 918 | 3.8% | 953 |
| Outside & Consulting | 998 | 4.4% | 1042 | 5.0% | 1094 | 4.8% | 1146 |
| Office Expense | 1385 | 3.9% | 1439 | 4.8% | 1508 | 4.8% | 1581 |
| Other Marketing Expense | 980 | 3.2% | 1011 | 4.5% | 1057 | 6.1% | 1122 |
| Utilities & Depreciation | 3435 | 7.5% | 3691 | 1.5% | 3746 | 1.5% | 3803 |
| Taxes & Rent | 2124 | 5.3% | 2236 | 5.9% | 2368 | 6.0% | 2509 |
| Other | 1090 | 4.9% | 1143 | -6.8% | 1065 | 16.3% | 1239 |
| TOTAL EXPENSES | 29916 | 6.9% | 31993 | 4.3% | 33369 | 4.6% | 34892 |
| Headcount | 303 | | 312 | | 318 | | 319 |

## Manufacturing Capacity Costs
## ($ 000)

**TOTAL DIVISION**

| Description | 1991 3QFC | Cost % Incr | 1992 | Cost % Incr | 1993 | Cost % Incr | 1994 |
|---|---|---|---|---|---|---|---|
| Wages | 3105 | 7.1% | 3327 | 5.9% | 3523 | 6.1% | 3737 |
| Incentive | | 0.0% | | 0.0% | | 0.0% | |
| Fringes | 776 | 22.7% | 952 | 5.6% | 1005 | 6.2% | 1067 |
| Travel & Entertainment | 36 | 2.8% | 37 | 2.7% | 38 | 2.6% | 39 |
| Automotive Expense | 7 | 0.0% | 7 | 0.0% | 7 | 0.0% | 7 |
| Outside & Consulting | 292 | 5.1% | 307 | 4.9% | 322 | 5.0% | 338 |
| | | 0.0 | 0 | 0.0 | 0 | 0.0 | 0 |
| Office Expense | 152 | 4.6% | 159 | 4.4% | 166 | 4.8% | 174 |
| | | 0.0 | 0 | 0.0 | 0 | 0.0 | 0 |
| Other Marketing Expense | | 0.0% | 0 | 0.0% | 0 | 0.0% | 0 |
| Utilities & Depreciation | 2879 | 8.9% | 3135 | 1.2% | 3174 | 1.3% | 3215 |
| Taxes & Rent | (64) | 6.3% | (68) | 7.4% | (73) | 5.5% | (77) |
| Other | 1458 | 4.1% | 1518 | 4.0% | 1579 | 4.1% | 1643 |
| TOTAL EXPENSES | 8641 | 8.5% | 9374 | 3.9% | 9741 | 4.1% | 10143 |
| Headcount | 60 | | 62 | | 63 | | 64 |

## Selling Capacity Costs
($ 000)

### TOTAL DIVISION

| Description | 1991 3QFC | Cost % Incr | 1992 | Cost % Incr | 1993 | Cost % Incr | 1994 |
|---|---|---|---|---|---|---|---|
| Wages | 6215 | 3.9% | 6457 | 4.8% | 6767 | 3.5% | 7003 |
| Incentive | 894 | -1.7% | 879 | 4.4% | 918 | 3.5% | 950 |
| Fringes | 1460 | 19.2% | 1740 | 4.7% | 1822 | 3.5% | 1885 |
| Travel & Entertainment | 1658 | 3.3% | 1713 | 4.0% | 1781 | 4.0% | 1852 |
| Automotive Expense | 805 | 3.2% | 831 | 4.0% | 864 | 3.9% | 898 |
| Outside & Consulting | 314 | 4.5% | 328 | 5.2% | 345 | 4.6% | 361 |
| | | 0.0 | 0 | 0.0 | 0 | 0.0 | 0 |
| Office Expense | 738 | 3.7% | 765 | 5.0% | 803 | 4.7% | 841 |
| | | 0.0 | 0 | 0.0 | 0 | 0.0 | 0 |
| Other Marketing Expense | 940 | 3.1% | 969 | 4.6% | 1014 | 6.1% | 1076 |
| Utilities & Depreciation | 175 | 2.3% | 179 | 4.5% | 187 | 4.3% | 195 |
| Taxes & Rent | 648 | 5.1% | 681 | 5.9% | 721 | 6.0% | 764 |
| Other | (226) | 4.0% | (235) | 56.6% | (368) | -31.2% | (253) |
| TOTAL EXPENSES | 13621 | 5.0% | 14307 | 3.8% | 14854 | 4.8% | 15572 |
| Headcount | 151 | | 153 | | 155 | | 155 |

## DIVISION
## Administrative Capacity Costs

**TOTAL DIVISION**

| Description | 1991 3QFC | Cost % Incr | 1992 | Cost % Incr | 1993 | Cost % Incr | 1994 |
|---|---|---|---|---|---|---|---|
| Wages | 2062 | 8.1% | 2229 | 6.5% | 2373 | 4.6% | 2481 |
| Incentive | 234 | 11.5% | 261 | 0.4% | 262 | 0.0% | 262 |
| Fringes | 559 | 20.4% | 673 | 5.9% | 713 | 4.8% | 747 |
| Travel & Entertainment | 112 | 4.5% | 117 | 4.3% | 122 | 4.1% | 127 |
| Automotive Expense | 20 | 0.0% | 20 | 0.0% | 20 | 0.0% | 20 |
| Outside & Consulting | 288 | 4.2% | 300 | 5.0% | 315 | 4.8% | 330 |
| | | 0.0 | 0 | 0.0 | 0 | 0.0 | 0 |
| Office Expense | 436 | 4.4% | 455 | 4.8% | 477 | 5.0% | 501 |
| | | 0.0 | 0 | 0.0 | 0 | 0.0 | 0 |
| Other Marketing Expense | 6 | 16.7% | 7 | 0.0% | 7 | 14.3% | 8 |
| Utilities & Depreciation | 374 | -1.1% | 370 | 2.2% | 378 | 2.1% | 386 |
| Taxes & Rent | 524 | 4.2% | 546 | 6.0% | 579 | 5.9% | 613 |
| Other | (366) | 3.0% | (377) | 4.0% | (392) | 3.8% | (407) |
| TOTAL EXPENSES | 4249 | 8.3% | 4601 | 5.5% | 4854 | 4.4% | 5068 |
| Headcount | 58 | | 61 | | 63 | | 63 |

## Engineering Capacity Costs
## ($ 000)

**TOTAL DIVISION**

| Description | 1991 3QFC | Cost % Incr | 1992 | Cost % Incr | 1993 | Cost % Incr | 1994 |
|---|---|---|---|---|---|---|---|
| Wages | 1484 | 8.8% | 1614 | 5.9% | 1710 | 4.4% | 1785 |
| Incentive | 11 | 9.1% | 12 | 8.3% | 13 | 7.7% | 14 |
| Fringes | 334 | 27.8% | 427 | 6.3% | 454 | 4.4% | 474 |
| Travel & Entertainment | 105 | 2.9% | 108 | 3.7% | 112 | 3.6% | 116 |
| Automotive Expense | 27 | 0.0% | 27 | 0.0% | 27 | 3.7% | 28 |
| Outside & Consulting | 104 | 2.9% | 107 | 4.7% | 112 | 4.5% | 117 |
| | | 0.0 | 0 | 0.0 | 0 | 0.0 | 0 |
| Office Expense | 59 | 1.7% | 60 | 3.3% | 62 | 4.8% | 65 |
| | | 0.0 | 0 | 0.0 | 0 | 0.0 | 0 |
| Other Marketing Expense | 34 | 2.9% | 35 | 2.9% | 36 | 5.6% | 38 |
| Utilities & Depreciation | 7 | 0.0% | 7 | 0.0% | 7 | 0.0% | 7 |
| Taxes & Rent | 1016 | 6.0% | 1077 | 5.9% | 1141 | 6.0% | 1209 |
| Other | 224 | 5.8% | 237 | 3.8% | 246 | 4.1% | 256 |
| TOTAL EXPENSES | 3405 | 9.0% | 3711 | 5.6% | 3920 | 4.8% | 4109 |
| Headcount | 34 | | 36 | | 37 | | 37 |

## SALES AND STANDARD MARGINS
## 1991 STRATEGIC PLAN

### TOTAL DIVISION

SALES

| Code | 3rd QFC | 1992 | 1993 | 1994 |
|---|---|---|---|---|
| U20-25 | 38835 | 40096 | 42363 | 44696 |
| U20-36 | 15920 | 16232 | 16799 | 17387 |
| U20-39 | 6025 | 6392 | 6740 | 7098 |
| U20-42 | 5917 | 7088 | 7856 | 8567 |
| U20-61 | 1966 | 3038 | 3283 | 3503 |
| TOTAL | 68663 | 72846 | 77041 | 81251 |

MARGINS

| | 3rd QFC | 1992 | 1993 | 1994 |
|---|---|---|---|---|
| | 14057 | 14557 | 15205 | 15851 |
| | 24778 | 25539 | 27158 | 28845 |
| % | 63.8% | 63.7% | 64.1% | 64.5% |
| | 5231 | 5381 | 5523 | 5669 |
| | 10689 | 10851 | 11276 | 11718 |
| % | 67.1% | 66.8% | 67.1% | 67.4% |
| | 1561 | 1647 | 1717 | 1786 |
| | 4464 | 4745 | 5023 | 5312 |
| % | 74.1% | 74.2% | 74.5% | 74.8% |
| | 2088 | 2438 | 2696 | 2936 |
| % | 35.3% | 34.4% | 34.3% | 34.3% |
| | 1116 | 1337 | 1471 | 1571 |
| | 850 | 1701 | 1812 | 1932 |
| % | 43.2% | 56.0% | 55.2% | 55.2% |
| TOTAL | 42869 | 45274 | 47965 | 50743 |
| % | 62.4% | 62.2% | 62.3% | 62.5% |

## SUMMARY BY PRODUCT

| | 1991 | 1992 | 1993 | 1994 |
|---|---|---|---|---|
| NET SALES | | | | |
| Domestic | 23825 | 24659 | 25902 | 27207 |
| Export | 2000 | 2070 | 2174 | 2284 |
| Mexico | 2324 | 2405 | 2526 | 2653 |
| Netherlands | 594 | 585 | 614 | 645 |
| Germany | 7096 | 7021 | 7375 | 7747 |
| Canada | 2700 | 2795 | 2936 | 3084 |
| Interco-Canada | 1200 | 1242 | 1305 | 1371 |
| Interco-Europe | 3450 | 3660 | 3844 | 4038 |
| Interco-Other (France) | 300 | 565 | 840 | 1080 |
| Eliminations | -4654 | -4906 | -5153 | -5413 |
| TOTAL SALES | 38835 | 40096 | 42363 | 44696 |
| | | | | |
| STANDARD MARGINS | | | | |
| Domestic | 14815 | 15424 | 16341 | 17309 |
| % | 62.2% | 62.5% | 63.1% | 63.6% |
| Export | 1333 | 1386 | 1466 | 1551 |
| % | 66.6% | 67.0% | 67.4% | 67.9% |
| Mexico | 1394 | 1452 | 1539 | 1631 |
| % | 60.0% | 60.4% | 60.9% | 61.5% |
| Netherlands | 301 | 278 | 292 | 307 |
| % | 50.7% | 47.5% | 47.6% | 47.6% |
| Germany | 3308 | 3046 | 3200 | 3362 |
| % | 46.6% | 43.4% | 43.4% | 43.4% |
| Canada | 1149 | 1190 | 1250 | 1313 |
| % | 42.6% | 42.6% | 42.6% | 42.6% |
| Interco-Canada | 588 | 615 | 656 | 699 |
| % | 49.0% | 49.5% | 50.3% | 51.0% |
| Interco-Europe | 1740 | 1863 | 1984 | 2112 |
| % | 50.4% | 50.9% | 51.6% | 52.3% |
| Interco-Other (France) | 150 | 285 | 430 | 561 |
| % | 50.0% | 50.4% | 51.2% | 51.9% |
| Eliminations | 0 | 0 | 0 | 0 |
| TOTAL STD MARGIN | 24778 | 25539 | 27158 | 28845 |
| % | 63.8% | 63.7% | 64.1% | 64.5% |

# Index